MW00560591

"In what is perhaps his most important book so far, John Piper demonstrates with great cogency and exegetical skill that God's providence 'is his purposeful sovereignty in which he will be completely successful in the achievement of his ultimate goal for the universe.' This book will enlarge your vision of God and thereby strengthen your faith."

D. A. Carson, Theologian-at-Large, The Gospel Coalition

"John Piper, with his characteristic clarity and focus on the biblical text, shows us the pervasiveness of God's providence in the Scriptures. Piper lingers over the biblical text, and we see in text after text that God rules over all of reality, from the smallest atom to horrific disasters. As we have come to expect from Piper, he turns our eyes to the infinite greatness and beauty of God, while reminding us that God's providence constitutes amazing good news for those of us who know Jesus Christ."

Thomas R. Schreiner, James Buchanan Harrison Professor of New Testament Interpretation, The Southern Baptist Theological Seminary

"There are many books by John Piper that I would recommend to believers because of the depth and freshness of thought in his writings. *Providence* will rank among the highest on the list. The breadth of God's providence that is covered here is breathtaking. Piper leaves no stone unturned! Read it and see for yourself. This is a landmark work!"

Conrad Mbewe, Pastor, Kabwata Baptist Church, Lusaka, Zambia

"While some see God's hand only in miracles, and others don't see his hand at all, providence is the wonderful truth that God is sovereign in and over everything that happens. Combining passion with a curious spirit, John Piper has cherished and proclaimed this truth throughout his ministry. This engaging book is not just about one doctrine, but ranges throughout the alpine vistas of God's work in our world, our redemption, and our lives today. It is deeply faith invigorating."

Michael Horton, Professor of Systematic Theology and Apologetics, Westminster Seminary California

"In this remarkable book, John Piper reveals the personal side of sovereignty, helping us glimpse the intricate complexity, winsome beauty, and ultimate purpose of God's plans in action. Piper is able to write about a multifaceted doctrine in a way that is easy to grasp and so practical!"

Joni Eareckson Tada, Founder and CEO, Joni and Friends International Disability Center

"John Piper's magisterial book is a robust antidote to the weak view of God's providence held by many Christians today. His exposition of the subject is thorough in scope and saturated with biblical insight. Piper is a model of the pastor-theologian as he not only describes providence but also shows how our understanding of providence can deepen our lives."

Tremper Longman III, Distinguished Scholar and Professor Emeritus of Biblical Studies, Westmont College

"With the publication of *The Justification of God* in 1988, John Piper showed that he was a man unflinching in his adherence to the sovereignty of God's grace. Now, half a generation later, that adherence remains. This massive book affords food for thought in a way that will stretch the minds and hearts of its readers."

 Paul Helm, Former Professor of the History and Philosophy of Religion, King's College London

"This is a book about the providence of God, written by a man who has spent his life expounding the glory of God. This volume is substantial, as its subject matter demands. Piper moves from the time before creation to the second coming of Christ, showing that the providential acts of God are pervasive through time, circumstances, and people as he explains the staggering power of the self-sufficient God."

 Miguel Núñez, Senior Pastor, International Baptist Church, Santo Domingo, Dominican Republic; Founding President, Wisdom and Integrity Ministries

"By nurturing humility and assisting us to tremble at God's word, John Piper's *Providence* helps our eyes to catch the eye of the King in his awesome and terrifying beauty (Isa. 33:17; 66:2). He is not a safe lion, but he is good."

 Jason S. DeRouchie, Research Professor of Old Testament and Biblical Theology, Midwestern Baptist Theological Seminary

"John Piper's careful exposition is coupled with insightful theological reflection and pastoral application. Here is hope when health fails, enemies assail, dreams unravel, relationships crumble, and calamities destroy. Here is strength for enduring difficulty, facing uncertainty, and overcoming anxiety. Here is the sweet experience of our Father's bountiful goodness in the special care and conduct of his providence."

 J. Stephen Yuille, Vice President of Academics, Heritage College and Seminary; Associate Professor of Biblical Spirituality, The Southern Baptist Theological Seminary

"Piper has the gift of making complex ideas easily understandable. Under the general theme of providence, he deals with some of the most difficult themes of the Christian faith—the relation of God's sovereignty to man's decisions, the origin of evil, God's use of evil people and the devil to accomplish his goals, and election. From a South American standpoint, where so many questions about God's ways arise from a context of rampant neopentecostalism, health-and-wealth gospel, poverty, and corruption, this book is much needed."

 Augustus Nicodemus Lopes, Assistant Pastor, First Presbyterian Church, Recife, Brazil; Vice President, Supreme Council, Presbyterian Church of Brazil

"In our profusely man-centered age, John Piper's book heals the mind and soul with gospel truth. This is not just a theological work on God's providence, but also pastoral guidance full of biblical yet practical wisdom. This book will help the modern generation of Christians enjoy the truth of God's sovereign power and help those around them to stand on the solid foundation of the gospel instead of the shaky ground of human pride. Piper lights a radiant flame of God's glory in the lighthouse of God's love where people will find true hope in a raging ocean of errors and fears. His book is very relevant for residents of post-Soviet countries, who need to see the greatness and beauty of the true King and ruler of this world while committing themselves to building his kingdom for the spiritual prosperity of their nations for the glory of Christ!"

Evgeny Bakhmutsky, Pastor, Russian Bible Church, Moscow, Russia

"John Piper helps us see and savor God's purposeful sovereignty by inductively demonstrating what the whole Bible teaches about its ultimate goal, its nature, and its extent."

Andy Naselli, Associate Professor of Systematic Theology and New Testament, Bethlehem College & Seminary; Elder, Bethlehem Baptist Church, Minneapolis

"Through this magnum opus, John Piper leads hearts to joyful worship by unfolding the often-neglected doctrine of God's providence. This book is both a textbook for serious students of theology as well as devotional reading for the layman. Read this book and worship the God who will achieve all his purposes for his glory and for the best of his elect."

Matthias G. Lohmann, Chairman, Evangelium21; Pastor, Free Evangelical Church Munich-Central, Germany

"In my estimation, this book represents the most mature and the fullest biblical-theological reflections of John Piper. As a pastor and teacher, I'm often asked, 'How can I reconcile what I know about God, man, and creation in the Bible with how I experience them?' Thanks to Piper, I now have a definitive work to help me answer these questions. This book will move readers to delight in God and in his revealed reality as they wonder at God's intended purpose for his creation."

Biao Chen, Chinese Project Coordinator, Third Millennium Ministries

"John Piper's works have always emphasized the glory of God and the joy of his people. Now Piper offers us a masterful treatise on the consoling doctrine of God's providence, moving between biblical theology and systematic theology with precision and a deep knowledge of Scripture without losing focus on the pastoral aspects of such important biblical teaching. May the Lord of glory use this book for the edification and joy of his people!"

Franklin Ferreira, Academic Director, Martin Bucer Seminar, São José dos Campos-SP, Brazil

"John Piper skillfully shows how the truth of providence directly relates to diverse areas of theology. *Providence* mixes his thorough theological and biblical insights with more than forty years of pastoral ministry. It is a real treasure for the global church and will be a valuable resource for the church of God for years to come."

Sherif A. Fahim, Lecturer in Systematic Theology and Biblical Studies, Alexandria School of Theology, Egypt; General Director, El-Soora Ministries

Other books by John Piper

Battling Unbelief

Bloodlines

Brothers, We Are Not Professionals

Coronavirus and Christ

The Dangerous Duty of Delight

Desiring God

Does God Desire All to Be Saved?

Don't Waste Your Life

Expository Exultation

Fifty Reasons Why Jesus Came to Die

Finally Alive

Five Points

Future Grace

God Is the Gospel

God's Passion for His Glory

A Godward Heart

A Godward Life

A Hunger for God

Lessons from a Hospital Bed

Let the Nations Be Glad!

A Peculiar Glory

The Pleasures of God

Reading the Bible Supernaturally

Seeing and Savoring Jesus Christ

Spectacular Sins

A Sweet and Bitter Providence

Taste and See

Think

This Momentary Marriage

What Jesus Demands from the World

When I Don't Desire God

Why I Love the Apostle Paul

PROVIDENCE

John Piper

WHEATON, ILLINOIS

Cover Design: Jordan Singer

First printing 2020

Printed in China

Unless otherwise indicated, Scripture quotations are from the ESV® Bible (The Holy Bible, English Standard Version®), copyright © 2001 by Crossway, a publishing ministry of Good News Publishers. Used by permission. All rights reserved.

Scripture quotations marked HCSB® are taken from *The Holman Christian Standard Bible*®. Copyright © 1999, 2000, 2002, 2003, 2009 by Holman Bible Publishers. Used by permission. HCSB® is a federally registered trademark of Holman Bible Publishers.

Scripture quotations marked KJV are from the *King James Version* of the Bible.

Scripture quotations marked NASB are from *The New American Standard Bible*®. Copyright © The Lockman Foundation 1960, 1962, 1963, 1968, 1971, 1972, 1973, 1975, 1977, 1995. Used by permission.

Scripture quotations marked NIV are taken from The Holy Bible, New International Version®, NIV®. Copyright © 1973, 1978, 1984, 2011 by Biblica, Inc.™ Used by permission. All rights reserved worldwide.

Scripture quotations marked NKJV are taken from the *New King James Version*®. Copyright © 1982 by Thomas Nelson. Used by permission. All rights reserved.

Scripture quotations marked NRSV are from *The New Revised Standard Version*. Copyright © 1989 by the Division of Christian Education of the National Council of the Churches of Christ in the U.S.A. Published by Thomas Nelson, Inc. Used by permission of the National Council of the Churches of Christ in the U.S.A.

Scripture quotations marked TNIV are taken from the Holy Bible, Today's New International Version. TNIV®. Copyright © 2001, 2005 by International Bible Society. Used by permission of Zondervan. All rights reserved.

All emphases in Scripture quotations have been added by the author.

Hardcover ISBN: 978-1-4335-6834-3
ePub ISBN: 978-1-4335-6837-4
PDF ISBN: 978-1-4335-6835-0
Mobipocket ISBN: 978-1-4335-6836-7

Library of Congress Cataloging-in-Publication Data

Names: Piper, John, 1946- author.
Title: Providence / John Piper.
Description: Wheaton, Illinois : Crossway, 2020. | Includes bibliographical references and index.
Identifiers: LCCN 2019059562 (print) | LCCN 2019059563 (ebook) | ISBN 9781433568343 (hardcover) | ISBN 9781433568350 (mobi) | ISBN 9781433568367 (pdf) | ISBN 9781433568374 (epub)
Subjects: LCSH: Providence and government of God–Christianity.
Classification: LCC BT135 .P536 2020 (print) | LCC BT135 (ebook) | DDC 231/.5–dc23
LC record available at https://lccn.loc.gov/2019059562
LC ebook record available at https://lccn.loc.gov/2019059563

Crossway is a publishing ministry of Good News Publishers.

RRDS		30	29	28	27	26	25	24	23	22	21	20
15	14	13	12	11	10	9	8	7	6	5	4	3	2	1

To all the missionaries
who have given their lives,
or will yet give their lives,
to gather God's elect from all the peoples of the world,
in the confidence that the saving purposes
of Providence
in Christ Jesus
cannot fail.

Contents

Introduction: Four Invitations 13

PART 1: A DEFINITION AND A DIFFICULTY

1   What Is Divine Providence? 29
2   Is Divine Self-Exaltation Good News? 39

PART 2: THE ULTIMATE GOAL OF PROVIDENCE

Section 1: The Ultimate Goal of Providence before Creation and in Creation

3   Before Creation 51
4   The Act of Creation 59

Section 2: The Ultimate Goal of Providence in the History of Israel

5   Overview: From Abraham to the Age to Come 71
6   The Exodus Unfolds 87
7   Remembering the Exodus 99
8   The Law, the Wilderness, and the Conquest of Canaan 111
9   The Time of the Judges and the Days of the Monarchy 125
10 The Protection, Destruction, and Restoration of Jerusalem 137

Section 3: The Ultimate Goal of Providence in the Design and Enactment of the New Covenant

11 The Designs of the New Covenant 155

12 Christ's Foundational Act in Establishing the New Covenant 165

13 The Entrance of Sin into Creation and the Glory of the Gospel 175

14 The Glory of Christ in the Glorification of His People 187

PART 3: THE NATURE AND EXTENT OF PROVIDENCE

Section 1: Setting the Stage

15 Knowing the Providence of the God Who Is 207

Section 2: Providence over Nature

16 The Loss and Recovery of a Theater of Wonders 221

17 Earth, Water, Wind, Plants, and Animals 233

Section 3: Providence over Satan and Demons

18 Satan and Demons 255

19 The Ongoing Existence of Satan 277

Section 4: Providence over Kings and Nations

20 Israel's Divine King Is King of the Nations 287

21 Human Kingship and the King of Kings 295

22 To Know and Rejoice That the Most High Rules 313

Section 5: Providence over Life and Death

23 A Bath of Truth and the Gift of Birth 337

24 The Lord Has Taken Away; Blessed Be the Name of the Lord 353

25 We Are Immortal till Our Work Is Done 371

Section 6: Providence over Sin

26 Natural Human Willing and Acting 385

27 Things We Know and Things We Do Not Need to Know 411

28 Joseph: God's Good Meaning in a Sinful Act 421

29 Israel Hated, Pharaoh Hardened, God Exalted, Helpless Saved 431

30 Broken Families 449

31 Deception and Dullness of Heart 463

32 Though He Cause Grief, He Will Have Compassion 475

33 A Wickedness God Especially Abhorred 497

Section 7: Providence over Conversion

34 Our Condition before Conversion 513

35 Three Biblical Pictures of How God Brings People to Faith 525

36 Saving Faith as the Gift of Providence 539

37 Driven Back to the Precious Roots of Election 559

Section 8: Providence over Christian Living

38 Forgiveness, Justification, and Obedience 577

39 God's Command-and-Warning Strategy 591

40 Those Whom He Called, He Also Glorified 609

41 Blood-Bought Zeal for Good Works 623

42 Working in Us That Which Is Pleasing in His Sight 635

43 Killing Sin and Creating Love—by Faith 647

Section 9: The Final Achievement of Providence

44 The Triumph of Missions and the Coming of Christ 661

45 New Bodies, New World, Never-Ending Gladness in God 673

Conclusion: Seeing and Savoring the Providence of God 691

General Index 713

Scripture Index 727

Desiring God Note on Resources 752

Four Invitations

God has revealed the goal and nature and extent of his providence. He has not been silent. He has shown us these things in the Bible. This is one of the reasons that the apostle Paul says, "All Scripture is . . . profitable" (2 Tim. 3:16). The profit lies not mainly in the validation of a theological viewpoint but in the revelation of a great God, the exaltation of his invincible grace, and the liberation of his undeserving people. God has revealed his purposeful sovereignty over good and evil in order to humble human pride, intensify human worship, shatter human hopelessness, and put ballast in the battered boat of human faith, steel in the spine of human courage, gladness in the groans of affliction, and love in the heart that sees no way forward.

What we find in the Bible is real and raw. The prizing and proclaiming of God's pervasive providence was forged in flames of hatred and love, deceit and truth, murder and mercy, carnage and kindness, cursing and blessing, mystery and revelation, and, finally, crucifixion and resurrection. I hope my treatment of God's providence will have the aroma of this shocking and hope-filled reality.

In this introduction, I would like to offer you four invitations.

Counterintuitive Wonders

First, I invite you into a biblical world of counterintuitive wonders. I will argue that these wonders are not illogical or contradictory, but they are different from our usual ways of seeing the world—so different that our first reaction is often to say, "That can't be." But the "can't" is in our *minds*, not in reality. "How unsearchable are his judgments and how inscrutable his ways!" (Rom. 11:33).

For example, in the justice of his judgment, God raises up a cruel shepherd for his people, and then he sends punishment on that shepherd:

> Behold, I am raising up in the land a shepherd who does not care for those being destroyed, or seek the young or heal the maimed or nourish the healthy, but devours the flesh of the fat ones, tearing off even their hoofs.
>
> "Woe to my worthless shepherd,
>   who deserts the flock!
> May the sword strike his arm
>   and his right eye!
> Let his arm be wholly withered,
>   his right eye utterly blinded!" (Zech. 11:16–17)

This jars us. For most of us, this is not how we usually think about the ways of God. First, that God *raises up* a brutal shepherd for his people seems to implicate God in sinful brutality. Second, that God judges the shepherd for his worthlessness seems like capriciously condemning what he himself ordained.

There are many such scenes in the Bible, and I will argue that in them all, God is neither sinful nor capricious. If we are prone to be critical rather than be changed, we should put our hands on our mouths and listen. We are sinful and finite. God is infinite and holy.

> My thoughts are not your thoughts,
>   neither are your ways my ways, declares the Lord.

For as the heavens are higher than the earth,
> so are my ways higher than your ways
> and my thoughts than your thoughts. (Isa. 55:8–9)

I am inviting you into a world of counterintuitive wonders. I hope that you will let the word of God create new categories of thinking rather than trying to force the Scripture into the limits of what you already know. When Paul calls us to be "transformed by the renewal of [our] mind" (Rom. 12:2), part of what he has in mind is the overcoming of our natural resistance to the strangeness of the ways of God. Immediately before calling for transformed minds, he writes:

Oh, the depth of the riches and wisdom and knowledge of God! How unsearchable are his judgments and how inscrutable his ways!

> "For who has known the mind of the Lord,
> or who has been his counselor?"
> "Or who has given a gift to him
> that he might be repaid?"

For from him and through him and to him are all things. To him be glory forever. Amen. (Rom. 11:33–36)

In the end, my invitation into the biblical world of counterintuitive wonders is an invitation to worship. God is vastly greater and stranger and more glorious and more dreadful and more loving than we realize. Immersing ourselves in the ocean of his providence is meant to help us know him, fear him, trust him, and love him as we ought.

Penetrating through Words into Reality
Second, I invite you to penetrate through words into reality. *Providence* is a word not found in the Bible. In that sense, it is like the words *Trinity, discipleship, evangelism, exposition, counseling, ethics, politics,* and *charismatics*. People who love the Bible and believe that it

is God's word want to know what the Bible teaches, not just what it says. They want to know the *reality* being presented, not just the *words* that were written.

The Bible itself makes clear that it is not enough just to say the words of the Bible. The Bible mandates that all churches have teachers. All churches are supposed to have elders (Titus 1:5), and elders are required to be teachers (1 Tim. 3:2). The task of a teacher is not just to *read* the Bible to his hearers, but to *explain* it. And explaining means using other words besides the ones in the text. Throughout the history of the church, heretics have frequently insisted on using only Bible words in defending their heresy. This was certainly the case for the fourth-century Arians, who rejected the deity of Jesus and were happy to use Bible words to do so.[1]

R. P. C. Hanson explained the process like this: "Theologians of the Christian Church were slowly driven to a realization that the deepest questions which face Christianity cannot be answered in purely biblical language, because the questions are about the meaning of biblical language itself."[2]

---

1 The Arians affirmed biblical sentences while denying biblical meaning. Here is a description of the proceedings: "The Alexandrians . . . confronted the Arians with the traditional Scriptural phrases which appeared to leave no doubt as to the eternal Godhead of the Son. But to their surprise they were met with perfect acquiescence. Only as each test was propounded, it was observed that the suspected party whispered and gesticulated to one another, evidently hinting that each could be safely accepted, since it admitted of evasion. If their assent was asked to the formula 'like to the Father in all things,' it was given with the reservation that man as such is 'the image and glory of God.' The 'power of God' elicited the whispered explanation that the host of Israel was spoken of as δυναμις κυριου [power of the Lord], and that even the locust and caterpillar are called the 'power of God.' The 'eternity' of the Son was countered by the text, 'We that live are alway (2 Corinthians 4:11)!' The fathers were baffled, and the test of ομοουσιον [same being], with which the minority had been ready from the first, was being forced upon the majority by the evasions of the Arians."

    See Archibald T. Robertson, "Prolegomena," in *St. Athanasius: Select Works and Letters*, ed. Philip Schaff and Henry. Wace, vol. 4, Select Library of the Nicene and Post-Nicene Fathers of the Christian Church, 2nd Series (New York: Christian Literature Company, 1892), *xix*.

2 R. P. C. Hanson, *The Search for the Christian Doctrine of God: The Arian Controversy* (Edinburgh: T. & T. Clark, 1988), *xviii–xix*.

The longer I have studied Scripture and tried to preach it and teach it, the more I have seen the need to encourage preachers and laypeople to penetrate through biblical words to biblical reality. How easy it is to think we have experienced communion with God when our minds and hearts have stopped with verbal definitions, grammatical relations, historical illustrations, and a few applications. When we do this, even Bible words themselves can become alternatives to what Paul calls "spiritual . . . understanding" (συνέσει πνευματικῇ, Col. 1:9).

I am going to use the word *providence* to refer to a biblical reality. The reality is not found in any single Bible word. It emerges from the way God has revealed himself through many texts and many stories in the Bible. They are like threads woven together into a beautiful tapestry greater than any one thread. We are using a word that is not in the Bible for the sake of this larger truth of the Bible.

Of course, there are dangers in doing this—just like there are dangers in using only Bible language, which can be twisted to carry false meanings while giving the impression of biblical faithfulness (cf. 2 Pet. 3:16). I will mention one danger, among others.

Since the word *providence* is not used in specific biblical texts, we have no biblical governor on its meaning. We can't say, "The Bible defines providence this way." We could say that only if the Bible actually used the word *providence*. Whenever you ask what a particular word means, there must be a mean*er* if the meaning is to have validity. So if the mean*er* is not one (or more) of the biblical writers, then when I use the word *providence*, I must assign a meaning. That is what I do in chapter 1. I don't assign an arbitrary meaning; I try to stay close to what others have meant by the word in the history of the church. But I do choose the meaning.

You can see what this implies. It implies that the issue before us in this book is *not* the meaning of the word *providence*. The issue is this: *Is the reality that I see in the Bible, and call* providence, *really there?* There is no point in quibbling over whether *providence* is the best word for the reality. That is relatively unimportant. The all-important truth is whether there is a reality in the Bible that corresponds to my description of the goal, nature, and extent of God's *purposeful sovereignty*. You will see in chapter 1 why I use the short definition "purposeful sovereignty" for providence. But for now, I am simply flagging the danger that it would be a sad mistake to miss the biblical reality by focusing on the word.

A God-Entranced World

Third, I invite you into a God-entranced world. Jesus said to look at the birds because God feeds them (Matt. 6:26) and to consider the lilies because God clothes them (Matt. 6:28–30). Jesus's aim was not aesthetic. His aim was to free his people from anxiety. He really considered it a valid argument that if our heavenly Father feeds the birds and clothes the lilies, how much more surely will he feed and clothe his children.

This is simply astonishing. The argument is valid only if God really is the one who sees to it that the birds find their worms and the lilies wear their flowers. If birds and lilies are simply acting by natural laws, with no divine hand, then Jesus is just playing with words. But he is *not* playing with words. He really believes that God's hand is at work in the smallest details of natural processes. This is even clearer in Matthew 10:29–31:

> Are not two sparrows sold for a penny? And *not one of them will fall to the ground apart from your Father.* But even the hairs of your head are all numbered. Fear not, therefore; you are of more value than many sparrows.

God does not just feed the birds and clothe the lilies; he decides when every bird (countless millions every year) dies and falls to the ground. His point is the same as in Matthew 6: "He is your Father. You are more precious to him than birds. Therefore, you don't need to be afraid." That kind of pervasive providence, combined with that kind of fatherly care, means he can and will take care of you. So seek the kingdom first, with radical abandon, and don't be anxious (Matt. 6:33).

CHARGED WITH GRANDEUR

This God-entranced view of the world was not peculiar to Jesus. The psalmist sings to the Lord of his specific care for the creatures he has made:

> These all look to you,
>   to give them their food in due season.
> When you give it to them, they gather it up;
>   when you open your hand, they are filled with good things.
> When you hide your face, they are dismayed;
>   when you take away their breath, they die
>   and return to their dust.
> When you send forth your Spirit, they are created,
>   and you renew the face of the ground. (Ps. 104:27–30)

God's involvement in nature is hands-on—the kind of closeness that causes the biblical writers to make declarations like, "He makes grass grow on the hills" (Ps. 147:8). "The LORD appointed a great fish to swallow up Jonah" (Jonah 1:17). "The LORD God appointed a plant" (Jonah 4:6). "God appointed a worm that attacked the plant" (Jonah 4:7). "He . . . brings forth the wind from his storehouses" (Ps. 135:7). "He it is who makes the clouds rise . . . who makes lightnings for the rain" (Ps. 135:7). "He . . . rebuked the wind and the raging waves" (Luke 8:24). This is not poetry for God-less naturalistic processes. This is God's hands-on providence.

God does not intend for us to see ourselves, or any part of the world, as cogs in the wheels of an impersonal mechanism. The world is not a machine that God made to run on its own. It is a painting, or a sculpture, or a drama. The Son of God holds it in being by the word of his power (Col. 1:17; Heb. 1:3). Gerard Manley Hopkins expressed it unforgettably in his sonnet "God's Grandeur":

> The world is charged with the grandeur of God.
>   It will flame out, like shining from shook foil;
>   It gathers to a greatness, like the ooze of oil
> Crushed. Why do men then now not reck his rod?
> Generations have trod, have trod, have trod;
>   And all is seared with trade; bleared, smeared with toil;
>   And wears man's smudge and shares man's smell: the soil
> Is bare now, nor can foot feel, being shod.
>
> And for all this, nature is never spent;
>   There lives the dearest freshness deep down things;
> And though the last lights off the black West went
>   Oh, morning, at the brown brink eastward, springs—
> Because the Holy Ghost over the bent
>   World broods with warm breast and with ah! bright wings.[3]

SEEING THE RISING SUN

I will never cease to be thankful that in my college days, Clyde Kilby was one of my literature professors. He gave a lecture once on the awakening of amazement at the strange glory of ordinary things. He closed the lecture with ten resolutions for what he called "mental health."[4] Here are two of them:

> I shall open my eyes and ears. Once every day I shall simply stare at a tree, a flower, a cloud, or a person. I shall not then be concerned

---

3   Gerard Manley Hopkins, "God's Grandeur," Poetry Foundation, accessed April 9, 2020, https://www.poetryfoundation.org/poems/44395/gods-grandeur.

4   You can read all of them here: John Piper, "10 Resolutions for Mental Health," Desiring God, December 31, 2007, https://www.desiringgod.org/articles/10-resolutions-for-mental-health. When Kilby speaks of "mental health," he is speaking generally, not clinically. He does not have clinically diagnosable mental illnesses in view.

at all to ask what they are but simply be glad that they are. I shall joyfully allow them the mystery of what [C. S.] Lewis calls their "divine, magical, terrifying and ecstatic" existence.

Even if I turn out to be wrong, I shall bet my life on the assumption that this world is not idiotic, neither run by an absentee landlord, but that today, this very day, some stroke is being added to the cosmic canvas that in due course I shall understand with joy as a stroke made by the architect who calls himself Alpha and Omega.

Because of Kilby's eye-opening influence, and because of what I now see in the Bible as an all-embracing, all-pervasive providence, I live more consciously in a God-entranced world. I see reality differently. For example, I used to look at sunrises when I was jogging and think that God has created a beautiful world. Then it became less general and more specific, more personal. I said, "Every morning God paints a different sunrise." He never gets tired of doing it again and again. But then it struck me. No, he doesn't do it again and again. He *never stops* doing it. The sun is always rising somewhere in the world. God guides the sun twenty-four hours every day and paints sunrises at every moment, century after century without one second of respite, and never grows weary or less thrilled with the work of his hands. Even when cloud cover keeps man from seeing it, God is painting spectacular sunrises above the clouds.

God does not intend for us to look at the world he has made and feel nothing. When the psalmist says, "The heavens declare the glory of God" (Ps. 19:1), he does not mean this only for the clarification of our theology. He means it for the exultation of our souls. We know this because of what follows:

In [the heavens] he has set a tent for the sun,
>   which comes out like a bridegroom leaving his chamber,
>   and, like a strong man, runs its course with joy. (Ps. 19:4–5)

What is the point of saying this? When we look at the handiwork of God in creation, we are to be drawn into bridegroom-like joy and into the joy of an Eric Liddell running with head back, elbows pumping, smile bursting in *Chariots of Fire*, basking in the very pleasure of God.

I am inviting you into a God-entranced world. No, we are not naïve about the miseries every sunrise meets. You will, perhaps, be shocked at the implications of God's pervasive providence in the suffering and death of this world. The Lord gives and the Lord takes away (Job 1:21). And the exulting sun dawns on 150,000 new corpses every morning. That's how many people die every day. In a world with this much God-entranced beauty, and this much God-governed horror, the biblical command to "rejoice with those who rejoice, weep with those who weep" (Rom. 12:15) means that we will continually be "sorrowful, yet always rejoicing" (2 Cor. 6:10).

To Know God

Fourth, and finally, I am inviting you to know, maybe as you never have known, the God whose involvement in his children's lives and in the world is so pervasive, so all-embracing, and so powerful that nothing can befall them but what he designs for their glorification in him and his glorification in them (2 Thess. 1:12).

The death of the Son of God ransomed a people for God from every tribe and language and nation (Rev. 5:9). The transaction between the Father and the Son in the death of Christ was so powerful that it secured absolutely, for all time and eternity, everything needed to bring the bride of Christ safely and beautifully to everlasting joy.

Romans 8:32 may be the most important verse in the Bible, because it establishes the unshakable connection between the greatest event in the universe and the greatest future imaginable: "He who did not spare his own Son but gave him up for us all, how will he not also with him graciously give us all things?"

Indeed. How will he not! All things. All things!

Let no one boast in men. For all things are yours, whether Paul or Apollos or Cephas or the world or life or death or the present or the future—all are yours, and you are Christ's, and Christ is God's. (1 Cor. 3:21–23)

All things ours. Because the Father did not spare the Son. When Christ died, everything—absolutely everything—that his people need to make it through this world in holiness and love was invincibly secured. God the Father predestined it—everything we need—and promised it to us (Ezek. 36:27; Rom. 8:29). God the Son purchased it for us (Titus 2:14). God the Spirit performs it in us (Gal. 3:5; Heb. 13:21). Nothing can separate us from the love of God in Christ (Rom. 8:35–39).

I would like to help as many as I can to know the God of all-embracing, all-pervasive, invincible providence. His word is spectacularly full of knowledge about God's ultimate goal. Cover to cover, it rings with the riches of his grace toward his undeserving people. Page after page tells the stunning story of the nature and extent of his providence. Nothing can stop him from succeeding exactly when and how he aims to succeed.

> I am God, and there is no other;
>   I am God, and there is none like me,
> declaring the end from the beginning
>   and from ancient times things not yet done,
> saying, "My counsel shall stand,
>   and I will accomplish all my purpose."
>   (Isa. 46:9–10)

Goal, Nature, Extent

The book is divided into three parts. Part 1 defines *providence* and then illuminates a difficulty, namely, the self-exaltation involved in God's aim to display his own glory. Part 2 focuses on the ultimate goal of providence. Part 3 focuses on the nature and extent of providence. I have chosen this order (goal before nature and extent) because I think we understand more clearly what a person is doing if we know the end he is pursuing. If I know your goal is to build a house in Minnesota, I will understand what you are doing when you dig a massive hole in the ground. Basements are important in this climate. Otherwise, without knowing your aim, I won't know what the hole in the ground means. The nature and extent of the hole is explained by the goal.

I refer to the *ultimate* goal of providence because God is always doing ten thousand things in every act of providence. (That is an understatement.) Each of those ten thousand things is intended. Which means that God has millions and millions of goals every hour. He accomplishes all of them. We don't know most of them. (That too is an understatement.) So part 2 of this book is not about trying to know all those goals. That is impossible. What I want to know is where everything is going. What is the goal that guides everything?

Then we can grasp more fully the nature and extent of his providence. By the question of *extent*, I mean, How much and how completely does God control things, including human beings? By the question of *nature*, I mean, for example, What *means* does God use to control things? Is the word *control* even the right word? It is not my default word to describe providence. Not because the word is false, but because it tends to carry connotations of mechanical processes and coercive strategies. I will use it. But I hope to continually show why these connotations do not attach to God's providence.

Providence is all-embracing and all-pervasive, but when God turns the human will, there is a mystery to it that causes a person to experience God's turning as his own preference—an authentic, responsible act of the human will. God is sovereign over man's preferences. Man is accountable for his preferences. God's hidden hand in turning all things and his revealed commands requiring all obedience are in perfect harmony in the mind of God, but not in our visible experience. We are obliged to follow his revealed precepts, not his secret purposes.[5] We will see that such is the nature of providence.

---

5   I have adapted here the words of John Owen: "The holiness of our actions consisteth in a conformity unto his precepts, and not unto his purposes." John Owen, *The Works of John Owen*, vol. 10, ed. William H. Goold (Edinburgh: T&T Clark, n.d.), 48.

PART 1

A DEFINITION AND
A DIFFICULTY

1

What Is Divine Providence?

The reason this book is about the providence of God rather than the sovereignty of God is that the term *sovereignty* does not contain the idea of *purposeful* action, but the term *providence* does. Sovereignty focuses on God's right and power to do all that he wills, but in itself, it does not express any design or goal.

Of course, God's sovereignty *is* purposeful. It *does* have design. It *does* pursue a goal. But we know this, not simply because God is sovereign, but because he is wise, and because the Bible portrays him as having purposes in all he does. "My counsel shall stand, and I will accomplish all my purpose" (Isa. 46:10).

The focus of this book is on God's sovereignty considered not simply as powerful but as purposeful. Historically, the term *providence* has been used as shorthand for this more specific focus.

The Building Blocks of Providence

Why was the English word *providence* chosen to capture this biblical teaching? In reference to God, the word does not occur in most English versions of the Bible (e.g., ESV, KJV, HCSB, NRSV).[1] It is

---

1 The word *providence* occurs once in reference to human action in Acts 24:2 in the KJV and NASB. And it occurs once in reference to God's action in Job 10:12 in the NIV and TNIV.

difficult to be certain about the history of a word and why it came to carry its present meaning. But here is a suggestion.

The word *providence* is built from the word *provide*, which has two parts: *pro* (Latin "forward," "on behalf of") and *vide* (Latin "to see"). So you might think that the word *provide* would mean "to see forward" or "to foresee." But it doesn't. It means "to supply what is needed"; "to give sustenance or support." So in reference to God, the noun *providence* has come to mean "the act of purposefully providing for, or sustaining and governing, the world."

Why is this? There are two interesting reasons, one based on an English idiom and the other based on a biblical story.

God "Sees to It"

We have an English idiom that goes like this: "I'll see to it." Like all idioms, it means more than the words, taken individually, seem to signify. "I'll see to it" in English means "I'll take care of it" (which is itself an idiom!). I'll provide for it. I'll see (or make sure) that it happens. So it could be that putting the Latin *vide* ("see") together with the Latin *pro* ("to," "toward") produced "see to" and came to mean more than "foresee," but to mean "see to it" in the sense of "take care of it" or "see that it happens." That would be what we mean by God's providence: he sees to it that things happen in a certain way.

Providence on Mount Moriah

Then, even more interestingly, there is the biblical story of Abraham's offering of his son Isaac. Before they went up Mount Moriah, Isaac said to his father, "Where is the lamb for a burnt offering?" (Gen. 22:7). Abraham answered, "God *will provide* for himself the lamb for a burnt offering, my son" (22:8). And when God had shown Abraham a ram caught in the thorns, "Abraham called the name of that place 'The LORD will provide'" (22:14).

What is striking is that whenever the word *provide* occurs in Genesis 22, the Hebrew word is simply "to see." Very simply, Abraham says to Isaac, "God *will see* for himself the lamb" (יִרְאֶה־לֹּו הַשֶּׂה 22:8). Similarly in verse 14: "'The LORD will provide' [the Lord will *see* יְהוָה יִרְאֶה]; as it is said to this day, 'On the mount of the LORD it shall be provided' [it shall be *seen* בְּהַר יְהוָה יֵרָאֶה]."

The old King James Version preserves this literal rendering of Genesis 22:14, even transliterating the Hebrew of "the Lord sees" as *Jehovahjireh*: "Abraham called the name of that place Jehovahjireh: as it is said to this day, In the mount of the LORD it shall be seen." The New King James Version has joined virtually all other contemporary versions by translating *see* as *provide*: "Abraham called the name of the place, The-LORD-Will-Provide; as it is said to this day, 'In the Mount of the LORD it shall be provided.'"

With regard to the doctrine of God's *providence*, the question is this: Why does God's *seeing* in Genesis 22 actually refer to his *providing*—his providence?

The answer I suggest is that in the mind of Moses, and other authors of Scripture, God does not simply *see* as a passive bystander. As God, he is never merely an observer. He is not a passive observer of the world—and not a passive predictor of the future. Wherever God is looking, God is acting. In other words, there is a profound theological reason why God's *providence* does not merely mean his *seeing*, but rather his *seeing to*. When God sees something, he sees to it. Evidently, as Moses wrote Genesis 22, God's purposeful engagement with Abraham was so obvious that Moses could simply refer to God's perfect *seeing* as implying God's purposeful *doing*. His *seeing* was his *seeing to*. His *perception* implied his *provision*—his *providence*.

Catch-22 in Writing a Book Like This

Those are my suggestions for how the English word *providence* has come to mean "the act of God's providing for or sustaining and governing the world." Of course, it is of minor importance whether I am right about that. When it comes to words, what matters is not that we know where they came from or how they got their meaning. What matters is that we grasp truly what a writer or speaker intends to communicate with his words.

Then the real task begins: Does what an author intends to communicate with words conform to reality? Is the conception of providence that an author describes true? Or, in the case of this book, since I take the Bible to be the touchstone of truth: Do we grasp truly what the Bible teaches about God's providence?

So as I turn to clarify more specifically what I mean by God's providence, it should be clear that I am caught in a kind of catch-22. On the one hand, I should give my evidence from the Bible first, in order to support my understanding of God's providence. On the other hand, I have to use the term *providence* all along the way as I lay out that evidence, and the term should have a clear meaning for my readers, which can only come from that evidence. I can either give you a clear sense of what I mean by *providence* before I give you the evidence for it, or I can use the word *providence* ambiguously throughout the book and wait for a clear conception until the end.

I don't like ambiguity. I think it is the source of much confusion and error. So I choose the first option. Here at the beginning, I'm going to give you as clear a conception as I can of what I mean by divine providence, knowing that it is based on evidence not yet provided. Then you may view the rest of the book as biblical support and explanation and application and celebration for this conception of providence.

My aim in this book is not to develop a new meaning of providence that the church has not embraced in its historic statements of faith. Instead, I aim to gather from the Scriptures some very old kindling of truth, pile it up in plain view, and put a match to it. This is not because I want to consume it, but because I want to release its incendiary properties for the intensifying of true worship, the solidifying of wavering conviction, the strengthening of embattled faith, the toughening of joyful courage, and the advance of God's mission in this world.

Some Good, Old Views of Providence

Let's reach back a few centuries for some definitions of providence that I am very happy with, because I think they express biblical truth.

Heidelberg Catechism (1563)

Question 27. What do you understand by the providence of God?

Answer. The almighty, everywhere-present power of God, whereby, as it were by his hand, He still upholds heaven and earth with all creatures, and so governs them that herbs and grass, rain and drought, fruitful and barren years, meat and drink, health and sickness, riches and poverty, indeed, all things come not by chance, but by his fatherly hand.

As in virtually all confessions, divine providence signifies an "almighty, everywhere-present power of God." This power "upholds" and "governs" all things. But what gives this definition its twist toward providence (and not just sovereignty) is the phrase "by his fatherly hand." This carries massive implications about the design of God's governing of all things. It implies that everything in the universe is governed with a view of the good of God's children! But we must wait to see this more fully.

The Belgic Confession (1561)

Article 13. The Doctrine of God's Providence

We believe that this good God, after creating all things, did not abandon them to chance or fortune but leads and governs them according to his holy will, in such a way that nothing happens in this world without God's orderly arrangement.

Again God "leads and governs" all things so that nothing is left to "chance or fortune." And again, what focuses the doctrine on providence, not just sovereignty, is that "nothing happens . . . without God's *orderly arrangement.*" Which, of course, begs for an explanation of the word *orderly.* Order implies design and purpose. Order to what end? That is what we will focus on in part 2 of this book.

Westminster Larger Catechism (1648)

Question 18. What are the works of providence?

Answer. God's works of providence are his most holy, wise, and powerful preserving and governing all his creatures; ordering them, and all their actions, to his own glory.

God's providence not only "preserves" and upholds the existence of "all his creatures," but also "[orders] . . . all their actions." The purpose of all this preserving and ordering is made explicit: "to his glory." This is purposeful sovereignty, which we call *providence.*

Westminster Confession of Faith (1646)

Chapter 5. Of Providence

5.1. God the great Creator of all things doth uphold, direct, dispose, and govern all creatures, actions, and things, from the greatest even to the least, by his most wise and holy providence, according to his infallible foreknowledge, and the free and immutable counsel of his own will, to the praise of the glory of his wisdom, power, justice, goodness, and mercy.

This is the fullest definition we have seen so far. God upholds, directs, disposes, and governs "all creatures, actions, and things." This is pervasive sovereignty. Then come all the providential colors: sovereignty governed by wisdom and holiness—and all "to the praise of the glory of his wisdom, power, justice, goodness, and mercy."

This way of expressing God's aim in providence will prove to be critical in being faithful to Scripture. Some views of providence focus so fully on God's aim in displaying his mercy that the rest of his glory is obscured. I think the Westminster resistance to that reduction is wise and biblical. The aim of God's providence, so says the confession, is "to the praise" of God's glory—not just one aspect, or one facet, of his glory (such as love or grace or mercy) but *all* of it: "the glory of his wisdom, power, justice, goodness, and mercy."

What Is the Difference between Providence and Fate?

Sometimes these strong statements of God's directing, disposing, and governing of all creatures, actions, and things raise the question of how the biblical view of God's providence differs from fate. The idea of fate has a long history—from Greek mythology to modern physics. What troubles people in general is that fate and providence imply a kind of fixedness to the future that seems to make life meaningless. Here is Charles Spurgeon's (1834–1892) response to this concern.

First, he gives us his astonishing conviction about the minute pervasiveness of divine providence. This is from a sermon on God's providence based on Ezekiel 1:15–19:

> I believe that every particle of dust that dances in the sunbeam does not move an atom more or less than God wishes—that every particle of spray that dashes against the steamboat has its orbit, as well as the sun in the heavens—that the chaff from the hand of the winnower is steered as the stars in their courses. The creeping of an aphid over the rosebud is as much fixed as the march of the devastating pestilence—the fall of . . . leaves from a poplar is as fully ordained as the tumbling of an avalanche.[2]

2 Charles Spurgeon, "God's Providence," sermon on Ezek. 1:15–19, Bible Bulletin Board, accessed April 9, 2020, http://www.biblebb.com/files/spurgeon/3114.htm.

That's astonishing. Every tiny, popping bubble in the foam at the top of a newly poured can of Coke. Every floating dust mote which you can see only in the early-morning bedroom beam of light. Every tip of every stalk of grain stretching across the endless Nebraska plains. All of them, with all their slightest movements, specifically governed by God.

So Spurgeon foresees the objection and continues on in the same sermon:

> You will say this morning, Our minister is a fatalist. Your minister is no such thing. Some will say, Ah! he believes in fate. He does not believe in fate at all. What is fate? Fate is this—*Whatever is, must be.* But there is a difference between that and Providence. Providence says, *Whatever God ordains must be*; but the wisdom of God never ordains anything without a purpose. Everything in this world is working for some one great end. Fate does not say that. Fate simply says that the thing must be; Providence says, God moves the wheels along, and there they are.
>
> If anything would go wrong, God puts it right; and if there is anything that would move awry, he puts his hand and alters it. It comes to the same thing; but there is a difference as to the object. There is all the difference between fate and Providence that there is between a man with good eyes and a blind man. Fate is a blind thing; it is the avalanche crushing the village down below and destroying thousands. Providence is not an avalanche; it is a rolling river, rippling at the first like a rill down the sides of the mountain, followed by minor streams, till it rolls in the broad ocean of everlasting love, working for the good of the human race. The doctrine of Providence is not: *what is, must be*; but that what is works together for the good of our race, and especially for the good of the chosen people of God. The wheels are full of eyes; not blind wheels.[3]

---

3 Spurgeon, "God's Providence."

I hope it will become obvious in what follows, particularly in part 2, that God's ultimate purpose in his pervasive providence is so purposeful, so wise, so holy, so gracious, and so joyful that the last thing anyone would think to call it is *fate*.

For the Ever-Increasing Enjoyment of All Who Love God

I agree with all of the descriptions of God's providence that we have seen above from the historic confessions of faith and from Spurgeon. I think they are coherent with each other and faithful to Scripture. This is what I will mean by the term *providence* in this book. But it might be helpful to quote one more affirmation of faith to clarify my own view.

During my thirty-three years as pastor of Bethlehem Baptist Church, the elders carefully crafted a document called *The Bethlehem Baptist Church Elder Affirmation of Faith.* Since I was part of that process, the statement on God's providence in this affirmation captures some emphases that will unfold in this book. Here are the key quotes on providence:

> 3.1. We believe that God, from all eternity, in order to display the full extent of His glory for the eternal and ever-increasing enjoyment of all who love Him, did, by the most wise and holy counsel of his will, freely and unchangeably ordain and foreknow whatever comes to pass.
>
> 3.2. We believe that God upholds and governs all things—from galaxies to subatomic particles, from the forces of nature to the movements of nations, and from the public plans of politicians to the secret acts of solitary persons—all in accord with his eternal, all-wise purposes to glorify Himself, yet in such a way that He never sins, nor ever condemns a person unjustly; but that his ordaining and governing all things is compatible with the moral accountability of all persons created in his image.[4]

4 "Elder Affirmation of Faith," Bethlehem Baptist Church (website), October 18, 2015, https://bethlehem.church/elder-affirmation-of-faith/.

This claim that God communicates his glory "for the eternal and ever-increasing enjoyment of all who love Him" is, I believe, implicit in the historic creeds, as, for example, when the Westminster Catechism says that the chief end of man is "to glorify God and *enjoy* him forever."[5] But I regard this goal of the enjoyment of God, and its relationship to the glorification of God, as so crucial to the purpose of God in providence that I make it explicit and prominent. It will, I hope, become clear in part 2 that this is not just what *I* do. It is what Scripture does.

Before we turn to the task of part 2 and the question of God's *goal* in providence, it will be helpful to deal with what many see as a stumbling block—namely, the self-exaltation involved in God's aim to display his own glory. That is what we take up in chapter 2.

---

5   For the exegetical defense of this idea of ever-increasing joy in the age to come, see the discussion of Eph. 2:7 in chap. 14.

2

Is Divine Self-Exaltation
Good News?

I am tempted to say that modern people find it almost impossible to receive with thankfulness and joy the relentless witness of the Bible that God consistently acts for the sake of his own glory. I have in mind texts such as Isaiah 48:9–11:

> For my name's sake I defer my anger;
>> for the sake of my praise I restrain it for you,
>> that I may not cut you off.
> Behold, I have refined you, but not as silver;
>> I have tried you in the furnace of affliction.
> For my own sake, for my own sake, I do it,
>> for how should my name be profaned?
>> My glory I will not give to another.

I wrote that I'm tempted to say *modern* people resist this divine self-exaltation rather than rejoicing in it. But upon further reflection, I realize that this resistance is not unique to modern people. It is human. And it is complex.

Our Resistance to God's Self-Glorification

On the one hand, human beings know all too well the experience of self-exaltation. We know it up close and personal. We have all done it. We all have a built-in reflex to love praise, and we enjoy, at some level, being made much of. On the other hand, it is an almost equally universal trait that we don't like this about people, including ourselves (in our best moments, anyway). We have a love-hate relationship with the desire for our own glory.

Our resistance to the pervasive biblical witness to God's self-glorification is made even more complex by the fact that, in general, we (Americans at least) seem to love cinematic or fictional heroes marked by arrogance and swagger and cocky self-assurance. We give them rousing cheers if they show off their ability to win when vastly outnumbered. We seem to love their smug, egotistical self-exaltation. It's cool. And being cool, self-exaltation (with all its cultural mutations over the decades) endures as a deep aspiration of the human heart as well as an admirable trait in our heroes. It is the feel-good counterpart of being shamed. We hate being seen as foolish. We love being seen as smart and competent. And we want our heroes to be the same, even if they push the envelope of cockiness.

And yet it's not that simple. If these cocky heroes begin to use their clever skills to act unjustly and hurt innocent people—or people we like—our empathetic admiration winces. Before long, the mental shrewdness, physical adroitness, and verbal wit that made them cool makes them evil. They lose their appeal. The self-exalting braggadocio that once pleased now repulses.

The complexity of human resistance to God's self-exaltation is further increased by the fact that Jesus himself said, "If I glorify myself, my glory is nothing" (John 8:54). And the apostle Paul said, "Love . . . seeks not its own" (1 Cor. 13:4–5 NKJV) and, "Let no man seek his own" (1 Cor. 10:24 KJV).

Not Just a Self-Exalting God, but Any God

But feeding our resistance to God's self-exaltation is something deeper. On the surface, we might mount a self-justifying moral case against God's supposed egotism, but in reality there is a much deeper rebellion in us that resists not just a self-exalting God, but any God—any real God who exists and who has authority over the world and us. Paul tells us that this is the mark of the human heart without the transforming death of Christ and the work of God's Spirit:

> The mind of the flesh is hostile to God, for it does not submit to God's law; indeed, it cannot. Those who are in the flesh cannot please God. (Rom. 8:7–8, my translation)

Paul contrasts those who have the "mind of the flesh" with those who have the mind of the Spirit (8:6). Then he describes those with the mind of the Spirit: "You, however, are not in the flesh but in the Spirit, if in fact the Spirit of God dwells in you" (8:9). We change from having the *mind of the flesh* to having the *mind of the Spirit* when the Spirit of God comes to dwell in us through faith in Christ (Gal. 3:2). Apart from the Spirit, received through faith, we are naturally insubordinate to God and resistant to his authority.

So the deepest problem we have in dealing with God's self-exaltation is not that we don't like some kinds of self-exalting authority but that fallen human nature does not like *any* kind of divine authority over our lives. The idea that God is unattractive to us because he acts for his own glory cloaks a deeper resistance: he is unattractive because he is God.

But What If?

But what if God's continual acting for his own glory proved to be less like an insecure, self-enhancing, needy bully and more like the star professional basketball player who drives his Porsche into the neighborhood because he genuinely loves inner-city kids and wants to give them the unimaginable pleasure of playing with their hero?

What if God's calling attention to his glory turned out to be less like a quack doctor who hangs out a sign that he's the best and more like a real doctor hanging out a sign because he is, in fact, the best, and he alone can do the procedure that will save the community from the spreading disease?

What if God's making known his superiority is less like an anxious college art teacher touting the greatness of his classes to shore up his reputation by attracting more students and more like the best artist in the world going to the poorest college and announcing that he is going to give an absolutely free course so that he can show the lowliest student the secrets of his superior skill?

What if God's public promotion of his power is less like a narcissistic, fame-hungry, military general who seeks victory by sacrificing thousands of soldiers from his safe position behind the lines and more like the truly greatest general who wins both victory and fame by willingly dying at the front line for the troops he loves?

In other words, what if, in the end, we discovered that the beauty of God turns out to be the kind that comes to climax in being shared? And what if the attitude we thought was mere self-promotion was instead the pursuit of sharing the greatest pleasure possible for all who would have it?

What if things turn out something like Jonathan Edwards believed they would?

> Doubtless the happiness of the saints in heaven shall be so great, that the very majesty of God shall be exceedingly shown in the greatness, and magnificence, and fullness of their enjoyments and delights.[1]

---

1   Jonathan Edwards, *The Miscellanies (Entries 833–1152)*, ed. Amy Plantinga Pauw (New Haven, CT: Yale University Press, 2002), 189 (#934).

The Great and Last End of God's Works

I have addressed God's self-exaltation toward the beginning of this book because, when we turn to the question of God's final goal in providence, we find in Scripture that his own glory—the beauty of the full panorama of his perfections—is God's most recurring and all-embracing aim. All the efforts I have made to survey and think through the Scriptures have confirmed that Jonathan Edwards's conclusion in his *Dissertation Concerning the End for Which God Created the World* is correct.[2] This is one of the most important and influential books I have ever read. Here Edwards piles reason upon reason and Scripture on Scripture to make this point:

> Thus we see that the great and last end of God's works which is so variously expressed in Scripture, is indeed but *one*; and this *one* end is most properly and comprehensively called "the glory of God"; by which name it is most commonly called in Scripture.[3]

In other words, as soon as we focus on the question about God's goal in his works of providence, we must face the fact that the Bible repeatedly and pervasively points us to God's doing these works for his own glory. And if Edwards is right (in both the quotes given above), "for his glory" does not mean to *get* glory which he doesn't already have, but rather to display and vindicate and communicate his glory for the everlasting enjoyment of his people—that is, for all those who, instead of resenting God's self-exaltation, receive him as their supreme treasure.

That is a big *if*—*if* Edwards is right. Part 2 of this book will put that *if* to the test of Scripture. We will focus in part 2 not mainly on

---

2   For an introduction to the life of Edwards, the implication of his theology for evangelicalism, and the complete text of *The End for Which God Created the World*, see John Piper, *God's Passion for His Glory: Living the Vision of Jonathan Edwards* (Wheaton, IL: Crossway, 1998).

3   Jonathan Edwards, *Ethical Writings*, ed. Paul Ramsey and John E. Smith, vol. 8, *The Works of Jonathan Edwards* (New Haven, CT: Yale University Press, 1989), 530. Or see John Piper, *God's Passion for His Glory*, 246.

the nature or the extent of divine providence, but on the ultimate goal of all that God does in his providence over the world. It will become increasingly clear why God's aim to communicate his glory is not at odds with his aim to make us fully and eternally happy. We will see from the Scriptures, not just from Jonathan Edwards, why the majesty of God shines in the fullness of the saints' enjoyments of his glory.

Glory as the Whole Panorama of God's Excellencies

Let's be clear about Edwards's meaning (and mine). When he says that God's one end, or goal, in providence "is most properly and comprehensively called 'the glory of God,'" he does not mean that the glory of God is one divine attribute among others. For example, he does not mean that the glory of God is vying with the love of God or the grace of God as the end of providence. God's glory does not vie with his love; it includes his love.

Above I used the phrase "the beauty of the full panorama of his perfections" to define the glory of God. In other words, God's glory is not any one of his perfections but the beauty of all of them, and the perfectly harmonious way they relate to each other, and the way they are expressed in creation and history.

This is important to emphasize because some scholars choose to make one perfection of God so prominent in their understanding of his providence that other perfections are, so to speak, deactivated. This is most often done with God's love. For example, someone may believe that the love of God would not allow a particular act of God's providence—say, the fact that "the angel of the Lord went out and struck down 185,000 in the camp of the Assyrians" (Isa. 37:36). They may ask, "If love seeks the good of the beloved, how could God allow, let alone perform, an act that created hundreds of thousands of Assyrian orphans and widows overnight?"

This is why I drew attention in chapter 1 to the wise and biblical way the Westminster Confession expressed the goal of God in his works of providence. They all exist, it says, "to the praise of the glory of his wisdom, power, justice, goodness, and mercy." Not just one of these excellencies. All of them. I agree. So when I say that God's final goal in providence is the fullest display and vindication and communication of his glory for the everlasting enjoyment of his redeemed people, I don't mean to reduce this goal to any one aspect of his glory. I mean that the greatness and beauty of his glory is all of his excellencies working in perfect harmony.[4]

4   Elsewhere I have tried to show from Scripture that "the glory of God is the infinite beauty and greatness of his manifold perfections." John Piper, "What Is God's Glory?," Desiring God, July 6, 2009, https://www.desiringgod.org/interviews/what-is-gods-glory.

PART 2

THE ULTIMATE GOAL
OF PROVIDENCE

SECTION 1

The Ultimate Goal of Providence
before Creation and in Creation

3

Before Creation

We do not ordinarily use the word *providence* to describe God's action before creation. But since our focus here in part 2 is on God's *purpose* in providence, we will see a fuller, more faithful picture of that purpose if we listen to the biblical witness about how it existed before God made the world. Scripture pulls back the curtain on eternity past and gives us a glimpse of God's act in choosing a people for himself before creation. God's goal is clearly stated:

> [God] chose us in [Christ] before the foundation of the world, that we should be holy and blameless before him. In love he predestined us for adoption to himself as sons through Jesus Christ, according to the purpose of his will, *to the praise of the glory of his grace.* (Eph. 1:4–6, my translation)

One express purpose of God's choosing a people "before the foundation of the world" is that we would be "holy and blameless before him" (1:4). But how will that holiness express itself? Is there a more ultimate goal? Yes. Our being chosen carries with it a God-given destiny—a *predestination*—planned *before* creation. It's found in verses 5 and 6: "He predestined us for adoption to himself as sons through Jesus Christ, according to the purpose of his will, *to the praise of the glory of his grace.*"

If you divide this act of *predestination* (1:5–6) into its four parts and relate them to each other in order from the deepest root to the most ultimate fruit, the progression moves like this: (1) the purpose of God's will gives rise to (2) a plan that through Jesus Christ (3) God's elect would receive adoption as sons with (4) the ultimate goal that they would praise the glory of God's grace.

The ultimate goal of God in initiating the entire plan of salvation before creation was that he would be praised for the glory of his grace.

Not Just Glory, but the Praise of Glory

Five decades ago, when I first saw this statement of God's ultimate purpose in our salvation, what riveted my attention was not only how unmistakably clear the purpose statement is ("to the praise of the glory of his grace"), but also the fact that Paul circles back to these very words two more times in Ephesians 1.

In Ephesians 1:11–12 he says that we have been "predestined according to the purpose of him who works all things according to the counsel of his will, so that we who were the first to hope in Christ might be *to the praise of his glory.*" Existence for the praise of God's glory! And two verses later, he says that the Holy Spirit is "the guarantee of our inheritance until we acquire possession of it *to the praise of his glory*" (1:14). Inheritance for the praise of God's glory! Notice: his purpose is that we might *be*, and his purpose is that we might *possess.* *Be in existence* to the praise of his glory. *Possess* the inheritance to the praise of his glory. In other words, God's goal from before creation was that *what we are* and *what we have* would give rise to praise for his glory.

So in this first chapter of Ephesians, we see God *choosing* us for his glory (1:4), *predestining* us for his glory (1:5), *adopting* us for his glory (1:5), destining us to *be* for his glory (1:12), and securing our *inheritance* for his glory (1:14). Or, to be more clear and precise, his goal, expressed three times, is not simply "God's glory" but "the *praise of his glory*" (1:6, 12, 14).

Calling attention to the goal of *praise* clarifies how we should understand what Jonathan Edwards meant when he said "that the great and last end of God's works . . . is most properly and comprehensively called 'the glory of God.'"[1] God's goal is not simply that the glory of his perfections shine, but that we find God's glory *praiseworthy*.

No, not just *find* it as praiseworthy, but *feel* it as praiseworthy—feel its value—because otherwise our "praise" would be hypocrisy. God is really pursuing the exaltation of his beauty in the *enjoyment* of his praising people. To the degree that our praise is without feeling, to that degree it falls short of commending the preciousness of what we praise. Half-hearted praise is poor commendation. But God does not intend for the final praise he seeks to be a poor commendation. His glory is of infinite value. It is infinitely beautiful. Therefore, God, in all his glory, will prove to be more satisfying than anything or anyone else.

The Discovery of C. S. Lewis

I linger over the implications of the word *praise* in Ephesians 1:6, 12, and 14 because it really does contain a key part of the solution to the problem raised in chapter 2 of this volume concerning God's self-exaltation in Scripture. C. S. Lewis, like so many others, stumbled over this reality in Scripture, and it was his own lingering over the nature of praise that provided the breakthrough for him.

At first, he complained that the way the Scriptures command us to praise God seemed to him like "a vain woman who wants compliments." But instead of turning away in disgust, Lewis looked more

---

1   Cited in the previous chap., p. 43. Jonathan Edwards, *Ethical Writings*, ed. Paul Ramsey and John E. Smith, vol. 8, *The Works of Jonathan Edwards* (New Haven, CT: Yale University Press, 1989), 530.

deeply, as he did with so many things, into the reality of praise. Oh, that we all would penetrate through words to the reality behind them. Here is what Lewis found:

> The most obvious fact about praise—whether of God or anything—strangely escaped me. I thought of it in terms of compliment, approval, or the giving of honor. I had never noticed that all enjoyment [note well!] spontaneously overflows into praise. . . . The world rings with praise—lovers praising their mistresses, readers their favorite poet, walkers praising the countryside, players praising their favorite game—praise of weather, wines, dishes, actors, horses, colleges, countries, historical personages, children, flowers, mountains, rare stamps, rare beetles, even sometimes politicians and scholars.
>
> My whole, more general difficulty about the praise of God depended on my absurdly denying to us, as regards the supremely Valuable, what we delight [!] to do, what indeed we can't help doing, about everything else we value.
>
> I think we delight to praise what we enjoy because the praise not merely expresses but completes the enjoyment; it is its appointed consummation. It is not out of compliment that lovers keep on telling one another how beautiful they are; the delight is incomplete till it is expressed.[2]

God's Goal: The Consummation of Our Joy in God

With this in mind, let's return to Ephesians 1 and the way Paul expressed the goal for God's plan to choose, predestine, and adopt a people. He says three times that the goal is the praise of God's glory (1:6, 12, 14). Now, if Lewis is right (and I think he is), then God's pursuit of our praise for his glory is his pursuit of *the consummation of*

2   C. S. Lewis, *Reflections on the Psalms* (New York: Harcourt, Brace & World, 1958), 93–95.

our enjoyment of that glory. "We delight to praise what we enjoy because the praise not merely expresses but completes the enjoyment; it is its appointed consummation."[3]

This means that *God's* self-exaltation is utterly different from all *human* self-exaltation. When humans exalt themselves, they call attention to something that can never satisfy the people they want to impress: themselves. No mere human, no matter how exalted, can be the all-satisfying treasure of another human. Nor is such satisfaction of others even a typical human motive for self-exaltation. For humans, self-exaltation is typically a way of getting, not giving—using people, not serving them. But it is otherwise with God.

In exalting himself—that is, in upholding and communicating his glory—God aims to *give* enjoyment to all who will have him as their supreme treasure. And since praise is the appointed consummation of such enjoyment, God is not indifferent to our praise. If he aims at our joy in him, he will aim at our praise—joy's consummation. He will not limit our joy by discouraging our praise.

God's Self-Exaltation vs. Human Self-Exaltation

So *God's* self-exaltation is different from *human* self-exaltation in that, by exalting himself, he is not distracting us from what is ultimately satisfying, but displaying it and inviting us into the enjoyment of it. When *we* exalt ourselves, we misdirect the hearts of others. We try to get their attention and praise for ourselves. We are thus not only encouraging idolatry but encouraging misery. We are luring people away from joy. We are saying, in effect, that it is better for them to admire us than to admire God—to enjoy our glory rather than God's.

Paradoxically, then, God is the one being in the universe for whom self-exaltation is a form of love. For he is the only being whose worth and beauty can satisfy the human soul fully and forever. When God

---

3 Lewis, *Reflection on the Psalms*, 95.

makes his praise the goal of his providence, he is pursuing our full and lasting pleasure. That is love.

This is why God's self-exaltation does not contradict those Scriptures we saw in the previous chapter that treat self-exaltation as sin (John 8:54; 1 Cor. 10:24; 13:5). God never sins (1 John 1:5). Nor did Jesus (Heb. 4:15). Yet people thought Jesus sinned when he exalted himself to forgive sins. "Who is this who speaks blasphemies? Who can forgive sins but God alone?" (Luke 5:21). But he was not sinning, because he was more than man. He really could forgive sins against God, for he was God. The point is this: there are things that are sinful for *man* to do that are not sinful for *God* to do. Such as forgive sins—or uphold and communicate his glory for the enjoyment of the world.

The Massive, Omitted Place of Grace

I realize that so far in this chapter I have totally omitted any discussion of the word *grace* as part of God's goal in Ephesians 1:6. Yet the key phrase that expresses the ultimate goal of God's providence terminates on *grace*. God chooses, predestines, and adopts "to the praise of the glory of *his grace*." My omission is not owing to the unimportance of grace, nor to the fact that Paul omits the word in his repetition of this purpose in verses 12 and 14, where he writes, "to the praise of his glory." My reason for the omission is not that grace is minor in God's goal, but because it is massive. It will be pervasive in the chapters to come.

Let me give just a taste of what I mean by *massive*. The implications of God aiming at the "praise of the glory of his grace" *before* the foundation of the world are staggering. For grace is God's merciful response to *undeserving* people. But sin had not yet entered the world when there was no world! There were no undeserving people. To say that praising *grace* is God's goal seems to imply that there had to be sin and rebellion against God. Seems? No. This passage does more than *seem* to imply that God is assuming the existence of sin in his creation—a creation that does not yet exist.

The Blood of the Beloved before Creation?

The praising of grace that God aims at before the foundation of the world will be accomplished "through Jesus Christ." "He predestined us for adoption to himself as sons *through Jesus Christ* . . . to the praise of the glory of his grace" (Eph. 1:5–6). What does that mean? Paul tells us plainly in verse 7: "In [the Beloved—Jesus!] we have redemption through his blood, the forgiveness of our trespasses, according to the riches of his grace."

This takes your breath away. Before the foundation of the world, before there were any human beings who had sinned, before any human needed to be *redeemed*, God planned that the goal of creation and providence would be "the praise of the glory of his *grace*," and that this grace would come to people through "the forgiveness of . . . trespasses," "through [the] blood" of "the Beloved"—the beloved Son of God (cf. Col. 1:13). In other words, not only was grace for undeserving people planned as the capstone of God's glory, but God planned for that grace to be expressed through the blood shedding of his beloved Son for trespasses that he never committed.

You can see, perhaps, why I say that my omission of an extended treatment of grace in this chapter is owing not to the fact that grace is minor but to the fact that it is massive. In the coming chapters, we will see repeatedly that God's purpose is to exalt his glory through the exercise of his grace. His aim is the greatness of his name and the gladness of his *undeserving* people. That is, his aim is the God-exalting, soul-satisfying praise of the glory of *his grace*.[4]

---

4 Treating the praise of the glory of "grace" as the ultimate end of God's providence does not imply that the glory of his other attributes, such as wisdom and justice (expressed in wrath against sin), are muted or minimized. Rather, in their proper biblical proportions, they ultimately serve to magnify the glory of God's grace toward the redeemed.

And the glory of that grace will be seen most beautifully in the suffering of the beloved Son of God for undeserving sinners. Therefore, we will deal much more fully with the centrality of the Son of God in God's pursuit of "the praise of the glory of his grace."[5] It will become plain concerning Christ that "all things were created through him and *for him*" (Col. 1:16). But we turn now to the purpose of God's providence that comes to expression in the act of creation itself.

5   See especially chap. 12, where I deal with 2 Tim. 1:9 and Rev. 13:8.

4

The Act of Creation

God's purposeful government of the world presumes not only a plan for the world before creation, as we have seen in Ephesians 1, but also the coming into existence of the world. Providence presumes creation. Since creation sets the stage where the works of providence will take place, it is likely that the ultimate purpose of creation is the same as the ultimate purpose of the works of providence that will be performed in the theater of creation. We may test this likelihood by the biblical texts dealt with in this chapter.

God Created All Things "for God"

In 1 Corinthians 8:6 Paul says, "There is one God, the Father, from whom are all things and *for whom* we exist." Similarly, the author of Hebrews writes, "It was fitting that he, *for whom* and by whom all things exist, in bringing many sons to glory, should make the founder of their salvation perfect through suffering" (Heb. 2:10). In other words, God created the world for God. He is the one "*for whom* we exist." He is the one "*for whom* . . . all things exist."

The phrase "for God" is ambiguous. Without any context, it could imply that God is needy—that he created the world because he was hungry and needed something to eat, or because he was bored and needed something to entertain him, or because he was lonely and needed companionship from men. Paul repudiates such views. He says, "The God who made the world and everything in it, being Lord of heaven and earth . . . is not served by human hands, as though he needed anything, since he himself gives to all mankind life and breath and everything" (Acts 17:24–25). God does not create out of need. He is a *giver* in creation, not a *taker*. He is a self-sufficient benefactor, not a dependent beneficiary: "He himself *gives* to all mankind life and breath and everything."

In Romans 11:34–36 Paul underscores this point and then makes clear what "for God" means as the purpose of creation:

> "Who has known the mind of the Lord,
>   or who has been his counselor?"
> "Or who has given a gift to him
>   that he might be repaid?"

> For from him and through him and to him are all things. To him be glory forever. Amen.

Those two rhetorical questions ("Who has known the mind of the Lord?" "Who has given a gift to him?") expect an answer: no one. In other words, no one can make any contribution to God's wisdom by counseling him. And no one can expect a repayment from God, as if we could put him in our debt by giving him something he did not already own. This is what we mean by saying that God is self-sufficient.

What then does "for God" mean when Paul says that everything was created and exists "for God"? Romans 11:36 clarifies. The reason no one can add to God's wisdom or give him a gift he doesn't already own—that is, the reason God is self-sufficient—is that "from him and through him and to him are all things." As the Creator, he is the source of all being ("from him"). Not only do all things come "from him," but their activity is also carried out "through him." He brought all things into being, and in his providence, he holds all things in being and governs them so that their movements and designs are "through him"—through his willing and acting.

Paul concludes that the upshot of God's creating ("from him") and governing ("through him") all things is that all things are "to him." This phrase in Greek (εἰς αὐτὸν) is identical with the phrase "for him" in 1 Corinthians 8:6 ("There is one God . . . for whom [εἰς αὐτὸν] we exist"). But here in Romans 11:36 Paul virtually defines for us what he means by the phrase: ". . . *to him* [εἰς αὐτὸν] are all things. *To him be glory forever. Amen.*" That all things were created and exist "for God," or "to God," means that they exist and are designed and governed in such a way that God would be seen and known and worshiped as glorious forever.

The Praises of Heaven for the Creator of All Things

Therefore, the meaning of the statement that God created the world *for God* (Rom. 11:36; 1 Cor. 8:6; Heb. 2:10) is that God created the world with the goal that it would display his glory and find an echo in the praises of his people—as it did in Paul's words "To him be glory forever." This is Paul's exultation in the power and wisdom and self-sufficiency of God. To awaken and intensify and perfect that exultation was God's goal in creating the world.

Therefore, in the book of Revelation, when we are granted a glimpse into the perfected exultation of heaven, we hear the words

Worthy are you, our Lord and God,
> to receive glory and honor and power,
for you created all things,
> and by your will they existed and were created. (Rev. 4:11)

Heaven surely responds to God's act of creation the way God intended when he created. And its response is praise. "Worthy are you . . . to receive glory . . . *for you created all things.*" To say that God "receives" glory, honor, and power does not mean that God was formerly deficient in glory, honor, and power. It means that he received the *acknowledgment*, the *ascription*, and the *celebration* of the glory, honor, and power he always had. His act of creation put this glory on display ("The heavens declare the glory of God," Ps. 19:1). The creatures made in God's image see this glory, joyfully embrace the beauty and preciousness of it, and give it back in the form of praise, exultation, and lives built on his supreme worth—all of which ascribes to God what he already is.

Goal at the End, Goal from the Beginning

Since the *last* book of the Bible gives us a glimpse of the final effect of creation in producing echoes of God's glory in the songs of heaven, we should not be surprised when we read in the *first* chapter of the Bible how God prepared for that very outcome. He created man—the capstone of his creation—in his own image and commissioned him to multiply and fill the earth with images of God:

> God created man in his own image,
>   in the image of God he created him;
>   male and female he created them.

> And God blessed them. And God said to them, "Be fruitful and multiply and fill the earth." (Gen. 1:27–28)

Whatever else it means to be created in the image of God, this much is clear: the purpose of images is to image! We carve images of people and build statues of them in order to portray those people—to put them on display. Thus when God creates human beings *in his image*, puts himself on display, and commands that the earth be full of such images of himself, it is clear that God's goal in creation is the display of God.

To be sure, nonhuman creation—the world of nature—is everywhere revealing the glory of God (Pss. 19:1; 104:31; Rom. 1:20). And this is manifestly God's idea, since nature does not invent its own purpose. Nevertheless, in creation God is aiming at a display of his glory far greater than the wonders of nature—amazing as they are. He is aiming at a world filled with worshiping human beings. We can see this in the promise of Numbers 14:21: "The earth shall be filled with the glory of the LORD." Then, more precisely, we see it in the similar promise of Habakkuk 2:14: "The earth will be filled with the *knowledge* of the glory of the LORD as the waters cover the sea" (cf. Isa. 11:9).

In one sense, nature itself fills the earth with the glory of the Lord. But that is not the ultimate goal. In order for God's purpose in creation to be attained, there must be a world filled with the "*knowledge* of the glory of the LORD." Trees may clap their hands for God (Isa. 55:12), but they do not *know* what they are doing. Such conscious, joyful knowing and loving and praising is the destiny of man, not nature. The goal of creation is not simply the echo of God's excellence in the exulting fields (Ps. 96:12), the rejoicing crocuses (Isa. 35:1), the singing mountains (Isa. 55:12), and the hand-clapping rivers (Ps. 98:8). The goal is the echo of God's excellence in the perceiving minds and praising hearts of human beings created in his image.

When the angel of God cries out to the world in Revelation 14:7, "Worship [God] who made heaven and earth, the sea and the springs of water," he is not crying out to trees and hills and rivers, but to human beings. We are the ones destined to fill the earth with worship—worship of the God who made heaven and earth.

Old Creation for Christ, New Creation in Christ

In chapter 3 I postponed a focus on the massive place of Christ-centered grace while discussing the goal of God before creation. I am aware that I am doing the same thing in this discussion of God's goal in creation itself. I have not yet focused on the role of Christ and his saving work in the final goal of creation. I am saving that for part 2, section 3, where it will become evident that the whole universe exists for the glory of Christ and his achievement on the cross and in the resurrection.

But let me give you a foretaste.

The First Creation Is through Christ and for Christ

First, Paul teaches that "all things were created through [Christ] and for [Christ]" (Col. 1:16). In other words, when we saw that all things were created for God, Paul did not mean God the Father minus God the Son. The glory of the Son and the glory of the Father are both purposes of creation. Later, we will ponder more fully how they are related.[1]

Christ's Glory Supremely Displayed in Suffering to Save Sinners

Second, the Christ-exalting aim of creation comes to climax in the greatest work in creation—namely, the work of salvation. No creation, no salvation. And the most glorious part of that saving work is what Jesus Christ achieved on the cross. So in saying that creation exists for the glory of Christ (Col. 1:16), we mean, mainly, the glory of who he was and what he did on Good Friday.

The book of Revelation makes this clear: because of the slaying of Jesus on Good Friday, the final worship of heaven will not simply, or even primarily, be an echo of God's excellence in *creation*, but also, and mainly, an echo of Christ's excellence in *salvation*. This is what heaven sings:

> Worthy are you to take the scroll
>   and to open its seals,
> for you were slain, and by your blood you ransomed
>   people for God
>   from every tribe and language and people and
>   nation,
> and you have made them a kingdom and priests to
>   our God,
>   and they shall reign on the earth. . . .

---

1   See chap. 14, where we will see that "the glory of Christ, who is the image of God" and "the glory of God in the face of Christ" are one glory (2 Cor. 4:4–6).

Worthy is the Lamb who was slain,

to receive power and wealth and wisdom and might

and honor and glory and blessing! (Rev. 5:9–10, 12)

Yes, we will sing, "Worthy are you . . . for you *created* all things"
(Rev. 4:11). But we will move through this glory (without leaving it
behind) to the even greater glory of the slaying of the Son of God to
ransom sinners. "Worthy are you . . . for you were slain, and by your
blood you ransomed people for God" (Rev. 5:9).

Let it not go unspoken that everything we said in chapters 2 and 3
about praising Christ as the consummation of enjoying Christ is
implicit here in the praises of the glory of Christ in Revelation 4 and 5.
The ultimate purpose of God in magnifying the glory of his Son in his
sufferings will reach its climax when the excellence of Christ finds its
echo in the unbridled joy of his praising people.

A New Blood-Bought Creation in Christ by the Spirit

Third, this ransom results in the outpouring of the Holy Spirit on
God's ransomed people so that they are made a new creation in the
image of Christ. The first creation was corrupted and made futile
(Rom. 8:20–21) in the catastrophe of man's fall into sin (Gen. 3:1–6;
Rom. 5:13–21). But in falling short of providing a flawless picture of
God's beauty, the first creation became the theater for an even greater
display of glory—the glory of saving grace through Christ.

The glory of this grace is seen not only in the actual beauty of Christ
and his atoning work on the cross, but also in the achievement of the
blood-bought work of the Holy Spirit's transforming ransomed sinners
into the image of Christ.

[God] saved us . . . by the washing of regeneration

and *renewal of the Holy Spirit*,

whom he poured out on us richly

through Jesus Christ our Savior. (Titus 3:5–6)

Because of Christ's ransom, the Holy Spirit is poured out on the ransomed people with the result that they are *renewed*.

That renewal is another name for the "new creation." "If anyone is in Christ, he is a new creation" (2 Cor. 5:17). "Neither circumcision counts for anything, nor uncircumcision, but a *new creation*" (Gal. 6:15). Every person ransomed by Christ, when the Holy Spirit brings him to faith and *renews* him, is a "new self . . . renewed in knowledge after the image of its *creator*" (Col. 3:10). This image is the image of Christ, who is the image of God (2 Cor. 3:18; 4:4). We will see, when we take up this transformative work of the Spirit in the New Testament, that the radiance of the glory of Christ in the life of the new creature is, at its heart, the radiance of a life of joy in Christ so satisfying that it empowers all the sacrifices that reveal the beauty of the love of Christ (see part 3, section 8).

New Creation, Not Just Restoration

This new creation is not a simple restoration of the image mankind had at the first. It is greater because it is "in Christ." Henry Alford points out:

> Whatever may have been God's image in which the first Adam was created, it is certain that the image of God, in which Christ's Spirit recreates us, will be as much more glorious than that, as the second man is more glorious than the first.[2]

One difference is that our calling as new creatures in Christ is to consciously reflect the specific beauties of the incarnate Christ. "We are [God's] workmanship, *created in Christ Jesus* for good works" (Eph. 2:10). For all eternity, the calling of the redeemed will be to live as images of Christ Jesus—not just to image God in general, as at the

---

2   Henry Alford, *Alford's Greek Testament: An Exegetical and Critical Commentary*, vol. 3 (Grand Rapids, MI: Guardian Press, 1976), 234.

first, but to image Christ. "We all, with unveiled face, beholding the glory of the Lord, are being transformed into the same image from one degree of glory to another" (2 Cor. 3:18).

So Much More to Say of the Glory of Christ and His Suffering

Thus, the aim of creation, and the aim of the salvation accomplished in the theater of creation, is the glorification of Jesus Christ. And what we have seen is that he is glorified both in the joy-consummating praises of his people and in the newly created lives of love in conformity to Christ's image. There is more to say—much more—about Christ and his suffering for undeserving sinners as the consummate expression of God's glory, and about its reflected radiance in the rejoicing of God's new creatures. But we are moving through Scripture along the history of God's unfolding revelation. So we will save the fuller focus on the glory of Christ for the moment when he arrives to the shout:

> Glory to God in the highest,
>> and on earth peace among those with whom he is pleased!
>> (Luke 2:14)

The glory of God and the glory of the Son of God in creation are one glory, just as the goal of the first creation through Christ and the goal of the new creation in Christ are one glory.

When Insights from All of Scripture Are Inexhaustible

In part 2, section 2, we trace God's ultimate purpose of God's providence in the history of Israel. Therefore, we are passing over without comment the chapters in between (Gen. 4–11). This is not because they have nothing to contribute to the question of God's ultimate purpose in the world. In fact, the story of the building of the tower of Babel is designed to show how man's sin is diametrically the opposite for God's ultimate purpose:

> Then they said, "Come, let us build ourselves a city and a tower with its top in the heavens, and *let us make a name for ourselves*, lest we be dispersed over the face of the whole earth." (Gen. 11:4)

Man was put on the earth to make a name for God, not for himself. So, in an indirect way, God's ultimate purpose is trumpeted by the debacle of this God-belittling, man-exalting tower. So I don't pass over these chapters because they have nothing to contribute but simply because I must be selective, since the possible insights from Scripture for our purpose are inexhaustible.

In the chapter that follows, we will look at the history of Israel from beginning to end—from a 30,000-foot elevation, so to speak. What was God's ultimate purpose in choosing an ethnic people for himself and then, in all the mysterious providences, even to this day, dealing with Israel in such a unique way? Then in chapters 6–10, we will descend from that 30,000-foot elevation and land in several specific periods of Israel's history to see more closely how God expresses his ultimate purpose in providence in the history of Israel.

SECTION 2

The Ultimate Goal of Providence
in the History of Israel

5

Overview

From Abraham to the Age to Come

Before we narrow the lens of our focus to particular periods of Israel's history (the exodus, the giving of the law, the conquest of Canaan, the judges, the monarchy, the exile), this chapter opens the lens of our focus to all of Israel's history—from Abraham to the age to come—as we ask, What is the ultimate goal in this amazing story of God's providence?

Jewish History and Jesus Christ for the Nations

In chapter 12 of the first book of the Bible, the story is told of God's choosing Abram (now four thousand years ago) to become the father of a great nation that would bring blessings to all the peoples of the earth. This was the beginning of the history of Israel as God's chosen people, through which would come the Messiah, Jesus Christ, whose death and resurrection would bring the blessings of Abraham to the whole world. God planned that his remedy for the universal problem of sin and suffering would come through Israel and her Messiah.

It is important to see that God's election of Israel, and his making her the focus of his saving blessings in the Old Testament, sets the stage in world history for the global impact of Jesus Christ and his saving work for the sake of the nations. Israel's history is not an abortive attempt to achieve his saving purposes through Israel alone, which God abandoned and replaced with Jesus and the history of Christianity. From the beginning, God planned to make the history of Israel serve all the nations of the world through the coming of the Messiah. There are not two stories. There is one story of redemption in history. And this single story will prove to have one overarching purpose.

Before we focus on that purpose in the history of Israel, let's first see the biblical basis for the claim that God's plan for Israel and his plan for the saving, global impact of Jesus on all nations are, in fact, one plan.

"In You All the Families of the Earth Shall Be Blessed"

God did not choose Abraham (at first called Abram) because he was a worshiper of the true God. He was a pagan worshiping other gods. We read this in Joshua 24:2–3:

> Joshua said to all the people, "Thus says the LORD, the God of Israel, 'Long ago, your fathers lived beyond the Euphrates, Terah, the father of Abraham and of Nahor; and *they served other gods.* Then I took your father Abraham from beyond the River and led him through all the land of Canaan, and made his offspring many.'"

In spite of Abram's serving other gods, God chose him and "gave him the name Abraham" (Neh. 9:7). In that initial encounter, God says to him these all-important words:

> I will make of you a great nation, and I will bless you and make your name great, so that you will be a blessing. I will bless those who bless you, and him who dishonors you I will curse, and in you all the families of the earth shall be blessed. (Gen. 12:2–3)

I call these words "all-important" because, in the New Testament, Paul cites this last clause ("in you all the families of the earth shall be blessed") in Galatians 3 to make the point that even Gentiles who have faith in the Jewish Messiah will inherit the blessing of Abraham:

> It is those of faith who are the sons of Abraham. And the Scripture, foreseeing that God would justify the Gentiles by faith, preached the gospel beforehand to Abraham, saying, "In you shall all the nations be blessed" [Gen. 12:3]. So then, those who are of faith are blessed along with Abraham, the man of faith. (Gal. 3:7–9)

In other words, the Jewish Messiah's death on behalf of all sinners who will put their faith in him resulted in a stunning mystery coming true. "This mystery is that the Gentiles are fellow heirs, members of the same body, and partakers of the promise in Christ Jesus through the gospel" (Eph. 3:6). Or, as Paul puts it later in Galatians 3 (vv. 13–14): "Christ redeemed us from the curse of the law by becoming a curse for us . . . so that in Christ Jesus the blessing of Abraham might come to the Gentiles." God's saving purpose for Israel through the Messiah becomes a saving purpose for the world—for everyone who "shares the faith of Abraham" (Rom. 4:16).

Wild Olives In, Natural Branches Out

Paul puts all this in a picture in Romans 11. He pictures Israel as an olive tree with a rich, life-giving root—the covenant of promise made with Abraham (Rom. 11:17). He argues that participation in this rich root of salvation is enjoyed not by a mere ethnic connection to the tree, but by faith, which implies that Jews may be cut off because of unbelief, and Gentiles may be grafted in through faith. So Paul says to the Gentiles:

> If some of the [Jewish] branches were broken off, and you [Gentiles], although a wild olive shoot, were grafted in among the others and

now share in the nourishing root of the olive tree, do not be arrogant toward the branches. If you are, remember it is not you who support the root, but the root that supports you. (Rom. 11:17–18)

In other words, from the beginning of Israel's existence, there has always been a *true* Israel (elsewhere referred to as a *spiritual* Israel or *inward* Israel, Rom. 2:28–29), as well as a cultural and ethnic Israel. This true Israel is marked by faith, and therefore Gentiles who share the faith of Abraham may be part of it:

It depends on faith, in order that the promise may rest on grace and be guaranteed to all his offspring—not only to the adherent of the law but also to the one who shares the faith of Abraham, who is the father of us all. (Rom. 4:16)

This also means that Jewish people who reject the Messiah, Jesus, are not part of the true Israel:

For not all who are descended from Israel belong to Israel, and not all are children of Abraham because they are his offspring, but "Through Isaac shall your offspring be named." This means that it is not the children of the flesh who are the children of God, but the children of the promise are counted as offspring. (Rom. 9:6–8)

So being "children of the flesh"—that is, being ethnically Jewish—does not make you a child of God. Being physical "offspring" of Abraham does not make people "children of Abraham" in the spiritual, saving sense. Not all Israel is Israel. But some Gentiles may be "counted as offspring" through faith in the Messiah. They then belong to the true Israel.

For no one is a Jew who is merely one outwardly, nor is circumcision outward and physical. But a Jew is one inwardly, and circumcision is a matter of the heart, by the Spirit, not by the letter. His praise is not from man but from God. (Rom. 2:28–29)

How Much More Their Full Inclusion!

This participation of the Gentiles in the saving blessing of Abraham does not mean that there is no longer any divine purpose for ethnic Israel, even today. In Romans 11 Paul foresees the day when ethnic Israel, as a corporate reality, will be grafted back into the olive tree of Abraham's covenant blessing. This will be through faith in Jesus the Messiah. "If they do not continue in their unbelief, [they] will be grafted in, for God has the power to graft them in again" (Rom. 11:23).

This "if" will, in fact, become a reality. For "if [Israel's] failure means riches for the Gentiles, how much more will their full inclusion mean!" (Rom. 11:12, see all of 11:11–16). God will lift the veil from their eyes (2 Cor. 3:12–16) and remove the hardening of unbelief (Rom. 11:25), and they will look "on him whom they have pierced . . . [and] mourn for him, as one mourns for an only child" (Zech. 12:10), and so "all Israel will be saved" (Rom. 11:26).

The Sweep of God's Focus on Israel

We turn now to focus on statements in Scripture that express God's purpose in choosing Israel and dealing mainly with Israel, rather than the other nations, for two thousand years, until the Messiah came. When I say God was dealing mainly with Israel, I imply two things. One is that God was, in fact, doing millions of works of providence in the world at large, both in nature and in world affairs (see part 3, sections 2–6). The other implication is that "in past generations [God] allowed all the nations to walk in their own ways" (Acts 14:16). Paul called these past generations "times of ignorance" that God has now, in Christ, brought to an end with his mission to the world. He is now commanding "all people everywhere to repent" (Acts 17:30) and believe in the name of Jesus, since "there is no other name under heaven given among men by which we must be saved" (Acts 4:12).

Nevertheless, until Christ came, the history of God's redeeming work in the world was mainly the history of Israel. To be sure, through all of that two-thousand-year history there were repeated pointers toward God's saving purpose for all the nations (for example, Rahab, Ruth, Jonah, Psalm 67). Yet the record of God's saving dealings with the world—dealings that led men out of the ruin of sin into a relationship with God—was a record of God's focus on Israel. This is what the Old Testament is.

God's Pervasive Plan and Hand in Israel's History

Before we ask, What was God's ultimate purpose in this history of Israel? it would be good to remind ourselves that the story of Israel's history really is a story of God's providential action. The Bible is radically oriented on God as the decisive actor in the history of Israel. I am not aware of any narration of history outside the Bible that compares with the way the Bible narrates the history of Israel. In the Old and New Testaments, history is portrayed as pervasively performed by God. In spite of real human agency at almost every turn, God is treated as the one who brings Israel's history to pass. This is why we can speak of a purpose of God's providence in Israel's history.

To take only one example, consider Paul's first sermon in the book of Acts—the one he preached in the synagogue in Antioch of Pisidia in Acts 13. I include the lengthy text here so that you can check my bullet points below as they appear in the sermon. Perhaps we are so familiar with this biblical way of writing history that we overlook how astonishing it is. No one writes history like this today. In the list below this Bible passage, I highlight with italics how God is portrayed (seventeen times) as the actor in Israel's history.

So Paul stood up, and motioning with his hand said:
"Men of Israel and you who fear God, listen. The God of this people Israel chose our fathers and made the people great during their stay in the land of Egypt, and with uplifted arm he led them out of it. And for about forty years he put up with them in

the wilderness. And after destroying seven nations in the land of Canaan, he gave them their land as an inheritance. All this took about 450 years. And after that he gave them judges until Samuel the prophet. Then they asked for a king, and God gave them Saul the son of Kish, a man of the tribe of Benjamin, for forty years. And when he had removed him, he raised up David to be their king, of whom he testified and said, 'I have found in David the son of Jesse a man after my heart, who will do all my will.' Of this man's offspring God has brought to Israel a Savior, Jesus, as he promised. Before his coming, John had proclaimed a baptism of repentance to all the people of Israel. And as John was finishing his course, he said, 'What do you suppose that I am? I am not he. No, but behold, after me one is coming, the sandals of whose feet I am not worthy to untie.'

"Brothers, sons of the family of Abraham, and those among you who fear God, to us has been sent the message of this salvation. For those who live in Jerusalem and their rulers, because they did not recognize him nor understand the utterances of the prophets, which are read every Sabbath, fulfilled them by condemning him. And though they found in him no guilt worthy of death, they asked Pilate to have him executed. And when they had carried out all that was written of him, they took him down from the tree and laid him in a tomb. But God raised him from the dead, and for many days he appeared to those who had come up with him from Galilee to Jerusalem, who are now his witnesses to the people. And we bring you the good news that what God promised to the fathers, this he has fulfilled to us their children by raising Jesus." (Acts 13:16–33)

Here's my condensed version of this sermon to draw attention to the relentless focus on God as the one who is the decisive actor in Israel's history.

- "The *God* of this people Israel chose our fathers" (13:17a).
- "[*God*] made the people great during their stay in the land of Egypt" (13:17b).
- "With uplifted arm [*God*] led them out of it" (13:17c).
- "For about forty years [*God*] put up with them in the wilderness" (13:18).
- "[God destroyed] seven nations in the land of Canaan" (13:19a).
- "[*God*] gave them their land as an inheritance" (13:19b).
- "After that [*God*] gave them judges until Samuel the prophet" (13:20).
- "Then they asked for a king, and *God* gave them Saul" (13:21).
- "[*God*] . . . removed him" (13:22a).
- "[*God*] raised up David to be their king" (13:22b).
- "Of this man's offspring *God* has brought to Israel a Savior, Jesus" (13:23a).
- ". . . as [*God*] promised" (13:23b).
- "Brothers, . . . to us has been sent [by *God*] the message of this salvation" (13:26).
- "Because [the rulers] did not recognize [Jesus] nor understand the utterances of the prophets, [they] fulfilled them [by *God's* guiding hand] by condemning him" (13:27).
- "But *God* raised him from the dead" (13:30).
- "We bring you the good news that what *God* promised to the fathers . . ." (13:32).
- "This [*God*] has fulfilled . . . by raising Jesus" (13:33).

The pervasive action of God is portrayed in this narrative not just by the frequency and consistency of God's action, but also by the remarkable way Paul speaks about the fulfillment of this story in Jesus. For example, in verse 27, Paul goes out of his way to show that even those who did not know God—who were out of step with God and did not grasp the prophecies of Scripture—nevertheless fulfilled those very prophecies. They did what God planned and prophesied:

> For those who live in Jerusalem and their rulers, because *they did not recognize him nor understand the utterances of the prophets*, which are read every Sabbath, *fulfilled them* by condemning him.

This is amazing. Precisely *because* the rulers did not know the prophecies, they fulfilled them! What's the point of saying such a thing? The point is this: if a person reads and understands God's prophecies and then fulfills them, we might conclude that he chose to partner with God to get them done. But if the rulers do *not* know the prophecies, and yet they act precisely in accord with them, who is at work *seeing to it* that this happens? God is. That's the point. Paul is on a mission here to make sure we see that the history of Israel is God's work.[1] It is divine providence.

What Was God's Ultimate Purpose in the History of Israel?

In view of that kind of narrative, we see how warranted we are in asking the question about God's ultimate purpose in the history of Israel. If Israel's history were guided decisively by human hands, or satanic hands, rather than God's hand and plan (Acts 4:28), it would be futile to ask what goal God was accomplishing in this history of Israel. But it is not futile. It is essential.

---

1 For a similar God-saturated recounting of Israel's history, see Josh. 24:1–13, where God himself narrates Israel's history in which humans were indeed acting, but in which God declares himself to be the decisive cause: "I took your father Abraham from beyond the River and led him through all the land of Canaan, and made his offspring many. I gave him Isaac. And to Isaac I gave Jacob and Esau. And I gave Esau the hill country. . . . I sent Moses and Aaron, and I plagued Egypt with what I did in the midst of it, and afterward I brought you out. . . . [The Lord] put darkness between you and the Egyptians and made the sea come upon them. . . . Then I brought you to the land of the Amorites . . . and I gave them into your hand . . . and I destroyed them before you. . . . I delivered you out of [the hand of Balaam]. . . . And I gave [the peoples] into your hand. And I sent the hornet before you; . . . it was not by your sword or by your bow. I gave you a land on which you had not labored."

What we are about to see (in the rest of section 2) is that God's over-arching purpose in these dealings with Israel was *that he would be glorified.* "You are my servant, Israel," he says in Isaiah 49:3, "in whom I will be glorified." In Jeremiah 13:11 he puts it this way: "I made the whole house of Israel and the whole house of Judah cling to me, declares the LORD, *that they might be for me a people, a name, a praise, and a glory.*"

Creating the World and Choosing Israel Have the Same Goal

God brought Israel into being, he says, "for myself" (Isa. 43:21). Then he explains what he means by "for myself": Israel is the "people whom I formed *for myself* that they might declare my praise." The language of creation ("whom I formed") links the purpose of Israel's election with the purpose of creation. They are the same. God has one ultimate purpose in creation and in the election and history of Israel. We see this especially in Isaiah 43:6–7:

> I will say to the north, Give up,
>   and to the south, Do not withhold;
> bring my sons from afar
>   and my daughters from the end of the earth,
> everyone who is called by my name,
>   whom I created for my glory,
>   whom I formed and made.

God's creation of Israel and then the widening of his redemptive action through the Messiah to include the Gentiles have one and the same ultimate purpose. This continuity between God's purpose in creating Israel and creating the New Testament church is seen in the way the apostle Peter uses similar language to describe God's purpose for the church as Isaiah did to describe God's purpose for Israel:

> You are a chosen race, a royal priesthood, a holy nation, a people for his own possession, that you may proclaim the excellencies

of him who called you out of darkness into his marvelous light. (1 Pet. 2:9)

Israel is destined to "declare my praise" (Isa. 43:21). The church is destined to "proclaim [his] excellencies" (1 Pet. 2:9).

The Distant Future of Israel for the Glory of God

When Isaiah lifts up his prophetic eyes to the more distant future of Israel's glory, the purpose of God remains the same:

> Your people shall all be righteous;
> > they shall possess the land forever,
> the branch of my planting, the work of my hands,
> > *that I might be glorified.* (Isa. 60:21)

From this same context in Isaiah, Jesus applies Isaiah 61:1 to himself in Luke 4:18–19 to show that he will be the means of Israel's final attainment of this future condition. The Spirit of the Lord will be on the Messiah, Jesus,

> to grant to those who mourn in Zion—
> > to give them a beautiful headdress instead of ashes,
> the oil of gladness instead of mourning,
> > the garment of praise instead of a faint spirit;
> that they may be called oaks of righteousness,
> > the planting of the LORD, *that he may be glorified.* (Isa. 61:3)

So if we consider simply the general statements about God's purpose for Israel's creation and consummation, the final, overarching purpose is consistent. The purpose is for Israel to be a servant in whom God will be *glorified* (Isa. 49:3); to be a people, a name, a praise, and *a glory* (Jer. 13:11); to be a people to declare *God's praise* (Isa. 43:21), created for *God's glory* (Isa. 43:7), the work of God's hands *that he may be glorified* (Isa. 60:21; 61:3).

One Goal: God's Name and Our Joy in It

In other words, God's ultimate purpose for Israel is the same as the purpose we saw while focusing on God's plans before the creation of the world (chapter 3) and God's work in creation (chapter 4). And there is another crucial consistency. The purpose of God's glorification in Israel's final condition will come to pass through her joy in God, and this joy will be the very sign of God's glorious reputation— his name:

> You shall go out in joy
>   and be led forth in peace;
> the mountains and the hills before you
>   shall break forth into singing,
>   and all the trees of the field shall clap their hands.
> Instead of the thorn shall come up the cypress;
>   instead of the brier shall come up the myrtle;
> and it shall make a name for the LORD,
>   an everlasting sign that shall not be cut off.
>   (Isa. 55:12–13)

What does "it" refer to in verse 13? "*It* shall make a name for the LORD, an everlasting sign." The Hebrew is no more specific than the English translation. But I don't think the meaning is unclear. "It" refers to the whole situation: Israel going out in joy and peace; mountains and hills singing; trees clapping their hands; cypresses replacing thorns; myrtles replacing briers. All of that will be "a name for the LORD." That will be his reputation, the display of his glory.

But what is all of that? So many commentators pass over the utterly crucial connection between God's name and man's joy. Calvin comments:

> When he says that it shall be to God "for a name," he shews what is the design of the restoration of the Church. It is, that the name

of God may be more illustrious among men, and that the remembrance of him may flourish and be maintained.[2]

Yes. But what will make his name "more illustrious"? What will make the "remembrance of him . . . flourish"? E. J. Young comments:

The subject of *it shall be* ["It shall be a name to the Lord"] is the glorious change itself. The preposition before *Lord* may be rendered either *for* or *to*; possibly the latter is preferable ["a name *to* the Lord"]. The prophet is stating, now that he has dropped his figurative language, that the change will exist for the glory of its author. It will be a *name* or *memorial* in that it will ever call to mind and exalt the Name of its author.[3]

Yes. But what is this "change" that "will exist for the glory of its author"?

The utterly crucial point is not about mountains and hills and trees. The utterly crucial point is about the *joy and peace of God's people.*

> *You* shall go out in joy
>   and be led forth in peace; . . .
>   and *it* shall make a name for the LORD,
>   an everlasting sign that shall not be cut off. (Isa. 55:12–13)

God's securing a *name* for himself and God's securing *joy* for his people are one.

That joy is his name—his reputation, his glory. The reason Israel's joy is God's glory is that all her joy in God's gifts is, in essence, joy in God himself. The redeemed Israel cries out, "I will greatly rejoice *in the*

2 John Calvin and William Pringle, *Commentary on the Book of the Prophet Isaiah*, vol. 4 (Bellingham, WA: Logos Bible Software, 2010), 174.
3 Edward Young, *The Book of Isaiah, Chapters 40–66*, vol. 3 (Grand Rapids, MI: Eerdmans, 1972), 385–86.

Lᴏʀᴅ; my soul shall exult *in my God*" (Isa. 61:10). And the promise is made to Judah, "You shall rejoice *in the* Lᴏʀᴅ; *in the Holy One of Israel* you shall glory" (Isa. 41:16).

Joy in His Gifts as Joy in His Goodness

To be sure, there is nothing evil about rejoicing in God's personal and material blessings. God does not make a new creation simply to be a temptation:

> Behold, I create new heavens
>   and a new earth,
> and the former things shall not be remembered
>   or come into mind.
> But be glad and rejoice forever
>   *in that which I create*;
> for behold, I create Jerusalem to be a joy,
>   and her people to be a gladness. (Isa. 65:17–18)

Israel's joy—our joy—will consist partly in joy over what God creates. The things of creation are good gifts to be received with thanksgiving and rejoicing. But joy *in God himself*—in and through (and, if necessary, without) his gifts—is what makes our final joy a sign of his glory.

We see this most clearly in Habakkuk 3:17–18:

> Though the fig tree should not blossom,
>   nor fruit be on the vines,
> the produce of the olive fail
>   and the fields yield no food,
> the flock be cut off from the fold
>   and there be no herd in the stalls,
> yet I will rejoice *in the* Lᴏʀᴅ;
>   I will take joy *in the God* of my salvation.

The point here is to show that, as good and precious and joy-inspiring as God's gifts are, they are not the ultimate goal of the human soul, or of the redeeming work of God. This is why I conclude from Isaiah 55:12–13 that the final and ultimate sign of God's glory—the final and ultimate demonstration of God's glorious name—will be the joy of God's people *in God*. "You shall go out in joy" because you will hear in the singing hills and the clapping trees the glory of God. You will see in the magnificent cypresses, replacing the miserable thorns, the beautiful power and wisdom and justice and mercy of your God. And you will exult with Habakkuk in God himself. "I will rejoice *in the Lord*; I will take joy *in the God* of my salvation." You will taste and see that, in and through all God's gifts, *God himself* is the all-satisfying treasure of life: "In your presence there is fullness of joy; at your right hand are pleasures forevermore" (Ps. 16:11).

God's Joy in Ours in God

It gets even better. God's ultimate goal in the history of Israel is not only the exaltation of his glorious name in the joy of his people; it is also his own joy in their joy in him:

> I will rejoice in Jerusalem
>   and be glad in my people;
> no more shall be heard in it the sound of weeping
>   and the cry of distress. (Isa. 65:19)

The weeping of his people ceases; the rejoicing of his heart soars. That is not a coincidental pair. God's final joy in us is our joy in him:

> The Lord your God is in your midst,
>   a mighty one who will save;
> he will rejoice over you with gladness;
>   he will quiet you by his love;
> he will exult over you with loud singing. (Zeph. 3:17)

The joy moves in both directions: from us toward God and from God toward us. God's glory is our joy. And our joy in God's glory is his joy. In this way, God's glorification is the final and ultimate goal of Israel's existence, and that goal is one with our exultation in God's glory and his joy in this.

From Wide Angle to Narrow

In the coming chapters of part 2, we move from the wide-angle focus on Israel's history to the narrow-angle focus on key periods of that history as presented in Scripture. The event of the exodus and its reverberations throughout the rest of Israel's history and the Bible are the focus of chapters 6 and 7. Aside from the incarnation of the Messiah Jesus, no other event in Israel's history has so many statements of purpose attached to it. The impact of God's goal in the exodus is felt through the rest of Scripture, including a profound impact on the apostle Paul.

6

The Exodus Unfolds

More than any other event in Israel's history, the exodus out of Egypt shaped Israel's worship of God as their redeemer who chose them, saved them, and made them a people for himself. Not surprisingly, therefore, Scripture expresses God's ultimate goal in the events of the exodus more clearly and more frequently than in any other event in Israel's history. That is what this chapter focuses on—the expressions of God's goal in the exodus embedded in the very story of the exodus itself. Then in chapter 7, we will broaden the focus and look at the ultimate goal of God for the exodus expressed throughout the history of Israel and into the New Testament.

Liberation of God's People, Identification of Israel's God

One of the reasons God's ultimate goal in the history of Israel receives such emphasis and repetition in the story of the exodus is that here in this story God reveals his unique name, Yahweh, which sets him off from all other gods. Yahweh is translated with small caps, "Lord," in most modern English translations of the Bible, and it occurs in the Old Testament over 6,800 times in reference to Israel's God.

The reason the revelation of this name not only elicits a surge of purpose statements about the exodus, but also unleashes a lineage of such statements throughout the Old Testament, is that this name carries the very essence of who God is and how he wants to be known. In other words, the name Yahweh exists in part because the name itself expresses God's goal for all God's action in the history of Israel, and, as we will see, all his action in the history of the world.

Setting for Revelation and Liberation

To see this, let's put the story of the exodus in its historical setting and then look at it more closely. For generations, the people of Israel— God's chosen people—have lived as aliens in Egypt. And for a long time, they have been treated as slaves. Now the time of God's deliverance is drawing near. A Jewish child is born and named Moses. He is providentially rescued from the edict of death by Pharaoh's daughter and raised in the Egyptian court.

As an adult, he defends one of his kinsmen by killing an Egyptian and then flees to the land of Midian. There God appears to him in a burning bush and tells him that he is God's chosen instrument to lead his people out of bondage: "Come, I will send you to Pharaoh that you may bring my people, the children of Israel, out of Egypt" (Ex. 3:10). Moses is stunned. He shrinks back. "Moses said to God, 'Who am I that I should go to Pharaoh and bring the children of Israel out of Egypt?'" God answers, "But I will be with you, and this shall be the sign for you, that I have sent you: when you have brought the people out of Egypt, you shall serve God on this mountain" (Ex. 3:11–12).

Then Moses brings us to one of the most important statements God ever made—the revelation of his name, Yahweh:

> Moses said to God, "If I come to the people of Israel and say to them, 'The God of your fathers has sent me to you,' and they ask me, 'What is his name?' what shall I say to them?" God said to Moses, "I am who I am." And he said, "Say this to the people of Israel: 'I am has sent me to you.'" God also said to Moses, "Say this

to the people of Israel: 'The LORD [Hebrew *Yahweh*], the God of your fathers, the God of Abraham, the God of Isaac, and the God of Jacob, has sent me to you.' This is my name forever, and thus I am to be remembered throughout all generations." (Ex. 3:13–15)

Notice three aspects of what God says about himself.

Absolute Being before Name

First, in Exodus 3:14a "God said to Moses, 'I AM WHO I AM.'" He did not say that was his name. He said, in effect, "Before you concern yourself with my name and where I line up among the many gods of Egypt or Babylon or Philistia, and before you wonder about conjuring me with my name, and even before you wonder if I am the God of Abraham—before all of that—be stunned by this: 'I AM WHO I AM.'"[1] In other words, "Before you hear my name, grasp my unique, absolute being over against all other being." This is of first, foundational, and infinite importance.

Second, in Exodus 3:14b God adds, "Say this to the people of Israel: 'I AM has sent me to you.'" Even here he has not yet told Moses his name. He is building a bridge between his being ("I AM WHO I AM") and his name (Yahweh). Here he simply puts the statement of his being in the place of his name. Tell the leaders of Israel, "I AM has sent me to you." The one who is—who absolutely is—sent me to you.

Third, in Exodus 3:15 God also says to Moses, "Say this to the people of Israel: 'The LORD [Yahweh], the God of your fathers, the God of Abraham, the God of Isaac, and the God of Jacob, has sent me to you.' This is my name forever." God finally gives us his name: Yahweh (the LORD).

This name, Yahweh, is a Hebrew word built on the Hebrew verb "I am." This is why the ESV translates "I AM WHO I AM" and "I AM"

---

1   See below for why the ESV puts this clause in small caps as with the name of God, LORD—that is, Yahweh.

with small caps the way it does the name Yahweh—LORD. The point is that every time Israel hears or reads the word *Yahweh* (or the short form *Yah*, which we hear every time we sing hallelu-*jah*—"praise Yahweh"), or every time we see "the LORD" in our English Bible, we should think, "This is a proper name (like Peter or James or John), and it has a meaning given by God himself. It means 'I AM WHO I AM' with all that this implies."

What God Tells Us about Himself 6,800 Times

In other words, God's name is a message. And the message is about how he intends to be known. Every time his name appears—all 6,800 times—he means to remind us of his utterly unique being. As I have pondered the meaning of the name Yahweh, built on the phrase "I AM WHO I AM" and pointing to God's absolute being, I see at least ten dimensions to its meaning:

1. God's absolute being means he never had a beginning. This staggers the mind. Every child asks, "Who made God?" And every wise parent says, "Nobody made God. God simply is and always was. No beginning."

2. God's absolute being means God will never end. If he did not come into being, he cannot go out of being, because he *is* absolute being. He is what is. There is no place to go outside of being. There is only God. Before he creates, that's all that is: God.

3. God's absolute being means God is absolute reality. There is no reality before him. There is no reality outside of him unless he wills it and makes it. He is not one of many realities before he creates. He is simply there, as absolute reality. He is all that was, eternally. No space, no universe, no emptiness. Only God, absolutely there, absolutely all.

4. God's absolute being means that God is utterly independent. He depends on nothing to bring him into being or support him

or counsel him or make him what he is. That is what absolute being means.

5. God's absolute being means that everything that is not God depends totally on God. All that is not God is secondary and dependent. The entire universe is utterly secondary—not primary. It came into being by God and stays in being moment by moment on God's decision to keep it in being.

6. God's absolute being means all the universe is by comparison to God as nothing. Contingent, dependent reality is to absolute, independent reality as a shadow to its substance, as an echo to a thunderclap, as a bubble to the ocean. All that we see, all that we are amazed by in the world and in the galaxies, is, compared to God, as nothing. "All the nations are as nothing before him, they are accounted by him as less than nothing and emptiness" (Isa. 40:17).

7. God's absolute being means that God is constant. He is the same yesterday, today, and forever. He cannot be improved. He is not becoming anything. He is who he is. There is no development in God. No progress. Absolute perfection cannot be improved.

8. God's absolute being means that he is the absolute standard of truth, goodness, and beauty. There is no law book to which he looks to know what is right. No almanac to establish facts. No guild to determine what is excellent or beautiful. He himself is the standard of what is right, what is true, what is beautiful.

9. God's absolute being means God does whatever he pleases, and it is always right, always beautiful, and always in accord with truth. There are no constraints on him from outside him that could hinder him from doing anything he pleases. All reality that is outside of him he created and designed and governs. So he is utterly free from any constraints that don't originate from the counsel of his own will.

10. God's absolute being means that he is the most important and most valuable reality and the most important and most valuable person in the universe. He is more worthy of interest and attention and admiration and enjoyment than all other realities, including the entire universe.

This is the message of his name. And in the exodus, he establishes a link forever between his name and his mighty rescue of Israel from bondage. The timing of the revelation of his name is not coincidental. God is coming to save. Israel will want to know who this saving God is. God says in effect, "Tell them that my name is Yahweh, and make clear what this means. I am absolutely free and independent. And I choose freely to save my people. The freedom of my being and the freedom of my love are one."

Now we are in a position to listen as Moses presents us with a surge of statements that tell us God's ultimate purpose in the exodus. Why the ten plagues? Ten! Why the defeat of Pharaoh and his army in the Red Sea? Why the protection and rescue of Israel through it all? Why the command to remember this forever?

To Show His Name to Israel and Egypt

God's purpose in multiplying his wonders in Egypt at the exodus was to make known his name and his power in such a way that he would be glorified by Israel, by Egypt, and eventually by the nations.

Moses comes to the leaders of Israel and delivers God's message:

> I am the Lord, and I will bring you out from under the burdens of the Egyptians, and I will deliver you from slavery to them, and I will redeem you with an outstretched arm and with great acts of judgment. I will take you to be my people, and I will be your God, and *you shall know that I am the Lord your God*, who has brought you out from under the burdens of the Egyptians. (Ex. 6:6–7)

He has *revealed* his name, "the Lord," and its meaning, "I am who I am."
Now he will *show* them, "with great acts of judgment" and deliverance,
that he is "the Lord." "You shall know that I am the Lord your God."

God's purpose is not only that *Israel* know who her God really is,
but also that *Pharaoh and the Egyptians* know as well. "Pharaoh will not
listen to you, *that my wonders may be multiplied* in the land of Egypt"
(Ex. 11:9; cf. 10:1). To what end? "The Egyptians *shall know that I am
the Lord*, when I stretch out my hand against Egypt and bring out the
people of Israel from among them" (Ex. 7:5).

And all the plagues leading up to that deliverance have the same
purpose. The frogs: "that you may know that there is no one like the
Lord our God" (Ex. 8:10). The flies: "that you may know that I am
the Lord in the midst of the earth" (Ex. 8:22). All the plagues: "I will
send all my plagues on you yourself [Pharaoh], and on your servants
and your people, *so that you may know that there is none like me in all
the earth*" (Ex. 9:14). And at the final deliverance through the Red Sea
"the Egyptians *shall know that I am the Lord*. . . . The Egyptians *shall
know that I am the Lord*" (Ex. 14:4, 18).

For His Name among All the Nations

But not even Egypt is a large enough audience for what God is doing
in the exodus. So God says to Pharaoh, "For this purpose I have raised
you up, to show you my power, *so that my name may be proclaimed in
all the earth*" (Ex. 9:16). The exodus is for the sake of the nations. One
example of the saving effects of God's reputation from the exodus is
Rahab, the harlot in Jericho. She befriended the spies from Israel and
eventually made her way into the list of believers in Hebrews 11:31
and the teaching on justification in James 2:25. How did that happen?
Here is what she said to the spies:

> I know that the Lord has given you the land. . . . For we have heard
> how the Lord dried up the water of the Red Sea before you when

you came out of Egypt. . . . And as soon as we heard it, our hearts melted, and there was no spirit left in any man because of you, for the LORD your God, he is God in the heavens above and on the earth beneath. (Josh. 2:9–11)

So when God said to Pharaoh in Exodus 9:16, "I have raised you up . . . *so that my name may be proclaimed in all the earth,*" we may believe that God had Rahab's faith in mind, as well as a million other effects. His purpose was to enlarge his own reputation—to make his name known among the nations—with the effect that those who saw his name as glorious would worship him with hope and joy.

Not Just Known, but Known and Acknowledged as Glorious

When God repeatedly says that his goal is that his name (and power, Ex. 9:16) might be known, we know that this aim was not that his name be known and despised, but known and *glorified.* God makes this clear in two statements about the climax of his victory at the Red Sea:

> I will harden Pharaoh's heart, and he will pursue them, and *I will get glory over Pharaoh* and all his host, and the Egyptians *shall know that I am the LORD.* (Ex. 14:4)

> I will harden the hearts of the Egyptians so that they shall go in after them, and *I will get glory over Pharaoh* and all his host, his chariots, and his horsemen. And the Egyptians shall *know that I am the LORD,* when *I have gotten glory over Pharaoh,* his chariots, and his horsemen. (Ex. 14:17–18)

The word translated three times as "I will get glory" is more literally translated, "I will be glorified." This passive construction ("be glorified") leaves unspecified who it is that is glorifying God. There is no reason to limit it to Israel or the Egyptians. He has already stated his aim: "so that my name may be proclaimed in all the earth" (Ex. 9:16).

Therefore, we may assume that this aim to be glorified is as wide as the aim for his name to be known.

Even More than Known and Acknowledged: Worshiped

So God's overarching purpose—his ultimate goal—in the exodus was that he would be seen and worshiped as glorious. I say, "worshiped," not just "admired reluctantly by his enemies," for several reasons.

One reason we have already seen—namely, the effect of God's design for the exodus (Ex. 9:14) in the salvation of Rahab (Josh. 2:8–11; Heb. 11:31). Another is the very meaning of the word *glorify*. While it is possible for an unbeliever to "glorify" God by ascribing terrifying power to him, that is not God's ultimate aim in doing what the Scripture writers call "wondrous things." In doing his wonders, God's ultimate aim is *worship*. That is what "glorify" aims at, which we can see, for example, in Psalm 86:9–10:

> All the nations you have made shall come
>   and *worship* before you, O Lord,
>   and shall *glorify* your name.
> For you are great and do wondrous things;
>   you alone are God.

When God aims, as he does in Exodus 14:4 and 17, to "be glorified" for his wondrous triumph over Pharaoh, his aim is that his "name be proclaimed in all the earth" (Ex. 9:16)—that is, that "all the nations you have made shall come and *worship* before you, O Lord, and shall *glorify* your name."

Worship Includes Joy in God's Glorious Greatness

Of course, worshiping God—glorifying God—for his wondrous deeds includes a great *gladness* in the hearts of God's people. The call for Israel and all the nations to worship God is a call to *rejoice* in the Lord:

> Shout for joy to God, all the earth;
> sing the glory of his name;
>> give to him glorious praise!
> Say to God, "How awesome are your deeds!
>> So great is your power that your enemies come
>> cringing to you." (Ps. 66:1–3)

> Let the nations be glad and sing for joy. (Ps. 67:4)

Another reason I say that God's ultimate aim in the exodus is to be *joyfully* worshiped, not just reluctantly admired by his enemies, is that this is what Moses and Israel and Miriam did in immediate response to God's drowning of Pharaoh at the Red Sea.

God said, I "have gotten glory over Pharaoh, his chariots, and his horsemen" (Ex. 14:18). And twelve verses later, the response of the people of Israel, when they "saw the great power that the LORD used against the Egyptians," was that they "feared the LORD, and they believed in the LORD and in his servant Moses" (Ex. 14:31). This fear was not paralyzing dread, but trembling faith (like what a child feels when his father scoops him into his arms out of a frightening ocean undertow). It trembles and laughs at the same time.

Moses and the people of Israel sang this song to the LORD, saying,

> "I will sing to the LORD, for he has triumphed
>> gloriously;
>> the horse and his rider he has thrown into
>> the sea.
> The LORD is my strength and my song,
>> and he has become my salvation;
> this is my God, and I will praise him,
>> my father's God, and I will exalt him.
> The LORD is a man of war;
>> the LORD is his name." (Ex. 15:1–3)

They *sing* to the Lord. They *praise* the Lord. They *exalt* the Lord. And when this song is complete, "Miriam . . . took a tambourine in her hand, and all the women went out after her with tambourines and dancing" (Ex. 15:20).

And Miriam sang to them:

> "Sing to the Lord, for he has triumphed gloriously;
> the horse and his rider he has thrown into the sea." (Ex. 15:21)

All this singing to the Lord, and praising the Lord, and exalting the Lord in response to the horse and rider being thrown into the sea is intended to show us what God was aiming at when he said, "I have gotten glory over Pharaoh, his chariots, and his horsemen" (Ex. 14:18). He was aiming at *joyful worship of the greatness of his glory.* That's why he multiplied his wonders in the land of Egypt (Ex. 11:9). That's why the exodus happened.

The Endless Echo of the Exodus

One of the things that makes the exodus unique is that expressions of its ultimate goal are not restricted to the story itself as it unfolds in the first chapters of the book of Exodus. There are reverberations of its purpose for centuries in the history of Israel and the history of the Christian church. In the next chapter we will look at the joyful faith and worship that the exodus was designed to unleash (and did often unleash) in the history of Israel and into the New Testament—indeed into eternity.

7

Remembering the Exodus

Chapter 6 closed with the argument that God's goal in the exodus was not only that his great name (Yahweh, with all it implies) be known and acknowledged but that it be gladly worshiped. The exodus was aiming not only at grudging admiration from Pharaoh and the nations but, even more, at joyful praise for the whole panorama of God's excellencies. We know this not only for the reasons given in chapter 6, but also because, in God's providence, the exodus unleashes centuries of joyful, worshiping responses in the history of Israel that reach all the way through the Old Testament and into the New—even into eternity. This chapter is a sampling of those responses.

David's Humble Amazement

Four hundred years after the exodus, King David prays with amazement and thankfulness that God has had such great mercies on Israel and on him in particular. "Who am I, O LORD God, and what is my house, that you have brought me thus far?" (1 Chron. 17:16). When the author of Psalm 105 considers the hundreds of years of blessings on Israel, he focuses on the exodus as the source of joy that should mark the worship of God's remembering people:

He remembered his holy promise,
and Abraham, his servant.
And he brought his people out with joy,
his chosen ones with singing. (Ps. 105:42–43,
my translation)

He brought them out with joy! God did this. This was his goal. He would make for himself a global name (Ex. 9:16), and his people would exult in this divine self-exaltation with joy. That was the purpose of the exodus, and it was still bearing the fruit of glad worship four hundred years later.

Wonders of Power, Wonders of Grace

Then come the psalms that exult in the exodus. Take Psalm 106 as just one example. What is amazing about this celebration of the exodus is that it makes clear that Israel was a sinful people and did not deserve to be delivered. This means that the most discerning Israelites knew that the wonders of the exodus were not only wonders of power, but also wonders of grace.

Both we and our fathers have sinned;
we have committed iniquity; we have done
wickedness.
Our fathers, when they were in Egypt,
did not consider your wondrous works;
they did not remember the abundance of your
steadfast love,
but rebelled by the sea, at the Red Sea.
Yet he saved them *for his name's sake,*
that he might make known his mighty power.
He rebuked the Red Sea, and it became dry,
and he led them through the deep as through
a desert.

So he saved them from the hand of the foe
> and redeemed them from the power of the enemy.
>> (Ps. 106:6–10)

Here is the essence of what we are seeing repeatedly in the ultimate purpose of God's providence: They "rebelled . . . at the Red Sea. Yet *he saved them for his name's sake, that he might make known his mighty power*" (106:7–8). So whom was the exodus for: Israel or God? He saved *them*. For *his* name's sake! To make known *his* power! Both. It was for Israel. It was for God.

But it was not for Israel and for God in the same sense. It was for Israel's *salvation*. It was for God's *reputation*. It showed Israel's desperate neediness and undeserving position. It showed God's mighty power and astonishing grace. It satisfied Israel with the thankful ecstasy that their need was met by God. It magnified God in that he was able and willing to meet that need. Israel got the blessing of help. God got the honor of being the strong helper. Israel got the joy. God got the glory.

As we have seen before, *our joy* and *God's glory* are not separable goals of God's providence. They are woven into one goal. The ongoing reverberation of God's glory in the exodus happens in the joyful worship of God's people for that glory. The gladness of Israel in her gracious, mighty, delivering God is the echo of God's exodus glory. God's aim to be glorified and his aim for his people to be satisfied in that glory are not separate aims. Israel's being satisfied in the God of the exodus is the essence of how the God of the exodus is glorified in Israel. That is the ultimate goal of God's providence that we are seeing again and again.

Isaiah's Celebration of the Arm of God's Glory

The prophets bear witness to this same goal of God's providence in the exodus. Consider Isaiah's witness:

> Then he remembered the days of old,
>> of Moses and his people.

Where is he who brought them up out of the sea
  with the shepherds of his flock?
Where is he who put in the midst of them
  his Holy Spirit,
who caused this arm of his glory
  to go at the right hand of Moses,
who divided the waters before them
  to make for himself an everlasting name,
who led them through the depths?
Like a horse in the desert,
  they did not stumble.
Like livestock that go down into the valley,
  the Spirit of the LORD gave them rest.
So you led your people,
  to make for yourself a name of glory. (Isa. 63:11–14,
  my translation)

God bared the arm of his *glory* (תִּפְאֶרֶת) to make for himself a name of *glory* (תִּפְאֶרֶת)—not the usual word of *glory* (כָּבוֹד), but signifying beauty, ornament, radiance, splendor. Why? "To make for himself an everlasting name" (63:12). Or, as Isaiah says at the end: "To make for yourself a name of glory" (63:14).

And what was he doing to make himself such a name? Bringing his people out of the sea. Shepherding them like a flock. Giving them his Holy Spirit. Leading them through the depths. Not letting them stumble. Giving them rest. In other words, the same pattern as we have seen: they get the *salvation*; he gets the *reputation*. They get the *joy* of being helped; he gets the *glory* of helping. The name he was making for himself was *Yahweh*—I am who I am—absolute, all-sufficient, all-glorious being! And yet all of this was in the service of a people who were desperate and undeserving. For those who had eyes to see, God was making a name for the glory of his *grace*.

From Bondage to Bounty for His Name

The prophet Jeremiah saw the same goal of divine providence in the exodus:

> You have shown signs and wonders in the land of Egypt, and to this day in Israel and among all mankind, *and have made a name for yourself,* as at this day. You brought your people Israel out of the land of Egypt with signs and wonders, with a strong hand and outstretched arm, and with great terror. And you gave them this land, which you swore to their fathers to give them, a land flowing with milk and honey. (Jer. 32:20–22)

God's aim in the exodus was to make a name for himself. What is that name? From this context, we could say that God's name is his character as a God who exerts a strong hand and an outstretched arm with great terror to show signs and wonders to bring his people from a land of misery into a land flowing with milk and honey. The glory of God's name is his power and wisdom and justice and mercy to bring a people from bondage to bounty. His aim is that his people see this glory and worship with gladness.

A Name of Justice and Grace

A thousand years after the exodus, some of the exiles of Israel were returning to Jerusalem from captivity in Babylon. At one point in the book of Nehemiah, the Levites rehearse the history of Israel in prayer (chapter 9), confessing the sins of the nation and thanking God for his mercies. When they come to the exodus, they include with it the same goal we have seen repeatedly:

> You saw the affliction of our fathers in Egypt and heard their cry at the Red Sea, and performed signs and wonders against Pharaoh and all his servants and all the people of his land, for you knew that they acted arrogantly against our fathers. *And you made a name for yourself,*

as it is to this day. And you divided the sea before them, so that they went through the midst of the sea on dry land, and you cast their pursuers into the depths, as a stone into mighty waters. (Neh. 9:9–11)

The insight that the Levites make explicit for us is that part of what it meant for God to make himself a name at the exodus was to deal justly with the arrogance of Egypt's leaders: "for you knew that they acted arrogantly against our fathers." Not only does this clarify the *justice* of God in the way he dealt with Pharaoh, but it also throws into stark relief the *grace* that God was showing to Israel in the exodus, because *they* were arrogant as well. Recall from Psalm 106:7–8:

> They did not remember the abundance of your steadfast love,
>   but *rebelled by the sea*, at the Red Sea.
> Yet he saved them *for his name's sake*,
>   that he might make known his mighty power.

The situation was not that Egypt deserved to be judged for its arrogance and Israel deserved to be saved for her righteousness. *Neither* deserved to be saved. But God freely chose to save Israel.

The Roots of Exodus Grace in Covenant Grace

To be sure, God was remembering his covenant with Abraham when he saved Israel from Egypt (Ex. 2:24; 6:5). But that covenant was made just as freely and graciously as the grace of the exodus:

> Behold, to the LORD your God belong heaven and the heaven of heavens, the earth with all that is in it. Yet the LORD set his heart in love on your fathers [literally: the Lord *delighted* in your fathers to love them] and chose their offspring after them, you above all peoples, as you are this day. (Deut. 10:14–15)

The election of Abraham at the very beginning of Israel's history was not owing to any constraints God felt from outside. He did not *have* to choose Israel. He could have chosen another nation. He could have chosen none. That is the point of saying, "To the LORD your God belong heaven and the heaven of heavens, the earth with all that is in it" (10:14). He owns every people, and could have chosen any he pleased. The point is that his choice of Israel was utterly free. He simply *delighted* to love them. It was not because of their superior faith or righteousness. Faith was a response to God's choice, not the cause (Gen. 15:6).

So at the exodus, when God chose to save Israel and not Egypt, even though both were rebellious (Neh. 9:10; Ps. 106:7), his choice was an extension of that same free grace that he gave to Israel at the beginning when he chose Abraham from all the peoples of the world. God's covenant does not oblige him to save any particular generation of unbelieving Israelites.

Any generation that presumes on God's covenant mercies, as though that generation cannot be condemned, should hear the word of John the Baptist to those who said (presumptuously), "We have Abraham as our father!" John replied, "I tell you, God is able from these stones to raise up children for Abraham" (Matt. 3:9). In other words, God's sovereignty frees him from being manipulated or coerced by his own covenant. That was as true in Egypt at the exodus as it was later in Jerusalem at the first coming of Christ. The exodus was a work of free grace to make a name for Yahweh. Or, as Paul would say it, the exodus was "to the praise of the glory of God's grace" (Eph. 1:6, my translation).

The name that God made for himself at the exodus had its roots in the name he revealed: "I AM WHO I AM." That name means freedom: "I am not bound by anything outside myself. I am who my own wise, self-consulting counsel determines I will be (Eph. 1:11). I am free." At the exodus, God made a name for himself by acting as a God of absolutely free grace. That is, he showed his saving power for a people (Israel) who were no more deserving of salvation than the Egyptians. He is who he is, and he saves whom he saves—that is the freedom of grace. Beneath the name he *makes for himself* is the name he *is in himself.* "I AM WHO I AM."

Romans 9 and Perishing Israelites

This is exactly where the apostle Paul goes with his application of the freedom of God in the exodus. Romans 9 begins with Paul's heart-rending lament that his kinsmen, the Israel of his day, are by and large "accursed and cut off from Christ" (Rom. 9:3). This is the staggering problem that defines how Romans 9 develops. How can God's chosen people—who have "the adoption, the glory, the covenants, the giving of the law, the worship, and the promises" (9:4)—be cursed and cut off from the Messiah? It seems unthinkable. This is the issue Romans 9 deals with (indeed, it's the issue behind all of Romans 9–11).

Paul's answer is that the promises of God have not failed, "for not all who are descended from Israel belong to Israel" (9:6). Or to put it another way, "It is not the children of the flesh [that is, merely *ethnic* Israel] who are the children of God, but the children of the promise are counted as offspring [that is, those whom God freely chooses to count as the heirs of the promise of life]" (9:8). In other words, even though many in ethnic Israel are "accursed and cut off from Christ," nevertheless the promises to Israel have not failed because not everyone who is physically an Israelite is counted by God as a true Israelite, that is, a true heir of the promise.[1]

To support this argument, Paul points out that, of Abraham's physical children, Isaac was chosen, not Ishmael (9:9). And of Isaac's physical children, Jacob was chosen, not Esau (9:10–13). Then Paul makes explicit what the *purpose* of such a divine, electing providence is. Why did God choose one son over the other, even though "they were not

---

1 See chap. 5 for a fuller discussion of Paul's understanding of the difference between true Israel and ethnic Israel and how this true, or inward, or spiritual Israel (Rom. 2:28–29) relates to Gentile believers in the Messiah.

yet born and had done nothing either good or bad" (9:11)? Answer: "in order that God's purpose of election might continue, not because of works but because of him who calls" (9:11).

In other words, the ultimate, decisive cause of Isaac being chosen, not Ishmael, and Jacob being chosen, not Esau, was not anything in them, but rather God's call. This should sound very much like *Israel*, not *Egypt*, being saved at the exodus, even though both were rebellious and undeserving.

Paul and the Exodus: The Freedom of God's Grace

In fact, Paul turns now to the book of Exodus to clarify the freedom of God in choosing the beneficiaries of his mercy. First, he cites Exodus 33:19 in Romans 9:15: "[God] says to Moses, 'I will have mercy on whom I have mercy, and I will have compassion on whom I have compassion'" (which is an echo of "I AM WHO I AM"). In other words, "I am absolutely self-determining and free in dispensing my mercy." From which Paul draws out this truth: "So then it depends not on human will or exertion, but on God, who has mercy" (9:16). In other words, God's freedom in having mercy on whom he wills means that his mercy is not governed decisively by human will or human exertion. It is governed finally and decisively by God's will.

Then, for further support, Paul turns to the purpose of God's providence in the event of the exodus itself. He calls to mind the purpose statement in Exodus 9:16 and quotes it in Romans 9:17: "For this very purpose I [God] have raised you up, that I might show my power in you, and that my name might be proclaimed in all the earth." In other words, God's will, his purpose, is final and decisive for why Pharaoh is raised up as the adversary of Israel.

Then Paul steps back from these two quotations from Exodus (33:19 and 9:16) and draws this conclusion in Romans 9:18: "So then [God] has *mercy* on whomever he wills, and he *hardens* whomever he wills." In other words, Paul sees in Exodus 33:19 and 9:16 the same thing we have been seeing in the name God made for himself in the exodus. God was making a name for his free, complete self-sufficiency. "I AM WHO I AM."

In his freedom and self-sufficiency, God aims to be known for freedom in grace toward an undeserving Israel (Ps. 106:7–8) and freedom in justice toward an arrogant Egypt (Neh. 9:10). "He has *mercy* on whomever he wills, and he *hardens* whomever he wills." His ultimate goal is that those who have eyes to see will come to tremble at his justice and treasure the glory of his grace—his self-determined, absolutely free grace.

To Make Known the Riches of Glory for Vessels of Mercy

Let's consider one more step in Paul's argument in Romans 9. Paul draws out something amazing from the lesson of Pharaoh. Pharaoh was raised up, God says, "that I might show my power in you, and that my name might be proclaimed in all the earth" (9:17). In verse 22 Paul begins a sentence about this desire of God to show his power, but he never finishes it. He says:

> *What if* God, desiring to show his wrath and *to make known his power*, has endured with much patience vessels of wrath prepared for destruction, in order to make known the riches of his glory for vessels of mercy, which he has prepared beforehand for glory? (9:22–23)

Actually, the word "what" in the phrase "what if" is not there. The sentence is a long *if* clause with no *then* clause. We are expected to supply the part that is missing. Here's my suggestion of what to supply: "*If* God, desiring to show his wrath and to make known his power, has endured with much patience vessels of wrath prepared for destruction, in order to make known the riches of his glory for vessels of mercy, which he has prepared beforehand for glory . . . *then no legitimate objection can be raised.*" That is what the translation "what if" implies as well. "*What if* I have this purpose in showing my wrath and power?"

If I do, will you fault me? This is the point Paul has been making in verses 20–21: the potter has a right to show his power and wisdom in any way he considers best for accomplishing his purposes.[2]

So Paul's ultimate argument for why it is right for God to act in freedom—having mercy on whomever he wills, and hardening whomever he wills (9:18)—is that the ultimate purpose of showing wrath and power (as in the defeat of Pharaoh) is *"in order to make known the riches of his glory for vessels of mercy."* The free justice of God in Pharaoh's hardening makes the freedom of God's mercy shine the more brightly for the vessels of mercy.

In the case of the exodus, this means that since neither Israel nor Egypt deserved anything but judgment, God's demonstration of wrath and power against the Egyptians was both *just*, because of Egypt's arrogance (Neh. 9:10), and *merciful*, because of Israel's rebellion (Ps. 106:7). God was free to harden whom he chose and have mercy on whom he chose (Rom. 9:18). Because God judged Pharaoh justly in his freedom, the riches of the glory of God's mercy shone all the more intensely for Israel. They did not deserve anything better than Pharaoh. But they received it—freely.

The Ultimate Goal of the Exodus: Free Grace for God's Glory

We, then, would be justified in saying that the ultimate purpose of God in the exodus is that he be glorified (Ex. 14:4, 17) for making a

---

2   I realize this has been a very brief overview of Rom. 9:1–23. If you would like to see the fuller argument, I wrote an entire book on these 23 verses: John Piper, *The Justification of God: An Exegetical and Theological Study of Romans 9:1–23* (Grand Rapids, MI: Baker Academic, 1983). Many scholars claim that these verses have nothing to do with individuals or eternal destinies but only with temporal experiences and corporate groups. I regard these claims as exegetically mistaken. They simply do not come to terms with the first and central problem raised in verse 2, namely, that individual Israelites are "accursed and cut off from Christ." The issue is indeed eternal destinies and individuals within Israel, not just the peoples as a whole. In fact, Paul's solution to God's seeming failure to keep his promises is to insist that not all of corporate Israel are truly children of God. The text begins (vv. 2 and 6) and ends (v. 24) with an emphasis on God's choosing individuals *"from* the Jews and *from* the Gentiles." The text is stunningly about individuals and their eternal destinies.

name for himself (Ex. 9:16; Neh. 9:10; Isa. 63:14; Jer. 32:20). More specifically, he made this name for himself by acting out the meaning of the name he revealed at the beginning of the story (Yahweh): "I AM WHO I AM" (Ex. 3:14). "I AM WHO I AM" becomes "I save whom I save" and "I judge whom I judge." Or as Romans 9 puts it, "I will have mercy on whom I have mercy" (9:15), and "he hardens whomever he wills" (9:18).

In other words, God's providence in the exodus (or any other event) is finally and decisively governed not by man's will or exertion (9:16), but by his own self-determining will. He is free. He is who he is—not what others make him. And he does what he does—not what others constrain him to do. In this freedom, he is never unjust, for he never treats anyone worse than they deserve. And his grace is always free, absolutely free. This is the name he aims to glorify. His name—his essential character—is that he is the God who saves for his own sake, that is, for the glory of his grace. His goal in the exodus—and in all his saving work—is to be praised for the glory of his grace "in all the earth" (Ex. 9:16; Rom. 9:17).

8

The Law, the Wilderness, and the Conquest of Canaan

"On the third new moon after the people of Israel had gone out of the land of Egypt, on that day they came into the wilderness of Sinai" (Ex. 19:1). If the exodus reverberated through the history of Israel's worship as the great exaltation of God's glory in gracious deliverance, then the giving of the law at Mount Sinai reverberated even more through Israel's common life as the all-encompassing constitution of her existence.

The God-Exalting Link between Law and Exodus

The time spent at Mount Sinai was an epoch-making moment in the life of Israel—indeed, in the life of the world, in view of how influential the Ten Commandments have been for human history. When God called to Moses on Mount Sinai, the first thing he said created a connection between the giving of the law and the exodus:

> You yourselves have seen what I did to the Egyptians, and how I bore you on eagles' wings and brought you to myself. Now therefore, if you will indeed obey my voice and keep my covenant, you shall be my treasured possession among all peoples, for all the earth is mine. (Ex. 19:4–5)

In other words, Israel, your crossing the Red Sea by my intervention was as miraculous and wonderful as if you had flown out of Egypt on the wings of an eagle. You were as helpless as baby eaglets, and I was powerful enough to fly an entire nation on my wings. That is how amazing my deliverance was. And add to this two other wonders: first, you deserved none of it (Ps. 106:7). Second, I brought you out to enjoy the best treasure in the universe: myself. "I bore you on eagles' wings and brought you *to myself*" (Ex. 19:4). Remember the words I spoke through Moses at the exodus:

> I will take you to be my people, and I will be your God, and you shall know that I am the LORD your God, who has brought you out from under the burdens of the Egyptians. (Ex. 6:7)

The exodus was a kind of ratification of God's original choosing of Abraham and his descendants (Gen. 12:1–3) to be "my treasured possession" (Ex. 19:5). Forty years later, on the brink of the promised land, God will say to Israel, "The LORD has taken you and brought you out of the iron furnace, out of Egypt, to be a people of his own inheritance" (Deut. 4:20).

Then when God actually gave to Moses the heart of the law at Mount Sinai—the Ten Commandments—his first words reasserted the connection between the exodus and the commandments:

> I am the LORD your God, who brought you out of the land of Egypt, out of the house of slavery. You shall have no other gods before me. (Ex. 20:2–3)

God's First Priority in the Law: His Supremacy

In view of what we saw in chapters 6 and 7 about the ultimate goal of providence in the exodus, we are not surprised that God's first priority in his constitution for Israel's life is that he be their supreme God. "You shall have no other gods before me." God's ultimate goal in the exodus was that Israel (Ex. 6:7) and Egypt (Ex. 7:5) would know that he is the supreme and only God—Yahweh, the one who absolutely is (Ex. 3:14). "The Egyptians shall know that I am the LORD [Yahweh], when I have gotten glory over Pharaoh" (Ex. 14:18).

This divine purpose is now enshrined in Israel's law and made the cornerstone of the nation's life together. This is not *man* demanding that God be supreme; it is *God* demanding that God be supreme. The self-exaltation of God could not be more intimately woven into the fabric of Israel's corporate life than it is in this first commandment. "You shall have no other gods before me."

Supreme in the Happy Affections of His Wife

But the nature of that self-exaltation in the first commandment does not become clear until we bring it into relationship to the second commandment:

> You shall not make for yourself a carved image, or any likeness of anything that is in heaven above, or that is in the earth beneath, or that is in the water under the earth. You shall not bow down to them or serve them, for I the LORD your God am a jealous God. (Ex. 20:4–5)

The first commandment was "You shall have no other gods before me" (20:3). But in what sense did God mean "before me"? The second commandment clarifies: "I the LORD your God am a *jealous* God" (20:5). In other words, "You, Israel, are my wife (Jer. 2:2; Ezek. 16:8). If your heart goes after another, I get angry, and it is part of my holiness for me to do so (Josh. 24:19; Ezek. 39:25). Your heart, your supreme loyalty, your love, your affection, your devotion, your enjoyment belong supremely to me."

Thus, the aim of the first commandment ("You shall have no other gods before me") was not only a call for God to be supremely exalted in Israel, but for Israel to be supremely satisfied in God. When a wife is satisfied in her husband and never looks for satisfaction elsewhere, she magnifies the worth of her husband, and his jealousy is never stirred. Her supreme enjoyment of her husband is her exaltation of his worth. That exaltation is the point of the first two commandments of the law.

How the First and Last of the Ten Commandments Are One

This understanding of the first two commandments is confirmed by the last one. The tenth commandment is "You shall not covet" (Ex. 20:17). The word for *covet* in Hebrew means simply "desire." So the question in defining what *covet* means is the question, When does desire for something—such as money, or what money can buy—become a bad desire? When does legitimate desire become covetousness?

The answer appears when we put the tenth commandment together with the first two. The first two commandments say, "No gods before me. Nothing in your heart should compete with me. Desire me so fully that when you have me, you are content." And then the tenth commandment says, "Don't covet. Don't have any illegitimate desires." That is, don't desire anything in a way that would undermine your contentment in God. So covetousness—or wrong desire—is desiring anything in such a way that you lose your contentment in God.[1]

In essence, then, the first and last of the Ten Commandments demand the same thing. Paul made this connection explicit in Colossians 3:5: "Covetousness [the tenth commandment] . . . is idolatry [the first commandment]." The first commandment ("You shall have no other gods before me") demands, "You shall always have me as supreme in your affections. You shall delight in me more than any

[1] These reflections on the first and last of the Ten Commandments are not new here. I have written and spoken about this relationship on several occasions. The wording used here was borrowed in part from John Piper, *Living in the Light with Money, Sex, and Power* (Charlotte, NC: Good Book Company, 2016), chap. 3.

suitor who comes along. Nothing shall appeal to you more than I do. Embrace me as your supreme treasure and be content in me."

The tenth commandment ("You shall not covet") demands, "Don't desire anything besides me in such a way that the desire would undermine your satisfaction in me. Let all your other desires for my gifts be expressions of your desire for more of me." Saint Augustine's way of saying this was to pray, "He loves thee too little who loves anything together with Thee, which he loves not for thy sake."[2]

The Goal of Providence and the Path of All Obedience

From this understanding of the Ten Commandments, I would draw two conclusions relevant for our purpose in this book. The first is that God saw to it that his ultimate goal in providence was embedded at the center of Israel's written constitution. That goal is that his worth and beauty be magnified above all things in his people's heartfelt worship of his excellence. Or to say it another way, the goal of God's providence, now established at the center of his law, is that he be exalted as the greatest treasure in the glad affections of his people—that he be supremely glorified through our being supremely satisfied in him.

The second conclusion I would draw from this understanding of the first and last of the Ten Commandments is that God's intention is for the other commandments to be obeyed on the basis of the first and last. The fact that the other commandments are sandwiched between the first and the last is not insignificant. The beginning and the ending of the law of Israel is that God should be exalted as supreme in the deepest satisfaction of his people in him.

I am arguing, therefore, that God's point in beginning and ending the Ten Commandments with this glad, God-exalting heart is that all other obedience flows from this kind of heart. Begrudging obedience does not make God look great. Or to say it another way: "Serve the

2 Augustine, *Confessions*, bk. 10, chap. 29.

LORD with gladness!" (Ps. 100:2) is a summary of the law. Only such service shows that God is our highest treasure and sweetest pleasure. Therefore, embedded at the center of the law is the ultimate goal of providence.

Wilderness Grace for the Glory of God

Israel's disobedience to God's law marked her history from the beginning. It was the bleak backdrop at the Red Sea, which made the exodus such an amazing display of grace (Ps. 106:7–8). It continued through the incident of the golden calf (Ex. 32) and on through the wandering in the wilderness. On the brink of the promised land, just before God turned the people away for forty more years of wandering, he said:

> But truly, as I live, and as all the earth shall be filled with the glory of the LORD, none of the men who have seen my glory and my signs that I did in Egypt and in the wilderness, and yet have put me to the test these ten times and have not obeyed my voice, shall see the land that I swore to give to their fathers. And none of those who despised me shall see it. (Num. 14:21–23)

> From the day you came out of the land of Egypt until you came to this place, you have been rebellious against the LORD. (Deut. 9:7)

Why then was Israel not destroyed in the wilderness? For the same reason she was not destroyed in Egypt. Eight hundred years after the exodus, as the prophet Ezekiel was looking back over the providence of God in Israel's history, he traced the purpose of God in the exodus to the purpose of God in Israel's experience in the wilderness. He described them in identical ways. His point was that Israel was sinful and undeserving, but that God saved them in the exodus and in the wilderness for the same reason—for the same ultimate goal. He saved them for his name's sake.

Quoting God, Ezekiel describes the purpose of God's providence in the exodus as we have seen:

> They rebelled against me and were not willing to listen to me. . . . Then I said I would pour out my wrath upon them and spend my anger against them in the midst of the land of Egypt. But *I acted for the sake of my name, that it should not be profaned in the sight of the nations among whom they lived, in whose sight I made myself known to them in bringing them out of the land of Egypt.* So I led them out of the land of Egypt and brought them into the wilderness. (Ezek. 20:8–10)

Then he quotes the Lord again, with almost identical words to describe the purpose of his providence in Israel's experience in the wilderness:

> The house of Israel rebelled against me in the wilderness. . . . Then I said I would pour out my wrath upon them in the wilderness, to make a full end of them. But *I acted for the sake of my name, that it should not be profaned in the sight of the nations, in whose sight I had brought them out.* (Ezek. 20:13–14)

Then eight verses later, he repeats himself to make sure the point is clear and forceful:

> The children rebelled against me. . . . Then I said I would pour out my wrath upon them and spend my anger against them in the wilderness. But I withheld my hand and *acted for the sake of my name, that it should not be profaned in the sight of the nations, in whose sight I had brought them out.* (Ezek. 20:21–22)

Ezekiel intends for us to see the connection between God's grace—not pouring out his wrath on Israel, though they deserved it—and his commitment to the glory of his name. The connection is that his wrath-restraining grace flowed to Israel *because* of his unwavering commitment to his name. In this case, specifically, he had concern for the glory of his name among the nations—"that it should not be profaned in the sight of the nations" (20:9, 14, 22).

We are cautioned again, therefore, not to think of God's purpose of self-exaltation as somehow at odds with his purpose to be merciful. It is precisely the opposite. God's self-exaltation was the ground of Israel's undeserved exultation. If they had eyes to see, they would be rejoicing in the glory of God's grace that moved him to spare them.

Divided Sea, Divided River, to Show That the Lord Is Mighty

We move next from the goal of God's providence in the wilderness wanderings of Israel to his goal in the brutal conquest of Canaan, the land of promise, the land flowing with milk and honey. In a kind of reenactment of the exodus, God divides the waters of the Jordan River so that Israel crosses into the promised land on dry ground (Josh. 3:15–17). They erect a memorial with twelve stones. The meaning of these stones establishes for us the connection between God's purpose in the exodus and his purpose for the imminent conquest:

> When your children ask their fathers in times to come, "What do these stones mean?" then you shall let your children know, "Israel passed over this Jordan on dry ground." For the LORD your God dried up the waters of the Jordan for you until you passed over, as the LORD your God did to the Red Sea, which he dried up for us until we passed over, *so that all the peoples of the earth may know that the hand of the LORD is mighty, that you may fear the LORD your God forever.* (Josh. 4:21–24)

In the exodus, God divided the Red Sea and defeated Pharaoh "to show you my power, so that my name may be proclaimed in all the earth" (Ex. 9:16). Similarly, God divided the Jordan and brought his people to a new land "so that all the peoples of the earth may know that the hand of the LORD is mighty" (Josh. 4:24).

Victory for Israel, Glory for God

As Israel engages the peoples of the land, one event in particular rivets our attention on this purpose of God to be known as the great and mighty God. Because of Achan's deceit, the people of Israel are defeated in battle for the city of Ai. Joshua was dismayed. He "tore his clothes and fell to the earth on his face before the ark of the LORD" (Josh. 7:6). He knew what the memorial stones signified and what God's purpose was in these battles. So his main controversy with the Lord was God's concern for his own name:

> Joshua said, "Alas, O Lord GOD, why have you brought this people over the Jordan at all, to give us into the hands of the Amorites, to destroy us? Would that we had been content to dwell beyond the Jordan! O Lord, what can I say, when Israel has turned their backs before their enemies! For the Canaanites and all the inhabitants of the land will hear of it and will surround us and cut off our name from the earth. *And what will you do for your great name?*" (Josh. 7:7–9)

Joshua's two concerns are inseparable in Israel's history and in the purpose of God's providence: Your people are about to be destroyed, and your name is about to be demeaned. Implicit in Joshua's prayer is the twofold longing "Save us, O God. And do it for your name's sake." Get *yourself* great glory in getting *us* the victory. The purpose of God in this conquest was "that all the peoples of the earth may know that the hand of the LORD is mighty" (Josh. 4:24), and that Israel might inherit the land and receive all God's mercies and cling to him and serve him with joy.

Free Grace for Israel, Deserved Judgment for Canaan

Before they crossed the Jordan, God had warned the people of Israel that this conquest was not a tribute to their righteousness. They do not deserve a land flowing with milk and honey. They are not destroying the inhabitants because of Israel's superior righteousness, but because of God's justice toward the nations and God's utterly undeserved grace toward Israel:

> Do not say in your heart, after the LORD your God has thrust them out before you, "It is because of my righteousness that the LORD has brought me in to possess this land," whereas it is because of the wickedness of these nations that the LORD is driving them out before you. Not because of your righteousness or the uprightness of your heart are you going in to possess their land, but because of the wickedness of these nations the LORD your God is driving them out from before you, and that he may confirm the word that the LORD swore to your fathers, to Abraham, to Isaac, and to Jacob.
>
> Know, therefore, that the LORD your God is not giving you this good land to possess because of your righteousness, for you are a stubborn people. Remember and do not forget how you provoked the LORD your God to wrath in the wilderness. From the day you came out of the land of Egypt until you came to this place, you have been rebellious against the LORD. (Deut. 9:4–7)

Time after time God reminds Israel that they do not deserve his blessings any more than the Egyptians or the Canaanites do. They deserve to be judged and destroyed as much as the pagan peoples do—perhaps even more because of rebelling against God in spite of all their benefits (Num. 14:11). But God chose freely to make a name for himself by pouring out undeserved *grace* on Israel and well-deserved *justice* on the wicked nations of Canaan, whose sins had, at last, been filled up (Gen. 15:16). Or as the apostle Paul would say, God was making known his wrath and power in order to make known the riches of his glory on the vessels of mercy (Rom. 9:22–23).[3]

---

3 When we ponder the fact that "many are called, but few are chosen" (Matt. 22:14; cf. Luke 13:23–24), we would do well to keep in mind what a great mercy it is that anyone is saved. John

God Fought for Them So That They Would Cling to Him

Oh, how valiantly did God fight for Israel, and how lavishly did he bless them! There was no mistaking. God fought for them. The victories belonged to the Lord:

> *The* Lord *has driven out before you great and strong nations.* And as for you, no man has been able to stand before you to this day. One man of you puts to flight a thousand, since it is *the* Lord *your God who fights for you,* just as he promised you. Be very careful, therefore, to love the Lord your God. (Josh. 23:9–11)

And what experience in the hearts of his people was God aiming at in all this judgment on his enemies and all this blessing on his people? What was his purpose for Israel in this new land, where "not one word has failed of all the good things that the Lord your God promised concerning you" (Josh. 23:14; cf. 21:45)?

The answer is that they would love him! "Be very careful, therefore, *to love the* Lord *your God*" (Josh. 23:11). Yes, he intended that they would "observe the commandment and the law" (Josh. 22:5)—which, as we saw above in dealing with the Ten Commandments, means "serving the Lord with gladness." The heart of God's goal for the experience

---

Owen reflects on this mercy: "Those who pretend a great difficulty at present, in the reconciliation of the eternal perishing of the greatest part of mankind with those notions we have of the divine goodness, seem not to have sufficiently considered what was contained in our original apostasy from God, nor the righteousness of God in dealing with the angels that sinned. For when man had voluntarily broken all the relation of love and moral good between God and him, had defaced his image—the only representation of his holiness and righteousness in this lower world—and deprived him of all his glory from the works of his hands, and had put himself into the society and under the conduct of the devil; what dishonour could it have been unto God, what diminution would there have been of his glory, if he had left him unto his own choice—to eat for ever of the fruit of his own ways, and to be filled with his own devices unto eternity? It is only infinite wisdom that could find out a way for the salvation of any one of the whole race of mankind, so as that it might be reconciled unto the glory of his holiness, righteousness, and rule. Wherefore, as we ought always to admire sovereign grace in the few that shall be saved, so we have no ground to reflect on divine goodness in the multitudes that perish, especially considering that they all voluntarily continue in their sin and apostasy." John Owen, *The Works of John Owen,* vol. 1, ed. William H. Goold (Edinburgh: T&T Clark, n.d.), 191.

of his people was in this great inference: because God so mercifully fights for you, "guard your souls exceedingly to love Yahweh your God" (Josh. 23:11, my translation). Or as Joshua 22:5 says, "Cling to him and . . . serve him with all your heart and with all your soul."

Loving, clinging, serving—this is the description not of a miserable slave but of a happy son.

> Happy are you, O Israel! Who is like you,
>> a people saved by the LORD,
> the shield of your help,
>> and the sword of your triumph!
> Your enemies shall come fawning to you,
>> and you shall tread upon their backs. (Deut. 33:29)

The purpose of God's providence in the conquest of Canaan was to put his power and his name on display in justice and mercy so that his people would be stunned at the freedom and glory of his grace. Then, in that stunned and humble amazement at his mighty grace, they would cling to him as their life (Deut. 30:20) and serve him forever *in a way that makes clear he is an all-satisfying treasure.* The purpose of God's providence was that his glory would be exalted as his people treasured and enjoyed him as their supreme portion (Ps. 73:26). This is what it would mean to "cling to him and to serve him with all your heart and with all your soul" (Josh. 22:5).

From the Ten Commandments to the Conquest of Canaan

Nothing would shape the corporate life of Israel for her entire history like the law given at Mount Sinai. Therefore, God embedded at the heart of it an unmistakable expression of his self-exaltation: "You shall have no other gods before me" (Ex. 20:3). This commandment was to be no more burdensome than the satisfied experience of a wife who has a perfect husband. That satisfaction would make the difference between desires that magnify the husband's greatness and those that are known as covetousness. God's ultimate goal in the law was that the supremacy of his worth and beauty be reflected in the supreme satisfaction of his people in him.

Just as the exodus and the giving of the law were designed by God to exalt the incontestable greatness of his glory in a God-satisfied and God-exalting people, so God's unparalleled patience with disobedient Israel in the wilderness was designed to magnify his name and keep it from being profaned among the nations (Ezek. 20:9, 14, 22). God's wonders in the wilderness were performed again and again for a people who rebelled against him. Therefore, the glory that God exalted among the nations was the glory of his mighty grace.

At last, in his mercy, God brought Israel into the promised land and dispossessed the nations in his justice on *their* wickedness and in his grace on *Israel's* wickedness (Deut. 9:4–7). Neither Israel nor the Canaanites deserved the land. God was acting in freedom ("I AM WHO I AM," Ex. 3:14; "I will have mercy on whom I have mercy," Rom. 9:15). His aim was "that all the peoples of the earth may know that the hand of the LORD is mighty" (Josh. 4:24), and that Israel would love him and cling to him with all their heart and soul (Josh. 22:5; 23:11). This global glory of God and this gladness of God's people in his grace are not separable. The perfection of glory stands forth at last in the perfection of gladness in the glory of grace. This is where all providence is leading. This means it is leading to Jesus Christ and his cross, as we saw in chapter 3 and will see again.

9

The Time of the Judges and the Days of the Monarchy

Alas, God's aim that his name be magnified among the nations through Israel's clinging to him in satisfied love (Josh. 4:24; 22:5) is not the way history goes. Not yet. The power of sin seems unstoppable. It cries out for a solution that never arises in the Old Testament. There are only foretastes and previews that point to a coming Messiah who would deal with sin in the most unthinkable, yet decisive, way (Isa. 53:4–6). But for now, with the end of Joshua's generation, Israel spiraled down into anarchy during the time of the judges. "In those days there was no king in Israel. Everyone did what was right in his own eyes" (Judg. 17:6; 21:25). "And the people of Israel did what was evil in the sight of the LORD and served the Baals" (Judg. 2:11).

Bleak Backdrop for Beautiful Mercies

In our trek through the history of Israel, we pause only briefly in this period, where it seems as if God's only purpose is to expose the depths of human sin. This is not the only goal of his providence in the time of the judges. We will linger over one event to show a greater purpose.

Reading the book of Judges is like having the insanity of sin rubbed in your face while God returns again and again with mercy, which was repeatedly forgotten. Here's a summary of that dark period of Israel's history:

> The LORD raised up judges, who saved them out of the hand of those who plundered them. Yet they did not listen to their judges, for they whored after other gods and bowed down to them. . . . Whenever the LORD raised up judges for them, the LORD was with the judge, and he saved them from the hand of their enemies all the days of the judge. For the LORD was moved to pity by their groaning because of those who afflicted and oppressed them. But whenever the judge died, they turned back and were more corrupt than their fathers. (Judg. 2:16–19)

Nevertheless, God did intend to make his patience and mercy and power crystal clear. We focus on one remarkable instance in which God reveals his unrelenting zeal for his own glory in the execution of his saving mercy—the story of Gideon.

God's Self-Exaltation in Gideon's Surprising Victory

In the sad refrain of the book of Judges we read, "The people of Israel did what was evil in the sight of the LORD, and the LORD gave them into the hand of Midian seven years" (Judg. 6:1). In spite of the disobedience of Israel (6:10), God sent an angel to Gideon to conscript him for a great work of deliverance: "The LORD said to him, . . . 'I will be with you, and you shall strike the Midianites as one man'" (6:16). So "the Spirit of the LORD clothed Gideon, and he sounded the trumpet" (6:34), and thirty-two thousand people assembled to fight the Midianites (7:3). At this point, God's zeal for his glory becomes plain. He says to Gideon:

> "The people with you are too many for me to give the Midianites into their hand, *lest Israel boast over me, saying, 'My own hand has*

saved me.' Now therefore proclaim in the ears of the people, saying, 'Whoever is fearful and trembling, let him return home and hurry away from Mount Gilead.'" Then 22,000 of the people returned, and 10,000 remained. (7:2–3)

The essence of sin is minimizing God and making much of self. In other words, the essence of sin is pride. What makes human self-exaltation so evil is the double tragedy that God is demeaned and humans are destroyed. Jesus made this clear:

Truly, I say to you, unless you turn and become like children, you will never enter the kingdom of heaven. Whoever humbles himself like this child is the greatest in the kingdom of heaven. (Matt. 18:3–4)

Of course, this most basic of all messages was made clear countless ways in the Old Testament. In the face of Pharaoh's arrogance (Neh. 9:10), the Lord had said, "How long will you refuse to humble yourself before me?" (Ex. 10:3). Pharaoh is one of many examples of this truth:

Pride goes before destruction,
  and a haughty spirit before a fall.
It is better to be of a lowly spirit with the poor
  than to divide the spoil with the proud. (Prov. 16:18–19)

After the pride of Egypt was punished in the exodus, God cared for his sinful people in the wilderness, and Moses made plain to them that God's aim was "that he might humble you and test you, to do you good in the end" (Deut. 8:16). That was what God was about to do through Gideon in the book of Judges. He intended by his power through Gideon to silence the pride of Israel.

He had reduced Gideon's army from thirty-two thousand to ten thousand "lest Israel boast over me, saying, 'My own hand has saved me'" (Judg. 7:2). But ten thousand was still too many. So God told Gideon to take the ten thousand down to the water and have them drink. Then he said, "With the 300 men who lapped I will save you and give the Midianites into your hand" (7:7). This was not because the Midianites were a small army. Their number was beyond estimation: "The Midianites and the Amalekites and all the people of the East lay along the valley like locusts in abundance, and their camels were without number, as the sand that is on the seashore in abundance" (7:12).

With these three hundred, God routed the Midianites (7:22). He had made his point—for those who had ears to hear. God says, in essence, "I oppose the arrogance of Israel as they exult in their greatness and not mine. My name and my power and my glory will be exalted in my people. I do not save you in order for you to forget me. I save you in order for you to praise me. If you do not see this in my merciful and mighty and repeated return to you in your sin, then see it at least this once in the victory of Gideon."

God says, in effect, "Your enemies were as innumerable as locusts, yet I delivered you with three hundred men. Do you understand, Israel? This was to shut the mouth of your boasting ('Lest Israel boast over me, saying, "My own hand has saved me,"' v. 2). My aim was to humble you so that you would see that I am your hope, your shield, your sword, your portion. If you will cling to me and love me for who I am, 'Happy are you, O Israel! . . . A people saved by the LORD' (Deut. 33:29). You will get the joy. I will get the glory." That was God's ultimate goal in the period of the judges—to point Israel beyond their anarchy and pride to the hope of humble, happy worship under the omnipotent, redeeming hand of God.

The Strange Rise of a Monarchy in Israel

The period of the judges came to an end with the rise of the monarchy in Israel, a period of the united Israel with Saul, David, and Solomon as kings, followed by a period of a divided kingdom with kings in the north (Israel) and the south (Judah). The northern kingdom was brought to an end in 722 BC with the Assyrian victory over the leading city of Samaria (2 Kings 17:6–8). The southern kingdom came to an end in 586 BC with the Babylonian exile (2 Kings 25:1–12).

The emergence of the kingship in Israel after about a thousand years of Jewish history without a king is one of the strange providences of the Bible. I say *strange* because the actual movement to install the first king was an act of rebellion against God, even though God had already prophesied that Israel would have a king. Adding to the strangeness is that God warned that having a king would be trouble for Israel, even though God's prophetic plan was that there be a glorious Messiah who would be the final and eternal king—the "King of kings" (1 Tim. 6:15; Rev. 17:14; 19:16).

The God-Ordained Roots of the Reign of Man

Early on, in Genesis 14, we meet a mysterious figure named Melchize-dek, to whom Abraham pays tribute (14:20). His name means "*king* of righteousness," and both Psalm 110:4 and Hebrews 7:10–11 treat him as a forerunner of Christ. So from the earliest biblical times, God's purpose was that there would be a final "king of righteousness" over his people. Kingship was not an afterthought or a plan B conceived after the kingless plan A had failed.

In Deuteronomy 17:14–20 God tells his people that they may install a king when they come into the promised land. But then he tells them that this king, in order to be a legitimate king, must live under the law, not above it. He must not acquire many horses, many wives, or much silver and gold, and his heart must not "be lifted up above his brothers" (17:20). These commands would be disobeyed in Israel for centuries of God's patience.

As the period of the judges was coming to an end, Hannah was granted to speak prophetically concerning a coming king in Israel:

> The adversaries of the LORD shall be broken to pieces;
>   against them he will thunder in heaven.

> The LORD will judge the ends of the earth;
> *he will give strength to his king*
> and exalt the power of his anointed. (1 Sam. 2:10)

Not long after Hannah's prophecy, Samuel warns that not all of the coming kings are going to be as circumspect as Deuteronomy required, or as Hannah's prophecy promised:

> These will be the ways of the king who will reign over you: he will take your sons and appoint them to his chariots. . . . And he will appoint for himself commanders . . . to plow his ground and to reap his harvest, and to make his implements of war and the equipment of his chariots. He will take your daughters to be perfumers and cooks and bakers. He will take the best of your fields and vineyards and olive orchards and give them to his servants. He will take the tenth of your grain and of your vineyards and give it to his officers and to his servants. He will take your male servants and female servants and the best of your young men and your donkeys, and put them to his work. He will take the tenth of your flocks, and you shall be his slaves. And in that day you will cry out because of your king, whom you have chosen for yourselves, but the LORD will not answer you in that day. (1 Sam. 8:11–18)

The Great Wickedness of Fulfilling God's Will

Nevertheless, the people insist on a king. They take Saul and make him king (1 Sam. 11:15). It was not a godly act. Nevertheless, God puts his royal seal on Saul as he sends Samuel to anoint him (1 Sam. 15:1). But Samuel makes sure that the people realize what a "great wickedness" they have committed in asking for a king:

> "You said to me, 'No, but a king shall reign over us,' when the LORD your God was your king. . . . And you shall know and see

that your wickedness is great, which you have done in the sight of the Lord, in asking for yourselves a king." . . . And Samuel said to the people, "Do not be afraid; you have done all this evil. Yet do not turn aside from following the Lord, but serve the Lord with all your heart. And do not turn aside after empty things that cannot profit or deliver, for they are empty. For the Lord will not forsake his people, *for his great name's sake*, because it has pleased the Lord to make you a people for himself." (1 Sam. 12:12, 17, 20–22)

We have seen this before—God's acting "for his great name's sake" (12:22). We have seen it in the purposes of God before creation (Eph. 1:4–6), and in the act of creation (Heb. 2:10), and at the exodus (Ps. 106:8), and in the wilderness (Ezek. 20:9), and in the conquest of Canaan (Josh. 4:24), and in the deliverances in the time of the judges (Judg. 7:2). What is so stark here is that the people have just committed great wickedness in asking for a king (1 Sam. 12:17). It was treason: they *had* a king—namely, God (1 Sam. 12:12)! So in the very act of dethroning their God, God says, "It is precisely for *my name's sake* that I will not destroy you, though that is what you certainly deserve."

A Kingship through Sin to Show God's Grace

In other words, the strange providence by which Israel becomes a monarchy is designed at least to show that the rule of this king over his people is based on absolutely free and sovereign grace. In making themselves a king, they acted wickedly. Their rightful king in heaven may justly put down this rebellion with a great judgment. Instead, he says, "I will not forsake my people." In other words, "I will act in lavish grace toward these rebels. I will confirm their king and not destroy them." And the ground of this grace? He says it explicitly: "for [God's] great name's sake" (1 Sam. 12:22). God's commitment to the glory of his name is the ground of his gracious commitment to his people—and their king.

The Undeserved Blessings of a Kingship Conceived in Sin

This story has far-reaching implications. The grace of affirming a monarchy conceived in sin signals that every blessing that comes from this kingship is undeserved. Every blessing that flows from this kingship is grace. In one sense, the kingship is a standing witness to Israel's mutiny. In another sense, it is a standing witness to the grace of God, who planned the kingship as a source of (literally endless) blessing. And all this gracious blessing will rest on this foundation: God is committed to uphold the glory of his name (1 Sam. 12:22).

We call to mind just three of those unspeakably great blessings that flow from this kingship.

A Poet-King for the Sake of God's Praise and the People's Joy

First, King David is portrayed as the great model of a king after God's own heart (1 Sam. 13:14; Acts 13:22). And what is he best known for? His songs:

> The oracle of David, the son of Jesse,
> the oracle of the man who was raised on high,
> the anointed of the God of Jacob,
> the sweet psalmist of Israel. (2 Sam. 23:1)

Though he did not write all the psalms of Israel, his name is so identified as the great psalmist of Israel that one can't help but see here a great irony of grace: the treasonous installation of a human king over Israel has been turned by God, within one generation, into a fountain of God-exalting praise. In other words, this kingship existed "for God's great name's sake." Why else would God make sure that a praising poet is installed as the paradigm of kingly faithfulness? David did more than anyone to solidify poetic praise as central to Israel's life. The psalms have one great message: God is worthy to be praised. And this praise is the pleasure humans were made for:

> Praise the LORD, for the LORD is good;
> sing to his name, for it is *pleasant*! (Ps. 135:3)

God gets the praise. We get the pleasure. This was central to David's achievement as a king. Without him there would probably be no book of Psalms. This was the greatest fruit of his kingship. Thus, the kingship was a providence of amazing grace.

A Builder-King for the Name of God and the Mercy of Forgiveness

Second, because of King David's planning and King Solomon's execution, the temple for Yahweh was erected in Israel. When Solomon prays the prayer of dedication (2 Chron. 6), we see clearly what this building signifies. Of course, it is not God's house in the sense that the Creator of the universe can live in a house: "Behold, heaven and the highest heaven cannot contain you, how much less this house that I have built!" (6:18).

The way Solomon prays shows that the house gives a kind of physical position for a spiritual transaction between man and God. And the heart of that transaction is this: sinful man acknowledges the holy God and his mercy and cries for help, and God forgives. For example, here is how Solomon put that into a prayer of dedication:

> Listen to the pleas of . . . your people Israel, when they pray toward this place. . . . And when you hear, forgive. (6:21)

> If your people Israel are defeated before the enemy because they have sinned against you, and they turn again and *acknowledge your name* . . . then hear from heaven and forgive. (6:24–25)

> When heaven is shut up and there is no rain because they have sinned against you, if they pray toward this place and *acknowledge your name* and turn from their sin . . . then hear in heaven and forgive. (6:26–27)

In other words, the temple stands for "God's name"—his essential character and greatness. This name is the glory of his justice and grace. The sacrifices happening here are evidence that he aims to be a forgiving God, but not without sacrifice—not without justice (as Rom. 3:23–25 will reveal when Christ is put forward as the great sacrifice behind all sacrifices).

So when a sinner looks to the temple and acknowledges this name and pleads for forgiveness because of this name, as David says ("For your name's sake, O LORD, pardon my guilt," Ps. 25:11), then Solomon's plea is that the sinner be forgiven. That is the meaning of this house—*the exaltation of the name of Yahweh in the forgiveness of sin.*

This mingling of God's exaltation and his grace toward sinners reaches its climax in Solomon's prayer with his plea for the *foreigner.* It is amazing:

> Likewise, when a foreigner, who is not of your people Israel, comes from a far country *for the sake of your great name and your mighty hand and your outstretched arm,* when he comes and prays toward this house, hear from heaven your dwelling place and do according to all for which the foreigner calls to you, *in order that all the peoples of the earth may know your name and fear you,* as do your people Israel, and *that they may know that this house that I have built is called by your name.* (2 Chron. 6:32–33)

Notice the structure of Solomon's prayer for these foreigners. First, they are coming to the temple "for the sake of your great name." Second, Solomon asks that God's response be gracious: "Do according to all for which the foreigner calls to you." Third, the aim of this grace is "that all the peoples of the earth may know your name" and that this house is "called by your name" and that they may "fear you."

Zeal for God's name leads the foreigner to seek God's mercies. Receiving his mercies leads him to know and fear God's name. What shall we say, then, about the relationship between the glory of God's name and the greatness of his mercies? We shall say that the mercies of God are designed to exalt the name of God. The foreigner was drawn to God's mercies "for the sake of your great name" (6:32). And the result of tasting those mercies was that the foreigner would know and revere the name of God even more.

So the kingship of Israel unleashed not only an era of poetic praises through King David to the glory of God's name, but also the building of a temple through King Solomon, whose purpose was the exaltation of God's name in the experience of divine mercy.

A Savior-King for the Father's Glory and the Joy of His People

Third, most wonderfully, and perhaps most obviously, without the existence of a kingship in Israel—no matter how wickedly it came to be—there would be no final kingship of Jesus the Messiah. There would be no cry, "Have mercy on us, Son of David" (Matt. 9:27); no confession from Nathanael, "You are the Son of God! You are the King of Israel!" (John 1:49); no king entering Jerusalem humble and riding on a donkey (Matt. 21:5); no crucified Savior with a sign over his head reading, "King of the Jews" (Matt. 27:37); no returning sovereign called "King of kings" (1 Tim. 6:15).

In other words, all the kingly dimensions of the incarnation of the Son of God as the Messiah were in the making when God ordained the establishment of the kingship in Israel. And as we will see, virtually all of Jesus's kingly work on earth and in heaven is designed to display and magnify the glory of his Father, especially the glory of his grace.

The Word became flesh and dwelt among us, and we have seen his glory, glory as of the only Son from the Father, full of grace and truth. (John 1:14)

That final and decisive revelation of the glory of God's grace—the revelation of the incarnation of Christ, the anointed Son of David—was the ultimate design of the monarchy of Israel. That is, it was ultimate if we include, in the *revelation* of the glory of King Jesus, the *experience* of his people seeing that glory, savoring that glory, and shining with that glory.

The ultimate goal of providence in establishing a monarchy in Israel will not be attained until the redeemed people of King Jesus see in it *their* perfection and *his* perfection. That is what Jesus prayed for in John 17:24: "Father, I desire that they also, whom you have given me, may be with me where I am, *to see my glory.*" Yes. But not even *seeing* his glory is the ultimate goal. It is a seeing *with joy.* When Jesus welcomes us into the presence of his final glory, he will say, "Enter into the *joy* of your master" (Matt. 25:21). When the Master's joy becomes the joy of his perfected people, their joy will be full (John 15:11). And they will be transformed into the likeness of the one they see with complete joy (1 John 3:2; 2 Cor. 3:18).

The ultimate purpose of the monarchy of Israel will be finally realized as Jesus sits on "the throne of his father David" (Luke 1:32–33) and reigns not only over a redeemed Israel but over a kingdom of worshipers from all nations (Rev. 5:10). They will see him exalted as "Lord of lords and King of kings" (Rev. 17:14). They will be satisfied under this gracious rule:

> He who sits on the throne will shelter them with his presence. They shall hunger no more, neither thirst anymore; the sun shall not strike them, nor any scorching heat. For the Lamb in the midst of the throne will be their shepherd, and he will guide them to springs of living water, and God will wipe away every tear from their eyes. (Rev. 7:15–17)

And in their joy they will "shine like the sun in the kingdom of their Father" and "of his Christ" (Matt. 13:43; Rev. 11:15). In that joyful, transformed likeness to Christ, the glory of the "King of the ages" (1 Tim. 1:17) will fill all creation. That is the ultimate goal of providence in establishing the monarchy of Israel.

10

The Protection, Destruction, and Restoration of Jerusalem

The monarchy of Israel, as an independent nation, ended with the sack of Jerusalem and the captivity of the nation in Babylon. According to the prophecy of Jeremiah, the Babylonian exile would last seventy years: "This whole land shall become a ruin and a waste, and these nations shall serve the king of Babylon seventy years" (Jer. 25:11). This was a devastating experience for Israel, and for Jerusalem in particular, perhaps best described in the book of Lamentations:

> How lonely sits the city
>   that was full of people!
> How like a widow has she become,
>   she who was great among the nations!
> She who was a princess among the provinces
>   has become a slave.
> She weeps bitterly in the night,
>   with tears on her cheeks. (Lam. 1:1–2)

For the biblical authors who tell the story, God was acting *for the sake of his name* from beginning to end in dealing with Jerusalem.

First, he was protecting Jerusalem for the sake of his name, then he gave Jerusalem into the hands of the Babylonians for the sake of his name, and then again he rescued his people from exile for the sake of his name. The Scriptures show us each of these phases of God's providence and draw specific attention to God's purpose in the exaltation of the glory of his name.

Defending Jerusalem "For My Own Sake"

In his patience, God had endured the unfaithfulness and sins of Jerusalem for a long time (Isa. 40:2; Lam. 1:8; Dan. 9:6; Mic. 1:5). Now Sennacherib, the king of Assyria, had come up against the fortified cities of Judah. He took them and threatened to take Jerusalem. He sent his emissary to King Hezekiah at Jerusalem with a great army and taunted the king, mocking his trust in the Lord (Isa. 36:1–10).

But God delivered Jerusalem from the hands of Sennacherib, and the prophet Isaiah tells us what God's purpose was in this amazing mercy: "I will defend this city to save it, *for my own sake and for the sake of my servant David*" (Isa. 37:35). God's patience and mercy toward sinful Jerusalem was owing finally and decisively not to their faith or their righteousness. It was owing to God's zeal for the glory of his name, which included the covenant he had freely made with David. "I will defend this city to save it, *for my own sake and for the sake of my servant David*" (Isa. 37:35; cf. 2 Kings 19:34; 20:6).

God's Rescuing Response to Faith

When I say that the deliverance of Jerusalem was owing finally or decisively not to their faith or their righteousness, I don't mean to imply that there is never a correlation between the faith of God's people and the divine rescue they experience. There often is. From the beginning of God's covenant with Abraham, the Lord has established a correlation between the obedience of faith and many of the blessings we receive: "In your offspring shall all the nations of the earth be blessed, *because you have obeyed my voice*" (Gen. 22:18). This *obedience* was the fruit of Abraham's faith—what the apostle Paul calls the "obedience of faith" (Rom. 1:5; 15:18; 16:26) or the "work of faith" (1 Thess. 1:3; 2 Thess. 1:11)—for Abraham "*believed* the LORD, and he counted it to him as righteousness" (Gen. 15:6). Many blessings flow to God's people because of such obedience.

Hence, David says to God:

> In you our fathers trusted;
> *they trusted, and you delivered them.* (Ps. 22:4)

And when Daniel was rescued in the lion's den, the author says, "So Daniel was taken up out of the den, and no kind of harm was found on him, *because he had trusted in his God*" (Dan. 6:23).

Other stories of God's mercies carry the same message: "The Reubenites . . . prevailed over them, the Hagrites and all who were with them . . . for they cried out to God in the battle, and he granted their urgent plea *because they trusted in him*" (1 Chron. 5:18, 20). Jehoshaphat, the king of Judah, says to the people, "Hear me, Judah and inhabitants of Jerusalem! *Believe in the LORD your God, and you will be established; believe his prophets, and you will succeed*" (2 Chron. 20:20).

And David says again, "The LORD . . . delivers [the righteous] from the wicked and saves them, *because they take refuge in him*" (Ps. 37:40). So with the other kings after David: "*As long as [Uzziah] sought the LORD, God made him prosper*" (2 Chron. 26:5). "Jotham became mighty, *because he ordered his ways before the LORD his God*" (2 Chron. 27:6).

The reverse is also true: judgment often follows unbelief and sin. "*If you transgress the covenant of the LORD your God . . .* the anger of the LORD will be kindled against you, and you shall perish quickly from off the good land that he has given to you" (Josh. 23:16). "*You have rejected me*, declares the LORD; . . . *so* I have stretched out my hand against you and destroyed you" (Jer. 15:6). The enemy "killed 120,000 from Judah in one day . . . *because they had forsaken the LORD*"

(2 Chron. 28:6). So, clearly, God often responds to faith with deliverance and to faithlessness with judgment.

Nevertheless, the book of Job and other places (e.g., Ps. 44:22; cf. Rom. 8:36) make plain that sometimes God lets his godly ones go through great affliction. He does not always deliver them *from* affliction, but often *through* affliction (Ps. 34:19). The author of Hebrews confirms this observation as he looks back over the Old Testament history of faith. On the one hand, faith is the way great triumphs were enjoyed:

> Through faith [they] conquered kingdoms, enforced justice, obtained promises, stopped the mouths of lions, quenched the power of fire, escaped the edge of the sword, were made strong out of weakness, became mighty in war, put foreign armies to flight. Women received back their dead by resurrection. (Heb. 11:33–35a)

On the other hand, that same faith was the way that believers endured great affliction:

> [By faith] some were tortured, refusing to accept release, so that they might rise again to a better life. Others suffered mocking and flogging, and even chains and imprisonment. . . . And all these [were] commended through their faith. (11:35b–36, 39)

Because Hezekiah Prayed and Because of God's Zeal for His Glory

When I say that God's mercy toward sinful Jerusalem was owing finally or decisively not to their faith or their righteousness but to God's zeal for the glory of his name, I don't mean that God did not respond to Hezekiah's prayer of faith, or to Isaiah's prophecy. For Hezekiah had indeed prayed for deliverance, and Isaiah, in response to that prayer, delivered a word of devastation for Sennacherib. Rather, I mean that Hezekiah's prayer for the deliverance of Jerusalem was a prayer of God-pleasing faith (Ps. 147:10–11) precisely because *it looked away from the ill-deserving sins of God's people and based his appeal squarely on God's zeal for his glory.* That divine commitment to his own name is decisive in the deliverance.

Here is how Hezekiah prayed when the city of God was threatened:

> O LORD of hosts, God of Israel, enthroned above the cherubim, you are the God, you alone, of all the kingdoms of the earth; you have made heaven and earth. Incline your ear, O LORD, and hear; open your eyes, O LORD, and see; and hear all the words of Sennacherib, which he has sent to mock the living God. . . . So now, O LORD our God, save us from his hand, *that all the kingdoms of the earth may know that you alone are the LORD.* (Isa. 37:16–17, 20)

Hezekiah's prayer did not appeal to the worthiness of Jerusalem to be rescued but to the worthiness of God to be worshiped. To this kind of God-exalting prayer, Isaiah responded this way:

> Thus says the LORD, the God of Israel: *Because you have prayed to me* concerning Sennacherib king of Assyria, this is the word that the LORD has spoken concerning him: . . . "I will defend this city to save it, *for my own sake and for the sake of my servant David.*" (37:21–22, 35)

And then we read: "The angel of the LORD went out and struck down 185,000 in the camp of the Assyrians" (37:36).

There is no contradiction between saying that Sennacherib's army was destroyed *because Hezekiah prayed* (37:21) and saying that it was destroyed *because of God's zeal for his own name.* The reason there is no contradiction is that Hezekiah's prayer appealed precisely to God's zeal for his name. "O LORD our God, save us from his hand, *that all the kingdoms of the earth may know that you alone are the LORD*" (37:20).

This is why, throughout the history of Israel (and the history of the church), God responds to the faith-filled prayers of his people with help. Faith, by its very nature, looks away from ourselves and our sinfulness and bases all our help on God's zeal for his name. Pardon us for your name's sake (Ps. 25:11). Save us for your name's sake (Ps. 106:8). Preserve us for your name's sake (Ps. 143:11). Lead us in righteousness for your name's sake (Ps. 23:3). This is the way faith prays. For faith despairs of self as sufficient and looks away to the all-sufficiency of God. That is why Paul says in Romans 4:20 that Abraham's faith "gave glory to God."

When Jesus made the first petition of the Lord's prayer, "Our Father in heaven, hallowed be your name" (Matt. 6:9)—that is, see to it that your name be revered and treasured and honored—he was showing us that the touchstone of all believing prayer is zeal for God's glory. Jesus taught us that, first and foremost, we should ask God to make sure he is seen and revered as great. We should want this and love this above all.

Therefore, when Isaiah says that God will rescue Jerusalem *because Hezekiah prayed* (Isa. 37:21) and that he will rescue Jerusalem *for his own sake* (37:35), these are the same motive because Hezekiah's prayer appealed to the Lord to act for his own sake. Thus, for generations Jerusalem was saved from destruction because the ultimate goal of God's providence is "that all the kingdoms of the earth may know [and exult in the glorious reality] that you alone are the Lord" (37:20).

God's Name Exalted in the End of His Patience

But the days would come when it would be plain that God's patience with Jerusalem, and his everlasting love (Jer. 31:3) toward the people of his covenant, would not exclude his judgment on the generations that forsake him and find their pleasure in other things.

> Your evil will chastise you,
>   and your apostasy will reprove you.
> Know and see that it is evil and bitter
>   for you to forsake the Lord your God. (Jer. 2:19)

The patience of God toward the idolatries of Jerusalem comes to a wise and holy end. His zeal for the glory of his name turns from the demonstration of the glory of his patience to the demonstration of the glory of his holiness and justice in terrible judgments against Jerusalem. This too is part of the glory of his name:

> As I live, declares the Lord GOD, surely, because you have defiled my sanctuary with all your detestable things and with all your abominations, therefore I will withdraw. My eye will not spare, and I will have no pity. A third part of you shall die of pestilence and be consumed with famine in your midst; a third part shall fall by the sword all around you; and a third part I will scatter to all the winds and will unsheathe the sword after them. Thus shall my anger spend itself, and I will vent my fury upon them and satisfy myself. *And they shall know that I am the LORD—that I have spoken in my jealousy*—when I spend my fury upon them. (Ezek. 5:11–13)

> *They shall know that I am the LORD*, when I disperse them among the nations and scatter them among the countries. (Ezek. 12:15)

> I will set my face against them. Though they escape from the fire, the fire shall yet consume them, and *you will know that I am the LORD*, when I set my face against them. (Ezek. 15:7)

When God judges Jerusalem "in [his] jealousy" (Ezek. 5:13) and says that his aim is that they "know that I am the LORD," the implication is that Jerusalem, like a faithless wife, has gone after other lovers as if the Lord is unworthy of her affections—as if greater pleasures can be found in the arms of another husband:

> You have played the whore with many lovers;
>> and would you return to me?
>> declares the LORD. (Jer. 3:1)

> All your lovers have forgotten you;
>> they care nothing for you;
>> for I have dealt you the blow of an enemy,
>> the punishment of a merciless foe,

because your guilt is great,
  because your sins are flagrant. (Jer. 30:14; cf. Ezek. 16:31–34)

Double Evil: Adultery against God

What makes this "whoring," or this adultery against "the Lord," especially wicked is that the name "Lord," as we saw in chapter 6, is not the generic name of God, but the personal name of Israel's God, Yahweh. Judgment is coming on Jerusalem because the people have treated the most precious reality, and the most precious relationship, with contempt. Jeremiah calls this a double evil:

> My people have committed two evils:
> they have forsaken me,
>   the fountain of living waters,
> and hewed out cisterns for themselves,
>   broken cisterns that can hold no water. (Jer. 2:13)

Evil one: despise God. Evil two: prefer dirt. This is the very essence of evil: to assess the infinitely valuable, all-satisfying God and then turn away from him as unworthy and unsatisfying in order to seek satisfaction by scratching in the dirt to make a broken cistern. There is no greater scorn against no greater name. This is why judgment is coming on Jerusalem.

Ezekiel's Relentless Reminder

The jealousy of God is not a personal tantrum because of a resented rival. It is the measured, fitting, and holy outrage of one who knows that scorning what is infinitely good and satisfying is blasphemous and suicidal. It is treason and tragedy. God's jealous judgment is the active revelation of the soul-satisfying worth and beauty of the person being spurned for broken cisterns.

When Ezekiel says that judgment is coming on Jerusalem so that "[they] *will know that I am the Lord*" (5:13; 12:15; 15:7), he intends for us to see the magnitude of God's name, "the LORD"—Yahweh—in the divine motivation. Seventy-two times in the book of Ezekiel, the prophet says that God does what he does "so that you might know that I am the LORD." Ten other times he says, "I am the LORD." Both terrible punishments (33:29) and thrilling salvation (20:44) are rooted in this motivation: "that you may know that I am the LORD." The words "I am the LORD" are meant to remind us of the great "I AM" of Exodus 3:14.

In other words, over eighty times Ezekiel reminds us: never, never forget that you are dealing with the God who absolutely *is*.[1] He is who he is. He does what he does. He wills what he wills. He does not conform to anything outside himself. He is not striving to become something he would like to be. He is ultimate, unoriginated, absolute, independent, self-sufficient, final reality.

Ezekiel would remind us that this ultimate, absolute, all-important, primary reality should dominate our consciousness more than anything else. When we look at our watches, we should be aware of the amazing fact that this watch is dependent on God. When we let our eye scan the galaxies at night, we should be glad that they were flicked out with God's little finger (Ps. 8:3), and are totally dependent for every millisecond of their existence on his thought (Heb. 1:3).

The point of Ezekiel's prophesying over and over and over again, "You shall know that I am the LORD," is that we should live in the conscious awareness that the supreme reality in the universe—in America, in China, in Brazil, in Nigeria, in Brussels, in our bedrooms, in our minds—is *Yahweh*, the God who absolutely is. Nothing is more important. Nothing is more pervasive. Nothing is more relevant. Nothing is more glorious. Nothing is more beautiful. Nothing is more satisfying.

---

1 Recall the meaning of the name Yahweh when God gave himself this name in Ex. 3:14 ("I AM WHO I AM"), as we saw in chap. 6.

God's centuries-long patience (Ezek. 2:3–5) with rebellious Jeru-salem, and his finally handing them over to Babylonian captivity, are both part of God's providential purpose. Both were guided by this aim: "They shall know that I am the LORD." They shall be shown that God is unwaveringly committed to the worth and beauty of his holy name—whether in merciful patience or in just punishment.

Restoration for Their Joy and "Evangelical Humiliation"
But mercy will have the last word toward his people. God's name is the great treasure he offers Israel for their everlasting joy, and for his glory. God is committed to the joy of his people in savoring his name, in a way that brings to an end the judgment of Jerusalem for scorning his name:

> This city shall be to me a *name of joy*, a praise and a glory before all the nations of the earth who shall hear of all the good that I do for them. (Jer. 33:9)

But there is something extraordinary about the way God reveals his commitment to his people in restoring them from exile. He magnifies the supremacy of his own name—the holiness of his name—by mak-ing clear that his mercy is not owing to Israel's righteousness. Three times in the book of Ezekiel, the Lord exalts his holiness and his name as the motive of his mercy in rescuing Israel from exile. He makes this motive all the more stark because, at the same time, he draws explicit attention to the fact that this restoration is "not for your [Israel's] sake" (Ezek. 36:22). Their restoration was doubly gracious: it was in spite of the presence of sin, and in spite of the absence of righteousness.

This means that God was at pains to make clear to us that the ground of his mercy—the ground of his restoration after exile—was zeal for his holiness and his name. Below are the three passages that exalt the holiness of God's name in saving Jerusalem. I recall feeling the force of these passages for the first time when I was reading Jonathan Edwards's book *Religious Affections*, where he gives twelve signs of being a true Christian—or in his words, twelve signs of "truly gracious affections"—that is, affections created and shaped by grace, not by mere human emotion. The sixth sign is this: "Gracious affections are attended with evangelical humiliation."[2]

I recoiled at the word *humiliation* until I read his exposition of these texts. In his mind, "evangelical humiliation" is not inconsistent with, but a part of, the most exquisite joy in the mercies of God. Edwards explains:

> Although Christ hath borne our griefs, and carried our sorrows, so that we are freed from the sorrow of punishment, and may now sweetly feed upon the comforts Christ hath purchased for us; yet that hinders not but that our feeding on these comforts should be attended with the sorrow of repentance.[3]

Saved and Confounded—by Grace

The passages that follow are the ones that Edwards ponders in coming to that conclusion. I invite you to ponder them with him. They are all about God's self-exalting motive in mercifully saving Israel from exile and restoring the fortunes of Jerusalem.

> I will accept you, when I bring you out from the peoples and gather you out of the countries where you have been scattered. And I will manifest my holiness among you in the sight of the nations. And *you shall know that I am the* Lord, when I bring you into the land of Israel, the country that I swore to give to your fathers. And there you shall remember your ways and all your deeds with which you

2 Jonathan Edwards, *Religious Affections*, ed. John E. Smith and Harry S. Stout, vol. 2, *The Works of Jonathan Edwards* (New Haven, CT: Yale University Press, 2009), 311.

3 Edwards, *Religious Affections*, 366.

have defiled yourselves, and you shall loathe yourselves for all the evils that you have committed. And *you shall know that I am the* L*ORD*, when I deal with you *for my name's sake*, not according to your evil ways, nor according to your corrupt deeds, O house of Israel, declares the Lord G*OD*. (Ezek. 20:41–44)

When [Israel] came to the nations, wherever they came, they profaned my holy name, in that people said of them, "These are the people of the L*ORD*, and yet they had to go out of his land." But *I had concern for my holy name*, which the house of Israel had profaned among the nations to which they came. Therefore say to the house of Israel, Thus says the Lord G*OD*: *It is not for your sake*, O house of Israel, that I am about to act, *but for the sake of my holy name*, which you have profaned among the nations to which you came. And *I will vindicate the holiness of my great name*, which has been profaned among the nations, and which you have profaned among them. And *the nations will know that I am the* L*ORD*, declares the Lord G*OD*, when through you *I vindicate my holiness before their eyes*. (Ezek. 36:20–23)

I will establish my covenant with you, and you shall know that I am the L*ORD*, that you may remember and be confounded, and never open your mouth again because of your shame, when I atone for you for all that you have done, declares the Lord G*OD*. (Ezek. 16:62–63)

When I read these texts and Jonathan Edwards's reflection on them, I felt like I was in a different world of God-centered grace than the world of my own century (the twentieth, at the time). I still feel that way. That's one of the reasons I am writing this book. As shocked as most modern people feel in being told that they should "be confounded" and have their mouths shut—*not* by God's righteous terror *but* by his atoning mercy—the fact is, this is profoundly right, and the brokenhearted soul who has been healed by grace knows it. It is cheap grace, not genuine grace, that thinks life in Christ is without remorse for past sin and for remaining corruption.

Humble, Brokenhearted Joy

But this remorse (which leads to life, 2 Cor. 7:9–11) is not at all inconsistent with the profoundest and most satisfying joy. In fact, our joy in God's mercy is intensified by the realization of how undeserving we were, and are. This sense of being undeserving is a real experience, not just a bare intellectual notion. It is felt. And God has so designed the new creation—the new person in Christ—that what seems utterly contradictory to the world is a paradox of profound, experienced pleasure for the true Christian. Edwards describes this experience in one of the most beautiful paragraphs I have ever read:

> All gracious affections that are a sweet odor to Christ, and that fill the soul of a Christian with a heavenly sweetness and fragrancy, are brokenhearted affections. A truly Christian love, either to God or men, is a humble brokenhearted love. The desires of the saints, however earnest, are humble desires: their hope is a humble hope; and their joy, even when it is unspeakable, and full of glory, is a humble, brokenhearted joy, and leaves the Christian more poor in spirit, and more like a little child, and more disposed to a universal lowliness of behavior.[4]

My main point here is that in restoring the fortunes of Jerusalem—and promising an even greater future for Israel than what they experienced in returning from Babylon (Ezek. 36:24–36)—God was acting to vindicate the holiness of his name. His commitment to his own glory was the ground of Israel's hope and joy. The name that God was making for himself in restoring his humiliated city—Zion, "the apple

---

4   Edwards, *Religious Affections*, 339–40.

of his eye" (Zech. 2:8)—was ultimately a *name of joy*. "This city shall be to me a *name of joy*" (Jer. 33:9).[5]

Not a Threat to Joy but Its Basis

My hope is that every reader will see that God's God-centeredness— God's commitment to magnify his name, his holiness, and his glory as the ultimate aim of his providence—is not a threat to our joy but the basis of it. Of course, if we feel that our joy comes from our own self-exaltation rather than from God's self-exaltation, none of this will be good news. But the design of God for his people is that his name and our joy rise together:

> Spread your protection over them,
>   that those who love your *name* may *exult* in you. (Ps. 5:11)

> May we shout for *joy* over your salvation,
>   and in the *name* of our God set up our banners! (Ps. 20:5)

> Your words became to me a *joy*
>   and the *delight* of my heart,
> for I am called by your *name*,
>   O Lord, God of hosts. (Jer. 15:16)

The All-Encompassing Promise of How the
Purpose of Providence Unfolds

The bridge from the Old Testament to the New Testament is built out of countless connecting components. It is a beautiful bridge and worthy of close inspection and admiration. More than once Jesus encouraged this admiring inspection:

> You search the Scriptures because you think that in them you have eternal life; and it is they that bear witness about me. (John 5:39)

---

5 See the final pages of chap. 5 for a fuller treatment of the joy of Israel's more distant future.

Beginning with Moses and all the Prophets, he interpreted to them in all the Scriptures the things concerning himself. (Luke 24:27)

Prominent among the connecting components of this bridge is what Jeremiah and Jesus call the "new covenant" (Jer. 31:31; Luke 22:20). As this covenant is promised in the Old Testament, and enacted in the New Testament, we see it as an all-encompassing description of how God finally accomplishes the ultimate goal of providence through Jesus Christ. That is what we turn to in the rest of part 2 (chapters 11–14).

The Ultimate Goal of Providence in the Design and Enactment of the New Covenant

11

The Designs of the New Covenant

The bridge between the Old and New Testaments is built largely on the promise that God would one day enact a new covenant. The enactment of this covenant through Jesus Christ would prove to be the all-encompassing path on which the ultimate goal of God's providence is attained. The rest of part 2 (chapters 11–14) traces the goal of providence on that path. In this chapter we focus not primarily on Christ's enactment of the new covenant (which we unfold in the remaining chapters of part 2), but rather on the inner designs of the covenant. Or, we might say, the particular promises of the covenant as they were expressed in the Old Testament.

Statement of the Covenant

The classic Old Testament expression of the new covenant—the text quoted in Hebrews 8 and 10 to show that Christ is a mediator of a "better covenant" (Heb. 7:22; 8:6)—is Jeremiah 31:31–34:

> Behold, the days are coming, declares the Lord, when I will make a new covenant with the house of Israel and the house of Judah, not like the covenant that I made with their fathers on the day when I took them by the hand to bring them out of the land of Egypt, my

covenant that they broke, though I was their husband, declares the Lord. For this is the covenant that I will make with the house of Israel after those days, declares the Lord: I will put my law within them, and I will write it on their hearts. And I will be their God, and they shall be my people. And no longer shall each one teach his neighbor and each his brother, saying, "Know the Lord," for they shall all know me, from the least of them to the greatest, declares the Lord. For I will forgive their iniquity, and I will remember their sin no more.

This new covenant is contrasted with the Sinai or Mosaic covenant described here as "the covenant that I made with their fathers on the day when I took them by the hand to bring them out of the land of Egypt" (31:32). We know this earlier covenant refers to the law of Moses given on tablets of stone at Mount Sinai because the apostle Paul says that he is a minister of this "new covenant" (2 Cor. 3:6) and contrasts it with "letters on stone" given to Moses (2 Cor. 3:7).

Three Massive Realities

The newness of the new covenant consists in three massive promised realities. First, God will forgive the sins of those in this covenant relationship (Jer. 31:34). Second, God will put his law within them and write it on their hearts—meaning that the will of God will not simply be experienced as an imposition from outside on tablets of stone but will be felt inside as a new disposition of the heart, inclining us to do what God requires (31:33). Third, God will be their God in such a way that "they shall all know me, from the least of them to the greatest" (31:34).

I put these three new-covenant realities in this order because this is the order in which God brings his ultimate purpose to pass. First, God cancels the sins of his people in such a way that, without any compromise to his justice, his mercy is free to flow in rivers with no wrath whatsoever. Second, this mercy moves from the legal cancellation of sins to the inward triumph over sinning. That is the meaning of the law being written on the heart.

Third, this inner transformation of obedience is the contrast with the old covenant. It is "not like the covenant that I made with their fathers . . . that they broke" (31:32). God's people will never be severed from God in the new covenant because the terms of the covenant are not only external *words* of God, but also internal *works* of God. He doesn't just require obedience; he creates it. This is why the goal of God's providence moves toward fulfillment along the path of the new covenant. Providence penetrates the heart and performs what it commands.

New Covenant as the Way Providence Moves toward Its Ultimate Goal

The heart of this newness that God works in the hearts of his people in the new covenant is that "they shall all know me" (Jer. 31:34). This promise has vast implications. It implies more than mere intellectual ideas of God. That is why it says God writes his law *on their hearts*. This is a true heart-knowing—the kind Paul prays for in Ephesians 1:18 when he asks that "the eyes of *your hearts*" would be enlightened so that you would know the hope, the riches, and the power of God (Eph. 1:17–18). This prayer is answered as the new covenant is fulfilled—God's word is written on the heart.

What we have seen in all the stages of providence—before creation, through the works of creation, and in the election of Israel, the exodus, the conquest of the promised land, the period of the judges, the monarchy, and the exile and its reversal—is that the ultimate purpose of God's providence is that God be known and enjoyed and praised for who he really is: "You shall know that I am the LORD." Now we see that this overarching purpose will be attained through the new covenant.

This is even more obvious from Ezekiel 36, where the prophet places the new covenant within God's purpose to "vindicate the holiness of [his] great name":

I had concern for my holy name, which the house of Israel had profaned among the nations to which they came. . . . It is not for your sake, O house of Israel, that I am about to act, but for the sake of my holy name. . . . And I will vindicate the holiness of my great name. . . . And the nations will know that I am the Lord. . . . I will sprinkle clean water on you, and you shall be clean from all your uncleannesses, and from all your idols I will cleanse you. And *I will give you a new heart, and a new spirit I will put within you. And I will remove the heart of stone from your flesh and give you a heart of flesh. And I will put my Spirit within you, and cause you to walk in my statutes and be careful to obey my rules.* (36:21–27)

Verses 26–27 are the words of the new covenant, and they are promised as God's strategy for vindicating the holiness of his great name and his purpose that the nations know that he is the Lord. In other words, the new covenant is God's way of achieving his ultimate purposes from the beginning—that the glory of who he really is be exalted for the enjoyment and praise of all who will have him as their greatest treasure (cf. Jer. 24:7).

New Covenant as the Creation of Joy in God

The reason I say that his purpose is to be exalted in *the enjoyment and praise of his people* is that his explicit strategy in the new covenant for vindicating "the holiness of [his] great name" is (1) to take out the heart of stone (Ezek. 36:26), and (2) to put his Spirit in his people (Ezek. 36:27a), and (3) to cause them to obey his word (Ezek. 36:27b). Each of these three strategies points to joy in God.

First, the heart of stone is the heart that feels nothing precious or beautiful or pleasing in the holiness of God. It will be replaced with a heart of living, feeling, sensitive flesh that feels the true preciousness and beauty and pleasantness of the Lord's holy name (Ezek. 36:26; cf. Ps. 135:3). Second, to put his own Spirit in his people means that from within they will assess and value the name of the Lord the way the Lord himself does (Isa. 63:14; John 16:14). Third, God causes his people to obey his word, and the essence and pinnacle of that word is the call to love the Lord and cling to him with all their heart (Josh. 22:5), which includes treasuring him and delighting in him above all else (Ps. 37:4; Matt. 13:44).

In other words, God's plan in the new covenant is to achieve what he has been pursuing in creation and redemption from the beginning, namely, to communicate his glory in such a way that it is exalted in the way his people enjoy and reflect his excellencies. This is why he moves history forward from the old covenant to the new—from the "oldness of the letter" to the "newness of the Spirit" (Rom. 7:6 NASB), from commanding love (Deut. 6:5) to creating love (John 17:26; Gal. 5:22; 1 Thess. 3:12), from beckoning joy (Ps. 37:4) to begetting joy (John 15:11; 17:13; Gal. 5:22).

He Won't Turn Away, or Let Us Turn Away, for His Full-Souled Joy

In the new covenant, we can see the final goal of all things more clearly than ever. We see it in the fact that God himself is moving in a new way to bring the goal to pass in the transformed hearts of his people. Then we see it in the fact that God intends to make this heart transformation permanent. Finally, we see it in the fact that God will rejoice over this transformed people with all his heart and with all his soul. These three aspects of the new covenant are found in Jeremiah 32:39–41:

> I will give them one heart and one way, that they may fear me for-
> ever, for their own good and the good of their children after them.
> I will make with them an everlasting covenant, that I will not turn

away from doing good to them. And I will put the fear of me in their hearts, that they may not turn from me. I will rejoice in doing them good, and I will plant them in this land in faithfulness, with all my heart and all my soul.

This expression of the new covenant contains some of the most amazing, hope-filled, precious promises in the Bible. Notice four things. First, God underlines the permanence of the blessings of this covenant: "I will make with them an *everlasting* covenant." Second, he secures the permanence of these blessings by pledging himself never to stop doing good to his people: "I will *not turn away from doing good to them.*" Third, he makes the blessings more secure by pledging never to let his people turn away from him: "I will put the fear of me in their hearts, that *they may not turn from me.*" Fourth, and perhaps most amazing and wonderful, he pledges to secure these blessings with overflowing joy: "*I will rejoice in doing them good . . .* with all my heart and all my soul." God is not begrudging in the everlasting blessings of the new covenant. He is doing what he loves to do.

Delight to Fear

Lest anyone stumble over the word *fear* in verse 40 ("I will put the *fear* of me in their hearts, that they may not turn from me"), thinking that God may be rejoicing over us in the new covenant as we cower before him, consider this: the beneficiaries of the new covenant will not be cowering. The fear of the Lord is not the opposite of joy in the Lord; it is the depth and seriousness of it.

We can see this in the connection between joy and fear, for example, in Isaiah 11:3. The prophet says of the promised Messiah, "His *delight* shall be in the *fear* of the LORD." We see the connection again in Nehemiah 1:11, where the servants of the Lord "delight to fear your name." When God promises in the new covenant to keep his people from turning away from him, the cords that bind our hearts to him are not cords of cowering but cords of fulfilled desire. What we "fear" is the failure to see God in Christ as supremely enthralling (cf. Rom. 11:20). God promises to hold us fast by not letting this happen. This means that the final goal of the new covenant is *the overflowing joy of God himself in the joy of his people in the glory of his name.*

New Covenant in Deuteronomy: God's Delight in Our Delight in Him

This purpose was evident from one of the earliest expressions of the new covenant. In Deuteronomy 29:4 Moses says to the people of Israel on the brink of entering the promised land, "To this day the LORD has not given you a heart to understand or eyes to see or ears to hear." This seems to portend a hopeless future for their joy and for God's purposes. They don't have the right *heart.*

But in Deuteronomy 30:6 Moses points the people to their only hope. Without using the phrase *new covenant*, he promises the reality: "The LORD your God will circumcise your heart and the heart of your offspring, so that you will love the LORD your God with all your heart and with all your soul, that you may live."

In other words, the day is coming when loving the Lord will be not just a command in writing, but a creation in the heart. God will give what he commands. And three verses later, we see what God is pursuing—not just his people's love for him, but his delight in their loving him. "The LORD will again take delight in prospering you, as he took delight in your fathers . . . when you turn to the LORD your God with all your heart and with all your soul" (Deut. 30:9–10). This new-covenant act of creating love in the hearts of his people is God's way of completing the great purpose of creation: God's delight in our delight in him. For that is the essence of what love for God is—delight in him. God's ultimate purpose is the beautification of his people by his own hand for his own glory. For their beauty is their delight in and reflection of his beauty.

The Spirit of the Lord is upon me . . .
> to give them a beautiful headdress instead of ashes,
> the oil of gladness instead of mourning,
>> the garment of praise instead of a faint spirit;
> that they may be called oaks of righteousness,
>> *the planting of the* LORD, *that he may be glorified.* (Isa. 61:1, 3)

The joyful praises of God's people are what he is creating in the new covenant. This is their beauty, their gladness, and their strength—and all of it "the planting of the LORD, that he may be glorified." Their beautification is his glorification, because their beautification is their exultation in God's beauty. Therefore, *the goal of God in his pervasive providence is the glorification of his own grace in beautifying an undeserving people whose beauty is their enjoyment and reflection of God's beauty.*

Glimpse of How Christ Effects the New Covenant

We will see this with stunning clarity as we turn to the enactment of the new covenant through the sufferings of Christ, but let me make the connection here, lest we minimize how this great purpose comes to fulfillment through Christ. We are going to see that the new covenant is secured through the sacrifice of Jesus for the sins of his people. Here is the way Paul describes the purpose of Christ's death:

> Christ loved the church and gave himself up for her, that he might sanctify her, having cleansed her by the washing of water with the word, *so that he might present the church to himself in splendor*, without spot or wrinkle or any such thing, that she might be holy and without blemish. (Eph. 5:25–27)

In a word, God's goal in the new covenant through the death of Jesus is the beautification of a bride in whom the Son could rejoice forever. When Paul says that Christ died "that he might present the church to himself in splendor," he did not mean that Christ would be bored by his blood-beautified bride. No, he meant that Christ would be thrilled with his bride. That is why he died—to make her thrilling.

And what is this beautification? It is her sanctification, her holiness (5:26). That is, it is her joyfully obeying all the word of God, which means it is, most essentially, her love for God. Her delight in God. Her reflection of God. Therefore, the ultimate goal of God's providence is *to glorify his grace in beautifying, by the blood of his Son, an undeserving bride, who enjoys and reflects his beauty above everything.*

Turning to the Enactment of the New Covenant through Christ

In the remaining chapters of part 2 (12–14), we will try to follow the all-encompassing path along which Christ accomplishes the ultimate goal of providence by enacting the new covenant through his saving, sanctifying suffering. I call it an all-encompassing path because the "mystery of Christ" (Eph. 3:4–6) is just that: as the crucified, risen, reigning Messiah of Israel, Christ enacts the new covenant in a way that ransoms people from *every* nation (Rev. 5:9), transforms them as a new humanity into his image (2 Cor. 3:18; 1 John 3:2), and sets the entire created universe free from its bondage to corruption (Rom. 8:21). And this all-encompassing work is done so that God's providence would attain its ultimate goal—his bride's everlasting praise of the glory of God's grace, as she enjoys, and thus exalts, the excellencies of Christ.

12

Christ's Foundational Act
in Establishing the New Covenant

In one sense, the rest of human history, from the incarnation of the
Son of God to the eternal ages of the new earth, could be described
as the enactment of the new covenant. From first to last in that endless period of time, Jesus Christ proves to be both the foundation and
the final reward of the new covenant. He is its ground and goal. The
price and the prize. The gracious redeemer and the great reward. This
chapter focuses on Christ's foundational step of suffering to establish
the new covenant and the way this suffering fits him to be its reward,
and fits us to receive it.

New Covenant in His Blood

The night before his crucifixion, Jesus said that the blood that he
was about to shed—the death that he was about to suffer—was the
foundational step in enacting the new covenant. After they had
eaten, he took the cup and said, "This cup that is poured out for
you is *the new covenant in my blood*" (Luke 22:20). "In my blood"
(or just as likely "by my blood") means that in the shedding of his
blood, the sins of his people were covered (Rom. 4:7), or canceled

(Col. 2:13–14). That is what the new covenant promised: "I will forgive their iniquity, and I will remember their sin no more" (Jer. 31:34). Jesus's shed blood was the foundation of that promised forgiveness.

Matthew quotes Jesus more fully from the Last Supper and makes the connection with forgiveness explicit: "This is my blood of the covenant, which is poured out for many *for the forgiveness of sins*" (Matt. 26:28). The pattern established by God under the old covenant had been that "without the shedding of blood there is no forgiveness of sins" (Heb. 9:22). But it was always the case that "it is impossible for the blood of bulls and goats to take away sins" (Heb. 10:4). All the animal sacrifices were pointing to the better and final sacrifice of Christ. Indeed, any efficacy that they had was owing to the atonement in Christ which was effective even for believers who lived before Christ (Rom. 3:25–26).

Unlike the former priests, who offered animals repeatedly for their own sin and the sins of the people (Heb. 9:7), Jesus was without sin (Heb. 4:15). Therefore, "he has appeared once for all at the end of the ages to put away sin by the sacrifice of himself" (Heb. 9:26). In this way, Christ "is the mediator of a new covenant, so that those who are called may receive the promised eternal inheritance" (Heb. 9:15; cf. 8:6; 12:24).

Therefore, Jesus is the ground of the new covenant. He is the basis of it. It has taken effect because of the sacrifice he made. He is responsible for putting it into effect.

Christ, the Ground and Goal of His Own New-Covenant Achievement

To speak of Christ's relationship to the new covenant in this way is a great honor to Christ. His sacrifice was a glorious achievement in providing for the forgiveness of sins. But putting it this way is only half the truth of Christ's achievement. In his death and resurrection

(Rom. 4:25), Christ not only provided the *ground* of the new-covenant promises; he also became the *goal*. Jesus is both the *ground* of our salvation, and the *glory* we were saved to see and savor and share. He was the *price* that was paid for our deliverance, and the *prize* we were destined to enjoy. He redeemed us from hell, and he rewarded us with himself. The promise of the new covenant was "I will be their God, and they shall be my people" (Jer. 31:33). The surprising and incomprehensible reality of the new covenant is that we experience God as our God precisely in relationship with Christ. For Christ is God.

In Him the Whole Fullness of Deity Dwells Bodily

Jesus is able to be the ground and the goal of the new covenant because he is no mere man. He is fully man and fully God. "In him the whole fullness of deity dwells bodily" (Col. 1:19; see also 2:9). Before he took on a human nature, "*he was in the form of God,* [but] did not count *equality with God* a thing to be grasped, but emptied himself, by taking the form of a servant, being born in the likeness of men" (Phil. 2:6–7). "He is the radiance of the glory of God and the exact imprint of his nature, and he upholds the universe by the word of his power" (Heb. 1:3). God himself testifies that his Son is God: "Of the Son he says, 'Your throne, O God, is forever and ever'" (Heb. 1:8, citing Ps. 45:6).

The deity of Christ—his divine being as the eternal Son of God—made it possible for him to be the ground of the new covenant in dying for sinners. "God has done what the law, weakened by the flesh, could not do. By sending *his own Son* in the likeness of sinful flesh and for sin, he condemned sin in the flesh" (Rom. 8:3). The punishment owing to our sin could be paid by another because God sent his Son in the likeness of sinful flesh. He was the *divine* Son, and he was sinless in his *human* nature. Therefore he had both the divine worth and the human mortality to accomplish what no one else could—to offer an infinitely valuable sacrifice and die for the sins of his people (Heb. 2:14).

Glories of the God-Man's Achievement

This glory of Christ's achievement in dying for his undeserving enemies is a glory added to the eternal glory of his deity.[1] As human nature was taken to the divine person of the Son, so the glories of the achievements of the God-man were added to the eternal glories of the Son that he had before he was man. When Jesus rose from the dead and ascended to the Father in heaven, he was restored to his former glory. "Now, Father, glorify me in your own presence with the glory that I had with you before the world existed" (John 17:5). But not only his former glory. He now has the glory of a triumphant redeemer. He is now the victorious God-man who defeated Satan (Col. 2:15; Heb. 2:14) and death (1 Cor. 15:54–57). He satisfied the holy wrath of God (Rom. 3:25; Eph. 2:3–5). He ransomed a bride (Eph. 5:25–27) out of all the peoples of the world (Rev. 5:9). For these achievements of the cross, and dozens more,[2] Christ was exalted to a place of manifold glory at God's right hand:

> *Therefore* God has highly exalted him and bestowed on him the name that is above every name, so that at the name of Jesus every knee should bow, in heaven and on earth and under the earth, and every tongue confess that Jesus Christ is Lord, to the glory of God the Father. (Phil. 2:9–11)

He will be worshiped forever not only for the glory of his eternal deity, but also for his glorious achievements as the God-man in redeeming his people—as the mediator of the new covenant. Notice that in the

---

1   I don't mean to imply that the intrinsic, eternal glory of the Son of God was altered, as if it was defective or deficient or anything less than infinite before the incarnation. Rather, the "added glories" were new extrinsic manifestations of the greatness of that intrinsic glory.

2   See John Piper, *Fifty Reasons Why Jesus Came to Die* (Wheaton, IL: Crossway, 2006).

song of heaven, his worthiness to open the scroll of history is owing directly to his achievement on the cross:

> Worthy are you to take the scroll
>   and to open its seals,
> *for you were slain*, and by your blood you ransomed people
>   for God
>   from every tribe and language and people and nation,
> and you have made them a kingdom and priests to our God,
>   and they shall reign on the earth. (Rev. 5:9–10)

So the dimensions of the glory of Christ are many. Some stem from eternity as essential to his divine nature. Some belong to his incarnate state as both divine and human. He is peculiarly glorious because of the work that he was able to achieve because of being both God and man. It is the totality of this glory that I refer to when I say that Christ is the *goal* of the new covenant. Because of what Christ accomplished in his suffering and death and resurrection, he is not only the ground of the new covenant; he has become its supreme reward. The price of all the new-covenant promises has become their supreme prize.

In Fitting Us to See His Glory, Christ Became Even More Worth Seeing

If Christ had not become the ground of the new covenant in his suffering, he could never have been the reward of the new covenant in his glory. This is true for two reasons. First, if he had not suffered, no one's sins would be forgiven, and therefore all would still be under the wrath of God (Eph. 2:3), with hearts of stone (Ezek. 36:26), blind to the glory of Christ (2 Cor. 4:4). Second, a great part of Christ's glory consists in the very *way* he established the new covenant—namely, by his dreadful, innocent, and loving suffering. In other words, in becoming the ground of the new covenant, Christ not only built on the eternal glory of his deity but also was manifest as a glorious redeemer.

His saving work not only *fitted us* to see his glory; it also *fitted him* to be seen as glorious in his saving achievement as well as his eternal grandeur.

In other words, God's purpose in the new covenant was not only to make it possible for sinners to be forgiven and to know and enjoy the glory of God forever. His purpose was also that the *mediator* of the covenant would be that very God and would enact a redeeming glory that would become the most beautiful display of glory anyone could ever enjoy—the glory of God's grace.

Grace the Apex of Glory, Christ the Apex of Grace

In chapter 3 we saw that from before the foundation of the world the goal of God's providence was to have a people who would live for "the praise of the glory of his grace" (Eph. 1:6, 12, 14, my translation). Now we see more clearly that this purpose was radically focused on Christ. More specifically, it was focused on Christ in his triumphs through suffering. The implication of Ephesians 1:4–6 is that the grace of God is the apex of his glory. His goal is not just "the praise of his glory." It is "the praise of the glory *of his grace.*"

That is, the constellation of excellencies that make up the glory of God reach their most beautiful overflow in the expression of grace for undeserving sinners like us. And what has now become clear in the enactment of the new covenant "in his blood" is that the humble, willing, obedient *suffering* of Christ for sinners is the apex of God's grace—the place where that grace is most beautifully on display.

So grace is the consummate expression of God's glory, and Christ in his suffering is the consummate expression of grace. Three times in Ephesians 1:4–6 Paul clarifies that the aim of praising "the glory of God's grace" is achieved "through Jesus Christ":

> He chose us *in him* before the foundation of the world, that we should be holy and blameless before him. In love he predestined us

for adoption to himself as sons *through Jesus Christ*, according to the purpose of his will, *to the praise of his glorious grace*, with which he has blessed us *in the Beloved*.

"In him." "Through Jesus Christ." "In the Beloved." We know that these phrases are references to Christ's work on the cross because in the next verse Paul says, "In him we have redemption through his blood, the forgiveness of our trespasses, according to the riches of his grace" (1:7). Therefore, the ultimate goal of God in his saving providence—namely, the praise of the glory of his grace—was achieved through the suffering of the Son of God, who died to deliver us from eternal suffering (2 Thess. 1:9) and bring us into everlasting enjoyment of his glory (John 17:24).

Suffering Essential for the Most Glorious Act of Grace

Let us again make explicit the obvious, but often neglected, point from Ephesians 1:4–6: this was God's plan from the beginning—Christ suffering for undeserving sinners to display the glory of God's grace. This was not plan B. God's ultimate purpose in creation and providence was *not* that his glory would be displayed and praised through means that did not involve the suffering of his Son. The cross was not an afterthought. It was part of the plan from before the foundation of the world (cf. 2 Tim. 1:9; Rev. 13:8).

The implications of this are staggering. It means that suffering is essential to the ultimate purpose of creation and providence. Suffering is an essential part of the tapestry of the universe so that the weaving of grace, through Christ's suffering, may be seen for what it really is. Or to put it most simply and starkly, the ultimate reason that suffering exists is so that Christ might display the greatness of the glory of the grace of God by suffering himself to overcome our suffering. The suffering of the utterly innocent, and infinitely holy, Son of God in the place of utterly undeserving sinners to bring us to everlasting joy is the greatest display of the glory of God's grace that ever was or ever could be.[3]

The Book of Life of the Lamb That Was Slain

This is so breathtaking, and so different from the way so many people think, that we would do well to lay out the basis for it more widely than only what we have seen in Ephesians 1:4–7. Consider two other passages: Revelation 13:8 and 2 Timothy 1:9.

In Revelation 13:8 John writes:

> All who dwell on earth will worship [the beast], everyone whose name has not been written before the foundation of the world in the book of life of the Lamb who was slain.

The precise wording here matters, and this is a good, careful, literal translation: "the book of life of the Lamb who was slain." It means that before the world was created, there was in the mind of God a "Lamb who was slain."

The slain Lamb is Jesus Christ crucified. Thus, the book of names is the book of Jesus Christ crucified. Therefore, before God made the world, he had in view Jesus Christ slain, and he had in view a people purchased by his blood, written in the book. Therefore, the suffering of Jesus was not an afterthought, as though the work of creation did not go the way God planned. The slaying of the Lamb was in view *before* the work of creation began.

Grace in Christ before the Ages Began

In 2 Timothy 1:9 Paul looks back into eternity before the ages began and says:

---

3   The thoughts in these paragraphs are adapted from John Piper, "The Suffering of Christ and the Sovereignty of God," in *Suffering and the Sovereignty of God*, ed. John Piper and Justin Taylor (Wheaton, IL: Crossway, 2006), 81–90.

> [God] saved us and called us to a holy calling, not because of our works but because of his own purpose and *grace*, which he gave us [that is, he gave us this *grace*] *in Christ Jesus* before the ages began.

God gave us *grace*—undeserved favor toward sinners!—in Christ Jesus *before the ages began.* We had not yet been created. We had not yet existed so that we could sin. But God had already decreed that grace—an "in Christ" kind of grace, blood-bought grace, sin-overcoming grace—would come to us in Christ Jesus. All that was in the mind of God before the creation of the world. So there is a "book of life of the Lamb who was slain," and there is grace flowing to undeserving sinners in Christ who are not yet created.

And don't miss the magnitude of that word *slain* (Greek *esphagmenou*): "the Lamb who was *slain*." It is used in the New Testament only by the apostle John and means literally "to slaughter." So here we have terrible suffering—the slaughter of the Son of God—in the mind and plan of God before the foundation of the world. The Lamb of God will suffer. He will be slaughtered. That's the plan.

Why? Because *the aim of God in creation and providence is to provide the fullest, clearest, surest display of the greatness of the glory of grace. And that display would be the slaughter of the best being in the universe in the place of millions of undeserving sinners.* The suffering and death of the Lamb of God in history is the consummate display of the glory of the grace of God. That is why God planned it before the foundation of the world. That is the aim and work and wonder of God's pervasive providence.

Slain Lamb, Centerpiece of Worship Forever

We have seen that the hosts of heaven focus their worship not simply on the Lamb, but on *the Lamb who was slain* (Rev. 5:9). And they are still singing this song in Revelation 15:3 ("They sing the song of Moses, the servant of God, *and the song of the Lamb*"). Therefore, we can infer that the centerpiece of worship in heaven *for all eternity* will be the display of the glory of the grace of God in the slaughtered Lamb.

Angels and all the redeemed will sing of the suffering of the Lamb forever and ever. The suffering of the Son of God will never be forgotten. The greatest suffering that ever was will be at the center of our worship and our wonder forever and ever. This is not an afterthought of God. This is the plan from before the foundation of the world.

Everything else is subordinate to this plan. Everything else is put in place by God's providence for the sake of this plan. *The display of the glory of God's grace, especially in the suffering of the Beloved, echoing forever in the all-satisfying praises of the redeemed,* is the goal of creation and the ultimate aim of all God's works of providence.

So Much More to See

In the new covenant, God promised forgiveness of sins, new hearts that treasure God above all, and that he himself would be our God in joyful fellowship forever (Jer. 31:33–34). In his suffering, death, and resurrection, Jesus became the foundation of these promises. And not only the foundation but also the goal. In the beauty of the love and wisdom and power of his triumphant suffering (1 Cor. 1:18–25; 2:7–9), Christ displayed the glory that his people will exult in forever. He became the price and the prize of the new covenant. The ground and the goal. The redemption and the reward. This was God's plan from before the foundation of the world.

There is more—so much more—to see in the beautiful achievements of Christ's sufferings and their inexhaustible implications. There are implications, for example, in how we understand the entrance of sin into the world, and how we understand the gospel. That will be the focus of chapter 13.

13

The Entrance of Sin into Creation and the Glory of the Gospel

In tracing the goal of providence back into the eternal plan of God, as we did in the previous chapter (Eph. 1:4–6; 2 Tim. 1:9; Rev. 13:8), we saw that the very existence of suffering—most explicitly, Christ's suffering—was part of the fabric of reality that God planned for human history, so that he might display the glory of his grace in the suffering of his Son for undeserving sinners. The amazing implications of this truth that we dealt with in chapter 12 do not exhaust its wonders. We have more to see in relation to the fall of man and the glory of the gospel.

Planned to Permit

If God planned the suffering of his Son before creation, and thus before the sin of Adam and Eve, as we saw in Revelation 13:8 and 2 Timothy 1:9, then he foresaw the coming of sin and planned to permit it to enter the world. I choose those words carefully: "planned to permit." Sometimes we say God permitted something. This is perfectly fitting, since God's providence does not govern all events in precisely the same way, and "permission" is one way to describe some of his acts of providence. For example, "Let us . . . go on to maturity. . . . And this we will do *if God permits*" (Heb. 6:1–3; see also Luke 8:32; 1 Cor. 16:7).

But what we sometimes overlook is that, since God foresees what he may or may not permit, he chooses whether to permit or not. And all God's choices accord with his perfect wisdom (Ps. 104:24; Isa. 28:9) and justice (Neh. 9:33; Ps. 145:17; Dan. 9:14) and goodness (Ps. 145:7, 9). God is not whimsical. He never chooses foolishly or sinfully. He chooses what to permit "according to the counsel of his will" (Eph. 1:11). He chooses in view of all the consequences (painful and pleasant) that will flow from whatever he permits. Therefore, we may speak properly of what he *planned* to permit. And thus we may, and should, speak of God's *purpose* in permitting.

God's Planned Permission of the Fall

God foresaw that Adam and Eve would sin and bring ruin on his creation. He took this reality into "the counsel of his will," considered all its consequences and all his purposes, and chose to permit their fall into sin. He did this in accord with his perfect wisdom, justice, and goodness. Since he could have chosen not to permit this first sin, just as he chose not to permit Abimelech's sin ("It was I who kept you from sinning against me," Gen. 20:6), we know that God had wise and just and good purposes in permitting it.

If God had wise and just and good purposes in permitting the fall of Adam and Eve, we may speak of God's *plan* in permitting it. That is, we may speak of God *planning* or *ordaining* the fall in this sense. By *planning* and *ordaining*, I simply mean that God could have chosen not to permit the fall, but, in choosing to permit it for wise purposes, he thus planned and ordained it. He considered everything (trillions of things) he would do with it and made it part of his ultimate plan.

This means that God plans and ordains that some things come to pass that he hates. God hates sin (Prov. 6:16–19). It dishonors him (Rom. 3:23) and destroys people (Rom. 6:23). Yet he planned to permit sin to come into his perfect creation. Therefore, in God's infinite wisdom and holiness, it is not sinful for him to plan that sin come to pass. There are, no doubt, countless wise and holy reasons God plans to permit sin. But we have been drawn into these reflections by only one: namely, that God's ultimate aim in creation and providence is *to display the glory of his grace, especially in the suffering of Christ, echoing forever in the all-satisfying praises of the redeemed.* That is the ultimate wise, just, and good purpose of God in planning to permit the fall.

Adam and Eve Meant It for Evil; God Meant It for Good

In other words, though there are mysteries in *how* God wills that sin exist, without himself sinning, we are given biblical guidance for how to think and talk about this. For example, we may fittingly speak of the sin of Adam and Eve with the words that Joseph spoke of the sin of his brothers, who sold him into slavery: "As for you, you meant evil against me, but God meant it for good" (Gen. 50:20). It does not say, "God *used* it for good." It says, God *meant* it for good—the same word used for the sinful intention of the brothers: they *meant* it for evil. They have *one* intention in the act. God has *another* intention in the act. Theirs is sinful. God's is saving—"to bring it about that many people should be kept alive, as they are today" (Gen. 50:20; see also 45:7; Ps. 105:17).

God has given us these words so that we can grasp, in some small measure, how his providence relates not only to Joseph's brothers' sin, but to *all* sin, including the first human sin. Thus we may say, "As for you, Adam and Eve, you meant it for evil, but God meant it for good. Your purpose in sinning was the vain pursuit of pleasure through self-exalting autonomy. God's purpose in permitting your sin was to give his people the pleasure of seeing and savoring the glory of his grace in the inexpressible suffering and triumphs of his Son."

Judgment of Suffering: Just and Gracious

Thus, this display of the glory of God's grace would happen supremely in and through the suffering of the Son of God for undeserving rebels against God. But for that to happen, there needed to be such a thing as suffering. Therefore, it was not only justice, but also mercy, that moved God to appoint suffering as the consequence of sin. To the woman he said, "I will surely multiply your pain in childbearing" (Gen. 3:16). To the man he said, "Cursed is the ground because of you; in pain you shall eat of it all the days of your life" (Gen. 3:17). These sufferings spread out over the entire inhabited creation:

> The creation was subjected [by God] to futility, not willingly, but because of him [God] who subjected it, in hope that the creation itself will be set free from its bondage to corruption and obtain the freedom of the glory of the children of God. For we know that the whole creation has been groaning together in the pains of childbirth until now. (Rom. 8:20–22)

The "futility" and "bondage to corruption" and "groaning" of the creation—with all the accompanying horrors of disease, natural disasters, and human atrocities—are physical and psychological consequences of the moral and spiritual outrage of sin. Their dreadfulness corresponds to the dreadfulness of rebellion against the Creator. They are a parable, as it were, of the unspeakable evil of belittling God by the rebellion of the heart. They are a trumpet blast of warning to the physical senses of fallen man, whose spiritual ability to discern the outrage of sin against God has been deadened. This was Jesus's interpretation of the atrocity of murdered worshipers (Luke 13:3) and deadly natural disaster (Luke 13:5): "Unless you repent, you will all likewise perish." Dying in a calamity does not mean you deserve death more than another (Luke 13:2). Rather, it is a message to all, for all deserve death: repent![1]

---

1   For more reflection on why God should appoint *physical* suffering as judgment on *moral* evil, and thus subject the entire creation to futility and corruption (Rom. 8:20–23), see chap. 33, pp. 503–7.

All sin and suffering on earth began with God's sentence of death after Adam's sin (Gen. 2:17; Rom. 5:12). And astonishingly, mingled with this judgment, in the very same breath, so to speak, God points to the ultimate triumph of grace through suffering: "I will put enmity between you [the serpent] and the woman, and between your offspring and her offspring; he shall bruise your head, and you shall bruise his heel" (Gen. 3:15). Ultimately, Christ, though bruised, will defeat the evil one (Col. 2:15; Heb. 2:14). This was the gospel of Romans 5:19, spoken in hope, thousands of years before Christ: "As by the one man's [Adam's] disobedience the many were made sinners, so by the one man's [Christ's] obedience the many will be made righteous."

What Has Been Woven in Chapters 12 and 13?

We have been drawing out the implications of the precreation origins of the new covenant and Christ's enactment of it. Let's step back and identify the threads of the tapestry we have been weaving in chapters 12 and 13. Then, with the threads clarified, we can complete our tapestry of the foundational enactment of the new covenant in unleashing "the gospel of the glory of Christ." Here's what we have seen:

1. The ultimate aim of God in promising and enacting the new covenant was to display the glory of God's grace, especially in the suffering of his Son, echoing forever in the all-satisfying praises of the redeemed.

2. No mere man could accomplish what the new covenant promised—the forgiveness of sins, the transformation of the human heart, and the revelation of God—to be enjoyed as our God forever. Therefore, the glory of Christ's enactment of the new covenant is immeasurably greater because he was, in fact, no mere man, but God incarnate. All the beauties of the saving work of Christ are intensified because he was the divine Son of God.

3. Within God's ultimate aim of the new covenant is the reality that God's grace is the consummate expression of his glory— the climactic overflow of the perfect cooperation of all his excellencies.

4. Also within the aim of the new covenant is the reality that the willing suffering and death of the Son of God for undeserving sinners is the most beautiful expression of God's grace. It will be sung with wonder forever (Rev. 5:9; 15:3).

5. This ultimate aim was planned by God before the foundation of the world (2 Tim. 1:9; Rev. 13:8).

6. Therefore, the sin of Adam and Eve did not take God off guard. His plan for the suffering of his Son for the sake of sinners already included his planned permission of human sin. He planned to permit the fall and, by its just consequences of suffering, set the stage for the work of redemption and the triumphant, grace-displaying suffering of his Son.

Good News of Christ's Glory

From these things we can see why Paul says that the good news, which Christ sent out into the world by enacting the new covenant, was the *good news of his glory*. In 2 Corinthians 4:4 Paul says, "The god of this world [Satan] has blinded the minds of the unbelievers, to keep them from seeing the light of *the gospel of the glory of Christ, who is the image of God*." This is an amazing phrase: "The gospel of the glory of Christ"—"the good news of the glory of Christ." Which implies that the greatest good of the good news is the glory of Christ.

We have already seen that the gospel tells the story of the glory of Christ in becoming the all-sufficient foundation for the forgiveness of sins—the most worthy person suffering the worst sufferings for the least deserving. This is the heart of the glory of the gospel. But now also see that by showing us the glory of what Christ has already done, "the gospel of the glory of Christ" goes on to accomplish two more wonders.

It creates a people who (1) enjoy *treasuring* the glory of Christ above all (Matt. 10:37) and (2) enjoy *being transformed* into Christ's glorious image (2 Cor. 3:18). The gospel brings about a new people who *rejoice* in the glory of Christ as their greatest treasure and who *reflect* the glory of Christ as their new identity. Christ is glorified by his glory being *enjoyed* and being *echoed*.

Both of these goals—joyfully treasuring the glory of Christ and joyfully being transformed by the glory of Christ—are explicit in Scripture.

Goal of Joyfully Treasuring Christ's Glory

The night before he died, Jesus prayed, "Father, I desire that they also, whom you have given me, may be with me where I am, *to see my glory* that you have given me because you loved me before the foundation of the world" (John 17:24). This was his ultimate prayer. Almost. There is one more request that, when combined with this one, makes them together the ultimate prayer. In John 17:26 Jesus adds this request: that we would not only see, but be able to *love* the glory of the Son the way the Father does—not the way we do now, with our sin-corrupted vision of Christ, but with the very love of the Father working in us in our perfected state.

Here's the way Jesus makes this request: "I made known to them your name, and I will continue to make it known, *that the love with which you have loved me may be in them*, and I in them." He asks that the Father's love for the Son be in us. In other words, "Father, let the purity and intensity of your love be the purity and intensity with which my people will see and treasure and be satisfied with my glory."

Goal of Joyfully Being Transformed by Christ's Glory

God's aim in the death of Christ included the transformation of his people. "[Christ] himself bore our sins in his body on the tree, *that we might die to sin and live to righteousness*" (1 Pet. 2:24). Christ died to secure the pardon of our sin, and to sever the power of our sinning. In his new covenant–establishing death, he dethroned the inclination to sin and implanted the preference for holiness. He secured both justification and sanctification. How does this transforming power of "the gospel of the glory of Christ" become effective?

The clearer and fuller our sight of Christ's glory, the more we will be transformed into its likeness. Four verses before saying that Satan blinds unbelievers to "the light of the gospel of the glory of Christ," Paul says that believers (who are no longer blind, 2 Cor. 4:6), by "beholding the glory of the Lord, are being transformed into the same image from one degree of glory to another. For this comes from the Lord who is the Spirit" (2 Cor. 3:18).

This is where seeing and savoring the glory of Christ leads, even now in this life. Beholding leads to becoming. Focused regarding of Christ leads to faithfully reflecting Christ. This is also how God will eventually fulfill his command that the earth be filled with his glory (Gen. 1:27–28; Num. 14:21; Hab. 2:14). By the Spirit (2 Cor. 3:18b) our satisfied gaze on the glory of Christ in his triumphant suffering transforms us into his likeness.

This is a process that reaches its perfection at the second coming of the Lord Jesus: "We know that when he appears we shall be like him, because we shall see him as he is" (1 John 3:2). In this way, God will fill the new earth with beautiful images of his Son's glory, and "the creation itself will be set free from its bondage to corruption and obtain the freedom of the glory of the children of God" (Rom. 8:21). And thus the new covenant will be finally and fully achieved.

Every Achievement of Christ's Suffering Leads to Cherishing His Glory

So when Paul calls the Christian message "the gospel of the glory of Christ" (2 Cor. 4:4), he implies that all the other precious achievements of the sufferings of Christ are means to this great and final goal: a redeemed people who enjoy treasuring the glory of Christ above all and enjoy being transformed into his glorious image. What makes the good news finally and ultimately good is that it secured eternal joy for God's people in treasuring and reflecting Christ's glory.

All the other achievements of Christ's suffering are glorious. But their glory resides ultimately in bringing undeserving, justified, forgiven, transformed sinners into the all-satisfying presence of God forever. "Christ also suffered once for sins, the righteous for the unrighteous, that he might bring us to God" (1 Pet. 3:18), where there is "fullness of joy [and] pleasures forevermore" (Ps. 16:11). All the other achievements of the cross serve this end.

Wonder of Propitiation for Seeing Christ's Glory

Take one example of "all the other achievements of Christ's suffering": the most basic achievement of propitiation—that is, the removal of God's wrath for all who believe on him, so that God is no longer against us but is 100 percent for us forever. How did Christ do that? Paul explains it this way:

> Christ redeemed us from the curse of the law by becoming a curse for us—for it is written, "Cursed is everyone who is hanged on a tree." (Gal. 3:13)

> God put [Christ] forward as a propitiation [wrath-remover, justice-satisfier] by his blood, to be received by faith. This was to show God's righteousness, because in his divine forbearance he had passed over former sins. (Rom. 3:25)

> If while we were enemies we were reconciled to God by the death of
> his Son, much more, now that we are reconciled, shall we be saved
> by his life [from God's wrath, cf. v. 9]. (Rom. 5:10)

Notice that God himself is the one who puts Christ forward to deal
with his own wrath. There is no thought that Jesus is merciful but God
the Father is not. No. God the Father takes the initiative to satisfy the
demands of his own righteous wrath. Christ bears the wrath so we
don't have to.

And notice that God does this "because in his divine forbearance
he had passed over former sins" (Rom. 3:25). One might think that
God could just forget the millions of sins of all the saints in the Old
Testament whom he had forgiven. But his righteousness will not allow
that. God-belittling sin must be justly punished if God's glory is to be
upheld as infinitely precious. It could be dealt with justly by sending
all sinners to hell. But God, in his grace (Rom. 3:24), plans to save
hell-deserving sinners by putting forward his Son to bear their punishment and satisfy his holy wrath.

In this way, the worth of God's glory, which has been demeaned for
all of history in trillions of ways, is upheld, his righteousness is vindicated, and sinners are saved. Or to say it in a way that expresses what
we have been seeing all through the Scriptures, God's ultimate aim in
the sufferings of Christ was to exalt the glory of his own righteousness
in the very act of saving sinners who will spend eternity praising the
glory of God's grace.

Therefore, this propitiation—this removal of the wrath of God—
was a means to the ultimate end of redeeming a people who exalt
the glory of Christ by enjoying God in Christ forever. Propitiation
is not an end in itself. It removes a massive obstacle to the enjoyment of the glory of God. That God-exalting joy is the ultimate
goal of propitiation—and the ultimate goal of all the other wonders
of providence.

Every Achievement of the Cross Removes Obstacles to Glory

The same can be shown of all the other achievements of Christ's sufferings. They all are means to the end of enabling undeserving people to spend eternity in the all-satisfying presence of God (Ps. 16:11; 1 Pet. 3:18). *Forgiveness* removes the barrier of our guilt-producing sins (Eph. 1:7). *Justification* provides a perfect righteousness that makes us legally acceptable to God (Rom. 5:19). *Adoption* provides legal standing in the family of God (Eph. 1:5). The *defeat of death* and the gift of *eternal life* secure the endlessness of our joy in God's presence (Rom. 6:23; 1 Cor. 15:56–57). The *disarming of demonic powers* ensures that our fellowship with God will never be invaded by hostile powers (Col. 2:15; Heb. 2:14). The *final healing* of all disease means that our enjoyment of God's presence will never be hindered by distracting pain (Isa. 53:5; Rev. 7:17).

In other words, when Paul calls the gospel "the gospel of the glory of Christ," he means not only that all these achievements of his suffering *reveal* the glory of Christ, but also that they are all *leading* to this ultimate goal—God's blood-bought people enjoying and reflecting the glory of God in Christ as their supreme treasure. The providence of God in sending his Son as a suffering substitute for sinners accomplishes everything necessary to bring his people into his presence with everlasting, soul-satisfying praises of the glory of his grace. God gets the glory of praise. We get the pleasure of praising. The glory of God's grace and the gladness of our souls are consummated together in this eternal praise.

Present and Future Enactment of the New Covenant

In the next chapter, we come to the end of our first journey through the Scriptures, searching out the *goal* of providence. In this final chapter of part 2, the focus shifts from the foundational achievement of Christ in the new covenant by his sufferings to the ongoing enactment of the new covenant in the transformation of God's people and finally of the created world. The new covenant promised not only the forgiveness of sins, but also the writing of the law on our hearts (Jer. 31:33)—a transformed people whose hearts delight to do the will of God. "I delight to do your will, O my God; your law is within my heart" (Ps. 40:8).

This blood-bought, Spirit-wrought transformation is, in the end, the creation of a new humanity (Eph. 2:10) whose affection *for* God and reflection *of* God will fill the earth the way the waters cover the sea (Num. 14:21; Ps. 72:19; Hab. 2:14; Eph. 1:22–23). This is the ultimate goal of providence—a glorified people, whose glory is their rejoicing in God and their reflection of God, who himself delights with all his heart (Jer. 32:41) in their delight in him. This is the enactment of the new covenant, which is happening even as I write these words and which will be completed in due time through the wisdom and power and justice and grace of God's providence.

14

The Glory of Christ in the Glorification of His People

Since the *final* glorification of God's people (Rom. 8:17, 30) will consist largely in their gladness in, and reflection of, the glory of God himself, the Scriptures remind us repeatedly that the *progressive* glorification of the saints in this life is for the glory of God. I know *progressive glorification* is not a common phrase. More common is *progressive sanctification*—that is, the process of being made more and more holy in this life by the work of the Holy Spirit (Rom. 15:16; 2 Thess. 2:13). That process proves to be the Christ-purchased, Spirit-empowered transformation that leads finally to the fulfillment of the purpose of providence in this age and the age to come.

Progressive Glorification

I use the phrase *progressive glorification* because it is such an apt paraphrase of 2 Corinthians 3:18: "We all, with unveiled face, *beholding the glory* of the Lord, are being transformed into the same image *from one degree of glory to another*. For this comes from the Lord who is the Spirit." This progressive change "from one degree of glory to another," which "comes from the Lord who is the Spirit," is what I mean by *progressive glorification*. And it is virtually the same experience as Paul describes in 2 Thessalonians 2:13, namely, being saved "through *sanctification* by the Spirit.*"

I suspect that when Paul wrote, "Those whom he predestined he also called, and those whom he called he also justified, and *those whom he justified he also glorified*" (Rom. 8:30), he omitted "those whom he *sanctified*" because in his mind the word *glorified*, at this point in his argument, included God's work of sanctifying. So he did not write, "Those whom he justified he also sanctified, and those whom he sanctified he also glorified." This is not because sanctification is optional (as we shall see), but, I am suggesting, because it is included in "glorified." Another way of describing *progressive sanctification* is to call it *progressive glorification*.

One of the good effects of using the phrase *progressive glorification* is that it draws attention to the fact that the purpose of God's sanctifying providence in our lives is to display the glory of God by working in us the kind of thoughts and affections and behaviors that point to the beauty and worth of God as our supreme treasure. Our progressive glorification is the experience of growing in ways of thinking and feeling and behaving that reflect the glory of God in Christ.

Progressive Glorification Fulfills the New Covenant

Such progressive glorification is what the new covenant promised when God said:

> I will give you a new heart, and a new spirit I will put within you. And I will remove the heart of stone from your flesh and give you a heart of flesh. (Ezek. 36:26)

> I will put my law within them, and I will write it on their hearts. (Jer. 31:33)

This new spirit and new heart, where God's law is made our inward desire, is the experience of progressive glorification. The Scriptures remind us again and again that this transformation is *from* the work of God's Spirit and *for* the glory of God's grace. It is *from* God's providence, *for* God's splendor. Consider four illustrations (from Jesus, Peter, Hebrews, and Paul) of how God expresses the goal of his providence in the progressive glorification of his people.

The Lord's Prayer for Progressive Glorification

In the Lord's Prayer, before Jesus tells his disciples to pray that they might do his will, forgive their debtors, and be delivered from temptation, he tells them to pray, first and foremost, that God's name would be hallowed (Matt. 6:9). In all God's providence in helping us do his will is the goal that his name be revered and cherished as our most precious treasure.

The fact that Jesus doesn't just command us to revere God's name, but tells us to *pray* that it be revered, shows that *God* is the decisive cause in the glorification of God. We are praying that God would cause us, and others, to revere God. And this revering is in and through our doing his will. Increasingly conforming to God's revealed will so that his name is hallowed, or glorified, is the same as progressive glorification. And Jesus is teaching us, in the Lord's prayer, that *God* is decisive in bringing this about. Providence is pursuing its goal through the progressive glorification of believers as they pray, "Hallowed be your name." In fact, it is precisely because God brings about our God-hallowing transformation that he gets the glory for it.

Serving in the Power God Supplies

That's what Peter means when he says:

> Whoever serves, [let him do it] as one who serves by the strength that God supplies—*in order that in everything God may be glorified*

through Jesus Christ. To him belong glory and dominion forever and ever. Amen. (1 Pet. 4:11)

The key to the new way of serving God in the new covenant (in the newness of the Spirit, not the oldness of the letter, Rom. 7:6) is that we look away from our own resources and trust the blood-bought strength that God supplies. Peter says that when we do this, "God [is] glorified through Jesus Christ." That is, our progressive glorification, in serving God by faith, reflects the worth of his glory that we enjoy through the work of Jesus.

Pleasing God through Christ to His Glory

The writer to the Hebrews says the same thing a different way:

> Now may the God of peace who brought again from the dead our Lord Jesus, the great shepherd of the sheep, by the blood of the eternal covenant, *equip you with everything good* that you may do his will, *working in us that which is pleasing in his sight*, through Jesus Christ, *to whom be glory forever and ever.* Amen. (Heb. 13:20–21)

The logic of this benediction goes like this: God decisively equips us to do his will; through Jesus, he actually works in us so that we do what he equips us to do. The result is that, in our doing what pleases him, it is not we who get the glory but Jesus Christ, because through him God worked our progressive glorification.

Works of Faith according to Christ's Grace for His Glory

The same logic of new-covenant sanctification (or progressive glorification) is seen in the apostle Paul:

> To this end we always pray for you, that our God may make you worthy of his calling and may fulfill every resolve for good and every work of faith by his power, so that the name of our Lord Jesus may

be glorified in you, and you in him, according to the grace of our God and the Lord Jesus Christ. (2 Thess. 1:11–12)

This is an amazing sentence! God makes us "worthy of his calling"— that is, he enables us to live a life that shows the supreme worth of our calling. To accomplish this, he fulfills our good resolves. They are accomplished "by his power." This power accords with the grace of God. In other words, it is free and undeserved.

Our part in this is to trust his grace and power, and then, in that faith, to use our hearts and minds and hands to work so that our deeds become works *of faith*. The final goal of living this way is "so *that the name of our Lord Jesus may be glorified in you,* and you in him." In other words, Christ is shown to be glorious as we reflect his glory in this amazing God-sustained pattern of progressive glorification.

Asking God to Glorify God

Something so obvious that it goes unnoticed is that Paul is *praying* in 2 Thessalonians 1:11–12 (as Jesus was praying the Lord's Prayer, and the author of Hebrews was praying his benediction). This means he is asking God to bring all this to pass, which means that he is asking God to glorify Christ, who is the image of God. He is asking God to glorify God. This is what Jesus told us to do in the first sentence of the Lord's Prayer: ask God to see to it that his name be hallowed. It is what the author to the Hebrews was doing when he prayed that God would work in us for the glory of Christ.

And it is what Paul does again in Philippians 1:9–11:

It is my prayer that your love may abound more and more, with knowledge and all discernment, so that you may approve what is excellent, and so be pure and blameless for the day of Christ, filled with the fruit of righteousness that comes through Jesus Christ, *to the glory and praise of God.* (Phil. 1:9–11)

Paul *prays* that the Philippians would bear the fruit of righteousness "to the glory and praise of God." So, by praying this way, he is asking *God* to glorify *God*. The reason I draw out this obvious fact, which usually goes unnoticed, is to remind us that from before creation this fact has been central: things don't just happen for God's glory; they happen for God's glory because the pervasive providence of God sees to it that they happen that way. This is the goal of providence.

God is supremely committed to the display of his glory for the admiration and enjoyment of all who will have it as their supreme treasure. If we do not feel at home with this radical God-centeredness of God, we will not feel at home with the biblical story of God's providence. We will not feel at home in God's God-exalting presence.

New-Covenant Reconciliation Releases God-Glorifying Transformation

Progressive glorification (or sanctification) is the *work of God* (Heb. 13:20–21) through Jesus Christ (Phil. 1:11) by the Holy Spirit (2 Thess. 2:13). The phrase "through Jesus Christ" reminds us that the transformation we are talking about is part of Christ's enactment of the new covenant. The new covenant promised that the law would be written on the heart (Jer. 31:33). That is, it would be made part of our desire so that we would joyfully do God's will. This is what God is doing "by the Holy Spirit" "through Jesus Christ."

In other words, when Christ suffered to provide the foundation of the new covenant in the forgiveness of sins, he also unleashed by his blood the mighty work of the Holy Spirit to fulfill the new-covenant transformation promised in the words "I will put my law within them, and I will write it on their hearts" (Jer. 31:33).

Peter makes explicit this connection between the foundational suffering of Christ *for* us and the resulting transformation *in* us. "He himself bore our sins in his body on the tree, *that we might die to sin and live to righteousness*" (1 Pet. 2:24). Christ founded the new covenant in dying for us. Then the achievement of this reconciliation with God (Rom. 5:10) unleashes the power of the Spirit in the process, and eventual triumph, of our progressive glorification.

God's Design in Every Human Duty—the Glory of God in Christ

Since the new-covenant transformation of God's people was thought out in eternity by the wisdom of God, and bought by the blood of Christ, and wrought by the Spirit of God—all for the glory of Christ and his Father—it is clear that the repeated biblical requirement that human beings glorify God and Christ in all they do is not a mere *human duty* but a *divine design*. That is true for all the following biblical requirements, and the design of God's providence in each of them is the glory of God.

Bearing fruit:
> *By this my Father is glorified*, that you bear much fruit.
> (John 15:8)

Doing good works:
> Let your light shine before others, so that they may see your good works and *give glory to your Father who is in heaven*.
> (Matt. 5:16; cf. 1 Pet. 2:12)

Acting with your body:
> You were bought with a price. So *glorify God in your body*.
> (1 Cor. 6:20)

Eating, drinking, and everything:
> Whether you eat or drink, or whatever you do, *do all to the glory of God*. (1 Cor. 10:31)

Living in harmony with believers:
> May the God of endurance and encouragement grant you to live in such harmony with one another, in accord with Christ

Jesus, that together you may with one voice *glorify the God and Father of our Lord Jesus Christ.* (Rom. 15:5–6)

Welcoming other believers:
Welcome one another as Christ has welcomed you, *for the glory of God.* (Rom. 15:7)

Being led in paths of righteousness:
He leads me in paths of righteousness *for his name's sake.* (Ps. 23:3; 31:3; Isa. 61:3)

Enduring hardship patiently:
You are enduring patiently and bearing up *for my name's sake.* (Rev. 2:3)

Suffering as a Christian:
If anyone suffers as a Christian, let him not be ashamed, but *let him glorify God in that name.* (1 Pet. 4:16)

Christ's Zeal for the Glory of His Father

This divine design, that God be glorified in all human action, not only was purchased and empowered by Christ, but also was perfectly exemplified in his life. Consider Christ's purpose in two passages about his ministry. What they show is that the Son of God came into the world to glorify the name of God and to redeem a people who do the same:

"Now is my soul troubled. And what shall I say? 'Father, save me from this hour'? But *for this purpose* I have come to this hour. *Father, glorify your name.*" Then a voice came from heaven: "I have glorified it, and I will glorify it again." (John 12:27–28)

Christ became a servant to the circumcised [he was born as the Jewish Messiah] to show God's truthfulness, in order to confirm the promises given to the patriarchs, and *in order that the Gentiles might glorify God for his mercy.* (Rom. 15:8–9)

These two passages express the two great goals of Christ's incarnation: first, that Jesus himself, in his work, would glorify the name of his Father; second, that Jesus would then bring the nations to join him in doing the same—glorifying God for his mercy. Or, putting the two together, as we have seen so often before, the aim of Christ was the praise of the glory of God's grace (Eph. 1:6). His enactment of the new covenant was in pursuit of this goal.

Glory of the Father and of the Son Are One

But as we move toward the climax of history, the consummation of the new covenant, and the final goal of providence, we should make clear that the glory of God the Father and the glory of God the Son are one glory. This means that when Christ aims to magnify the glory of the Father, and when he aims to magnify the glory of the Son, he is not double-minded, and he is not blasphemous.

Jesus said, "I and the Father are one" (John 10:30). He was not blaspheming when he prayed, "Father, glorify *me* in your own presence with the glory that I had with you before the world existed" (John 17:5). He was not distracting his followers from the glory of the Father when he prayed, "I desire that they . . . may be with me where I am, to see *my* glory" (John 17:24). The glory of the Father and the glory of the Son are profoundly one glory.

Paul taught this when he said that the gospel was the good news of "the glory of *Christ*, who is the image of God," and then said that it was the good news of "the glory of *God* in the face of Jesus Christ" (2 Cor. 4:4, 6). Note the parallel:

"the glory of *Christ*, who is the image of *God*"
"the glory of *God* in the face of *Jesus Christ*"

These are not two gospels and two glories. The glory of God is known in the face of Christ. It is Christ's glory. The glory of Christ is God's glory shining in him as God's perfect image. It is God's glory. Therefore, the divine design and the human duty of the perfect God-man was to magnify his own glory—the glory of the Father and the Son.

For example, when he knew that his friend Lazarus was ill, Jesus delayed an extra two days and let Lazarus die (John 11:1–15). Why? He answers: "This illness does not lead to death. *It is for the glory of God, so that the Son of God may be glorified through it*" (John 11:4). Notice how the glory of God and the glory of the Son are now the combined aim of Jesus's action.

Coming of the Spirit to Glorify Christ

Therefore, we must not stumble over the aim of Christ to glorify Christ. We must not be offended by how Christ-exalting Christ is. When Jesus was about to leave his disciples and return to the Father, he said that he would come to them. "I will not leave you as orphans; I will come to you" (John 14:18). He was referring to the Holy Spirit—*his own* Spirit. "I will ask the Father, and he will give you another Helper, to be with you forever, even the Spirit of truth, whom the world cannot receive, because it neither sees him nor knows him. You know him, for *he dwells with you and will be in you*" (John 14:16–17). Christ dwelt with them (in the flesh) and would be in them (by the Spirit).

Christ himself will send the Spirit: "When the Helper comes, whom I will send to you from the Father, the Spirit of truth, who proceeds from the Father, *he will bear witness about me*" (John 15:26). The mission that the Spirit has from the Father and the Son—but especially from the Son ("I will send to you")—is to bear witness to the Son. More specifically, Jesus says of the Spirit whom he himself sends, "He will glorify *me*" (John 16:14). This Son-glorifying Spirit is the Spirit of the Son. So God's design for the Son of God and the duty he embraced, both during and after his earthly ministry, was to glorify himself, which is not in conflict with his mission to glorify the Father (John 12:27–28).

Coming of Christ to Glorify Christ

This is how history comes to its climax. Christ returns from heaven for this very purpose—to be glorified in his people. This is his intention and aim in the climactic acts of divine providence:

> [Those who do not obey the gospel] will suffer the punishment of eternal destruction, away from the presence of the Lord and from the glory of his might, when he comes on that day *to be glorified in his saints, and to be marveled at among all who have believed*, because our testimony to you was believed. (2 Thess. 1:9–10)

Paul states this as the purpose for Christ's coming: "to be glorified in his saints, and to be marveled at among all who have believed." These two statements ("to be glorified" and "to be marveled at") strike two slightly different notes in the same music of magnifying Christ. "To be glorified in [the] saints" puts the emphasis on Christ's own experience of receiving glory. "To be marveled at" puts the emphasis on the heart experience of the saints in their marveling at that glory. These two experiences are not separable. As we have seen so often, the ultimate goal is the united experience of God in Christ being exalted as supreme and our being thrilled to see and reflect that supremacy.

But let me note again the obvious truth that is so often overlooked: the glorification of Christ is not only the *result* of his coming. It is the *purpose* of his coming. *His* purpose. He is coming *in order to* be glorified and marveled at. If we are not glad that Christ is Christ-exalting, we will not be glad at his coming. If there lurks in us a resistance to God's zeal for his glory and Christ's commitment to his own exaltation, all our reading will be out of tune with the tenor of Scripture. We will not know God or ourselves or the world aright.

Eternal Purpose

This Christ-exalting purpose of Christ's second coming is not a momentary purpose. It is an eternal one. From eternity past to eternity future, the purpose of creation and providence has been, and always will be, the communication of the glory of Christ. "All things were created through him and *for him*" (Col. 1:16). That purpose—the exaltation of Christ in all creation and providence—does not come to an end in the new creation. God's providence does not vanish in the age to come. And its ultimate design will not change—"that in everything [Christ] might be preeminent" (Col. 1:18). To be sure, the event of the second coming will be like none other before or after it. There will be a stunning, once-for-all turning point at the climax of human history as we know it:

> Then will appear in heaven the sign of the Son of Man, and then all the tribes of the earth will mourn, and they will see the Son of Man coming on the clouds of heaven *with power and great glory.* (Matt. 24:30)

But we have seen at every point of history (even before history) that this universe is designed in God's wisdom—and governed by God's providence—to be a theater for the glory of God, manifest consummately in the glory of his grace, enacted through the glory of Christ, which shines most brightly in his suffering for undeserving rebels.

God's Most Lavish Promise?

This has been the ultimate purpose from the beginning. And it is the ultimate purpose of the eternal ages in the future. Paul exults as he expresses this in one of the most lavish promises in Scripture:

> [God] seated us with him in the heavenly places in Christ Jesus, that in the coming ages he might show the immeasurable riches of his grace in kindness toward us in Christ Jesus. (Eph. 2:6–7)

This is glorious verbal piling on. It will take eternal "ages" for God to exhaust the demonstration of his "riches" to those who are in Christ. For these riches are "immeasurable." They also are "riches of . . . grace." And lest we think of grace too vaguely, Paul says that this grace is "in kindness." And lest we think too generically about this gracious kindness, he says it is "toward us." And lest we think that these are the riches of the Father and not the Son, he concludes that these riches of kindness come to us from the Father "in Christ Jesus." In him are all the treasures. This means that God in Christ will be seen as increasingly rich in glory for all eternity, and we will be ever more fully satisfied with increasing measures of fresh kindness.

Every day for all eternity—without pause or end—the riches of the glory of God's grace in Christ will become increasingly great and beautiful in our perception of them. We are finite. They are "immeasurable"—infinite. Therefore, we cannot ever take them in fully. Let that sink in. There will *always* be more. Gloriously more. Forever. Only an infinite being can fully take in infinite riches. But we can, and we will, spend eternity taking in more and more of these riches. There is a necessary correlation between eternal existence and infinite blessing. It takes the one to experience the other. *Eternal* life is essential for the enjoyment of *immeasurable* riches of grace.

Experience is an absolutely essential word here—it takes the one to *experience* the other. Paul has already said in the previous chapter that from before creation God planned to make the universe—including the new creation and the age to come—a theater not only for the *display* of "the immeasurable riches of his grace" (Eph. 2:7), but also for the joyful "*praise* of the glory of his grace" (Eph. 1:6, 12, 14). This is the *experience* implied in Ephesians 2:7. What does it mean for us—for our experience—when God lavishes on us forever "the immeasurable riches of his grace in kindness toward us in Christ Jesus"? It means *joy.* To use the words of the apostle Peter, "joy that is inexpressible and glorified" (1 Pet. 1:8, my translation).

Supernatural, Everlasting, God-Glorifying, Christ-Exalting Joy

This is no merely natural joy that we could produce on our own, even at our perfected best. This will be the very joy of God in his Son, as we saw in John 17:26.[1] The delight that God has in Christ will dwell in us. His joy in the Son will be our joy in the Son. And our joy will be Christ's joy in the Father.

This is what Jesus will say to us at the second coming: "Enter into the joy of your master" (Matt. 25:21, 23). He is the master. We enter *his* joy. This will be the eternal work of the Holy Spirit—taking the joy of the Father in the Son and the joy of the Son in the Father and making them *our* joy, by revealing to us the glory of the Father and the Son in ever-increasing measures. This will be the all-satisfying, God-glorifying, Christ-exalting, Spirit-dependent *experience* of "the immeasurable riches of his grace in kindness toward us in Christ Jesus."

God's Delight in the Joyful Echo of His Excellencies in the Praises of His People

This experience of ever-increasing joy in all that God is for us in Christ will be the *essence* of God's eternal glorification in the coming ages. To be sure, the heavens will be glad. The sun and moon and shining stars will praise the Lord. The earth will rejoice. The seas will roar with praise. The rivers will clap their hands. The hills will sing for joy. The field will exult and everything in it. The trees of the forest will chant their praise. The desert will blossom like the crocus (Ps. 96:11–13; 98:7–9; 148:3; Isa. 35:1). The created world—liberated and perfected (Rom. 8:21)—will never cease to declare the glory of God (Ps. 19:1; Rom. 1:20).

Nevertheless, all this God-revealing, God-exalting beauty in nature will not perform its highest purpose until it finds a reverberation in the praising hearts—the *experience*—of the blood-bought children of

---

1   When Jesus says, "The love with which you [Father] have loved me may be in them" (John 17:26), he does not mean a kind of love that must overcome obstacles of sin and ill-desert, as when God loves us. Jesus is infinitely and perfectly worthy of the Father's love, so that this love is essentially delight, enjoyment, joyful approval. "This is my beloved Son, with whom I am *well pleased*" (Matt. 3:17).

God (Rom. 8:21). The glory of God will be the all-pervading light of that new country, but the lamp of that glory will be the Lamb (Rev. 21:23)—the remembered suffering, the eternal spectacle.

The perfected theater of creation will be glorious, radiant with God. But the drama—the human experience of God in Christ—not the theater, will be foremost in magnifying the God of all-pervasive providence. And the unparalleled beauty and worth of the Lamb who was slain will be the main song of eternity. And the joy of the children of God will be the main echo of the infinite excellencies of God—and the focus of his eternal delight.

PART 3

THE NATURE AND
EXTENT OF PROVIDENCE

Setting the Stage

15

Knowing the Providence of the God Who Is

The aim of part 3 of this book is to show from Scripture not the *goal* of providence but its *nature* and *extent*. The new question is not *Where* is God taking the world? but *How* does he see to it (providentially!) that it gets there? Nevertheless, the goal of providence will still be prominent, since that is where everything is moving. And *how* God brings the world to its appointed climax clarifies along the way the meaning of that climax.

In part 2 we saw from Scripture the ultimate goal of providence. In all the works of providence, God's ultimate aim is to be glorified in bringing about a new humanity—a church, a bride of Christ, a people of God—who through Jesus Christ exist *for the praise of the glory of his grace* (Eph. 1:6, 12, 14, my translation).

Since joyful prizing is the essence of *praising*, and since free grace is the apex of God's *glory*, and since Jesus Christ, slain for undeserving rebels, is the consummate display of *grace*, therefore we may also express the ultimate goal of providence as the perfected and irrepressible joy of God's people in the glory of God's grace, supremely radiant in the triumphant suffering of the Son of God. The goal of providence is expressed in the joyful exultation "Worthy is *the Lamb who was slain,* to receive power and wealth and wisdom and might and honor and glory and blessing!" (Rev. 5:12).

For God's Sake—and Ours

The fact that *praise* is God's ultimate goal shows that all the works of providence are for God's own sake. *"For my own sake, for my own sake,* I do it. . . . My glory I will not give to another" (Isa. 48:11). "I am he who blots out your transgressions *for my own sake"* (Isa. 43:25). "He leads me in paths of righteousness *for his name's sake"* (Ps. 23:3).

And the fact that this very praise is also the completion of our *joy* in the one we most admire[1] shows that all the works of providence are also *for our sake. "It is all for your sake,* so that as grace extends to more and more people it may increase thanksgiving to the glory of God" (2 Cor. 4:15; cf. 8:9).

This is not a contradiction—for *his* sake and for *our* sake. To be sure, the display of the worth and beauty of God's glory is the ultimate goal. But God has so constituted the created world, and human nature in particular, that the worth and beauty of God shine forth most clearly in a people who joyfully prize him above all. *He is the one being in the universe for whom self-exaltation is an act of supreme love.*

Implications of God's Self-Revealed Name

That last sentence, together with the name God revealed for himself in Exodus 3:14, shapes the way I have conceived of part 3 of this book. Let me try to explain how this is so. As we saw in chapter 6, God's self-revealed name in Exodus 3:14 was prominent in explaining God's ultimate purpose in the exodus. "God said to Moses, 'I AM WHO

---

1   See chap. 3 and the insights of C. S. Lewis concerning how praise not only expresses the joy of admiration but completes it.

I AM.'" I mentioned ten dimensions of this self-identification of God. Included in those dimensions were these three:

1. God is absolute being, absolute reality. Nothing existed before him. He never had a beginning. He is not becoming. He simply is, and always has been. Before he created other reality, he was all there was—eternally.

2. God is utterly independent. He depends on nothing to bring him into being or support him or counsel him or make him what he is. Therefore, everything that is not God depends totally on God. All that is not God is secondary and dependent. The entire universe is utterly secondary. It came into being by God and stays in being moment by moment because of God's decision to keep it in being.

3. God is the most important and most valuable reality in existence. He is more worthy of interest and attention and admiration and enjoyment than all other realities, including the entire universe.

This brings us back to this sentence: *He is the one being in the universe for whom self-exaltation is an act of supreme love.* God did not *decide* to be a being who is supremely valuable, supremely beautiful, supremely interesting, supremely admirable, and supremely enjoyable. He is who he is. That is what he *is*. He didn't ponder alternative kinds of being and then become one. He didn't decide to be "the blessed and only Sovereign" (1 Tim. 6:15). Therefore, God did not decide among various options what the *greatest gift* he could give would be.

Love's Greatest Gift

Nothing exists that is greater or better or more beautiful or more satisfying than God *himself*. It would be idolatrous and blasphemous for God to even contemplate the existence of a better gift than himself. If being supremely loving includes giving what is supremely valuable and beautiful and satisfying, then God's very *being* established the aim of his love. *The ultimate aim of the greatest love would be God's gift of himself for the everlasting enjoyment of the beloved.* When God upholds and displays and exalts and gives himself for the enjoyment of the beloved, he is loving supremely. Therefore, *God is the one being in the universe for whom self-exaltation is an act of supreme love.*

To be sure, *how* the supremely valuable gift of himself would be given, so that the whole panorama of his glorious attributes would be known with the greatest clarity and enjoyed with the greatest intensity—*that question* he did indeed contemplate and decide "according to the counsel of his will" (Eph. 1:11). And that contemplation, rooted in his wise, gracious, and just *being*, led to the whole history of providence and salvation through Christ that we see in Scripture.

How God's Being Shapes Part 3 of This Book

I linger over the implications of God's name ("I AM WHO I AM," Ex. 3:14) because they profoundly shape the way I approach the question being posed in part 3 of this book. I said above that the aim of part 3 is to show from Scripture not the *goal* of providence but its *nature* and *extent*.

By *extent* I mean, how extensive, or far-reaching, is God's governance or control of created reality? Does it reach *out to* the farthest galaxies? Does it reach *in to* subatomic particles? Does it include all the processes of nature (like weather systems and mutations of viruses)? Does it include the movement of kings and nations and the smallest choices of the human will?

By the *nature* of providence, I mean not so much the extent but *how* he influences whatever it is that he governs. Is his control always exerted in the same *way*? If his control reaches to the extent of governing the sinful actions of human beings, *how* does he do this in such a way that does not make him a sinner? If his control reaches to the extent of governing all the winds and waves, how does he do that in such a way that, when a tsunami sweeps away two hundred thousand people, it is consistent with his mercy?

There may or may not be comprehensive answers to these questions in Scripture. That's not my point at the moment. My point here is two-fold: (1) to say that the question posed in part 3 concerns the *nature* and *extent* of providence; and (2) to say that the reality of God in the absoluteness of his existence ("I AM WHO I AM") and the centrality of himself in the nature of his love (1 Pet. 3:18) profoundly shape my approach to those two concerns.

High-Flying Banner: God Is God, We Are Not

We do not share God's absolute existence. We do not say, "I am who I am." We say with the apostle Paul, "*By the grace of God* I am what I am" (1 Cor. 15:10). We know the truth implied in Paul's questions: "What do you have that you did not receive? If then you received it, why do you boast as if you did not receive it?" (1 Cor. 4:7). We are not God. We are creatures. We are ultimately dependent on God for everything.

We depend on him for our being and for our knowing—especially our knowing of him. We *are* because he *is*. We *know* because he *reveals*. We do not originate our existence or our knowledge. He is the ultimate source and foundation of both. And since God's absolute being and revealing is essential to his glory, and since his glory is the greatest gift he could give, we are happy for *him* to be the all-glorious, self-giving God rather than to be God ourselves.

That is the all-influencing banner flying over part 3 of this book. God is God, and we are not. He is totally self-sufficient. We are totally dependent. Our being comes from him. Our knowing him comes from him. We know the *extent* and *nature* of God's providence, to the degree that we know it at all, because he *reveals* it to us, partly in nature (Rom. 1:19–21) but most fully, indeed infallibly, in his word, the Scriptures. "Have I not *told* you from of old and declared it? . . . Is there a God besides me?" (Isa. 44:8). "I am God, and there is none like me, *declaring* the end from the beginning . . . *saying*, 'My counsel shall stand, and I will accomplish all my purpose'" (Isa. 46:9–10). God *speaks* to us about his providence. That is how we know it for what it is.

Biblical Observation vs. Philosophical Speculation

Therefore, part 3 is not a philosophical analysis about the extent and nature of God's providence. It is, rather, an attempt to rivet our attention on what God has told us about his providence in his word. My experience in reading analyses of God's providence that prioritize philosophical questions over exegetical ones is that unbiblical assumptions easily take over and mute or distort what the Scriptures teach. Not only that, but it seems to me that our minds easily become so tangled in the ambiguities and subtleties of philosophical words and categories that we come away with less clarity and less courage to risk our lives for the one who says, "Some of you they will put to death. . . . But not a hair of your head will perish" (Luke 21:16–18).

Example of Unwarranted Assumptions

When it comes to how *much* God controls, and *how* he controls, we must *be told* by him. We dare not bring to him, or to his word, governing assumptions that are alien to his word, no matter how widely held they are in any given culture. For example, I think it is an alien and biblically unwarranted assumption that human accountability is canceled out by God's ultimate and decisive control over the human will. Or to say it another way: I don't think we should bring to the Bible the governing assumption that humans must have ultimate self-determination in order to act responsibly and do things that are praiseworthy or blameworthy.

I know the term *ultimate self-determination* runs the risk of being one of those confusing philosophical terms I just complained about. But actually I'm trying not so much to clarify a philosophical assumption as I am an ordinary, everyday assumption of the average person. I think average Western people today assume the very thing that I am warning us not to assume, namely, that when it comes to *God's* possible control over their decisions or *their* control over their own decisions, it is their control, not God's, that is ultimate. That's what many people assume. By *ultimate*, I simply mean the control that finally decides the outcome. That's what I mean by the assumption of ultimate self-determination.

My point here is not that this assumption (that we must have ultimate self-determination in order to act responsibly) is false (though I think it is), but that it should not be brought to our Bible reading as a governing assumption. We should wait and see if God *tells us* in his word whether such an understanding of ultimate self-determination is true.

Defining Free Will

So, yes, I concede that the term *ultimate self-determination* crosses over into the use of philosophically loaded terminology. But my aim is not mainly philosophical, but practical. Millions of ordinary people carry in their minds the culturally (not biblically) informed assumption that ultimate self-determination is essential to their morally responsible humanity. To be sure, almost none of them use that very term. Rather, the term they use is *free will*. This term is viewed with such positive feelings and associations in our culture that it is virtually unchallenged as an accepted assumption.

But very few people pause to define it. If they do, they start sounding like a philosopher. That's why philosophers exist. It is unavoidable. And I'm not complaining that they exist. What I complained about above was prioritizing philosophical questions over exegetical ones and the inevitable danger of getting entangled in the ambiguities and subtleties of philosophical words. I stand by these two concerns, even if I have to risk the danger as well. So I am not against philosophy. In fact, I pray for more God-centered, Christ-exalting, Bible-saturated philosophers!

When we pause to define *free will*, I think people simply mean, at one level, something like this: "I do something of my own free will when my choice is not coerced, say, by someone putting a gun at my head (or my child's head)." But at a deeper level, if you ask people about who finally or ultimately controls their choices, they would, I think, ordinarily say something like, "If I don't have the final control, then I don't have free will." Then they would probably add: "And if I don't have free will, then I am not responsible. I'm a robot."

Since this deeper (and almost universal) understanding of free will contains the assumption of ultimate self-determination (I have final, decisive control in the moment when I prefer something and act on it), you can see how often this assumption would be brought into our Bible reading. My point is that we should not do that. We should wait and see what *God says* about his providence. We should wait to see if God's word leads us to the assumption that we must have ultimate self-determination in order to be responsible human beings.

Are You Denying the Use of Logic?

If someone says, "Wait, this is simply an issue of logic. It's like saying, 'Two plus two equals four.' It's like saying, "'A' cannot be 'not A' in the same way at the same time. Are you saying that we have to throw away all ordinary logic when we come to the Bible?" My answer is, first, no, we don't. The ordinary laws of logic are on clear display in the Bible. But, second, no, I don't agree that the statement "Ultimate self-determination is necessary for human accountability" is the logical equivalent of the statement "Two plus two equals four." The relationship between divine providence and human accountability is not a matter of logic in this way. We can see this by noticing how different the two statements are.

Consider the statement "Two plus two equals four." The answer to the question "What must be added to two in order to make it four?" is contained in the question itself. That's what four *is*. By definition, it *is* another two added to two. This number of asterisks (* * * *) is the *same* as this number of asterisks (* * + * *). But the relationship between ultimate human self-determination and human accountability is *not* like that. The definition of the one is not contained in the other. How they relate is not settled by logical laws. It is settled by what God tells us in his word.

How Shall We Know the Providence of God?

It is impossible that all readers of the Bible be philosophically sophisticated. Some readers should be. That is their God-given calling. But for millions, this is unrealistic and undesirable. Only certain kinds of minds and hearts can navigate the complexities of philosophy safely (Col. 2:8). How then shall these millions of ordinary readers who want to know the truth and embrace it and live by it come to reasonable and justified convictions about the extent and nature of God's providence? By humble, Spirit-dependent, careful, extensive reading of the whole Bible. Or, if they don't have access to the whole Bible, then as much of it as they have.

There are convictions behind this answer that I have explained and defended in the book *A Peculiar Glory*.[2] They lead me to the position that God intends for ordinary, faithful Christians to be able to discern, in his word, with warranted confidence, the truth of his providence. By reading or listening regularly to all of God's word, Christians may grasp the reality of God's providence in such a way that it becomes a soul-satisfying *treasure* to sweeten our worship, a love-empowering *energy* to sustain our sacrifices, and a perfectly weighted *ballast* in our souls to keep our boats from tipping over in the lashing waves of life.

"The Place Where You Are Standing Is Holy"

Therefore, the main task of part 3 of this book is to listen to what God says about his providence and to draw the reader's attention to it. The

---

2 John Piper, *A Peculiar Glory: How the Christian Scriptures Reveal Their Complete Truthfulness* (Wheaton, IL: Crossway, 2016).

burdens of this chapter may be summed up by a story in the life of Joshua:

> When Joshua was by Jericho, he lifted up his eyes and looked, and behold, a man was standing before him with his drawn sword in his hand. And Joshua went to him and said to him, "Are you for us, or for our adversaries?" And he said, "*No; but I am the commander of the army of the Lord. Now I have come.*" And Joshua fell on his face to the earth and worshiped and said to him, "What does my lord say to his servant?" And the commander of the Lord's army said to Joshua, "Take off your sandals from your feet, for the place where you are standing is holy." And Joshua did so. (Josh. 5:13–15)

If I come to the word of God and say, "Are you for me, or for my theological adversaries?" I may expect to hear God say, "No; but I am the commander." In other words, God does not meet us in his word as a partisan advocate, but as a commander. He is not governed by our partisan assumptions. He is who he is. And he reveals what he reveals. Our job is to listen, bow down in trusting worship, and obey. Our calling, as we come to God's word, is to receive the *treasure*, the *energy*, and the *ballast* of the reality of providence. We take off our shoes—the symbols of our self-sufficiency to tread the heights of the mysteries of providence—and we say, "Speak, Lord, for your servant hears" (1 Sam. 3:9).

Where Do We Go from Here?

Part 3 of this book aims to answer the question about the nature and extent of providence in achieving the ultimate goal discovered in part 2. That is, how extensively does God rule the world? And what sort of rule does he exert, for example, over nature and life and death and especially over the wills of Satan and unbelievers and those whom he saves? This all-embracing rule is relevant for God's ultimate goal. That goal is to have a transformed, God-centered, Christ-exalting,

Spirit-empowered, love-saturated, joyful people magnifying the riches of his grace in a new world that has been renovated in perfect harmony with these glorified saints. Therefore, the progress of part 3 moves toward the work of providence in creating this new people and new world.

But it does not go straight there. On the way to our focus on the creation and transformation of a new people, we focus on earth, water, wind, plants, animals, Satan, demons, kings, nations, birth, life, death, and sin. The reason for this wider treatment of providence, before we get to its most crucial work in saving and sanctifying and glorifying the bride of Christ, is threefold.

First, this wider providence permeates God's word. And our aim is to see what God has to say about his providence. Second, this is the world, and these are the sinful powers, from which God's people will be saved. This world and these powers—*around* us and, sadly, still very much *in* us—are the battleground where providence does its saving, sanctifying, glorifying work. Everything hangs on whether God's providence holds sway in this world—the world of nature, and nations, and Satan, and sin. We are not saved immediately out of this world. We are saved and transformed in and through it. These powers are such that we will not be saved if God's providence does not hold sway over them. Therefore, seeing that providence in the Bible matters.

Third, this vast world of earth, water, wind, plants, animals, Satan, demons, kings, nations, birth, life, death, and sin is not only a battleground, but also a theater for the glory of God's providence. Here is where we see the hand of God. And if God's providence guides the tiniest speck of dust floating in the air, that will be an occasion of worship in this life and forever. As Jonathan Edwards writes:

> Every atom in the universe is managed by Christ so as to be most to
> the advantage of the Christian, every particle of air or every ray of

the sun; so that he in the other world, when he comes to see it, shall sit and enjoy all this vast inheritance with surprising, amazing joy.[3]

This world of nature and beauty and sin and sorrow is the theater into which God himself enters history in Jesus Christ. And it is the theater where we experience the triumphs of our own salvation. Knowing if and how God's providence holds sway in this world—this *whole* world—matters more to our perseverance than most Christians realize.

Therefore, to give us courage and competence in the battle, and to give us eyes in the theater, we turn now to the nature and extent of God's providence.

3   Jonathan Edwards, *The "Miscellanies": (Entry Nos. A–z, Aa–zz, 1–500)*, ed. Thomas A. Schafer and Harry S. Stout, vol. 13, *The Works of Jonathan Edwards* (New Haven, CT: Yale University Press, 2002), 184.

Providence over Nature

16

The Loss and Recovery of
a Theater of Wonders

The picture presented in the Bible, cover to cover, is not one of God creating the natural world to run on its own while he maintains his distance. What we find instead is a picture of God creating, sustaining, owning, and governing the world of nature. His providence is not, so to speak, by proxy, but present and hands-on—the kind of closeness that causes the biblical writers to say such things as "He makes grass grow on the hills" (Ps. 147:8), "God appointed a worm that attacked the plant" (Jonah 4:7), and "He brings forth the wind from his storehouses" (Ps. 135:7). This chapter is about the close attentiveness—the pervasive involvement—of God's providence in nature to make it a theater of wonders.

Present Work of the Creator
Modern science has made us more aware of patterns of causality and regularity in nature, which we have come to call "laws of nature." But the picture in the Bible reveals God's ongoing relation to nature in such a way that he may be called an ongoing Creator, and in such a way

that no natural process or event is so insignificant that it lies outside his pervasive and purposeful providence.

> O LORD, how manifold are your works!
>   In wisdom have you made them all;
>   the earth is full of your creatures.
> Here is the sea, great and wide,
>   which teems with creatures innumerable,
>   living things both small and great.
> There go the ships,
>   and Leviathan, which you formed to play in it.
> These all look to you,
>   to give them their food in due season.
> When you give it to them, they gather it up;
>   when you open your hand, they are filled with good
>   things.
> When you hide your face, they are dismayed;
> when you take away their breath, they die
>   and return to their dust.
> When you send forth your Spirit, they are created,
>   and you renew the face of the ground.
> May the glory of the LORD endure forever;
>   may the LORD rejoice in his works (Ps. 104:24–31)

The earth and sea are full of creatures that *God has made* (Ps. 104:24–25). This "making" did not just happen at the beginning of the world (Gen. 1:25). Rather, every time an animal comes into being, God is active in that creation: "When you send forth your Spirit, they are created" (Ps. 104:30), which may mean either that God's Holy Spirit is active in the creation of each new animal, or, more metaphorically, that God's life-imparting breath gives the animal life. The point is essentially the same in either case. And even though most of the "teeming creatures" of the sea have no breath, the point remains the same: the psalmist wants us to attribute the ever-recurring emergence of animal life to the ongoing creator-work of God.

Sustaining Work of the Creator

Not only is God active in giving life to all animals (and taking it away, Ps. 104:29), but he is also involved in the processes by which they are kept alive:

> You make springs gush forth in the valleys;
>> they flow between the hills;
> they give drink to every beast of the field;
>> the wild donkeys quench their thirst.
> Beside them the birds of the heavens dwell;
>> they sing among the branches.
> From your lofty abode you water the mountains;
>> the earth is satisfied with the fruit of your work.
> You cause the grass to grow for the livestock
>> and plants for man to cultivate,
>> that he may bring forth food from the earth.
>>> (Ps. 104:10–14)

God makes this provision for his creatures with such care and intentionality that the psalmist speaks of his actually feeding them, just as Jesus does when he says of the birds, "Your heavenly Father feeds them" (Matt. 6:26):

> These all look to you,
>> to give them their food in due season.
> When you give it to them, they gather it up;
>> when you open your hand, they are filled with good things.
> When you hide your face, they are dismayed. (Ps. 104:27–29)

The psalmist has not lost sight of the fact that there was a beginning when God created the heavens and the earth (Gen. 1:1):

The mountains rose, the valleys sank down
    to the place that you appointed for them.
You set a boundary that they may not pass,
    so that they might not again cover the earth. (Ps. 104:8–9)

Nevertheless, the focus of this psalm is on the amazing immediacy of God's wisdom. "You cause the grass to grow" (Ps. 104:14). And, as it says in Psalm 147:8–9:

He covers the heavens with clouds;
    he prepares rain for the earth;
    he makes grass grow on the hills.
He gives to the beasts their food,
    and to the young ravens that cry.

The psalmists do not want us to think or talk like modern naturalists, who think of the natural world as formed and sustained by mindless physical processes. Whether with clouds, grass for the animals, or eyes and ears for man, God's providence is up close and powerful in his ongoing creating and sustaining. "The hearing ear and the seeing eye, the LORD has made them both" (Prov. 20:12). All the billions of eyes and ears on this planet were made by God—not just designed at the beginning of the world, but *made* in the womb. "You formed my inward parts; you knitted me together in my mother's womb" (Ps. 139:13). The biblical view of the world is that grass and rain and springs and ears and eyes are the work of God's hands as they come into being and do their God-appointed work.

Losing a Theater of Wonders and the Purpose of Providence

It is a tragic fact of the modern world that most contemporary, scientifically minded people think it is more true and significant to speak of the technicalities of photosynthesis than to say, "God makes the grass grow." This is not just a sentence for children. It is a sentence—

a reality—desperately needed by the soul-shrunken modern man whose world has been reduced from a theater of wonders to a machine running mindlessly on mechanical laws.

Of course, a God-entranced Christian may happily go about his scientific work on photosynthesis and put technical names on the ways of God. But woe to us if we follow the secular spirit of the age into a frame of mind where God is out of sight, out of mind, and out of our everyday conversation about the wonders of growing grass.

The main reason it is tragic to lose sight of the pervasive and intimate providence of God in the natural world is that it means we also lose sight of the purposes for this providence that God intends for us to see. The writer of Psalm 104 is wonderfully clear on the purposes he has in meditating on God's created world. And these purposes are the same ones that resound throughout Scripture as God's great ends in creating and sustaining and owning and governing the natural world.

God's Joy in the Greatness of His Work

First, it is God's purpose to overflow with glorious, God-revealing wonders for the sake of his own enjoyment. The psalmist joins in affirming God's joy in his own handiwork:

> May the glory of the LORD endure forever;
>   may the LORD rejoice in his works. (Ps. 104:31)

I am assuming that the psalmist is not out of touch with reality here in voicing his desire that the Lord would rejoice in his works. He is not wishing for something God is reluctant to do. He is not praying for God to commit idolatry by rejoicing in creation rather than only in himself. No, he is joining God in affirming what he knows from his own God-breathed insight: this is what God actually does—he rejoices in the works of his hands.

If, at every point in his creation, God saw that it was good (Gen. 1:4, 10, 12, 18, 21, 25), it would be very strange if he were disappointed rather than rejoicing. And it would be doubly strange if, at the moment of creation, all the angels of heaven shouted for joy, but God didn't share their joy.

> Where were you when I laid the foundation of the earth?
>   Tell me, if you have understanding. . . .
>   Who laid its cornerstone,
> when the morning stars sang together
>   *and all the sons of God [angels] shouted for joy?*
>   (Job 38:4, 6–7)

In other words, one of God's purposes in creating the natural world was the enjoyment he would take in it. The fact that he rejoices in the works of his hands gives a partial explanation for the countless glories of the natural universe that no human being ever sees and no angel fully comprehends. God made the Leviathan to "play" in the sea: "Here is the sea, great and wide . . . and Leviathan, which *you formed to play in it*" (Ps. 104:25–26). There are millions of such playful wonders that no human ever sees:

> Behold, Behemoth,
>   which I made. . . .
> The mountains yield food for him
>   *where all the wild beasts play.* (Job 40:15, 20)

All of this utterly fascinating play fills the humanly unseen creation. But it is not wasted. The angels grasp some of it. Someday we may grasp more of it. But God grasps and rejoices in all of it. It is part of God's glory that he misses none of it and that he values it according to its true nature as a revelation of himself.

God's Joy in Creation Is Joy in His Glory

God's enjoyment of the natural world (like his enjoyment of his redeemed people, Isa. 62:5; Jer. 32:41; Zeph. 3:17) is not an enjoyment *added to* the joy he has in his own all-satisfying glory. Notice the way the psalmist speaks of God's joy in his works:

May the glory of the LORD endure forever;
 may the LORD rejoice in his works. (Ps. 104:31)

The psalmist knows that it would be blasphemous to suggest that God *needed* creation in order to be glorious or to be happy—like a frustrated child who needs a toy to play with. No. God's joy in creation is the fullness of his joy in the glory of his own power and wisdom and goodness coming to expression in creation. This will become clearer if we turn to the second purpose of God in the creating, sustaining, owning, and governing of the natural world.

Happy, Eternal Purpose of the Theater of Wonders
The second purpose (which we can see clearly in Psalm 104) is God's display of his glory for the enjoyment of his people—an enjoyment that comes to consummation in praising the God whose kindness overflows with such tastes of himself. God created the natural world as a theater for his glory and a joyful habitation for his beholding people, who, to all eternity, will live in glorified bodies in a profoundly pleasing glorified world of nature.

When Jesus returns to establish his eternal kingdom, he "will transform our lowly body to be like his glorious body, by the power that enables him even to subject all things to himself" (Phil. 3:21). Then "the creation itself will be set free from its bondage to corruption and obtain the freedom of the glory of the children of God" (Rom. 8:21).

It is true that Paul says of our resurrection body, "It is sown a *natural* body; it is raised a *spiritual* body. If there is a natural body, there is also a spiritual body" (1 Cor. 15:44). And he says, "I tell you this, brothers: flesh and blood cannot inherit the kingdom of God, nor does the perishable inherit the imperishable" (1 Cor. 15:50). But his point is not that we become bodiless, but that our natural, created, physical bodies undergo a profound change that suits them for a glorified world and a radically new, yet still embodied, spiritual life. Perishable flesh and blood would be ill-suited for such a world and such a life.

In describing the final resurrection, Paul calls the transformation of our bodies a *putting on*, rather than a *taking off*. The thought of a dis-embodied soul was untrue and undesirable: "While we are still in this tent [fallen, natural bodies], we groan, being burdened—not that we would be unclothed [without any body], but that we would be further clothed, so that what is mortal may be swallowed up by life" (2 Cor. 5:4). The point is not that Paul wants to take off the body; rather, he wants to put on a new kind of body, suited for immortal life.

This was also the point of 1 Corinthians 15:53: "This perishable body must *put on the imperishable*, and this mortal body must *put on immortality*." Put on, not take off. In other words, in the new earth we will not be "unclothed"—with no body. We will not be disembodied spirits. There will be a created world of glorified physical matter in which we dwell with glorified physical bodies "like [Jesus's] glorious body" (Phil. 3:21).

That new world and this one we live in now are both intended to be theaters for the glory of God and joyful habitations for God's children, even though this present world, with its fallenness and futility and corruption (Rom. 8:20–22), causes us to be "grieved by various trials" (1 Pet. 1:6). Joy and sorrow always mingle in this fallen world that is radiant with God-revealing wonders and ruined with body-destroying, soul-threatening evils. Therefore, the demeanor of the Christian, as Paul said, is "sorrowful, yet always rejoicing" (2 Cor. 6:10). We "groan inwardly as we wait eagerly for adoption as sons, the redemption of our bodies" (Rom. 8:23). But mingled with our groaning is joy, because we know that there is no condemnation for those in Christ (Rom. 8:1), that the sting of death is removed (1 Cor. 15:55), and that our afflic-tions are "preparing for us an eternal weight of glory" (2 Cor. 4:17), so "we rejoice in hope of the glory of God" (Rom. 5:2).

But those are not the only reasons we rejoice. Every sight, every sound, every fragrance, every texture, every taste in this world that is not sin, points to something of the glory of God that Christ died to obtain for sinners like us. This "something" is what I was referring to above where I said that God's kindness overflows in creation with "tastes of himself." The God-revealing glories of the natural world and its redeemed, future perfection are not separate from the "glorious inheritance" (Eph. 1:18) that Christ died to secure for his people. That's the point of Romans 8:21: "The creation itself will be set free from its bondage to corruption and obtain the freedom of the glory of the children of God." But even now there are foretastes—glorious foretastes displayed onstage in the theater of his glory for the joy of his people.

Our Joy in Creation Is Finally Joy in the Lord

Return with me now to Psalm 104, where I said we could see clearly the purpose of God to make the world a theater for his glory for the enjoyment of his people:

> O Lord, how manifold are your works!
> In wisdom have you made them all. (Ps. 104:24)

> May the glory of the Lord endure forever. . . .
> I will sing to the Lord as long as I live;
> I will sing praise to my God while I have being.
> May my meditation be pleasing to him,
> for I rejoice in the Lord. (Ps. 104:31, 33–34)

The psalmist calls his psalm a "meditation" (or meditative praise: "May my meditation be pleasing to him"). He has been meditating on the world God creates and sustains and governs. The world of providence. What he has seen moved him to exult in God's unparalleled *wisdom* in the countless natural wonders God creates and controls.

"In wisdom have you made them all." The glory of this wisdom, and its execution in power and goodness, causes the psalmist to sing and praise and rejoice in the Lord.

This is crucial to note: he rejoices "in the LORD" (104:34). Yes, he rejoices in the *works* of the Lord (as God himself does, 104:31). It would be an ungrateful sin not to. They are gifts and blessings. But when all is said and done and the psalmist hopes his meditation will be pleasing to God, the ground of his hope is this: "For I rejoice *in the LORD*"[1]—not finally or fully in his works, but in *himself*. That is what creation is for.

All of creation—in the skies above and on the earth beneath— is designed to reveal the glory of God. His glory, including his power, his divine nature, his understanding, his goodness—all these and more—is put on display in the theater of God's glory called the natural world:

The heavens declare the *glory* of God,
    and the sky above proclaims his handiwork. (Ps. 19:1)

[God's] *invisible attributes*, namely, his *eternal power* and *divine nature*, have been clearly perceived, ever since the creation of the world, in the things that have been made. (Rom. 1:20)

The LORD is the everlasting God,
    the Creator of the ends of the earth.
He does not faint or grow weary;
    his *understanding* is unsearchable. (Isa. 40:28)

The LORD is *good* to all,
    and his *mercy* is over all that he has made. (Ps. 145:9)

1' There is no Hebrew word in this verse for "for." But I think the ESV properly interprets the implicit logical link between the two clauses: (1) "May my meditation be pleasing to him"; (2) "I rejoice in the LORD" (Ps. 104:34).

All Glory in Creation Is the Glory of Christ

The apostle Paul makes clear that every aspect of this revelation of the glory of God is, in fact, for the glory of *Christ*. "All things were created through [Christ] and *for* [*Christ*]" (Col. 1:16). Indeed, "*in him* all things hold together" (Col. 1:17). "He upholds the universe by the word of his power" (Heb. 1:3). Everything God reveals of himself in nature is revealed for the glory of Christ and for our enjoyment of his greatness.

But no spiritually blind (2 Cor. 4:4) and dead (Eph. 2:5) sinner would see or savor the glory of Christ in creation without the new-covenant work of Christ that we saw in chapter 12—the sin-covering, wrath-absorbing, blindness-removing purchase of Christ in his death and resurrection. Therefore, every good gift in this world and the next (including innumerable wonders to enjoy in nature) was purchased by Christ for us at the cost of his life. Therefore, every sight, every sound, every fragrance, every texture, every taste in this world that is not sin is meant to intensify our admiration and love for Jesus (as creator, sustainer, upholder, and redeemer) and move us to "boast . . . in the cross of our Lord Jesus Christ" (Gal. 6:14). The theater of wonders that we call the natural world is through Christ and for Christ.

We Need a Closer Look

When it comes to God's actual governance of the natural world, this chapter may be seen as a kind of introduction and overview of God's pervasive involvement and design in making the world of nature a theater of wonders. But it is not extensive or detailed enough to show what I want us to see in Scripture, namely, how pervasive and exhaustive God's providence is in governing every aspect of the natural world. For that, we pursue a closer look in chapter 17.

17

Earth, Water, Wind,
Plants, and Animals

In chapter 16 we inferred an extensive and detailed divine governance of all natural processes, mainly from a few verses in Psalm 104: "You cause the grass to grow" (v. 14); "You make springs gush forth in the valleys" (v. 10); "When you take away [your creatures'] breath, they die and return to their dust" (v. 29). But the biblical testimony to God's providence over the natural world is far more vast and specific. It addresses the largest and smallest events of nature, and it shows God's close attentiveness in directing every aspect of this natural world.

Three Reasons We Need A Closer Look

There are at least three reasons why we need this closer look at the extensiveness and detailed attentiveness of God's providence in every part of nature.

First, because it is the natural world that threatens to harm us more constantly than any danger from human accident or assault or war. Dangers from other people are real and may be prevalent in some times and places. But the dangers of heart attack, stroke, cancer, pneumonia, diabetes, malaria, and viruses are ever present, no matter how peaceful our relationships are with other people—not to mention perilous natural disasters (such as hurricanes, earthquakes, and flooding) and countless possibilities of freak accidents. We need to know the measure of God's providence over the parts of reality that threaten our lives most.

Second, in order for us to have a deep and unshakable, life-stabilizing conviction about God's providence over the natural world, we need to take into account the vastness and specificity of the biblical description of God's macro and micro rule in nature.

The third reason for taking a closer, more detailed look at God's providence in nature is that if we don't see the close attentiveness of his governance of the natural world in Scripture, we will not see his purposes in that governance. One may have a purpose for a stone, namely, that it knock out Goliath. But if one has no control over the stone, the purpose becomes a *hope*, not a *certainty*. My point in this chapter is that while David with his slingshot, on the one hand, may have only hoped his stone would bring down Goliath, because his control was not complete, God, on the other hand, has *more* than a hope for his purposes in the natural world because his control is complete. Therefore, our confidence in the purposes of his providence in nature can be total.

Providence over the Earth

Although God creates the stars (Isa. 40:26), puts each one in place (Ps. 8:3), and gives each its name (Ps. 147:4) so that he can call them to do his bidding (Isa. 40:26), it is the earth and its inhabitants that he attends to with unusual closeness.

"I made the earth," the Lord says (Isa. 45:12; cf. Job 38:4). Therefore, he owns the earth. It belongs to him to do with as he pleases. "The earth is the Lord's and the fullness thereof" (Ps. 24:1). "To the Lord your God belong . . . the earth with all that is in it" (Deut. 10:14; cf. Ps. 89:11). Or, as the Lord himself says, "All the earth is mine" (Ex. 19:5). "The world and its fullness are mine" (Ps. 50:12). Therefore, the earth exists to serve the purposes of its maker and owner, and God governs it to that end.

He causes it to do his bidding. He removes mountains, shakes the earth, and opens it with earthquakes at his will:

> . . . he who removes mountains, and they know it not,
>   when he overturns them in his anger,
> who shakes the earth out of its place,
>   and its pillars tremble. (Job 9:5–6)

> . . . who looks on the earth and it trembles,
>   who touches the mountains and they smoke! (Ps. 104:32)

> You have made the land to quake; you have torn it open;
>   repair its breaches, for it totters. (Ps. 60:2)

One instance where we see God move from his ordinary processes of ruling the earth to an extraordinary act of control is when Korah and Dathan and Abiram rebel against Moses. God sentences them and their households to death. And he takes their lives by causing the earth to open and swallow them:

> [Moses said,] "If the LORD creates something new, and the ground opens its mouth and swallows them up with all that belongs to them, and they go down alive into Sheol, then you shall know that these men have despised the LORD." And as soon as he had finished speaking all these words, the ground under them split apart. And the earth opened its mouth and swallowed them up. (Num. 16:30–32; cf. Deut. 11:6)

Based on God's creating the earth for his purposes, and his absolute ownership of the earth and everything on it, and his continuously shaping its terrain (as when mountains are "removed," Job 9:5), and his causing it to tremble and tearing it open, we may conclude that whatever natural processes happen in the earth, God is acting in them to bring about his purposes. I am not yet dealing with what Satan and man may be able to do to the earth. That comes later, in chapter 18.

I am simply concluding that all natural processes in the earth, such as earthquakes, are in God's control, for if God causes them (as we have seen he does), he also can stop them. The earth is not autonomous. It does not have a will of its own.[1] Its processes do not proceed independently of their maker, owner, and ruler. God is "Lord of heaven and earth" (Acts 17:24). He "shakes the earth" (Job 9:6). Or he does not. It moves, or stands fast, at the bidding of the one who "works all things according to the counsel of his will" (Eph. 1:11). He is the one of whom Job says, at the end of his troubles, "I know that . . . no purpose of yours can be thwarted" (Job 42:1). He is the one who says, "My counsel shall stand, and I will accomplish all my purpose" (Isa. 46:10). For "all things are your servants" (Ps. 119:91). Therefore, if an earthquake destroys a city, this was of the Lord. For the Lord has said, "Does disaster come to a city, unless the LORD has done it?" (Amos 3:6). He expects the answer no. If disaster comes, the Lord has done it.

Providence over Water

When it comes to the impact on human life, there is a close connection between earth and water. An earthquake may destroy a dam, but it is the raging water downstream that destroys the village. An earthquake may happen at the bottom of the Indian Ocean, but it was the tsunami of December 26, 2004, that took the lives of over two hundred thousand people. What does the Bible have to say about God's control of water—floods, seas, rivers, waves, rain, hail, snow, ice, dew?

There is no reason to think that Jesus, from his throne in heaven today, cannot command the waves the way he did when he was here.

---

1   For how I understand a figure of speech such as in Acts 12:10 that says the iron gate "opened for them of its own accord," see John Piper, "The Prison Gates Opened of Their Own Accord— Really?," Desiring God, August 25, 2011, https://www.desiringgod.org/articles/the-prison-gates -opened-of-their-own-accord-really.

"He . . . rebuked the wind and the raging waves, and they ceased, and there was a calm" (Luke 8:24). From that, the disciples inferred correctly, "Even winds and sea obey him" (Matt. 8:27). This is still true today: the seas obey Jesus. They do not move without his instruction, either by command or by his wisely planned permission.[2] With a single rebuke, the Lord Jesus can make all raging waves become calm. He can stop tsunamis. If he does not, we put our hands over our mouths and trust the justice and goodness and wisdom of God's plan. "I lay my hand on my mouth. I have spoken once, and I will not answer; twice, but I will proceed no further" (Job 40:4–5).

Seas and Rivers Split, Bear, and Freeze at His Command

The seas not only obey God's command to be calm; they also obey his command to split. "He rebuked the Red Sea, and it became dry" (Ps. 106:9). "You divided the sea before [the Israelites], so that they went through the midst of the sea on dry land" (Neh. 9:11). Then, when they were safely through, "the LORD brought back the waters of the sea upon [the Egyptians]" (Ex. 15:19; see also Deut. 11:4; Josh. 24:7).

The sea also obeys Christ's command to hold him up when he walks on it. "He came to them, walking on the sea" (Matt. 14:25). This was not because the sea was frozen! Peter sank in the same water that Jesus walked on (Matt. 14:30). But it is true that God causes water to freeze by his own breath: "By the breath of God ice is given, and the broad waters are frozen fast" (Job 37:10). "He gave them hail for rain" (Ps. 105:32).

> He gives snow like wool;
> he scatters frost like ashes.

---

2 See chap.13 where I discussed this idea of "planned permission," making the point that God does all things wisely, and, therefore, every time he permits an event, he has a purpose for it and a plan for all that will flow from the event. A permitted event may have more God-governed secondary causes between God and the event, but the permitted event is no less governed and guided by God's all-embracing purposes and plan.

He hurls down his crystals of ice like crumbs;
  who can stand before his cold? (Ps. 147:16–17)

Water also obeys God's command to flow where there is no stream
(2 Kings 3:17, 20), and to turn to blood (Ps. 105:29), and to flow
out of a bone-dry rock (Num. 20:8; Ps. 105:41; 114:17), and to
make an axe head float (2 Kings 6:6–7), and to stop being poisonous
(2 Kings 4:41).

He Rules Rain, Drought, and Famine

Most importantly, water obeys the command of God to fall as rain to
bring forth crops, or not to fall and bring drought and famine. God
commands both. "I sent rain on one city, and sent no rain on another
city; one field would have rain, and the field on which it did not rain
would wither" (Amos 4:7, my translation). The all-important, life-
sustaining rains are sent by God. "The Lord will open to you . . . the
heavens, to give the rain to your land in its season and to bless all the
work of your hands" (Deut. 28:12). "He makes his sun rise on the evil
and on the good, and sends rain on the just and on the unjust" (Matt.
5:45; cf. Acts 14:17). And the drought and famine are from the Lord.
"I shut up the heavens so that there is no rain" (2 Chron. 7:13). "I . . .
command the clouds that they rain no rain upon it" (Isa. 5:6). "I have
called for a drought on the land" (Hag. 1:11; cf. Deut. 28:22).

Elihu tells Job that all the seemingly random turnings of the clouds,
giving and withholding their rain, are, in fact, *by God's guidance*, and
are purposeful through and through. They *accomplish his commands*.
They express *correction* and *love* for God's creatures.

He loads the thick cloud with moisture;
  the clouds scatter his lightning.
They turn around and around *by his guidance*,
  to accomplish all that he commands them
  on the face of the habitable world.

Whether for *correction* or for his *land*,
  or for *love*, he causes it to happen. (Job 37:11–13)

The providence of God in rain is not random. Nor is any other action of water anywhere in the world. The Bible presses us toward a worldview where no natural element or natural event exists or operates randomly or by the so-called laws of nature alone. The biblical worldview is God-entranced.[3] Nothing in nature happens without God's wise and just and gracious providence. Nothing falls outside his concern and guidance. To be sure, his ways are, for us, often inscrutable (Rom. 11:33). But the biblical picture of the natural world is radiant with the reality that "from him and through him and to him are all things. To him be glory forever" (Rom. 11:36).

Providence over the Wind

I recall a deep-sea fishing trip off the coast of Florida with my father when I was a boy. We were trawling for big-game fish, not bottom fishing. When dark clouds gathered over our boat, which was out of sight of land, and it began to rain, I asked the captain if this was dangerous for us. He said, "Rain is no problem; the boat is designed for the water to just run off the deck." Then he added, "Wind is what's dangerous." Of course, wind makes waves.

Indeed, when Jesus removed the danger of the raging waves from threatening the disciples on the Sea of Galilee, it was ultimately the wind that he commanded. As we have seen, he rules the waters. But one of the ways he rules the waters is by ruling the winds:

He rose and rebuked the *winds* and the sea, and there was a great calm. And the men marveled, saying, "What sort of man is this, that even *winds* and sea obey him?" (Matt. 8:26–27)

---

3 See John Piper and Justin Taylor, eds., *A God-Entranced Vision of All Things: The Legacy of Jonathan Edwards* (Wheaton, IL: Crossway, 2004).

He Raises the Stormy Winds and Makes Them Still

God governs the winds. They do his bidding. When he wanted to cover the land of Egypt with locusts, "*The Lord brought an east wind upon the land all that day and all that night. When it was morning, the east wind had brought the locusts*" (Ex. 10:13). And when his purposes were complete, "the Lord turned the wind into a very strong west wind, which lifted the locusts and drove them into the Red Sea" (Ex. 10:19). And when he had finished walling up the waters of the sea so his people could pass through on dry ground, he summoned the wind to finish his judgment on Pharaoh's army: "You blew with your wind; the sea covered them; they sank like lead in the mighty waters" (Ex. 15:10).

Stormy winds are the deadly threats to those who go out to sea in ships. And the ceasing of those storms is sweet. The Lord commands both:

> Some went down to the sea in ships,
>   doing business on the great waters;
> they saw the deeds of the Lord,
>   his wondrous works in the deep.
> *For he commanded and raised the stormy wind,*
>   which lifted up the waves of the sea. . . .
> Then they cried to the Lord in their trouble,
>   and he delivered them from their distress.
> *He made the storm be still,*
>   and the waves of the sea were hushed. (Ps. 107:23–25, 28–29)

Clouds, flashes of lightning, every gust of wind—these are kept by the Lord, as it were, in his storehouses, and brought out as he sees fit for his purposes:

> Whatever the Lord pleases, he does,
>   in heaven and on earth,

in the seas and all deeps.
He it is who makes the clouds rise at the end of the earth,
who makes lightnings for the rain
and *brings forth the wind from his storehouses.* (Ps. 135:6–7)

And when he brings them from his storehouses, he commands them and they *fulfill his every word*:

Praise the LORD from the earth,
you great sea creatures and all deeps,
fire and hail, snow and mist,
stormy wind *fulfilling his word*! (Ps. 148:7–8)

Ten Thousand Unthanked Providences—Daily

I can't help but pause here to make an observation about the way the world responds to God's providence. If there is a storm at sea and an ocean liner is sunk, or if a hazardous weather condition brings down a commercial airliner and lives are lost, there is often an outcry—both publicly and in the personal grief of family members—about the failure of God to prevent this disaster ("Where was God?"). Intense grief is real and painful and understandable from all who experience loss in these disasters. And very often, even the most mature saints speak ill-advised words for the wind (Job 6:26). Wise counselors let them pass without judgment in the moment of crisis.

But where is the corresponding emotional intensity, or even mild recognition, of God's providence when one hundred thousand airplanes land safely every day? That is roughly how many scheduled flights there are every day in the world. And that does not include general aviation, air taxis, military, and cargo. Where is the incessant chorus of amazement and thanks that today God provided ten million mechanical and natural and personal factors to conspire perfectly to keep these planes in the air and bring them to their desired destination safely—and most of them carrying people who neglect and demean God every day?

Even when a plane with no functioning engines lands on the Hudson River, and every passenger walks out on the floating wings of this 80-ton airliner, or when a plane with ninety-seven passengers crashes in Mexico and bursts into flames *after* every passenger and the entire crew are safely off the plane, where is the public outpouring of thankfulness to the God of wonders? Where is the heart's cry of thankfulness to God that we hear in Psalm 107:31 for the rescue on the sea?

Let them thank the Lord for his steadfast love,
    for his wondrous works to the children of man!

The world and even thousands of Christians give no praise and thanks to God for millions of daily, life-sustaining providences because they do not see the world as the theater of God's wonders. They see it as a vast machine running on mindless natural laws, except where our heart's rebelliousness and self-exaltation find a suitable opportunity to find fault with God and justify our blindness to a billion acts of kindness toward his defiant creation. One of my aims in writing this book is to help us see the world another way.

Providence over Plants

God not only governs inanimate elements of nature, such as earth, water, and wind (not to mention fire[4]), but he also commands plants, and they obey him. "Now the Lord God *appointed a plant* and made it come up over Jonah, that it might be a shade over his head" (Jonah 4:6). But more important than such an extraordinary intervention in Jonah's case is the daily work of God in sustaining millions of people by making food for man and the animals:

You cause the grass to grow for the livestock
    and plants for man to cultivate,

---

4   See Gen. 19:24; 1 Kings 18:38; 2 Kings 1:10; Ps. 97:3; Jer. 49:27; Lam. 4:11; Ezek. 22:31; Dan. 3:17; Amos 1:14; Luke 3:16–17.

> that he may bring forth food from the earth
> > and wine to gladden the heart of man,
> oil to make his face shine
> > and bread to strengthen man's heart. (Ps. 104:14–15)

The grain of the field obeys the Lord's summons, whether to perish in famine or to prosper as famine is restrained:

> He summoned a famine on the land
> > and broke all supply of bread. (Ps. 105:16; cf. 2 Kings 8:1;
> > Ezek. 5:16–17; 14:13)

> I will summon the grain and make it abundant and lay no famine upon you. (Ezek. 36:29; cf. Ruth 1:6)

If We Don't See Providence over Plants, How Can We Savor God's Care?

The Lord Jesus taught us that observing these processes of providence in the earth's plant life is not only for the purpose of marveling, or for aesthetic comparisons to a lover's lips (Song 5:13), but it is also for the purpose of buttressing our faith in the providential care of our heavenly Father:

> Why are you anxious about clothing? *Consider the lilies of the field,* how they grow: they neither toil nor spin, yet I tell you, even Solomon in all his glory was not arrayed like one of these. But if God so clothes the grass of the field, which today is alive and tomorrow is thrown into the oven, will he not much more clothe you, O you of little faith? (Matt. 6:28–30)

This really is astonishing. God intends for us to look at flowers and be encouraged and strengthened to be done with anxiety about having clothing to wear. How can that possibly work? I mean, if we are poor and have scarcely any clothing and no shoes, how can a blooming lily have the power to quiet our hearts from the fear of shame and exposure?

The answer is that it can't—*unless* we are deeply persuaded by a robust, biblically informed doctrine of God's detailed providence over plants, and over our lives. One of the reasons I am writing this book is to help Christians live in the radical, free devotion to seeking the kingdom first (Matt. 6:33), because our doctrine of providence moves us to really believe God's control is detailed and powerful and merciful enough to clothe every lily on the planet and give us all we need to live out his righteousness.

Providence over Animals

Jesus expects us to overcome fear by using the same lily-based logic when we look at the birds. He uses this kind of argument in two different settings in the Gospel of Matthew. First, in the Sermon on the Mount he says:

> Look at the birds of the air: they neither sow nor reap nor gather into barns, and yet your heavenly Father feeds them. Are you not of more value than they? (Matt. 6:26)

Jesus took seriously a pervasive and detailed view of providence when he looked at the world and when he read his Old Testament. He, no doubt, read in Psalm 147:9, "[God] gives to the beasts their food, and to the young ravens that cry." And he knew the answer to God's question when he asked Job, "Who provides for the raven its prey, when its young ones cry to God for help, and wander about for lack of food?" (Job 38:41). Indeed, he knew that his Father holds all of life in his hands: "In his hand is the life of every living thing" (Job 12:10).

Does a robin need a worm to survive? God governs the underground world of worms and commands them to be where he wants them to be for his purposes. For example, when he wanted to rebuke Jonah for sitting in the shade with his ethnocentric anger, "God *appointed a worm* that attacked the plant, so that it withered" (Jonah 4:7). Does a pelican need a fish to survive? God governs the underwater world of fish and commands them to do his bidding, as when Jonah needed saving from the deep: "The LORD *appointed a great fish* to swallow up Jonah" (Jonah 1:17). And when the disciples needed awakening, Jesus saw to it that the fish came along at the appointed time and filled their nets (Luke 5:5–6; John 21:5–6). And if necessary, one of these fish will have a shekel in its mouth (Matt. 17:27), not to mention that when the fish are all dead, Jesus can see to it that two of them (with five loaves) can feed five thousand (Matt. 14:17–21).

So Jesus takes his all-embracing view of providence and reasons this way in Matthew 6:26:

Premise 1: God feeds the birds of the air.
Premise 2: You are more valuable to him than birds are.
Conclusion: He will give you everything you need to accomplish all his purposes, which is the foundation of the command, "Seek first the kingdom of God and his righteousness" (Matt. 6:33).

Jesus does not intend to do this reasoning for us all the time. He is setting an example. He is telling us to apply the doctrine of providence as we look at the natural world: "Look at the birds of the air" (Matt. 6:26). "Consider the ravens" (Luke 12:24). "Consider the lilies" (Luke 12:27).

Jesus Believed the Picture of Providence in His Bible
Jesus's remarkable confidence in his Father's all-encompassing, detailed providence was, of course, shaped by the fact that he shared in it as the Son of God. "All things have been handed over to me by my Father" (Matt. 11:27). But it was also shaped by how seriously he took his Bible—what we know as the Old Testament. "Scripture cannot be broken" (John 10:35), not even the smallest detail. "Not an iota, not a dot, will pass from the Law until all is accomplished" (Matt. 5:18).

Therefore, Jesus took to heart the astonishing providence of God over animals as he read the story of the exodus. The animals were central to the story. The Lord said that they did his bidding, "that you may know that I am the LORD in the midst of the earth" (Ex. 8:22). When God said, "I will stretch out my hand and strike Egypt with all the wonders that I will do in it" (Ex. 3:20), most of what he was about to do was to command animals to perform his judgments. He began with a snake that came from a rod, and he turned back into a rod, to set the stage for the wonders they were about to see (Ex. 4:3–4). Then he summoned frogs (Ex. 8:1–15) and gnats (Ex. 8:16–19) and flies (Ex. 8:20–32) and locusts (Exodus 10:4) to devastate rebellious Egypt.

As Jesus read on in his Bible, he saw that God commanded quail to come and feed his people after their escape from Egypt (Ex. 16:11–13) to prove to them that, even in their rebellion, God could indeed "spread a table in the wilderness" (Ps. 78:19). Jesus read how God commanded ravens to feed his depressed prophet Elijah (1 Kings 17:4). He read how God promised that, for an obedient people, he would "remove harmful beasts from the land" (Lev. 26:6; cf. Ezek. 14:15). He read how God delivered the shepherd boy David "from the paw of the lion and from the paw of the bear" (1 Sam. 17:37), and how he shut the mouth of ravenous lions so that Daniel could spend the night with them unhurt (Dan. 6:22).

Attending to the Least Significant Natural Events

It is not surprising that Jesus would have a keen eye for God's providence through the animals he himself created. He wants us to share this keen eye and this view of providence. He gives us one other illustration. He says we should consider the birds, not just when they flourish, but also when they fall. Ponder the robin when she gets her worm. And ponder the sparrow when she drops dead from old age. Ponder how utterly insignificant that death is. Ponder how many millions of such dying birds there are globally every year. Ponder God's providence in relation to each of these millions of utterly insignificant bird deaths. Then draw your conclusions and be fearless for Christ in the face of those who can kill only the body!

> Do not fear those who kill the body but cannot kill the soul. Rather fear him who can destroy both soul and body in hell. Are not two sparrows sold for a penny? And *not one of them will fall to the ground apart from your Father.* But even the hairs of your head are all numbered. Fear not, therefore; you are of more value than many sparrows. (Matt. 10:28–31)

We Attend and Believe; He Decides and Directs

This reasoning is useless if it has to do only with God's *awareness* of birds and disciples rather than with his control—as if Jesus were only saying, "Not one of them will fall to the ground apart from *your Father's awareness.*" It is not encouraging to hear the news "God watches all birds die, so he will watch you die." No. That is not the point. The point is that "apart from your Father" (ἄνευ τοῦ πατρὸς ὑμῶν)—that is, "without the knowledge *and consent*"[5] of your Father, no bird falls. God's all-governing *will* is the point, not just his all-knowing *awareness.* God's knowledge is of little help to the fearing Christians, if God does not also *govern* both dying birds and endangered disciples. So Jesus reasons from providence over bird deaths to the power of fearless faith. And he expects us to do the same—to strengthen our faith by looking at God's detailed, all-embracing providence as we look at the world. So we reason this way:

> Premise 1: God governs the least significant events in the world, such as bird deaths.
>
> Premise 2: You disciples are far more precious to him than birds.

---

5 William Arndt et al., *A Greek-English Lexicon of the New Testament and Other Early Christian Literature* (Chicago: University of Chicago Press, 2000), 78; emphasis added.

Premise 3: Your Father attends to you with meticulous care, counting your hairs.

Conclusion: Be fearless in my glorious cause in this world.

It Is Good to Scratch the Surface

We have barely scratched the surface of God's providence over the natural world. We have not considered God's sovereign rule over chariot wheels (Ex. 14:24–25), manna from the sky (Ex. 16:4), the sun standing still (Josh. 10:12–13), the voice of thunder (1 Sam. 7:10; Ps. 29), the inexhaustible oil and flour (1 Kings 17:14–16), the opening of prison doors (Acts 5:19) and iron gates (Acts 12:10), or the falling off of prison chains (Acts 12:7).

Nor have we inquired into the depth and vastness of the implications that Christ is not only the creator of all things but also the one who holds everything in existence. "He is before all things, and in him *all things hold together*" (Col. 1:17). "He upholds the universe by the word of his power" (Heb. 1:3; cf. Acts 17:28). If you thought we were advocating too much directness for God's governance when we said, "He makes grass grow" (Ps. 147:8), what do you think of the claim that every electron in every molecule in every cell of every blade of grass everywhere in the world not only is governed by God for growth but *exists* because of God every second? This is a control that is as close as it gets. The directness of God's engagement cannot be closer than existence-sustaining, growth-causing engagement.

To the Praise of the Glory of God's Grace

We circle back now to the question, What is God's purpose in the way he governs the natural world? We saw in chapter 16 that his ultimate purpose in the natural world is the same as his purpose in all his other works of providence, including the redeeming work of Jesus Christ—the communication of the glory of God for the enjoyment of his people:

The heavens declare the glory of God,
and the sky above proclaims his handiwork. (Ps. 19:1)

God's aim is that in all that he has made his "eternal power and divine nature" might be glorified from thankful hearts (Rom. 1:20–21). His aim is that we might turn *to him* from the wonders of his world and say:

May the glory of the LORD endure forever. . . .
I will sing to the LORD as long as I live;
I will sing praise to my God while I have being. . . .
I rejoice in the LORD. (Ps. 104:31, 33–34)

The ultimate purpose of God's providence over the natural world is that the glory of God, which we see and hear and taste and feel and smell in it, might be joyfully, thankfully, admiringly experienced as part of the inheritance purchased for us by the blood of Jesus. The horrors of natural calamities and the pleasures of natural wonders are part of a perfectly wise, just, and loving providence that leads to Jesus Christ, whose death and resurrection secure a future where the glorified natural world will be all mercy without pain, to the praise of the glory of God's grace.

How Does God Bring Job to Silent Blessedness?

Until that day, one central purpose of the natural world is to confront fallen man (all of us) with so many God-governed mysteries that our mouths are shut and we cease to find fault with God.

This was the point of Job 38–41, where God finally speaks to Job, who had put God in the wrong (Job 40:8). And what does God do in these chapters in response to Job's indictments, and the failures of Eliphaz, Bildad, and Zophar to answer him with truth? He takes him into the mysteries of the natural world.

"Where were you when I laid the foundation of the earth?" (Job 38:4). "Who shut in the sea with doors?" (Job 38:8). "Have you commanded the morning since your days began, and caused the dawn to know its place?" (Job 38:12). "Have the gates of death been revealed to you?" (Job 38:17). "Where is the way to the dwelling of light, and where is the place of darkness?" (Job 38:19). "Have you entered the storehouses of the snow?" (Job 38:22). "Can you bind the chains of the Pleiades or loose the cords of Orion?" (Job 38:31). "Can you send forth lightnings, that they may go and say to you, 'Here we are'?" (Job 38:35). "Can you . . . satisfy the appetite of the young lions?" (Job 38:39). "Who has let the wild donkey go free?" (Job 39:5). "Do you give the horse his might? Do you clothe his neck with a mane?" (Job 39:19). "Is it by your understanding that the hawk soars?" (Job 39:26).

Whether we focus on the earth, the sea, the dawn, the snow, the constellations, the prey of lions, the birth of mountain goats, the freedom of the wild donkey, the insubordination of the wild ox, the stupidity of the ostrich, the might of the war horse, or the flight of the hawk and the eagle, the upshot is that Job is ignorant and impotent. He did not make them. He does not know where they came from. He cannot see what they are doing. He does not know how to make them work. He does not know how to control them.

He is utterly surrounded, above and below, by mysteries. And so are we. Science has not changed this. The scientific advancements of the last two hundred years are like sand pails of saltwater hauled up from the ocean of God's wisdom and dumped in a hole on the beach while the tide is rising. God is not impressed. And we should be more overwhelmed with our ignorance, and amazed at countless God-governed wonders and mysteries, than we are impressed with science.

Job, You Are in No Place to Judge My Competence

The point of God's interrogation was not to punish Job or push him away. The point was just what, in fact, happened. Job answered the Lord:

> Behold, I am of small account; what shall I answer you?
> I lay my hand on my mouth.
> I have spoken once, and I will not answer;
> twice, but I will proceed no further. (Job 40:4–5)

Job got the message: Job, there are ten million things about running the world of which you don't know the first thing, but which I know perfectly. You are a finite, sinful creature who has no wisdom to run this world and is utterly ignorant of 99.99 percent of its processes. And that is an understatement. So it is presumptuous to assume you can counsel me about how to run a more just world. You can't begin to know all that has to be taken into account in making decisions about how to run a wise and just and merciful world for my glory and for the joy of my people!

Job's final words concede the absoluteness of God's purposeful, wise, all-embracing providence:

> I know that you can do all things,
> and that no purpose of yours can be thwarted. . . .
> therefore I despise myself,
> and repent in dust and ashes. (Job 42:2, 6)

This is a fitting response for any of us who has put God in the dock and accused him of wrong. But Job's self-despising did not lead to a life of misery. In the New Testament, James draws out the lesson of God's mercy and Job's final happiness:

> Behold, we consider those *blessed* [happy] who remained steadfast. You have heard of the steadfastness of Job, and you have seen the purpose of the Lord, how the Lord is compassionate and merciful. (James 5:11)

God has been "compassionate and merciful" in all his designs for his servant Job. At last, Job comes to see this and finds the "blessedness"

God finally intends for his people. There is an irony in the way God brought Job to this final awakening. In Job 38–41 God turned to the world of nature—the very world that had devastated Job's family and health. Wind had killed his children (Job 1:19), and "loathsome sores" had almost driven Job mad (Job 2:7). But God used that same natural world to silence Job's blaming mouth and to open his eyes to the countless God-governed wonders which brought him to repentance (Job 42:6) and blessedness (Job 42:10; James 5:11). The point is that God's providence in nature should have the same effect on us.

How Does Satan Fit In?

The story of Job raises a question for us, as we close this chapter: What about Satan? It certainly appears that he has some kind of control over the natural world. "Satan went out from the presence of the LORD and struck Job with loathsome sores from the sole of his foot to the crown of his head" (Job 2:7). If Satan can control the physical processes that cause "loathsome sores" and the pain they bring, then where is God's providence in relation to that? That is the question we turn to in chapter 18. If, as we have seen, God's providence over the natural world is pervasive and complete, how does the will of Satan and the demonic world fit into this picture?

SECTION 3

Providence over Satan and Demons

18

Satan and Demons

There are other wills in the universe besides God's. Satan and his angels (Matt. 25:41; Rev. 12:9) have wills. Humans have wills. Animals, in one sense, have wills, in that they "decide" to come or go or to do this or that. But I don't include animals in the willing agents that I have in mind. Even though they "choose" a path of action, they do not contemplate with reason and moral concerns and spiritual perception the wise or virtuous path of action.

This is what David was getting at in Psalm 32:9 when he said, "Be not like a horse or a mule, *without understanding*, which must be curbed with bit and bridle, or it will not stay near you." In other words, the "understanding"—the powers of moral reasoning and spiritual perception—is not granted to animals. Their "choices" are dictated by impulses and instincts. Their choosing faculty is not created in the "image of God" (Gen. 1:27), with Godlike capacities for reasoning and moral contemplation and spiritual perception. David's point is that the more we forsake true reason, and the more we are unconcerned with moral considerations and blind to spiritual reality, the less human-like and the more animal-like we are.

In pondering the extent and nature of God's providence, we must consider the way demonic and human wills relate to the will of God.

The book of Job, as we saw in the previous chapter, perhaps more directly than any other book of Scripture, poses for us the question about how God's will and Satan's will relate to each other. In this chapter, we will address that question, in view of the whole of Scripture. What is the biblical picture, as a whole, of God's providence over Satan's will and actions?

Satan's Strategies for Modern and Nonmodern Cultures
Most people who live where modern science has shaped everyday life have little awareness of Satan and the demonic forces of the world. Other cultures live with profound and daily awareness of demonic reality. Secular people will attribute this difference largely to the fact that demons are not real and to the belief that more primitive peoples are still in the illusion of prescientific explanations of reality. A more biblical explanation for this modern obliviousness to demonic reality is that Satan is by nature a deceiver, and he uses different deceptions to get modern and nonmodern cultures to fall in with his designs.

In Revelation 12:9 the "ancient serpent," who tricked Adam and Eve in the garden of Eden, "is called the devil and Satan, *the deceiver of the whole world.*" At one level, he is as stupid and senseless as is imaginable, in that he continues on in his headlong, suicidal opposition to omnipotence. But at another level, he is shrewd beyond all human powers to resist. In nonmodern cultures, his shrewdness plays on people's true awareness of his reality and controls them with fear. In modern cultures, he holds people in his sway incognito, happy with their disbelief in his reality, as he leads them by the illusion that their deification of self is an experience of autonomy and freedom, when, in fact, they are in perfect sync with his desires.

Both Strategies Already in the New Testament
We can see both these strategies in the New Testament. On the one hand, Satan openly assaults people in supernatural ways that cause

terror. For example, there was the man who was filled with demons who identified themselves as "Legion" (Luke 8:30). The man was so fearsome in his behavior that people tried to keep him in chains (Luke 8:29). And there was the boy who from birth would often foam at the mouth and cast himself into the fire and into the water (Mark 9:22). On the other hand, Jesus described the ordinary sinful religious behavior of the Pharisees as slavery to the devil:

> You are of your father the devil, and your will is to do your father's desires. He was a murderer from the beginning, and does not stand in the truth, because there is no truth in him. When he lies, he speaks out of his own character, for he is a liar and the father of lies. (John 8:44)

Similarly, the apostle Paul pointed out that not just religious hypocrites but more secular libertines were also in lockstep with Satan as they thought they were living their free and autonomous lives:

> You were dead in the trespasses and sins in which you once walked, following the course of this world, *following the prince of the power of the air*, the spirit that is now at work in the sons of disobedience— among whom we all once lived in the passions of our flesh, *carrying out the desires of the body and the mind*, and were by nature children of wrath, like the rest of mankind. (Eph. 2:1–3)

This passage could scarcely be more relevant to the modern, scientific, post-Christian world, where people don't believe in Satan but serve him all day. Paul says that they were "carrying out the desires of the body and the mind." What could be more free, more autonomous, more modern and scientific? But, in fact, unbeknownst to them, they were "following the prince of the power of the air" who was at work in them.

Corresponding Strategies for Deliverance

Corresponding to these two strategies of Satan (frontal supernatural attack and incognito control through "deceitful desires," Eph. 4:22;

cf. 2 Thess. 2:10) are two strategies for deliverance that we see in the New Testament. One we might call "exorcism" or "power encounter," which involves confronting Satan's demonic presence directly and driving the demonic forces out by faith in Christ's blood and in the power of his word (Rev. 12:11). For example, when the young woman with a "spirit of divination" was interfering with Paul's gospel ministry, he said to the spirit, "'I command you in the name of Jesus Christ to come out of her.' And it came out that very hour" (Acts 16:18).

A second strategy of deliverance in the New Testament is less dramatic but more pervasive in the normal ministry of the church (I say normal, meaning typical and everyday, but not less supernatural):

> The Lord's servant must not be quarrelsome but kind to everyone, able to teach, patiently enduring evil, correcting his opponents with gentleness. God may perhaps grant them repentance leading to a knowledge of the truth, and *they may come to their senses and escape from the snare of the devil*, after being captured by him to do his will. (2 Tim. 2:24–26)

These people who repent and "escape from the snare of the devil" are no less endangered ultimately than those who foam at the mouth or see apparitions or hear voices or go into convulsions. But in this case, the path to deliverance is by means of the gloriously powerful, ordinary, everyday ministry of teaching God's word in the power of God's fruit-bearing Spirit.

Turning from the Power of Satan to God

I have seen firsthand and been a part of both of these kinds of deliverances. Sooner or later, you may be also. I believe that all Christians, in some measure, and especially vocational ministers of the word, may take Paul's commission as their own:

> I am sending you to open their eyes, so that they may turn from darkness to light and *from the power of Satan to God*, that they may

receive forgiveness of sins and a place among those who are sanctified by faith in me. (Acts 26:17–18)

Setting people free from the "power of Satan" is our calling—
whether secular people, who don't even believe there is such a power,
or animistic people, who build their lives around appeasing evil spirits.
And God's "divine power has granted to us all things that pertain to
life and godliness" in helping people escape "from the [demonic] corruption that is in the world because of sinful desire" (2 Pet. 1:3–4).

Whether we are involved in power encounters where demons are
cast out dramatically, or in the more typical, but just as supernatural, work of deliverance by Spirit-empowered preaching and teaching
and counseling, the summons for faith is the same. Both strategies of
deliverance call for humble, courageous use of God's full armor (Eph.
6:10–18), especially faith in God's promises and in the power of his
Spirit to do what we are utterly helpless to do. Both call us to a life of
earnest prayer (Mark 9:29), purity of heart and life (Matt. 5:8), and
closeness to Jesus (John 14:21–23).

Our Fundamental Confidence

Both strategies of deliverance call also for a deep, unshakable confidence that Satan is not in control of this world. We are called in
Scripture to have confidence that Satan will never have the final say.
God wants his children to be confident that God's will is final and
decisive, when his will and Satan's will clash, which they always do,
since, even when they will the same act, they differ radically in how
it should be done and to what end. Divine providence is never frustrated by Satan in its plan for this world—for the everlasting good
of God's people in the all-satisfying praise of the glory of his grace.
That is what this chapter aims to show. Then in chapter 19 we will
show how the ongoing existence of Satan actually serves the ultimate
purpose of providence.

Ten Powers of Satan That Are Not Final or Decisive

My approach here is not to minimize the power and pervasive activity of Satan. Just the opposite. My strategy is to take seriously Satan's power in ten different spheres and show how this power is not final and not decisive.[1] In other words, while God has his reasons for why he permits Satan to exist and to pursue his evil path (which we will see in chapter 19), he never has given, and never will give, to Satan any freedom that God himself does not restrain and decisively direct for his wise, just, and good purposes.

In these ten exposures of Satan's ultimate powerlessness under God's providence, I realize that I will be touching on many aspects of God's providence that are yet to be treated with more detail in the remainder of this book. So wherever it seems to you that I may have passed over a dimension of God's control too quickly, I hope you will await the later treatment of that dimension to see whether things become more clear and compelling.

1. Providence over Satan's Delegated World Rule

Satan is sometimes called in the Bible "the ruler of this world" (John 12:31; 14:30; 16:11), or "the god of this world" (2 Cor. 4:4), or "the prince of the power of the air" (Eph. 2:2), or a "cosmic [power] over this present darkness" (Eph. 6:12). This means that we should take him seriously when we're told in Luke 4:5–7:

> The devil took [Jesus] up and showed him all the kingdoms of the world in a moment of time, and said to him, "To you I will give all this authority and their glory, for it has been delivered to me,

---

[1]   The substance of these ten aspects of God's providence over Satan's power were part of a message I gave at the 2005 Desiring God National Conference in Minneapolis. This message then was made part of the collection of messages from that conference. John Piper, "Suffering and the Sovereignty of God: Ten Aspects of God's Sovereignty over Suffering and Satan's Hand in It," in *Suffering and the Sovereignty of God*, ed. John Piper and Justin Taylor (Wheaton, IL, Crossway, 2006), 17–30.

and I give it to whom I will. If you, then, will worship me, it will all be yours."

Of course, that is strictly true: if the sovereign of the universe bows in worshipful submission to *anyone*, he elevates that one as the sovereign of the universe. But Satan's claim that he can give the authority and glory of world kingdoms to whomever he wills is actually only a half-truth. No doubt he does play havoc in the world by maneuvering a Stalin or a Hitler or an Idi Amin or a Bloody Mary or a Genghis Khan or a Saddam Hussein into murderous power. But he does this only at God's permission and within God's appointed limits.

This is made clear over and over again in the Bible. For example, Daniel 2:21: "[God] removes kings and sets up kings," which means he could today remove any tyrant anywhere, any time he chooses. And he could have done so at any time in history. And Daniel 4:17: "The Most High rules the kingdom of men and gives it to whom he will." And Romans 13:1: "There is no authority except from God, and those that exist have been instituted by God." And when the kings are in their God-appointed place, with or without Satan's agency, they are in the sway of God's sovereign will, as Proverbs 21:1 says: "The king's heart is a stream of water in the hand of the LORD; he turns it wherever he will."

Evil nations rise and set themselves against the Almighty: "The kings of the earth set themselves, and the rulers take counsel together, against the LORD and against his anointed, saying, 'Let us burst their bonds apart and cast away their cords from us.' He who sits in the heavens laughs; the Lord holds them in derision" (Ps. 2:2–4). Do they think that their rebellion against God can thwart the counsel of the Lord? Psalm 33:10–11 answers, "The LORD brings the counsel of the nations to nothing; he frustrates the plans of the peoples. The counsel of the LORD stands forever, the plans of his heart to all generations." So when they rage against him, he laughs. That is not his only response. But it is the one that makes this clear: you are not in charge!

Therefore, the satanic power behind the nations, which God grants in some measure, is governed by God. Satan and his rulers do not move without his permission, and they do not move outside God's decisive providence.

2. Providence over Demons and Evil Spirits

Satan has thousands of cohorts in supernatural evil. They are called "demons" (James 2:19) or "evil spirits" (Luke 7:21) or "unclean spirits" (Matt. 10:1) or "the devil and his angels" (Matt. 25:41). We get a tiny glimpse into demonic warfare in Daniel 10, where the angel who is sent in response to Daniel's prayer says, "The prince of the kingdom of Persia withstood me twenty-one days, but Michael, one of the chief princes, came to help me" (Dan. 10:13). So apparently the demon, or evil spirit, over Persia fought against the angel who was sent to help Daniel, and a greater angel, Michael, came to his aid. But the Bible leaves us with no doubt as to who is in charge in all these skirmishes. Martin Luther got it right:

> And though this world with devils filled should threaten to
> undo us,
> We will not fear, for God hath willed His truth to triumph
> through us.
> The prince of darkness grim, we tremble not for him;
> His rage we can endure, for lo, his doom is sure.
> One little word shall fell him.[2]

We see glimpses of those "little words" at work, for example, when Jesus comes up against thousands of demons in Matthew 8:29–32. They were oppressing a man and making him insane. The demons cry out, "What have you to do with us, O Son of God? Have you come here to torment us before the time?" They realize that a time is set for

---

2   Martin Luther, "A Mighty Fortress Is Our God," 1529.

their final destruction. What they did not know was that that final destruction has, in one sense, arrived in history. It is present decisively in Jesus.

Jesus spoke to them *one little word*: "Go." And they came out of the man. There is no question who is sovereign in this battle. Readers of the New Testament have seen this before in Mark 1:27, where the people were amazed and said, "He commands even the unclean spirits, and they obey him." They *obey* him. Yes, they do—no exceptions. As for Satan: "We tremble not for him; his rage we can endure." But as for Christ: even though they slay him, even *that* is by plan (Acts 4:27–28). Though demons *disobey* God's written commandments in Scripture, they do not disobey when he addresses them directly with the decisive command of his power. "He commands the unclean spirits, and they obey him" (Mark 1:27). God's providence holds sway over Satan's angels. This is as true today as it was when Jesus walked the earth.

3. Providence over Satan's Hand in Persecution

The apostle Peter describes the suffering of Christians this way: "Your adversary the devil prowls around like a roaring lion, seeking someone to devour. Resist him, firm in your faith, knowing that the same kinds of suffering are being experienced by your brotherhood throughout the world" (1 Pet. 5:8–9). So the sufferings of persecution are like the jaws of a satanic lion trying to consume and destroy the faith of believers in Christ.

But do these Christians suffer in Satan's jaws of persecution apart from God's governing providence? When Satan crushes Christians in the jaws of their own private Calvary, does God not govern those jaws for the good of his precious child? Listen to Peter's answer in 1 Peter 3:17: "It is better to suffer for doing good, *if that should be God's will*, than for doing evil." Or again: "Let those who suffer *according to God's will* entrust their souls to a faithful Creator while doing good" (1 Pet. 4:19). In other words, *if God wills* that we suffer for doing good, we will suffer. And if he does not will that we suffer for doing good, we will not. The lion does not have the last say. Providence does.

The night Jesus was arrested, satanic power was in full force for persecution (Luke 22:3; 22:31). And Jesus spoke into that situation one of his most sovereign words. He said to those who came to arrest him in the dark: "Have you come out as against a robber, with swords and clubs? When I was with you day after day in the temple, you did not lay hands on me. But *this is your hour, and the power of darkness*" (Luke 22:52–53). In other words, "The jaws of the lion close on me tonight no sooner and no later than my Father planned. 'No one takes [my life] from me, but I lay it down of my own accord' (John 10:18). Boast not over the hand that made you, Satan. You have *one hour*. This is your hour. What you do, do quickly." God decides when the hour begins and when it ends. Until the God-appointed hour came, "no one laid a hand on him, because his hour had not yet come" (John 7:30; cf. 8:20). God's providence governs Satan's hand in persecution.

4. Providence over Satan's Life-Taking Power

The Bible does not take lightly or minimize the power of Satan to kill people, including Christians. Jesus said in John 8:44, "You are of your father the devil, and your will is to do your father's desires. He was a murderer from the beginning." Jesus tells us, in fact, that Satan does indeed take the lives of faithful Christians. "Do not fear what you are about to suffer. Behold, the devil is about to throw some of you into prison, that you may be tested, and for ten days you will have tribulation. *Be faithful unto death*, and I will give you the crown of life" (Rev. 2:10).

Is God not the Lord of life and death? He is. No one lives and no one dies but by God's sovereign decree. "See now that I, even I, am he, and there is no god beside me; I kill and I make alive; I wound and I heal; and there is none that can deliver out of my hand" (Deut. 32:39). There is no god, no demon, no Satan that can snatch to death any person that God has decided will live (1 Sam. 2:6). James the brother of Jesus says this in a stunning way in James 4:13–16:

> Come now, you who say, "Today or tomorrow we will go into such and such a town and spend a year there and trade and make a profit"—yet you do not know what tomorrow will bring. What is your life? For you are a mist that appears for a little time and then vanishes. Instead you ought to say, "*If the Lord wills, we will live and do this or that.*" As it is, you boast in your arrogance. All such boasting is evil.

If the Lord wills, we will live. And if he doesn't, we will die. God, not Satan, makes the final call. When Job lost his ten children, he said, "The LORD gave, and the LORD has taken away; blessed be the name of the LORD" (Job 1:21; see more on this text in the next section). Our lives are in God's hands ultimately, not Satan's. God's providence rules over Satan's life-taking power.

5. Providence over Satan's Hand in Natural Disasters

Hurricanes, tsunamis, tornadoes, earthquakes, blistering heat, deadly cold, drought, flood, famine—we can easily imagine that these deadly forces are in the hands of "the god of this world" (2 Cor. 4:4), who is a "murderer from the beginning" (John 8:44). In fact, when Satan approached God in the first chapter of Job, he challenged God, "Stretch out your hand and touch all that he has, and he will curse you to your face" (Job 1:11). And then the LORD said to Satan, "Behold, all that he has *is in your hand.* Only against him do not stretch out your hand" (Job 1:12).

The result was two human atrocities and two natural disasters. The atrocities were that "the Sabeans . . . struck down [Job's] servants with the edge of the sword" (Job 1:15), and that "the Chaldeans . . . struck down [another group of] servants with the edge of the sword" (Job 1:17). The first of the two natural disasters is reported to Job in verse 16: "The fire of God [probably lightning] fell from heaven and burned up the sheep and the servants and consumed them." Then came the report of the second natural disaster—the worst report of all—in verses 18–19: "Your sons and daughters were eating and drinking wine in their oldest brother's house, and behold, a great wind came across the wilderness and struck the four corners of the house, and it fell upon the young people, and they are dead."

Even though God had loosened the leash of Satan to do this (". . . all that he has is in your hand"), when Job responded, he did not focus on Satan as the one God loosed or permitted to destroy. He traced the cause back to God himself. "Job arose and tore his robe and shaved his head and fell on the ground and worshiped. And he said, 'Naked I came from my mother's womb, and naked shall I return. *The Lord gave, and the Lord has taken away*; blessed be the name of the Lord'" (Job 1:20–21). Lest we think Job erred in this worship, the inspired writer added: "In all this Job did not sin or charge God with wrong" (Job 1:22).

Job had discovered with many of us that it is small comfort to focus on the freedom of Satan to destroy. In the academic classroom and in an apologetics discussion, the agency of Satan in our suffering may lift a little of the burden of God's providence for some, but for others, like Job, there is more security and more relief and more hope and more support and more glorious truth in despising Satan's hateful hand and looking straight through him to God for the cause of our trouble and for his mercy (see below on James 5:11).

We saw in the previous chapter how Elihu helped Job see providential mercy in seemingly random events. In Job 37:11–14 he said:

He loads the thick cloud with moisture;
    the clouds scatter his lightning.
They turn around and around *by his guidance*,
    to accomplish all that he commands them

on the face of the habitable world.

Whether for *correction* or for his *land*,

or for *love*, he causes it to happen.

Hear this, O Job;

stop and consider the wondrous works of God.

Job's first impulses in Job 1:21 were exactly right: "The LORD gave, and the LORD has taken away; blessed be the name of the LORD." When James wrote in the New Testament about the purpose of the book of Job, this is what he said: "You have heard of the steadfastness of Job, and you have seen the purpose of the Lord, how the Lord is compassionate and merciful" (James 5:11). God, not Satan, is the final ruler of wind. What are "stormy winds" doing when they rampage? They are, the psalmist says, "fulfilling [God's] word!" (Ps. 148:8).[3]

Satan is real and terrible. All his designs are hateful. But he is not sovereign. Whatever he does, God governs in his all-wise providence. It is right to sing with Isaac Watts:

There's not a plant or flower below,

But makes Thy glories known;

And clouds arise, and tempests blow,

By order from Thy throne.[4]

If you find little comfort in the biblical truth that God is the final and decisive governor of the winds that destroy property and take life, be sure that you ponder whether more comfort comes from any alternative ideas. Is it more comforting to think that the powers of life and death are ultimately in the hands of one who hates us rather than loves us? Is it more comforting to think that there is no guide and ruler at all, neither for mercy nor misery, but that the events of nature are random—meaningless, without design or purpose—and not even

3   See the treatment of God's providence over the wind in chap. 17.
4   Isaac Watts, "I Sing the Mighty Power of God," 1715.

God can turn the course of things for the good of his children? Is it more comforting to think that there is simply no revelation about these things, and we are left in ignorance about God's and Satan's relation to our calamities? For many of us, the biblical teaching is a rock of stability and hope—namely, that, in our worse calamities, "the purpose of the Lord" (James 5:11) is wise and good and merciful for all who trust him.

6. Providence over Satan's Sickness-Causing Power

The Bible is vivid with the truth that Satan can cause disease. Acts 10:38 says that Jesus "went about doing good and healing all who were *oppressed by the devil*, for God was with him." The devil had oppressed people with sickness. In Luke 13 Jesus finds a woman who had been bent over, unable to stand up for eighteen years. He heals her on the Sabbath, and in response to the criticism of the synagogue ruler he says, "Ought not this woman, a daughter of Abraham *whom Satan bound for eighteen years*, be loosed from this bond on the Sabbath day?" (Luke 13:16). There is no doubt that Satan causes much disease.

This is why Christ's healings are a sign of the in-breaking of the kingdom of God and its final victory over all disease and all the works of Satan. It is right and good to pray for healing. God has purchased it in the death of his Son, with all the other blessings of grace, for all his children (Isa. 53:5; Rom. 8:32). But he has not promised that we get the whole inheritance in this life. And *he* decides how much, and when.

THE PARADOX OF ANSWERED, UNANSWERED PRAYER

Jesus tells us to pray. And we are to trust that he really hears, and that his answer is good for us, even if not exactly what we ask for or when we ask for it. If you ask your Father for bread, he will not give you a stone. If you ask him for a fish, he will not give you a serpent (Matt. 7:9–10). But the answer may not be bread. And it may not be a fish. Yet it will be good for you. That is what he promises (Rom. 8:28). This may sound paradoxical. Not bread, when you asked for bread?

Not fish, when you asked for fish? But good? I wrote a poem about this paradox that for some of you may shed light on this perplexity:

The Stone and the Snake

> My Father bade me come, and said,
>> "Ask me for what you need. And spread
> Before me all your heart. Seek me
>> For ev'ry true desire, and see
> If I will ever fail to love
>> You perfectly with treasures of
> My boundless store, my heart. And keep
>> On knocking. Though I do not sleep,
> I have my reasons for delay,
>> And I delight to hear you pray.
>
> If you should need an anchor for your boat,
> But, lured by hunger, ask for bread,
>> I'll mark your need, and lest you seaward float,
>> Give you a heavy stone instead.
>
> Or if you need to drain a viper's fang,
>> A healing antidote to make,
> But ask for useless fish to ease the pang,
>> I will discern, and give the snake.
>
> O precious child, think not, because
>> I meet your needs with love by laws
> Beyond your grasp: It is in vain
>> For you to pray, as if the gain
> Of snake and stone were no reply
>> To your desire. Dear Child, your cry
> *Does* open treasuries, and shake
>> The heavens. I bid you come and take

These keys, and all my store unlock,
My heart: to ask, and seek, and knock."

IN HIS DISEASE, JOB WOULD NOT CONCEDE
THE SOVEREIGNTY OF SATAN

Beware lest anyone say that Satan is sovereign in our diseases. He is not. When Satan went to God a second time in the book of Job, God gave him permission this time to strike Job's body. Then the author of the book says, "Satan went out from the presence of the LORD and struck Job with loathsome sores from the sole of his foot to the crown of his head" (Job 2:7). When Job's wife despaired and said, "Curse God and die" (Job 2:9), Job responded exactly as he did before. He looked past the finite cause of Satan to the ultimate cause of God and said, "Shall we receive good from God, and shall we not receive evil?" (Job 2:10).

And lest we attribute error or irreverence to Job, when he traces his "loathsome sores" back to the will of God, the inspired writer does two things. First, the writer says, "In all this Job did not sin with his lips" (Job 2:10). In other words, it was not sin to treat God as the ultimate cause of the loathsome sores with which Satan struck Job. And, second, the writer of Job closes his book in the last chapter by referring back to Job's terrible sufferings this way: "Then came to him all his brothers and sisters . . . and comforted him for *all the evil that the LORD had brought upon him*" (42:11).

Satan is real and full of hate, but he is not sovereign in sickness. God will not give him even that tribute. As he says to Moses at the burning bush, "Who has made man's mouth? Who makes him mute, or deaf, or seeing, or blind? Is it not I, the LORD?" (Ex. 4:11; see also 2 Cor. 12:7–9).

I have been preaching and teaching these things for about fifty years. My files are now laden with letters from people who thank God for the biblical discovery of God's purposeful, wise, merciful, and painful sovereignty in the suffering of disease. I'll give you one example here. It's from a twenty-seven-year-old father whose newfound trust in the pervasive providence of God was put to the test. Writing two years after the event he mentions below, he said:

> My wife and I packed the car to go to our first ultrasound. We would get the news (boy or girl), then grab smoothies and celebrate. . . . But as we sat in our appointment, we watched as the happy chatter of the tech quieted to a focused, silent gaze at the screen. Why was she looking so intently at the images? . . . She got up and left the room, making some excuse about printing something off. . . . Finally the doctor entered. He said he regretted to inform us that the ultrasound was quite conclusive. . . . Our daughter had Spina bifida. There was also the potential of genetic disorders known as trisomy 21 (Down syndrome) and 18 (infant death syndrome). . . .
>
> This is not theory anymore; this was a real-life-I-need-some-answers-now moment.
>
> Did God "allow" this? Worse yet, design it? Certainly He could not be the architect of so much pain.
>
> And then I read of your mother's death. You wrote, "I took no comfort from the prospect that God could not control the flight of a four-by-four. For me there was no consolation in haphazardness," and it hit me . . . neither did I [find comfort in God's inability to control the flight of a four-by-four]. No matter what I had thought I believed in the past . . . the only place where hope was found, in that moment, was in the hands of a sovereign God who is in control and ordains the falling of a sparrow and the electing of kings and the flights of four-by-fours and the spinal development of our precious daughter. It was here that hope was found. And hope, being the seed-bed for joy, began growing in our hearts, a joy that could truly be shaken by no pain.[5]

5 Personal letter dated May 2007.

7. Providence over Satan's Use of Animals and Plants

The imagery of Satan as a "roaring lion" in 1 Peter 5:8 and as a "great dragon" in Revelation 12:9 and as the serpent of old in Genesis 3 makes us aware that in his destructive work, Satan can, and no doubt does, employ animals and plants—from the lion in the Colosseum, to the black fly that causes river blindness, to the birds that carry the avian flu virus, to the pit bull that attacks a child, to the bacteria in your belly that doctors Barry Marshall and Robin Warren discovered causes ulcers (winning for them the Nobel Prize in medicine). If Satan can kill and can cause disease, no doubt he has at his disposal many plants and animals—both large and microscopic—to make his weapons.

But he cannot make them do what God forbids them to do. We saw this in some detail in the previous chapter. So just a summary paragraph here will suffice. From the giant Leviathan that God made to sport in the sea (Ps. 104:26) to the tiny gnats that he summoned over the land of Egypt (Ex. 8:16–17), God commands the world of animals and plants.

The most vivid demonstrations of God's control over animals and plants are in the book of Jonah. "The LORD appointed a great fish to swallow up Jonah" (Jonah 1:17). And the fish did exactly as he had been appointed. "And the LORD spoke to the fish, and it vomited Jonah out upon the dry land" (Jonah 2:10). "Now the LORD God appointed a plant and made it come up over Jonah" (Jonah 4:6). "But when dawn came up the next day, God appointed a worm that attacked the plant, so that it withered" (Jonah 4:7). Fish, plant, worm—all appointed, all obedient. Satan can have a hand here, but it is not a decisive hand. Satan is not sovereign over plants and animals. God's providence holds final sway.

8. Providence over Satan's Temptations to Sin

Satan is called in the Bible "the tempter" (Matt. 4:3; 1 Thess. 3:5). This was the origin on earth of all the misery that we know. Satan tempted

Eve to sin, and sin brought with it the curse of God on the natural order (Gen. 3:14–19; Rom. 5:12–14; 8:20–22). Ever since that time, Satan has been tempting all human beings to do what will dishonor God, hurt themselves, and damage others.

But the most famous temptations in the Bible do not portray Satan as sovereign in his tempting work. Take Satan's temptation of Judas to betray Jesus. Luke 22:3–4 says that "Satan entered into Judas called Iscariot. . . . He went away and conferred with the chief priests and officers how he might betray him to them." But Luke tells us that the betrayal of Jesus by Judas was the fulfillment of Scripture: "The Scripture had to be fulfilled, which the Holy Spirit spoke beforehand by the mouth of David concerning Judas" (Acts 1:16). Therefore, Peter said that Jesus was "delivered up according to the definite plan and foreknowledge *of God*" (Acts 2:23). Satan had his role to play on this deadly and wonderful stage of history, but he was not in charge. He was not the director or the author of this soul-saving drama.

Even more famous than the temptation of Judas is the temptation of Peter. We usually think of Peter's three disavowals as *denials*, not as *temptations*. But Jesus says something to Peter in Luke 22:31–32 that makes plain the tempter is at work here: "Simon, Simon, behold, Satan demanded to have you, that he might sift you like wheat, but I have prayed for you that your faith may not fail. And *when* you have turned again [not *if* you turn, but *when*], strengthen your brothers."

Sifting Peter means putting him through the sieve of fearful danger, with the aim of straining out his faith. It's the same thing we see in 1 Thessalonians 3:5, where Paul says, "I sent to learn about your *faith*, for fear that somehow the tempter had tempted you and our labor would be in vain." That's what the tempter is aiming at: the destruction of faith. God was giving Satan enough leash so that he would help fulfill Jesus's prediction: "Before the rooster crows, you will deny me three times" (Matt. 26:34). But Jesus's prayer for Peter shows who is in charge. In essence he says, "I have prayed for you. You *will* fall, but not utterly. *When* you repent and turn back—not *if* you turn back—strengthen your brothers."

Both Judas's and Peter's temptations by the devil are examples of Satan's deadly reality, but also of his limitations. God uses him to accomplish the purposes of his judgment toward Judas, and his preparation for ministry toward Peter. The providence of God governs even the primary bent of Satan—as a tempter to sin.

9. Providence over Satan's Mind-Blinding Power

Satan's final defeat is to be thrown into the lake of fire, where he will suffer forever. Revelation 20:10 says, "The devil who had deceived them was thrown into the lake of fire and sulfur where the beast and the false prophet were, and they will be tormented day and night forever and ever." Satan's aim is to take as many there with him as he can. To do that he must keep people blind to the gospel of Jesus Christ, because the gospel "is the power of God for salvation to everyone who believes" (Rom. 1:16). No one who is justified by the blood of Christ goes to hell. "Since, therefore, we have now been justified by his blood, much more shall we be saved by him from the wrath of God" (Rom. 5:9). Only those who fail to embrace the wrath-absorbing substitutionary work of Christ will suffer the wrath of God.

Therefore, Paul says in 2 Corinthians 4:4, "in their case the god of this world [Satan] has blinded the minds of the unbelievers, to keep them from seeing the light of the gospel of the glory of Christ, who is the image of God." This blinding is the deadliest weapon in Satan's arsenal. If he succeeds with a person, that person's suffering will be endless.

But at this most critical point, Satan is not sovereign; God is. And, oh, how thankful we should be! Two verses later, in 2 Corinthians 4:6, Paul describes God's blindness-removing power over against Satan's blinding power. "For God, who said, 'Let light shine out of darkness,' has shone in our hearts to give the light of the knowledge of the glory of God in the face of Jesus Christ." The comparison is between God's creating light at the beginning of the world and God's creating light in the darkened human heart. With total sovereignty, God said at the beginning of the world, and at the beginning of our new life in Christ, "Let there be light." And there was light. Satan has the power to blind hearts to the gospel. But that power is limited, because God can overcome it for anyone he chooses (see chapters 35–36).

10. Providence over Satan's Spiritual Bondage

Satan enslaves people in two ways. One is by misery and suffering, making us think there is no good God worth trusting. The other is by pleasure and prosperity, making us think we have all we need so that God is irrelevant. His two great strategies of deceit are pain and pleasure. Pain luring us to say, "God is evil." Pleasure luring us to say, "God is not needed." When he succeeds in either deception, we are in bondage.

To be freed from this bondage, we must repent. We must confess that God is good and trustworthy, not evil and cruel. And we must confess that the pleasures of this world (both the sinful and the innocent) are not worth comparing to the value of knowing Christ (Matt. 10:37; Phil. 3:8). But Satan hates this repentance and does all he can to prevent it. This is how Satan holds a person in bondage.

But when God chooses to overcome our rebellion, bring us to repentance, and save us from Satan's bondage, nothing can stop him. When God overcomes Satan's bondage and our complicity, we repent and Satan's power is broken. That's what we saw in 2 Timothy 2:24–26 at the beginning of this chapter. It is so important that it is worth quoting again:

> The Lord's servant must not be quarrelsome but kind to everyone, able to teach, patiently enduring evil, correcting his opponents with gentleness. God may perhaps *grant them repentance* leading to a

knowledge of the truth, and they may . . . *escape from the snare of the devil*, after being captured by him to do his will.

Notice the key words: "God may perhaps *grant* them repentance." Repentance is a gift. God *grants* it. To be sure, repentance is something *we* do. It is *our* act. But it is a miracle-act—a free gift from God. Satan is not sovereign over his captives. God is. When God grants repentance, we are set free from the snare of the devil. We had been "captured by him to do his will," but we are not in bondage to him anymore.

Satan Subject to Providence

My conclusion from these ten spheres of Satan's power is that, in all his acts, Satan is subject to God's overruling and guiding providence. Since Satan is uniformly evil, we may use the words of Genesis 50:20 for every one of his acts in this world: "He meant it for evil, but God meant it for good." When Satan wills something, he always intends to diminish God's glory and ultimately ruin God's people. When God permits Satan to act with that design, God's design in doing so is for his glory and the ultimate good of his people. We have shown before that all God's wise permissions have good designs.[6] They are *planned* permissions, and all God's plans are good.

But given the amount of evil and pain that Satan causes in the world, we inevitably ask, Why does God permit Satan to go on working, or even existing? Why not destroy him with one word, or throw him into the lake of fire *now*? I do assume God could do that without any injustice to Satan or man. We already saw in point 9 above that God is, in fact, going to throw Satan into the lake of fire at the end of this age (Rev. 20:10). So why not now? That is what we turn to in the next chapter.

---

6   See chap. 13, and chap. 17n2.

19

The Ongoing Existence of Satan

The point of the previous chapter was that none of Satan's powers, great as they are, is final and decisive. God's providence holds final and decisive sway in all of Satan's acts. This then raised the question, If God rules Satan so thoroughly, why does he not use his power and wisdom to put Satan out of existence now? Why not cast him into the lake of fire now, which Revelation 20:10 says he will eventually do? That is the question we try to answer in this chapter. The Bible does not answer this question directly. But there are pointers. So let me venture four answers for you to test. Even though these suggestions are not given in Scripture as explicit answers to our question, nevertheless, I think they do give a partial answer.

Four Indirect Answers from Scripture

I would sum up why God permits Satan to go on living and working by saying that God intends to defeat Satan not with one initial blow of power, but through four processes:

- He is defeating Satan with *showing*.
- He is defeating Satan with *suffering*.

- He is defeating Satan with *Satan.*
- He is defeating Satan with *savoring.*

I. GOD IS DEFEATING SATAN WITH *SHOWING* MORE OF HIS OWN ATTRIBUTES.

Consider the lamentable condition of the woman in Luke 13:10–17, who "was bent over and could not fully straighten herself" for eighteen years (Luke 13:11). Luke tells us more specifically that "*Satan* [had] bound [her] for eighteen years" (Luke 13:16). Jesus is going to heal her completely, which means that God could have healed her at any time during those eighteen painful years. He was powerful and compassionate enough to do it at any time. But instead he permitted Satan to have his ugly way in her body for eighteen years.

The upshot of healing her was that Jesus's "adversaries were put to shame, and all the people rejoiced at all the glorious things that were done by him" (Luke 13:17). We do not know why God permitted this woman to endure Satan's "binding" for eighteen years. But what we do know is this: Jesus defeated Satan in exposing the hypocrisy of his adversaries and in showing his compassion and authority and power so that people rejoiced at his glorious deeds.

It seems to me, then, that this one incident gives a glimpse into God's larger purpose for his timing in defeating Satan. From this story, we may infer that part of God's purpose is to *show* more aspects of Christ's glory by the manifold demonstrations of his superiority over Satan than would be shown if he had put Satan out of existence all at once, at some earlier point in redemptive history. I think this same point could be made in relation to each of the ten ways shown in the previous chapter that God is superior over Satan.

2. GOD IS DEFEATING SATAN WITH *SUFFERING*.

The most central and staggering reality about Satan's eventual defeat is not that he will be thrown into the lake of fire but that Jesus was thrown into the lake of fire, as it were (Luke 12:50), to defeat Satan's hold on his people. Both Paul and the writer to the Hebrews teach that Jesus defeated Satan by means of his suffering and death:

> You, who were dead in your trespasses and the uncircumcision of your flesh, God made alive together with him, having forgiven us all our trespasses, by canceling the record of debt that stood against us with its legal demands. This he set aside, nailing it to the cross. *He disarmed the rulers and authorities and put them to open shame, by triumphing over them in him.* (Col. 2:13–15)

> Since therefore the children share in flesh and blood, he himself likewise partook of the same things, *that through death he might destroy the one who has the power of death,* that is, the devil, and deliver all those who through fear of death were subject to lifelong slavery. (Heb. 2:14–15)

It is more beautiful, more glorious and excellent and wonderful, that the greatest person in the universe should defeat the most despicable being in the universe by choosing to suffer and die in an act of liberating love—love for those who were in fact "following the prince of the power of the air . . . like the rest of mankind" (Eph. 2:2–3). When Jesus throws Satan into the lake of fire, Jesus's justice and power will be on full display. But at the cross, his grace and mercy and patience and love and wisdom were on full display as he conquered Satan's claim on God's people by paying their debts.

Colossians 2:14 makes clear how Satan lost his claim on God's people when Christ died. Christ canceled "the record of debt that stood against us with its legal demands. This he set aside, nailing it to the cross." This is followed by its effect on Satan: "He [in canceling their debts] disarmed the rulers and authorities and put them to open shame, by triumphing over them in him" (Col. 2:15). In other words, the only damning indictments Satan can bring against us at the last day is unforgiven sin. But Christ nailed those to the cross. This stripped from Satan's hand his only damning weapon. He was disarmed. Indeed, he was shamed because, in all his vaunted strength and pride and hate, he lost his prize—God's elect—to an act of omnipotent weakness and humility and love.

We saw in part 2 of this book that the ultimate goal of providence is the joyful praise of the glory of God's grace (Eph. 1:6, 12, 14) and that the consummate demonstration of that glorious grace is the freely chosen suffering and death of the infinitely worthy Son of God for unworthy sinners like us. Now we see some small glimpse of why Satan is given such a role in the theater of God's wonders. At every point, Christ proves superior, and at the most important moment in history, the beauty of Christ shines most brightly as the ugliest being is undone by the greatest act of beauty.

3. GOD IS DEFEATING SATAN WITH *SATAN*.

The wisdom of God appears more fully, and his superiority over Satan in every way, not just in sheer power, shines more brightly in the manifold ways he brings Satan to ruin. One of those ways is to make Satan serve God's sanctifying purposes in the lives of his children. It must infuriate Satan that God's ways are so pure and brilliant that Satan not only fails to obstruct them but unwittingly serves them.

What I have in mind is Paul's "thorn in the flesh," which he tells us about in 2 Corinthians 12:1–10. Paul had been granted a supernatural glimpse into heaven (2 Cor. 12:1–4). God had granted Paul this privilege, knowing it would tempt Paul to be conceited. God deemed the gift worth the troubles to come. His answer to this dangerous temptation of pride was to see to it (providence) that Paul would have a thorn in the flesh. Paul tells us this with a stunning sentence about God's aim to sanctify him, and Satan's unwitting hand in it!

To keep me from becoming conceited because of the surpassing greatness of the revelations, a thorn was given me in the flesh, *a messenger of Satan* to harass me, *to keep me from becoming conceited.*
(2 Cor. 12:7)

At the beginning and the ending of this verse, the purpose of the
thorn is mentioned: "to keep me from becoming conceited . . . to
keep me from becoming conceited." Now that is *not* the design of
Satan. Satan does not *hinder* conceit; he *helps* it. This is *God's* design
for Paul's thorn—humility and trust. Nevertheless, the thorn is called
"a messenger of Satan." In ways that exceed our full comprehension,
God is able to harness Satan's hatred of Paul and make it serve God's
own purposes of Paul's humility and purity and joy.

If this makes Satan look like a fool, it should. But be careful. Every
sin you commit is equally idiotic and self-destructive. Sin and Satan
are, in their essence, irrational. Satan suicidally puts it in the heart of
Judas to betray Jesus, with the result that Satan himself is disarmed
(Luke 22:3; Col. 2:15), and Satan acts in the same self-defeating way
in giving Paul a thorn in the flesh so that Satan's own designs for Paul's
hurt inadvertently humble Paul and make him rely more gladly on the
grace of Jesus.

So the upshot of Satan's attack on Paul is not only the exposure of
his self-defeating folly, but also the revelation of Christ's all-satisfying
grace:

Three times I pleaded with the Lord about this, that it should leave
me. But he said to me, "*My grace is sufficient for you,* for my power
is made perfect in weakness." Therefore I will boast *all the more
gladly* of my weaknesses, so that *the power of Christ may rest upon me.*
(2 Cor. 12:8–9)

I think this gets close to the heart of why God allows Satan to exist
and bring short-term harm on God's people. It becomes an occasion

not only to show the greater glory of Christ's wisdom and power and worth, but also to show the *superior satisfaction* that this glory gives his people compared to what Satan can give. This leads to the final divine strategy for defeating Satan.

4. GOD IS DEFEATING SATAN WITH *SAVORING*.

Notice that the climax of Paul's experience of the thorn in the flesh is not Paul's awareness of Christ's grace as sufficient. Rather, the awareness and experience of this sufficiency brings Paul to "boast *all the more gladly* of my weaknesses." When Paul experiences the all-sufficient grace of Jesus as a "glad" (ἥδιστα, 2 Cor. 12:9, the word from which we get *hedonism*!) boast, this experience makes the grace and the power of Christ stand forth all the more clearly.

I call this "gladness" *savoring*. And my point is that God intends for Satan to be defeated in this age not merely by showing him to be weaker than Christ, but also by showing him to be *less savory than Christ*—less desirable, less satisfying. If this sounds superficial or marginal to you, you and I are not yet on the same page. In my understanding of God's purposes in the universe, the ultimate goal is that the beauty and worth of Christ be magnified as the supreme treasure of the universe *through being savored above all other reality*. Providence over Satan and all other created reality reaches its ultimate goal when the intensity of human savoring corresponds to the infinite beauty and worth of Christ.

Satan's most essential role in achieving that goal is to offer us every conceivable *pleasure* to entice us away from savoring, desiring, and being satisfied with Christ, and every conceivable *pain* to turn us against the goodness of Christ. When God's people face these temptations to *prefer* the world and to *repudiate* Christ, but instead "gladly" boast in their weaknesses and losses because of *the surpassing value of Christ* (2 Cor. 12:9; Phil. 3:8), Satan is defeated in the most wonderful and thorough way.

Satan is not only shown to be weaker than Christ, but, more importantly, he is shown to be less desirable than Christ. Satan is less satisfying because he is not only weak compared to Christ's power, but also ugly compared to Christ's beauty and disgusting compared to Christ's sweetness. Nothing he is and nothing he offers can compare with Christ.

The *savoring* of Christ above all that Satan can give in riches, or all he can take in suffering, magnifies Christ's beauty and worth in ways that could never have happened if God had banished Satan from the world before his weakness and folly and ugliness were fully exposed, and before Christ was shown to be infinitely more desirable. In this way, God's plan to allow Satan's ongoing existence and influence serves the ultimate goal of providence.

How the Next Chapter Relates to This One

We turn in the next chapter to the providence of God over kings and nations. There is a crucial connection between these two chapters. In Ephesians 6:12 Paul says:

> We do not wrestle against flesh and blood, but against the *rulers*, against the *authorities*, against the cosmic powers over this present darkness, against the spiritual forces of evil in the heavenly places.

Those two words *rulers* and *authorities* appear to refer to demonic beings since they are adversaries and Paul distinguishes them from "flesh and blood." That also would appear to be the meaning of these two words in Colossians 2:15: "[God] disarmed *the rulers and authorities* and put them to open shame, by triumphing over them in [Christ]." And yet Paul uses the very same pair of words in Titus 3:1 to refer to human institutions of authority: "Remind them to be submissive *to rulers and authorities*."

It is likely, therefore, that Paul saw human governments and demonic powers in such a relationship that very often, the human authority and demonic authority were woven inextricably together. This means that the following chapter on God's providence over kings and nations continues to buttress the good news of God's purposeful sovereignty over Satan and all his work among the nations of the world.

SECTION 4

Providence over Kings and Nations

20

Israel's Divine King Is King of the Nations

God's providence over kings and nations is prominent in the Old Testament primarily because God's plan for history, until the Messiah came, was that the nation of Israel would be the central focus of God's saving work. This meant that God's people, as an ethnic, political, and geographic nation, would be in constant relationship, and often conflict, with other nations. How God dealt with Israel and those nations is a thread of providence running through the entire Old Testament.

Israel the Nation and the Church of Jesus Christ

Before God called Abraham as the father of the nation of Israel and established his covenant with him, God had dispersed all the peoples of the world "over the face of all the earth" (Gen. 11:7–8), thus creating a world of nations and languages. According to the apostle Paul:

> [God] made from one man every nation of mankind to live on all the face of the earth, having determined allotted periods and the boundaries of their dwelling place. (Acts 17:26)

So God's concern with nations did not begin with Abraham. However, with the call of Abraham into perpetual covenant relationship with God, Israel became the focus of God's involvement with the nations. Israel would become a "great nation" (Gen. 12:2), which inevitably would have political, territorial, and military interactions with other nations.

More mysteriously, God promised not only that Abraham would become a great nation but also that he would be "the father of a *multitude of nations*" (Gen. 17:4–5). How would Abraham be the father of one unique nation but also the father of a multitude of nations? In the New Testament, Paul took this promise as a pointer to the inclusion of the non-Jewish nations in the Abrahamic covenant by faith in the Messiah (Rom. 4:13–17). "Abraham . . . is the father of us all [Jew and Gentile believers in the Messiah Jesus], as it is written, 'I have made you the father of many nations'" (Rom. 4:16–17).

According to Paul, then, the eventual consummation of God's concern with the nations would mean that his ransomed people would come from *all* the peoples of the world, as John saw in his vision:

> Worthy are you to take the scroll
>   and to open its seals,
> for you were slain, and by your blood you ransomed people
>   for God
>   *from every tribe and language and people and nation,*
> and you have made them a kingdom and priests to our God,
>   and they shall reign on the earth. (Rev. 5:9–10)

This means that the people of God today, the Christian church, made up of those who trust the Messiah, Jesus Christ, does not have a single ethnic, political, or national identity. "Our citizenship is in heaven, and from it we await a Savior, the Lord Jesus Christ" (Phil. 3:20). "Here [in the global Christian church] there is not Greek and Jew, circumcised and uncircumcised, barbarian, Scythian, slave, free; but Christ is all, and in all" (Col. 3:11).

This accounts for why there is such a difference in focus between the Old Testament and the New Testament in regard to nations. In the Old Testament, the visible people of God (as distinct from those who were truly the children of God) was an ethnic, political, and geographic nation (Rom. 9:6–8). God had promised that they would have their own kings (Gen. 17:6; Deut. 17:15) and their own land (Gen. 12:7).

But in the New Testament, the visible people of God includes people from thousands of ethnic, political, and geographic groups. The church is not a political state. It has no king but Jesus (1 Cor. 8:6) and no land but the promise to inherit the earth (Matt. 5:5; Rom. 4:13; 1 Cor. 3:21–23) at the second coming of the Lord Jesus (Matt. 25:31–34). The church is not a nation, and therefore does not relate to nations the way Israel did.

Relevance Today of Providence over Old Testament Nations

Circling back to the beginning of the chapter, this is why there is such prominence given in the Old Testament to God's providence over the nations, and their relation to Israel, while in the New Testament there is a dramatically different picture. What we learn from the Old Testament about God's providence over nations and kings is, nevertheless, relevant for us. God's providence over the nations today is just as inclusive and pervasive as it was in the Old Testament. This has huge implications for the faith and courage of God's people today, who are charged to "make disciples of all nations" (Matt. 28:19), and who are told by Jesus that we will "be hated by all nations for my name's sake" (Matt. 24:9).

Not only that, but God's providence over the nation of Israel in the Old Testament is relevant for the Christian church because the royal line of national kings stemming from David was promised to issue in a "Son of David" whose kingdom would endure forever and would encompass all the nations:

> He will be great and will be called the Son of the Most High. And the Lord God will give to him the throne of his father David, and he will reign over the house of Jacob forever, and of his kingdom there will be no end. (Luke 1:32–33)

> I, Jesus, . . . am the root and the descendant of David, the bright morning star. (Rev. 22:16)

This same Jesus, who is the "King of kings" (Rev. 17:14) and will rule all the nations of the earth (Rev. 19:15–16), is head of the Christian church and the central person of the Christian gospel (Rom. 1:1–4). By faith in him, people from all the nations of the world are granted "entrance into the eternal kingdom of our Lord and Savior Jesus Christ" (2 Pet. 1:11). Therefore, for these and other reasons we shall see, the Old Testament record of God's providence over nations and kings is relevant—even urgent—for Christians today.

The Lord Is King and Rules over All Kings

Implicit in God's foundational self-identification "I AM WHO I AM" (Ex. 3:14)[1] is the truth that "The LORD is king forever" (Ps. 10:16). "Kingship belongs to the LORD" (Ps. 22:28). It "belongs" to him not because anyone anointed him or authorized him or chose him or instated him. It belongs to him because he is what he is—and that includes ruler of all. To be God is to be King: "The LORD is the *true God*; he is the living God and the *everlasting King*" (Jer. 10:10). His kingship has no beginning and can have no ending. He is "the King of the ages, immortal, invisible, the only God," and so to him belong "honor and glory forever and ever" (1 Tim. 1:17; cf. Pss. 145:13; 29:10; 93:2).

---

1   See chap. 6 for a fuller discussion of this text.

Therefore, when Jehoshaphat prayed, "O Lᴏʀᴅ, . . . *you rule over all the kingdoms of the nations*" (2 Chron. 20:6), he did not mean that the nations had elected him or appointed him. God did not find the nations without a king and figure out a way to be their king. He *created* them as nations under his authority, and one day he will have the fullness of his elect from all of them in joyful submission: "All the nations *you have made* shall come and worship before you" (Ps. 86:9; cf. Rev. 5:9; Rom. 11:12, 25). Therefore, "God reigns over the nations" (Ps. 47:8) whether they choose him or not.

Indeed, if they do not acknowledge him as their king, we are shown in the book of Daniel, in graphic detail, what will happen. In fact, Daniel's narrative of what God taught Nebuchadnezzar and Belshazzar is so rich with insight into God's providence that it can provide the structure of the next two chapters. Nebuchadnezzar, the king of Babylon, was given a vision from the Lord to show him what his arrogance would cost him. In the vision, a spokesman says:

> Let his mind be changed from a man's, and let a beast's mind be given to him . . . to the end that the living may know that the Most High rules the kingdom of men and gives it to whom he will and sets over it the lowliest of men. (Dan. 4:16–17)

Nebuchadnezzar had been given a dream. To find out what God was revealing in the dream, he called for Daniel to interpret it. Daniel gives the interpretation:

> This is the interpretation, O king: It is a decree of the Most High, which has come upon my lord the king, that you shall be driven from among men, and your dwelling shall be with the beasts of the field. You shall be made to eat grass like an ox, and you shall be wet with the dew of heaven, and seven periods of time shall pass over you, till you know that the Most High rules the kingdom of men and gives it to whom he will. (Dan. 4:24–25)

The vision was accordingly fulfilled:

> [Nebuchadnezzar] was driven from among men and ate grass like
> an ox, and his body was wet with the dew of heaven till his hair
> grew as long as eagles' feathers, and his nails were like birds' claws.
> (Dan. 4:33)

Astonishingly, the effect was redemptive rather than hardening:

> At the end of the days I, Nebuchadnezzar, lifted my eyes to heaven,
> and my reason returned to me, and I blessed the Most High, and
> praised and honored him who lives forever,
>
>> for his dominion is an everlasting dominion,
>>   and his kingdom endures from generation to generation;
>> all the inhabitants of the earth are accounted as nothing,
>>   and he does according to his will among the host of heaven
>>   and among the inhabitants of the earth;
>> and none can stay his hand
>>   or say to him, "What have you done?"
>
> At the same time my reason returned to me, and for the glory of
> my kingdom, my majesty and splendor returned to me. . . . Now
> I, Nebuchadnezzar, praise and extol and honor the King of heaven,
> for all his works are right and his ways are just; and those who walk
> in pride he is able to humble. (Dan. 4:34–37)

Then to underline all of that, and to show how disinclined most
rulers are to embrace the truth that Nebuchadnezzar had learned,
Daniel tells us how Nebuchadnezzar's son Belshazzar responded foolishly (and suicidally) to his father's experience. Daniel tells Belshazzar
the consequences of pride all over again:

> When [your father's] heart was lifted up and his spirit was hardened
> so that he dealt proudly, he was brought down from his kingly

throne, and his glory was taken from him. He was driven from among the children of mankind, and his mind was made like that of a beast, and his dwelling was with the wild donkeys. He was fed grass like an ox, and his body was wet with the dew of heaven, until he knew that the Most High God rules the kingdom of mankind and sets over it whom he will. (Dan. 5:20–21)

Then Daniel interprets the handwriting on the wall (Mene, Mene, Tekel, and Parsin) that God has sent to bring Belshazzar down:

"And you his son, Belshazzar, have not humbled your heart, though you knew all this, but you have lifted up yourself against the Lord of heaven. . . . The God in whose hand is your breath, and whose are all your ways, you have not honored. . . . This is the interpretation [of the writing on your wall]: MENE, God has numbered the days of your kingdom and brought it to an end; TEKEL, you have been weighed in the balances and found wanting; PERES, your kingdom is divided and given to the Medes and Persians." . . . That very night Belshazzar the Chaldean king was killed. (Dan. 5:22–23, 26–28, 30)

These two stories about Nebuchadnezzar and Belshazzar condense so many essentials of the Old Testament vision of God's providence over kings and nations that we may take them as headings for the unfolding of providence over kings and nations. In summary, they are:

1. The Most High rules the kingdom of men (Dan. 4:17, 25, 32).
2. All the inhabitants of the earth are accounted as nothing (Dan. 4:35).
3. He does according to his will among the host of heaven and among the inhabitants of the earth, and none can stay his hand (Dan. 4:35).
4. The breath and the ways of the king are in the hand of God (Dan. 5:23).

5. The Most High gives the kingdom to whom he will, even to the lowliest of men (Dan. 4:17).

6. Those who walk in pride he is able to humble (Dan. 4:37).

7. All his works are right and his ways are just (Dan. 4:37).

8. God's aim is that the living may know and rejoice that the Most High rules in all these ways (Dan. 4:17).

9. He aims for us to know that when we fail to submit to, and rejoice in, God's kingship, we are acting like animals, not the way humans are meant to act (Dan. 4:32–33; 5:21).

These nine aspects of God's providence over kings and nations form the outline of the next two chapters.

21

Human Kingship and
the King of Kings

The fall and rise of King Nebuchadnezzar followed by the uncompre-
hending arrogance of his son Belshazzar are narrated in the book of
Daniel with graphic detail and force. They are intended to have a humbling impact on kings and nations, as well as the rest of us. I identified
nine truths God is showing us from these stories about his providence
over kings and nations. We will deal with the first four in this chapter,
and the remaining five in chapter 22. In each of these nine aspects of
God's providence, we will widen the aperture of our lens and see if they
appear in the wider biblical terrain.

1. The Most High Rules the Kingdom of Men (Dan. 4:17, 25, 32)
We have already taken note of this fundamental fact, that the Most
High rules the kingdom of men, and need only to focus here on the
phrase "kingdom of *men*." Some facts are so obvious they often go
unnoticed. One of those is the fact that God has chosen, in the way he
orders the world, to enact most of his purposes not by his immediate

kingly action but through human agents, in this case human kings—
"the kingdom of men."

ULTIMATE REASON HUMAN KINGSHIPS EXIST

God did not need to create nations or set up kings. But he has done
both (Ps. 86:9; Dan. 2:21). God could have planned a world in
which there would be no nations and no kings. But that is not what
he planned. Instead, he planned that there be a "kingdom of men,"
that is, that human beings assume roles of kingship over nations.
Therefore, in saying God rules human kingships (Dan. 4:17), let us
not overlook that there are, in fact, such kingships. This is the outworking of God's all-wise providence.

We will see that this is not a superfluous observation when we realize that the ultimate purpose of God's providence in the creation of
the "kingdom of men" is that one day his divine Son become one of
these men, and that he rule, as the God-man, over an "eternal kingdom" (2 Pet. 1:11; cf. Luke 1:32–33). In view of this final purpose,
we may say that the reason God created human kingships was for the
sake of the kingly glory of his Son.

God did not plan the incarnation of the Son *after* there were
human kings on the earth. On the contrary, his ultimate purpose
from before creation was "the praise of the glory of his grace," manifest supremely in the redemption that came through the blood of his
loved Son (Eph. 1:6–7). The plan was that his Son take on human
flesh (Heb. 2:14), make purification for sins, and take his seat at the
right hand of the Majesty on high (Heb. 1:3) and reign as King of
kings forever (Rev. 17:14; 19:16). Then, with that goal in view, God
planned that there be such a thing as human kingship so that he
might make kingship part of the glory of his Son. "Of the Son he says,
'Your throne, O God, is forever and ever, the scepter of uprightness
is the scepter of your kingdom'" (Heb. 1:8). "He shall reign forever
and ever" (Rev. 11:15).

PATH OF THE CHRIST'S KINGSHIP THROUGH ISRAEL'S MONARCHY

More specifically, God planned that the human kingship of his chosen people Israel would be the human line through which his Son would enter the world as the King of Israel and finally as the everlasting King of all nations. God established a covenant with King David and pledged himself to make the line of his kingship everlasting:

> I will establish the throne of his kingdom *forever.* I will be to him a father, and he shall be to me a son. When he commits iniquity, I will discipline him with the rod of men, with the stripes of the sons of men, but my steadfast love will not depart from him, as I took it from Saul, whom I put away from before you. And your house and your kingdom shall be made sure *forever* before me. Your throne shall be established *forever.* (2 Sam. 7:13–16)

This threefold *forever* contained a divine plan that was not yet clear to the saints in the Old Testament. How would the human factor ("when he commits iniquity"), with its consequent failures and mortality, issue in an eternal kingdom? Nevertheless, the covenant was seen as sure. A Son of David would rise and reign, and his kingdom would last forever.

The prophet Isaiah heightened the mystery by promising that this coming Davidic king would be "Mighty God" and "Everlasting Father" in his endless kingdom:

> To us a child is born,
>   to us a son is given;
> and the government shall be upon his shoulder,
>   and his name shall be called
> Wonderful Counselor, Mighty God,
>   Everlasting Father, Prince of Peace.

Of the increase of his government and of peace
    there will be no end,
on the throne of David and over his kingdom,
    to establish it and to uphold it
with justice and with righteousness
    from this time forth and forevermore.
The zeal of the Lord of hosts will do this.
        (Isa. 9:6–7)

And Daniel adds to the drama with his vision of the humanity of the coming King, who is somehow unlike any other human king:

I saw in the night visions,
and behold, with the clouds of heaven
    there came *one like a son of man,*
and he came to the Ancient of Days
    and was presented before him.
And to him was given dominion
    and glory and a kingdom,
that all peoples, nations, and languages
    should serve him;
his dominion is an *everlasting dominion,*
    which shall not pass away,
and his kingdom one
    that shall not be destroyed. (Dan. 7:13–14)

This is the promised kingship that the angel announced to Mary the mother of Jesus:

He will be great and will be called the Son of the Most High. And the Lord God will give to him the throne of his father David, and he will reign over the house of Jacob forever, and of his kingdom there will be no end. (Luke 1:32–33)

This throne of David turns out to be the very throne of God, as Jesus, the God-man, is raised from the dead and sits with his Father on his divine throne: "I also conquered and sat down with my Father on his throne" (Rev. 3:21). He is "the Lamb in the midst of the throne" (Rev. 7:17). The throne of the universe is "the throne of God and of the Lamb" (Rev. 22:1).

Therefore, through all eternity, the song of heaven will be:

Worthy is the Lamb who was slain,
to receive power and wealth and wisdom and might
and honor and glory and blessing! . . .
To him who sits on the throne and to the Lamb
be blessing and honor and glory and might forever
    and ever! (Rev. 5:12–13)

This was the ultimate goal of God's providence in bringing about a "kingdom of men" and in guiding the thousand-year history of the kingship of Israel—the glorification of the reigning Lamb in the joyful praises of his people.

Therefore, as we continue to flesh out the essentials of God's providence over kings and nations, which is summarized in Daniel 4 and 5, we should keep in mind that all the glories of this providence are meant, ultimately, to help us see and savor the worth and beauty of the eternal kingship of Jesus Christ.

2. All Earth's Inhabitants Are Accounted as Nothing (Dan. 4:35)

The immediate and all-embracing implication of what Daniel writes in chapters 4 and 5 is: "[God] does according to his will among the host of heaven and among the inhabitants of the earth; and none can stay his hand" (Dan. 4:35).

His dominion is an everlasting dominion,
    and his kingdom endures from generation to generation;

all the inhabitants of the earth are accounted as nothing,
    and he does according to his will among the host of
        heaven
    and among the inhabitants of the earth;
and none can stay his hand
    or say to him, "What have you done?" (Dan. 4:34–35)

In relation to Nebuchadnezzar and Belshazzar, the point was to humble them. It is designed to silence their boasts: "Is not this great Babylon, which I have built by my mighty power as a royal residence and for the glory of my majesty?" (Dan. 4:30). To which God says, in effect, "Your little Babylon is as *nothing* to me, and it is *my* will that holds sway in your infinitesimal kingship, not yours."

MAGNIFYING GRACE, NOT NULLIFYING MAN

The point of saying that earth's inhabitants are counted as nothing was not that God takes no interest in the world of human kingships or that he shows no kindness to them. The point is that when he does, he is absolutely free and unconstrained by any power or right or worth in "the inhabitants of the earth."

In other words, earthly kingdoms and their inhabitants are *not* impressive. *God* is impressive. And when he takes interest in these insignificant creatures, his grace, not their glory, is amazing. In fact, he does take interest in them. And the absolute, majestic sovereignty of his providence over the nations and their inhabitants is not meant to make his grace inconceivable but to make it spectacular. Watch how Isaiah weaves together the condescension of God and the exaltation of God in this same way:

He will tend his flock like a shepherd;
    he will gather the lambs in his arms;
he will carry them in his bosom,
    and gently lead those that are with young. . . .

Behold, *the nations are like a drop from a bucket,*
>   and are accounted as the dust on the scales;
>   behold, he takes up the coastlands like fine dust. . . .
All *the nations are as nothing before him,*
>   they are accounted by him as *less than nothing and*
>   *emptiness.* . . .
It is he who sits above the circle of the earth,
>   and *its inhabitants are like grasshoppers*; . . .
who brings princes to nothing,
>   and *makes the rulers of the earth as emptiness.* . . .
Lift up your eyes on high and see:
>   who created these [stars]?
He who brings out their host by number,
>   calling them all by name;
by the greatness of his might
>   and because he is strong in power,
>   not one is missing. . . .
Have you not known? Have you not heard?
The LORD is the everlasting God,
>   the Creator of the ends of the earth. . . .
He gives power to the faint,
>   *and to him who has no might he increases strength.* . . .
They who wait for the LORD shall renew their strength;
>   they shall mount up with wings like eagles;
they shall run and not be weary;
>   they shall walk and not faint. (Isa. 40:11, 15, 17,
>   22–23, 26, 28–29, 31)

This passage begins with God gathering his lambs in his arms (40:11) and ends with his giving strength to the faint who have no might (40:29–31). Between these two pictures of God's stooping to help the helpless are the most exalted glimpses of his majesty:

"the nations are like a drop from a bucket" (40:15); "the nations are as nothing before him" (40:17); "[earth's] inhabitants are like grasshoppers" (40:22); "[he] makes the rulers of the earth as emptiness" (40:23); he created the stars and calls all their billions by name (40:26).

This juxtaposition of God's self-exaltation and self-humbling is pervasive in the biblical picture of God's providence and is near the essence of his peculiar and wonderful glory. Here it is again:

> Thus says the One who is high and lifted up,
>   who inhabits eternity, whose name is Holy:
> "I dwell in the high and holy place,
>   and also with him who is of a contrite and lowly spirit,
> to revive the spirit of the lowly,
>   and to revive the heart of the contrite." (Isa. 57:15)

The effect that Daniel and Isaiah (and God) intend for these portraits of providence is at least threefold. First, they should silence every whiff of objection we might raise to the way God governs the nations and their inhabitants: "None can stay his hand or say to him, 'What have you done?'" (Dan. 4:35). Second, they should amaze us that God pays any attention to us at all, and especially that he would carry us like lambs, or give us strength, or revive our spirit. My sense is that in the twenty-first-century church, we are more likely to feel God's mercy as a presumed right rather than a mind-blowing surprise. Third, they should prepare us for the incomprehensible mystery of how the Son of God pursued his role as Redeemer-King:

> Though he was in the form of God, [Christ] did not count equality with God a thing to be grasped, but emptied himself, by taking the form of a servant, being born in the likeness of men. And being found in human form, he humbled himself by becoming obedient to the point of death, even death on a cross. (Phil. 2:6–8)

From the infinite majesty of "equality with God" to the lowest shame of "death on a cross," this was God's plan for the kingship of his Son. If we have eyes to see, we notice pointers to the peculiar glory of this kind of divine dominion throughout the Old Testament.

3. He Does according to His Will in Heaven and on Earth, and None Can Stay His Hand (Dan. 4:35)

With the words "none can stay his hand," the text draws out the veiled counterclaim against God's providence that God aims to nullify. That false claim is this: there are powers present in God's creation, especially in his human creatures, and in the great national and military forces that humans build, that can indeed "stay God's hand." God is intent in Scripture on exposing that claim to be false.

For example, when the Syrians were defeated by Israel in the hills, the Syrians said it was because the Lord was a god of the hills, not of the valleys (1 Kings 20:23). So they thought, *If we can fight Israel in the valleys, we will win.* In other words, we can "stay God's hand" by our superior numbers in the right terrain. God did not approve that analysis of the situation. It was absurd, which he would show them:

> The people of Israel encamped before them like two little flocks of goats, but the Syrians filled the country. And a man of God came near and said to the king of Israel, "Thus says the LORD, 'Because the Syrians have said, "The LORD is a god of the hills but he is not a god of the valleys," *therefore* [to refute that slander against God] I will give all this great multitude into your hand, and you shall know that I am the LORD.'" . . . And the people of Israel struck down of the Syrians 100,000 foot soldiers in one day. (1 Kings 20:27–29)

Neither terrain nor numbers can thwart the purposes of God for nations and kings. "Nothing can hinder the LORD from saving by many or by few" (1 Sam. 14:6). Over and over, God aims to show that he holds decisive sway in national and military conquests. He does this often by giving victory to his people when they are outnumbered. He says explicitly that the purpose of this strategy is to prevent human beings from claiming the power to thwart his aim or do what only he can do.

For example, when Gideon, whom God had raised up to rescue Israel (Judg. 6:36), was about to fight the Midianites with twenty-two thousand soldiers, God said to him, "The people with you are too many for me to give the Midianites into their hand, *lest Israel boast over me, saying, 'My own hand has saved me'*" (Judg. 7:2). In other words, God's purpose in his providence is not only to show that no power can thwart what he intends to do, but also to show that every victory is *his* victory. "In your hand are power and might, so that none is able to withstand you" (2 Chron. 20:6). "The horse is made ready for the day of battle, but the victory belongs to the LORD" (Prov. 21:31; cf. 2 Chron. 20:15; 32:8).

God is intent on showing these two truths: first, his plans cannot be nullified by man. They stand:

> The LORD of hosts has purposed,
>   and who will annul it?
> His hand is stretched out,
>   and who will turn it back? (Isa. 14:27)

> I know that you can do all things,
>   and that no purpose of yours can be thwarted. (Job 42:2)

And, second, no plans of man will ever be fulfilled unless they are part of God's plan. God's plans determine which human plans succeed, whether we are talking about the plans of the most powerful nations or of individual kings or their subjects:

> The LORD brings the counsel of the nations to nothing;
>   he frustrates the plans of the peoples. (Ps. 33:10; cf. Isa. 19:3)

Many are the plans in the mind of a man,
> but it is the purpose of the LORD that will stand. (Prov. 19:21)

4. *The Breath and Ways of the King Are in The Hand of God (Dan. 5:23)*

This is the underlying truth that enables God to frustrate human plans and accomplish his own plans infallibly. His providence is not merely a general influence in the world that constantly confronts lives and behaviors that he did not govern from their start. God's providence is not the management of unforeseen or unplanned lives or behaviors. This was what Belshazzar, Nebuchadnezzar's son, failed to reckon with.

> You have praised the gods of silver and gold, of bronze, iron, wood, and stone, which do not see or hear or know, but the God *in whose hand is your breath, and whose are all your ways,* you have not honored. (Dan. 5:23)

In other words, the God you are dealing with in reality is not just superior to your stone gods, in that he can see and hear and know, and they can't. Far, far more than that: the God you are dealing with holds "your breath" and "your way" in his hand. He doesn't just *see* you breathing; he gives every breath (until he doesn't). He doesn't just *hear* your footsteps; he holds them—your foot falls where he plans. He doesn't just *know* what you are about to do, so he can get ready for it; he guides every move you make. And, O king, when you inhale and exhale, every movement of your diaphragm is a free and undeserved gift of God for which you owe perpetual humble thankfulness. "In [God's] hand is the life of every living thing and the breath of all mankind" (Job 12:10).

If God had wanted to be more specific, he could have said to Belshazzar, "Your breath ends tonight"—which it did (Dan. 5:30). And he could have told him what was to become of the great kingdom of Babylon: "The LORD has stirred up the spirit of the kings of the Medes, because his purpose concerning Babylon is to destroy it" (Jer. 51:11). This means that not only are the breath and the ways of Israel's kings in the hands of the Lord, but so are the breath and the ways of all kings.

> The king's heart is a stream of water in the hand of the LORD;
>   he turns it wherever he will. (Prov. 21:1)

Israel found this to be the case again and again, both to their dismay, when God sent foreign kings against them, and to their joy, when he raised up kings to save them.

PROVIDENCE TURNING FOREIGN KINGS AGAINST ISRAEL

Repeatedly God whistled for the nations to come and do his bidding in bringing judgment and correction on his people: "[The LORD will] . . . whistle for them from the ends of the earth; and behold, quickly, speedily they come!" (Isa. 5:26; cf. 7:18).

Notice in the following texts how many different verbs are used to describe God's turning the hearts of foreign kings and nations against his people.

He *sold* them into the hands of enemies:

> The anger of the LORD was kindled against Israel, and he *sold* them into the hand of Cushan-rishathaim king of Mesopotamia. (Judg. 3:8)

He *raised up* nations against Israel:

> "Behold, I will *raise up* against you a nation,
>   O house of Israel," declares the LORD, the God of hosts.
>   (Amos 6:14)

He made foreign kings his *axe* and *saw* and *rod*, and *commanded* them against Israel:

Woe to Assyria, the rod of my anger;
 the staff in their hands is my fury!
Against a godless nation I send him,
 and against the people of my wrath I command him.
  (Isa. 10:5–6)

Shall the axe boast over him who hews with it,
 or the saw magnify itself against him who wields it?
As if a rod should wield him who lifts it,
 or as if a staff should lift him who is not wood!
  (Isa. 10:15)

He *brings* nations against Israel:

The Lord will bring a nation against you from far away, from the end of the earth, swooping down like the eagle. (Deut. 28:49)

Behold, I am bringing against you
 a nation from afar, O house of Israel,
 declares the Lord. (Jer. 5:15)

He *sends* nations against Israel:

In those days the Lord began to send Rezin the king of Syria and Pekah the son of Remaliah against Judah. (2 Kings 15:37)

He makes nations *his servants* against Israel:

Behold, I will send for . . . Nebuchadnezzar the king of Babylon, my servant, and I will bring them against this land and its inhabitants. (Jer. 25:9; cf. 43:10)

He *gives* his people into the hands of foreign nations:

The anger of the Lord was kindled against Israel, and he gave them continually into the hand of Hazael king of Syria. (2 Kings 13:3)

He gave them into the hand of the nations,
    so that those who hated them ruled over them. (Ps. 106:41)

Now I have given all these lands into the hand of Nebuchadnezzar, the king of Babylon, my servant, and I have given him also the
beasts of the field to serve him. (Jer. 27:6)

Thus says the Lord: "Behold, I am giving this city into the hand
of the king of Babylon, and he shall burn it with fire." (Jer. 34:2)

You gave them into the hand of their enemies, who made them
suffer. (Neh. 9:27)

He *gathers* nations against Israel:

I will gather all the nations against Jerusalem to battle, and the city
shall be taken. (Zech. 14:2)

PROVIDENCE TURNING FOREIGN KINGS TO HELP ISRAEL

To her joy, Israel found the truth of Proverbs 21:1 ("The king's heart
is a stream of water in the hand of the Lord; he turns it wherever he
will") to work for her deliverance at key points in her history. God
turned the hearts of foreign kings to oppose Israel's enemies (Isa. 9:11)
and to help Israel recover from destruction.

After God had used Nebuchadnezzar to be God's judgment against
Jerusalem, God raised up the Medes to bring judgment on Nebuchadnezzar and his Babylonian kingdom:

Behold, *I am stirring up the Medes* against them,
    who have no regard for silver
    and do not delight in gold. . . .
And Babylon, the glory of kingdoms,
    the splendor and pomp of the Chaldeans,
will be like Sodom and Gomorrah
    when God overthrew them. (Isa. 13:17, 19; cf. 14:22)

This defeat would unleash a sequence of events that, in God's providence, would restore the Jewish captives to Jerusalem:

> Thus says the LORD of hosts, the God of Israel: I have broken the yoke of the king of Babylon. Within two years I will bring back to this place all the vessels of the LORD's house, which Nebuchadnezzar king of Babylon took away from this place and carried to Babylon. . . . *I will break the yoke of the king of Babylon.* (Jer. 28:2–4)

More clearly than anyone else, Ezra celebrates the turning of the heart of the pagan king to serve Israel in her time of need:

> In the first year of Cyrus king of Persia . . . *the LORD stirred up the spirit of Cyrus* king of Persia, so that he made a proclamation . . . : "Thus says Cyrus king of Persia: The LORD . . . has charged me to build him a house at Jerusalem." (Ezra 1:1–2)

Later the people rejoice that

> the LORD had . . . *turned the heart of the king of Assyria to them,* so that he aided them in the work of the house of God. . . . "Blessed be the LORD . . . who *put such a thing as this into the heart of the king.*" (Ezra 6:22; 7:27)

GREATEST GOOD CAME THROUGH
PROVIDENCE OVER EVIL RULERS

Without God's providence over wicked authorities, there would be no gospel. The murder of the Son of God is pivotal in providing our salvation. Christ did not die randomly. It was planned. His death was a God-orchestrated travesty of justice that his enemies hoped would get rid of his influence. But in all of that sin and injustice, providence was pursuing the salvation of those who plotted his death—and millions more who don't deserve it. There would be no salvation without this kind of God-planned, God-orchestrated death.

At the merely human level, Jesus's death was owing to a wicked king and expedient governor and brutal soldiers and a bloodthirsty mob. But they were all acting in accord with a perfectly wise, just, and gracious providence:

> Truly in this city there were gathered together against your holy servant Jesus, whom you anointed, both Herod and Pontius Pilate, along with the Gentiles and the peoples of Israel, to do whatever your hand and your plan had predestined to take place. (Acts 4:27–28)

The kind of pervasive providence over the hearts of evil kings that we have seen in the Old Testament is the kind of providence to which we owe our hope of forgiven sins and eternal life.

PROVIDENCE OVER KINGS FOR THE SAKE OF MISSIONS

Not only is the accomplishment of our salvation at the cross of Christ possible because of God's providence over evil rulers, but the news of this salvation reached us (all over the world) because of God's providence over thousands of secular authorities. The spread of the gospel is often hindered or advanced by the actions of kings and rulers and those in authority. This is why Paul told Timothy to pray for kings:

> I urge that supplications, prayers, intercessions, and thanksgivings be made for all people, *for kings and all who are in high positions*, that we may lead a peaceful and quiet life, godly and dignified in every way. This is good, and it is pleasing in the sight of God our Savior, who desires all people to be saved and to come to the knowledge of the truth. (1 Tim. 2:1–4)

The flow of thought in this passage shows that praying for rulers can advance the fulfillment of God's desire for "all people to be saved and to come to the knowledge of the truth." History has shown this to be true. It is generally more difficult to penetrate all the peoples of the world with the gospel if war is raging, and laws (or lawlessness) stand in the way. Therefore, God's providence over "kings and all who are in high positions" affects the spread of the gospel.

To be sure, "the word of God is not bound" (2 Tim. 2:9), and Paul himself showed us that we must be willing to be imprisoned and beaten by rulers for the sake of the gospel (2 Cor. 11:23–29). Nevertheless, it remains true that we are to pray for kings and rulers, because the heart of the king is in the hand of the Lord (Prov. 21:1), and he can turn it for the advance of the gospel.

22

To Know and Rejoice That
the Most High Rules

Failing to know and rejoice in the absolute rule of God over the kings of the earth is a sign that we are becoming like animals, not humans. The story of Nebuchadnezzar's beast-like experience is a graphic reminder that self-exaltation is the exact opposite of what it seems to be. "He was driven from among men and ate grass like an ox" (Dan. 4:33). Why? Because he said, "Is not this great Babylon, which I have built by my mighty power?" (4:30). At the very moment of his self-exaltation, he was about to eat grass like a beast. God's word to us is this: don't descend into the perversion of humanity; delight in providence.

We continue unfolding the nine aspects of providence over kings and nations that we saw in the stories of Nebuchadnezzar and Belshazzar. We dealt with the first four in chapter 21 and deal with the final five in this chapter.

5. The Most High Gives the Kingdom to Whom He Will, Even to the Lowliest (Dan. 4:17)

God's providential ordering of every kingdom is what Nebuchadnezzar was to learn by being turned into a beast for his pride. To use the words of the apostle Paul, "There is no authority except from God, and those that exist have been instituted by God" (Rom. 13:1). Jesus himself made this clear in the powerful testimony at his trial. Pilate said, "Do you not know that I have authority to release you and authority to crucify you?" But Jesus answered, "You would have no authority over me at all unless it had been given you from above" (John 19:10–11). So whether it is Paul under the wicked Nero or Jesus under self-serving Pilate, the testimony of God's providence over evil rulers stands: no authority but from God. The Most High gives the kingdom to whom he will:

> He changes times and seasons;
>> he removes kings and sets up kings. (Dan. 2:21)

> [The Lord] makes nations great, and he destroys them;
>> he enlarges nations, and leads them away. (Job 12:23)

> It is God who executes judgment,
>> putting down one and lifting up another. (Ps. 75:7;
>>> cf. 2 Chron. 25:8)

PECULIAR GLORY THREADED THROUGH PROVIDENCE'S BEAUTY

Woven into this indestructible fabric of providence over all human authority are the golden threads of God's peculiar glory. The fabric itself is glorious. When Nebuchadnezzar returned to his senses after being humbled, he praised the glory of God's absolute providence over all human authority—that's the fabric:

> I, Nebuchadnezzar, lifted my eyes to heaven, and my reason returned to me, and I blessed the Most High, and praised and honored him who lives forever,
>
>> for his dominion is an everlasting dominion,
>>> and his kingdom endures from generation to generation;

all the inhabitants of the earth are accounted as nothing,
    and he does according to his will among the host of
        heaven
    and among the inhabitants of the earth;
  and none can stay his hand
    or say to him, "What have you done?" (Dan. 4:34–35)

But the golden threads of God's peculiar glory—his exaltation of his own greatness by showing mercy to the weak—are even brighter than the fabric of God's absolute, pervasive providence over human kings and nations. In fact, the colors of this indestructible fabric of absolute power are designed precisely to make these golden threads of mercy glow the more brightly (Rom. 9:22–23).

The peculiar glory of these threads is seen in the last phrase of Daniel 4:17: "The Most High rules the kingdom of men and gives it to whom he will *and sets over it the lowliest of men.*" God is not just *sovereign* in power. He is *surprising* in power. His delight is not only in the exercise of his power, but in lifting up the lowest to make them high:

He sets on high those who are lowly,
  and those who mourn are lifted to safety. (Job 5:11)

When they are diminished and brought low
  through oppression, evil, and sorrow,
he pours contempt on princes
  and makes them wander in trackless wastes;
but he raises up the needy out of affliction
  and makes their families like flocks. (Ps. 107:39–41;
    cf. Ps. 147:5–6; Ezek. 21:26)

And so, as God inaugurated the kingship of Israel—sinful as it was for them to wish to be like the other nations (1 Sam. 12:17)—the fabric of his king-choosing power was on display. And his peculiar glory was woven in. In the books of Acts and Kings and Chronicles, the fabric of sovereign power over kings is laid out: "God gave them Saul . . . for forty years" (Acts 13:21). Then "the Lord put him to death and turned the kingdom over to David the son of Jesse" (1 Chron. 10:14). Then the Lord made Solomon king in place of David (1 Kings 3:7). The Most High gives the kingdom to whom he will.

Through all the sin and all the intrigue that led to the enthronement of these first three kings of Israel, it was God's providence that held sway. He raised them up and put them in office. But woven into this fabric of sovereignty were the golden threads of counterintuitive surprise. He sets over the kingdom "the lowliest of men."

Even though Saul's kingship was marred by arrogance and disobedience, he does express rightly the connection between God's selection and his own insignificance. Saul cries out to Samuel as he prepares him for kingship: "Am I not a Benjaminite, from the least of the tribes of Israel? And is not my clan the humblest of all the clans of the tribe of Benjamin? Why then have you spoken to me in this way?" (1 Sam. 9:21).

In a similar spirit, David's father, Jesse, cannot imagine that Samuel would want to consider his youngest son, the shepherd boy, as the next king of Israel (1 Sam. 16:11). The Lord himself reminds David of these humble origins:

> Thus says the Lord of hosts, I took you from the pasture, from following the sheep, that you should be prince over my people Israel. . . . And I will make for you a great name, like the name of the great ones of the earth. (2 Sam. 7:8–9)

And Solomon felt the same unworthiness and prayed, "O Lord my God, you have made your servant king in place of David my father, although I am but a little child. I do not know how to go out or come in" (1 Kings 3:7).

GOLDEN THREADS LEAD TO THE MOST PECULIAR GLORY OF ALL

These golden threads of counterintuitive mercy, as God rejects the way of the world and exalts the lowly, lead finally to Jesus as the greatest of kings from the lowest disgrace. The apostle Peter said that the Old Testament prophets "searched and inquired carefully, inquiring what person or time the Spirit of Christ in them was indicating when he predicted *the sufferings of Christ and the subsequent glories*" (1 Pet. 1:10–11). First, the lowest shame and suffering. Then, after suffering, the glory of kingship.

So when Mary the mother of Jesus sings over the child in her womb, this is the thread she weaves into her song:

He has shown strength with his arm;
　he has scattered the proud in the thoughts of their hearts;
*he has brought down the mighty from their thrones
　and exalted those of humble estate.* (Luke 1:51–52;
　　cf. 1 Sam. 2:6–8)

And so it came to pass. Born to lie in a feeding trough but worshiped as a king (Matt. 2:16; Luke 2:16). Son of a carpenter, but Son of David (Mark 6:3; Luke 18:39). No place to lay his head, but owner of every palace (Luke 9:58; John 13:3). Supplied with food by women who traveled with him, but able to make five loaves feed thousands (Matt. 14:13–21; Luke 8:3). Without any formal education, but spoke like no one else in history (John 7:15, 46). More worthy of allegiance than any man, but forsaken by all his closest followers (Matt. 10:37; Mark 14:50). Suffered the most painful and shameful death, but exalted by God to be King over all other kings (Phil. 2:6–8; Rev. 1:5).

THREADS OF PECULIAR GLORY STILL BEING WOVEN

This was the plan from the beginning. And the pattern of providence over kings and nations throughout Israel's history prepared the way.

The pattern still holds true in our day. The golden thread of God's peculiar glory is woven through the fabric of his all-embracing, all-pervasive, indestructible providence over the great affairs of nations and kings. His church is the focus of this peculiar glory. Here is how Paul and Jesus and James describe the peculiar glory of the people of Christ:

> Consider your calling, brothers: not many of you were wise according to worldly standards, not many were powerful, not many were of noble birth. But God chose what is foolish in the world to shame the wise; God chose what is weak in the world to shame the strong; God chose what is low and despised in the world, even things that are not, to bring to nothing things that are, so that no human being might boast in the presence of God. And because of him you are in Christ Jesus, who became to us wisdom from God, righteousness and sanctification and redemption, so that, as it is written, "Let the one who boasts, boast in the Lord." (1 Cor. 1:26–31)

> Jesus declared, "I thank you, Father, Lord of heaven and earth, that you have hidden these things from the wise and understanding and revealed them to little children; yes, Father, for thus it was well-pleasing before you." (Matt. 11:25–26, my translation)

> Has not God chosen those who are poor in the world to be rich in faith and heirs of the kingdom, which he has promised to those who love him? (James 2:5)

One could say, with clear warrant from Scripture, that the vastness and depth and completeness of God's providence in history over kings and nations is designed by God to give joyful confidence to his children as he calls us to humble ourselves, take the low place of service (Matt. 20:26), and wait patiently, knowing that "whoever exalts himself will be humbled, and whoever humbles himself will be exalted" (Matt. 23:12; cf. Matt. 18:4; James 4:6; 1 Pet. 5:5).

6. Those Who Walk in Pride He Is Able to Humble (Dan. 4:37)

This aspect of God's providence over kings and nations, his humbling of them, was implicit in the previous point: the Most High gives the kingdom to whom he will, even to the lowliest of men. But there the focus was on his work of lifting up those whom he chooses—often the least likely—to be rulers. Here the focus is on taking rulers down.

God hates the pride of kings in proportion to how he loves to exalt the lowly to positions of greatness:

> Pride and arrogance and the way of evil
>   and perverted speech I *hate*. (Prov. 8:13)

> There are six things that the LORD *hates*,
>   seven that are an abomination to him:
> haughty eyes . . . (Prov. 6:16–17)

> The Lord GOD has sworn by himself, declares the LORD, the God of hosts:

> "I *abhor* the pride of Jacob
>   and hate his strongholds." (Amos 6:8)

Therefore "God opposes the proud" (James 4:6; 1 Pet. 5:5). There is nothing more fearful than to have a God of omnipotent power (Job 42:2; Matt. 19:26), perfect justice (Isa. 5:16), and all-encompassing providence (Eph. 1:11) *oppose* us. Therefore, human pride is a great adversary not only to God, but to man himself. If God leaves it unpunished, he denies his own supreme worth (which he cannot do, 2 Tim. 2:13) and sends a false and destructive message to man (which he also cannot do, Heb. 6:18). If God sanctions the self-exaltation of human pride, he would contradict this all-important truth: man's greatest happiness can be found only as he ceases to be supreme in his own estimation and God becomes his greatest treasure. In the pursuit of such happiness, God opposes human pride.

God "opposes the proud" in many different ways. He rebukes nations (Ps. 9:5) and kings (Ps. 105:14). He executes judgment among nations (Ps. 110:6) and disciplines them (Ps. 94:10). He tramples on rulers (Isa. 41:25) and breaks their scepters (Isa. 14:5). "[He] brings princes to nothing, and makes the rulers of the earth as emptiness" (Isa. 40:23). The haughty eyes he brings down (Ps. 18:27).

PROVIDENCE AND PRIDE

The history of Israel and the nations carries an unmistakable message about providence and pride. Pride is the preference for man over God—the man in the mirror, the man who knows better than God where pleasure and significance are to be found, the man with power who can provide better security than God. Pride is every form of self-exaltation, preferred above joyful God-exaltation. Therefore, pride is the destruction of the glad-hearted praise of the glory of God's grace (Eph. 1:6)—which is the ultimate goal of the rightful ruler of the universe (see chapter 14). Therefore, pride is the height of treason and the end of human happiness. It is opposition to the ultimate purpose of providence.

Therefore, every story of God's judgment on the pride of nations is a message of warning and love to the world.

The story of judgment on *Israel* is a warning against pride:

> Your renown went forth among the nations because of your beauty, for it was perfect through the splendor that I had bestowed on you, declares the Lord God. But you trusted in your beauty and played the whore because of your renown. . . . Therefore, behold, I will gather all your lovers . . . against you from every side and will uncover your nakedness to them. . . . And I will give you into their hands, and they shall throw down your vaulted chamber and break down your lofty places. (Ezek. 16:14–15, 37, 39)

The story of judgment on *Moab* is a warning against pride:

We have heard of the pride of Moab—
 he is very proud—
of his loftiness, his pride, and his arrogance,
 and the haughtiness of his heart.
I know his insolence, declares the LORD. . . .
Gladness and joy have been taken away
 from the fruitful land of Moab;
I have made the wine cease from the winepresses;
 no one treads them with shouts of joy;
 the shouting is not the shout of joy. (Jer. 48:29–30, 33)

The story of judgment on *Tyre* is a warning against pride:

Son of man, raise a lamentation over the king of Tyre,
 and say to him. . . .
Your heart was proud because of your beauty;
 you corrupted your wisdom for the sake of your splendor.
I cast you to the ground;
 I exposed you before kings,
 to feast their eyes on you. (Ezek. 28:12, 17)

The story of judgment on *Assyria* is a warning against pride:

Behold, Assyria was a cedar in Lebanon,
with beautiful branches and forest shade,
 and of towering height,
 its top among the clouds. . . .

Therefore thus says the Lord GOD: Because it towered high and set its top among the clouds, and its heart was proud of its height, I will give it into the hand of a mighty one of the nations. He shall surely deal with it as its wickedness deserves. I have cast it out. (Ezek. 31:3, 10–11)

The story of judgment on *Babylon* is a warning against pride:

Summon archers against Babylon, all those who bend the bow. Encamp around her; let no one escape. . . . For she has proudly defied the LORD, the Holy One of Israel. Therefore her young men shall fall in her squares, and all her soldiers shall be destroyed on that day, declares the LORD. (Jer. 50:29–30)

The story of judgment on *man* is a warning against pride:

The haughty looks of man shall be brought low,
　　and the lofty pride of men shall be humbled,
and the LORD alone will be exalted in that day.
For the LORD of hosts has a day
　　against all that is proud and lofty,
　　against all that is lifted up—and it shall be brought low. . . .
And the haughtiness of man shall be humbled,
　　and the lofty pride of men shall be brought low,
　　and the LORD alone will be exalted in that day.
　　　　(Isa. 2:11–12, 17)

The story of judgment on the *world* is a warning against pride:

I will punish the world for its evil,
　　and the wicked for their iniquity;
I will put an end to the pomp of the arrogant,
　　and lay low the pompous pride of the ruthless. (Isa. 13:11)

PRIDE-OPPOSING PROVIDENCE IS LOVE

Every warning, through the mighty works of pride-opposing providence, is an act of love for those who have ears to hear and eyes to see:

Give thanks to the LORD, for he is good,
　　for his steadfast love endures forever. . . .
To him who struck down great kings,
　　for *his steadfast love endures forever;*

and killed mighty kings,

    for *his steadfast love endures forever.* (Ps. 136:1, 17–18)

God has not ceased to love when he kills the mighty kings of pride. The ultimate aim of providence is the exaltation of the worth and beauty of God in the soul-satisfying praises of God's people. Where pride exists, this purpose is not yet fulfilled. Therefore, pride-opposing providence is love.

7. All His Works Are Right, and His Ways Are Just (Dan. 4:37)

When Nebuchadnezzar came to his senses (Dan. 4:34), he praised not only the *sovereignty* of God's providence over kings and nations, but also the *justice* and *righteousness* of it:

> Now I, Nebuchadnezzar, praise and extol and honor the King of heaven, for all his works are *right* and his ways are *just* [כָּל־מַעֲבָדֹ֫והִי קְשֹׁט וְאֹרְחָתֵהּ דִּין]; and those who walk in pride he is able to humble. (Dan. 4:37)

The words for *right* and *just* are not the ones widely used in Old Testament Hebrew. They occur only in Daniel and Ezra. They mean, more literally, *truth* and *judgment.* But when you think this through to the reality behind these words, the English translation is not misleading.

TO WHAT IS GOD ULTIMATELY AND ALWAYS TRUE?

To call God's works of providence *truth* (קְשֹׁט) suggests that they correspond to something firm and ultimate. And to call his ways of providence *judgment* (דִּין) suggests that they provide the criteria of judgment among the ways of man. God's ways stand as judges (according to some standard) that measure human events. Therefore, both truth and judgment presuppose a standard to which God's works and ways are always true.

I have argued in great detail in *The Justification of God* that this standard to which God is ultimately committed is the infinite worth and beauty of his own being—sometimes simply referred to as his own *name*.[1] So I will argue for this only briefly here. My point is that God's righteousness or his truth or his justice is most fundamentally God's holding *true* to his commitment to treat as most valuable what is most valuable, namely, himself. This is what Paul meant when he said that God cannot deny *himself*. He must always be *true* to his own infinite worth and beauty:

> If we deny him, he also will deny us;
> if we are faithless, he remains faithful—
> for he cannot deny himself. (2 Tim. 2:12–13)

This cannot mean, "If we are faithless, he remains faithful *to us*." For he has just said, "If we deny him, he will *deny* us." What God remains faithful to is explained in the next clause: "He remains faithful—for he cannot deny *himself*." God is faithful to himself. He is unwaveringly committed to uphold and display what is infinitely valuable, beautiful, and satisfying, namely, his own perfect and glorious being. This means that God acts in righteousness when his actions accord with his own infinite worth and beauty. If he acts in a way that diminishes his worth and beauty, his action is *unrighteous*. It is not *right*. It is not *true* to the ultimate standard of the universe, God himself.

HOW SHALL THE UNRIGHTEOUS APPEAL TO GOD IN HIS RIGHTEOUSNESS?

This understanding of God's righteousness is plain in the Old Testament as well. Consider Psalm 143. It begins:

> Hear my prayer, O LORD;
> give ear to my pleas for mercy!

---

[1] John Piper, *The Justification of God: An Exegetical and Theological Study of Romans 9:1–23* (Grand Rapids, MI: Baker Academic, 1993), chap. 6.

> In your faithfulness answer me, in your *righteousness*!
>
> Enter not into judgment with your servant,
>
> > for no one living is righteous before you. (Ps. 143:1–2)

This is puzzling at first. David is pleading for help and asks that God answer him "in [his] righteousness." But then he confesses that "no one living is righteous" before God. How can a person who is not righteous appeal for help to God on the basis of God's righteousness? The most typical way of answering this is to argue that in the Old Testament God's righteousness regularly refers to his faithfulness to Israel or to his covenant. In other words, David would be saying, in effect, "Answer me in your merciful, covenant-keeping faithfulness to me."

Although I agree that God's righteousness will, of course, prevent him from being a covenant breaker, I think it is wrong to *define* God's righteousness as covenant keeping. That is one of the things righteousness *does*, but not what God's righteousness most fundamentally *is*. God did not become righteous when the covenant came into being. Righteousness was the *foundation* of the covenant—indeed the foundation of his very reign as God (Ps. 89:14; 97:2). Therefore, it is more basic than covenant keeping. "You have kept your promise, *for* you are righteous" (Neh. 9:8).

How, then, are we to make sense of David's appeal to God's righteousness as a basis for his help, when he himself is unrighteous? The clue is found in verse 11. Notice the parallel between God's acting *for his name's sake* and his acting *in his righteousness*:

> *For your name's sake*, O LORD, preserve my life!
>
> > *In your righteousness* bring my soul out of trouble!
> >
> > > (Ps. 143:11)

In the mind of David, the foundational meaning of God's acting *in righteousness* is that he is acting *for his name's sake*. In other words, what is *right* for God is not to conform to a standard outside himself, but rather to treat his own name—his own nature or character or essence or worth or beauty—as the ultimate standard of his conduct.

So the reason David, who is not righteous, can appeal to God's righteousness as the basis for being helped is that the very mercy and pardon David needs is rooted most deeply not in God's allegiance to David or to his covenant, but in God's allegiance to his own name. This is why David can pray in Psalm 25:11, "*For your name's sake*, O Lord, pardon my guilt, for it is great." God's commitment to the worth of his name inclines him to help those who look away from themselves to the infinite worth of God as the foundation of their hope.

HOW THIS DIVINE RIGHTEOUSNESS APPEARS IN THE NEW TESTAMENT

The New Testament supplies the missing link in understanding how it is just for the unjust to appeal to justice for mercy. The understanding of God's justice in Psalm 143 is at the root of how we are forgiven in Christ. "I am writing to you, little children, because your sins are forgiven *for his name's sake*" (1 John 2:12). In other words, because of Christ's *name*—his infinitely valuable person and his flawless substitutionary work—we who believe in him are forgiven. This is why in 1 John 1:9 God is called faithful and *just* in forgiving us. "If we confess our sins, he is faithful *and just* to forgive us our sins and to cleanse us from all unrighteousness."

Paul confirms this by showing in Romans 3 that when Christ died for our sins, he vindicated the righteousness of God in passing over God-belittling sins (Rom. 3:23). How can God be righteous in upholding the beauty and worth of his own glory if he simply passes over sins which demean his glory? Paul's answer is that God does *not* simply pass over sins. He puts Christ forward to die for them, and thus shows that his glory is infinitely precious and his justification of sinners is just:

God put [Christ] forward as a propitiation by his blood, to be received by faith. This was *to show God's righteousness,* because in his divine forbearance *he had passed over former sins.* It was *to show his righteousness* at the present time, so that he might *be just* and the justifier of the one who has faith in Jesus. (Rom. 3:25–26)

The righteousness of God is vindicated by the death of Christ because it shows that God does not treat his name, his glory, as anything less than infinitely valuable and beautiful. It cost the life of his Son! Sin, which exchanges the glory of God for the glory of creation (Rom. 1:23), and thus belittles God's glory (Rom. 3:23), is not swept under the rug of the universe, as though it (and God's name) were insignificant. God's righteousness is upheld in the sacrifice of Christ, because the infinite value of his glory is upheld. For his righteousness is most fundamentally his unwavering allegiance to the worth and beauty of his perfect and glorious being.

RIGHTEOUS IN ALL HIS WORKS AND WAYS

With this understanding of righteousness, we may, therefore, say that all of God's works of providence over kings and nations are perfectly righteous. They are true to the highest standard in existence—namely, God himself. He cannot deny himself (2 Tim. 2:13). He cannot, and does not, act in ways that treat his name, his glory, as anything less than infinitely valuable and beautiful. This is the rock under our feet when all else seems shifting and uncertain. This is certain. God is righteous. And all his works are done in righteousness:

All his ways are justice. (Deut. 32:4)

The LORD is righteous; he loves righteous deeds. (Ps. 11:7)

The heavens declare his righteousness. (Ps. 50:6)

Righteousness and justice are the foundation of his throne. (Ps. 97:2)

He will judge the world with righteousness. (Ps. 98:9)

His righteousness endures forever. (Ps. 111:3)

Righteous are you, O Lord, and right are your rules. (Ps. 119:137)

The Lord is righteous in all his ways. (Ps. 145:17)

The Lord our God is righteous in all the works that he has done. (Dan. 9:14)

He will judge the world in righteousness by a man whom he has appointed. (Acts 17:31)

Is there unrighteousness on God's part? By no means! (Rom. 9:14, my translation)

Therefore, all God's works are right, and his ways are just.

8. God Aims That the World Know and Rejoice That He Rules in All These Ways (Dan. 4:17)

God put the king of Babylon through his humbling experience of becoming like a beast because he wanted him—and us—to *know* something and to *feel* something:

> Let his mind be changed from a man's, and let a beast's mind be given to him; and let seven periods of time pass over him . . . *to the end that the living may know* that the Most High rules the kingdom of men and gives it to whom he will and sets over it the lowliest of men. (Dan. 4:16–17)

God wants the world *to know* the scope of his providence—that it extends to the greatest and smallest kings and nations on earth. God is "the Most High [who] rules the kingdom of men" (Dan. 4:17)— from the greatest to the smallest. People need to know this. "Let seven periods of time pass over him . . . *to the end that the living may know.*" This is why God calls some people to write books on providence. God aims for the scope and nature of his providence to be *known*.

GOD'S AIM IN OUR KNOWING PROVIDENCE
IS OUR PLEASURE IN IT

I also infer from this story of Nebuchadnezzar's humbling that God is aiming at his and our *joy* in showing us his providence. I infer this because Nebuchadnezzar's experience ends with him *praising* the God of heaven:

> At the end of the days I, Nebuchadnezzar, lifted my eyes to heaven, and my reason returned to me, and *I blessed the Most High, and praised and honored him* who lives forever. . . . Now I, Nebuchadnezzar, *praise and extol and honor* the King of heaven. (Dan. 4:34, 37)

We know that authentic praise is a pleasing experience, not a displeasing experience. If we are displeased with the one we are praising and do not like to praise him, we are hypocrites—as when we give a standing ovation to a mediocre performance because everyone else is standing. Genuine praise is something we love to do, or we are not doing the real thing.

As we learned from C. S. Lewis in chapter 3, "We delight to praise what we enjoy because the praise not merely expresses but completes the enjoyment; it is its appointed consummation."[2] God did not take Nebuchadnezzar through his humbling experience to produce a sense of boredom or indifference concerning divine providence. He was transforming Nebuchadnezzar's affections as well as his convictions.

This is God's design for his people in all his works—that sooner or later, when we see them in relation to the totality of his redemptive work, we will rejoice in the wisdom and justice and goodness and love

---

2   C. S. Lewis, *Reflections on the Psalms* (New York: Harcourt, Brace & World, 1958), 93–95.

of his providence. "You, O LORD, have made me glad by your work; at the works of your hands I sing for joy" (Ps. 92:4). "The LORD has done great things for us; we are glad" (Ps. 126:3).

In Psalms 103 and 145, David pictures the works of the Lord as causing thanks to the Lord, and he calls those very works to bless the Lord. What is happening is the overflow of a heart thrilled with the works of God's providence:

> Bless the LORD, all his works,
>   in all places of his dominion.
> Bless the LORD, O my soul! (Ps. 103:22)

> All your works shall give thanks to you, O LORD,
>   and all your saints shall bless you! (Ps. 145:10)

The works of God are not reluctant to praise their maker. They are brimming with tributes to the God of providence. David is eager to join them. That is God's design for all his works. That is the goal of providence—the gladness of man in the glory of God, revealed in all his ways and works.

9. God Aims for Us to Know That When We Fail to Submit to and Rejoice in God's Kingship, We Are Acting Like Animals, Not Humans (Dan. 4:32–33; 5:21)

> "You [Nebuchadnezzar] shall be driven from among men, and your dwelling shall be with the beasts of the field. And you shall be made to eat grass like an ox, and seven periods of time shall pass over you, until you know that the Most High rules the kingdom of men and gives it to whom he will." Immediately the word was fulfilled against Nebuchadnezzar. He was driven from among men and ate grass like an ox, and his body was wet with the dew of heaven till his hair grew as long as eagles' feathers, and his nails were like birds' claws. (Dan. 4:32–33)

God's purpose in this humiliation of Nebuchadnezzar is not only that we "*know* that the Most High rules the kingdom of men," but also that we be shocked into wakeful reality—that not to know and rejoice in God's rule is to become like beasts. We are meant to see and feel how graphic and humiliating this was: he ate grass like an ox, his hair was like eagles' feathers, and his fingernails were like birds' claws.

These are graphic illustrations not of mere physical changes, but rather of something far more serious. Nebuchadnezzar's return from becoming beast-like was the recovery of his *reason*, not the cutting of his fingernails:

> At the end of the days I, Nebuchadnezzar, lifted my eyes to heaven, and my reason [מַנְדַּע, power of knowing] returned to me, and I blessed the Most High, and praised and honored him who lives forever. (Dan. 4:34)

The point of his humiliation is to help us not follow the same course. God is warning us not to become beast-like in failing to use our distinctively human powers to know God—particularly, in this case, to know the true meaning of the providence of God. This story is not just about providence and pride but also about providence and dehumanization.

SUICIDAL IRONY: FEELING SIGNIFICANT WITHOUT GOD

There is an irony that God aims to expose, namely, that self-exaltation is, in fact, dehumanization. God is adding to the all-important truth that self-exaltation dethrones God. He is revealing the additional truth that self-exaltation dehumanizes man. The irony is that human autonomy feels like we have gained significance, when in fact we have lost sanity. Freedom from God feels exhilarating. But it's the exhilaration of skydiving without a parachute. Apart from the Holy Spirit, all humans fall for this lie. The truth, over against this lie, is that the glory of man is not to *be* God but to *know* God. Nebuchadnezzar's humiliation is a graphic portrayal of this truth. Until you "*know* that the Most High rules the kingdom of men," you have lost your reason and become like a beast, not a human.

In the end, beastly men do not treat other humans well. I do not claim that those who have right ideas about providence always treat others the way they should. But I do claim that those who are not humbled by the providence of God, and who do not embrace their true God-exalting humanity, will never be able to pursue anyone's *eternal* good—their greatest good. God was not aiming only at Nebuchadnezzar's knowing, but at the fruit of knowing—humility, faith, wisdom, justice, and love. Knowing the infinite *sovereignty* of God, and the glory and graciousness of its *purposefulness* (which together are his providence), and being humbled in heart by this power, and satisfied in soul by this glory, and emboldened in love by this grace, is the highest dignity of human personhood.

GOOD NEWS FOR BELEAGUERED EXILES

Daniel is not the only biblical writer who wants us to see this. David says that when we turn away from the instruction and counsel of God, we become "like a horse or a mule, without understanding" (Ps. 32:8–9). Isaiah says that when we do not embrace God's truth, we are more foolish than the ox (Isa. 1:3). Jeremiah says that when we reject the ordinances of God, we have less sense than the stork and turtledove and crane (Jer. 8:7). Both Peter and Jude lament the presence of those who blaspheme what they don't understand "like unreasoning animals" (Jude 10; cf. 2 Pet. 2:12). And Paul warns the Philippians, "Look out for the dogs. . . . Their end is destruction, their god is their belly, and they glory in their shame, with minds set on earthly things" (Phil. 3:2, 19).

The humanizing truth that *Daniel* was most concerned about was the pervasive providence of God over kings and nations. This was probably because he and his band of Jewish exiles seemed utterly small and insignificant in the belly of pagan Babylon. But, in reality, it is the nations who are a drop in a bucket. To know that your covenant-keeping God rules the mightiest king on earth and makes him eat straw like an ox is essential to exile survival (then and now). It protects the believing exiles not only from desecrating God's name, but also from dehumanizing their own souls.

There have always been, and always will be, until Jesus returns, seasons of oppression and persecution of God's people. The great twin dangers will always be doubt and dehumanization. When humans are treated like animals by ruthless overlords—whether in Nero's Rome, or Nazi concentration camps, or the Middle Passage of Atlantic slave trading—the perpetrators are living as if God is not God and they are not human. The book of Daniel was written for believers in such oppressive conditions. And the God-exalting, soul-ennobling message is that God rules the overlords for the good of his people (Rom. 8:28, 36–37), and it is the Nebuchadnezzars of the world, not we, who have lost their reason and their humanity.

No Fabric without Threads

As we close this chapter, we would do well to step back and take note of something obvious but unmentioned. In order for God to remove kings and set up kings (Dan. 2:21), and to make nations great and destroy them (Job 12:23), he must orchestrate thousands upon thousands of human decisions, events of nature, and immeasurably vast webs of causes and effects. Don't be naïve and affirm the fabric of God's providence over kings and nations while doubting whether he holds all the threads and weaves with perfection.

Among those threads are the bright and dark colors of life and death. Who can measure or fathom the depth of the wisdom and the vastness of the dominion of one who holds in his hands the breath of every being? That is the measure of God's providence over life and death to which we now turn.

Providence over Life and Death

23

A Bath of Truth and the Gift of Birth

We are enveloped in a murky haze of misperceptions about life and death. This noxious mist is invisible and inescapable. It penetrates our minds and hearts. It is formed partly by Satan ("You will not surely die," Gen. 3:4), partly by sin ("Let us eat and drink, for tomorrow we die," 1 Cor. 15:32), and partly by culture ("We hold these truths to be self-evident, that all men . . . are endowed by their Creator with certain unalienable Rights, that among these are Life . . . ," Declaration of Independence). The assumptions that life primarily consists in this present vapor's breath of threescore and ten and that when the body dies, it's over, and that life belongs to us to do with as we please, make it hard for man to see life the way the Bible does. Chapters 23–25 will come as a profound shock to those who have not been delivered from the illusions of the world and set free into the bracing air of God's word.

Entering through a Bath of Bible Truth

Assuming that we are all coated with misleading mists where we walk in this world, perhaps it would be good for us to begin this chapter by simply diving into a purifying pool of biblical truth and splashing about for a few moments. Perhaps some of the real splendors of life might cut through the coating of folly that has formed over the years. Here's a small pond of biblical reality that would be a safe place to start bathing:

"O death, where is your victory? O death, where is your sting?" The sting of death is sin, and the power of sin is the law. But thanks be to God, who gives us the victory through our Lord Jesus Christ. (1 Cor. 15:55–57)

Since the children share in flesh and blood, [Christ] himself likewise partook of the same things, that through death he might destroy the one who has the power of death, that is, the devil, and deliver all those who through fear of death were subject to lifelong slavery. (Heb. 2:14–15)

You guide me with your counsel,
   and afterward you will receive me to glory.
Whom have I in heaven but you?
   And there is nothing on earth that I desire besides you.
My flesh and my heart may fail,
   but God is the strength of my heart and my portion forever.
      (Ps. 73:24–26)

Father, I desire that they also, whom you have given me, may be with me where I am, to see my glory that you have given me because you loved me before the foundation of the world. (John 17:24)

O God, . . . your steadfast love is better than life. (Ps. 63:1, 3)

To me . . . to die is gain. . . . My desire is to depart and be with Christ, for that is far better. (Phil. 1:21, 23)

We know that while we are at home in the body we are away from the Lord. . . . We would rather be away from the body and at home with the Lord. (2 Cor. 5:6, 8)

Do not fear those who kill the body but cannot kill the soul. (Matt. 10:28)

If the Spirit of him who raised Jesus from the dead dwells in you, he who raised Christ Jesus from the dead will also give life to your mortal bodies through his Spirit who dwells in you. (Rom. 8:11)

[He] will transform our lowly body to be like his glorious body, by the power that enables him even to subject all things to himself. (Phil. 3:21)

The creation itself will be set free from its bondage to corruption and obtain the freedom of the glory of the children of God. (Rom. 8:21)

In your presence [O Lord] there is fullness of joy;
    at your right hand are pleasures forevermore. (Ps. 16:11)

When we come up out of this pool of biblical truth, if the Spirit of God has caused it to penetrate our hearts, the sweetness that pierces will be at least sevenfold. Though death is real, (1) Christ has defeated it by his death and resurrection, so that (2) those who treasure him need not fear what kills the body, because (3) in that moment we will be with Christ, seeing his glory, savoring his love, feeling at home, until the day of his appearing, when (4) he will raise our bodies from the dead, and (5) give us a body like his glorious body, and (6) renew all creation as our eternal habitation, and (7) bring us to fullness of joy and pleasures forever in the radiance of his glorious presence. That is bracing reality.

Death's Ultimate Goal and Its Defeat

For all eternity, the redeemed will sing the praises of the glory of the grace of a death-experiencing, death-defeating sovereign. In one of his visions, the apostle John fell as though dead before this sovereign, who said to him:

Fear not, I am the first and the last, and the living one. I died, and behold I am alive forevermore, and I have the keys of Death and Hades. (Rev. 1:17–18)

This will be a great part of Christ's glory forever—that he died, that he lives, and that therefore the keys of eternal life and death are in his hands. We will sing of his death, and his triumph over death, forever. "They sang a new song, saying, 'Worthy are you . . . for you were slain, and by your blood you ransomed people'" (Rev. 5:9). Forever Jesus will be "crowned with glory and honor because of the suffering of death, so that by the grace of God he might taste death for everyone" (Heb. 2:9). The Father loves the Son with a special delight because he endured and defeated death: "For this reason the Father loves me, because I lay down my life that I may take it up again" (John 10:17). For this suffering and death for sinners, the Father "highly exalted him and bestowed on him the name that is above every name" (Phil. 2:9).

The glory of the Son of God is not that death broke in and snatched him and that he overcame the intruder. Death did not snatch him. It did not intrude upon his plans. He snatched death. Death served his plans. He destroyed death—not by escaping its intrusion upon his life, but by intruding himself into death's life and killing it from the inside and walking out victorious:

I lay down my life that I may take it up again. No one takes it from me, but I lay it down of my own accord. I have authority to lay it down, and I have authority to take it up again. (John 10:17–18)

Destroy this temple, and in three days I will raise it up. (John 2:19)

Christ walked into death of his own accord. And he walked out of his own accord. He chose when to die (Luke 13:32), and he chose when to rise (Mark 10:34). Death never had the upper hand. It only looked that way to the world (1 Cor. 2:8). This choice to die, as we showed more fully in chapter 12, was not made *after* sin and death entered the world through Adam's fall (Rom. 5:12); it was made "*before the foundation of the world.*" We know this, among other reasons, because there was a book in eternity past whose name was "the book of life of the Lamb *who was slain*" (Rev. 13:8). The plan that the Lamb of God be slain for sinners, and thus slay death, was not plan B, as if sin and death had nullified plan A. The praise of the glory of Christ, manifest supremely in dying and destroying death for his people, was the plan of the ages, and the purpose of all that has ever come to pass in the all-encompassing providence of God.

Death's Reality and Revulsion

Let us not lose sight of the end where this death-ruined, anguish-wracked, horror-stricken creation is moving. It is moving toward the fullness of the glorification of Christ. "All things were created through him and *for him*" (Col. 1:16). This end cannot fail, because Christ is already "the head of all rule and authority" (Col. 2:10). In the end, it will be manifest that the Father "put *all things under his feet* and gave him as head over all things to the church" (Eph. 1:22).

But in the meantime, we gain nothing, and lose much, by being naïve and oblivious about the terrors of death and suffering. I write this chapter with trembling, lest I make light of the ghastly experience of death for millions. To be sure, there are sweet and peaceful deaths as believers step into the arms of Jesus. I have seen them. I recall one old saint, in the nursing home a block from our house, who had been part of our church for decades. He was peacefully awake and conscious and communicating, and within five seconds was gone. It was astonishing and beautiful—and rare.

I also have seen the most seasoned and faithful saints suffer in ways I dread. One of the great old prayer warriors (as they used to be called) of our church named Ruth had horrible hallucinations of lewd figures dancing around her bed, as her tongue dried up in her mouth and turned almost black as she pleaded with me to pray that the Lord would take her. And there was the young mother of four who in her last half hour with cancer did not die peacefully, but was so wracked with pain that she convulsed with vomiting, and died in the smell and mess, as her young children waited in the next room for news. And there was the infant, born with his liver outside his body. Swaddled in a blanket, he looked perfectly normal. He lived about nine hours.

Those illustrations of the horrors of death took place under the best medical care, with as much palliative help as possible. Multiply those deaths a million times over every year, only in most cases with no medical relief, in the poorest places of earth. Unlike most of those deaths, the deaths of my friends were deaths in hope. They were believers. They had profound confidence in Christ, that they would see him face-to-face. The terrors were mainly of dying, not death. But for millions every year, this is not the case. Their suffering leads only to worse suffering forever (Matt. 25:46; Rev. 14:11). Only if we keep such appalling reality in mind will the matrix of misery in this world and the love of Christ who endured it for sinners become part of our wisdom, brokenness, healing, and courage.

God Made and Owns Every Soul

God is the original possessor of life. Therefore, life is a gift from God—both *spiritual* life by new birth and *natural* life by the creation of the soul. "As the Father has life in himself, so he has granted the Son also to have life in himself" (John 5:26). The Son gives this life to whom the Father chooses, as Jesus prays in John 17:2: "You have given him authority over all flesh, to give eternal life to all whom you have given him." Christ purchased the gift of life for believing sinners at the cost of his own life, which means our life belongs to him. "*You are not your own*, for you were bought with a price" (1 Cor. 6:19–20). "[He] gave himself for us . . . to purify for himself a people *for his own possession*" (Titus 2:14). "I have redeemed you; I have called you by name, *you are mine*" (Isa. 43:1).

Thus, believers in Jesus are doubly his. Because not only are we his by redeeming purchase but also, along with all mankind, by creation of the soul. Not only is spiritual life by new birth a divine gift, but so is natural life by the creation of each soul. One could argue (without biblical support) that our bodies come into being by physical processes alone, through the union of sperm and egg and cellular multiplication. But for those who embrace the teaching of Jesus—that we are a soul, not only a body (Matt. 10:28)—all talk of merely natural origins for each life misses the mark. If each human life is the life of a soul as well as a body, then each human life is created by God. Humans may act as participants in the making of a new body, but humans do not create the soul. God does.

The summons of the psalmist "Let us kneel before the LORD, *our Maker!*" (Ps. 95:6) is a call to acknowledge that our existence as individual persons is owing to God, not just man. "Your hands have made and fashioned me" (Ps. 119:73). "Know that the LORD, he is God! It is he who made us, and we are his" (Ps. 100:3). The psalmists see human life in its totality—body and soul—as a work of God and therefore a possession of God:

The earth is *the LORD's* and the fullness thereof,
   the world and *those who dwell therein.* (Ps. 24:1)

The world and its fullness *are mine.* (Ps. 50:12)

All the earth is *mine.* (Ex. 19:5)

Behold, *to the LORD your God belong* . . . the earth with *all that is in it.* (Deut. 10:14)

Whatever is under the whole heaven is *mine.* (Job 41:11)

You formed my inward parts;
   you knitted me together in my mother's womb.
I praise you, for I am fearfully and wonderfully made.

> Wonderful are your works;
>   my soul knows it very well. (Ps. 139:13–14)

Every Life Has Always Been a Gift of God

From the beginning of history, the Scripture portrays human offspring as a gift of God, not in general but individually. The portrait is not as if God merely designed procreation and let it run with no sustaining, no guiding, no plan for each child. God's involvement is much more personal and hands-on. He upholds (Heb. 1:3) and holds together (Col. 1:17) all things.

After Cain had killed Abel, Scripture tells us that "Adam knew his wife again, and she bore a son and called his name Seth, for she said, '*God has appointed for me another offspring* instead of Abel, for Cain killed him'" (Gen. 4:25). The word *appointed* is a common word for "putting" or "setting" or "establishing." The name Seth happens to be a wordplay on this verb because they are pronounced similarly. But the point is that God brought about (put, set, established, appointed) this child.

This is the way Eve announced her son Cain as well: "I have gotten a man with the help of the LORD" (Gen. 4:1). Literally it says, "I have gotten a man *with the LORD*." This does not mean that the Lord was the father, since the text had just said, "Now Adam knew Eve his wife, and she conceived and bore Cain." It means that the Lord was decisive in causing this conception and birth.

That is the way the Bible views all conception and birth. Each one of them is a gift of God. When Job lost his children, he bowed and worshiped God and said, "*The LORD gave*, and the LORD has taken away; blessed be the name of the LORD" (Job 1:21). And the inspired writer added, "In all this Job did not sin or charge God with wrong" (1:22). He was not wrong in *giving* them or in *taking* them. But it was indeed the Lord who *gave*. Neither Job, nor any other Old Testament believer, doubted that. Nor should we. "[God] gives the barren woman a home, making her the joyous mother of children" (Ps. 113:9). "Children are a heritage from the LORD, the fruit of the womb a reward" (Ps. 127:3).

Conception and Birth Are God's Work

Opening and closing the womb, giving and preventing (or taking) life, were seen as the infallible, efficacious prerogatives of God. "When Rachel saw that she bore Jacob no children, . . . she said to Jacob, 'Give me children, or I shall die!' Jacob's anger was kindled against Rachel, and he said, '*Am I in the place of God*, who has withheld from you the fruit of the womb?'" (Gen. 30:1–2). In other words, to open and close the womb—to grant and withhold conception—was to be "in the place of God." That was Jacob's view. He was not alone.

When Hannah bore no children to her husband, Elkanah, the inspired author of 1 Samuel said, "The LORD had closed her womb" (1 Sam. 1:5). This was not pictured as any kind of punishment. It was simply the reality: God governs conception. Therefore, Hannah cried out to the Lord that he would "give to your servant a son" (1 Sam. 1:11). In his mercy, "the LORD remembered her. And in due time Hannah conceived and bore a son" (1 Sam. 1:19–20). When Hannah offered up her prayer of worship and thanks, she ascribed absolute authority and power to God to give life and to take it:

> Those who were full have hired themselves out for bread,
>   but those who were hungry have ceased to hunger.
> The barren has borne seven,
>   but she who has many children is forlorn.
> *The LORD kills and brings to life*;
>   he brings down to Sheol and raises up. (1 Sam. 2:5–6)

Hannah is not exaggerating when she generalizes from her experience to the sweeping statement that "the LORD kills and brings to life." She is simply acknowledging, as Job and Jacob did, that this is what it means for God to be God. God's providence extends to this: life is in his hands.

What It Means for God to Be God

I say that God's sheer God-ness includes his effective authority and power to give life and to take it, not only because of the wording that we have seen ("The LORD gave, and the LORD has taken away"; "Am I in the place of God?"), but also because Moses uses wording that is even more set on forging this link between God's God-ness and his giving and taking life:

> See now that I, even I, am he,
>   and there is no god beside me;
> I kill and I make alive;
>   I wound and I heal;
> and there is none that can deliver out of my hand. (Deut. 32:39)

This is also the way the prophet Isaiah talks (41:4; 43:10, 13, 25; 48:12; 51:12) when he is reaching for verbal emphasis on God's unique being as God—his unique prerogatives. Isaiah and Moses agree: God is God. There is none besides him. No one can deliver from his hand. Therefore, it belongs to God, and God alone, to have absolute sway over life and death.

Joram, the king of Israel in the time of Elisha, responded like Jacob (Gen. 30:1–2) and revealed the same view of God's authority over life and death. Naaman, a commander in the army of Syria, was a leper. With the encouragement of a Jewish servant girl, he came to Israel, seeking healing. He approached King Joram with a letter from the king of Syria. When Joram read the letter, "he tore his clothes and said, '*Am I God, to kill and to make alive?*'" (2 Kings 5:7). In the king's mind, as in the minds of Hannah, Job, Jacob, and Moses, that is what it means to be God: life is in his hands. He gives and he takes. He opens the womb and he closes it. The idea that these were merely natural processes ungoverned by providence was not part of their God-permeated worldview.

When Paul was trying to make plain to the philosophers on the Areopagus the nature of the true God, he argued not only that "God . . . made the world and everything in it" (Acts 17:24), but also that this God, moment by moment, maintains his Creator role as utterly self-existent and self-sufficient. "[He is not] served by human hands, as though he needed anything, since he himself gives to all mankind life and breath and everything" (Acts 17:25). In Paul's view, this is what it meant for God to be God: totally self-sufficient, having all life in himself, and being the ultimate, decisive cause of all human life and breath.

Infallible Promises of Offspring

This is the reality behind the promises of God, which he makes over and over, that he will give offspring. No one else can make such promises. And the promises he makes, he himself fulfills. As when God said to Jacob, "I will not leave you until I have done what I have promised you" (Gen. 28:15). God's promises are not mere predictions of what fate may bring about. They are statements of what he himself intends to do. "The LORD will *do* this thing that he has *promised*" (Isa. 38:7). "The former things I declared of old; they went out from my mouth and I *announced* them; then suddenly I *did* them and they came to pass" (Isa. 48:3). "With his hand [the LORD] has fulfilled what he promised with his mouth" (2 Chron. 6:4). "I am watching over my word to perform it" (Jer. 1:12).

Therefore, when God says to Abraham, "I will make your offspring as the dust of the earth" (Gen. 13:16), and as numerous as the stars of heaven (Gen. 15:5), so that "they cannot be numbered" (Gen. 16:10), and even "nations and kings shall come from you" (Gen. 17:6), it did not matter that his wife Sarah had always been barren (Gen. 11:30), and that even now she was beyond childbearing age (Gen. 18:11).

It did not matter, because God is God, and he had spoken. So it came to pass:

> The LORD said, "I will surely return to you about this time next year, and Sarah your wife shall have a son." (Gen. 18:10)

> The LORD said to Abraham, ". . . Is anything too hard for the LORD?" (Gen. 18:13–14)

> The LORD visited Sarah as he had said, and the LORD did to Sarah as he had promised. And Sarah conceived and bore Abraham a son in his old age at the time of which God had spoken to him. (Gen. 21:1–2)

When the apostle Paul read this story, he saw to the bottom of it, namely, that God is God and nothing can stop him from giving life where he pleases, even if no human resources exist at all. "The God in whom [Abraham] believed . . . *gives life to the dead* and *calls into existence the things that do not exist*" (Rom. 4:17). And lest we think the Lord had simply found Sarah in this barren condition, Sarah has a deeper, truer view than that. The Lord did not *find* her barren. The Lord *made* her barren: "Sarai said to Abram, 'Behold now, the LORD has prevented me from bearing children'" (Gen. 16:2). She knew that the processes of nature are within God's providence. Conception and birth are in the hands of the Lord.

Wherever We Turn in Scripture, God Shuts and Opens the Womb

We could draw out this point in great detail in Scripture. But let it suffice just to mention briefly five more instances.

Isaac:

> Isaac prayed to the LORD for his wife, because she was barren. And the LORD granted his prayer, and Rebekah his wife conceived. (Gen. 25:21)

The Lord appeared to [Isaac] and said, ". . . I will multiply your offspring as the stars of heaven." (Gen. 26:2, 4)

Jacob:

Your offspring shall be like the dust of the earth. . . . For I will not leave you until I have done what I have promised you. (Gen. 28:14–15)

When the Lord saw that Leah was hated, he opened her womb, but Rachel was barren. (Gen. 29:31)

Then God remembered Rachel, and God listened to her and opened her womb. (Gen. 30:22)

I will bring forth offspring from Jacob, and from Judah possessors of my mountains. (Isa. 65:9)

Ruth:

Boaz took Ruth, and she became his wife. And he went in to her, and the Lord gave her conception, and she bore a son. (Ruth 4:13)

David:

Solomon said, ". . . You have kept for [David] this great and stead-fast love and have given him a son to sit on his throne this day." (1 Kings 3:6)

John the Baptist:

The angel said to him, "Do not be afraid, Zechariah, for your prayer has been heard, and your wife Elizabeth will bear you a son, and you shall call his name John." (Luke 1:13)

Elizabeth conceived, and for five months she kept herself hidden, saying, "Thus the Lord has done for me in the days when he looked on me, to take away my reproach among people." (Luke 1:24–25)

Her neighbors and relatives heard that the Lord had shown great mercy to her, and they rejoiced with her. (Luke 1:58)

No Birth Is Impossible with God

Most dramatically, the birth of Jesus illustrates the absolute sovereignty of God over the natural and supernatural realms in governing the process of birth. When the angel Gabriel announced to Mary that she would have a son without having sexual intercourse, Mary humbly said, "How will this be, since I am a virgin?" (Luke 1:34). Gabriel's answer was beyond amazing: "The Holy Spirit will come upon you, and the power of the Most High will overshadow you; therefore the child to be born will be called holy—the Son of God" (Luke 1:35).

Gabriel knew that this announcement pushed the boundaries of the believable. So he gave two helps to her faith. First, he pointed her to her relative Elizabeth, who "in her old age has also conceived a son, and this is the sixth month with her who was called barren" (Luke 1:36). Second, he directed her to the most sweeping biblical promise of God's all-governing providence: "Nothing will be impossible with God" (Luke 1:37).

God Decides When Life Comes and When It Departs

With a worldview rooted in the words "nothing will be impossible with God," neither the Old Testament saints, nor those in the New Testament, nor any of the biblical writers believed that life could or would ever come into being, or go out of the world, apart from the conception-governing, death-ruling providence of God. It was inconceivable. If God is God, life belongs to him. He created every soul; he holds all life in being moment by moment. He decides when it comes into being and when it ends:

> If he should set his heart to it
>   and gather to himself his spirit and his breath,

all flesh would perish together,
and man would return to dust. (Job 34:14–15)

Thus says God, the LORD,
who created the heavens and stretched them out,
who spread out the earth and what comes from it,
who gives breath to the people on it
and spirit to those who walk in it:
"I am the LORD . . ." (Isa. 42:5–6)

The Lord gives and the Lord takes away. Blessed be the name of the Lord (Job 1:21). That is what it means to be God, when life and death are at stake. And that is what it means to worship and to trust in his sovereign wisdom and goodness: "Blessed be the name of the Lord."

The Lord Has Taken Away; Blessed Be the Name of the Lord

In the previous chapter, we focused largely on the first half of Job's worshipful statement, "the Lord gave" (Job 1:21). We have seen that this providence is the cause of great joy, as millions of sons and daughters are "given." According to UNICEF, about 250 births happen every minute globally, about 350,000 per day, about 127 million a year. Though these births are usually accompanied with a mother's pain, it is not uncommon that "when she has delivered the baby, she no longer remembers the anguish, for joy that a human being has been born into the world" (John 16:21).

But we have also seen that the same providence that gives life also withholds that gift. God opens and shuts the womb (Gen. 16:2; 20:18; 30:2; 1 Sam. 1:5). When providence yields conception and birth and life, it is sweet. When providence yields infertility and miscarriage and stillbirth, it is bitter.[1]

---

1 For the working out of these terms in the book of Ruth, see John Piper, *A Sweet and Bitter Providence: Sex, Race, and the Sovereignty of God* (Wheaton, IL: Crossway, 2010).

Physical and Satanic Causes of Harm Are Real but Not Decisive

Of course, in speaking of *bitter* providence, as Naomi does when she has lost her homeland, her husband, and her two sons ("It is exceedingly *bitter* to me . . . that *the hand of the* LORD *has* gone out against me," Ruth 1:13), we are not denying other causes of such bitter losses, natural or demonic. But we *are* denying that physical and satanic causes thwart the wise and merciful purposes of providence. Physical and satanic causes of death are real. But they are not ultimate or decisive (see chapters 18–19).

When all ten of Job's children died, the wind that blew the house down was real physical wind (Job 1:19), and the stones that fell on them were real physical stones brought down with life-crushing, real physical gravity. And when Job's body was covered with sores (2:7), they were real physical sores with real physical worms crawling in them (7:5). Nature was highly active—as was Satan. The inspired writer of this story says that "*Satan* . . . struck Job with loathsome sores" (2:7). These physical and satanic causes were real. But they were not ultimate or decisive. They did not thwart the wise and merciful purposes of God's providence. We know this for four reasons from the text of the story itself.

1. Though he heard that the wind had taken his children, Job said, "*The* LORD *gave, and the* LORD *has taken away; blessed be the name of the* LORD" (1:21). And the inspired writer says, "In all this Job did not sin or charge God with wrong" (1:22).

2. When Job saw the sores on his body and heard his wife's challenge to curse God and die (2:9), Job gave counterchallenge: "Shall we receive good from God, and shall we not receive evil?" (2:10). And again the inspired writer assures us that this was not a sinful way of talking: "In all this Job did not sin with his lips" (2:10).

3. When Job is finally brought to repentance for some of his ill-advised criticism of God (41:6), he admits to God, "I know

that you can do all things, and that *no purpose of yours can be thwarted*" (42:2).

4. One last time, the inspired writer of the story gives his God-breathed (2 Tim. 3:16) interpretation of all these painful events in Job 42:11: "All his brothers and sisters . . . comforted [Job] for all *the evil that the LORD had brought upon him.*"

The point of lingering over Job's bitter experiences—which James says, in the end, show "the purpose of the Lord, how the Lord is compassionate and merciful" (James 5:11)—is to simply help us see (1) why it is biblical, and true to experience, to speak of bitter providences from the Lord, and (2) why treating the purpose of the Lord as ultimate and decisive does not nullify the reality or horror of natural and demonic causes.

Broadening Our Perspective on the Rights of God over All Life

We return now to our transition from our emphasis on God's providence in opening and closing the womb to God's providence over *all* life and death. God holds the same divine ownership of life, and prerogative over life, at the end of life on earth as at the beginning. The second half of Job's worshipful confession is just as true as the first half: "The LORD gave, and *the LORD has taken away*" (Job 1:21). Since God owns all life, as its Creator and sustainer (Ps. 24:1–2; Job 41:11; Acts 17:25), he may give it and take it at any time and in any way he pleases, as he acts in the fullness of his wisdom and goodness and justice.

When God asserts, "I kill and I make alive" (Deut. 32:39), he is not merely declaring his power. He is declaring his right. He is declaring how he acts in his total uniqueness as God—as always in perfect righteousness (Ps. 96:13; Isa. 5:16; Jer. 4:2; Acts 17:31; Rev. 19:11).

Is Life an Unalienable Right?

You may have wondered why I began the last chapter by citing the American Declaration of Independence. I cited it as an illustration of the way our culture forms the murky haze of misperceptions that engulfs our minds every day, unless we use the word of God to blow it away. "We hold these truths to be self-evident, that all men . . . are endowed by their Creator with certain unalienable Rights, that among these are Life . . ." Not many Americans pause to ponder whether this implies that we have an unalienable right to life in relation to God or only to man.

My sense is that there is a deep assumption in the hearts of most modern people that we have a right to life in relation to God. That is, he has no right to take our life. And, if he exists at all, he is obliged to do what he can to preserve our lives. Our life, most people feel, is ours. It does not belong to anyone else. And no one, not even God, has the right to take my life when I do not choose. I should be sovereign over my life. And if anyone takes my life, including God, he has done me wrong. That, I think, is the often unspoken form of our view of the "unalienable" right to life.

But that is not God's view. It is not the view of the Bible. To be sure, there is a human right to life *in relation to other humans*. No human has a right to take my life. But this right to life, which each of us has, is not a mere effect of genetic superiority to animals. It is owing to God's commandment and rooted in our relation to God as created in his image. God commanded, "You shall not murder" (Ex. 20:13). With that command, he endowed human beings with a right to life *in relation to other people*. That was the meaning, I suppose, of the Declaration of Independence: "*endowed by their Creator* with certain unalienable Rights . . ."

This command and endowment was rooted in our relation to God as created in his image. This is shown paradoxically by the fact that a human life may be taken from one who takes a human life:

> For your lifeblood I will require a reckoning. . . . From his fellow man I will require a reckoning for the life of man.

Whoever sheds the blood of man,
　　by man shall his blood be shed,
for God made man in his own image. (Gen. 9:5–6)

The creation of man in the image of God makes the taking of human life so serious that one who takes it will lose it. In other words, a just application of capital punishment reflects not the minimizing of life but the massive value of human life in the image of God. The right to life, in relation to other human beings, is so great and precious that it can be honored suitably only by taking that right from the one who takes it from another.

My point here is not a defense of capital punishment. There are many factors, biblically and experientially, that affect the justice of that punishment from case to case. My point here is that we should not confuse a right to life *in relation to other people* with a right to life *in relation to God.* In relation to people, God himself has established that right. In relation to himself, he has not. We have no right to life in relation to God. God has absolute rights over our lives. He gives and takes life according to the principle Jesus laid down in Matthew 20:15: "Am I not allowed to do what I choose with what belongs to me?"

We have seen that life does, in fact, belong to God. Not only does this follow from Job 41:11; Psalm 24:1; Acts 17:25; Ecclesiastes 12:7; Isaiah 57:16; and Zechariah 12:1, but also from Job 12:10:

In his hand is the life of every living thing
　　and the breath of all mankind.

So also Job 33:4:

The Spirit of God has made me,
　　and the breath of the Almighty gives me life.

Therefore, since life belongs to God, and we have it only as a stewardship to be used while he pleases for his glory, God may take it at any time and in any way he pleases, as he acts in the fullness of his wisdom and goodness and justice.

Christians' Strange Reaction to God's Authority over Death

Few truths have a greater effectiveness in cleansing our minds from the presumptuousness of thinking we own our lives than to read in Scripture of all the groups and individuals whose lives God took. It is astonishing to me how many people who claim to be Bible-believing Christians react angrily to the statement, no matter how carefully timed or caringly spoken, that deadly catastrophes are part of God's providence—that they are finally in the control of his wise and just and good and purposeful sovereignty. For example, on December 26, 2004, a massive tsunami killed over two hundred thousand people in Indonesia and India and neighboring countries. Not immediately, but several days later (timing is pastorally important), I wrote an article that contained this paragraph:

> God claims power over tsunamis in Job 38:8, 11 when he asks Job rhetorically, "Who shut in the sea with doors when it burst out from the womb . . . and said, 'Thus far shall you come, and no farther, and here shall your proud waves be stayed'?" Psalm 89:8–9 says, "O Lord . . . you rule the raging of the sea; when its waves rise, you still them." And Jesus himself has the same control today as he once did over the deadly threats of waves: "He . . . rebuked the wind and the raging waves, and they ceased, and there was a calm" (Luke 8:24). In other words, even if Satan caused the earthquake, God could have stopped the waves.[2]

Since God did not stop them, though he could have done it with a single word, he had reasons for not stopping them. He does not act

<hr/>

2   John Piper, "Tsunami, Sovereignty, and Mercy," Desiring God, December 29, 2004, https://www .desiringgod.org/articles/tsunami-sovereignty-and-mercy.

whimsically or randomly or aimlessly. If he permits, he has a purpose. This viewpoint elicited angry responses. In fact, my impression is that whenever there is a natural disaster causing human suffering and death, most Christians seem allergic to any claim that the Lord gave and now *the Lord has taken.* It is as though somewhere they were taught that God does not take human life. It is as though they have never read their Bible.

So let's take an overview of the biblical picture not just of God's *right* to take human life but of his *actual* taking of it.

All Life Taken in the Fall

First, there is the fall of all humanity in the sin of Adam and the entrance of death into the world, with the result that every human being is under the condemnation of death. "In Adam all die" (1 Cor. 15:22). God had warned Adam, "In the day that you eat of [the tree of the knowledge of good and evil] you shall surely die" (Gen. 2:17). The judgment of death fell on that terrible day of disobedience (Gen. 3), though the fullness of the sentence was delayed. But it has come relentlessly: "Because of one man's trespass, death reigned through that one man" (Rom. 5:17). It has reigned over old people and infants, rich and poor, men and women, every race and ethnicity. Whatever your position on whether babies who die go to heaven,[3] the biblical truth remains: all die in Adam, including infants.

Therefore, the biblical view of death is that every human being dies because of God's judgment on sin. Not only is that the picture of

---

3 My view is that infants who die do go to heaven. But this is my view not because of any sentimental notion that infants are not participants in Adam's original sin. In fact, I'm inclined to think Paul has infants in mind in Rom. 5:13–14 when he says, "Sin indeed was in the world before the law was given, but sin is not counted where there is no law. Yet death reigned from Adam to Moses, *even over those whose sinning was not like the transgression of Adam,* who was a type of the one who was to come." In Paul's view, sin is the cause of all infant mortality because it is part of human mortality. For my argument for how Scripture points to the rescue of infants from final judgment, see John Piper, "Why Do You Believe That Infants Who Die Go to Heaven?," January 30, 2008, Desiring God, https://www.desiringgod.org/interviews/why-do-you-believe-that-infants-who-die-go-to-heaven.

Genesis 2:17, but Paul uses judgment language, not naturalistic language. It is not as though death were a kind of disease that broke out from a virus. Paul said, "One trespass [Adam's] led to *condemnation* for all men" (Rom. 5:18). *Condemnation* is a legal term—a sentence delivered by a judge. It is not a consequence of nature; it is a rendering of the court of heaven—God's just decision.[4] This doctrine is theologically and historically so basic to Christianity that it is strange how many Christians today treat death as though it is utterly foreign to God's plan for the world.

Since the fall, death is not a surprise, and it is not merely an aspect of nature. It is God's judgment. One may say, as we often hear, that death was not the original design for humanity. That is true in the sense that when God created man as male and female, told them to multiply on the earth (Gen. 1:27–28), and pronounced the creation "very good" (Gen. 1:31), he did not mean that death was part of this goodness. But it is not wise or faithful to Scripture, in saying that death was not the original design, to imply that death intruded into creation against God's plan, and that God was compelled by some outside force to contend with this unwilled intruder. It was not unwilled by God. It was his judgment.

Of course, death is an enemy. "The last enemy to be destroyed is death" (1 Cor. 15:26). And, yes, it would eventually prove to be the desecration of the Son of God (Phil. 2:8). But let us beware of using one biblical truth to cancel out another. Rather, let us experience the renewal of our minds (Rom. 12:2) by holding together what God puts together. God brings the judgment of death onto all humanity, *and* he calls that judgment an enemy—both of man and of himself. Death is a judgment from the hand of God, *and* it is murder in the hand of

---

4   The best explanation I have read for how all of humanity is viewed by God as so united to Adam that his death sentence passes justly to them is found in Jonathan Edwards, *Original Sin*, ed. John E. Smith, vol. 3, *The Works of Jonathan Edwards* (New Haven, CT: Yale University Press, 1970).

Satan (John 8:44). God governs death as owner of life and judge of the world, *and*, under God, Satan "has the power of death" (Heb. 2:14). The shame of crucifixion swallowed up the Son of God (Matt. 12:40), *and* in that apparent defeat Christ was undeterred by shame (Heb. 12:2), abolished death (2 Tim. 1:10), and put the glory of God's grace on display in a way that would never have been possible if God had not subjected the whole creation to death and corruption and futility (Rom. 8:20–21).

All That Breathes Taken in the Flood

Next, let us remember and be appalled at the flood that God sent to bring death to the world of mankind. This too was a judgment because of the sinfulness of humanity:

> The LORD saw that the wickedness of man was great in the earth, and that every intention of the thoughts of his heart was only evil continually. And the LORD regretted[5] that he had made man on the

---

5 Sometimes this statement, and others like it, are used to argue that God did not foresee the sin that would enter the world when he created humanity. Why else, they say, would he *regret* something he did in the full awareness of what would happen? There are three responses that uphold the teaching of Scripture that God foreknows all things (Isa. 46:10; 41:26; 42:9): (1) There are indications in Scripture that before creation God did foresee that sin would enter the world (Eph. 1:4–7; 2 Tim. 1:9; Rev. 13:8; see chap. 13). (2) The word *regret* in English may carry implications that the Hebrew (נחם) did not. The Hebrew can mean "feel sorry" or "repent" or "change the mind" or "relent." Each of these carries a slightly different set of connotations. (3) Most importantly, in the story of God's "regretting" (or being sorry) that he had made Saul king, we are shown how to understand such statements. In 1 Sam. 15:11, God says, "I regret [same word as Gen. 6:6] that I have made Saul king, for he has turned back from following me and has not performed my commandments." But then, in verse 29, as if to clarify for us, Samuel says to Saul, "The Glory of Israel will not lie or have regret [same word], for he is not a man, that he should have regret." The point of this verse seems to be that, even though there is a sense in which God does regret or feel sorry about some of his own actions (v. 11), there is another sense in which he does not regret or feel sorry (v. 29). The difference, Samuel says, is that God "is not a man that he should have regret." In other words, his way of regretting in verse 11 is not the way a human would. The difference would most naturally be that God's regret happens in spite of perfect foreknowledge, while most human repentance happens because we lack foreknowledge. I conclude, therefore, that Gen. 6:6 does not call God's foreknowledge into question but shows the complexity of God's emotional life that is far above our ability to question or comprehend. Even in our own experience, there are

earth, and it grieved him to his heart. So the Lord said, "I will blot out man whom I have created from the face of the land, man and animals and creeping things and birds of the heavens, for I am sorry that I have made them." (Gen. 6:5–7)

The point I am making here does not depend on the flood being global or local, though it seems to me that the Scriptures treat the flood as global (Gen. 6:13, 17; 8:21; Heb. 11:7; 2 Pet. 2:5). The point here is simply that God took the life of thousands, perhaps millions, of people—men, women, and children:

I will blot out man whom I have created. (Gen. 6:7)

I have determined to make an end of all flesh. (Gen. 6:13)

I will bring a flood of waters upon the earth to destroy all flesh in which is the breath of life under heaven. (Gen. 6:17)

Everything on the dry land in whose nostrils was the breath of life died. He blotted out every living thing that was on the face of the ground, man and animals. . . . They were blotted out from the earth. Only Noah was left, and those who were with him in the ark. (Gen. 7:22–23)

This was a judgment on the human race (or at least a huge portion of it). It was so fierce and thorough that it defies imagination. Even the greatest hurricanes and tsunamis we have witnessed are small by comparison. Few events in the history of the world show more clearly God's rights over life and death. To underline the horror of it, God promises never to do it like this again:

---

times when we look back on difficult decisions we made and feel both sorrow at making them and yet approve making them. See a fuller wrestling with these things in John Piper, "God Does Not Repent Like a Man," Desiring God, November 11, 1998, https://www.desiringgod.org/articles /god-does-not-repent-like-a-man; and in John Piper, *The Pleasures of God: Meditations on God's Delight in Being God* (Colorado Springs, CO: Multnomah, 2012), 41–46.

I will never again curse the ground because of man, for the intention of man's heart is evil from his youth. Neither will I ever again strike down every living creature as I have done. (Gen. 8:21)

But even in the pledge never to repeat the flood, God takes direct accountability for its execution: "Neither will I ever again strike down every living creature *as I have done.*" God himself, he says, struck down "every living creature." This is not a mere matter of nature, nor is it an impersonal outworking of moral laws. It is God's judgment. From one person (the Judge) to other persons (every human). God struck down every living creature, except for the eight he saved by grace (1 Pet. 3:20).

Firstborn Taken in the Passover

Next, we call to mind the decisive judgment that God brought on Egypt just before he brought out his people through the Passover and the dividing of the Red Sea. God had already devastated the land of the Egyptians with various plagues.[6] But then God showed that he had absolute rights over life and death in Egypt. Even before Moses arrived in Egypt to tell Pharaoh that Israel is God's chosen people and should be enslaved no more, God told Moses to say to him:

Thus says the LORD, Israel is my firstborn son, and I say to you, "Let my son go that he may serve me." If you refuse to let him go, behold, *I will kill your firstborn son.* (Ex. 4:22–23)

That was a true statement. Only the actual judgment on Egypt was far worse. In Exodus 11:4–8 Moses delivers the final warning that if the Egyptian leaders do not let the people of Israel go, "every firstborn in the land of Egypt shall die" (v. 5). At this point, God establishes what came to be known as the Passover. God's angel of death would pass through the land, and wherever a household had put the blood of the

6   See chap. 6.

Passover lamb on the doorposts and the lintel of the house (12:7), no one would die.

> The blood shall be a sign for you, on the houses where you are. And when I see the blood, I will pass over you, and no plague will befall you to destroy you, when I strike the land of Egypt. (Ex. 12:13, cf. 12:23)

So it came. "At midnight *the LORD struck down all the firstborn* in the land of Egypt" (12:29). This was remembered through all the history of Israel as the night when "the LORD makes a distinction between Egypt and Israel" (Ex. 11:7). The lessons were stunning. The point of the blood of a lamb was presumably to show that there was sin in these blood-covered houses as there was in all the Egyptian houses. But the sin of these houses is covered by the sacrifice of a lamb. This means that the passing over of the sentence of death was not because Israel deserved better treatment than the Egyptians, but because of God's free grace (as we saw before in chapter 7).

Israel sang in its poetry about this judgment on Egypt:

> He *struck down all the firstborn* in their land,
>   the firstfruits of all their strength. (Ps. 105:36)

> Whatever the LORD pleases, he does,
>   in heaven and on earth,
>   in the seas and all deeps. . . .
> *He it was who struck down the firstborn of Egypt,*
>   both of man and of beast. (Ps. 135:6, 8)

The point I am making here is that the Lord "struck down the firstborn." Their death was not some natural outworking of the folly of sin (like smoking causing lung cancer or selfishness causing loneliness). It was God's judgment. And he was not only the Judge but also the executioner. "He struck down all the firstborn."

This shows with painful, graphic forcefulness that the life of all humans, including children, is in the hands of God to do with according to his wisdom. The firstborn who died may have been an adult. But many would have been children. Perhaps thousands. This was not because the firstborn were worse sinners than their parents. The firstborn of Pharaoh himself died (Ex. 12:29). If God were thinking only of who deserves most to die, Pharaoh himself would have been near the top of the list. God's judgment *on Pharaoh* was to take his firstborn son. It was a graphic rebuke: You withhold my son, Israel, from me. I will withhold your son from you (see Ex. 4:22–23).

God is free to perform graphic, symbolic judgments like this because the life of the firstborn belongs to him. He owns all life. The infants are not their own. They are God's. He brought them into being (Isa. 42:5; Acts 17:25). He holds them freely in being (Col. 1:17; Heb. 1:3). They have no independent or autonomous existence. When God takes them, he does not steal or murder. He takes back what is his own (Luke 12:20). And if there is any suffering that God thinks should be set right with joy, it will be rectified in the resurrection (Matt. 19:29; Luke 6:20–21; 14:14; 16:25).

Canaanite Nations Taken in the Conquest

Next, we focus on God's taking the life of Israel's enemies. There are examples of this throughout the history of Israel, but perhaps most dramatically during the conquest of the land of Canaan. God had said to Abraham hundreds of years earlier that his judgment on these peoples would be delayed because their sin had not reached the fullness that would provide a suitable public warrant for the destruction God would bring. "[Israel] shall come back here in the fourth generation, for the iniquity of the Amorites is not yet complete" (Gen. 15:16). When that time was complete, God said to Israel through Moses, "When my angel goes before you and brings you to the Amorites . . . and *I blot them out*, you shall not bow down to their gods nor serve them" (Ex. 23:23–24).

Though there will be many battles for Israel to fight, God makes clear well ahead of time that he is the one who "blots them out." He takes the life of the Amorites and the other peoples of the lands:

> The LORD said to Joshua, "Do not be afraid of them, for tomorrow at this time *I will give over all of them, slain*, to Israel." (Josh. 11:6)

> It was the LORD's doing to harden their hearts that they should come against Israel in battle, in order *that they should be devoted to destruction* and should receive no mercy but be destroyed, just as the LORD commanded Moses. (Josh. 11:20)

> Manasseh led them astray to do more evil than the nations had done whom *the LORD destroyed before the people of Israel*. (2 Kings 21:9)

> You shall consume all the peoples that *the LORD your God will give over to you*. Your eye shall not pity them, neither shall you serve their gods, for that would be a snare to you. (Deut. 7:16)

God warns Israel, and he warns us, not to think that his judgment on the nations was owing to Israel's superior righteousness:

> Do not say in your heart, after the LORD your God has thrust them out before you, "It is because of my righteousness that the LORD has brought me in to possess this land," whereas it is because of the wickedness of these nations that the LORD is driving them out before you . . . and that he may confirm the word that the LORD swore to your fathers, to Abraham, to Isaac, and to Jacob. Know, therefore, that the LORD your God is not giving you this good land to possess because of your righteousness, for you are a stubborn people. . . . From the day you came out of the land of Egypt until you came to this place, you have been rebellious against the LORD. (Deut. 9:4–7)

God judged the wickedness of the nations by "[giving] over all of them, *slain*" (Josh. 11:6). He took thousands of lives in battle. This is his prerogative as God—as Creator, sustainer, and judge. The Lord gives in birth, and the Lord takes away in battle. And his name is blessed.

185,000 Taken in One Night

Later in Israel's history, we are confronted with God's taking life in defense of his people and in the punishing of his people. For example, when Jerusalem was besieged, God struck a blow of staggering proportions. He struck down 185,000 Assyrian soldiers—not in battle but while they slept:

> "Thus says the Lord concerning the king of Assyria: . . . I will defend this city to save it, for my own sake and for the sake of my servant David." And that night the angel of the Lord went out and struck down 185,000 in the camp of the Assyrians. And when people arose early in the morning, behold, these were all dead bodies. (2 Kings 19:32, 34–35)

I say this was staggering not only because the number was huge and the directness of the Lord's dealings was dramatic, but also because we may surmise that in this one night God created perhaps one hundred thousand widows in Assyria and hundreds of thousands of fatherless children. These are not just numbers. They were real people with real families. This calls for great trust in the wisdom and justice and goodness of God. The same sovereignty that can kill 185,000 soldiers in one night can work a million circumstances of widows and fatherless children for their eternal good if they look away from the false gods of Assyria and from themselves to the God of Israel and call on him for mercy.

If we think that killing fathers and husbands is not the most effective way of winning the hearts of Assyrian wives and mothers, we should be very careful not to presume to know what justice and mercy call for in countless cases of which we are almost totally ignorant. God has sent the world more mercy than anyone knows (Acts 14:17; Rom. 2:4), and his severe summonses to repentance, like those described in Revelation 9:20 and 16:9, are not foolish. Recall that Rahab was saved by hearing about the destruction of Egypt (Josh. 2:8–10; Heb. 11:31; James 2:25 in chap. 6).

Countless Israelites Themselves Taken in Judgment

Perhaps the most appalling descriptions of God's taking life are not his destruction of Israel's enemies but the punishment of Israel herself, and Jerusalem in particular:

> Even if they bring up children,
>> I will bereave them till none is left. (Hos. 9:12)

> I sent among you a pestilence after the manner of Egypt;
>> I killed your young men with the sword. (Amos 4:10)

> If they go into captivity before their enemies,
>> there I will command the sword, and it shall kill them.
>>> (Amos 9:4)

> I will strike down the inhabitants of this city, both man and beast. (Jer. 21:6)

> You [O Lord] have wrapped yourself with anger and pursued us,
>> killing without pity. (Lam. 3:43)

> The Lord said to [the angel visitant], "Pass through the city, through Jerusalem, and put a mark on the foreheads of the men who sigh and groan over all the abominations that are committed in it." And to the others he said in my hearing, "Pass through the city after him, and strike. Your eye shall not spare, and you shall show no pity. Kill old men outright, young men and maidens, little children and women, but touch no one on whom is the mark. And begin at my sanctuary." So they began with the elders who were before the house. (Ezek. 9:4–6)

I will give their dead bodies for food to the birds of the air and to the beasts of the earth. . . . And I will make them eat the flesh of their sons and their daughters. (Jer. 19:7, 9; cf. Deut. 28:53)

You shall eat the flesh of your sons, and you shall eat the flesh of your daughters. (Lev. 26:29)

I will make them a horror to all the kingdoms of the earth, to be a reproach, a byword, a taunt, and a curse in all the places where I shall drive them. And I will send sword, famine, and pestilence upon them, until they shall be utterly destroyed from the land that I gave to them and their fathers. (Jer. 24:9–10; cf. Deut. 28:37; Jer. 15:4)

If you see that God's decisions to destroy life sometimes include using the sinful acts of man to accomplish his judgments, keep in mind that he has told us how to think about this. When he worked through the sinful acts of Joseph's brothers to accomplish his purposes for Israel in Egypt, the explanation he gave through the words of Joseph to his brothers was this: "As for you, you meant evil against me, but God meant it for good" (Gen. 50:20).

This is how we should think about all the instances in Scripture where God's purposes include the sinful actions of those who are accomplishing his good purposes (as when Pilate and Herod accomplished the infinitely horrible and precious death of Jesus, Acts 4:27–28). Sin remains sin. Judgment remains judgment. Humans remain morally accountable. And God remains righteous.

25

We Are Immortal till
Our Work Is Done

The previous chapter closed with a focus on God's judgments on Jerusalem and Israel. These are so horrifying that the question rises repeatedly: Why has the Lord done this? We will address that here and then personalize the issue, and then lay hold on the preciousness of the providence of God in life and death.

Why Such Judgments on Israel?

Concerning the reason for judgments on Israel, here are some of God's responses:

> Many nations will pass by this city, and every man will say to his neighbor, "Why has the LORD dealt thus with this great city?" And they will answer, "Because they have forsaken the covenant of the LORD their God and worshiped other gods and served them." (Jer. 22:8–9)

> When your people say, "Why has the LORD our God done all these things to us?" you shall say to them, "As you have forsaken me and served foreign gods in your land, so you shall serve foreigners in a land that is not yours." (Jer. 5:19)

All the nations will say, "Why has the LORD done thus to this land? What caused the heat of this great anger?" Then people will say, "It is because they abandoned the covenant of the LORD, the God of their fathers, which he made with them when he brought them out of the land of Egypt." (Deut. 29:24–25)

This house will become a heap of ruins. Everyone passing by it will be astonished and will hiss, and they will say, "Why has the LORD done thus to this land and to this house?" Then they will say, "Because they abandoned the LORD their God who brought their fathers out of the land of Egypt and laid hold on other gods and worshiped them and served them. Therefore the LORD has brought all this disaster on them." (1 Kings 9:8–9; cf. 2 Chron. 7:20–22)

The answer given is that *God regards faithfulness to him as more important than life.* Repeatedly, God shows that forsaking him is to forfeit life. This is a radical God-centeredness that is intellectually and emotionally foreign, it seems, to much of the contemporary Christian church. The instincts of many of today's preachers and churchgoers seem to go in the other direction: to treat life on earth as the great central value and the honor of God as subservient to that. If God does not serve our comforts here, then he is unworthy. This is a great sorrow and weakness in the church—and in her mission.

One by One, Taken by the Hand of God

Since most of us experience the sorrows of death not because of statistics of wars or pestilence but because of the loss of individuals we love, we should give serious consideration to the fact that God takes the lives of individuals. It would be a mistake to think that God's providence over life and death comes into exercise only in battles and great judgments of multitudes. No. Every death, as with every life, is in God's hands. As James says, "If the Lord wills, we will live" (James 4:15).

Therefore, the Scriptures awaken us to this fact again and again with specific stories where this universal fact is made explicit in individual lives. I will simply mention a few. It is sobering and steadying to hear the very words of inspired Scripture declare God's actual taking of individual lives.

Er, Judah's son:

> Er, Judah's firstborn, was wicked in the sight of the LORD, and the LORD put him to death. (Gen. 38:7)

Eli's sons:

> They would not listen to the voice of their father, for it was the will of the LORD to put them to death. (1 Sam. 2:25)

King Saul:

> Saul died for his breach of faith. . . . The LORD put him to death. (1 Chron. 10:13–14)

Nabal, Abigail's foolish husband:

> The LORD struck Nabal, and he died. (1 Sam. 25:38)

Uzzah, who put out his hand to touch the ark:

> The anger of the LORD was kindled against Uzzah, and God struck him down there because of his error. (2 Sam. 6:7)

King Jeroboam and his house:

> Jeroboam did not recover his power in the days of Abijah. And the LORD struck him down, and he died. (2 Chron. 13:20)

Sennacherib, king of Assyria:

> Thus says the LORD: . . . "I will make him fall by the sword in his own land." . . . Then Sennacherib king of Assyria departed and went

home and lived at Nineveh. And as he was worshiping in the house
of Nisroch his god, Adrammelech and Sharezer, his sons, struck him
down with the sword. (2 Kings 19:6–7, 36–37)

Ananias and Sapphira:

> Peter said, ". . . Why is it that you have contrived this deed in your
> heart? You have not lied to man but to God." When Ananias heard
> these words, he fell down and breathed his last. (Acts 5:3–5)

> Peter said to her, "How is it that you have agreed together to test
> the Spirit of the Lord? Behold, the feet of those who have buried
> your husband are at the door, and they will carry you out." Imme-
> diately she fell down at his feet and breathed her last. (Acts 5:9–10;
> cf. 1 Cor. 11:30)

Herod, who did not give glory to God:

> Immediately an angel of the Lord struck him down, because he did
> not give God the glory, and he was eaten by worms and breathed
> his last. (Acts 12:23)

Better Taken by God than by Satan or Fate

Whether we consider all breathing creatures perishing in the flood, or
all the firstborn of Egypt dying in the Passover, or an army of 185,000
perishing in a single night, or nations of Canaan slain under the ban of
God's condemnation, or the starving people of Jerusalem under siege,
or the ten children of Job crushed in a windstorm, or the return of
all breath to God, the biblical truth is the same: God is the author of
every life (Isa. 57:16; Zech. 12:1), the agent of every deliverance from
death (Ps. 68:20), the one who decides the length of every lifetime
(Ps. 139:16) and the moment of every death (Job 1:21). In one final act
of absolute authority over life and death, he will, in the last day, raise
every life from the dead—"both the just and the unjust" (Acts 24:15)—

and assign the eternal destiny of each: "some to everlasting life, and some to shame and everlasting contempt" (Dan. 12:2; cf. John 5:28–29).

Let me ask you, my reader: in whose power would you want your life and death to lie? In whose hands would you prefer the destiny of your loved ones to rest? Would you want the length of your life and theirs to be in the hands of Satan? Or in the hands of aimless fate? Or in the hands of mindless and haphazard natural forces? Surely not. Nor are they! Every breath is in the hands of God (Job 12:10; Isa. 42:5; Dan. 5:23; Acts 17:25).

In Whose Hands Would You Have Your Martyrdom?

God's rule of every life is not bad news. It is glorious news, for in Christ Jesus nothing befalls us but what is good for us (Rom. 8:28–32). Even in death we are "more than conquerors" (Rom. 8:35–39). As history draws to a close, and seasons of mounting death sweep the globe (Rev. 6:4, 8), and God allows the saints to be conquered (Rev. 13:7), and the great powers of earth become drunk with the blood of the saints (Rev. 17:6), what will your confidence be? Not that God will spare your life. He has made no such promise. "We are being killed all the day long" (Rom. 8:36). No. Our confidence will be that God, in perfect wisdom and mercy and goodness, will appoint for us the death with which we will glorify God.

That is the gift Jesus gave to Peter as a parting encouragement:

> "When you are old, you will stretch out your hands, and another will dress you and carry you where you do not want to go." (This he said *to show by what kind of death he was to glorify God*.) And after saying this he said to him, "Follow me." (John 21:18–19)

Peter's death was planned and appointed. It was not finally and decisively in Satan's hands, in the hands of Roman authorities, or in the hands of fate. It was in God's hands. So is yours. If you are to be a martyr for Christ, who would you want to be in charge in those last days? John left us in no doubt who would be in charge, because he said that God had already planned who, and how many, would perish as martyrs before the end comes:

> [The martyrs under the altar in heaven] cried out with a loud voice, "O Sovereign Lord, holy and true, how long before you will judge and avenge our blood on those who dwell on the earth?" Then they were each given a white robe and told to rest a little longer, *until the number of their fellow servants and their brothers should be complete, who were to be killed as they themselves had been.* (Rev. 6:10–11)

Such merciful providence over life and death is the rock of stability in the unpredictable upheaval of every generation. Unless Jesus comes back first, we all will die. For those who belong to him, the timing and outcome of that death is mercy, not wrath.

Immortal till My Work Is Done

That kind of rock-solid confidence in the face of death has emboldened missionaries for two thousand years. The truth of God's providence has been the stabilizing power for thousands of Christ's emissaries. Believing that God holds life and death and always works mercy for his children has freed them to embrace the dangers of the mission and has sustained them when death came.

Henry Martyn, missionary to India and Persia, who died when he was thirty-one (on October 16, 1812), wrote in his journal in January 1812:

> To all appearance, the present year will be more perilous than any I have seen; but if I live to complete the Persian New Testament, my life after that will be of less importance. But whether life or death be mine, may Christ be magnified in me! If he has work for me to do, I cannot die.[1]

---

1 Henry Martyn, *Journal and Letters of Henry Martyn* (New York: Protestant and Episcopal for the Promotion of Evangelical Knowledge, 1851), 460.

This has often been paraphrased as "I am immortal till Christ's work for me to do is done." This is profoundly true. And it rests squarely on Martyn's confidence that life and death are in the hands of a sovereign God. Indeed, the entire cause of Christ is in his hand. Seven years earlier, at twenty-four, Martyn had written:

> What a world this would be, if there were no God! Were God not the sovereign of the universe, how miserable I should be! But the Lord reigneth, let the earth be glad. And Christ's cause shall prevail. O my soul, be happy in the prospect.[2]

Sovereign Bullet

Sometimes the greatest challenge to our faith in pursuing Christ's mission is not the question of the final outcome, or even the possibility of our own death, but rather the death of our family members. Again, thousands of faithful servants have been sustained by the certainty that God's merciful providence governs the life and death of loved ones.

One of the most striking, and well publicized, examples of this in the last twenty years is the case of the shooting down of a missionary plane and the killing of a young mother and her baby. On April 20, 2001, the Peruvian Air Force mistook the missionary plane for a drug plane and opened fire. Missionary Veronica Bowers, age thirty-five, was holding her seven-month-old daughter, Charity, in her lap behind pilot Kevin Donaldson. With them were Veronica's husband, Jim, and six-year-old son, Cory. The pilot's legs were shot. He put the plane into an emergency dive and, amazingly, crash landed it on a river where it sank just as they all got out. One bullet had passed by Jim's head and made a hole in the windshield. Another bullet passed through Veronica's back and stopped inside her baby, killing them both.

---

2 Martyn, *Journal and Letters of Henry Martyn*, 210.

What does a young husband do when this happens? What does he believe and say? There are many Christians ready to tell him not to embrace the purposeful and merciful providence of God. One popular writer would counsel him:

> When an individual inflicts pain on another individual, [one should not] go looking for "the purpose of God" in the event. . . . Christians frequently speak of "the purpose of God" in the midst of tragedy caused by someone else. . . . But this I regard to simply be a piously confused way of thinking.[3]

In other words, God had no particular purpose for the taking of Veronica and Charity Bowers and the leaving of Jim and Cory. And all the words of Elisabeth Elliot and Steve Saint and Jim Bowers at the memorial service for Veronica and the baby were a "piously confused way of thinking," and no true ground for comfort and strength?

One of the points of this book—and chapters 23–25 in particular—is to say, no, what we are about to hear is not confused. It is biblical. It is the rock of hope when waves of sorrow are crashing against you. The memorial service was held at Calvary Church in Fruitport, Michigan, on April 29, 2001. Let's look at the testimony of this young husband, who lost his wife and daughter, as he spoke to the twelve hundred people gathered for the service, with his six-year-old son, Cory, sitting at the front.[4]

> Most of all I want to thank my God. He's a sovereign God. I'm finding that out more now. . . . Could this really be God's plan for Roni and Charity; God's plan for Cory and me and our family? I'd like to tell you why I believe so, why I'm coming to believe so.

3 Greg Boyd, *Letters from a Skeptic* (Colorado Springs, CO: Chariot Victor, 1994), 46–47.
4 All the quotes from the memorial service were taken from a full transcript of the memorial service on May 12, 2001, http://www.abwe.org/family/memorials/service_michigan.htm. The transcript has since been removed.

Then he gave a long list of unlikely events in and after the shooting, and refers to God's sending his Son to the cross. Here are some of the key sentences that only those who trust in God's sovereign care for his own can truly understand. He said:

> Roni and Charity were instantly killed by the same bullet. (Would you say that's a stray bullet?) And it didn't reach Kevin [the pilot] who was right in front of Charity; it stayed in Charity. That was a sovereign bullet.

He spoke of his forgiveness to those who shot at the plane. "How could I not," he said, "when God has forgiven me so?" Then he adds:

> Those people who did that, simply were used by God. Whether you want to believe it or not, I believe it. They were used by Him, by God, to accomplish His purpose in this, maybe similar to the Roman soldiers whom God used to put Christ on the cross.

Words for the Child and a Poem from Elisabeth Elliot

Steve Saint and Elisabeth Elliot both spoke at the memorial service. Steve is the son of Nate Saint, who was speared to death by the Huaorani Indians in Ecuador on January 8, 1956, along with Ed McCully, Peter Fleming, Roger Youderian, and Jim Elliot. Elisabeth Elliot was Jim's wife.

Steve Saint came to the microphone and looked down at Cory, the six-year-old boy, whose mother and sister had been killed. He said:

> Cory, my name is Steve. You know what? A long time ago when I was just about your size, I was in a meeting just like this. I was sitting down there and I really didn't know completely what was going on. . . . But you know, now I understand it better. A lot of adults used a word then that I didn't understand. They used a word that's called tragedy. . . . But you know, now I'm kind of an old guy, and now when people come to me and they say, "Oh I remember when that tragedy happened so long ago," I know, Cory, that they were wrong.

You see, my dad, who was a pilot like the man you probably call Uncle Kevin, and four of his really good friends had just been buried out in the jungles, and my mom told me that my dad was never coming home again. My mom wasn't really sad. So, I asked her, "Where did my dad go?" And she said, "He went to live with Jesus." And you know, that's where my mom and dad had told me that we all wanted to go and live. Well, I thought, isn't that great that Daddy got to go sooner than the rest of us? And you know what? Now when people say, "That was a tragedy," I know they were wrong.

Then he looked up at the people and told them the difference between the unbelieving world and the followers of Jesus. He said, "For them, the pain is fundamental and the joy is superficial because it won't last. For us, the pain is superficial and the joy is fundamental."

What would Elisabeth Elliot say to the family? She had already lifted her flag for the all-governing providence of God in the death of her husband and the other four missionaries. In her book *Shadow of the Almighty*, published in 1958, she had said that the world could see these deaths only as a tragedy. But she protested, "The world did not recognize the truth of the second clause in Jim Elliot's credo":

He is no fool who gives what he cannot keep to gain what he cannot lose.[5]

Now what would she say?

You wonder what God is doing, and of course, we know that God never makes mistakes. He knows exactly what He is doing, and suffering is never for nothing. . . . He has given to you, Jim, the cup of suffering, and you can share that with the Lord Jesus who said, "The cup the Father has given to me, I have received."

5   Elisabeth Elliot, *Shadow of the Almighty: The Life and Testament of Jim Elliot* (New York: Harper & Brothers, 1958), 19.

She ended with a poem by Martha Snell Nicholson, whose last couplet is pure gold:

I stood a mendicant of God before His royal throne
And begged him for one priceless gift, which I could call my own.

I took the gift from out His hand, but as I would depart
I cried, "But Lord this is a thorn and it has pierced my heart."

This is a strange, a hurtful gift, which Thou hast given me.
He said, "My child, I give good gifts, and gave My best to thee."

I took it home and though at first the cruel thorn hurt sore,
As long years passed I learned at last to love it more and more.

I learned He never gives a thorn without this added grace,
He takes the thorn to pin aside the veil which hides His face.

In the end, this is the final mercy of God's painful providences: "to pin aside the veil which hides" the face of Christ. God always means for us to know him and treasure him more deeply through the losses in our lives. The confidence that there is no condemnation for his children and the confidence that there are no maverick bullets from a jet fighter give us the courage to embrace God's calling, no matter how dangerous.

God has not destined us for wrath, but to obtain salvation through our Lord Jesus Christ, who died for us so that *whether we are awake or asleep* we might live with him. Therefore encourage one another and build one another up, just as you are doing. (1 Thess. 5:9–11)

Indeed, let us encourage each other with the glorious truth that life and death, now and forever, are in the hands of God. His merciful, all-encompassing providence is our strength while we live and our hope when we die. Blessed be the name of the Lord (Job 1:21).

Providence over Sin

26

Natural Human Willing and Acting

In the preceding chapters of this book, we have seen so many instances of God's governing the details of nature's events, Satan's action, the deeds of kings, the movements of nations, and the moments of life and death that we are led naturally to think of God's providence as all-encompassing—all-pervasive. In other words, after seeing the extent and nature of God's providence portrayed in chapters 16–25, our expectation is that there is no sphere of life—no matter how ordinary or seemingly insignificant—where providence is suspended or limited in its ultimate and decisive dominion.

In this chapter we will find this expectation confirmed as we focus on natural human willing and doing. By the word *natural*, I am distinguishing ordinary human inclinations and preferences and decisions from those that Christians experience under the influence of the Holy Spirit. Paul calls persons outside Christ "natural" persons. "The natural person does not accept the things of the Spirit of God" (1 Cor. 2:14). In one sense, natural people are capable of good decisions and good deeds, as such deeds are beneficial to others in earthly ways (1 Pet. 2:14). But in another sense, unbelievers are acting in rebellion against God at all times and therefore are sinning in all they do. "For whatever does not proceed from faith is sin" (Rom. 14:23). This is why I include this chapter in part 3, section 6, "Providence over Sin." Toward the end of the chapter, we will turn briefly to God's providence over the countless circumstances that hinder that willing and doing, or give it success.

God Turned Pharaoh's Heart to Bless Joseph

From the earliest days of Israel's national history in Egypt to the final days of captivity in Babylon, God showed his power and willingness to turn the hearts and minds of ordinary individuals and kings, and even whole nations, so that they were willing to treat Israel with beneficence, even when they were adversaries. When Joseph was sold into slavery in Egypt, the favor that he found in the eyes of his master, Potiphar (Gen. 39:3–4), and then in the sight of the jailer after he had been put in prison, was not a mere outcome of social forces or human nature. It was a work of God upon the hearts and minds of Joseph's captors:

> The LORD was with Joseph and showed him steadfast love and *gave him favor in the sight of the keeper of the prison.* And the keeper of the prison put Joseph in charge of all the prisoners who were in the prison. Whatever was done there, he was the one who did it. (Gen. 39:21–22)

This "favor" that God gave to Joseph was a disposition in the heart and mind of the jailer (as it was in Potiphar's) to treat Joseph well. This means that God acted on the mind and heart—the will—of the jailer (we are not told how) so that he had an inclination to treat Joseph this way. The effect was astonishing. We are meant to feel the wonder of this. The jailer put all the prisoners in the charge of a prisoner! And everything that happened in the prison was in the charge of Joseph. The picture of this incredible trust is designed to make us feel how thoroughly God is able to govern the hearts and minds of his people's adversaries. The focus is not on Joseph's winsome personality, but on

God: "The LORD . . . gave him favor in the sight of the keeper of the prison" (39:21).

The same amazing influence is seen in God's providence over Pharaoh's disposition toward Joseph. The jailer put Joseph in charge of the whole *prison*. Pharaoh put Joseph in charge of the whole *nation*. The description of Pharaoh's lavish trust in Joseph, whom he scarcely knew, is meant to take our breath away and cause us to wonder why:

> "You shall be over my house, and all my people shall order themselves as you command. Only as regards the throne will I be greater than you. . . . See, I have set you over all the land of Egypt." Then Pharaoh took his signet ring from his hand and put it on Joseph's hand, and clothed him in garments of fine linen and put a gold chain about his neck. And he made him ride in his second chariot. And they called out before him, "Bow the knee!" Thus he set him over all the land of Egypt. Moreover, Pharaoh said to Joseph, "I am Pharaoh, and without your consent no one shall lift up hand or foot in all the land of Egypt." (Gen. 41:40–44)

This is an incredible cluster of choices made by one of the most powerful people in the world toward a man who days before had been a foreign slave and imprisoned criminal. From the Egyptian standpoint, Pharaoh's behavior seemed reckless. What accounted for it? Stephen's answer in Acts 7:9–10 was that God had turned Pharaoh's will to act this way:

> God was with [Joseph] and rescued him out of all his afflictions and *gave him favor* and wisdom before Pharaoh, king of Egypt, who made him ruler over Egypt and over all his household.

God *gave* Joseph favor with Pharaoh. Pharaoh *decided* to treat Joseph with such trust because God *inclined Pharaoh's heart* to that decision. This was what Joseph's brothers eventually reported back to their father. The upshot was that when Jacob decided to send them back with his youngest son, Benjamin, he knew God had the power and the right to incline Pharaoh's heart again, the way he did toward Joseph, only this time toward his other sons: "May God Almighty grant you mercy before the man" (Gen. 43:14). In other words, Jacob was praying that God would put in Pharaoh's heart an effective resolve to treat his sons with mercy. Or, to say it another way, he was praying that God would *give* the brothers *favor* with Pharaoh. Jacob believed God had the right and the power to do this—to turn the will of Pharaoh.

God Turned the Hearts of Egyptians to Favor the Israelites

The same prerogative and power of God to incline the hearts of the Egyptians became evident not only when Israel arrived in Egypt in the time of Joseph, but also as they were leaving in the time of Moses. God's purpose was that the Israelites, as they left Egypt in the exodus, would plunder the Egyptians as part of God's judgment for their hardness of heart (Ex. 14:4). So before Moses even arrived in Egypt, God said to him:

> *I will give this people favor in the sight of the Egyptians*; and when you go, you shall not go empty, but each woman shall ask of her neighbor, and any woman who lives in her house, for silver and gold jewelry, and for clothing. You shall put them on your sons and on your daughters. So you shall plunder the Egyptians. (Ex. 3:21–22)

And so it came to pass, as God had said:

> The people of Israel . . . asked the Egyptians for silver and gold jewelry and for clothing. And *the LORD had given the people favor in the sight of the Egyptians*, so that they let them have what they asked. Thus they plundered the Egyptians. (Ex. 12:35–36)

God *gave* Israel favor in the hearts of the Egyptians. He inclined the hearts of their overlords to treat them favorably. Remember, every firstborn among the Egyptians had just died, while none of the Jewish sons had died. It is not readily obvious that giving silver and gold and jewelry and clothing to the Israelites, who seemed responsible for such a catastrophe, would be the natural response.

One can easily imagine fury and retaliation in a popular uprising against Israel. It didn't happen. The reason given by the Scripture for why it didn't happen is that "the LORD had given the people favor in the sight of the Egyptians" (Ex. 12:36). In other words, God turned the hearts of the Egyptians to favor Israel rather than fight them. So "the Egyptians were urgent with the people to send them out of the land in haste" (Ex. 12:33).

So with Many Nations and the Hearts of Daniel's Masters

The same picture is painted at the end of Old Testament history as Israel finds itself in exile in Babylon. Before this decisive captivity, there had been other defeats and foreign dominations along the way. During some of these, God did for Israel what he did for Joseph and his brothers in Egypt:

> He gave them into the hand of the nations,
> so that those who hated them ruled over them. . . .
> *He caused them to be pitied*
> *by all those who held them captive.* (Ps. 106:41, 46)

God's providence over the hearts and minds of Israel's enemies turned their hearts to pity rather than to destruction. He did the same for Daniel as a captive in Babylon: "God gave Daniel favor and compassion [same word as *pity* in Ps. 106:46 in Hebrew] in the sight of the chief of the eunuchs" (Dan. 1:9). Then in an amazing parallel with Pharaoh and Joseph in Egypt, Nebuchadnezzar responded to Daniel the same way that Pharaoh responded to Joseph:

> King Nebuchadnezzar fell upon his face and paid homage to Daniel,
> and commanded that an offering and incense be offered up to him.
> . . . Then the king gave Daniel high honors and many great gifts,

and made him ruler over the whole province of Babylon and chief
prefect over all the wise men of Babylon. (Dan. 2:46, 48)

Again, this is meant to take our breath away. A young Jewish captive,
who just a few weeks earlier was nothing more than a foreign exile
from an enemy state, now made "ruler over the whole province of
Babylon"! Unthinkable! How could such a thing happen? Though it
is not said explicitly that God gave favor to Daniel with King Nebuchadnezzar, it does say that God gave Daniel favor with his immediate
superior (Dan. 1:9), who brought him to the king; and the parallel
with Pharaoh's response to Joseph is remarkable. The design of Scripture is that we discern the hand of God when we have been given such
clues. Daniel rose to great authority in Babylon because *God* gave him
favor. God turned the heart of the king.

God Turns Animosity to Peace

Besides such specific illustrations as Joseph, Moses, and Daniel, Scripture gives us general statements of God's providence over the hearts
of our enemies:

> When a man's ways please the LORD,
>   he makes even his enemies to be at peace with him.
>   (Prov. 16:7)

The author of this proverb does not intend for us to infer that righteous people never have long-term enemies (Ps. 44:22; Prov. 25:26;
John 15:20; Rom. 8:36). His point is that God does this sort of thing
for those who please him. He can do it. And he will do it if it would
bring the greatest good for his people. The point here is that this lies
in God's prerogative and power. He can and will turn the hearts of our
adversaries from animosity to peace when he pleases. The disposition
of the heart and the behavior of the mouth and hand are in the sway
of God's providence.

God Turns Hearts to Dread and Panic and Confusion

This is true not only in regard to creating *favor* in the hearts of Israel's adversaries, but also in regard to creating *dread* and *panic*. As Israel prepared to advance on the trans-Jordan and then Canaan, God promised, "This day *I will begin to put the dread and fear of you on the peoples* who are under the whole heaven" (Deut. 2:25). And so it came to pass. For example, as Joshua approached the Amorites: "*The Lord threw them into a panic* before Israel" (Josh. 10:10). Later, in the case of Gideon's preparations for battle with his three hundred men against the countless Midianites, "*The Lord set every man's sword against his comrade* and against all the army" (Judg. 7:22). And in the days of king David, "*The Lord brought the fear of him upon all nations*" (1 Chron. 14:17). Finally, Zechariah prophesied a similar work of God in the future: "On that day *a great panic from the Lord shall fall on them*, so that each will seize the hand of another, and the hand of the one will be raised against the hand of the other" (Zech. 14:13; cf. Ezek. 30:13).

God put dread in the adversaries. He threw the Amorites into a panic. He set soldiers' swords against their comrades. He brought the fear of David on the nations. And in the distant future, panic among the nations will come from God. The implication of these texts is that God holds the right and power to bring about emotions in human hearts that have the effect of creating behaviors that serve God's purposes, like causing an army to self-destruct (Judg. 7:23–25).

God Makes Pagan Kings His Hammer and Rod

God's directing the emotions and decisions of Israel's enemies extends to the hearts of the kings and the commanders who rule them. Again and again God turned the hearts of pagan rulers to do his bidding. And then he turned the hearts of other kings to deliver his blows of judgment against the sins of the very ones he had used as his hammer of judgment.

For example, when Israel rejected God and went after other "lovers," God said, "Therefore, behold, *I will gather all your lovers* with whom you took pleasure, all those you loved and all those you hated. *I will gather them against you* from every side" (Ezek. 16:37). This means that God turned the hearts of those lovers to come and fight against Israel. The text does not say he was predicting. It says he was gathering. They were deciding to oppose Israel. This deciding was the Lord's gathering.

A specific instance was the apostasy of the Reubenites and the Gadites and the half-tribe of Manasseh. When they "whored after the gods of the peoples of the land, . . . *the God of Israel stirred up the spirit of Pul king of Assyria*, the spirit of Tiglath-pileser king of Assyria, and he took them into exile" (1 Chron. 5:25–26). By this stirring up and this gathering, God directs the hearts and minds of pagan rulers to bring judgment on Israel.

When God did this with the king of Babylon, he called Babylon his "hammer" and the rod of God:

> *You are my hammer* and weapon of war:
> with you I break nations in pieces;
>   with you I destroy kingdoms;
> with you I break in pieces the horse and his rider;
>   with you I break in pieces the chariot and the charioteer;
> with you I break in pieces man and woman;
>   with you I break in pieces the old man and the youth;
> with you I break in pieces the young man and the young woman;
> with you I break in pieces the shepherd and his flock;
> with you I break in pieces the farmer and his team;
>   with you I break in pieces governors and commanders.
>   (Jer. 51:20–23)

> I will send for . . . Nebuchadnezzar the king of Babylon, my servant, and I will bring them against this land and its inhabitants, and against all these surrounding nations. (Jer. 25:9)

God's providence over Nebuchadnezzar's purposes to devastate Israel was such that he called the king his "servant." Though Nebuchadnezzar was acting according to his own plans, he was fulfilling God's plans. Again, we are not told *how* God does such a thing—how he guides the decisions of a pagan king, while the king acts as a responsible decision maker.

We know that God regards Nebuchadnezzar as a responsible person and not as a nonmoral robot, because God holds him accountable and brings judgment on him for his sinfulness in the very work God led him to do:

> The LORD has stirred up the spirit of the kings of the Medes, because his purpose concerning Babylon is to destroy it. . . . I will repay Babylon and all the inhabitants of Chaldea before your very eyes for all the evil that they have done in Zion, declares the LORD.
>
> Behold, I am against you, O destroying mountain,
>   declares the Lord,
>   which destroys the whole earth;
> I will stretch out my hand against you. . . .
>
> The land trembles and writhes in pain,
>   for *the LORD's purposes against Babylon stand,*
> to make the land of Babylon a desolation,
>   without inhabitant. (Jer. 51:11, 24–25, 29)

God rules over the hearts of pagan rulers so that they become his hammer of judgment. And he rules over others so that they discipline the ones who acted sinfully even while God wielded them in his hand.

God Turns the Hearts of Cyrus, Darius, and Artaxerxes

One of the most remarkable reversals in the history of Israel was owing to God's "turning the heart" of pagan kings near the end of the exile of

Israel. We touched on this in passing in chapter 20, but it is worthy of fuller attention. The book of Ezra begins:

> In the first year of Cyrus king of Persia, that the word of the LORD by the mouth of Jeremiah might be fulfilled, *the LORD stirred up the spirit of Cyrus* king of Persia, so that he made a proclamation throughout all his kingdom and also put it in writing: "Thus says Cyrus king of Persia: The LORD, the God of heaven, has given me all the kingdoms of the earth, and he has charged me to build him a house at Jerusalem, which is in Judah. Whoever is among you of all his people, may his God be with him, and let him go up to Jerusalem, which is in Judah, and rebuild the house of the LORD." (Ezra 1:1–3)

In a stunning reversal, the very gold and silver vessels that Nebuchadnezzar had plundered from the Jewish temple before it was destroyed are now returned by a different king of Babylon:

> In the first year of Cyrus king of Babylon, Cyrus the king made a decree that this house of God should be rebuilt. And the gold and silver vessels of the house of God, which Nebuchadnezzar had taken out of the temple that was in Jerusalem and brought into the temple of Babylon, these Cyrus the king took out of the temple of Babylon, and they were delivered to one whose name was Sheshbazzar, whom he had made governor; and he said to him, "Take these vessels, go and put them in the temple that is in Jerusalem, and let the house of God be rebuilt on its site." Then this Sheshbazzar came and laid the foundations of the house of God that is in Jerusalem, and from that time until now it has been in building, and it is not yet finished. (Ezra 5:13–16)

It gets even better. After the surrender of the Babylonians to the Persians, Darius not only supports the return of the exiles to Israel and the rebuilding of the temple but also decrees that it would be paid for by the Persian treasury in full:

Moreover, I make a decree regarding what you shall do for these elders of the Jews for the rebuilding of this house of God. The cost is to be paid to these men in full and without delay from the royal revenue. (Ezra 6:8)

At the completion of the temple, what brought the people of Israel to joyful celebration was the providence of God over the heart of a pagan king:

They kept the Feast of Unleavened Bread seven days with joy, for the LORD had made them joyful and *had turned the heart of the king of Assyria to them, so that he aided them in the work of the house of God, the God of Israel.* (Ezra 6:22)

Finally, when the next king, Artaxerxes, added his overflowing support to the temple services, the people blessed the Lord for his amazing, heart-turning providence:

I, Artaxerxes the king, make a decree to all the treasurers in the province Beyond the River: Whatever Ezra the priest, the scribe of the Law of the God of heaven, requires of you, let it be done with all diligence, up to 100 talents of silver, 100 cors of wheat, 100 baths of wine, 100 baths of oil, and salt without prescribing how much. (Ezra 7:21–22)

With this the praises rose:

Blessed be the LORD, the God of our fathers, *who put such a thing as this into the heart of the king,* to beautify the house of the LORD that is in Jerusalem. (Ezra 7:27)

God Turns the Hearts of Kings Where He Will

This would not be the last such blessing on the restoration of Jerusalem (Neh. 2:8), but it is enough to illustrate the heart-turning authority and power of God's providence over the wills of rulers. From such experience throughout their history, Israel's wise men formulated a proverb under God's inspiration:

> The king's heart is a stream of water in the hand of the LORD;
>> he turns it wherever he will. (Prov. 21:1)

If one wanted to make the case that this is not always true—that there are situations when the king's heart is not in the hands of the Lord to turn it where he will—it would be difficult to come up with criteria for when this is true and when it's not. We have seen above, and in chapter 20, that God turns the hearts of kings and rulers when they are acting sinfully as well as righteously, and we will focus on this again in chapter 29. So that would not be the criterion one would use to decide when the king's heart is not in the hands of the Lord.

Not only that, but if the Lord only sometimes holds the king's heart in his hand, turning it where he will, then the times when he does *not* do so would be for perfectly wise, all-knowing purposes. He would already know what the king is about to do, and he would choose purposefully to permit that to happen[1]—or not. If God does not step in and turn the king's heart another way, when he has the right and power to do so, then his choosing not to do so is to decide that the king's decision will happen. This is as much to govern the king's behavior as if God more immediately turned the king's heart.

But, in fact, it would be unwarranted to restrict Proverbs 21:1. Even though the nature of a proverb is that it is often a general rule rather than a universal truth, this is certainly not always the case. Many proverbs are meant to be taken absolutely without exception. For example:

> The fear of the LORD is the beginning of knowledge. (1:7)

> Trust in the LORD with all your heart,
>> and do not lean on your own understanding.

---

1   See the discussion in chap. 13 on God's "planned permission."

In all your ways acknowledge him,
  and he will make straight your paths. (3:5–6)

The LORD by wisdom founded the earth;
  by understanding he established the heavens. (3:19)

The fear of the LORD is hatred of evil.
Pride and arrogance and the way of evil
  and perverted speech I hate. (8:13)

Lying lips are an abomination to the LORD,
  but those who act faithfully are his delight. (12:22)

The fear of the LORD is a fountain of life,
  that one may turn away from the snares of death.
    (14:27)

The name of the LORD is a strong tower;
  the righteous man runs into it and is safe. (18:10)

To do righteousness and justice
  is more acceptable to the LORD than sacrifice. (21:3)

Proverbs 21:1 is part of a larger theme in Scripture that inclines us to see God's heart-turning power as unrestricted: the king's heart is *always* in the hand of the Lord, and he *always* turns it wherever he will. This larger theme is brought to mind with this proverb because of its virtually identical wording to that which we find in Psalm 115:3 and Psalm 135:6:

Our God is in the heavens;
  he does *all that he pleases* [כֹּל אֲשֶׁר־חָפֵץ]. (Ps. 115:3)

Whatever the LORD pleases [כֹּל אֲשֶׁר־חָפֵץ] he does,
  in heaven and on earth,
  in the seas and all deeps. (Ps. 135:6)

The king's heart is a stream of water in the hand of the LORD;
he turns it *wherever he will* [כָּל־אֲשֶׁר יַחְפֹּץ]. (Prov. 21:1)

The English phrases "all that he pleases" (Ps. 115:3), "whatever the
LORD pleases" (Ps. 135:6), and "wherever he will" (Prov. 21:1) are
identical in Hebrew.[2] In other words, the use of the phrase "[unto]
whatever he pleases" (translated "wherever he will") in Proverbs 21:1
brings the proverb verbally into alignment with the larger theme
in Scripture, namely, that God does "whatever he pleases," or as
Paul says, he "works *all things* according to the counsel of his will"
(Eph. 1:11). I conclude, therefore, that it is unwarranted to restrict
the meaning of Proverbs 21:1 by saying that there are situations
in which God's providence does not hold sway over the heart of
the king.

What about All Ordinary Human Willing and Doing?

Our focus in this chapter is on God's providence over the human
mind and heart and the actions that flow from their thoughts and
inclinations. Till now in this chapter, our attention has been on the
heart and mind of rulers. Our conclusion so far is that God does
indeed direct the hearts of rulers, and there appear to be no exceptions. This confirms the picture we saw in chapters 20–22. By looking
in this chapter at God's providence over rulers' *hearts* and *decisions*,
we see confirmed what we saw there by looking at God's providence
over the sweeping *events* of kings and nations.

But it would be a mistake to think that God's providence is concerned only with the hearts of kings and not with the hearts of ordinary
folks like us. This will be most clearly seen—and most importantly

---

2   The reason Prov. 21:1 is translated "wherever he will" is that the Hebrew word "unto" (עַל) is pre-
fixed to the phrase "whatever he pleases" making it "unto whatever he pleases," which is translated
"wherever he pleases [or wills]." But the same phrase, for "all he pleases," is present in Pss. 115:3
and 135:6 (כָּל־אֲשֶׁר יַחְפֹּץ).

seen—when we turn to God's providence over saving faith and the works of faith in the Christian life (part 3, sections 7 and 8). But there are significant biblical pointers to God's decisive providence, not just over faith and its fruits but over all human willing and doing. Paul makes a foundational statement about human willing and doing in Romans 9:16.

He has just referred to God's declaration of his own freedom in showing mercy to whomever he wills: "I will have mercy on whom I have mercy, and I will have compassion on whom I have compassion" (Rom. 9:15). This refers most immediately to mercy in salvation. But it is more all-encompassing than that, as we saw in chapter 7, because this freedom, and the very way it is expressed, is rooted in God's name, "I AM WHO I AM" (Ex. 3:14). "I AM WHO I AM" leads to "I am merciful to whom I am merciful."

Then comes the foundational statement about human willing and doing. It is an inference from God's freedom in verse 15: "So then (ἄρα οὖν) it depends not on human will or exertion, but on God, who has mercy" (Rom. 9:16). Literally: "Therefore, [how God shows his mercy is] not of the one who wills, nor of the one who runs, but of the mercy-showing God." Human willing and doing are pictured as willing and running. And the point is this: human willing and doing are not finally decisive in determining the way God's mercy is shown. God, in his absolute freedom—rooted in his being as God—is finally decisive, not human willing or doing.

The Arrogance James Sees in Failing to See Providence

Someone might disagree that Romans 9:16 is a foundational statement about willing and doing in general, the way I have taken it. We could linger here while I build my case on the way Paul roots this statement in the freedom of God, which is deeper and more comprehensive than its application to election or salvation. But it might be more helpful to turn to a passage in James where human willing and doing are treated in a sweeping way beyond the processes of salvation. James 4:13–16 deals with the most ordinary events of daily life:

> Come now, you who say, "Today or tomorrow we will go into such and such a town and spend a year there and trade and make a profit"—yet you do not know what tomorrow will bring. What is your life? For you are a mist that appears for a little time and then vanishes. Instead you ought to say, "If the Lord wills, we will live and do this or that." As it is, you boast in your arrogance. All such boasting is evil.

We touched on this text briefly in chapters 18 and 21, but its implications for God's providence over ordinary human life are so significant that we need to pay closer attention to its details.

James's burden is to help us overcome our bent to arrogance: "As it is, you boast in your arrogance. All such boasting is evil" (4:16). What makes this burden relevant for this book is that the arrogance he has in mind is our failure to embrace God's pervasive providence and to bring our attitudes and words into sync with it. What is out of sync? Answer: the simple presumption that in our everyday life, our willing and doing are decisive:

> Come now, you who say, "Today or tomorrow we will go into such and such a town and spend a year there and trade and make a profit." (4:13)

- "*Today or tomorrow* . . ." We'll decide which one. When we go is *our* choice.
- "Today or tomorrow *we will go* . . ." Or stay. Our choice. This or that, stay or go.
- "Today or tomorrow we will go *into such and such a town* . . ." This town or that one. It will be our choice.
- ". . . *and spend a year* . . ." Or two. Or six months. Our choice. This duration or that duration. We'll decide.

- "We'll spend a year there . . ." Or move around from town to town. Different business strategies. This kind or that kind. We'll choose.
- "We'll spend a year there and trade . . ." Or take some time off. We'll decide how much we work. This amount or that.
- "We'll spend a year there and trade *and make a profit.*" We know how to turn a profit. This much or that much. *We'll* make it happen.

What's the problem here? Verse 13 is a pretty ordinary way of talking. The whole world thinks and talks this way.

Don't Act as If Tomorrow Is Knowable, Durable, and Controllable

Here is James's response. First, verse 14: "Yet you do not know what tomorrow will bring. What is your life? For you are a mist that appears for a little time and then vanishes." The first thing James does is focus on the fact that they are utterly ignorant about *everything* they just presumed to know and plan. "You do not know what tomorrow will bring."

- You don't know when you will leave for such and such a town.
- And if you leave, you don't know if you will get there.
- And if you get there, you don't know if you will spend a year or a minute there.
- And if you spend a year there, you don't know if you will trade or be flat on your back, paralyzed from a fall.
- And if you do trade, you don't know if you will make a profit or fail completely.

And then James zeroes in on one of the reasons they don't know what tomorrow may bring: "What is your life? For you are a mist that appears for a little time and then vanishes."

They are as fragile and as temporary as the vapor that comes out of their mouths on a cold morning. They can't control it. And they can't make it stay. It's not in their power, and before they can try to shape it, or guide it, it's gone.

So behind the words of verse 13 ("Today or tomorrow we will go into such and such a town and spend a year there and trade and make a profit"), there is an operating belief that our future life is knowable, durable, and controllable. James says that all three of those beliefs are false. Tomorrow is unknown. Life is a vapor. And you don't have decisive control over anything.

Missing: Belief in Providence, Not Agnosticism, Not Fatalism

One could be an agnostic and a fatalist and yet agree with James so far. But James explains himself in a totally different direction—providence, not agnosticism, not fatalism.

Verse 15: "Instead, you ought to say, 'If the Lord wills, we will live and do this or that.'" We already focused in chapters 18 and 21 on the words "If the Lord wills, we will live." We are focusing here on the words "If the Lord wills, we will . . . *do this or that.*"

- "*Today or tomorrow . . .*" God will decide whether you leave today or tomorrow.
- ". . . *we will go . . .*" Or not. God will decide.
- ". . . *into such and such a town . . .*" This one or that one—God will decide.
- ". . . *and spend a year . . .*" Or two, or none. God will decide.
- ". . . *there . . .*" Or be flooded out, or driven out, or not. God will decide.
- ". . . *and trade . . .*" Or maybe lie paralyzed from a fall. God will decide.
- ". . . *and make a profit*" Maybe. Maybe we'll fail. God will decide.

That is what James means by "this or that." "If the Lord wills, we will . . . do this or that" (4:15), which I take to mean that our willing and doing are not decisive in our ordinary living. God is. This is pervasive providence. It is so counterexperiential for most people that we should linger here to make clear how wonderful and practical this is and how different it is from, say, what Muslims believe.

Islam Does Not Make the Connections

I am aware that Islam believes in the absolute sovereignty of God. Muslims would have no problem with James 4:13–17, considered in isolation. So it is utterly crucial that we remind ourselves that no biblical doctrine, and no attribute of God, should ever be considered in isolation from other biblical doctrines and other attributes of God. If we don't see the pervasive providence of God in relation to the fuller picture of God in the Bible, it may make us a suicide bomber instead of a sacrificial lover.

So let's consider four such connections with the bigger biblical picture to prevent that tragedy: the connections of God's pervasive providence with (1) gospel joy, (2) sacrificial love, (3) fearless witness, and (4) confident planning.

1. THE PROVIDENCE OF GOD AND GOSPEL JOY

Christians pass through so many difficulties, doubts, temptations, and sins that we need to be consciously anchored in the gospel every day, if we are to "rejoice . . . always" (Phil. 4:4). That is, we need continual reassurance that our sins are forgiven for Jesus's sake, that God is for us and not against us because of Christ, and that we are not destined for wrath, but for everlasting joy, because of the death and resurrection of Jesus.

In other words, we need deep and ever-renewed confidence that the crucifixion of Jesus under Pontius Pilate was not a random, historical fluke of circumstance but was the outworking of God's pervasive providence. And that is exactly what Luke reports that it is in Acts 4:27–28:

> Truly in this city there were gathered together against your holy servant Jesus, whom you anointed, both Herod and Pontius Pilate,

along with the Gentiles and the peoples of Israel, to do whatever your hand and your plan had predestined to take place.

In other words, God planned and predestined everything that Pilate and Herod and the Jews and the soldiers did to bring about the death of Jesus. Therefore, we ought to say, "Since the Lord willed, they lived *and did this and that.*" The death of Jesus was not random. It was a sovereign plan to save our souls—and secure our unshakable joy.

2. THE PROVIDENCE OF GOD AND SACRIFICIAL LOVE

Christians are called to love their neighbor (Matt. 19:19) and their enemy (Matt. 5:44). Such love is costly. It requires sacrifice. Time. Inconvenience. Effort. Money. Risk of reputation, or your very life. It may be love for someone you don't even like and who has treated you badly.

Over and over in the New Testament, especially in 1 Peter, we are told to do good to people—to love people—even if it requires suffering. How are we to do this? Peter's answer—and he says it twice—is that we realize that whatever suffering love may require, we are to accept it as the sovereign will of our faithful Creator. We see our suffering as part of God's pervasive providence:

> Let those who suffer *according to God's will* entrust their souls to a faithful Creator while doing good. (1 Pet. 4:19)

> It is better to suffer for doing good, *if that should be God's will*, than for doing evil. (1 Pet. 3:17)

Suffering will come—especially for those committed to doing good and to loving their enemies. But take heart. God is sovereign. No suffering befalls you apart from the merciful providence of God. He is our Father (1 Pet. 1:17) and our maker (1 Pet. 4:19). He is faithful. Entrust your soul to a faithful Creator in doing good—to his faithful providence.

3. THE PROVIDENCE OF GOD AND FEARLESS WITNESS

As we walk into the future, the way James describes in James 4:13—today or tomorrow we will go—there will inevitably be fears. Some will be small. Others may be huge—a malignant tumor, a city blown to pieces with racial hatred, the explosion of a nuclear weapon, a terrorist kidnapping.

In all of this, Jesus calls us not to shrink back into security but to step forward in fearless witness. How does he support and motivate that? He does it with a reminder of God's pervasive providence:

> Do not fear those who kill the body but cannot kill the soul. . . . Are not two sparrows sold for a penny? And not one of them will fall to the ground apart from your Father. . . . Fear not, therefore; you are of more value than many sparrows. (Matt. 10:28–29, 31)

The pervasive providence of God over birds that fall dead to the forest floor is the foundation of your fearlessness. You are precious to him, and he is sovereign over you. Whatever happens in the world and whatever happens in your family, fear not.

4. THE PROVIDENCE OF GOD AND CONFIDENT PLANNING

Christians plan. They do not coast. At the end of Paul's life, he was still planning to go to Spain (Rom. 15:24). As our plans take shape, we can think like fatalists or Christians. We can say, "If I'm *lucky*, I will live and do this or that. By *chance*, I may live and do this or that. As *fate* may have it, I will live and do this or that." Or we can say, "If the Lord wills, I will live and do this or that."

Luck and chance and fate are nothing. They are not a foundation for any plans. They can do nothing because they are nothing. They are simply words that describe emptiness and meaninglessness. But when you make a plan and say, "I plan to do this, *if the Lord wills*," you build your life on an unshakable foundation: the sovereign will of God—his pervasive providence.

The Old Testament wise man said, "The heart of man plans his way, but the LORD establishes his steps" (Prov. 16:9). "Many are the plans in the mind of a man, but it is the purpose of the LORD that will stand" (Prov. 19:21). It is right to plan. The alternative to planning is not usually serendipitous fruitfulness but rather fruitless drifting. Nevertheless, the Christian plan, the humble plan, always includes, "If the Lord wills."

If we rest in the wise and good providence of God in all our plans, we will be confident people, and peaceful. Because we will know that whatever details of our plan don't happen, God's merciful providence holds sway. Because of the pervasive providence of God, Christians can be joyful in the gospel, sacrificial in our love, fearless in our witness, and confident in our planning. Providence does not make us fatalists, agnostics, or Muslims. It does not stand alone. It is what it is in relation to everything else the Bible tells us about God and his ways.

He Works All Things according to the Counsel of His Will

We have seen that man's willing and doing are not decisive in what comes to pass in this world. God is (Rom. 9:16). And we have seen that by God's decisive sway (not man's), human beings "live and do this or that" (James 4:15). It appears, then, that the pervasiveness of God's providence is not limited by human willing, but that our willing is encompassed within that providence. Another way to put it would be that the "all things" of Ephesians 1:11 should not be defined so as to exclude human willing. Paul says:

> In [Christ] we have obtained an inheritance, having been predes-tined according to the purpose of him who *works all things according to the counsel of his will*, so that we who were the first to hope in Christ might be to the praise of his glory. (Eph. 1:11–12)

Paul expresses a universal truth—God "works all things accord-ing to the counsel of his will" (1:11)—in order to support a more particular truth: that those who are predestined by God will, in fact, reach their predestined end, namely, to praise God's glory (1:12). The certainty of our hope that we will persevere to the end and attain our predestined goal of praising the glory of God's grace forever (Eph. 1:6) is supported by the universal truth that God's providence "works all things." And this working is guided decisively not by human willing but by "the counsel of his will" (1:11). Therefore, God's "working all things" cannot be thwarted by our willing. Rather, our willing is encompassed within his providence.

Even though the immediate focus of Ephesians 1:11–12 is the work of God in accomplishing the predestined goal of God's elect (1:4), my point here is that Paul appeals to a universal truth larger than this particular goal. Paul does *not* argue that the predestined will persevere because God governs the wills of his people and prevents them from committing apostasy. No. He argues that God's predestined people will persevere because God governs *all things*, which includes governing the wills of his people. Therefore, it is very likely that in Paul's mind, the "all things," which is greater than its application to Christians, includes *all* human willing. Indeed, it would be virtually pointless, it seems, for Paul to say that God "works all things according to the counsel of his will" if, in fact, the trillions of human decisions that shape most of what happens in the world were excluded from "all things."

With Man It Is Impossible, but Not with God

Jesus points us in the same direction as Paul, namely, that God's pervasive providence encompasses all human willing. A rich ruler asked Jesus how to inherit eternal life. Jesus penetrated through all his claims to righteousness and said, "Sell all that you have and distribute to the poor, and you will have treasure in heaven; and come, follow me" (Luke 18:22). The rich man did not comply, but turned away in sadness.

In response to this, Jesus said to his disciples, "How difficult it is for those who have wealth to enter the kingdom of God! For it is easier for a camel to go through the eye of a needle than for a rich person to enter the kingdom of God" (18:24–25). This stunned the disciples. They saw the implication of Jesus's illustration of a camel and the needle's eye. They said, "Then who can be saved?" (18:26). Jesus did *not* say, "Oh, you misunderstand. It was just a hyperbole. Don't overdo my words." No. On the contrary Jesus acknowledged that they got the implication exactly right. He said, "What is impossible with man is possible with God" (18:27).

They inferred, "Well, then, no one can be saved. It's impossible." Jesus said, in effect, "That's exactly what I am saying." The exercise of the human will to change itself from world loving to Jesus loving is not going to happen. It is impossible. That's the point of the camel and the needle! Impossible.

But he continues: "What is impossible with man is possible with God" (18:27). God's providence encompasses the human will in such a way that God can bring about compliance to his commands ("Sell all that you have and distribute to the poor," 18:22) when the human will cannot. The precise focus of God's power in this text is the focus on the human will: what needs to happen in the human will but cannot happen, because it is "impossible with man," is in the power of God's providence—"it is possible with God." Again, we have found it confirmed that the pervasiveness of God's providence is not limited by human willing, but our willing is encompassed within that providence.

Who Holds Decisive Sway over Success and Failure?

I mentioned at the beginning of this chapter that we would focus on God's providence over the human heart, "[turning] it wherever he will" (Prov. 21:1), and then conclude by a brief focus on God's providence over the circumstances that hinder or give success to human choices. God governs what happens in the world not only by holding sway over the decisions of human hearts, but also by giving success, or not, to the decisions he permits.

Concerning Joseph's experience as a captive in Egypt, we read, "The LORD caused all that he did to succeed in his hands" (Gen. 39:3). "The LORD was with him. And whatever he did, the LORD made it succeed" (39:23). In other words, God's providence extends not only to the processes of decision making about what we will do, but also to the circumstances that determine if our decisions will succeed or not.

When it comes, for example, to wealth and poverty, we may think that our shrewdness in working and saving and investing is decisive in whether we succeed. God says no. "The heart of man plans his way, but the LORD establishes his steps" (Prov. 16:9). God may grant you to be an excellent planner but then bring it all to ruin—or not. No matter how shrewd we are, "a man's steps are from the LORD; how then can man understand his way?" (Prov. 20:24). In the end, "the LORD makes poor and makes rich; he brings low and he exalts" (1 Sam. 2:7; cf. Ps. 113:7). As David acknowledges in prayer, "Riches and honor come from you, and you rule over all. In your hand are power and might, and in your hand it is to make great and to give strength to all" (1 Chron. 29:12).

So it is in all human endeavor—from the drawing of straws to the winning of battles, God's providence is decisive.

> The lot is cast into the lap,
>   but its every decision is from the LORD. (Prov. 16:33)

> The horse is made ready for the day of battle,
>   but the victory belongs to the LORD. (Prov. 21:31)

I Am God and Accomplish All My Purpose

I conclude, therefore, that the providence of God is pervasive. It encompasses, in its sway, all human willing and doing, from kings to paupers. And it superintends all circumstances that give that willing and doing success or not. It works all things according to the counsel of God's will (Eph. 1:11). Job confessed that he had learned this lesson through all his sufferings. No human willing and no circumstances surrounding that willing limit God's providence: "I know that you can do all things, and that no purpose of yours can be thwarted" (Job 42:2).

This is, as we have seen before, part of what it means to be God, which is why Isaiah says:

> I am God, and there is no other;
>   I am God, and there is none like me,
> declaring the end from the beginning
>   and from ancient times things not yet done,
> saying, "My counsel shall stand,
>   and I will accomplish all my purpose." (Isa. 46:9–10; cf. 43:13)

"I am God." "I accomplish all my purpose." That is what it means to be God. What we have seen in this chapter is that God's purpose, which is always accomplished, includes all human willing and doing and all the circumstances that govern whether that willing and doing succeed or fail—whether they lead to "this or that" (James 4:15).

Not a Hair of Your Head Will Perish

The effect of this vision of God's pervasive providence, for those who embrace it, is undaunted, joyful, contrite courage in the cause of God's mission. They see in the cross of Christ the final verdict: the all-governing God is for me and not against me. And they embrace Paul's reasoning: "If God is for us, who can be against us?" (Rom. 8:31). The enemy may put us to death all day long (Rom. 8:36), "but not a hair of your head will perish" (Luke 21:18). Sovereign bullets do not separate us from the love of Christ (Rom. 8:35). We are immortal till our work is done. Every need will be met (Matt. 6:33; Phil. 4:19). Every enemy will be restrained (Ps. 23:5; Jer. 29:11). So we embrace whatever cost love requires, and we say, "The LORD is on my side; I will not fear. What can man do to me?" (Ps. 118:6; see also Heb. 13:6). Man can do nothing but what the merciful purpose of providence ordains.

27

Things We Know and Things We Do Not Need to Know

We turn now to the extent and nature of God's providence over explicitly *sinful* human choices and their effects. This is an unavoidable and hope-filled topic because there are so many examples of it in Scripture, and because such all-inclusive providence brings hope for despairing, paralyzed sinners and their most wounded victims. Another reason for not avoiding this issue is that people stumble more easily over God's ordaining sinful choices than they do over his ordaining righteous choices.[1] So if the Bible shows that God's

---

1 A word about terminology: I don't think there is a verb (such as "ordain") or group of verbs, which, in reference to God's relation to human choices, can protect a writer from being misunderstood. In other words, whatever view we have regarding God's direct or indirect or nonexistent influence over human choices, the words we use to describe that relationship are all open to misunderstanding. Language is simply not precise enough to include or exclude all the connotations and implications we may or may not want our readers to include. So, in reference to human choices, we might say God *causes, ordains, governs, decrees, produces, authors, guides, leads into, brings about, rules, determines, controls, regulates, decides, defines,* and more. None of those words will avoid misunderstanding. My point is not to despair of clear communication. I think it is possible. I am aiming at it. My point is that we must regularly clarify with clear sentences what we mean by our words. Here is one of the most important clarifying sentences recurring in various forms throughout this book: Whatever verb I use to describe God's relation to human choices, I always mean a kind of divine "seeing to it" (providence) that never means God sins, or that

providence over sinful choices is all-encompassing and hopeful, then
the case for his providence over righteous choices will not seem as
problematic.

Holy, Holy, Holy

The very thought of God governing, or in any way controlling, the
occurrence of sinful human choices may rightly cause a Christian worshiper of God to become vigilant and cautious, for at the heart of
our worship is the adoration of God's unimpeachable holiness—his
transcendent purity. We join the perfect beings of heaven in singing,
"Holy, holy, holy is the LORD of hosts; the whole earth is full of his
glory!" (Isa. 6:3). We rejoice that "day and night they never cease to
say, 'Holy, holy, holy, is the Lord God Almighty, who was and is and is
to come!'" (Rev. 4:8). We are vigilant lest any false doctrine implicate
God in any unholiness.

We say with Moses and the psalmists and the prophets and the
apostles, "The Rock, his work is perfect, for all his ways are justice"
(Deut. 32:4). "The LORD is righteous in all his ways" (Ps. 145:17).
"Righteousness and justice are the foundation of your throne" (Ps.
89:14). "You are not a God who delights in wickedness; evil may
not dwell with you" (Ps. 5:4). "You . . . are of purer eyes than to see
evil and cannot look at wrong" (Hab. 1:13). "He does no injustice;
every morning he shows forth his justice; each dawn he does not fail"
(Zeph. 3:5). "God is light, and in him is no darkness at all" (1 John
1:5). "God cannot be tempted with evil" (James 1:13). "Let God be
true though everyone were a liar, as it is written, 'That you may be
justified in your words, and prevail when you are judged.' But if our
unrighteousness serves to show the righteousness of God, what shall

---

man is not accountable for his choices. To be specific, God can see to it that sin happens without
himself sinning or taking away the responsibility of the sinner. This is not a presupposition. It is
a conclusion from biblical texts, especially the kind we are about to see in chaps. 28–33.

we say? That God is unrighteous to inflict wrath on us? (I speak in a human way.) By no means! For then how could God judge the world?" (Rom. 3:4–6).

Indeed, as we stand before every human injustice, every human sin and cruelty, and every natural calamity, we say with Abraham, "Shall not the Judge of all the earth do what is just?" (Gen. 18:25). And we answer yes.

If the Scriptures Teach It, It Is True

How do we come to know this unimpeachably holy God? The only clear and infallible revelation we have is his inspired word, the Bible. Without this infallible revelation from God about his own flawless character, all our declarations of divine justice and goodness would be speculative at best. Maybe true. Maybe not. Therefore, the same Spirit-given capacity to see and love the holiness of God in Scripture inclines the Spirit-illumined reader of Scripture to see, reverence, and embrace those inspired portrayals of God's providence in governing the sinful choices of human beings.

My approach in reading the inspired Scriptures is not to silence the true meaning of one passage with the true meaning of another. If I find that two passages seem to contradict each other, my assumption is either that I have misconstrued the meaning of one (or both) of them, or that I am calling a contradiction what is, in fact, not a contradiction. In what follows, we will consider many biblical instances of God's providence in governing sinful human choices. At every point, my assumption is *not* "This cannot be." I think that claim is a philosophical prejudgment, not a biblical assessment of what is possible for God.

My assumption will be that if the Bible teaches clearly and repeatedly that God governs sinful human choices, then he can do it without becoming unholy or unjust or impure or evil. If finite humans can find ways to handle radioactive uranium to produce useful energy without being contaminated by the deadly radiation, it is likely that the infinitely wise God can handle the deadly evil of sin without contamination or harm in bringing about his wise and holy purposes. If finite humans searching for a preventive vaccine can handle the lethal viruses of new diseases without being infected themselves, it is likely that the infinitely wise and good God can handle the disease of sin without being infected. Whether he does or not, we will discover not from logical likelihoods but from what the Scriptures teach.

Entering Another World

When we enter the Bible, we enter a world of thought about God very different from our own. From beginning to end, we find believers, and the inspired spokesmen of Scripture, bowing without hesitation before God's rule over good and evil. God's all-encompassing providence over evil as well as good is expressed so many times, without any pause to question it, that we realize we are in a world of thought that assumes God's absolute right and power to direct human choices (good and evil) according to his holy purposes. There is a biblical mindset that seems to have a built-in presupposition that God, with perfect justice, holiness, goodness, and wisdom, guides the good and evil choices of all humans. This mindset is, by and large, foreign to our modern world.

We often cry, "Contradiction!" where the Bible sees none. Many insist that humans (not God) must provide the final and decisive cause in the instant of decision, or else the decision cannot be justly praised or blamed. That is, they insist on ultimate human *self*-determination in the act of choosing, if there is to be moral accountability. The Bible does not share this assumption.

This is a watershed issue. If we bring this alien assumption to the Bible, we will either reject parts of the Bible as unworthy of our trust, or we will twist the texts we are about to look at in such a way that they fit our assumptions.

Logic Is Not a Problem

This assumption—that ultimate self-determination is essential to moral accountability—is not an assumption about what *logic* demands, but about what infinite divine wisdom is capable of. We argued this before briefly in chapter 15. It is crucial that we press the matter again, particularly at this juncture in the book. The Bible does not require of anyone that we believe in four-sided triangles, or that we believe the following syllogism is valid:

> Premise 1: Cows have four legs.
> Premise 2: Fido has four legs.
> Conclusion: Therefore, Fido is a cow.

That syllogism is as logically invalid for God as it is for us. What the Bible requires is that we also see the following syllogism as invalid:

> Premise 1: God holds all human beings accountable for their
> moral choices.
> Premise 2: John is a human being.
> Conclusion: Therefore, John has ultimate self-determination.

That syllogism is invalid because the conclusion does not follow from the premises. Neither of those two premises contains, or leads to, that conclusion. That conclusion is *assumed* to be a part of premise 1. But that assumption is not demanded by logic. It is forced into premise 1 by a philosophical *assumption*—namely, that there is moral accountability *only* where humans have final, decisive self-determination in the act of choosing.

Seeing Assumptions That Are Not There

The Bible does not teach or share that assumption. In the passages of Scripture people usually point to in order to show the presence of that assumption, it is not there. If someone points to Revelation 22:17, "*Whosoever will*, let him take the water of life freely" (KJV), it is not

there. If someone points to Matthew 23:37, "O Jerusalem, Jerusalem!
. . . How often would I have gathered your children together as a hen
gathers her brood under her wings, and *you were not willing!*" it's not
there. If someone points to 1 Timothy 2:4, "[*God*] *desires* all people to
be saved," or 2 Peter 3:9, "*The Lord is . . . not wishing* that any should
perish," or Ezekiel 33:11, "As I live, declares the Lord GOD, I have
no pleasure in the death of the wicked," it is not there. These texts do
not assume that humans have ultimate self-determination in the act
of choosing. That assumption is read *into* the text, not read out of it.

There are two reasons we know it is read *into* the text and is not really
there. In the case of Revelation 22:17, the truth that *whosoever will may
come* does not tell us *why* one person wills one thing and another person
wills another. We are not told what the ultimate or decisive cause of the
act of willing is. Therefore, the statement that *anyone who wills may come*
tells us nothing about how the choice to come to Christ, in fact, happened. It may have come decisively from self-determination. Or it may
have come decisively from God. It is wrong to *assume* from these words
which is the case. We should not read into the text what is not there.

In the case of Ezekiel 33:11, Matthew 23:37, 1 Timothy 2:4, and
2 Peter 3:9, each text says that God or Christ desires someone's salvation and that the salvation does not happen.[2] In other words, God does
not carry his desire forward into the accomplishment of his desire.
Why? One possible answer is that he is hindered by ultimate human
self-determination. In other words, it is possible that God has given
man the power of decisive self-determination so that man, not God,
provides the final, decisive cause in the choice not to come to Christ.
That's one possible explanation for why God's desire is unrealized.

But there is another possible explanation. It is possible that God
does not carry his desire forward to its accomplishment, not because
people have the power of ultimate self-determination, but because

2 We will deal with these texts more fully in chaps. 36 and 44.

God has wise and holy and good purposes for not bringing his desire to fruition.[3] Which of these possible explanations is, in fact, true is not decided by *assuming* the texts can mean only that man's will is decisive in the moment of conversion. To assume one explanation or the other from the texts alone would be reading into the text the assumptions we already have, not reading out of them what is really there.

It is a mistake to *assume* that ultimate human self-determination is a feature of biblical thinking. Ultimate self-determination, as a trait of man's will, might be taught in Scripture, or it might not be. That needs to be decided from the *teaching* of Scripture, not from philosophical assumptions we bring to the text. This book is about what the Bible teaches. In the present chapter (as well as chapters 28–33), we ask, What does it teach about God's providence over the sinful human will? I am arguing that it teaches that God, in his infinite wisdom and goodness and holiness and justice, knows how to govern the good and evil choices of all humans without himself sinning and without turning human preferences and choices into morally irrelevant, robot-like actions.

Therefore, in what follows, we should make every effort not to *assume* that ultimate, divine control over evil makes God evil or strips man of moral accountability. The question we should be asking is, What does the text teach about reality? Let us not bring to the text our philosophical assumptions that dictate what God's wisdom and goodness and justice must do.

We Do Not Need to Know How *God's Providence* Preserves Human Accountability

Nor should we come to the text demanding that we be told *how* God can govern sin and not be a sinner. Or *how* God can govern sinful

---

3   For a fuller explanation and biblical defense of this point, see John Piper, *Does God Desire All to Be Saved?* (Wheaton, IL: Crossway, 2013), originally published as chap. 5 in *The Grace of God, the Bondage of the Will: Biblical and Practical Perspectives on Calvinism*, ed. Thomas Schreiner and Bruce Ware (Grand Rapids, MI: Baker, 1995).

human choices and not turn man into a robot. We do not need to know *how*. God may or may not give us insight into the mysteries of how he does this. If he reveals that his all-governing providence includes the sinful choices of all people, and if he reveals that in this he is wise, good, just, and holy, that should be enough for us to trust him and worship him.

It should be enough that he tell us, "No one—absolutely no one—will be judged unjustly. No one—absolutely no one—will be punished in ways or degrees that are undeserved. No one—absolutely no one—will ever be able to say truthfully to the infinitely wise, good, just, and holy God, 'You have treated me unjustly.'" On the contrary, we say with the apostle Paul: "Is there injustice on God's part? By no means!" (Rom. 9:14). It cannot be.

From Stumbling Stones to Rocks of Refuge

With these preparatory thoughts, I hope our minds and hearts are more inclined to let the Scriptures have their say in the next six chapters, which focus on God's providence over sin. What many of us have found, over decades of meditating on God's word and walking in his fellowship, is that his "unsearchable . . . judgments" and his "inscrutable . . . ways" (Rom. 11:33)—revealed in sufficient measure in Scripture—are often shocking at first and comforting later.

God's pervasive providence is like his discipline: "For the moment all discipline seems painful rather than pleasant, but later it yields the peaceful fruit of righteousness to those who have been trained by it" (Heb. 12:11). A steady stream of testimonies has come to me over the last fifty years—testimonies of people who say, "At first God's providence was a massive stumbling stone, but now it is a massive rock of refuge and stability and strength in the troubles and sorrows of life."

These testimonies have kept alive the flame of desire to write this book. My prayer is that such testimonies will multiply, and that the next six chapters, which, at first glance, contain some of the greatest stumbling blocks in the Bible, will, in time, become a pathway of great hope in a world of great evil. Stumbling stones can become great barriers, or they can be gathered, by grace, and built into indestructible pillars in the house of truth and love and joy.

28

Joseph

God's Good Meaning in a Sinful Act

If God's providence is all-pervasive in this world, seeing to it that everything happens in the pursuit of his ultimate goal to communicate the fullness of his divine perfections for the eternal enjoyment of his redeemed people, then, in principle, I could illustrate his providence over sin by looking at any sinful act recorded in the Bible. But it will accord more closely with God's intention in Scripture if we focus on those sins that God himself explicitly says he has governed or brought to pass. Our approach, therefore, in chapters 28–33, will be to focus on striking instances of such providences in the history of Israel, from the beginnings of the nation in Egyptian bondage to the Babylonian exile. Along the way, we also will make explicit connections with the New Testament and our own experience.

We will find that there is nothing merely theoretical in the biblical portrayals of God's providence over sin. The biblical authors do not bring up the issue of God's purposeful sovereignty over sin merely to validate a theological viewpoint, but rather to humble human pride, intensify human worship, shatter human hopelessness, and put ballast in the battered boat of human faith, steel in the spine of human courage, and love in the human heart that sees no possible human way forward. What we find is real and raw. The prizing and proclamation of God's pervasive providence was forged in flames of hatred and love, deceit and truth, murder and mercy, carnage and kindness, cursing and blessing, mystery and revelation, and, finally, crucifixion and resurrection. I hope my treatment of God's providence over human sins will have the aroma of this horrible and hope-filled reality.

"God Meant It for Good"

We begin with one of the most famous and hopeful stories of sin and sorrow in the Bible. The story of God's rescue of his chosen people from starvation (Gen. 47:1–12) by means of the enslavement of Joseph through the sins of his brothers contains one of the most important statements in all the Bible about the providence of God. The statement is made by Joseph to his brothers near the end of the story: "*As for you, you meant evil against me, but God meant it for good,* to bring it about that many people should be kept alive, as they are today" (50:20). We will look at this statement carefully and why it is so important, but first let's make sure we see how it fits in the story.

Favoritism, Jealousy, Hatred, and Greed Set Salvation in Motion

Before there was any hint of famine coming on the land of Canaan, strife was brewing among Jacob's twelve sons. Hatred for Joseph was intensifying from two sources: his father's playing favorites by loving Joseph more, and Joseph's dreams that predicted his brothers would bow down to him someday:

> When [Joseph's] brothers saw that their father loved him more than all his brothers, they hated him and could not speak peacefully to him. Now Joseph had a dream, and when he told it to his brothers they hated him even more. . . . "Are you indeed to reign over us? Or

are you indeed to rule over us?" So they hated him even more for his dreams and for his words. (Gen. 37:4–5, 8)

Thus, the sequence of events by which God would save this family from the coming famine was set in motion through a tangle of sins, including fatherly favoritism and brotherly jealousy and hatred. This hatred came to the brink of murder. Joseph was sent to his brothers in the field.

They saw him from afar, and before he came near to them they conspired against him to kill him. They said to one another, "Here comes this dreamer. Come now, let us kill him and throw him into one of the pits. Then we will say that a fierce animal has devoured him, and we will see what will become of his dreams." (37:18–20)

Reuben intervened by persuading them to throw him into a pit rather than shed his blood, hoping later to rescue him (37:22). While Reuben was away, the plan for murder was replaced by the power of greed, since there was no financial gain in mere murder.

They saw a caravan of Ishmaelites coming from Gilead, with their camels bearing gum, balm, and myrrh, on their way to carry it down to Egypt. Then Judah said to his brothers, "What profit is it if we kill our brother and conceal his blood? Come, let us sell him to the Ishmaelites, and let not our hand be upon him, for he is our brother, our own flesh." And his brothers listened to him. Then Midianite traders passed by. And they drew Joseph up and lifted him out of the pit, and sold him to the Ishmaelites for twenty shekels of silver. They took Joseph to Egypt. (37:25–28)

Then the brothers covered their tracks by dousing Joseph's coat with animal blood and convincing their father that he had been killed by a fierce animal. With this constellation of sins against Joseph and his father, the brothers had set in motion an astonishing sequence of events that would lead to their own deliverance from famine.

Thirteen Years of Perplexed Faithfulness

For thirteen years, Joseph was first a slave (Gen. 37:36) and then a prisoner (39:20) in Egypt. He was seventeen years old when his brothers sold him (37:2). When he turned thirty in prison, "where the king's prisoners were confined" (39:20), there was an astonishing reversal of his fortunes. Because Joseph interpreted Pharaoh's dream about the coming famine, Pharaoh set Joseph "over all the land of Egypt" (41:41). Joseph was responsible for gathering enough food during the seven prosperous years so that it would last during the seven lean years of famine.

After seven years of prosperity and food storage, the famine began. Two years into it, Joseph's brothers come to Egypt for help. They are running out of food. Joseph is now thirty-nine years old. They have not seen him for twenty-two years. They do not recognize him. Eventually Joseph reveals himself to them.

Sent

If we have not figured out the point of this beautifully told story by now, the narrator makes it plain at this moment. His brothers "were dismayed at his presence" (Gen. 45:3). Joseph could discern some of what was in their minds, and he gives them his interpretation of God's providence in all that had happened:

> Now do not be distressed or angry with yourselves because you sold me here, for *God sent me before you to preserve life.* For the famine has been in the land these two years, and there are yet five years in which there will be neither plowing nor harvest. And *God sent me before you to preserve for you a remnant on earth*, and to keep alive for you many survivors. So *it was not you who sent me here, but God.* (45:5–8)

Joseph had been given not only the ability to interpret dreams, but also the ability to interpret providence. The key word in his interpretation is the word *sent.* Three times:

God sent me before you to preserve life. (45:5)

God sent me before you to preserve for you a remnant on earth. (45:7)

It was not you who sent me here, but God. (45:8)

This is the same interpretation the psalmist gave to God's providence in Joseph's being sold into slavery:

> When he summoned a famine on the land
>> and broke all supply of bread,
> *he had sent a man ahead of them,*
>> *Joseph*, who was sold as a slave. (Ps. 105:16–17)

Sent by Means of Sin

We are close now to the crucial statement we mentioned earlier from Genesis 50:20. We can see it implied in Genesis 45:8: "It was not you who sent me here, but God." What does that mean? It means that their intention was not *sending* for future deliverance. Their intention was *selling* for selfish gain, not sending for salvation. But God's intention in this sinful selling was very different. It was not sinful; it was saving. Their selling was driven by lust for "twenty shekels of silver" (37:28). God's sending was driven by love for his chosen people (39:21).

It would be a mistake to infer from Joseph's gracious counsel to his brothers—"Do not be distressed or angry with yourselves" (45:5)—that they had not sinned. I say this for three reasons. First, in the way the story unfolded, the intention was indeed to present the brothers as hateful and murderous and greedy, with their sin climaxing in the kidnapping and sale of Joseph into slavery. Second, both Old and New Testament teaching on godly regret and repentance is that it should lead to life and hope and freedom, not to lasting distress and bitterness and paralyzing self-hate (Ps. 51; 2 Cor. 7:8–10). Joseph's words to ease his brother's self-recrimination need not imply that there was no sin. Third, what they did is called "evil" in Genesis 50:20: "You meant it for evil."

You Had a Sinful Intention; God Had a Holy One

Joseph's remark about God's intention is one of the most important statements on the providence of God in all the Bible. Jacob, the father of these twelve brothers, had died. The eleven are fearful that now that because Jacob is gone, Joseph will take vengeance on them for their sin against him. So they make their plea in the name of their father:

> They sent a message to Joseph, saying, "Your father gave this command before he died: 'Say to Joseph, "Please forgive the transgression of your brothers and their sin, because they did evil to you."'" And now, please forgive the transgression of the servants of the God of your father." (Gen. 50:16–17)

Joseph was moved to tears (50:17). They came in person and fell before him with the same pleas for mercy. Then Joseph says:

> "Do not fear, for am I in the place of God? *As for you, you meant evil against me, but God meant it for good,* to bring it about that many people should be kept alive, as they are today. So do not fear; I will provide for you and your little ones." Thus he comforted them and spoke kindly to them. (50:19–21)

"You meant evil against me, but God meant it for good" (וְאַתֶּם חֲשַׁבְתֶּם עָלַי רָעָה אֱלֹהִים חֲשָׁבָהּ לְטֹבָה). What makes this statement so important is that the very same verb for *meant* is used in both halves of the statement. You *meant* (חֲשַׁבְתֶּם). God *meant* (חֲשָׁבָהּ). And the direct object is the same for both assertions: "You meant evil. . . . God meant it . . ." The word *it* (a suffix in Hebrew) is third-person feminine singular. That means its antecedent is the feminine word *evil* (רָעָה). You don't have to know Hebrew to see this. It is clear in English: "You meant *evil* against me." "God meant *it* [that same evil] for good." The parallels are complete:

You	God
meant	meant
evil	it
against me	for good

The Intersection of Divine and Human Willing in One Act

Therefore, the text does *not* say, "As for you, you *meant* evil against me, but God *used* it for good." They *meant* their sinful acts. God *meant* their sinful acts. Their decisions were intended by *them* according to their sinful designs. But their decisions were intended by *God* according to his saving designs (cf. Isa. 10:5–7; Mic. 4:11–12).

Here is the intersection of divine and human willing—our intending and God's intending in one set of sinful decisions and their practical action. In this case, the intersection specifically concerns sinful human willing. I have said before, and reaffirm here, that we do not need to comprehend the mysteries of this intersection of divine and human. What we are called to affirm is that human sinful willing is not simply used or managed by God after it has happened; rather, this very sinful willing is meant or intended by God for righteous, saving purposes. Nevertheless, God means, or intends, or wills this sinful human willing in such a way that he does not sin but, in perfect wisdom and righteousness and goodness, aims at and achieves a good end and is himself doing good at every point.

What, then, is the relationship between the human willing and the divine willing in Genesis 5:20—the "you meant" and the "God meant"? To see the answer, it helps to consider that God's acts of will— his intentions and meanings and decisions—are in accord with his prior counsels and purposes. His acts of will do not arise randomly in the instant of their execution but are designed by his prior wisdom, which takes into account the trillions of factors (past, present, and future) that fit together to attain his perfectly just and gracious goals. "All his works are right and his ways are just" (Dan. 4:37).

Therefore, it follows that before God "meant it [the enslavement, which was also intended by the brothers] for good," his wisdom had provided the counsel and the purpose that he would, in that instant, "intend for good." I say this because of Isaiah 46:9–10:

> I am God, and there is no other;
> >I am God, and there is none like me,
> declaring the end from the beginning
> >and from ancient times things not yet done,
> saying, "My counsel shall stand,
> >and I will accomplish all my purpose." (Isa. 46:9–10)

The very deity of God ("I am God" 46:9) means that God acts with unwavering success according to his counsel and purpose. He fulfills his counsels and purposes infallibly, dependably, invincibly. "My counsel shall stand, and I will accomplish all my purpose." Not sometimes. Not maybe. Always. For certain.

So we arrive at the critical moment when Joseph's brothers decide to follow greed, instead of murder, by selling him for twenty shekels. God has, before this critical moment, taken counsel with his wisdom. And he has purposed to see to it that the brothers' sinful choice of greed will come to pass. Therefore, God's will, not the brothers' will, is ultimately decisive. God has ultimate sway. God has ultimate self-determination, not the brothers.

When it comes to *how* this works, I do not know. How do two acts of willing—one human and sinful, the other divine and righteous—work together to bring about the sinful deed so that the brothers are guilty and God is sinless? I do not know. And I argued earlier (in chapter 27) that no one knows such things. Except God.

In view of Genesis 50:20 ("As for you, you meant evil against me, but God meant it for good"), it would be presumptuous to bring, from outside the Bible, a presupposition that humans cannot be held accountable for sinful acts that God has planned. The brothers were accountable. They needed forgiveness (Gen. 50:17). And God planned and willed that their evil act come to pass. Yet in all of this, God did not sin or in any way defile his perfect holiness or diminish his perfect goodness.

Another Providence over Hatred, Four Hundred Years Later

Generations will go by in relative silence in the Scriptures. God had saved Israel from starvation through the sinful hatred of Joseph's brothers. But as time passes, this salvation turns into slavery. Stunningly, when the time comes for a new deliverance, it will come again through sinful hatred—the hatred of Pharaoh for Israel. In fact, as we watch God's providence unfold in the history of Israel, it is difficult not to see a pattern of salvation through being sinned against, which will come to a climax in the way Jesus accomplishes the greatest deliverance of all. We turn in the next chapter to the hatred and the hardening of Pharaoh—both of them from the Lord.

29

Israel Hated, Pharaoh Hardened, God Exalted, Helpless Saved

Lingering over God's providence in the exodus is warranted not only because of the forthright statements of God's turning and hardening human hearts in sinful purposes, but also because the apostle Paul makes God's freedom in hardening Pharaoh the paradigm for his freedom in dispersing all his mercy. "So then he has mercy on whomever he wills, and he hardens whomever he wills" (Rom. 9:18). Paul's understanding and application of God's providence in Israel's exodus from Egypt elevate this Old Testament event to supreme importance in our reflections on God's providence over sin.

Moses Catapulted into Prominence through Human Hatred
After the rescue of Israel through Joseph, the decades go by in Egypt. The favor that Israel enjoyed in the earliest days evaporated:

> There arose a new king over Egypt, who did not know Joseph. And
> he said to his people, "Behold, the people of Israel are too many and
> too mighty for us. Come, let us deal shrewdly with them, lest they

multiply, and, if war breaks out, they join our enemies and fight against us and escape from the land." (Ex. 1:8–10)

The favor Joseph received was replaced by hatred for the Jews. There are striking parallels between the emergence of Joseph and of Moses for the deliverance of Israel. Neither Joseph nor Moses began, in human eyes, as a deliverer. Seventeen-year-old Joseph was imperiled by the hatred of his brothers, and infant Moses was imperiled by the hatred of Pharaoh, who ordered the killing of Jewish infant boys (Ex. 1:16). In the lowest, most endangered moment of their lives, both Joseph and Moses were catapulted into the Egyptian court, one as coruler, the other as adopted grandson. In both cases, this was the utterly unexpected path to the role of savior.

But the most significant parallel for our purposes here, in dealing with God's providence, is that both Joseph and Moses were brought to Egyptian prominence through the sinful actions of human hatred. And most astonishing of all, the existence of this human hatred was willed by God in both cases. We have seen this in detail in Joseph's case from Genesis 45:7; 50:20 and Psalm 105:17. Now we see it in Moses's case from Psalm 105:23–26:

> Then Israel came to Egypt;
> Jacob sojourned in the land of Ham.
> And the Lord made his people very fruitful
> and made them stronger than their foes.
> *He turned their hearts to hate his people,*
> to deal craftily with his servants.
> He sent Moses, his servant,
> and Aaron, whom he had chosen.

Through the hatred of Joseph's brothers, Joseph became a deliverer. Through the hatred of the Egyptians, Moses became a deliverer. Concerning Joseph's brothers' sin, it was said, "God meant it for good"

(Gen. 50:20). Concerning Moses's adversaries in Egypt, it was said, "[God] turned their hearts to hate his people" (Ps. 105:25).

What Should I Say in Response to Providence over Hatred?

When the psalm says that God "turned their hearts to hate his people," it does not specify whether he turned their hearts from some other emotion to hatred or from some other object to hating Israel in particular. Either is grammatically possible. In either case, the point is that God governs the sinful hatred of the Egyptians in the sense that he sees to it that his people are hated. If I had been an Israelite, I would have been right to say, "Because of God's ultimate and decisive providence, we are hated by the Egyptians." I would not be able to say that the Egyptians are innocent. Nor would I be able to say that God is sinful or cruel.

I might be legitimately perplexed why God would plan such a painful plight for his people, but it would not be legitimate to criticize God or impute to him malevolent motives. I might say with the apostle Paul (so many centuries later), "We are afflicted in every way, but not crushed; perplexed, but not driven to despair" (2 Cor. 4:8). Or I might follow the advice of Jeremiah:

> Let him sit alone in silence
>   when it is laid on him;
> let him put his mouth in the dust—
>   there may yet be hope; . . .
> For the Lord will not
>   cast off forever. (Lam. 3:28–29, 31)

I will not demand that God reveal the mystery of how he can turn a heart to hate me without turning his hands into hateful hands. I will not assume he is a mere man with such human limitations (Num. 23:19; 1 Sam. 15:29). I will say with Moses, "The secret things belong to the Lord our God" (Deut. 29:29). And, "Your thoughts are very deep!" (Ps. 92:5). And, "How unsearchable are his judgments and how inscrutable his ways!" (Rom. 11:33).

And as one who reads Psalm 105:25 ("He turned their hearts to hate his people") today, I would take careful note how this psalm begins and ends. The farthest thing from the psalmist's mind is faultfinding with God:

> Oh give thanks to the LORD; call upon his name;
>> make known his deeds among the peoples!
> Sing to him, sing praises to him;
>> tell of all his wondrous works!
> Glory in his holy name;
>> let the hearts of those who seek the LORD rejoice!
>>> (105:1–3)

> So he brought his people out with joy,
>> his chosen ones with singing.
> And he gave them the lands of the nations,
>> and they took possession of the fruit of the
>>> peoples' toil,
> that they might keep his statutes
>> and observe his laws.
> Praise the LORD! (105:43–45)

God's strange providence in turning the hearts of the Egyptians to hate Israel was part of a much bigger picture of divine wisdom and power and covenant-keeping love. When we cannot see this, we wait in silence (Ps. 62:1). When we can, we "give thanks to the LORD" and "call upon his name" (Ps. 105:1).

The Relation between Hating and Hardness

We are not left to view Psalm 105:25 as an isolated act in God's deliverance in the exodus. This act of God was repeated over and over in the story of the exodus, namely, in the act of hardening Pharaoh's heart. Pharaoh's heart was hardened in a hateful purpose to keep Israel enslaved rather than to release the nation at Moses's command. This act of hardening is so pervasive in the story, and so critical in Paul's understanding of God's freedom, that we will focus on it now in more detail than we did in chapters 6 and 7.

In those two chapters, the focus was on the *goal* of God's providence in hardening Pharaoh's heart and on the way the divine hardening shaped Paul's thinking in Romans 9. The focus here is on the *fact* and *nature* of the divine hardening. One of the reasons this closer focus is needed is because of how many people draw attention to Pharaoh's *self*-hardening, as if this made God's hardening a mere response to Pharaoh's self-determination, and as if that "response" prevented God's hardening from confirming Pharaoh's will in evil. Neither proves to be true when we actually look closely at the texts. God is not merely responding. And his hardening does confirm Pharaoh's will in its evil course.

Hardened by God vs. Hardened by Self

You recall what is happening. God has sent Moses and Aaron to command Pharaoh to let his people go. Pharaoh refuses over and over, and God multiplies his wonders in Egypt with more and more miracles—ten plagues and then a great sea-splitting deliverance—to show that he is God and Pharaoh is nothing in his rebellion. Eighteen times Exodus refers to the hardening of Pharaoh's heart, so that he does not let the people go. Once, Exodus refers to the hardening of the Egyptians at the Red Sea (14:18), which probably includes Pharaoh. Hardening is sometimes described as *God's* hardening, sometimes as *Pharaoh's* self-hardening, and sometimes with a passive verb that does not specify who is doing the hardening (e.g., "Pharaoh's heart *was hardened*"). Here is a table of these occurrences so you can easily look at them in context.

God's Hardening	Being Hardened	Self-Hardening
4:21	7:13	8:15
7:3	7:14	8:32
9:12	7:22	9:34
10:1	8:19	
10:20	9:7	
10:27	9:35	
11:10		
14:4		
14:8		
14:17		

The Plan to Harden and the Purpose

One of the most important details to observe in the story of the exodus is that before Moses even arrives in Egypt to confront Pharaoh with God's command that he let Israel go, God's plan was to harden Pharaoh's heart. The earliest statement to this effect is Exodus 4:21: "The LORD said to Moses, 'When you go back to Egypt, see that you do before Pharaoh all the miracles that I have put in your power. But *I will harden his heart*, so that he will not let the people go.'" The next statement of God's plan to harden Pharaoh is found in Exodus 7:3:

> The LORD said to Moses, . . . "You shall speak all that I command you, and your brother Aaron shall tell Pharaoh to let the people of Israel go out of his land. But *I will harden Pharaoh's heart*, and though I multiply my signs and wonders in the land of Egypt, Pharaoh will not listen to you. (7:1–4)

Twice we are told explicitly why God planned to harden Pharaoh's heart and not let the people go:

> The LORD said to Moses, "Go in to Pharaoh, for I have hardened his heart and the heart of his servants, *that I may show these signs of*

mine among them, and that you may tell in the hearing of your son and of your grandson how I have dealt harshly with the Egyptians and what signs I have done among them, that you may know that I am the Lord." (10:1–2)

The Lord said to Moses, "Pharaoh will not listen to you, *that my wonders may be multiplied in the land of Egypt.*" (11:9)

God did not send Moses to Egypt wondering how many plagues it would take to bring Pharaoh to his knees. The plan from the beginning was to "multiply my signs and wonders in the land of Egypt" (7:3). God said this before leveling the first plague. This was the aim of God's hardening: "I have hardened his heart and the heart of his servants, that I may show these signs of mine among them" (10:1).

So the purpose of the hardening is linked to the purpose of the wonders and of the exodus itself in the future history of Israel and of the world. God hardens Pharaoh so that (1) he may multiply his wonders (7:3; 10:1; 11:9). He multiplies his wonders to (2) put Pharaoh in his place, (3) show the Egyptians that he is the absolute Lord, (4) establish himself as the center of Israel's worship for generations, and (5) make a name for himself in all the earth.

1. "I [will] show these signs of mine" (Ex. 10:1).

2. "I will harden the hearts of the Egyptians so that they shall go in after them, and *I will get glory over Pharaoh*" (Ex. 14:17).

3. "*The Egyptians shall know that I am the Lord,* when I have gotten glory over Pharaoh" (Ex. 14:18; cf. 11:9).

4. "I [will] show these signs . . . *that you may tell in the hearing of your son and of your grandson*" (Ex. 10:1–2).

5. "For this purpose I have raised [Pharaoh] up . . . *so that my name may be proclaimed in all the earth*" (Ex. 9:16).

438 *The Nature and Extent of Providence*

Self-Hardening under the Hand of God-Hardening

The point I am making is that God's hardening of Pharaoh's heart was not a mere response to Pharaoh's self-hardening. It was a plan from the beginning. Not only that, but it can be shown that Pharaoh's being hardened, and even his self-hardening, is the effect of God's hardening, not its cause. Many people deny this and point out that the explicit statement that God hardened Pharaoh's heart occurs first in Exodus 9:12, *after* Pharaoh had already twice hardened his own heart (8:15, 32). They infer from this that God's hardening is the effect of Pharaoh's self-hardening.

But there is a serious problem with that inference. We have seen that *before* the encounters with Pharaoh begin, God said to Moses, "I will harden his heart" (4:21). But what we have not yet seen, which is absolutely crucial to see, is that Moses (the author of Exodus) refers back to this promise four times as he describes Pharaoh's hardening. In other words, four times Moses tells us that the hardening is happening "as the LORD had said." And it is all-important to remember what, in fact, the Lord had said when it says, "as the LORD had said." What he said was "I will harden his heart." He had *not* said, "He will harden his own heart."

Here are these four occurrences of "as the LORD had said":

Before the first plague: "Still *Pharaoh's heart was hardened*, and he would not listen to them, *as the LORD had said*" (7:13).

After the first plague: "But the magicians of Egypt did the same by their secret arts. So *Pharaoh's heart remained hardened*, and he would not listen to them, *as the LORD had said*" (7:22).

After the second plague: "But when Pharaoh saw that there was a respite, *he hardened his heart* and would not listen to them, *as the LORD had said*" (8:15).

After the third plague: "Then the magicians said to Pharaoh, 'This is the finger of God.' But *Pharaoh's heart was hardened*, and he would not listen to them, *as the LORD had said*" (8:19).

Again, what the Lord had said was, "I will harden his heart, so that he will not let the people go" (4:21; cf. 7:3). What is remarkable is that, in Exodus 8:15, Pharaoh's self-hardening is traced back to God's hardening: "He hardened his heart . . . as the LORD had said." That is, he hardened his heart, as it was said, "[the Lord] will harden his heart."

The point is this: whether it says that Pharaoh hardened his own heart (8:15) or that his heart "was hardened" (8:19), in each case the hardening is happening "as the LORD had said." And what he had said was, "I will harden Pharaoh's heart." This means that behind the "self-hardening" and behind the "being hardened" were the plan and purpose of God to harden. God's hardening is not described as a response to what Pharaoh does. It's the other way around. What Pharaoh does—his self-hardening—is described as the effect of what God does.

What Paul Saw in the Story of Pharaoh's Hardening

The decisive impulse in this entire drama is not the self-determination of Pharaoh but the prior and ultimate purpose of God, namely, to display his power and make known his name (Ex. 7:3; 9:16; 10:1–2; 11:9; 14:17–18). This is precisely what the apostle Paul picks up on. Paul sees that God's unwavering commitment to make known the fullness of his glory (his name) governs his actions in such a way that God is never merely responding to what humans do. He is free to act always in accord with the counsel of his own will (Eph. 1:11). This freedom Paul expresses as God's showing mercy and hardening "whomever he wills." Here is how he makes the connection with Pharaoh:

> The Scripture says to Pharaoh, "For this very purpose I have raised you up, that I might show my power in you, and that my name might be proclaimed in all the earth." So then he has mercy on whomever he wills, and he hardens whomever he wills. (Rom. 9:17–18)

What Paul is doing here in verse 18 is reaching back, first to Romans 9:15–16, and summing up the freedom of God in mercy: "I will have mercy on whom I have mercy, and I will have compassion on whom I have compassion" (9:15). So he says in verse 18, "So then he has mercy on whomever he wills." In other words, he underscores God's freedom in showing mercy. Then Paul draws out of the exodus story the freedom of God in hardening. After quoting Exodus 9:16 (in Romans 9:17), he sums up God's freedom in hardening: "He hardens whomever he wills."

When I describe this as God's freedom in showing mercy and freedom in hardening, I mean that in choosing whom to treat with hardening and whom to treat with mercy, God is not constrained by anything outside himself. He consults "the counsel [or plan] of his will" (τὴν βουλὴν τοῦ θελήματος αὐτοῦ, Eph. 1:11). This is decisive. Nothing in man, good or bad, past, present, or foreseen, determines who is hardened and who is shown mercy.

To be sure, all human beings, in themselves, are unworthy of being shown mercy and deserve judgment. One could say, then, that human sinfulness is the cause of hardening. But that is not the question. The question is not why anyone might be hardened. The question is, Why this one and not that one, since both are sinful and undeserving? Why does one sinner receive hardening and another receive mercy? Paul's answer is, "[God] has mercy on whomever he wills, and he hardens whomever he wills" (Rom. 9:18).

A Demand That Will Not Succeed

Hardening whom he wills means that God freely decides who will experience the hardness of rebellion and unbelief and impenitence, and therefore deservingly be condemned. God's hardening does not make human fault impossible; it makes it certain. Here is our familiar mystery: people who are thus hardened against God are really guilty. They have real fault. They really deserve to be judged. There is no injustice with God (Rom. 9:14). And it was God who decided who would be in that condition and who would be rescued from it in mercy. If we demand an explanation for *how* this can be—that God freely chooses who is hardened, and yet they have real guilt—we will probably be disappointed in this life. I do not offer such an explanation. I say what I see in the word: God hardens whom he wills, and man is accountable. God's hardening does not take away guilt; it renders it certain.

Seven Contextual Evidences for Unconditional Hardening

What are the evidences that the words "he hardens whomever he wills" (Rom. 9:18) mean that God freely and unconditionally decides who will be hardened and who will not? That's what I mean by *unconditional*—not that there is no condition of unworthiness, but that nothing in any human—past, present, or future—makes the difference in God's decision who is hardened and who is shown mercy. I point very briefly to seven strands of evidence from the context of Romans 9 in the hope that you will follow them long enough to see if they are woven into a fabric of pervasive providence over the sin of human hardness.

1. *That is what the words most naturally mean.* "He hardens whomever he wills" says that his will, and not our will, is decisive in hardening whomever *he* wills. To be sure, our will rebels and is hard against God. But the natural meaning of these words is that God's will is decisive beneath and behind our willing, without nullifying the importance of our will.

2. *The exact parallel with mercy shows that the act of God in hardening is as unconditional as the act of God in having mercy.* Verse 18 says, "He has mercy on whomever he wills, and he hardens whomever he wills." So if we believe that God's showing mercy is unconditional, the most natural way to take the parallel is that the hardening is unconditional. Again, the point is not to deny that God sees us in our sinfulness, and

thus as deserving of judgment. The point is that since all are in the same hopeless condition, nothing in any person accounts for why one receives mercy and another hardening.

3. *This is in fact exactly what Paul infers from God's words in verse 15, "I will have mercy on whom I have mercy."* Paul draws out of this, in verse 16: "So then it depends not on human will or exertion, but on God, who has mercy." If that is what "I have mercy on whom I have mercy" means, then it is probably what "he hardens whomever he wills" means, namely, "It depends not on human will or exertion, but on God, who hardens."

4. *The parallel with Jacob and Esau shows that mercy and hardening are unconditional.* Paul said in verses 11–13, "Though they were not yet born and had done nothing either good or bad, . . . she was told, 'The older will serve the younger.' As it is written, 'Jacob I loved, but Esau I hated.'" In other words, the context demands that Paul address not just the love and mercy part of God's sovereignty but also the hate and hardening part of God's sovereignty. The parallel with Jacob and Esau in verse 13 shows that the hardening and the mercy are unconditional.

5. *The objection raised in Romans 9:19 and Paul's answer to it show that Paul did not deal with God's sovereignty the way many people deal with it today.* Paul raises the objection to his own position: "You will say to me then, 'Why does he still find fault? For who can resist his will?'" Now at this point many people today say, "God finds fault because human beings have ultimate self-determination and use it to rebel against God." So God's hardening, they say, is not free and unconditional but is caused by man's self-determined hardness.

If Paul agreed with that way of thinking, he could have so easily answered the objection of verse 19 that way. The objector hears Paul say, "[God] hardens whomever he wills," and then the objector responds, "Why does he still find fault? For who can resist his will?" How easily Paul could have answered the objection with an appeal to ultimate human self-determination! But he didn't. Because it is the wrong answer. It turns Paul's teaching on its head. Paul's point is that nothing in man explains why one is hardened and another is shown mercy. That distinction lies wholly in God, not man. So Paul turned away the question of verse 19, detecting a wrong spirit in it: "But who are you, O man, to answer back to God?" (9:20).[1]

6. *Verse 21 shows that Paul sees mercy and hardening as unconditional because he speaks of the objects of mercy and hardening as coming from the same lump of clay.* "Has the potter no right over the clay, to make out of the same lump [there's the crucial phrase!] one vessel for honorable use and another for dishonorable use?" The stress is that it was not the nature of the clay that determined what God would do with it. It was the free and wise and sovereign will of the potter. He has mercy on whom he wills, and he hardens whom he wills—from the same lump of clay.

7. *We read in Romans 11:7, "What then? Israel failed to obtain what it was seeking. The elect obtained it, but the rest were hardened."* In other words, the decisive issue in who is hardened, and who is not, is election, not some prior willing or running on our part. "The elect obtained it, but the rest were hardened," which is parallel to Romans 9:18: "He has mercy on whomever he wills, and he hardens whomever he wills."

Mystery Remains

Let me say again, after these seven reasons for believing in God's freedom in mercy and hardening, that I have not removed a mystery; I have stated a mystery. God makes the choice to treat one with mercy and one with hardening unconditionally. Nothing in any person provides a criterion for one being hardened and another receiving mercy. The distinction lies in the will of God. The distinction lies not in man. Yet those who are hardened are truly guilty and truly deserve judgment for the rebellious condition of their hearts. Their own consciences will

---

1   See chap. 7 (pp. 108–9) for a discussion of Rom. 9:20–23.

justly condemn them. If they perish, they will perish for real sin and real guilt. How God freely hardens and yet preserves human accountability, we are not told.

Hardening in Majestic Holiness

In this chapter we have focused on the foundational event in Israel's existence, the exodus. They were brought to desperation in Egypt by being *hated*, and they were delivered through multiplied wonders because Pharaoh was *hardened*. Both the hatred and the hardening, we have seen, were brought about by the all-embracing providence of God. The hatred of the Egyptians was sin. And the hardness of Pharaoh was sin. Nevertheless, in "[turning] their hearts to hate his people" (Ps. 105:25) and in hardening Pharaoh's heart, God did not sin or compromise his majestic holiness. On the contrary, he became the subject of a song of praise:

> Who is like you, O LORD, among the gods?
>   Who is like you, majestic in holiness,
>   awesome in glorious deeds, doing wonders? (Ex. 15:11)

Providence as the Foundation of Our Encouragement

I don't doubt that one of the reasons God records such amazing examples of salvation, coming through hatred against his people, is that we need great encouragement that painful and sinful circumstances are not out of control, but that God rules over the rise and fall of hatred against his people. In fact, he rules hateful circumstances in such a way that they regularly lead to a greater deliverance than otherwise possible.

It really does look like an intentionally encouraging pattern in Scripture. Besides Joseph (whom we studied in chapter 28) and Moses, recall the book of Esther and the way Mordecai was elevated in the pagan court and was able to turn Haman's hatred of the Jews into a stunning reversal and deliverance for Israel. And recall how the pattern comes to a climax in hatred against Jesus (Luke 19:14; John 7:7; 15:18), resulting in his crucifixion—and, stunningly, our salvation. Salvation through being hated and killed! This will be the Christian path to final deliverance: "You will be hated by all for my name's sake. But the one who endures to the end will be saved" (Matt. 10:22).

Already in the Old Testament this Christian path was foreseen, as, for example, by the psalmist in Psalm 44:22:

> For your sake we are killed all the day long;
> we are regarded as sheep to be slaughtered.

Paul quoted that as part of Christian experience in Romans 8:36:

> As it is written,
>
> > "For your sake we are being killed all the day long;
> > we are regarded as sheep to be slaughtered."

What is the basic biblical encouragement for God's people in this pattern of deliverance through being hated? One answer is this: the basic encouragement—the foundation of many other encouragements— is God's all-encompassing providence over the smallest and the largest adversaries, including their power to hate. In Romans 8 Paul encourages believers who are suffering. He does this with the promise that God works *all things* together for their good (Rom. 8:28). And he makes explicit that these "all things" include the hateful intentions behind "tribulation, or distress, or persecution, or famine, or nakedness, or danger, or sword" (Rom. 8:35). He goes so far as to say that even if we are slaughtered like sheep, "in all these things we are more than conquerors through him who loved us" (Rom. 8:37).

The rock-solid foundation of our encouragement is the all-governing providence of God. When we are in prison with Joseph or when our baby is in the crocodile-infested bulrushes with Moses or when we are despised by Pharaoh or when we receive 195 cumulative lashes with Paul (2 Cor. 11:24), or when we are on the cross with Jesus, the fact that God's all-wise providence governs even the hatred of our persecutors is meant to put steel in the backbone of our faith and help us endure everything for the joy set before us (Heb. 12:2).

We Need the Fact Established, Not the Mystery Fathomed

We have seen enough in this book so far so that hatred-governing (Ps. 105:25) and hardness-governing (Ex. 4:21) providence of God is not a surprise. My hope is that you will begin to reflexively say to such texts, "Yes, there it is—the perplexing providence of God—and, yes, he knows *how* to do this in a way that neither forces good people to be hateful against their will, nor diminishes any accountability for sin, nor tarnishes his own immaculate holiness and goodness and justice." *How* God governs the human heart in its acts of sinning, we are not told. *That* he does, we are told over and over.

What sustains us, when surrounded by hatred, is not our ability to *explain* God's providence, but the unshakable *fact* of God's providence. And that fact will sustain us to the degree that we believe that nothing—absolutely nothing—can happen to us but "by God's fatherly hand."[2] This is why stories of God's providence abound in Scripture, but explanations of the mystery of *how* it works do not. Our faith needs the certainty of the fact, not the fathoming of the mystery.

Between Exodus and Exile

As we move forward in our effort to come to terms with the extent and nature of God's providence over human sin, we will find that just as

---

2   Recall the beautiful answer to Question 27 of the Heidelberg Catechism from chapter 1: "What do you understand by the providence of God?" Answer: "The almighty, everywhere-present power of God, whereby, as it were by his hand, He still upholds heaven and earth with all creatures, and so governs them that herbs and grass, rain and drought, fruitful and barren years, meat and drink, health and sickness, riches and poverty, indeed, all things come not by chance, *but by his fatherly hand."*

God made great sin serve his purposes in the founding of the nation of Israel, so he will make great sin serve his purposes in the climactic judgment on Israel in the Babylonian destruction of Jerusalem. Some of the strongest and clearest demonstrations of God's providence over sin cluster around their glorious exodus and their tragic exile. It is as if God would say, "I will make sin serve your merciful creation, and I will make sin serve your just destruction."

We will devote chapters 32 and 33 to the providence of God over the tragedy of Jerusalem's destruction. But between the exodus and the exile, the providence of God over human sinning goes on without pause. In chapters 30 and 31 we will narrow the focus onto two kinds of sinning: the sins of family against family and the sins of deception and delusion. My choice of these among many other possibilities is partly owing to the explicit way Scripture attributes these sorrows to God and partly because our own experience makes them more pressing.

30

Broken Families

Family sorrows are the heaviest sorrows. One may have great compassion when someone else's family breaks down. We may weep with those who weep. That is a beautiful and Christlike reflex of the Christian heart (Mark 8:2; Luke 7:13). But the breakdown physically, and especially spiritually, of *one's own* family weighs on the heart like a great rock in our chest. There are many who feel as if the all-encompassing providence of God over such miseries is not a comfort or encouragement, but an added burden. But for others, while such family-governing providence is sobering (as is all ultimate reality), nevertheless it gives far more hope than the thought of Satan, sinful man, or mindless fate having the upper hand.

What Jesus Would Say
Jesus is incredibly blunt to his followers in warning them that there are going to be family divisions:

> Do you think that I have come to give peace on earth? No, I tell you, but rather division. For from now on in one house there will be five divided, three against two and two against three. They will be divided, father against son and son against father, mother against daughter and

daughter against mother, mother-in-law against her daughter-in-law
and daughter-in-law against mother-in-law. (Luke 12:51–53)

Brother will deliver brother over to death, and the father his child,
and children will rise against parents and have them put to death.
And you will be hated by all for my name's sake. But the one who
endures to the end will be saved. (Mark 13:12–13)

Does the all-encompassing providence of God rule in the lives
of disobedient children? There is a biblical story near the end of the
period of the judges, as God was about to raise up the prophet Samuel,
that gives the answer. Eli was a priest to God in those days, and to his
sorrow, his sons Hophni and Phineas were defiling the tabernacle of
God by their flagrant immorality:

Now Eli was very old, and he kept hearing all that his sons were
doing to all Israel, and how they lay with the women who were
serving at the entrance to the tent of meeting. And he said to them,
"Why do you do such things? For I hear of your evil dealings from
all these people. No, my sons; it is no good report that I hear the
people of the LORD spreading abroad. If someone sins against a
man, God will mediate for him, but if someone sins against the
LORD, who can intercede for him?" But they would not listen to
the voice of their father, *for it was the will of the LORD to put them to
death*. (1 Sam. 2:22–25; cf. Josh 11:20)

Why Would the Sons Not Listen?

There is no doubt here that Eli's sons were wicked. They did not
deserve any help from the Lord to change their ways and obey their
father's warnings not to sin "against the LORD." In fact, when their
father called for them to change, they "would not listen to [him]."
The inspired writer tells us why: "For it was the will of the LORD to
put them to death" (2:25). The word *for* (Hebrew, כִּי) gives us the

reason the sons did not obey. It was *because* God intended to put them to death, which he did, striking the brothers down on the same day (1 Sam. 2:34; 4:11).

The question here is not whether these sons were already guilty of high-handed sin against God and worthy of such punishment from the Lord. They were. Rather, the point is that the author goes out of his way to put their *final recalcitrance and disobedience* in the hands of God. God knew what it would take to bring these sons to repentance and obedience, and he chose not to let that happen. "They would not listen to the voice of their father, *for* it was the will of the LORD to put them to death" (2:25). They did not listen. They kept on disobeying. Why? Because God had decided that there would be no repentance and forgiveness but only punishment by early death.

Why Would the Young King Not Listen?

The sinful unwillingness of Eli's sons to listen to fatherly counsel is similar to Rehoboam's unwillingness to listen to the wisdom of the older men in Israel who advised him—after the death of his father, Solomon—to treat the people kindly (2 Chron. 10:7). Instead, he followed the folly of the younger men, with the result that the kingdom was divided with Jeroboam leading ten of the tribes away from Rehoboam.

Why did this happen? Why did Rehoboam not act wisely for the good of the people? The answer, as in the case of the sons of Eli, is, finally, the providence of God. "So the king [Rehoboam] did not listen to the people, *for it was a turn of affairs brought about by God that the LORD might fulfill his word*, which he spoke by Ahijah the Shilonite to Jeroboam the son of Nebat" (2 Chron. 10:15; cf. 1 Kings 12:15, 24). God's aim was to tear the kingdom from the hand of Solomon's son (1 Kings 11:11). This he accomplished by seeing to it that Rehoboam would not listen to the wisdom of his elders, just like the sons of Eli would not listen to their father. (See a similar case in 2 Chron. 25:20.)

In both cases (Eli's sons and Rehoboam), the reality of God's judgment is sobering. In one case, there were devastating effects for centuries because of the division of Israel into two kingdoms. In the other case, it was more personal, less national, but perhaps more devastating because God had decided that there would be no repentance and forgiveness for the sons of Eli. Disobedience and death were decreed.

Not an Irrelevant Story for Christians

This is a frightening prospect—that there may be a point of sinning in our lives after which God says, "There will now be no repentance and no forgiveness for you." Even today, we Christians are to feel this as a warning. We see this, for example, in 1 John 5:16:

> If anyone sees his brother committing a sin not leading to death, he shall ask, and God will give him life—to those who commit sins that do not lead to death. There is sin that leads to death; I do not say that one should pray for that.

The point is not that there is *a specific sin* that leads to death—as if one group of sins is forgivable and another not. The point, rather, is that there comes a point—and only God knows it—when God may say, "No more. I will not grant you repentance, and therefore you have forfeited forgiveness."

This was what happened in the case of Esau:

> See to it that no one fails to obtain the grace of God; that no "root of bitterness" springs up and causes trouble, and by it many become defiled; that no one is sexually immoral or unholy like Esau, who sold his birthright for a single meal. For you know that afterward, when he desired to inherit the blessing, he was rejected, for he found no chance to repent, though he sought it with tears. (Heb. 12:15–17)

What Esau could not find was "a place of repenting" (μετανοίας . . . τόπον). He had come to the point of sinning that could be called, to use John's language, "sin that leads to death" (1 John 5:16). No repentance would be given. And, therefore, no forgiveness. We will see in section 8 how God prevents this from happening in the lives of his children (e.g., Jude 24–25). One of the means he uses to keep it from happening is by causing us to take biblical warnings seriously. The story of Eli's sons, together with 1 John 5:16 and Hebrews 12:17, serve as such warnings.

Tyre and Sidon Would Have Repented

I said that God had decided not to give repentance to Eli's sons—or to Esau. I said that God knows what it would take to bring a person to repentance. He may bring about what it takes or not. This thought may be foreign to some readers—that God grants repentance and knows what it takes to bring it about, and may or may not lead a person to repent. So let's linger here and ponder some implications of God's providence in the disobedience of Eli's sons *"for it was the will of the LORD to put them to death"* (1 Sam. 2:25).

Jesus said that God knows what works are needed to bring people to repentance, and yet he leaves some of those people in the hardness of unrepentance by not showing those works. This is what we have seen in the case of Eli's sons. In this story about the mighty works of Jesus, the cities of Tyre and Sidon are like Eli's sons:

> He began to denounce the cities where most of his mighty works had been done, because they did not repent. "Woe to you, Chorazin! Woe to you, Bethsaida! For if the mighty works done in you had been done in Tyre and Sidon, they would have repented long ago in sackcloth and ashes. But I tell you, it will be more bearable on the day of judgment for Tyre and Sidon than for you. And you, Capernaum, will you be exalted to heaven? You will be brought

down to Hades. For if the mighty works done in you had been done in Sodom, it would have remained until this day. But I tell you that it will be more tolerable on the day of judgment for the land of Sodom than for you." (Matt. 11:20–24)

Jesus knows that if the works he had done in Chorazin and Bethsaida had been done in Tyre and Sidon, they would have repented. Nevertheless, such works were not done there. This is doubly astonishing to readers who do not reckon with the magnitude of what it means for God to be God—and for Jesus to be God. First, it is astonishing that Jesus can know what human beings would do under certain circumstances. Tyre and Sidon would have repented. He knows this. We don't. Second, even in his own day Jesus does not do the works in Tyre and Sidon that he knows would bring about repentance.

Jesus and his Father have their reasons for where and when they do the works they do. God is infinitely wise and just and good. Our response should be a trembling amazement that he has seen fit to grant repentance to us, when we are no more deserving than the people in Tyre and Sidon. Jesus is free to "[have] mercy on whomever he wills" (Rom. 9:18). "Am I not allowed to do what I choose with what belongs to me?" (Matt. 20:15).

What Is Our Hope for Dead People Repenting?

Alongside the response of trembling amazement, we should also feel *hope* for those we love who are outside Christ. Not because they are ultimately self-determining. That gives us little hope, since all people, including our family, are dead in trespasses (Eph. 2:5), not able to understand the things of the Spirit (1 Cor. 2:14), unable to submit to God's law (Rom. 8:7), and in the captivity of Satan (2 Tim. 2:26). If people must become the ultimate decisive cause of their own repentance, we have no hope of salvation. Rather, we should feel hope because God knows how to bring people to repentance, and when he decides to do it, it happens. Nothing can stop him. Not the longest pattern of sinning. Not the worst kind of sinning. If he decides for bondage to be broken, and for repentance to happen, it will. We see this in 2 Timothy 2:24–26:

> The Lord's servant must not be quarrelsome but kind to everyone, able to teach, patiently enduring evil, correcting his opponents with gentleness. *God may perhaps grant them repentance* leading to a knowledge of the truth, and they may come to their senses and escape from the snare of the devil, after being captured by him to do his will.

Repentance is a gift of God. He may give it. He may not. No one deserves it. He did not give it to Tyre and Sidon, and he did not give it to Eli's sons. But he has given it to millions upon millions. That he can give it to whomever he pleases means that no sin, no rebellion—in any family member—can escape the sway of his repentance-giving providence when he decides to grant repentance.

Therefore, our sacred calling in the work of salvation is to pray like Paul in Romans 10:1 ("My heart's desire and prayer to God for them is that they may be saved"); and to speak the gospel, since God causes the new birth "through the living and abiding word of God" (1 Pet. 1:23); and to be kind to everyone, patiently enduring evil, correcting our opponents with gentleness (as Paul says in 2 Timothy 2:24–26), for God may grant them repentance. That is our calling, our confidence, and our hope.

The Sorrows of a Man after God's Own Heart

The sin and death of Eli's sons was not the only prominent family brokenness in Israel. The most famous falling-out of all was the rebellion of David's son Absalom against his father. The whole affair is heartbreaking, and the cry of David at the end has often moved me deeply.

When word was brought to David that the rebellion was crushed and Absalom was dead, we read:

> The king was deeply moved and went up to the chamber over the gate and wept. And as he went, he said, "O my son Absalom, my son, my son Absalom! Would I had died instead of you, O Absalom, my son, my son!" (2 Sam. 18:33)

But these tragic and sinful events did not happen apart from God's providence. After David had committed adultery with Bathsheba and arranged for the killing of her husband, the prophet Nathan came to David and said:

> "Why have you despised the word of the Lord, to do what is evil in his sight? You have struck down Uriah the Hittite with the sword and have taken his wife to be your wife and have killed him with the sword of the Ammonites. Now therefore *the sword shall never depart from your house,* because you have despised me and have taken the wife of Uriah the Hittite to be your wife." Thus says the Lord, "Behold, *I will raise up evil against you out of your own house.* And I will take your wives before your eyes and give them to your neighbor, and he shall lie with your wives in the sight of this sun. For you did it secretly, but I will do this thing before all Israel and before the sun." (2 Sam. 12:9–12)

When we ponder all the evil that happened to David in the wake of his own sin, the seriousness of it is compounded by the words of God: "I will raise up evil against you" (12:11). These evils were not mere natural consequences of human sin. They were divine judgments from the hand of God. "I will raise up evil against you."

The Divine Cause of Shimei's Curse

During the uprising led by Absalom, David had to deal with heart-wrenching conflicts at every level. One of these that is described as specifically ordained by God is found in 2 Samuel 16:5–7, where Shimei pours out his curses on David as he leaves Jerusalem in tears over Absalom's conspiracy:

> When King David came to Bahurim, there came out a man of the family of the house of Saul, whose name was Shimei, the son of Gera, and as he came he cursed continually. And he threw stones at David and at all the servants of King David, and all the people and all the mighty men were on his right hand and on his left. And Shimei said as he cursed, "Get out, get out, you man of blood, you worthless man!"

Abishai, one of David's commanders, said, "Why should this dead dog curse my lord the king? Let me go over and take off his head" (2 Sam. 16:9). David did not allow this. He saw the hand of providence in the hateful treatment he was receiving.

> David said to Abishai and to all his servants, "Behold, my own son seeks my life; how much more now may this Benjaminite! Leave him alone, and let him curse, *for the* LORD *has told him to.*" (Literally: "Leave him. And he will curse, because the Lord spoke to him," 2 Sam. 16:11)

David sees God's providence in Shimei's hateful cursing. He speaks of it in language similar to the language of Lamentations 3:37:

> Who has *spoken* and it came to pass,
>   unless the Lord has *commanded* it?

David says that the Lord *spoke* to Shimei, and that is why Shimei is cursing David. This does not imply that God whispered in Shimei's ear that he should curse David. God does not give Shimei a revealed command to sin. God's *revealed* will for human beings (what he says they should do in his word) is always "You shall be holy, for I the LORD your God am holy" (Lev. 19:2; cf. 1 Pet. 1:16).

Nevertheless, if God's *sovereign* will ordains that someone act contrary to his *revealed* will (which indeed it does, as when he willed the murder of his Son for our salvation, Acts 2:23; 4:27–28), he always brings that sovereign will to pass in such a way that the human will makes a real choice and is morally accountable. God did not whisper in Shimei's ear that he was suspending the moral law and that it would now be righteous to curse the Lord's anointed. When it says, "The Lord has told him to" (2 Sam. 16:11), it likely means that God spoke in his Creator voice and brought his intended result to pass. In this sense, God's *speaking* is his *bringing about*. This is what Jeremiah means when he says, "Is it not from the *mouth* of the Most High that good and bad come?" (Lam. 3:38). This is the "mouth" of sovereign decree, not the mouth of revealed command.[1]

Shimei confesses openly and clearly that his cursing of David was *sin* and that he is responsible. When Absalom's rebellion had been quelled, David returned to Jerusalem. He met Shimei on the way back:

> Shimei the son of Gera fell down before the king, as he was about to cross the Jordan, and said to the king, "Let not my lord hold me guilty or remember how your servant did wrong on the day my lord the king left Jerusalem. Do not let the king take it to heart. For your servant knows that I have sinned." (2 Sam. 19:18–20)

I conclude, therefore, that Shimei's sin was real, and that he was truly guilty. His plea is not that God's providence took away his guilt. His plea is that David would forgive him for real sin and real guilt.

---

1   See chap. 27 note 3 for my essay where I explain and defend more fully the difference between the *revealed will* of and the *sovereign will* of God. This distinction is warranted by the Bible. The simplest way to see it is to notice that God's *revealed* will is "You shall not murder" (Ex. 20:13), while his *sovereign* will, in the case of Jesus, is that his Son be murdered. It was "the will of the Lord to crush him" (Isa. 53:10) "by the hands of lawless men" (Acts 2:23). In other words, God often wills that things come to pass that are sin, and therefore contrary to his "revealed will."

When God's providence brings about hate or cursing toward his people, it does not make the sinning person into a robot with no moral accountability.

Endless Stream of Evils against the Forgiven King

Perhaps David had learned to read the providence of God in situations like the one with Shimei because God had taught him through Nathan the prophet that God's decree was that David would be sinned against for the rest of his life. This was part of God's discipline for David's adultery with Bathsheba and for his murdering her husband Uriah. We already cited the word of God to David through Nathan:

> The sword shall never depart from your house, . . . and I will raise up evil against you out of your own house. And I will take your wives before your eyes and give them to your neighbor, and he shall lie with your wives in the sight of this sun. For you did it secretly, but I will do this thing before all Israel and before the sun. (2 Sam. 12:10–12)

"I will raise up." "I will take." "I will . . . give." "I will do." God is not nearly as squeamish as we are about asserting his active providence in bringing about evil. "I will raise up *evil* against you out of your own house" (2 Sam. 12:11). Evil like Absalom's murder of his brother Amnon (2 Sam. 13:28–29) and Solomon's murder of his brother Adonijah (1 Kings 2:23–25). Evil like Absalom's armed uprising against his father and Joab's killing of Absalom (2 Sam. 18:14). Evil like Absalom's sex with his father's concubines in a tent on the roof, in the sight of all Israel (2 Sam. 16:22)—just as God had promised (2 Sam. 12:12).

David had learned to live with these miseries, not because he believed God had no hand in causing his family sorrows, but because

all the paths of the Lord are steadfast love and faithfulness,
> for those who keep his covenant and his testimonies.
For your name's sake, O Lord,
> pardon my guilt, for it is great. (Ps. 25:10–11)

All his paths are steadfast love. Not just *some* of them. *All* the paths of his family's wreckage—just as Jeremiah is going to say in the midst of the horrors of Jerusalem's suffering, "[God's mercies] are new every morning" (Lam. 3:23). *Every* morning. And be sure to take note that it is not a contradiction in David's mind to say that this is true for "those who keep his covenant and his testimonies," *and* then pray, "For your name's sake, O Lord, pardon my guilt, *for it is great*" (Ps. 25:11). Covenant keeping does not mean sinlessness. Even in the midst of God's heavy and severe and painful providence that came to him and his family, David believed that God was loving and faithful to him, and that he—David himself—was a covenant keeper whose great guilt was forgiven.

No Family beyond the Wakening Work of Providence

On this side of the cross of Christ, such confidence is also how Christians endure the unremitting hardships and sorrows of life. We know that "through *many* tribulations we must enter the kingdom of God" (Acts 14:22). But we do not endure and thrive by thinking that man, Satan, or fate has decisive control over sin and evil in this world or in our lives. Rather, we press on and rejoice by trusting the sovereign God of the universe, who proved his love in Jesus Christ, and who governs all things, including family desolations like David's. We press on by believing that all God's paths are steadfast love and faithfulness to those who are in Christ Jesus (Rom. 8:28–39), and by believing that what is impossible with man is possible with God—including the great, impossible work of new birth (Mark 10:27).

From Precious Families to Priceless Word

If families are dear to us, so is God's word dear to him. We have seen how his providence reigns over the brokenness of the families of priests and kings. We will now see how his providence reigns over the rejection and distortion and suppression of his word. In spite of the abuses of his holy word, we may be sure that God's all-embracing providence secures this truth: "The word of God is not bound!" (2 Tim. 2:9).

31

Deception and Dullness of Heart

We have seen that God sometimes judges his sinful people by seeing to it that certain sinful actions come to pass that provide particularly suitable judgment. For example, because of David's adultery with Bathsheba in secret, God decrees that his son Absalom will lie with David's wives on the very rooftop. God says this to David through Nathan the prophet:

> I will take your wives before your eyes and give them to your neighbor, and he shall lie with your wives in the sight of this sun. For you did it secretly, but I will do this thing before all Israel and before the sun. (2 Sam. 12:11–12)

Providence of Withholding God's Word

In this chapter we focus on God's providence over the particular sin of withholding the true word of God. One way to say it is that God punishes those who do not want his word with the privation of his word. And that deprivation comes in different forms, including the delinquency of false shepherds, the dullness of human hearing, and the deception of false prophets.

For example, where the word of God is not cherished and faithful shepherding is not prized, we read,

> "Behold, the days are coming," declares the Lord GOD,
>> "when I will send a famine on the land—
> not a famine of bread, nor a thirst for water,
>> but of hearing the words of the LORD."
>> (Amos 8:11)

Behold, I am raising up in the land a shepherd who does not care for those being destroyed, or seek the young or heal the maimed or nourish the healthy, but devours the flesh of the fat ones, tearing off even their hoofs.

> Woe to my worthless shepherd,
>> who deserts the flock!
> May the sword strike his arm
>> and his right eye!
> Let his arm be wholly withered,
>> his right eye utterly blinded!
>> (Zech. 11:16–17)

It is sinful for shepherds not to feed the flock of God. But God may judge his people by giving them shepherds with sinful resistance to preaching and refusal to teach the truth. We see this repeatedly in the Old and New Testaments:

> You will give them dullness of heart;
>> your curse will be on them. (Lam. 3:65)

Go, and say to this people:

> "Keep on hearing, but do not understand;
> keep on seeing, but do not perceive."
> Make the heart of this people dull,

> and their ears heavy,
> > and blind their eyes;
> lest they see with their eyes,
> > and hear with their ears,
> and understand with their hearts,
> > and turn and be healed. (Isa. 6:9–10)

They know not, nor do they discern, for he has shut their eyes, so that they cannot see, and their hearts, so that they cannot understand. (Isa. 44:18)

Lest They See and Understand

Such was God's judgment on Israel in the time of the prophets. But not only during the time of the prophets; it was the same when Jesus came. He met with great resistance (John 1:11). And the apostle John said that this was not finally and decisively owing to human self-determination but to the design of God to fulfill Scripture.

> Though [Jesus] had done so many signs before them, they still did not believe in him, *so that the word spoken by the prophet Isaiah* might *be fulfilled*:
>
> > "Lord, who has believed what he heard from us,
> > > and to whom has the arm of the Lord been revealed?"
> > [Isa. 53:1].
>
> *Therefore* [on account of this divine purpose to fulfill prophecy] they could not believe. For again Isaiah said,
>
> > "He has blinded their eyes
> > > and hardened their heart,
> > *lest they see* with their eyes,
> > > and understand with their heart, and turn,
> > > and I would heal them" [Isa. 6:10]. (John 12:37–40)

At times, Jesus chose to speak in ways that were designed to keep people from understanding:

> Jesus declared, "I thank you, Father, Lord of heaven and earth, that *you have hidden these things from the wise and understanding* and revealed them to little children; yes, Father, for such was your gracious will." (Matt. 11:25–26)

> The disciples came and said to him, "Why do you speak to them in parables?" And he answered them, "To you it has been given to know the secrets of the kingdom of heaven, *but to them it has not been given*. For to the one who has, more will be given, and he will have an abundance, but from the one who has not, even what he has will be taken away." (Matt. 13:10–12)

> When his disciples asked him what this parable meant, he said, "To you it has been given to know the secrets of the kingdom of God, but for others they are in parables, *so that* 'seeing they may not see, and hearing they may not understand.'" (Luke 8:9–10)

Beware of minimizing the extent of God's providence in such words and strategies of Jesus. It is true that Jesus is not dealing with neutral people, but with sinful people who deserve judgment. But keep in mind that there are *no* neutral people. All of us are sinful and guilty and deserve judgment. No one *deserves* the truth from God. We will see in part 3, section 7 (chapters 34–38) that if there are, in fact, "little children" who submissively and thankfully receive the word of God (Matt. 11:25), it is because God has made them so (Matt. 16:17). But what should not be minimized is that Jesus is concealing the truth (Matt. 11:25; 13:11; Luke 8:10). He is confirming and solidifying the unrepentant, sinful condition of unbelievers when he joins his Father in "[hiding] these things from the wise and understanding" (Matt. 11:25).

God Sends Them a Strong Delusion

We see this again in Paul's prophecies about the last times:

> The coming of the lawless one is by the activity of Satan with all
> power and false signs and wonders, and with all wicked deception
> for those who are perishing, because they refused to love the truth
> and so be saved. Therefore *God sends them a strong delusion, so that
> they may believe what is false,* in order that all may be condemned
> who did not believe the truth but had pleasure in unrighteousness.
> (2 Thess. 2:9–12; cf. Rev. 17:16–17)

Paul introduces us here to an extent of God's providence that seems to
go beyond concealing truth to sending delusion (2:11). The reason I
say "seems" to go beyond concealing truth is that we do not know *how*
God sends this delusion. It is possible that he sends this delusion by
how much truth he withholds. We don't know *how* he does it.

But perhaps the most important words for discerning the extent of
God's providence in this text are the words "*so that* they may believe
what is false [εἰς τὸ πιστεῦσαι αὐτοὺς τῷ ψεύδει]" (2:11). These
words express God's design, his purpose, for sending the delusion. His
aim is their unbelief of the truth and their belief in a lie. Refusing to
"love the truth" (2:10) and preferring to "believe what is false" (2:11)
are sins. God, in his providence, has chosen not only that these people
be justly condemned (2:12), but that they be confirmed in the very sin
of unbelief that makes their condemnation just.

Making the Question of God's Truthfulness More Pressing

Does God's sending a strong delusion (2 Thess. 2:11) contradict the
biblical teaching that God never lies?

> Paul, a servant of God and an apostle of Jesus Christ, for the sake
> of the faith of God's elect and their knowledge of the truth, which
> accords with godliness, in hope of eternal life, which God, *who*

never lies [ὁ ἀψευδὴς θεὸς], promised before the ages began. (Titus 1:1–2; cf. Rom. 3:3–4; Heb. 6:17–18; 2 Tim. 2:12–13)

To make the question even more pressing, biblical passages describe God's arranging for people to be deceived. This is true not only in war strategies, where God commands the use of ambush, which deceives the enemy (e.g., Josh. 8), but also in cases where God intends to bring judgment on sinful persons through their being deceived. In Ezekiel 14:6–11, for example, God says:

> Say to the house of Israel, Thus says the Lord GOD: Repent and turn away from your idols, and turn away your faces from all your abominations. For any one of the house of Israel, or of the strangers who sojourn in Israel, who separates himself from me, taking his idols into his heart and putting the stumbling block of his iniquity before his face, and yet comes to a prophet to consult me through him, I the LORD will answer him myself. And I will set my face against that man; I will make him a sign and a byword and cut him off from the midst of my people, and you shall know that I am the LORD. *And if the prophet is deceived and speaks a word, I, the LORD, have deceived that prophet,* and I will stretch out my hand against him and will destroy him from the midst of my people Israel. And they shall bear their punishment—the punishment of the prophet and the punishment of the inquirer shall be alike—that the house of Israel may no more go astray from me, nor defile themselves any-more with all their transgressions, but that they may be my people and I may be their God, declares the Lord GOD.

A person separates himself from God by taking idols into his heart (14:7). That very person comes to a prophet to "consult" with God, as if to use God, while loving idols. God gives him an answer through the prophet (14:7)—namely, he sees to it that the man is deceived through the prophet: "*And if the prophet is deceived and speaks a word, I, the* L*ORD, have deceived that prophet"* (14:9). So there will be "punishment of the prophet and . . . punishment of the inquirer" (14:10). God's aim in this punishment through deception is "that the house of Israel may no more go astray from me" (14:11).

Sending a Lying Spirit

Before I try to show how this is reconciled with "God never lies" (Titus 1:2), consider one more example, namely, the encounter of King Ahab (of Israel) and King Jehoshaphat (of Judah) with the prophet Micaiah (1 Kings 22). The issue is whether these kings should go up together and fight against the Syrians at Ramoth-gilead. They inquire of the Lord, and four hundred prophets, led by Zedekiah (22:11), say, "Go up, for the Lord will give it into the hand of the king" (22:6; see also 22:12). This was a false prophecy, because the Lord intended for Ahab to perish in this very battle and for his blood to be licked up in the very place where innocent Naboth had been killed (1 Kings 21:19; 22:17, 34, 38). The false prophecy was designed to accomplish God's judgment on Ahab.

One prophet is not included in this chorus of false prophecy: Micaiah. When pressed by Ahab, he prophesied the truth, Ahab's defeat: "I saw all Israel scattered on the mountains, as sheep that have no shepherd" (1 Kings 22:17). Then Micaiah gives a glimpse into why the four hundred prophets had deceived Ahab and Jehoshaphat:

> Micaiah said, "Therefore hear the word of the LORD: I saw the LORD sitting on his throne, and all the host of heaven standing beside him on his right hand and on his left; and the LORD said, 'Who will entice Ahab, that he may go up and fall at Ramoth-gilead?' And one said one thing, and another said another. Then a spirit came forward and stood before the LORD, saying, 'I will entice him.' And the LORD said to him, 'By what means?' And he said, 'I will go out, and will be a lying spirit in the mouth of all his prophets.' And he said, 'You are to entice him, and you shall succeed; go out and do so.' Now therefore

behold, the LORD has put a lying spirit in the mouth of all these your prophets; the LORD has declared disaster for you." (1 Kings 22:19–23)

This picture of the transaction in heaven is not unlike the picture of heaven in Job 1:6: "Now there was a day when the sons of God came to present themselves before the LORD, and Satan also came among them." The upshot of the transaction in Job 1 was that Satan went out from the Lord's presence, with God's permission, on his way to kill Job's children (Job 1:12, 19), which Job saw as effectively God's taking his children—"*The LORD* has taken away" (Job 1:21)—which the inspired writer notes was not sinful for Job to say (Job 1:22; cf. 42:11).[1]

The upshot of the transaction in 1 Kings 22 was that "a spirit" volunteered to "be a lying spirit in the mouth of all his prophets" (22:22). The result was that four hundred prophets deceived Ahab into thinking he would triumph over the Syrians, when God intended for him to perish for his sins. Thus God used the deception of this "lying spirit" to accomplish his judgment on Ahab.

God Never Lies

Now back to the question: Does God's sending a strong delusion to those who refuse to love the truth (2 Thess. 2:10–11), or his deceiving a prophet as a judgment on idolatry (Ezek. 14:9), or his dispatching a "lying spirit" as a judgment on Ahab (1 Kings 22:22) contradict the biblical teaching that God "never lies" (Titus 1:2)?

On the one hand, I could simply say that the biblical texts brought forward in chapters 26–30 have established the fact that God can see to

---

1   It is likely that Satan is used by God in a similar way to test David and finally bring judgment on the people of Israel. We see this by comparing 1 Chron. 21:1 with 2 Sam. 24:1. "Then Satan stood against Israel and incited David to number Israel" (1 Chron. 21:1). "The anger of the LORD was kindled against Israel, and he incited David against them, saying, 'Go, number Israel and Judah'" (2 Sam. 24:1). One says Satan incited David to take the census. The other says that the Lord incited him. Both are true. Only in one of them, the incitement is traced back to God as decisive, without mentioning the intervening means.

it that sin happen without himself sinning. That's true. Applying that here, we could possibly say, "God can see to it that deception happen without being a deceiver." But the problem with such a statement is that God's hand in the deception is such that he himself says that he is deceiving—"I, the LORD, have deceived that prophet" (Ezek. 14:9). In other words, the text does not simply say that God saw to it that sin happened (believing a delusion), but also that in seeing to it, God used a means that Titus 1:2 says he never does, namely, deception or lying.

God Is Not a Man to Regret or Lie

In 1 Samuel 15 there is a pointer to a possible solution to this apparent contradiction in God's action. The situation is that God had commanded Saul to destroy the Amalekites, including their king Agag (1 Sam. 15:3). Saul disobeyed and knew it (1 Sam. 15:9, 24). The word of the Lord came to Samuel about this disobedience: "I regret [נִחַמְתִּי] that I have made Saul king, for he has turned back from following me and has not performed my commandments" (1 Sam. 15:11). Similarly, at the end of the story, we are told that the Lord "regretted" making Saul king: "Samuel did not see Saul again until the day of his death, but Samuel grieved over Saul. And the LORD regretted [נִחָם] that he had made Saul king over Israel" (1 Sam. 15:35).

This has caused some readers to think God did not know what would become of Saul when he made Saul king. Why would you speak of regret if you knew ahead of time that he would go bad? I have written answers to that question in various places.[2] Part of the answer relates to our present question of whether God is lying in 1 Kings 22, Ezekiel 14, and 2 Thessalonians 2.

---

2   Here are three of those places, all at the Desiring God website, regarding the question of God's "regret" and whether God lies: "God Does Not Repent Like a Man," November 11, 1998, https://www.desiringgod.org/articles/god-does-not-repent-like-a-man; "The Repentance of God," March 30, 1987, https://www.desiringgod.org/articles/the-repentance-of-god; and "Does God Lie?," July 23, 2008, https://www.desiringgod.org/articles/does-god-lie.

Even though it says twice in 1 Samuel 15 that God regretted making Saul king, it also says, amazingly, as Samuel speaks to Saul:

> The LORD has torn the kingdom of Israel from you this day and has given it to a neighbor of yours, who is better than you. *And also the Glory of Israel will not lie or have regret* [יִנָּחֵם], *for he is not a man, that he should have regret.* (1 Sam. 15:28–29)

My assumption is that the author of 1 Samuel 15 did not slip up and contradict verses 11 and 35 (God regretted) when he wrote verse 29 (God does not regret). These statements are too close together, and too similar, to think this is not intentional. The key, I think, is to notice that in verse 29 Samuel says, "The Glory of Israel will not lie or have regret, *for he is not a man,* that he should have regret." I take this to mean that God may "regret" but not like a man—not the way humans regret.

Human regret is based partly on lack of foreknowledge. But divine regret is not. God "[declares] the end from the beginning" (Isa. 46:10). His foreknowledge of human sin is part of what it means to be Yahweh, "I am" (John 13:19).[3] Therefore, I draw from 1 Samuel 15 that God does regret, but he does so in a way that does not compromise the completeness, or perfection, of his divine foreknowledge. We are not told how. One could suggest that the divine sorrow present in the "regret" at Saul's failure was already present in its peculiarly divine way when Saul was chosen in the first place.

Applying the Point to God's Acts of Deception

The link between God's regret and his truthfulness is explicit in 1 Samuel 15:29: "The Glory of Israel *will not lie* or have *regret.*"

---

3   See how John 13:19 connects the deity of Christ with his foreknowledge, thus showing that foreknowledge is part of God's goodness: John Piper, "Is the Glory of God at Stake in God's Foreknowledge of Human Choices?," Desiring God, July 3, 1998, https://www.desiringgod.org/messages/is-the-glory-of-god-at-stake-in-gods-foreknowledge-of-human-choices.

Therefore, we are led to think of God's deception in the same way we think about his regretting. Just as his regretting seems to compromise his divine omniscience, so his sending a lying spirit (1 Kings 22:22), or his deceiving a prophet (Ezek. 14:9), or his sending a delusion (2 Thess. 2:11) seems to compromise God's truthfulness ("God . . . never lies," Titus 1:2). But the point of 1 Samuel 15:29 is that what looks like sinful, human lying or regretting in God is, in fact, *not* that. God does regret, but he does *not* regret in such a way that his divine foreknowledge is compromised. God does send a lying spirit and deceive a prophet and send a delusion, but he does *not* do this in such a way that his divine veracity or truthfulness is compromised.

We are not told *how* God prevents his providence in deceit from being sinful. Only that his glory is such that his providence, in judging people by means of deception, guides his action in complete freedom from sin. "The Glory of Israel . . . is not a man" (1 Sam. 15:29). With God, there is a kind of regretting, and a kind of deceiving, that is not like man's regretting and man's deceiving. It is not prompted or guided by finiteness or sin. It is rooted, rather, in infinite wisdom. It is guided by perfect justice.

God's providence over the sin of deception and blindness comes to its judging and saving climax after three years of Judas's deceptions as a false apostle. Jesus had chosen him to be one of the twelve, knowing full well what would come (John 6:64; 13:11). The final, multiplying, God-ordained deceptions and dissimulations (Matt. 11:25; Acts 4:27–28; 13:27) brought the Son of God to the cross. In this way, God turned all the deceptions into a great act of salvation for sinners. Jesus's death was orchestrated by deception and falsehood (Matt. 26:60). And by that death he stamped every promise as *true* with the seal of his blood (2 Cor. 1:20). Although God's hand and God's plan conducted this orchestration of falsehood (Acts 4:27–28), he was true. Indeed, let every mouth confess, "Let God be true though every one were a liar" (Rom. 3:4).[4]

The Rape of the Apple of God's Eye

From the preservation of Jacob's family in Egypt (chapter 28), and the creation of Israel as a nation through the exodus (chapter 29), and the breakdown of families of priests and kings (chapter 30), and the judgment of Israel through a famine of the word (chapter 31), we turn now to the climax of Israel's horrors in the destruction of Jerusalem. Not surprisingly, we will see that God's providence in Israel's darkest hour provides unshakable hope for ours.

---

4   A number of other passages confirm God's truthfulness: "God is not man, that he should lie, or a son of man, that he should change his mind. Has he said, and will he not do it? Or has he spoken, and will he not fulfill it?" (Num. 23:19). "The word of the Lord is upright, and all his work is done in faithfulness" (Ps. 33:4). "This God—his way is perfect; the word of the Lord proves true" (2 Sam. 22:31). "Every word of God proves true" (Prov. 30:5). "The words of the Lord are pure words, like silver refined in a furnace on the ground, purified seven times" (Ps. 12:6).

32

Though He Cause Grief,
He Will Have Compassion

I argued in chapter 5 that even today, in the mercy of God's providence, there is a Christ-exalting future for the people of Israel, when God lifts the veil (2 Cor. 3:14), takes away the hardness of heart (Rom. 11:25), and grants them repentance and faith in Jesus as the Messiah (Acts 5:31; 2 Cor. 3:16). But in the years following the Babylonian rape of Jerusalem, it was almost impossible to believe there was a future.

How could this have happened? This was the place where the God of Israel had chosen to make his name dwell (Neh. 1:9). His love for Jerusalem was echoed in the songs of Israel:

If I forget you, O Jerusalem,
　　let my right hand forget its skill!
Let my tongue stick to the roof of my mouth,
　　if I do not remember you,
if I do not set Jerusalem
　　above my highest joy! (Ps. 137:5–6)

And now:

> How lonely sits the city
>   that was full of people!
> How like a widow has she become,
>   she who was great among the nations!
> She who was a princess among the provinces
>   has become a slave.
>
> She weeps bitterly in the night,
>   with tears on her cheeks;
> among all her lovers
>   she has none to comfort her;
> all her friends have dealt treacherously
>   with her;
>   they have become her enemies.
>   (Lam. 1:1–2)

Surely the destruction of this city, with the horrors of suffering and death and deportation, will bring down the judgment of God on Babylon. This city and her people were the "apple of [God's] eye" (Zech. 2:8). Yes. But, first, Israel will have to learn that this *was* the judgment of God. Providence was not suspended while Jerusalem was sacked.

"Besides Me There Is No God"

For hundreds of years—even as far back as Deuteronomy 28:49–57— God had prepared Israel to grasp this painful providence, the sacking of Jerusalem. Isaiah, prophesying hundreds of years earlier, spoke with stunning clarity about Israel's captivity and deliverance. He traced both to God's providence. And what makes Isaiah stand out among the prophets is that, more than any other, he argued that holding absolute sway over good and evil is part of what it means to be God.

In Isaiah 45 God addresses the Persian king Cyrus in the distant future. Cyrus would defeat Israel's captors, the Babylonians, and assist in the repatriation of the Jews to their homeland. In all of this, God identifies the pagan king Cyrus as one "whose right hand I have grasped" (Isa. 45:1). God's aim in wielding this pagan king for his purposes is "that you [Cyrus] may know that it is I, the LORD, the God of Israel, who call you by your name" (45:3). He makes clear to Cyrus that he is wielding Cyrus not for Persia's sake but for Israel's: "For the sake of my servant Jacob, and Israel my chosen, I call you by your name, I name you, though you do not know me" (45:4).

Then come the sweeping statements about God's providence over all nature and all history. In speaking to Cyrus, God intends to leave no suggestion that the God of Israel is one among many gods. He is the only God. And God's argument is that absolute rule over what happens in the world belongs only to such a deity, namely, to himself:

> I am the LORD, and there is no other,
>> besides me there is no God;
>> I equip you, though you do not know me,
> that people may know, from the rising of the sun
>> and from the west, that there is none besides me;
>> I am the LORD, and there is no other.
> I form light and create darkness;
>> I make well-being and create calamity;
>> I am the LORD, who does all these things. (45:5–7)

Four times: "There is no other." "Besides me there is no God." "There is none besides me." "There is no other." This is what the Lord wants Cyrus and Israel to take to heart. Then come two sweeping statements about God's providence:

> I form light and create darkness;
>> I make well-being and create calamity. (45:7)

Why Use the Language of Creating, Forming, and Making?

The two pairs present extreme opposites: light opposite dark, and well-being opposite calamity. The point seems to be that Cyrus should get out of his mind that there is one god behind the light and all that happens in the light, and another god behind the dark and what happens in the dark. Similarly, Cyrus should not think that the God of Israel can make only good things happen or only bad things. No. The God of Israel is behind everything. He has no competitors. He is not doing his best with the good while some other malevolent being is frustrating him with the bad.

The Hebrew words translated "well-being" and "calamity" are שָׁלוֹם (*shalom*, peace or well-being) and רַע (evil or calamity). Both words include human actions (e.g., peaceful behavior or hostile behavior) as well as natural processes (e.g., harvest or drought). There is no well-being (in the sense of Hebrew *shalom*) in which human behavior makes people destitute or miserable. Neither is the idea of calamity restricted to natural disasters; it also includes moral evil. The effort to limit these words only to natural processes so that God is not said to govern human actions does not fit the actual words, nor would it have been impressive to Cyrus, whose very action was being controlled by God as he spoke (Isa. 45:1). Moreover, the word רַע is used fourteen times in Isaiah, and all but one refer to the moral evil of human behavior—and the one instance that doesn't refers to a disaster caused by man, not nature (31:2).

The language of *forming* and *creating* and *making* light and dark and well-being and calamity goes beyond ideas of managing or guiding—as if God were saying, "I can turn evil once it's there, but I can't make sure it comes to pass." The idea of managing evil that is already there, or guiding what is already there, may leave the impression that while Yahweh may be the only God, nevertheless, he is limited in what he has to work with. If there is light, he can work with that. But if there is dark, he has to work with that. Similarly with well-being and calamity.

Some might think that if God is presented with the one or the other, he can manage it for his purposes. Isaiah's purpose is to rule out that way of understanding providence.

The language of *forming* and *creating* and *making* communicates something very different from managing or guiding what is already there. It communicates that *God is the one who decides what is there*. In other words, as Creator, God is never limited to managing what he finds at hand. Indeed, when thinking of the world in relation to the Creator, Isaiah would say it is wrongheaded to think of God's finding *anything* at hand. The Creator never "finds" what he has not first appointed to be put in place. That is the point of using the language of *creating* and *forming* and *making*. So Isaiah's point to Cyrus is that there is only one God, and it belongs to the meaning of being the only God that he relates to the world of natural events and human actions not just as manager, but as one who decides (like a creator) all that is there to manage.

No Disaster without the Lord

Another example of how God prepared Israel to understand God's providence in the destruction of Jerusalem was the ministry of the prophet Amos, a contemporary of Isaiah. Amos shared Isaiah's vison of God's providence over disaster. Drawing our minds in the same direction as Isaiah 45:5–7 is Amos 3:6:

> Does disaster come to a city,
> 　　unless the LORD has done it?

This rhetorical question is not meant to confuse or perplex. Like the six rhetorical questions that precede this one (3:3–6) the answer is plain, and the point is clear. These questions are like the jest of someone asking me if I like spaghetti and hearing me answer, "Is the Pope Catholic?" That is not a quiz. It is a strong statement about how I feel about spaghetti. Amos is making a statement, not posing a riddle: "No disaster comes to a city unless the LORD has done it."

This is an instance of a prophet applying a sweeping, all-inclusive truth to a particular disaster. Amos was one of the earliest writing prophets. He ministered during the reign of Uzziah, king of Judah, and Jeroboam, king of Israel (1:1). He warned that because of Israel's injustices (5:7, 15, 24; 6:12) and opulence (3:15), God would bring disaster. This will happen in spite of (and because of) Israel's being God's chosen people:

> You only have I known
> > of all the families of the earth;
> therefore I will punish you
> > for all your iniquities. . . .
> Does disaster come to a city,
> > unless the Lord has done it? (3:2, 6)

Amos reasons from the general truth to the specific instance: because no disaster comes to a city unless the Lord has done it, therefore, know for a certainty, Israel, that your disaster is from the Lord. This disaster is from the Lord, because all disasters are from the Lord. "Does disaster come to a city, unless the Lord has done it?" = "Disaster does not come to a city (any city!), unless the Lord has done it."

Countless Human Decisions Create the Disaster

Moreover, Israel's disaster is not an earthquake or a flood or a drought. It is not a natural disaster. It is "an adversary" surrounding Israel and plundering her. "An adversary shall surround the land and bring down your defenses" (Amos 3:11). Which means that this disaster involves thousands of human decisions which are in the sway of God's providence, accomplishing his purposes of just punishment: "I will punish you for all your iniquities" (3:2). These decisions are being made in the minds of the faithless adversaries, which means that they are pervasively sinful, since whatever is not from faith is sin (Rom. 14:23; cf. Heb. 11:6).

Viewing millions of sinful decisions as firmly in the hands of divine providence does not, however, imply that those hands are thereby defiled. We have seen this and will see it again. "The LORD is in the right" as he wields the plans of the nations in his wisdom (Lam. 1:18). Neither Amos nor Isaiah nor Jeremiah (as we will see) would have countenanced our modern sentiments that try to remove human decisions as part of God's appointed disasters, or to remove disasters as part of providence.

Only God-Ordained Military Commands Come to Pass

With Isaiah and Amos having prepared the way (for us and for Israel), we turn now to Jeremiah's witness in Lamentations. It is a witness to carnage, providence, and astonishing hope. He sounds remarkably like Isaiah in his sweeping view of God's providence: All things—every command in battle, every good and evil—are "from the mouth of the Most High."

> Who has spoken and it came to pass,
>   unless the Lord has commanded it?
> Is it not from the mouth of the Most High
>   that good and bad come?
> Why should a living man complain,
>   a man, about the punishment of his sins? (Lam. 3:37–39)

The rhetorical question "Who has spoken and it came to pass, unless the Lord has commanded it?" expects the answer "No one." Using a rhetorical question, which he expects us to answer, communicates that the speaker (Jeremiah) considers this an obvious point. Anyone can answer this. Our modern idiom might be "It's a no-brainer." That is Jeremiah's view. No human word has called for action and then that action happened, unless the Lord commanded it to happen. This is stunning, sweeping, and all-encompassing. Consider three observations about the effort to put limitations on this statement.

MISTAKE OF SEEING SPECIFIC APPLICATION AS LIMITATION

First, sometimes people limit a sweeping, all-encompassing statement by saying that the context provides a focus, and we should not go beyond the focus of the context. In this text, there are two contextual focuses. One is that Jeremiah is talking about the evils that have come upon *Jerusalem* (1:7, 8, 17; 2:10). The other is that he is thinking primarily about evils that have come because God is punishing sin. We see this in Lamentations 3:39: "Why should a living man complain, a man, about the punishment of his sins?"

So some would say that verse 37 ("Who has spoken and it came to pass, unless the Lord has commanded it?") is a sweeping statement not about *all things* spoken by the human mouth, but only about the words that came out of Babylonian mouths as they sacked the city. So the meaning would be this: "Who among these attacking Babylonians has spoken his commands to strike Jerusalem, and it came to pass, unless the Lord has commanded that his beloved city be punished in this way?" So, they would say, Lamentations 3:37 means only that, and no more, because that's the immediate application.

There are at least two problems with this approach. One is that we don't use universal statements that way. And there is no reason to think that Jeremiah did either. We might say, for example, "Does not the light of the sun reach every country? Are you, then, O China, unfavored by God?" What if someone said, "The focus of these two rhetorical questions is on China and God's blessing of that nation with sunshine. Therefore, that is the meaning of these questions, and one may not infer anything about the author's belief about whether the sun shines on other nations." We would respond, "That's absurd."

The reason it's absurd is that the very point of the questions is to start with a universal claim and then *apply* it to China, not *limit* it to China. That is the way universal statements work when applied to specific instances. We don't cancel out the universality of a statement by applying it to a specific case. The specific case in Lamentations is Jerusalem and the fact that for most of the people in it, this calamity was part of God's punishment. But Jeremiah is applying a universal statement in the form of a rhetorical question: "Who has spoken and it came to pass, unless the Lord has commanded it?" He starts with a rhetorically formed assertion: *Any event that happens because of a spoken human word happens only if God sees to it that it happens.* This universal claim is then applied to Jerusalem and the experience of God's punishment.

CONFIRMATION OF EXTENT IN THE NEXT VERSE

A second observation about the attempt to limit Jeremiah's sweeping claim is that the next verse repeats it and reemphasizes the universality of it: "Is it not from the mouth of the Most High that good and bad come?" (Lam. 3:38). No limitations. All good and bad come from the mouth of God. The reference to God's *mouth* ties back to the word *command* in the previous verse: "Who has spoken and it came to pass, unless the Lord has *commanded* it?" (3:37). The idea is that countless ideas and plans and words of man are thought and spoken—for good and for evil—but which of them become reality? Jeremiah says it ultimately depends on God's *mouth* or *command*. This is God's providence, or we might say, his decree.

This is Jeremiah's way of expressing Proverbs 19:21: "Many are the plans in the mind of a man, but it is the purpose of the LORD that will stand." Many *plans* are "spoken," as Lamentations 3:37 says, but which ones actually come to pass? The proverb says, "The ones the Lord *purposes*." Jeremiah says, "The ones the Lord *commands*." The words "the Lord has commanded it" in Lamentations 3:37 refer to God's giving active implementation to his purpose or his decree. Or as Isaiah 46:10 says, "My counsel shall stand, and I will accomplish all my purpose."

CALAMITY ONLY, OR ALSO MORAL EVIL?

The third observation about attempts to limit Jeremiah's sweeping claim about God's providence over all "good and bad" [הָרָעוֹת וְהַטּוֹב]" (Lam. 3:38) is that some people try to limit the word *bad* to bad events (calamities) rather than bad human choices (sin). You read this repeatedly in commentaries on Lamentations 3:38 and on Isaiah 45:7 ("I form light and create darkness; I make well-being and create calamity [or evil, רָע]; I am the LORD, who does all these things").

The aim of this distinction is usually to get God off the hook for commanding or purposing or decreeing moral evil. Behind this aim is the *assumption* that God would be evil to see to it that moral evil happen. I do not share that assumption. People bring that assumption *to* the Bible; they do not get it *from* the Bible. The Bible teaches that God absolutely *is* not evil, and never *does* evil. *And* the Bible teaches that God sees to it that evils happen (which we will see more fully in what follows). Therefore, I embrace both.

This is not a contradiction. If God hasn't revealed *how* he can do both, we don't need to see how. "The secret things belong to the LORD our God" (Deut. 29:29). There are countless things working all around us in the world, and we cannot begin to explain *how* they work. In fact, I would go so far as to say, when it comes to *ultimate* explanations of how things work, we don't know how *anything* works. That is, at the bottom of our explanations for anything, someone can always legitimately ask, "But how does *that* work?" There is always another layer of reality beneath what we have explained.

If common sense has not taught us this, then surely the arrival of quantum mechanics should expose our explanatory limitations. Of course, this ultimate ignorance about how everything works does not stop us from getting to the moon or building four-billion-dollar underwater floating tunnels or finding cures for diseases—or turning on a laptop. Nor does that same ignorance about how God governs sin, without sinning, stop us from rejoicing in his holiness and bowing to his sovereignty and trusting his promises.

God's Purpose in Judgment on Jerusalem Includes Sinful Acts against Her

There is another problem with this third effort to limit Jeremiah's claim that "from the mouth of the Most High . . . good and bad come" (Lam. 3:38). Limiting the word *bad* to the calamity that has befallen Jerusalem, in the hopes that this will not include moral evil, does not accomplish what is hoped for. What has befallen Jerusalem includes horrors that are perpetrated by people, and their perpetration is sinful. For example:

> All your enemies
>   rail against you;
> they hiss, they gnash their teeth,
>   they cry: "We have swallowed her!
> Ah, this is the day we longed for;
>   now we have it; we see it!"
> The Lord has done what he purposed;
>   he has carried out his word,
> which he commanded long ago;
>   he has thrown down without pity;
> he has made the enemy rejoice over you
>   and exalted the might of your foes. . . .
> Look, O Lord, and see!
>   With whom have you dealt thus?
> Should women eat the fruit of their womb,
>   the children of their tender care?
> Should priest and prophet be killed
>   in the sanctuary of the Lord?
>   (Lam. 2:16–17, 20)

Here we see the Babylonian enemy gloating over Jerusalem, with hissing and gnashing teeth, that they have finally attained their longed-for desire for the destruction of Israel. This is sinful. And it is going to be punished by the Lord (3:64–66). But for now, it is what God has "purposed" and "commanded."

> The LORD has done what he *purposed*;
>> he has carried out his word,
> which he *commanded* long ago. (2:17)

This word *commanded* occurs three times in Lamentations. Besides here, we read in Lamentations 1:17:

> Zion stretches out her hands,
>> but there is none to comfort her;
> the LORD has *commanded* against Jacob
>> that his neighbors should be his foes;
> Jerusalem has become
>> a filthy thing among them.

This command from the Lord in 1:17 is the same as the command in 2:17. It is the expression of God's purpose that Babylon devastate Jerusalem. This is the command referred to in the only other place the word is used:

> Who has spoken and it came to pass,
>> unless the Lord has *commanded* it? (3:37)

Which means that what was "spoken" ("Who has *spoken* and it came to pass?") refers to the expressed designs of the Babylonians—such as:

> They hiss, they gnash their teeth,
>> they cry: "We have swallowed her!
> Ah, this is the day we longed for;
>> now we have it; we see it!" (2:16)

Therefore, the Babylonian design of hateful destruction was spoken by them, but, Jeremiah says, it did not come to pass except by the command of the Lord. This means just what Jeremiah says it does in Lamentations 3:38—from the mouth of the Most High "good and bad come." The *mouth*—that is, the *command* of God—therefore, expresses his all-encompassing providence over the sins of the Babylonians that they committed in carrying out God's judgment on Jerusalem.

Not Cries of Rebellion against God, but of Agony under His Justice

God's providence in the enemy's evil is seen also in Lamentations 2:20:

> Look, O LORD, and see!
> > With whom have you dealt thus?
> Should women eat the fruit of their womb,
> > the children of their tender care?
> Should priest and prophet be killed
> > in the sanctuary of the Lord?

Here the women of Israel, in desperation, are eating their own children (see also 4:10). This is not only desperate and heartbreaking and horrific; it is also sinful. God had warned that it would come to this if Israel persisted in her idolatry (Lev. 26:29; Deut. 28:53–57; Jer. 19:9; Ezek. 5:10).[1] Of this, Jeremiah says to the Lord, "With whom have *you* dealt thus?" He traces this sinful horror back into the dealings of God. You *dealt* this. This is not a sinful slip by the inspired writer of this book. This is the same as saying, "From the mouth of the Most High . . . good and bad come" (Lam. 3:38). This is not an isolated slip. It is the theme of the whole book.

> The Lord has swallowed up without mercy. . . .
> He has cut down in fierce anger

---

1 This issue of the people of Jerusalem eating their own children is so horrible that we will devote a much fuller treatment to it in chap. 33.

all the might of Israel. . . .
He has burned like a flaming fire. . . .
He has bent his bow like an enemy . . . ;
  he has killed all who were delightful in our eyes . . . ;
He has poured out his fury like fire. . . .
The Lord has made Zion forget
  festival and Sabbath. . . .
He has delivered into the hand of the enemy. (2:2–4, 6–7)

Jeremiah's cries are not the misled cries of rebellion against an unrighteous God; they are cries of agony under God's justice:

The Lord is in the right,
  for I have rebelled against his word. (1:18)

Jerusalem sinned grievously;
  therefore she became filthy. (1:8)

The crown has fallen from our head;
  woe to us, for we have sinned! (5:16)

The punishment of your iniquity, O daughter of Zion, is accomplished. (4:22)

Therefore, I conclude from Lamentations 3:37–39, in the context of the whole book, that God's providence governs good and evil, whether they are thought of as events of prosperity and disaster or as human decisions of moral good and moral evil. God holds sway in what happens in this world, both good and evil (see also Eccles. 7:14). And he does so without becoming evil. "The Lord is in the right" (Lam. 1:18).

Crafting Carnage in Poetic Form

We must not leave this most sorrowful of all biblical books without seeing something even more amazing, perhaps, than God's providence over good and evil—namely, Jeremiah's expression of hope and the astonishing ground of it, expressed here, as nowhere else in Scripture.

Surprisingly, Lamentations is a carefully crafted book. I say *surprisingly* because, ordinarily, when there is an outpouring of such anguish and horror, one does not expect that the outpouring would flow through the confined banks of finely crafted poetry. But it does. There are five chapters. The first, the second, and the fourth are divided into twenty-two stanzas, the number of letters in the Hebrew alphabet. Each stanza begins with a different letter of the alphabet. In other words, there are three agony-laden acrostics.

Then chapter 3, the most personally intense of all, is still more tightly structured: again twenty-two stanzas, but here each stanza has exactly three lines, and all three in each stanza begin with the same letter—one stanza for each letter of the Hebrew alphabet. Finally, chapter 5 is the only chapter that is not an acrostic, though it is twenty-two lines long.

Why this form? Why do poets lay such difficult constraints upon themselves? Surely if there is any place for authentic, unencumbered spontaneity, it is here in the overflow of anguish. Why bind the heart with such a severe discipline of poetic form? Why work so hard to give such careful shape to suffering? I do not know for sure. But I will make a suggestion.

Could it be that the carefully structured form of the book is meant to communicate that ultimate reality in the hands of the Creator is like this? Could the book's form tell us that reality contains good and evil—horrible evil, unspeakable evil—but it is all moving within the infinitely wise and powerful and good hands of the perfect Poet of history?

New Mercies Every Morning—in the Midst of Misery

With that possible meaning of the form in mind, consider how Jeremiah expresses his hope. Chapter 3 is the central chapter. There are two chapters on either side. It is also, as I mentioned, the most thoroughly structured—an acrostic with twenty-two stanzas of three lines each (hence sixty-six verses), with each of the three lines of each stanza starting with the same letter of the Hebrew alphabet. Precisely in this most controlled section, we experience the most jarring shift of tone and focus in the entire book. Amid the carnage and the lament, we read this:

> Remember my affliction and my wanderings,
>> the wormwood and the gall!
> My soul continually remembers it
>> and is bowed down within me.
> But this I call to mind,
>> and therefore I have hope:
>
> The steadfast love of the LORD never ceases;
>> his mercies never come to an end;
> they are new every morning;
>> great is your faithfulness.
> "The LORD is my portion," says my soul,
>> "therefore I will hope in him."
>
> The LORD is good to those who wait for him,
>> to the soul who seeks him.
> It is good that one should wait quietly
>> for the salvation of the LORD. (3:19–26)

This is the same author that has said that the worst horrors imaginable in Jerusalem are owing ultimately to the way God has dealt with his people (2:20). And here he is saying that *not a day has gone by* but that God's steadfast love and mercy have been newly present. "The steadfast love of the LORD never ceases; his mercies never come to an end; they are new every morning" (3:22–23). Every morning!

Evidently, Jeremiah believes that when he says, "From the mouth of the Most High . . . good and bad come," he does not mean only *sequentially*, but somehow *simultaneously*. It will prove true that a season of exile and sorrow will be followed sequentially by a season of restoration and joy for Jerusalem. But it is also true that "every morning," during the worst of horrors God's mercies were newly present.

The Lord Is My Portion

One way to see this is to notice that Jeremiah says, "The LORD is my portion" (Lam. 3:24). This remains true for God's people on the worst mornings. And thousands of saints have witnessed that the Lord not only *remains* our portion in the worst of times, but *becomes* most real during the worst of times.

This was certainly the way the apostle Paul experienced the worst of his crises:

> We do not want you to be unaware, brothers, of the affliction we experienced in Asia. For we were so utterly burdened beyond our strength that we despaired of life itself. Indeed, we felt that we had received the sentence of death. But that was to make us rely not on ourselves but on God who raises the dead. (2 Cor. 1:8–9)

God's design (for it certainly was not Satan's) in bringing Paul and his comrades to the end of their strength, and placing them on the brink of eternity, was "to make us rely not on ourselves but on God who raises the dead." In other words, the misery of those terrible days was simultaneous with a new mercy every morning. The new mercy was Paul's deeper awareness of God as real beyond the grave and his deeper trust in God's care through it all.

Emotional Miracle We Cannot Perform

In view of the horrors of Babylonian slaughter, and Jerusalem's self-inflicted carnage, this may seem emotionally impossible—how could there be new mercies *every* morning? In fact, it is *impossible* for fallen human beings like us to experience sorrow this way. That's why Lamentations ends with this prayer: "Restore us to yourself, O Lᴏʀᴅ, that we may be restored!" (Lam. 5:21). The literal translation is "O Lᴏʀᴅ, cause us to turn to you, and we will turn." In other words, the kind of heart turning required for us to feel hope in God in the midst of God-ordained misery is a miracle that no human being can experience without God doing the turning.

Though He Cast Off, He Will Have Compassion

Now, after Jeremiah's amazing expression of hope in the middle of God-sent horrors, and in the middle of this God-inspired book, comes the astonishing *ground* of his hope, expressed in Lamentations 3:31–33 as nowhere else in Scripture. Why should we put our mouth in the dust (3:29) and still feel hope that God is for us?

> For the Lord will not
>   cast off forever,
> but, though he cause grief, he will have compassion
>   according to the abundance of his steadfast love;
> for he does not afflict from his heart
>   or grieve the children of men. (3:31–33)

This astonishing argument has two levels for why the Lord will not cast off forever. First, God will not cast off forever because his intent to make compassion follow grief is "according to the abundance of his steadfast love" (3:32). The final word is not destructive judgment, but forgiving compassion. Neither cancels out the other. But Jeremiah declares that the abundance of God's steadfast love will have the last word. God will exert his sovereign covenant prerogative and turn his people back to him. There will be a new covenant in which he performs the miracle of Lamentations 5:21: "O Lᴏʀᴅ, cause us to turn to you, and we will turn" (cf. Deut. 30:6; Jer. 32:39–41; Ezek. 36:26–27).

God Is Not Afflicting Jerusalem from His Heart

Then there is a second, even deeper level of the argument for why the Lord will not cast off forever, and why his dealing so harshly with them is not the last word:

> Though he cause grief, he will have compassion
> according to the abundance of his steadfast love;
> for *he does not afflict from his heart*
> *or grieve the children of men.* (Lam. 3:32–33)

There is nothing quite like this in all the rest of Scripture, though it is implied in many places. Jeremiah reveals explicitly that God has levels, or layers, of motivation.

God *does* indeed "afflict" and "grieve" the children of men ("Though he cause grief," 3:32). That is one level of motivation. And Jeremiah says that when God is motivated to do this, he "is in the right" (1:18). But then Jeremiah says that when God afflicts and grieves, this is "not . . . from his heart."[2] This phrase "from his heart" points to an unfathomable mystery in God. It would be blasphemous to think of God as double-minded or having a split personality. It would be equally blasphemous to think of God as at war with himself rather than as seeing perfectly at every moment the way of truth and righteousness.

Jeremiah is not blasphemous. He is saying rather that, while not disapproving of anything God does, some of God's acts are means to the ends that are more ultimately aimed at and more heartily desired as the final end. The means affliction and grief are exactly what God wills for that time and situation. They are perfect as means. And, as perfect, they are perfectly approved by God's perfect mind.

---

2 Some translations say, "For he does not willingly bring affliction or grief to anyone" (NIV). But this is misleading since it gives the impression that something outside of God is constraining him to do what he is not willing to do. The ESV is right to translate מִלִּבּוֹ quite literally as "from the heart."

But in God's overall view of history, and in view of the totality of his nature, there are acts which are preeminent and more suited for his ultimate goal. Causing affliction and grief has its place in the expression of God's justice and holiness against sin. But more central to God's nature is "the abundance of his steadfast love" (3:32). This is why he will make a new covenant to secure the enjoyment of this love for his redeemed, renewed, purified, and faithful people.

Glimpse of the Suffering and Glory of Christ

This deeper, more central motivation is the foundation of Jeremiah's hope. And though he had not seen Jesus Christ in the flesh, he was one of those prophets who, in the words of the apostle Peter, "[inquired] what person or time the Spirit of Christ in them was indicating when he predicted the sufferings of Christ and the subsequent glories" (1 Pet. 1:11). From where we stand on this side of the sufferings of Christ, it is difficult not to see a pointer to them in Lamentations 3:30, just before Jeremiah's grounding of hope in the deepest heart of God. He counsels the sufferer that "there may yet be hope" (3:29). And on the way to that hope,

> Let him give his cheek to the one who strikes,
> and let him be filled with insults. (3:30)

The pattern that runs all through Scripture is that God's people must pass through suffering on the way to glory. This pattern came to a peak of horror and glory in Jesus Christ. "They spit in his face and struck him. And some slapped him" (Matt. 26:67). His experience of suffering and subsequent glory became the perfect pattern and the perfect foundation of our hope in suffering.

How much of this Jeremiah glimpsed, we do not know. But it is a wonder of Scripture that Jeremiah would be granted a singular glimpse into what is and is not from the heart of God, and that it would correspond so remarkably with the purpose of the incarnation of Christ.

Affliction and grief are not from God's heart. Rather, from his heart of hearts (so to speak) come compassion and steadfast love. Therefore, we may say, "God did not send his Son into the world to condemn the world, but in order that the world might be saved through him" (John 3:17).

Where Angels Fear to Tread?

We passed over too quickly the lowest degradation of Jerusalem's condition under siege. "Look, O Lord! . . . Should women eat the fruit of their womb, the children of their tender care?" (Lam. 2:20). For many years this has felt, at times, overwhelmingly heavy to me. It is part of the larger issue of the suffering of children in this world. How shall we think about the all-embracing providence of God in the face of this? Going, perhaps, where angels fear to tread, we ponder this in the next chapter.

33

A Wickedness God
Especially Abhorred

We saw at the beginning of chapter 27 that God sometimes judges his people by seeing to it that certain kinds of sinful actions come to pass that provide particularly suitable judgment. For example, David's adultery was punished by adultery against him (2 Sam. 12:11–12). Throughout Scripture, God regularly expresses how fitting it is that punishments correspond to crimes not only in severity but also in kind. For example:

> If there is harm, then you shall pay life for life, eye for eye, tooth for tooth, hand for hand, foot for foot, burn for burn, wound for wound, stripe for stripe. (Ex. 21:23–25)

> With the judgment you pronounce you will be judged, and with the measure you use it will be measured to you. (Matt. 7:2)

> The day of the LORD is near upon all the nations.
> As you have done, it shall be done to you;
>   your deeds shall return on your own head. (Obad. 15)

He loved to curse; let curses come upon him!
> He did not delight in blessing; may it be far from him!
>> (Ps. 109:17)

Because you did not hate bloodshed, therefore blood shall pursue you. (Ezek. 35:6)

As your sword has made women childless, so shall your mother be childless among women. (1 Sam. 15:33)

How Would God Judge the Lowest Degradation?

This is how God often carries out his justice among men. One of the most horrifying sinful human acts is the sacrifice by fire of one's own children. The shedding of innocent blood was warned against in the law (Deut. 19:10). It included the shedding of the blood of adults who had not committed any crime (Deut. 19:13; 1 Sam. 19:5), the "guiltless poor" (Jer. 2:34), and children.[1] And it was the sacrifice of children that seemed to be the low point of wickedness:

> They sacrificed their sons
>> and their daughters to the demons;
> they poured out innocent blood,
>> the blood of their sons and daughters,
> whom they sacrificed to the idols of Canaan,
>> and the land was polluted with blood. (Ps. 106:37–38)

This level of wickedness God especially abhorred:

> Then the anger of the LORD was kindled against his people,
>> and he abhorred his heritage. (Ps. 106:40)

---

1 From this we can see that "innocent" does not mean without sin. All are born in a sinful condition. "Innocent blood" means the blood of a person who does not deserve to be punished by man—that no crime against man has been committed that deserves from man any punishment.

How would God punish the sacrifice of one's own children? He warned in the covenant threats of Leviticus 26 and Deuteronomy 28 that he would spend his fury on them in a horrific form of poetic justice—by making them eat their own children:

If . . . you will not listen to me, but walk contrary to me, then I will walk contrary to you in fury, and I myself will discipline you sevenfold for your sins. You shall eat the flesh of your sons, and you shall eat the flesh of your daughters. (Lev. 26:27–29)

All these curses shall come upon you . . . because you did not obey the voice of the LORD your God. . . . You shall eat the fruit of your womb, the flesh of your sons and daughters, whom the LORD your God has given you, in the siege and in the distress with which your enemies shall distress you. (Deut. 28:45, 53)

Then came the urgent warning from Ezekiel and from Jeremiah, who could see these threats about to come true in their own time:

Because of all your abominations I will do with you what I have never yet done, and the like of which I will never do again. Therefore fathers shall eat their sons in your midst, and sons shall eat their fathers. And I will execute judgments on you, and any of you who survive I will scatter to all the winds. (Ezek. 5:9–10)

Hear the word of the LORD, O kings of Judah and inhabitants of Jerusalem. . . . Behold, I am bringing such disaster upon this place that the ears of everyone who hears of it will tingle. Because the people have forsaken me and . . . have filled this place with the blood of innocents, and have built the high places of Baal to burn their sons in the fire as burnt offerings to Baal, . . . therefore, behold, . . . I will make them eat the flesh of their sons and their daughters . . . in the siege and in the distress. (Jer. 19:3–6, 9)

Then It Actually Happened

Then the unthinkable actually happened. The judgment fell, and the killers of children became the eaters of children, as the siege brought them to starvation:

> Look, O LORD, and see!
>   With whom have you dealt thus?
> Should women eat the fruit of their womb,
>   the children of their tender care? (Lam. 2:20)

> The hands of compassionate women
>   have boiled their own children;
> they became their food
>   during the destruction of the daughter of my
>   people.
> The LORD gave full vent to his wrath;
>   he poured out his hot anger. (Lam. 4:10–11)

The hatred of God for the murder of children, especially as a supposed act of worship, is matched by the shock of the words "I will make them eat the flesh of their sons and their daughters" (Jer. 19:9).

The Children! The Children!

If this were only a matter of wicked parents being made to endure the maddening moral stench of their own rotting consciences, we might put our hands over our mouths and stand silent with sickened, trembling approval at the Lord's providence.

But what makes the matter more complex is the children. What are we to think about the children? What about their suffering and death? We have had to face this question before, in section 5. We know that God took the life of countless children in the flood that he sent in Genesis 6. And he sent the angel of death and killed all the firstborn sons in the Passover in Exodus 12:29: "At midnight the LORD struck down all the firstborn in the land of Egypt."[2] But even though the suffering of helpless children is not new, the horrors of parental wickedness have reached a new low in the sufferings of Jerusalem.

Widening the Lens of Our Focus: The Origin of Death

Part of the biblical answer to the question about how to understand the suffering and death of children is found in the way Paul's letter to the Romans connects the spiritual outrage of Adam's first sin to the physical effects of human death and suffering. Paul connects Adam's sin to the history of human death. "Just as sin came into the world through one man, and death through sin, and so death spread to all men because all sinned . . ." (Rom. 5:12). Paul explains that in Adam, God saw the entire human race represented in such a way that all his descendants were counted sinners: "By the one man's disobedience the many were appointed sinners [ἁμαρτωλοὶ κατεστάθησαν]" (5:19, my translation). Paul saw this appointing as sinners not as a consequence of fate or physical inheritance, but as a legal condemnation by God: "One trespass led to *condemnation* for all men" (5:18).

The outcome of suffering and death was not a natural consequence; it was a divine judgment: "Judgment following one trespass brought condemnation" (5:16). And the effect of that legal condemnation, and that decree of judgment, was the reign of death over all human beings: "Because of one man's trespass, death reigned through that one man" (5:17). "Many died through one man's trespass" (5:15). "Sin reigned in death" (5:21).

Subjected in Hope

This is the background for Paul's devastating and gloriously hopeful words in Romans 8:20–22:

---

2   See chapter 24 for what I said about the fate of children in the night of the first Passover.

> The creation was subjected to futility, not willingly, but because of him who subjected it, in hope that the creation itself will be set free from its bondage to corruption and obtain the freedom of the glory of the children of God. For we know that the whole creation has been groaning together in the pains of childbirth until now.

This "[subjection] to futility" is what we saw in Romans 5:12–21. When sin entered the world, death entered the world as a condemnation and judgment. Death does not exist as an isolated judgment. The prelude to death for everyone is a life with much suffering, described in part in Genesis 3:14–19. Paul broadens the picture now in Romans 8 to include the whole creation in God's judgment because of sin.

The entire creation is "subjected to futility" (Rom. 8:20). Nothing escapes the brokenness of the world. The original goodness has been corrupted from the day when God pronounced his creation "very good" (Gen. 1:31). Things are painfully frustrating, again and again. Just when you think you have one thing fixed, another breaks. When one relationship is healed, another breaks down. When one disease is under control, another strikes. When one accident is avoided, another comes from a different direction.

Paul describes this fallen condition of creation as "bondage to corruption" (Rom. 8:21). It is slavery. The creation was subjected "not willingly" (8:20). Rather, the one who subjected it was God. We know this because Paul says he subjected it "in hope that the creation itself will be set free" (8:21). That was not Satan's design, nor Adam's. It was God's. This is why I called Romans 8:20–22 "devastating and gloriously hopeful words." The condemnation to futility and corruption and suffering and death is devastating. But the promise that the subjection is a path to liberation is gloriously hopeful.

The present sufferings are like "the pains of childbirth" (8:22), meaning something joyful is about to be born in creation. The subjection and condemnation were not the final word; the subjection was "in hope." It was labor pains. "The creation itself will be set free from its bondage to corruption" (8:21). First, the children of God are justified through faith in Christ (5:1), and then they will be glorified (8:30) with new resurrection bodies (8:23). And then the whole creation, as if to become the perfect habitation for eternal joy in the presence of God, will be glorified as the children have been: "the creation itself will obtain the freedom of the glory of the children of God" (8:21).

Why Is Moral Evil Judged with Physical Pain?

For now, the world is under God's judgment. It is subjected to natural (Rom. 8:20–23) and moral corruption (Rom. 1:24, 25, 28). This includes the physical horrors of natural calamity, disease, suffering, and death. It includes the suffering and death of children, both from natural causes and from human cruelty.

Have you ever pondered the question, Why does God judge moral evil with physical pain? Picture for a moment Adam and Eve in the garden of Eden before sin entered the world. Everything is perfect. Then they eat the forbidden fruit (Gen. 2:17; 3:6). God strikes the natural world with a curse. Physical things such as bodies and ground and vegetation are made slaves to corruption (Gen. 3:14–19; Rom. 8:20). But why? Physical things did not sin. The sin was between Adam's heart and God. The sin was not first wife abuse. That came soon—as a consequence (Gen. 3:12). But it was not first. First was God abuse. And it was not physical. It was spiritual.

Adam hit God. But not with his fist. He hit him with his heart. He said, in effect, "I don't trust you anymore to provide the best life. I think I know better than you what the best life is. I reject your love. I reject your wisdom. I reject you as my all-wise, all-providing Father. I vote for myself as the sovereign in this relationship. I will do it my way." That was man's derision of the greatness and beauty and worth of God, which was outrageous in proportion to the infinite worthiness of God to be treated otherwise.

Who Loses Sleep over the Outrage of God Abuse?

But here's the problem. Fallen human beings are oblivious to the magnitude of that outrage. God is so insignificant in the hearts of fallen people that they do not lose any sleep over the infinite outrage that holds sway every day in the world in every human heart where God is not the supreme treasure. God knows this. He knew, from the moment of the fall, that it would be this way.

This, I suggest, is one of the reasons God judged moral evil with physical pain. While fallen people do not value God, they do value being pain free. Therefore, to point them to the outrage of belittling God, God judges that belittling of God with physical pain and sorrow. He subjected the whole creation to futility and corruption. In other words, God puts the call to repentance in the language everyone can understand—the language of pain and death.

All Calamity Is a Call to Repentance

We can see this in Luke 13:1–5:

> There were some present at that very time who told him about the Galileans whose blood Pilate had mingled with their sacrifices. And he answered them, "Do you think that these Galileans were worse sinners than all the other Galileans, because they suffered in this way? No, I tell you; but unless you repent, you will all likewise perish. Or those eighteen on whom the tower in Siloam fell and killed them: do you think that they were worse offenders than all the others who lived in Jerusalem? No, I tell you; but unless you repent, you will all likewise perish."

People approached Jesus with two horrors, one from human cruelty (Pilate's brutality) and one from seemingly natural causes (the collapse of a tower). They were expecting Jesus to make some connection between specific human sins and specific suffering. Their assumption seems to be that if certain people experience such brutality or disaster, they must be worse sinners than others. In both situations, Jesus says no (13:3, 5).

Instead of connecting their suffering and death with specific sins that would make them worse sinners, Jesus connects their suffering with universal human sinfulness and interprets their suffering as a call for all of us to wake up and repent. He says in both cases, "Unless you repent, you will all likewise perish" (13:3, 5).

This is astonishing. Notice the word *all*. You will *all* likewise perish—unless you repent. In other words, wherever there is suffering in the world—whether from natural causes or human cruelty, we all are to hear a call: repent. How can this be? How can such random, or humanly caused, calamities be a call for every human being to repent?

God Made Physical Suffering a Parable of Moral Outrage

Surely part of the answer, as we saw from Romans 5 and 8, is that God himself has made physical human suffering a signpost, or a parable—a staggeringly realistic drama—of the horrors of the outrage of sin against God. This is why Jesus can take a random collapse of a tower with eighteen crushed bodies in the rubble and a hideous act of cruelty by Pilate and say that both of them are a divine call to repentance for *all*. All of us, in our sin, deserve the fate of these crushed and brutalized people. The shock we are to feel in looking at such suffering and death is not mainly that it happened, but that it hasn't yet happened *to us*. That's the point. We still have another undeserved hour to repent.

But Still They Did Not Repent

The last book of the Bible, Revelation, also puts the call to repentance in the language of pain and death. As the world shakes in the last throes of "childbirth" (Rom. 8:22), God and his angels pour out horrible suffering and death on the world, which, no doubt, will take away the lives of both children and adults, since we see a vision in which "a third of mankind was killed" (Rev. 9:18). Three times we are told that, similar to Jesus's point in Luke 13:1–5, the aim of this global suffering is repentance:

> By these three plagues a third of mankind was killed. . . . The rest of mankind, who were not killed by these plagues, *did not repent of the works of their hands* nor give up worshiping demons and idols. (Rev. 9:18, 20)

> They were scorched by the fierce heat, and they cursed the name of God who had power over these plagues. *They did not repent* and give him glory. (Rev. 16:9)

> People gnawed their tongues in anguish and cursed the God of heaven for their pain and sores. *They did not repent* of their deeds. (Rev. 16:10–11)

Children Too Are Swept Away in the Drama of Outrage

My point in directing our attention to Romans 5 and 8, Luke 13:1–5, and these texts in Revelation is to give God's creation-wide perspective on the moral horrors of eating one's own children (Jer. 19:9), and the unspeakable suffering and death of the children themselves. That perspective shows us that one of the reasons there is such moral revulsion, suffering, and death in the world is to provide an outrageous visible drama of an even more outrageous invisible reality.

The outrageous drama is century after century of global suffering and death. The invisible reality being dramatized is the universal human treatment of God as Adam and Eve did—neglecting, marginalizing, and disdaining him as an all-providing Father, a merciful Creator, an all-wise counselor, an all-powerful protector, an ever-present joy, and an infinitely valuable treasure.

Fallen human beings do not feel the outrage of this treatment of God. Very few people go to bed troubled by this universal human scandal. But, oh, how we feel physical pain and loss. We know this language—the language of suffering and death. It makes us rage, often against God. The Bible is written to help us interpret this language of pain. It is, Jesus said, a call to repentance. When you see carnage and "random" horror, hear the voice of God: "Unless you repent, you will all likewise perish" (Luke 13:3, 5). Children are swept away in this carnage. The outrage of demeaning God is that terrible. Their suffering too is part of the outrageous drama. Their suffering too is a call to repentance.

Will Infants Who Die Inherit Eternal Joy?

How will the suffering and death of children be set right? When I consider the final display of God's justice at the day of judgment, I see God exercising a standard of judgment that opens the door for infants who die in this world to be saved from condemnation. I do not deny the sinfulness of every human from the moment of conception. "Behold, I was brought forth in iniquity, and in sin did my mother conceive me" (Ps. 51:5). I believe that all humans are "appointed sinners" by Adam's disobedience (Rom. 5:19, my translation). I believe God does no wrong when he takes the life of any child (Job 1:21–22). He owns it (Ps. 100:3) and may take it when he pleases (Dan. 5:23).

Nevertheless, there is a standard of judgment that Paul expresses that causes me to think that God has chosen, and will save, those who die in infancy. That standard is expressed in Romans 1:19–20:

> What can be known about God is plain to them [all people], because God has shown it to them. For his invisible attributes, namely, his eternal power and divine nature, have been clearly perceived, ever since the creation of the world, in the things that have been made. So they are without excuse.

The words "*so* they are without excuse" show that God's principle of judgment is that someone who does not have access to the knowledge Paul speaks of will indeed "have an excuse." That access involves both the objective revelation in nature (which he says is fully adequate), and the natural ability in the observer to see and construe what God has revealed.[3] The words "have been clearly perceived" in verse 20 imply that this natural ability involves a perception through mental reflection (νοούμενα καθορᾶται).

What I am arguing is that infants don't have this perception through mental reflection, and therefore do not have access to the revelation of God, and therefore will be treated by God as having an excuse at the judgment day. Not in the sense of being guiltless (because of original sin), but in the sense that God has established a principle of judgment by which he will not condemn those who in this life lacked access to general revelation. *How* he will save these infants is a matter of speculation. But it will be in a way that glorifies Jesus's blood and righteousness as the only ground of acceptance with God (Rom. 3:24–25), and in a way that honors faith as the only means of enjoying this provision (Rom. 3:28; 5:1).[4]

---

3   The term *natural ability* is used to distinguish this capacity from *moral ability*, which fallen people do not have, and which is not a prerequisite for moral accountability. *Moral ability* is the capacity to see the glory of God for the beauty that it is and be drawn to esteem it for what it is worth. But in our natural condition we are blind and thus lacking in this moral ability (2 Cor. 4:4). More on this distinction between natural and moral inability can be found in Sam Storms's article "The Will: Fettered Yet Free," Desiring God, September 1, 2004, https://www.desiringgod.org/articles/the -will-fettered-yet-free. It is also clarifying to think of the term *inability* with the same contrasting modifiers, *natural* and *moral*. Here is how Jonathan Edwards distinguishes them: "We are said to be *naturally* unable to do a thing, when we can't do it if we will, because what is most commonly called nature don't allow of it, or because of some impeding defect or obstacle that is extrinsic to the will; either in the faculty of understanding, constitution of body, or external objects. *Moral* inability consists not in any of these things; but either in the want of inclination; or the strength of a contrary inclination; or the want of sufficient motives in view, to induce and excite the act of the will, or the strength of apparent motives to the contrary. Or both these may be resolved into one; and it may be said in one word, that moral inability consists in the opposition or want of inclination. For when a person is unable to will or choose such a thing, through a defect of motives, or prevalence of contrary motives, 'tis the same thing as his being unable through the want of an inclination, or the prevalence of a contrary inclination, in such circumstances, and under the influ-ence of such views." Jonathan Edwards, *Freedom of the Will*, ed. Harry S. Stout and Paul Ramsey, vol. 1, *The Works of Jonathan Edwards* (New Haven, CT: Yale University Press, 2009), 159–60.

4   For a fuller defense of this position of infant salvation, see Matt Perman, "What Happens to Infants Who Die?," Desiring God, January 23, 2006, https://www.desiringgod.org/articles/what -happens-to-infants-who-die.

A Closing Confrontation with My Worldliness

We are at the end of section 6 and our focus on the nature and extent of God's providence over sinful human choices and their effects. These chapters confront me with very serious questions about my life: Do I walk in a haze of worldliness that is oblivious to the vastness of the reality of God? Am I anesthetized by trivial excitements that keep me from seeing and feeling what is most terrible and glorious in this world? Have I lost soul capacities to live my life in the trembling and joyful awareness of God's all-embracing providence?

Can I see death and suffering with razor-sharp edges of lucidity, feel them with suitable empathy (Heb. 13:3), and draw near with tears of compassion, laden with riches of quiet hope, precisely *because of* God's providence and not *in spite of* it? Do I taste and see the wisdom and power and goodness of God in his all-embracing providence in such a way that I bring unshakable hope, irreversible healing, and the steadying ballast of truth for the stormy voyage to heaven?

Will I come to know this God, whose way is perfect, with such depth and intimacy that the pervasiveness of his providence over suffering and sin will be for me—and through me—a rock, a shield, a staff, a balm, a bed, a treasure, and a joy? Will I look most resolutely at the cross of Christ, where the worst human sins and the greatest divine love came together with perfect justice and mercy by the plan and hand of providence (Acts 4:27–28)? Will I realize that without this all-embracing providence, there is no gospel? And so will I rejoice and be glad that the providence of God governs everything?

I will, God helping me—God providentially and omnipotently helping me. This utterly essential divine help is where we turn next.

SECTION 7

Providence over Conversion

34

Our Condition before Conversion

Chapter 26 was focused on God's providence over ordinary, natural human willing and doing. Chapters 27–33 narrowed that focus onto providence over sinful willing and doing. The outcome of that wider and narrower focus was the sobering and hope-filled realization that there is no sphere of life, no human will or act, where God's majestic providence is suspended or limited in its ultimate and decisive dominion.

Turning to God's Providence in the Lives of His People

The words "ordinary, natural human willing" were intended to distinguish that vast ocean of human action from God's providence over saving faith, repentance, and the Christian walk of faith (2 Cor. 5:7). This is where we turn now. The conviction behind the distinction between *ordinary* human willing and *Christian* willing is that God is uniquely at work in the lives of his people in a way that he is not in the lives of others. In the case of true Christians, God's providence is an inexorably saving providence.

God is "seeing to it" that his people—his bride, the church (Eph. 5:25–27)—come to faith in Christ, repent of sin, experience forgiveness and justification and reconciliation with God as adopted children, walk by faith, be transformed into the image of Christ, live lives of love and good deeds, attain the resurrection of the dead, be perfected in glory, inhabit a renewed creation, and spend eternity glorifying God by treasuring him supremely with ever-increasing joy. The rest of this book aims to provide biblical foundation for that claim—namely, that God, not man, provides the decisive influence in the origin, preservation, and consummation of Christian existence. Man does not have ultimate self-determination. Only God does. In the moment of conversion to Christ, and at every moment of persevering faith, God's providence is the decisive cause of our Christian existence.

To be sure, we are commanded to do many things as part of our conversion, preservation, and the attainment of everlasting joy (see chapter 39). We are not passive in the process of our salvation. But what we learn from Scripture is that our doing is the acting of a miracle, of which God is the decisive cause. There will be no final salvation without our acting the miracle.[1] But when all is said and done, we will say, with lavish thankfulness, "It was not I, but the grace of God that is with me" (1 Cor. 15:10).

This is not our first look at God's providence in redeeming and renewing his people. Part 2 of this book reached its crescendo in chapters 11–14 by tracing the *goal* of God's providence in the way he saved—and is saving—his bride, the church, through Jesus Christ. So we have already taken one tour of God's providence in creating a redeemed people for himself. Our aim in that first tour was to clarify the *goal* of God's providence. Our focus in the remainder of the book is on the *nature* and *extent* of God's providence in saving his people, and bringing all of history and creation to serve that great goal.

We have stated that goal in several ways. For example, in all the works of providence from beginning to end, the ultimate goal has been

---

1   See John Piper and David Mathis, eds., *Acting the Miracle: God's Work and Ours in the Mystery of Sanctification* (Wheaton, IL: Crossway, 2013).

God's joyful glorification of his own grace in beautifying an undeserving people whose beauty is their enjoyment and praise and reflection of Christ now and forever in the new heaven and the new earth. We devoted twelve chapters to clarifying and supporting this claim (3–14). In what follows, the final goal of providence will never be far from our discussion of its nature and extent in the conversion and transformation of God's people.

But the question now is this: At the pivotal moments of human willing, when a person passes from the dominion of darkness to the kingdom of Christ (Col. 1:13), when inclinations hold sway to persevere in faith (John 8:31), and when good motivation triumphs in the pursuit of holiness (Heb. 12:14)—at those pivotal moments, *is God or man the final and decisive cause* of the conversion, the perseverance, and the holiness?

Starting in the Middle of Saving Providence

As we give our attention to the extent and nature of God's providence in saving his people, I am going to start in the middle. That is, I am not starting in eternity past with the question of divine election and tracing God's providence forward to the point of conversion. And I am not starting in eternity future with the final outcome of glorification and tracing God's providence backward to conversion. I am starting where the conscious human experience of salvation starts—the point when saving faith comes into being. My reason for this starting point is that election before time and glorification in the distant future often feel more theoretical, and therefore are more likely to be discussed in abstract terms with little immediate urgency. The question I am starting with is, What happened in your conversion?

What if I look you in the eye and ask, "Are you a Christian? Do you have saving faith in Jesus?" And what if you say, "Yes, I do," and I then ask, "How did that happen? How did you cease to be a person who preferred other things to God and become a person who treasures

516 *The Nature and Extent of Providence*

Christ?" Will you be able to give me a true, biblical answer? This is not theoretical. This is urgent. For most people, the answer presses for an answer with more urgency than the question of election. It feels like something great hangs in the balance. And it does.

I'm Not Asking What You Remember

Notice that I am not asking whether you remember the events surrounding your conversion to Christ. I do not remember those events in my own life. My mother told me that when I was six years old at a motel in Florida, I came to her and wanted to be forgiven for my sins and go to heaven to be with Jesus. She told me that I knelt by the bed and prayed with her and called on the Lord to save me. I have no recollection of this at all.

When I ask you about how you came to have faith, I am not asking about what you can remember about the circumstances—young or old, recent or distant. Those facts may be precious in memory or long forgotten. The genuineness of our conversion does not depend on its being remembered. If it did, people with dementia would be in a desperate spiritual plight. Salvation is not by works—including the work of memory.

Far more important than the human circumstances God used to bring you to faith is how God himself was involved at the moment when you passed from death to life (Eph. 2:5). And we learn *that* from Scripture, not from memory. In fact, many people must unlearn aspects of what they think happened, when they finally see in Scripture what truly happened in their conversion.

Sometimes we treat stories of dramatic conversions (say, from drugs and sexual bondage to freedom and purity in Christ) as amazing, and treat a conversion story like mine (at the age of six that I can't even remember) as boring. That's a problem. One of our wise youth leaders at the church I served loved to say to the young people who had grown up in the church, "Resurrections from the dead are *never* boring! So your conversion wasn't." Here's the basic problem with such thinking: we think the magnitude of the miracle of conversion is shown more clearly in our circumstances than in the Bible. That's not true.

Where to Learn What Happened to You: Scripture

In fact, I love to say that the person who understands from the Bible the power of sin (Rom. 6:17), the bondage of darkness (John 3:19), the hopelessness of spiritual deadness (Eph. 4:18), and the impotence of the unconverted mind (Rom. 8:7) will be more amazed at his conversion (at the age of six) than the person who is amazed only because of his amazing experience (at the age of twenty-six). If we are to know what really happened to us in conversion, we need Scripture more than memory.

So in trying to understand the extent and nature of God's providence in saving his people, I am starting in the middle—with conversion to Christ. *Your* conversion to Christ (which may still be future!). "How did that happen? How would it happen? How does one cease to be a person who prefers other things to God and become a person who treasures Christ?"

Painting the Backdrop of Saving Providence

To understand, and be properly dumbfounded, at the saving providence of God in our conversion, we need a clear view, and fearful realization, of how hopeless and dreadful our condition was before God broke into our lives. So we will spend the rest of this chapter making sure we know the backdrop for God's saving providence in salvation, namely, the seriousness of our former bondage to sin. A six-year-old does not grasp the full seriousness of our pre-conversion plight. Neither does the most amazed convert from drugs and sex and crime. Experience does not teach us the depth of our difficulty. Only God can do that. And he does it by his word and Spirit.

Slaves of Sin

Paul describes our condition before the liberating work of God as slavery to sin. "Thanks be to God, that you who were once *slaves of sin* have become obedient from the heart to the standard of teaching to which you were committed" (Rom. 6:17). "Thanks be to *God*" because God was the liberator. Not "Thanks be to *us*," as if we emancipated ourselves. If we know the meaning of slavery to sin, we know why he said, "Thanks be to *God!*"

Dead in Trespasses

Paul also describes our preconversion condition as dead in trespasses:

> You were dead in the trespasses and sins in which you once walked, following the course of this world, following the prince of the power of the air, the spirit that is now at work in the sons of disobedience—among whom we all once lived in the passions of our flesh, carrying out the desires of the body and the mind, and were by nature children of wrath, like the rest of mankind. (Eph. 2:1–3)

Dead in sin. Led by the devil. Sons of disobedience. Ruled by the passions of the flesh. By nature children of wrath. These are devastating descriptions of our trapped condition. "Dead" means we are insensible of the beauty and worth and attractiveness of spiritual reality. Without a spiritual resurrection—being made alive, as Paul says—we are not going to perceive Christ and his work and ways as compelling. But we are described not only as "dead," but also as "sons of disobedience" and "by nature children of wrath." I don't want to press the analogy too far, but it appears that one of our parents is disobedience, and one is wrath, which I take to mean that, left to ourselves and our own nature, our spiritual DNA is *disobedience*, and our destiny is God's *wrath*.

Loving the Darkness

In other words, we didn't just *do* sin; we *loved* it. It was in our nature. This is how Jesus described the world that he came to save:

> This is the judgment: the light has come into the world, and people *loved the darkness* rather than the light because their works were evil. For everyone who does wicked things *hates the light* and does not come to the light, lest his works should be exposed. But whoever does what is true comes to the light, so that it may be clearly seen that his works have been carried out in God. (John 3:19–21)

Our problem before God broke into our lives was not that we didn't have enough light but that we loved the dark. We were dead to the light and by nature had so much pleasure in the dark that we would not come to the light—until God stepped in, and we were able to say, "[Our] works have been carried out in [or by] God" (3:21).[2]

Under the Wrath of God

Until then, we were not only dead in our slavery to sin but also under the dreadful and righteous wrath of God. God was angry with us, and his just penalty for the dishonor he had received from us hung over us with terrifying and hopeless certainty. When people objected to the justice of God's wrath, Paul answered that God is righteous to inflict wrath on us:

2   Even though one could say that it is more literal to translate John 3:21b (ὅτι ἐν θεῷ ἐστιν εἰρ-γασμένα) "carried out *in* God," the meaning would remain similar to "carried out *by* God"—not in the sense that God did the works instead of the person who came to the light, but rather in the sense that the deeds done by the human person were enabled and brought to pass by the sovereign grace of God. For "carried out *in* God" would mean "in relation to God," or "in the sway of God," or "in union with God"—all of which point to God's crucial agency in bringing the deeds to pass. An analogy that shows the decisive influence of God would be John 15:5: "I am the vine; you are the branches. Whoever abides in me and I in him, he it is that bears much fruit, for apart from me you can do nothing." Being "in" implies that whatever fruit (deeds) appears on the branch is really owing to the vine.

If our unrighteousness serves to show the righteousness of God, what shall we say? That God is unrighteous to inflict wrath on us? (I speak in a human way.) By no means! For then how could God judge the world? (Rom. 3:5–6)

There is one remedy for God's wrath against the human race. God has seen to it in the death of Jesus. How? By punishing Christ in the place of his people:

> Surely he has borne our griefs
>> and carried our sorrows;
> yet we esteemed him stricken,
>> smitten by God, and afflicted.
> But he was pierced for our transgressions;
>> he was crushed for our iniquities;
> upon him was the chastisement that brought us peace,
>> and with his wounds we are healed.
> All we like sheep have gone astray;
>> we have turned—every one—to his own way;
> and *the* Lord *has laid on him*
>> *the iniquity of us all.* (Isa. 53:4–6)

"Smitten by God" (53:4) means that God was doing the punishing. But the sins he was punishing were not Christ's. "The Lord has laid on him *the iniquity of us all*" (53:6). We call this *substitution*. Christ substituted himself for us under the wrath of God, and absorbed it—drank the cup of God's wrath to the dregs, so to speak (Isa. 51:17, 22; Matt. 26:39). This is why Paul says, "There is therefore now no condemnation for those who are in Christ Jesus" (Rom. 8:1). Why? Because "by sending his own Son in the likeness of sinful flesh and for sin, [God] condemned sin in the flesh" (Rom. 8:3). Whose flesh? Christ's. Whose sin? Ours. This is penal substitution. Christ penalized in our place. Christ bearing our condemnation. "Christ redeemed us from the curse of the law by becoming a curse for us" (Gal. 3:13). That is the decisive work of saving providence in removing the wrath of God for all who are in Christ through faith.

So there is now one way out—and only one way among all the peoples of the earth—from under the omnipotent and horrifying wrath of God, a conversion that changes us in such a way that we trust Christ:

> Whoever believes in the Son has eternal life; whoever does not obey the Son shall not see life, but *the wrath of God remains on him.* (John 3:36)

Or as Paul says,

> Since . . . we have now been justified by [Christ's] blood, much more shall we be saved by him *from the wrath of God.* (Rom. 5:9)

Under Wrath and Loving What Held Us There

So there was a double horror to our condition before our conversion to Christ. We were under the wrath of God for our sin. And we loved our sin so deeply that we could not taste the glory of Christ. I use the words *could not* because that is what Paul says about us before we were converted.

> The natural person does not accept the things of the Spirit of God, for they are folly to him, and he is *not able to* [could not] understand them because they are spiritually discerned. (1 Cor. 2:14)

"The natural person" means simply the kind of ordinary person we all were until the Spirit of God broke in and took us beyond a merely "natural" condition. This natural person "is not able to understand" the glory of Christ for what it really is. To the natural mind, Christ is not a glorious Savior and supreme treasure. And his greatest achievement—namely, *salvation from wrath by substitutionary death*— is folly. Paul says the same thing in Romans 8:6–8, referring to the natural person as one who has the "mind of the flesh" not the "mind of the Spirit":

> The mind of the flesh is death, but the mind of the Spirit is life and peace. For the mind of the flesh is hostile to God, for it does not submit to God's law; indeed, *it cannot*. Those who are in the flesh *cannot* please God. (My translation)

Impossibility of Loving What We Do Not Love

Those two *cannots* include saving faith, because submission to God in his word is part of what faith does, and because Hebrews 11:6 says, "Without faith it is impossible to please [God]." The next verse in Romans 8 says, "You, however, are not in the flesh but in the Spirit, if in fact the Spirit of God dwells in you" (8:9). There is hope to break free from these dreadful *cannots*. The Spirit of God must move into our lives.

Humanly speaking, we were hopeless. Slaves of sin. Dead in trespasses. Unable to taste spiritual reality as sweet. Unable to submit to God or please him. By nature children of wrath. Paul summed up our condition this way:

> You were . . . separated from Christ, alienated from the commonwealth of Israel and strangers to the covenants of promise, having no hope and without God in the world . . . darkened in [your] understanding, alienated from the life of God because of the ignorance that [was] in [you], due to [your] hardness of heart. (Eph. 2:12; 4:18)

And Jesus, when he was dealing with the young man who would not give up his wealth for Jesus's sake, summed up our condition with an absolute "impossible":

> "I tell you, it is easier for a camel to go through the eye of a needle than for a rich person to enter the kingdom of God." When the

disciples heard this, they were greatly astonished, saying, "Who then can be saved?" But Jesus looked at them and said, "With man this is *impossible*, but with God all things are possible." (Matt. 19:24–26)

The extent of our bondage to sin and the impossibility of overcoming this bondage on our own are not seen or felt without God's revelation in Scripture and the Spirit's work to open our eyes. A six-year-old and a former drug user, based on their experiences, may have a glimpse (indeed a terrifying glimpse) of their true condition without Christ, but only with God's word do we really know the extent of the words *cannot* and *impossible*.

Those words do not mean that we are held in chains and prevented from doing what we would desperately love to do—trust and love Jesus. No, just the opposite: the chains are not external, preventing us from having our dearest wants; they are internal. They *are* our dearest wants. We do not stay in darkness because the door into light is locked. No. We stay in the darkness because we "[love] the darkness" and "[hate] the light" (John 3:19–20). The *cannot* is the impossibility of loving what you don't love and hating what you don't hate. We were slaves of sin, not of situations. That is, we were slaves of our strongest preferences, and we preferred sin to Christ.

Back to the Crucial Question

So I ask you again: How did you come to have faith in Jesus? How did you cease to be a person who preferred other things to God and become a person who treasures Christ? If we answer this question incorrectly, we may find ourselves trusting in things that did not happen or failing to trust in things that did happen. So what comes in the next chapter is crucial. What is the extent and nature of God's providence in bringing you to faith in Christ?

35

Three Biblical Pictures of How
God Brings People to Faith

We are focusing now on the extent and nature of God's providence in creating and preserving and perfecting a people who will live forever "to the praise of the glory of his grace" (Eph. 1:6, my translation). This providence has roots in eternity, because the grace we will praise forever is a "grace which [God] gave us in Christ Jesus *before the ages began*" (2 Tim. 1:9). But as I said in chapter 34, I am not starting where God's providence started in eternity or where it ends in eternal glorification, but rather in the middle, where providence penetrates our lives in our conversion to Christ.

So the question is, What is the extent and nature of God's providence in bringing you to faith in Christ? Experience cannot teach us this. Only Scripture can. The experience of chest pain cannot teach us the nature and extent of heart failure or of what a surgeon does in open-heart surgery. Only doctors can explain that. The realization that we are suffering heart failure, followed by successful heart surgery, has a transforming effect on real-life experience. That is because doctors know vastly more than we do and can do vastly more than we can do. So it is with God's word and Spirit. God alone knows the nature and extent of the disease of sin. And he alone knows how his providence works to bring us to faith. He tells us enough of this great work to humble our pride, exalt his grace, give us hope, empower our obedience, and preserve us to the end. That great work of providence is what we want to see in this chapter and the next.

Our Condition from Which God Saves Us

At least three biblical descriptions of God's providence in bringing people to faith relate to our condition apart from Christ as "dead." Recall from the previous chapter the biblical description of every person before conversion to Christ: "You were *dead* in trespasses and sins" (Eph. 2:1). This deadness includes blindness to the truth and beauty of Christ (2 Cor. 4:4). "Seeing they do not see" (Matt. 13:13). It includes an inability to grasp the things God communicates by the Spirit in Christ: "The natural person . . . *is not able* to understand them" (1 Cor. 2:14). In other words, this deadness is a condition of "hardness of heart" (Eph. 4:18) that cannot submit to God and "cannot please God" (Rom. 8:7–8).

We also saw in the previous chapter that this *cannot* is not a bondage that keeps us from doing what we really want to do—namely, submit to God. Rather, it is a bondage created by the strength of how much we really don't want to submit to God. Our good will is not imprisoned from outside; our rebellious will *is* the prison from inside. Our bondage is the overwhelming force of our heart's preference for self-exaltation over submission to God. If there is any hope that our hard, rebellious, insubordinate, dead hearts will ever come to trust and treasure Jesus, something so radical will have to happen to us that one could call it a new birth, or a life-giving call out of the grave, or a new creation. In fact, that is what God's saving providence is called when he brings us to faith.

New Birth

The first of these three biblical descriptions of God's providence in bringing people to faith is the picture of *new birth*. If the result of our first birth—our natural birth by our natural mothers—is a condition of spiritual deadness, then we are hopeless unless there is a new birth, a kind of miracle that replaces death with life, blindness with sight, and hard rebellion with tender submission. Jesus taught that a new birth is the only hope for seeing the kingdom of God:

> Truly, truly, I say to you, unless one is born again he cannot see the kingdom of God. . . . That which is born of the flesh is flesh, and that which is born of the Spirit is spirit. Do not marvel that I said to you, "You must be born again." The wind blows where it wishes, and you hear its sound, but you do not know where it comes from or where it goes. So it is with everyone who is born of the Spirit. (John 3:3, 6–8)

When Jesus says, "That which is born of the flesh is flesh, and that which is born of the Spirit is spirit," I take him to mean that by our first birth, we did not have spiritual life. Our "spirit" was dead. It may as well have not existed, as far as its usefulness in knowing and loving God is concerned. We were simply "flesh," in the sense that our capacities for connecting with God in a saving way did not exist. Flesh—including the human brain—may be amazing. It can create computers, find remedies for diseases, and send land rovers to Mars. But it cannot grasp the beauty of Christ or gladly submit to God's word. In that sense, none of us had life.

Jesus said, "It is the Spirit who gives life; the flesh is no help at all" (John 6:63). This is what the Spirit of God does in the new birth— he gives life. So when Jesus says, "That which is born of the Spirit is spirit" (3:6), he means, "God's Spirit gives life to our spirit so that it is now a living reality." We wake up, as if from death, to the truth and beauty of Christ.

He Blows Where He Wills

Then Jesus compares the Spirit's work in the new birth to the blowing of the wind: "The wind blows where it wishes, and you hear its sound, but you do not know where it comes from or where it goes. So it is with everyone who is born of the Spirit" (John 3:8). The point is that this new birth is not under our control. "He blows where *he* wishes." Not where *we* wish. I say *he* because Jesus presents the Spirit not as a thing or a mere force, but as a person (John 14:15–18, 26).

The point of John 3:8 is that the Spirit is free to give life to whomever he chooses. He does not move under our control. How could we cause him to act, when we are dead? Those who are born of the Spirit experience the miracle of life—as if one were standing in the absolutely still, humid heat, and suddenly, without doing anything to make it happen, a cool breeze is felt on the cheek. Or better—as if you were standing blind in the beautiful light of day, and suddenly, for no discernible cause, you could see. A miracle happened. But "you do not know where it comes from or where it goes." That is how free the Spirit is in giving life.

Commanding Us to Do What We Cannot Do

If you think, "How can Jesus command us to be born again, if the Spirit is the one who makes it happen?" there are two answers. One is that it is right and good and fitting for every human being to love what is lovely, enjoy what is enjoyable, admire what is admirable, worship what is infinitely worthy, and submit to infinitely wise and good authority. The fact that, apart from conversion, we all hate to do all these things is no excuse for not doing them. If my inability to love and enjoy and admire and worship and submit to God is because I prefer self-exaltation over God-exaltation, my obligation is not less. I am obliged to do what is right, even if the power of my selfish preferences keeps me from doing it. That's the first answer: Jesus has every right to command me to be the kind of person who does what is right, even if my love for what is wrong keeps me from it. Or to say it another way, Jesus is right to tell me to be born again, even if it takes a miracle of providence to make it happen.

The second answer is that there is a kind of command that creates the very response being commanded. We are answering the question, How can Jesus command us to be born again if the Spirit is the one who makes it happen? In other words, isn't it pointless to tell someone to be born when they are dead? Or to return to the metaphor of new birth, it does no good to give an unborn child a manual on midwifery. The child does not deliver himself. He is delivered. So what's the point of commanding an unborn infant to be born?

God's Life-Giving Call

The answer is found in the second biblical description of God's providence in bringing people to faith, namely, *the call of God.* The point here is that there is a kind of divine call that creates what it calls for. This is why it is not nonsense to call for a child to be born or a dead man to rise. Jesus illustrated this kind of call as he stood before the tomb of Lazarus, who had been dead four days:

> [Jesus] cried out with a loud voice, "Lazarus, come out." The man who had died came out, his hands and feet bound with linen strips, and his face wrapped with a cloth. (John 11:43–44)

Now, in one sense, it is perfectly pointless to command a dead man to come out of the grave—just like it is pointless to tell an unborn child to follow the instructions in the birth manual. But it is not pointless if the call itself contains the creative power to give life to the dead. Just as the Spirit blows where he wills and gives new life, so the command of Jesus is spoken where he wills and gives life.

The apostle Paul sees the condition of unbelievers as similar to Lazarus's. We were dead—or by all appearances, asleep. How do you awaken a sleeping person? You tell him to get up—loud enough for the command to create the obedience. That is the way Paul sees people rising from spiritual death:

Awake, O sleeper,
> and arise from the dead,
> and Christ will shine on you. (Eph. 5:14)

Death is like sleep. How pointless to tell such a "sleeper" to "arise from the dead." Yet that is exactly what Paul does, as he preaches from city to city. He calls out, "Wake up, sleepers! Rise from the dead! Open your eyes, and the light of Christ will shine into your soul!"

Call within the Call

We know Paul thinks this way because of the all-important text about God's call in 1 Corinthians 1:22–24:

> Jews demand signs and Greeks seek wisdom, but we preach Christ crucified, a stumbling block to Jews and folly to Gentiles, but to those who are called, both Jews and Greeks, Christ the power of God and the wisdom of God.

Notice that there are two kinds of calling in this text. In verse 23 Paul says, "We preach Christ." That is, he stands before Jews and Gentiles and heralds the good news that the gospel is the power of God unto salvation for all who believe (Rom. 1:16). His voice is a call. "If you confess with your mouth that Jesus is Lord and believe in your heart that God raised him from the dead, you will be saved" (Rom. 10:9). So "believe in the Lord Jesus, and you will be saved" (Acts 16:31).

Then Paul says that, in general, the response to this call produces ridicule. The preaching of Christ is "a stumbling block to Jews and folly to Gentiles" (1 Cor. 1:23). They hear the call of Paul's preaching and reject it.

But then come the amazing words. Among the Jews and Gentiles who are hearing Paul's call, there is a group who doesn't hear the gospel as offensive or foolish, but as the very power and wisdom of God. Their eyes are opened to the glory of the cross, and their hearts are made submissive to God's word. Who are these people? What made the difference? Paul answers: they were "called." "To those who are called, both Jews and Greeks, Christ [is seen as] the power of God and the wisdom of God" (1:24).

In other words, there is the outward, general call of preaching. And there is another kind of call. The first kind of call does not create what it calls for. But the second kind does. The first kind of call makes the hearers accountable to believe the truth they have heard. The second kind of call creates the belief itself. This second call is effective. It creates what it commands. It is the same as the call from Jesus to Lazarus: "Dead man, live!" (see John 11:43).

The Call Creates Saving Faith

We can see the connection between this kind of call and saving faith in Romans 8:28–30:

> We know that for those who love God all things work together for good, for those who are *called* according to his purpose. For those whom he foreknew he also predestined to be conformed to the image of his Son, in order that he might be the firstborn among many brothers. And those whom he predestined he also called, and *those whom he called he also justified, and those whom he justified he also glorified.*

Notice in verse 30 that everyone who is called is justified. It does not say that *some* of the called are justified. It says, "Those whom he called he also justified." What does that imply about the effectiveness of this call? It implies that the call is always accompanied by saving faith. We know this because in Paul's writings, justification is always and only by faith. "We hold that one is justified *by faith* apart from works of the law" (Rom. 3:28). "Since we have been justified *by faith*, we have peace with God through our Lord Jesus Christ" (Rom. 5:1). "We know that a person is not justified by works of the law but *through faith* in Jesus Christ" (Gal. 2:16; cf. 3:8, 24).

So when Paul says that "those whom he called he also justified," he implies that the call is effective in always bringing faith with it. This is not the general call of preaching. This is the invincible call of God in and through preaching, which creates what it commands. It causes blind and dead hearts to live and see and embrace the cross of Christ as wisdom and power (1 Cor. 1:24). This omnipotent and astonishing work of God's saving providence was so central to becoming a Christian that the early Christians virtually made "the called" another name for what it means to be a Christian (Rom. 1:7; 9:24; 1 Cor. 1:2, 8–9; Heb. 9:15; 1 Pet. 2:9; 5:10; 2 Pet. 1:3; Jude 1).

New Birth Also Creates Saving Faith

I said earlier that in the New Testament there are at least three biblical descriptions of God's providence in bringing people to faith that relate to our condition apart from Christ as "dead." We have seen two of those: new birth and God's calling from death to life. We saw the connection between God's call and the creation of faith. But I did not draw out the explicit connection between new birth and the creation of faith. So let's consider two passages that make that connection clear.

In John's first letter, he says, "Everyone who believes that Jesus is the Christ has been born of God" (1 John 5:1). The tenses of the verbs (in Greek and English) matter. "Believes" is in the present tense (πιστεύων) and refers to our ongoing trust in Jesus. "Has been born" is in the perfect tense (γεγέννηται) and refers to a past act with ongoing effect. This means that the new birth brings about belief, not the other way around. Unborn babies do not choose to be born. It is a gift. And dead people do not fulfill the condition of faith in order to live. Life brings the gift of faith. If we believe, we *have been* born again, not the other way around.

We see this again in John 1:11–13:

[Jesus] came to his own, and his own people did not receive him. But to all who did receive him, who believed in his name, he gave the right to become children of God, *who were born*, not of blood nor of the will of the flesh nor of the will of man, but of God.

In verse 12, those who are given the right to be the children of God are those who *receive* Christ and *believe* in his name. So being a child of God (one who is *born* into his family) is connected to believing. It doesn't say how it's connected—which causes which—it just says they are connected. If you *receive* Christ, if you *believe* in his name, you are a child of God. That is, you are born again and belong to God's family forever. So becoming a child of God is connected to our act of believing. What comes next in verse 13 shows *how* they are connected—which gives rise to the other: being born of God giving rise to believing, or believing giving rise to new birth.

In verse 13, being born again is connected not first with our act of believing but with God's act of begetting: ". . . who were born, not of blood nor of the will of the flesh nor of the will of man, but *of God*." The emphasis in verse 13 makes clear that the event of the new birth is not caused by ordinary human agency, but by God.

Here's how John says this with triple clarity. There are three negations: (1) not of blood (literally "bloods"), (2) not of the will of the flesh, and (3) not of the will of man (literally, of a male, that is, a husband). In other words, the emphasis falls on saying that membership in *God's* family is definitely *not* connected with being in any *human* family—including the Jewish family. Being born the second time does not depend on who gave birth to you the first time.

"Not of bloods" means that two people coming together from two bloodlines is irrelevant. Their union does not make a child of God. "[Not] of the will of the flesh" means that humanity as mere humanity (flesh) cannot produce a child of God. Remember, Jesus said in John 3:6, "That which is born of the flesh is flesh." That's all that flesh can produce. It can't produce a child of God. It can't cause the new birth. "Not of the will of a male" means that no husband, no matter how holy he is, can produce a child of God.

God, Not Man, Is Decisive in Causing the New Birth

The alternative to all three of these negated human causes is God himself. Verse 13: ". . . who were born, not of blood nor of the will of the flesh nor of the will of man, *but of God.*" Decisive over all human agency is *God.* Those who received Christ and believed in his name are born *of God.* They are the born-again ones.

Therefore, the emphasis of John 1:12–13 falls on new birth as the *work of God*, not of man. So how does John understand the relationship between our act of *believing* and God's act of *begetting?* Does God's begetting cause our believing, or does our believing bring about God's begetting? Does the new birth bring about faith, or does faith bring about the new birth? The answer is clear. The whole burden of these verses is to deny ("not . . . nor . . . nor") that human causes can bring about a child of God. Not human, *but God.* God's begetting, not man's believing, is decisive in bringing about the new birth. This is what John said in 1 John 5:1: "Everyone who believes . . . *has been* born of God"—not of blood, nor of flesh, nor of man.[1]

The Spirit Brings about New Birth through the Gospel

In the wisdom of his providence, God brings people to new birth, and thus to faith in Christ, through the gospel of Christ. In other words, God intends that the creation of faith come not only through the miracle of new birth, but also through the hearing of Christ-exalting truth. When the Spirit of God gives new life and new sight to the soul

---

1   For a much fuller treatment of the new birth, see John Piper, *Finally Alive: What Happens When We Are Born Again* (Fearn Rosh-shire, UK: Christian Focus, 2009). The preceding six paragraphs were adapted from pp. 117–18.

(John 6:63), his aim is that the soul see Christ as the true and glorious Savior and Lord and treasure that he is. This means that the Spirit gives life through the word, which reveals Christ. He does not open the eyes of the blind to see nothing. He sets Christ crucified before the soul in the preaching of the gospel and opens the blind eyes to see *that*. Both Peter and James make this clear. For example, Peter says:

> You have been born again, not of perishable seed but of imperishable, *through the living and abiding word of God*; for "All flesh is like grass and all its glory like the flower of grass. The grass withers, and the flower falls, but the word of the Lord remains forever." And this word is the good news that was preached to you. (1 Pet. 1:23–25)

Peter says that the new birth happens "through the living and abiding word of God," and then he defines that word: "This word is the good news that was preached to you." What does that good news contain? Peter had just written, "According to God's great mercy, he has caused us to be born again to a living hope *through the resurrection of Jesus Christ from the dead*" (1:3). And, "You were ransomed from the futile ways inherited from your forefathers, not with perishable things such as silver or gold, but with the precious blood of Christ" (1:18–19).

This is what the "good news" contains: Christ crucified as a ransom for sinners and raised from the dead. When this is preached, the Spirit (in his freedom, as the wind blowing where it wills) causes the new birth. With new eyes and a new submissive heart, we see the truth and the glory of Christ crucified and risen. And in that instant, faith is created—by the Spirit and the word.

Born Again by God's Own Will

James says it like this:

> Of his own will [God] brought us forth by the word of truth, that we should be a kind of firstfruits of his creatures. (James 1:18)

The phrase "brought us forth" (ἀπεκύησεν) refers to giving birth. And the phrase "of his own will" (as in John 1:13) puts the emphasis on God as the decisive cause of the birth: "Of *his* own will [βουλη-θείς]," not of "our own will." And as in 1 Peter 1:23, this God-caused birth happens "by the word of truth," the gospel (Eph. 1:13; cf. Col. 1:5).

So when the New Testament writers emphasize that the faith-awakening new birth is decisively owing to God's providence, they do not mean that this stupendous, life-giving miracle happens apart from human acting. There is no new birth where the gospel is not preached, heard, and believed. Saving faith comes not only by the Spirit, but by hearing the word of God. Paul is at pains to make this clear:

> How then will they call on him in whom they have not believed? And how are they to believe in him of whom they have never heard? And how are they to hear without someone preaching? And how are they to preach unless they are sent? . . . So faith comes from hearing, and hearing through the word of Christ. (Rom. 10:14–15, 17)

But we saw from 1 Corinthians 1:22–24 that there is much "hearing" that does not produce faith, but rather ridicule. So hearing is essential but not sufficient. The glorious work of the Spirit, blowing where he wills, must give life, new birth, so that as the word is heard, Christ is seen as true and glorious. This is how God, in his merciful providence toward his sinful people, brings about saving faith.

A New Creation

I said earlier that the New Testament gives at least three biblical descriptions of God's providence in bringing people to faith that relate to our condition apart from Christ as dead. We have seen two of them: new birth and the divine call of God. Both create life where there was spiritual deadness. And in giving life, both bring saving faith into being. The third of these biblical descriptions is the picture of conversion as a new creation.

In 2 Corinthians 4:4–6 Paul pictures people apart from the miracle of this new creation as blind—not blind to physical things, but blind to the glory of Christ. This blindness is part of the deadness all of us were in until God gave us life. But this third description of God's providence in bringing his people to faith is not a picture of *new birth* or of *being called* out of death, but of a *new act of creation* with the omnipotent words "Let there be light!"

> The god of this world [Satan] has blinded the minds of the unbe-lievers, to keep them from seeing the light of the gospel of the glory of Christ, who is the image of God. For what we proclaim is not ourselves, but Jesus Christ as Lord, with ourselves as your servants for Jesus' sake. For God, who said, "Let light shine out of darkness," has shone in our hearts to give the light of the knowledge of the glory of God in the face of Jesus Christ. (2 Cor. 4:4–6)

Notice the parallels between verses 4 and 6:

Verse 4: the light	of the gospel	of the glory of Christ	who is the image of God
Verse 6: the light	of the knowledge	of the glory of God	in the face of Jesus Christ

In verse 4, there is blindness to the light. And in verse 6, God over-comes that blindness with a kind of repetition of the way he created light at the very beginning in Genesis 1, namely, with the command "Let light shine out of darkness." He "has shone in our hearts to give the light of the knowledge of the glory of God in the face of Jesus Christ." So the biblical picture of conversion to Christ in this text is the picture of a new creation (cf. 2 Cor. 5:17; Gal. 6:15; Eph. 4:24; Col. 3:10).

What Must We See in Order to Believe and Be Saved?

It is hard to imagine a more important statement about how God brings us from the blindness of death and unbelief into the reality of life and faith than 2 Corinthians 4:4–6. The essence of our problem before the miracle of new creation was that we simply could not see Christ as the beautiful image of God. When we happened to look on Christ in the Bible or in preaching, we may have seen him as a myth or as an interesting historical figure, or as offensive, foolish, boring, or simply a nonissue. He did not shine in our hearts with the infinitely valuable beauty of God. But that is what we must see if we are to believe and embrace Christ for who he is. And that is what God creates, by his merciful providence, when he brings someone to faith in Christ.

Utterly Dependent on Faith-Creating Providence

We are focusing on the question, How does the providence of God see to it that his people come to faith in Christ? In this chapter, we looked at three biblical descriptions of such providence that relate to our condition apart from Christ as dead. In the *new birth*, God gives spiritual life where there was none (John 3:6–8). In the *call of God*, he awakens the dead and causes Christ crucified to be seen as the wisdom and the power of God (1 Cor. 1:24). In the *new creation*, God overcomes the blindness of the soul and gives the light of the knowledge of the glory of God in the face of Christ (2 Cor. 4:6).

In each case, the answer to our question is this: God's providence brings his people to faith in Christ by doing for them what they cannot do for themselves. We cannot cause our own birth. We cannot cause our own resurrection. And we cannot cause our own creation. These are divine miracles that must be done to us and for us. We are absolutely dependent on God's grace to make us alive to spiritual reality and to give us the sight of Christ's glory that embraces him in saving faith. Or we could say that saving faith is a *gift* of providence. That is what we will see in the next chapter.

36

Saving Faith as the Gift of Providence

In the conclusion of the previous chapter, we observed that God sees to it that his people come to saving faith in Christ by (1) causing them to be born again (1 Pet. 1:3), (2) calling them out of darkness into his marvelous light (1 Pet. 2:9), and (3) creating light in their hearts by which they see the truth and glory of Jesus Christ in the gospel (2 Cor. 4:6). He does this "through the . . . word of God" (1 Pet. 1:23; see also James 1:18), so that, even though the decisive cause of saving faith is God's merciful providence, such faith does not take place apart from the human agency of delivering and hearing the gospel (Rom. 10:17).

Repentance and Faith as Gifts of Providence

I said at the end of the previous chapter that another way of expressing this conclusion is to say that saving faith is a *gift* of providence. I would add now that so is repentance—the change of mind (μετάνοια) that includes faith (Acts 19:4) and remorse for sin (2 Cor. 7:9), and brings about a transformed life, described as "fruit worthy of repentance" (Matt. 3:8, my translation). Faith and repentance are free gifts of God. We do not earn them, merit them, or bring them about, as though we had such ultimate self-determination. This means that, from the first day we believed, we should wake up every morning with overflowing thankfulness to God that we believe in Jesus. Paul thanks God for the faith of his churches (Col. 1:3–4), and they should thank God too.

Inexhaustible Passage of Scripture

What follows is the biblical evidence for the claim that faith and repentance are gifts of God—which means that God, not we ourselves, was the decisive cause of our faith in the moment of our conversion. This is clear from Ephesians 2:4–10:

> God, being rich in mercy, because of the great love with which he loved us, even when we were dead in our trespasses, made us alive together with Christ—by grace you have been saved—and raised us up with him and seated us with him in the heavenly places in Christ Jesus, so that in the coming ages he might show the immeasurable riches of his grace in kindness toward us in Christ Jesus. For by grace you have been saved through faith. And this is not your own doing; it is the gift of God, not a result of works, so that no one may boast. For we are his workmanship, created in Christ Jesus for good works, which God prepared beforehand, that we should walk in them.

The riches of this passage are inexhaustible. Paul says as much. The salvation God brings about has this purpose: "so that in the coming ages [God] might show the *immeasurable* riches of his grace in kindness toward us in Christ Jesus" (2:7). Almost beyond belief! Let it sink in. It will take eternity for finite humans to discover and enjoy the immeasurable riches of grace in Christ. That is what providence has planned for God's people: an eternally increasing happiness, as more and more of the immeasurable riches of Christ open before us—forever!

He Made Us Alive with Christ

How did God see to it that his people would experience this future without fail? The pivotal answer Paul gives is "when we were dead

. . . [he] made us alive together with Christ" (Eph. 2:5). Then, before he adds that he also "raised us up with him and seated us with him in the heavenly places in Christ Jesus" (2:6), Paul does something very unusual—not unprecedented for him, but unusual. He breaks off the sentence, inserts a comment, and then picks up the sentence again. He says that when we were dead he made us alive with Christ. Then he breaks off mid-sentence and says, "By grace you have been saved." And then he picks up the sentence again: "and raised us up with him." Why?

Something Indispensable about Grace

I suggest that Paul inserts "by grace you have been saved" right after saying, "When we were dead . . . [he] made us alive," because he wanted us to see something indispensable about *grace*, as he is using the term here. He wants us to see that this grace is really free and uncaused by us. So he inserts it exactly at the point which makes that clear: we were dead. God made us alive. That is grace. Dead people don't make themselves alive. Dead people contribute nothing but death to their spiritual resurrection. They do not cause .001 percent of their new life in Christ. That is what we are to see about grace by Paul's inserting it here. This grace is not grace if in my deadness I contributed to my spiritual resurrection.

This is important for us to see because we are trying to answer the question of how God sees to it that his sinful, dead-in-trespasses people come to saving faith. That is the question Paul answers in verses 8–9. And what is crucial to see is that he now repeats the intruded phrase from verse 5, "by grace you have been saved." Having clarified how radical grace is in verse 5, he now uses it to describe how we come to faith: "by grace you have been saved *through faith*." By clarifying the radical meaning of grace in verse 5, Paul has prevented us from making the mistake of thinking that the words "through faith" in verse 8 mean that we, by faith, raised ourselves from spiritual death.

By Grace through Faith

"Through faith" in Ephesians 2:8 means that God raised us from the dead (that is, he saved us) by bringing faith into being. Dead people do not originate their faith. God raises dead people, and he makes faith part of his miracle. How? The rest of verse 8 gives the answer: "And this is not your own doing; it is the gift of God." What does "this" refer to when Paul says, "*This* is not your own doing"? And what does *it* refer to when Paul says, "*It* is the gift of God"? In the original Greek of verse 8, the words *grace* (χάριτί) and *faith* (πίστεως) are both feminine in gender: "By *grace* you have been saved through *faith*." But *this* is neuter in gender, and *it* is not in the Greek. Literally, the text reads, "And this is not from you, [but] the gift of God."

Ordinarily in New Testament Greek, pronouns agree in gender with their antecedents. But *this* is neuter, while *grace* and *faith* are feminine. So what does *this* refer back to? What is "not from you, but the gift of God"? I have two suggestions.

First, I suggest that the neuter gender of *this* is taken from the following word *gift* (δῶρον), which is neuter. This is not unusual in Greek. It is called "attraction." That is, the gender of the pronoun is attracted forward and agrees with its predicate ("This is . . . the gift of God"), rather than agreeing with its antecedents, grace and faith.

Second, I suggest that the word *this* refers to grace and faith together as part of a single act of God—"saved by grace through faith." That action as a whole is what *this* refers to. And that whole act of salvation from the dead, happening by grace through faith, is "not from you" but is a "gift of God."

Raised, Saved, Created

Ephesians 2:10 confirms that we are on the right track, because Paul describes these new raised (2:5) and saved (2:8) persons as "[God's] workmanship, created in Christ Jesus." Calling raised and saved people

God's workmanship and creation underscores how God, not man, has brought all this about.

Three descriptions in this passage stress that God, not man, is decisive in conversion. (1) We were raised with Christ and seated in the heavenly places when we were dead (2:5–6). (2) We were saved "by grace . . . through faith" in such a way that the whole process, including the awakening of faith, is not from us but is a gift of God (2:8). (3) We are God's workmanship, in the sense that he created us in Christ Jesus for good works (2:10). The resurrection was not from ourselves. The salvation through faith was not from ourselves. The creation was not from ourselves. That is the meaning of *grace*. We did not deserve it. And we did not cause it. Therefore, as Paul says in verse 9, there is no place for boasting in the indispensable role we played in our resurrection (2:5), salvation (2:8), or creation (2:10). Our role begins after this resurrection, salvation, and creation. We are raised, saved, and created "for good works" (2:10).

Two Gifts: Faith and Suffering

As crucial as Ephesians 2:4–10 is in clarifying God's providence in bringing about saving faith as a gift, this text does not stand alone in the use of such language. For example, Paul says in Philippians 1:27–30 that God has granted to us two gifts: faith and suffering:

> [Stand] firm in one spirit, with one mind striving side by side for the faith of the gospel, and not frightened in anything by your opponents. This is a clear sign to them of their destruction, but of your salvation, and that from God. For it has been granted to you that for the sake of Christ you should not only believe in him but also suffer for his sake, engaged in the same conflict that you saw I had and now hear that I still have.

Verse 29 could stand by itself to make the point I am stressing. Literally, it says, "It has been given to you on behalf of Christ to believe on him." Believing is a gift. But let's not see verse 29 standing by itself. Let's notice that it begins with *for* and thus provides the basis for what went before, namely, Paul's amazing claim that the unified and fearless stand of the Philippians for the gospel in the face of opposition is "a clear sign to them of their destruction, but of your salvation, and that from God."

Sign from God

Why is their fearless, unified courage for the gospel a "sign . . . *from God*"? That's what Philippians 1:29 answers: their fearless, unified stand for the gospel is a sign from God because God has given two gifts to the Philippians, faith and suffering. Their faith gives them the unity and fearlessness to endure suffering before their opponents. And the fact that this faith and suffering are gifts of God explains why the sign of unified courage in the face of opposition is a sign *from God*.

I have pressed into the context here because I want us to see that we are not playing academic games in arguing that saving faith is a gift of God. This truth, for Paul, was not marginal, minor, or irrelevant for real life. He wanted the Philippians to see how God was at work in their sufferings. And his explanation was that in their suffering, God himself had created a sign—"a sign . . . from God"—for them and for their opponents. And this sign will never be rightly understood where we ignore or reject the truth that our believing is a gift of God. In his providence, God sees to it that his people receive the gift of saving faith.

From Him You Are in Christ Jesus

Before we turn to repentance as a gift of God, consider briefly one more passage that highlights the fact that God gives faith to his people. In the first chapters of 1 Corinthians, Paul is eager to show the dangers of boasting in ourselves or in other human beings. God saves his people in such a way "that no human being might boast in the presence of God" (1 Cor. 1:29). One way God has done this is to choose for himself the least likely candidates for the honor of salvation:

> God chose what is foolish in the world to shame the wise; God chose what is weak in the world to shame the strong; God chose what is low and despised in the world, even things that are not, to bring to nothing things that are. (1:27–28)

But once God had chosen his people, how did they become united to Christ so that Christ could be their righteousness and the ground of their justification? The answer is that God himself took full responsibility for seeing to it that his people were united to Christ. Here's the way Paul puts it:

> Because of him [ἐξ αὐτοῦ] you are in Christ Jesus, who became to us wisdom from God, righteousness and sanctification and redemption, so that, as it is written, "Let the one who boasts, boast in the Lord." (1:30–31)

God has done all things to make sure that our boast is only in the Lord, not in ourselves. Not only does he see to it that Christ is our wisdom, our righteousness, our sanctification, and our redemption, but he also makes sure that we know how we were united to Christ so that he could be all that for us. He makes sure we know that God himself *gave* us union with Christ. "From him" we are in Christ Jesus. This is not our doing. We do not unite ourselves to Christ.

To be sure, God unites us to Christ *through faith*, as we can see especially in Philippians 3:9, where we are "found *in [Christ]*, not having a righteousness of [our] own . . . but that which comes *through faith in Christ*." But what Paul stresses when he is eliminating all boasting, except boasting in the Lord, is that this union with Christ through faith is "from God," not from you. You are the one who *acts* the faith, but God is the one who *gives* the action of faith and union with Christ.

God May Perhaps Grant Repentance

We turn now to God's gift of repentance. Not only is faith a free gift of God, start to finish, but so is repentance. I said earlier in this chapter that *repentance* refers to the change of mind (μετάνοια) that includes faith (Acts 19:4) and remorse for sin (2 Cor. 7:9), and that it brings about a transformed life, described as "fruit worthy of repentance" (Matt. 3:8, my translation). So it is not possible that faith could be given by God without repentance and vice versa. One never exists without the other.

Nevertheless, we will be helped in very practical ways to actually see how Paul teaches that repentance is a gift of God. This teaching is embedded in a pastoral word from Paul to Timothy about how to minister to people who are ensnared by the devil and need deliverance from his captivity. Paul's bottom line of hope—our hope for those we love—is that God may grant repentance:

> The Lord's servant must not be quarrelsome but kind to everyone, able to teach, patiently enduring evil, correcting his opponents with gentleness. God may perhaps grant them repentance leading to a knowledge of the truth, and they may come to their senses and escape from the snare of the devil, after being captured by him to do his will. (2 Tim. 2:24–26)

"God may perhaps grant them repentance." He may, or he may not. God is free. He owes no one the gift of repentance. If our sin has caused us to depart from the truth, lose our senses, and be ensnared by the devil and captured by him so that we prefer what he prefers, God is not obliged to save us by granting repentance. He may, in his mercy, but no one can demand it as a right. It is a gift. It is all mercy.

Truth Is Indispensable, God Is Decisive

But this gift is not disconnected from the effectiveness of faithful teaching. This passage is pastorally relevant for anyone who wants to be used by God to bring people to repentance, because Paul says very plainly that how we teach really matters. God uses the content of the teaching and the character of the teacher to bring people to repentance. That's why he says we must not be "quarrelsome but kind." We must teach with skill and be patient. We must correct opponents with gentleness (2 Tim. 2:24–25). Why? Because through these means "God may perhaps grant them repentance."

For those who realize how dreadful it is to be in the condition described in verse 26 (having lost our spiritual senses, in the snare of the devil, captured to do his will), Paul's promise in verse 25 is infinitely more hopeful than the teaching that humans must provide the final, decisive cause of their own repentance in order to be liberated. God may give repentance. That is our hope, and that is our earnest and continual prayer. As it was Paul's: "My heart's desire and prayer to God for them is that they may be saved" (Rom. 10:1).

God Desires All People to Be Saved

Perhaps you hear in the words "God may perhaps grant them repentance *leading to a knowledge of the truth*" an echo of 1 Timothy 2:4, where Paul says, "[God] desires all people to be saved and to come to *the knowledge of the truth*." This connection between these two texts is very important. Notice the desire of God for people to "be saved and to come to the knowledge of the truth [εἰς ἐπίγνωσιν ἀληθείας]" (in 1 Tim. 2:4), and the gift of God that people "repent unto a knowledge of the truth [εἰς ἐπίγνωσιν ἀληθείας]" (in 2 Tim. 2:25).

Why is this parallel so important? Because many people use 1 Timothy 2:4 ("God . . . desires all people to be saved") as an argument that God could not possibly choose that some people repent and be saved while not choosing to save others. But that is precisely what 2 Timothy 2:25 says. "God may perhaps grant them repentance." He gives repentance to some. The fact that these two texts are parallel in wording shows us how Paul might answer those who argue from 1 Timothy 2:4 that God cannot choose to give repentance only to some.

He might say something like this: God's desire (θέλει) for all to be saved (1 Tim. 2:4) is real, but it does not rise to the level of decisive action for all people. God can desire things at one level and choose not to act on those desires at another level. He desires all to be saved at one level, and he grants some to repent and be saved at another level.

Ezekiel, Deuteronomy, and Lamentations on the Levels of God's Desires

This way of viewing God's desire for all to be saved is similarly helpful in understanding texts such as Ezekiel 18:32 and 33:11:

> I do not have pleasure in the death of anyone, declares the Lord GOD; so turn, and live. . . . As I live, declares the Lord GOD, I do not have pleasure in the death of the wicked, but that the wicked turn from his way and live; turn back, turn back from your evil ways, for why will you die, O house of Israel? (my translation)

God does not delight in the death of the wicked. Yet we read in Deuteronomy 28:63, as God foresees his coming judgment on his sinful people, "As the LORD took delight in doing you good and multiplying you, so *the LORD will take delight in bringing ruin upon you and destroying you*" (Deut. 28:63).

Rather than impugn the Scriptures with contradiction, I think we should humbly impute to God complexity. These texts say that in some sense, or at some level, God does not delight in the death of the wicked, but in their salvation; and in another sense, or at another level, he does delight in their destruction. God does not disapprove of the wisdom and justice of his judgments on the wicked. In fact, the day will come when he will summon all of heaven to rejoice that judgment upon the wicked has come (Rev. 18:20; cf. Ps. 48:11; 58:10; 96:11–13; Rev. 19:1–3).

What I learn, therefore, from these texts is that there is a genuine inclination in God's heart to spare those who have committed treason against his kingdom. But his motivation is complex. Not every true element in it rises to the level of effective choice. In his great and mysterious heart, there are kinds of real longings and desires—they tell us something true about his character. Yet not all of his desires govern God's actions. He is governed by the depth of his wisdom through a plan that no ordinary human deliberation would ever conceive (Rom. 11:33–36; 1 Cor. 2:9). There are holy and just reasons for why the affections of God's heart have the nature and intensity and proportion that they do.

These texts (Ezek. 18:32; 33:11; 1 Tim. 2:4) show us that God loves the world with an authentic compassion that desires their salvation. But this does not contradict or nullify what we see in this chapter— that saving faith is a free gift of grace, and God decided before the foundation of the world which traitors would be spared.[1]

This is not owing to a split personality. It is the way Jeremiah spoke of God's heart in Lamentations 3:32–33:

> Though he cause grief, he will have compassion
>> according to the abundance of his steadfast love;
> for he does not afflict *from his heart*
>> or grieve the children of men.

Here we see a level of willing "from [God's] heart" that does *not* wish to cause grief and a level of willing that actually *does* cause grief. Similarly, there is a way for God's heart to desire the salvation of all, while at the same time granting repentance only to some.

The Peril of Alien Assumptions

This is a good example of what happens when we bring alien assumptions to the Bible rather than letting the Bible itself tell us what to

---

1 I dealt with Ezek. 18:32 and 33:11 more fully in John Piper, *The Pleasures of God* (Colorado Springs, CO: Multnomah, 2012), 130–33, from which this paragraph was adapted.

assume or not. If we bring the assumption to the Bible that *if God desires all people to be saved, he cannot refuse the gift of repentance to any*, then we will misinterpret the Bible. That assumption is not taught anywhere in the Bible. Nor is it demanded by the laws of logic. On the contrary, Paul protects us from making that assumption by saying very plainly, "God may perhaps grant them repentance" (2 Tim. 2:25).

Rich Mercy, Great Love, Saving Grace

I conclude from what we have seen in this chapter that both faith and repentance are free gifts of God, which he owes to no one because of our sin, but which he grants mercifully and lovingly and graciously to many. I say *mercifully* and *lovingly* and *graciously* because these are the words that Paul piles up to describe God's gift of bringing people from death to life and giving them faith. Recall how he said in Ephesians 2:4–5, "God, being rich in *mercy*, because of the great *love* with which he loved us, even when we were dead in our trespasses, made us alive together with Christ—by *grace* you have been saved." Some—not all—are made alive with Christ because of God's rich *mercy*, great *love*, and saving *grace*.

How Arminians Think about Prevenient Grace

Before leaving this chapter, there is a crucial issue that needs to be dealt with concerning the grace of God. What seems clear from what we just said in the previous paragraph is that the rich mercy, great love, and saving grace referred to in Ephesians 2:4–5 are not directed by God to all people the way they are to those who are "made . . . alive together with Christ." If God's mercy and love and grace made all people alive, then all people would be "seated . . . in the heavenly places in Christ Jesus" (Eph. 2:6). All would be saved. No one would perish under the wrath of God. But Paul does not teach that God makes everyone alive. In Ephesians 5:6 he says that "the wrath of God comes upon the sons of disobedience."

But there is a view of God's grace that is common and, I think, mistaken and harmful to the church and the mission of Christ. I think it is important enough to deal with, not only because of how widespread it is, but also because it contains a tendency to go against Paul's aim to exclude all boasting in human self-determination in our own conversion. I'm thinking of the way the term *prevenient grace* is used by historic Arminian and Wesleyan theologians. I don't think a person is right or wrong because of a theological label. I use these terms, in this case, simply as a shorthand for the way prevenient grace is understood. Whether we are right or wrong hangs not on our label but on whether our view is what the Bible teaches.

The term *prevenient grace* is a very good term. Prevenient simply means "coming before." It is used to refer to God's grace that *must* precede saving faith. The reason it must is that humans are so marred and enslaved by sin that without divine intervention no one would be saved. So far, we are agreed. Such grace is indeed necessary for saving faith to come into being.

The difference lies in what this divine grace does in the human heart and how it relates to the will of man. You can see why the issue is important to address right here at Ephesians 2:4–10, because that is exactly the issue Paul is addressing with the words "By grace you have been saved through faith. And this is not your own doing; it is the gift of God" (2:8).

Prevenient Grace in Their Own Words

What do historic Arminians say about prevenient grace? To be as fair as I can be, I will let a respected theologian, who self-identifies as a historic Arminian,[2] answer this question in his own words. Concerning prevenient grace Roger Olson says:

---

2 Roger Olson, *Arminian Theology: Myths and Realities* (Downers Grove, IL: IVP Academic, 2006).

If anyone comes to Christ with repentance and faith, it is only because they are enabled by God's "prevenient grace" to do so.[3]

Arminianism has always insisted that the initiative in salvation is God's; it is called "prevenient grace," and it is enabling but resistible.[4]

[Wesley] affirmed original sin, including total depravity in the sense of spiritual helplessness. But he also affirmed God's universal gift of prevenient or enabling grace that restores freedom of the will.[5]

Classical Arminian theology . . . attributes the sinner's ability to respond to the gospel with repentance and faith to prevenient grace—the illuminating, convicting, calling, enabling power of the Holy Spirit working on the sinner's soul . . . makes them free to choose saving grace (or reject it).[6]

In Arminian theology, a partial regeneration does precede conversion, but it is not a complete regeneration. It is an awakening and enabling, but not an irresistible force. . . . [Prevenient grace is] God's powerful attracting and persuading power that actually imparts free will to be saved or not.[7]

The Scriptures Point in a Different Direction

The question is whether that understanding of how grace works to bring about our faith is biblical. I don't think it is. I think what we saw in the previous chapter, and especially in Ephesians 2:4–10, shows that it is mistaken. What we have seen, and will see in the next chap-

---

3   Roger Olson, *Against Calvinism* (Grand Rapids, MI: Zondervan, 2011), 66.
4   Olson, *Against Calvinism*, 169.
5   Olson, *Against Calvinism*, 129.
6   Olson, *Against Calvinism*, 67. Just to be clear, the ability given by prevenient grace, in the Arminian view, is the ability to believe or not to believe.
7   Olson, *Against Calvinism*, 171.

ter as well, is that God's grace does *more* than just bring us up to a point of "partial regeneration" (Olson's term), and then stop and leave the outcome to our *ultimate self-determination*. This latter term is my term, not Olson's, but I think it is fair and illuminating. When he says that prevenient grace "makes them free to choose saving grace (or reject it)," he means that this final act in the moment of conversion is not decisively swayed by God. We are, at this moment, ultimately self-determining. By *ultimately*, I simply mean that there is nothing outside of our self-determining will that decisively sways whether we will believe or not at the point of conversion—that is, at the point where saving faith comes into being, or not.

The view I am trying to show from Scripture is that God does *more* in our conversion than make us able to use our wills to believe or not believe. Rather, what we have seen, I am arguing, is that God overcomes all our resistance, opens the eyes of our heart, and makes Christ so real and so beautiful and so compelling that our will gladly embraces Christ as our Savior and Lord and treasure.

The question is, which of those is the biblical view of how God's grace brings us to saving faith? Does God's grace make us "free to choose saving grace (or reject it)"? That is, does God's grace put us in a position of having *ultimate self-determination* in our conversion? Or does it overcome all our rebellion and blindness so that we are drawn triumphantly by the beauty of Christ to embrace what is true?

FOUR VERBS STAND IN THE WAY

I think Scripture as a whole, as we have seen, leads away from the historic Arminian limitation on the effect of grace in conversion. But more to the point, the text we are focusing on right now in Ephesians 2 does not fit with this view. Paul said in verses 4–5, "God, being rich in mercy, because of the great love with which he loved us, even when we were dead in our trespasses"—and then come four verbs describing what God does in this great love.

First, he *"made us alive together with Christ"* (2:5). Make alive—that's what he does for dead sinners. He makes them alive. But notice that this making alive is not a partial regeneration, as though the aim were to give a kind of *life* that, for some of the *living ones* results in faith and heaven and for others results in unbelief and hell. No. He says, "[He] made us alive *with Christ.*" This is not a halfway resurrection, leaving people in limbo to live or die as they choose. Such an idea is not in Paul's mind. Made alive "with Christ" is to have a life like his—an eternal life.

Then comes the second verb, *saved*: "By grace you *have been saved*" (2:5). "Have been saved" simply does not mean "given enough freedom from sin so that you choose to live or die." Both the verb and its tense refer to a great work that has happened decisively by grace. It is, as we have seen, a resurrection from the dead (2:5) and a new creation in Christ (2:10). These words do not refer to a partial regeneration enabling a person to possibly choose unbelief.

The third verb, *raised*, was just mentioned: God *"raised us up* with [Christ]" (2:6). This simply intensifies the verb *"made . . . alive* together with Christ." The making alive with Christ is specifically a union with him in his resurrection. And the glorious meaning of Christ's resurrection is that he can never die again. "Christ, being raised from the dead, will never die again; death no longer has dominion over him" (Rom. 6:9). That is the resurrection we have already decisively shared with him (Col. 3:1–3).

Finally, the fourth verb Paul uses is *seated*: *"seated* us with him" (Eph. 2:6). God "seated us with him in the heavenly places in Christ Jesus." The almighty grace of God in Ephesians 2:5 and 8 does not bring his people out of sin only to the point of being suspended between belief and unbelief and between hell and heaven. That is not what Paul teaches. When God saves by grace, he makes alive with Christ, he raises from the dead with Christ, and he seats us with Christ in heaven. We are not given freedom to perish. We are given a permanent home—seated with Christ in heaven.

No One Can Say "Jesus Is Lord" Except in the Holy Spirit

We could cite other texts to make the same point that when God converts his elect, he does it decisively and permanently. I will refer to one more. I choose this text because within the text there is a connection that makes the point very clear. I'm thinking of 1 Corinthians 12:3:

> I want you to understand that no one speaking in the Spirit of God ever says "Jesus is accursed!" and no one can say "Jesus is Lord" except in the Holy Spirit.

"No one can say 'Jesus is Lord' except in the Holy Spirit." Of course, the point is that no one can say this and mean it from the heart. Demons can say, "Jesus is Lord." For example, in Mark 1:24 an unclean spirit cries out in the presence of Jesus, "I know who you are—the Holy One of God." Paul's point is that genuine faith in Christ as the Lord of your life is not possible apart from the work of the Holy Spirit.

But suppose someone said, "Paul doesn't mean that the Holy Spirit's influence is decisive at the moment of conversion. He doesn't mean that the Spirit overcomes all obstacles in the human will and effectively brings a person all the way to saving faith. Rather, what he means is that prevenient grace from the Holy Spirit is necessary for every conversion, but does not secure any particular conversions. Paul is only saying that the Holy Spirit removes enough sinful resistance to the lordship of Jesus that a person is now free to become the decisive cause of his own faith at the point of conversion. And the Spirit does this for everyone."

Does Paul think that way? Is that what he means?

No. This is not what Paul means. We can see that it is not by comparing the two halves of 1 Corinthians 12:3. In the first half (12:3a), he says, "No one speaking in the Spirit of God ever says 'Jesus is accursed!'" In the second half (12:3b), he says, "No one can say 'Jesus is Lord' except in the Holy Spirit." So Paul pictures two instances of speaking "in the Holy Spirit"—or perhaps more clearly translated "by the Holy Spirit."[8] In the first instance, he says it is *impossible* to say, "Jesus is accursed" if that person is speaking by the Spirit (ἐν πνεύματι). In the second instance, he says the *only* way a person can say, "Jesus is Lord" is if he is speaking by the Spirit (ἐν πνεύματι). The very same phrase is used in both cases: "by the Spirit" (ἐν πνεύματι).

Consider the implications that both of these statements use the same phrase, "by the Spirit." In the first instance (12:3a), "by the Spirit" is a decisively effective influence. That is, under this influence, a person *cannot* say (and mean it), "Jesus is accursed." So in Paul's thinking, speaking "by the Spirit" refers to a decisively effective working by the Spirit. Speaking "by the Spirit" does *not* mean that the Spirit has given us freedom to go either way—cursing Jesus or trusting him. Such a notion of prevenient grace, which brings you partway out of sin and unbelief and leaves you with the self-determining power to call Jesus accursed, is not in Paul's mind.

Therefore, it is unwarranted to make the phrase "by the Holy Spirit" mean something so different in the second half of the verse. When Paul says, "No one can say 'Jesus is Lord' except by the Holy Spirit," he is using the same phrase with the same meaning: speaking *by the Spirit* means speaking under a decisively effective influence of the Spirit. That's the meaning the phrase has in the first half of the verse, and there is no reason to think it does not have that meaning in the second half of the verse.

Therefore, the notion that God's grace does not effectively bring his people *all the way* to saving faith in Jesus, but rather brings all people *only* to a point where they can curse Jesus or bless Jesus, is not what Paul teaches.

---

8   See John 3:21 for a similar instrumental use of "in": ". . . that it may be clearly seen that his works have been carried out in [that is, by] God."

My Difference with the Arminian View of Prevenient Grace

Therefore, the difference between my view and that of historic Arminian theology is not that one believes in *total depravity* and the other
doesn't. And the difference is not that one believes that *grace must
precede faith* and the other doesn't. The difference, rather, is this: what
I see in Scripture is that God's saving grace does *not* merely restore a
kind of free will that can accept or reject Christ, but rather opens our
blind eyes and grants us to see the compelling truth and beauty and
worth of Jesus in such a way that we find him irresistible, and so gladly
and willingly embrace him as our Savior and Lord and treasure. He
brings us all the way to saving faith so that we give him all the glory
for our receiving Jesus.

Turning to Eternity Past

As this chapter ends, a question is thrust to the front of our minds.
If God does as much unconditional saving work as we have seen (the
new birth, the new creation, the calling from death to life, the gift of
faith, the gift of repentance), when did he decide to do this? These
acts of God on our behalf are not dependent, in any way, on our
initiative. There are other acts of divine grace that are dependent on
our responses (e.g., James 4:6, "He gives more grace. Therefore it says,
'God opposes the proud but gives grace to the humble.'"). But not the
divine acts we have been looking at. So if God is not acting in response
to our initiative in these saving acts, what is prompting him, and when
did that prompt begin? That is where we turn in the next chapter.

37

Driven Back to the Precious Roots of Election

We did not begin our treatment of God's providence over conversion at the beginning, in God's eternal plan. We began it in the middle, with the question, How did you come to believe? Or, How might you come to believe? In other words, we began with the most immediate and urgent question—the point where God's saving providence intersects with our real existence. Are you, or is God, finally decisive in your conversion at the moment you trusted Christ?

But given the way the Bible describes our salvation, it is inevitable that, beginning in the middle of Christian existence, we will be driven back into the eternal roots of saving providence. In this chapter, we will let the reality of God's present, saving providence lead us down, through and out of time, into its eternal roots. It is not an arbitrary move demanded by the scope of this book. It is demanded by the reality and the wording of God's present providence in bringing his people to faith. There it is, embedded in the phrase *his people*. To speak of God bringing *his people* to faith implies they were his before they had faith. What does that mean? And should we even talk that way?

Pondering the Implications of the New Covenant

The plan of this chapter is to glance again at the nature and enactment of the new covenant (Jer. 31:31–34) and let that reality drive us back into the precious roots of election. In part 2, section 3 (chapters 11–14), we traced the inner designs and historical enactment of the new covenant. That covenant, in essence, promises that God will unfailingly cause his people to fulfill everything he requires in order that they might have their sins forgiven, walk in obedience, and enjoy his presence forever:

> I will make a new covenant. . . . I will put my law within them, and I will write it on their hearts. And I will be their God, and they shall be my people. And no longer shall each one teach his neighbor and each his brother, saying, "Know the LORD," for they shall all know me, from the least of them to the greatest, declares the LORD. For I will forgive their iniquity, and I will remember their sin no more. (Jer. 31:31, 33–34)

On the night before Jesus would die in fulfillment of this covenant, he said, "This cup that is poured out for you is the *new covenant in my blood*" (Luke 22:20). On the basis of Jesus's blood sacrifice for the sins of his people, God set in motion all the forces that would call a people out of darkness, bring them to faith, overcome their rebellion, cause them to walk in his ways, keep them from the evil one, bring them finally to glory, and make the universe a new and glorious habitation for his children. In other words, everything God does to fulfill his new-covenant promises was secured by the death of Jesus.

The Logic of Romans 8:32

The most comprehensive text to show this is Romans 8:32: "He who did not spare his own Son but gave him up for us all, how will he not also with him graciously give us all things?" If we change Paul's rhetorical question into the declaration he intends for it to make, it would go like this: "Since God did not spare his own Son but gave him up for his people, therefore it is certain that he will now provide everything they need to reach their final destiny." In other words, God's doing the hardest thing for his people—namely, not sparing his own Son—shows that God is totally committed to all the other promises of the new covenant.

He will take out their heart of stone (Ezek. 11:19). He will give them a new heart and put a new spirit within them (Ezek. 36:26), even his own Spirit (Ezek. 36:27). He will circumcise their heart so that they will love the Lord (Deut. 30:6). He will forgive their sins (Jer. 31:34). He will write the law on their hearts (Jer. 31:33). He will be their God (Jer. 31:33). They will all know him personally (Jer. 31:34). He will never turn away from doing good to them (Jer. 32:40).

Since we traced the nature and enactment of the new covenant in part 2, section 3, we do not need to do it again here. I refer to it here to make sure that we realize that all the acts of providence by which God brings his people to faith, works in them a new holiness, and finally brings them to glory—all of these acts were obtained and guaranteed by the blood of the new covenant. That is the point of the logic of Romans 8:32. He did not spare his Son. *Therefore*, he will absolutely see to it that our faith, our holy living, our glory will unfailingly come to pass. "All the promises of God find their Yes in [Christ]" (2 Cor. 1:20).

This is the point of one of the most precious and popular promises in the Bible, namely, Romans 8:28: "For those who love God all things work together for good, for those who are called according to his purpose." That "good" is our final glory in joyful conformity to Jesus Christ. The ground of this certainty is God's eternal plan and his providential rule of all things:

> [Romans 8:28 is true] *for* those whom he foreknew he also predestined to be conformed to the image of his Son, in order that he might be the firstborn among many brothers. And those whom he predestined he also called, and those whom he called he also justified, and those whom he justified he also glorified. (Rom. 8:29–30)

The word *for* at the beginning of verse 29 shows that what is coming is the foundation for Romans 8:28. It is true, because those whom God foreknew he predestined. And the predestined he will bring all the way to glory.

The Foreknown He Predestined

Beware of misconstruing the word *foreknew* in verse 29. It would be a serious mistake to think that the divine certainty and security that Romans 8:29–30 intend to give are hanging by the thread of our foreseen faith, as if verse 29 meant, "He predestined for glory those whose *decisively self-determined faith* he foresaw."

In chapters 34–36 I tried to show that there is no such thing as decisively self-determined faith—faith that has man, rather than God, as the deciding cause at the moment it comes into being. Saving faith is a gift of God. God foreknows what God creates. The point of Romans 8:28–30 is that the omnipotent God will not and cannot fail in bringing his people from rebellion to everlasting glory. Everything that must happen—their faith, their holiness, their perseverance—he will surely accomplish *for* them and *in* them. It is as certain as the fact that he did not spare his own Son.

God's *foreknowing* his people before they exist and before they have faith refers to his forming a clear view of them as his own, and thus choosing them. For example, the Hebrew word *know* (ידע) is translated as *chosen* in Genesis 18:18–19:

> Abraham shall surely become a great and mighty nation, and all the nations of the earth shall be blessed in [him.] For I have chosen [literally *known*] him, that he may command his children and his household after him to keep the way of the LORD.

"To choose" is the evident meaning of "to know" also in Amos 3:2: "You only [Israel] have I *known* of all the families of the earth." When God knows someone, or some group, in this distinguishing way, there is the double connotation of *select* and *look upon as a special possession.* We see this second connotation especially in Psalm 1:6: "The LORD *knows* the way of the righteous, but the way of the wicked will perish." Clearly, God knows *about* the wicked. He knows that they exist and everything about them. But the "way of the righteous" is known as what he approves and loves. We could say he knows the wicked "from afar," as he says of the haughty in Psalm 138:6: "Though the LORD is high, he regards the lowly, but the haughty *he knows from afar.*"

Inescapable, Priceless Reality of Election

Some discerning readers will have noticed that throughout the chapters of this book, especially in the more recent ones—even in the previous paragraph—I have repeatedly referred to God's providence in bringing *his people* to faith, giving *his people* the gift of repentance, and offering Christ as a blood sacrifice uniquely for *his people.* I understand that for many readers this way of speaking may sound strange and even wrong, because it implies that before people have faith, and before they repent, God has in mind individual people who are his, and to whom he will give faith and repentance, and for whom Christ will die in a unique way. I realize that many people have taught that this is not so and that God does not have specific people in mind to whom he will give faith and repentance.

What we are bumping into here is the question of *election*—the question of whether God chose people beforehand, even before creation (Eph. 1:4), to whom he would give saving faith and repentance. This is a biblical question, not just a theological one, because the reality of election pervades the New Testament. For example, Jesus said, "Many are called,[1] but few are *chosen*" (Matt. 22:14). And, "For the

---

1 This use of the word *called* does not refer to the effective call we discussed in chap. 32 from 1 Cor. 1:24. Rather, it refers to the general call that goes out in the preaching of the gospel to all people, which is what the context of invitations to the wedding feast implies (Matt. 22:1–14).

sake of the *elect* those days [of tribulation] will be cut short" (Matt. 24:22). And, "He will send out his angels with a loud trumpet call, and they will gather his *elect* from the four winds" (Matt. 24:31). And, "Will not God give justice to his *elect*, who cry to him day and night?" (Luke 18:7). And, "You did not choose me, but I *chose* you" (John 15:16).

And Paul said, "Who shall bring any charge against God's *elect*?" (Rom. 8:33). And, "Israel failed to obtain what it was seeking. The *elect* obtained it, but the rest were hardened" (Rom. 11:7). And, "God *chose* what is foolish in the world to shame the wise; God *chose* what is weak in the world to shame the strong" (1 Cor. 1:27). And, God "*chose* us in [Christ] before the foundation of the world, that we should be holy and blameless before him" (Eph. 1:4).

And James said, "Has not God *chosen* those who are poor in the world to be rich in faith and heirs of the kingdom?" (James 2:5). And Peter said, "You are a *chosen* race, a royal priesthood, a holy nation, a people for his own possession" (1 Pet. 2:9). And John said, "He is Lord of lords and King of kings, and those with him are called and *chosen* and faithful" (Rev. 17:14).

My aim here is not to treat the biblical teaching on election in a full or systematic way. Rather, my aim is to give a brief account for why I have been using language the way I have. That is, why have I repeatedly said things like, "God will bring *his people* to saving faith," or, "God will give *his people* the gift of repentance"? What is the biblical warrant for thinking this way?

New Hearts of Faith—for Whom?

I began this chapter by glancing back at the new covenant because I think the very nature of the new covenant is a partial answer to this question. If the new covenant promises that God will "give you a new heart, and . . . remove the heart of stone from your flesh" (Ezek. 36:26), then it implies there are people for whom he will do this and people for whom he will not. Taking out the heart of stone means removing the hard heart that refuses to repent and believe. So repenting and believing cannot *precede* the spiritual heart transplant promised in the new covenant. Therefore, this heart transplant means God chose, before there was faith, who would receive the new heart and who would not.

Or to change the imagery slightly, God actually does what John the Baptist said he could do: "God is able from these stones to raise up children for Abraham" (Luke 3:8). And when he does create children of Abraham out of stony hearts (Rom. 9:7–8; Gal. 3:7), it is clear that he has *chosen* which dead, unresponsive "stones" are his. And in this choosing, God does not act whimsically and without a wise plan. Therefore, this choosing (that is, election) must be part of a plan.

The Ordained to Life Believed

The reason I have written the way I have ("God sees to it that *his people* will have saving faith") is that there are even more explicit teachings in the New Testament that model for us this way of thinking. For example, Acts 13:48: "[The Gentiles] began rejoicing and glorifying the word of the Lord, and *as many as were appointed to eternal life believed*" (Acts 13:48). Luke could have simply said, "The Gentiles began rejoicing and glorifying the word of the Lord, *and many believed.*" But instead he said, "*As many as were appointed to eternal life* believed."

I take this to mean that he considers it important to speak of belief as happening to a group who are ordained to believe. This is why I have written the way I have written. Luke sets the example. The Gentiles did not just believe. They believed because they were in the group that was ordained to believe. This is what I mean when I say that God will see to it that *his people* have saving faith. "His people" are those ordained to believe. God has done the ordaining. And God gives the faith. God's providence in seeing to it that his people believe includes his choosing them for this.

Unlikely Treasure Chest of Election: Gospel of John

One of the most remarkable supports and explanations for why I have talked this way comes from an unlikely place, namely, the Gospel of John.[2] I say this is an unlikely place because this Gospel has the reputation of being simple and wonderfully universal in its offer of the gospel. Both of those points of reputation are true. Is it not simple and wonderful that "God so loved the world, that he gave his only Son, that whoever believes in him should not perish but have eternal life" (John 3:16)?

The Gospel of John does not have the reputation of being permeated with a massive and weighty doctrine of election and a pervasive emphasis on God's invincible providence in bringing *his people* to faith. But that is what we find, along with simple and wonderful words of life. I have written the way I do because of spending years soaking in John's vision of how God saves his people.

"Yours They Were, and You Gave Them to Me"

Let's start with Jesus's prayer in John 17:

> I have manifested your name to the *people whom you gave me* out of the world. *Yours they were, and you gave them to me.* . . . I am praying for them. I am not praying for the world but for *those whom you have given me, for they are yours.* (17:6, 9)

Here are two stupendous statements. One is that God *gave* the disciples to Jesus. The other is that before he gave them to Jesus, they were

---

2 Some of the following paragraphs are based on my article "Before You Believed, You Belonged," Desiring God, January 14, 2018, https://www.desiringgod.org/articles/before-you-believed-you-belonged.

already his. The Father's giving them to Jesus refers to the experience of repentance and turning to Jesus in faithful discipleship. Before this happened, these people were already God's people. "Yours they were, and you gave them to me" (17:6). That is the way I have been writing. God has a people; they are his; and he gives them to Jesus. We will return to this in a moment.

Belonging to the Father before Faith

There are at least three other ways that Jesus talks about people belonging to the Father *before* the Father gives them to Jesus:

> You do not believe because you are not *among my sheep.* (John 10:26)

> Whoever is *of God* hears the words of God. The reason why you do not hear them is that you are not *of God.* (8:47)

> Everyone who is *of the truth* listens to my voice. (18:37)

Each of these three phrases—"among my sheep," "of God," and "of the truth"—describes people *before* the Father gives them to Jesus.

- People are "among my sheep" or not, *before* they believe, because Jesus says that not being of his sheep is *why* they "do not believe" (10:26).

- People are "of God" *before* they truly "[hear] the words of God," because Jesus says that not being "of God" is *why* people don't hear (8:47).

- And people are "of the truth" *before* they "[listen] to my voice," because Jesus says that being "of the truth" is *why* they listen (18:37).

So these are three ways of describing the disciples' *belonging to the Father* before he gives them to Jesus (17:6).

He Was Praying for All Believers

Let's ponder this for a moment. In John 17 Jesus was praying for those who believed on him (17:9) and for those "who will believe in me through their word" (17:20). In other words, he was praying for all of us who have become Christians.

Therefore, what he says about those who belong to him, he says about us. Let this be personal. How is it that *you* came to belong to Jesus? In John 17:6 and 9, Jesus says it is because God the Father *gave* you to Jesus. And how is it that the Father could give you to his Son? Jesus answers in verse 9: *because* you already belonged to the Father. "I am praying . . . for those whom you [Father] have given me, *for* they are yours."

Did All Belong to Him?

What does it mean to belong to the Father before we are given to Jesus? Does it mean simply that God possesses all humans, including us? Does it mean that we belonged to the Father because everybody belongs to the Father? Probably not. Because those who belong to the Father would be those who are "of God," and Jesus says in John 8:47 that there are those who are "*not* of God." So being "of God" can't include all humans. So belonging to God before being given to Jesus does not include everyone.

Who, then, does it include? Or a more personal way to ask the question is this: Why does it include me? Why am I among those who belonged to the Father before he gave me to the Son? Was it because I had some quality, and God saw this quality and chose me to be in the group that he would give to Jesus? Did he see that I was willing to come to Jesus or willing to believe on Jesus, and for that reason counted me to be part of those who were his?

No, because in John 6:44 Jesus says, "No one can come to me unless the Father who sent me draws him." In other words, being willing to come to Jesus was not something God *saw* in me, but something God *worked* in me. No one is willing to come to Jesus on his own. Only those who are drawn by the Father come.

Does He Draw Everyone to Jesus?

But what about the possibility that *all* humans are drawn by the Father, but only some prove willing to come? After all, doesn't Jesus say in John 12:32 that he draws *all people* to himself? Well, actually no, it doesn't exactly say that. He says, "I, when I am lifted up from the earth, will draw *all* [πάντας] to myself." This could mean *all* people who are his sheep (John 10:16), or *all* people who are the children of God (John 11:52), or *all* people who belong to the Father (John 17:6).

Actually, we know Jesus did not mean that the Father's drawing applies to every person when he said, "No one can come to me unless the Father who sent me draws him." The reason we know this is that, later in John 6, Jesus explicitly explains his meaning. He says:

> "There are some of you who do not believe." (For Jesus knew from the beginning who those were who did not believe, and who it was who would betray him.) And he said, "*This is why I told you that no one can come to me unless it is granted him by the Father.*" (6:64–65)

That's an explanation of verse 44 ("No one can come to me unless the Father who sent me draws him"). But now Jesus gives Judas as an example of someone who would not believe. Then he explains Judas's unbelief by saying, "This is why [back in verse 44] I told you that no one can come to me unless it is granted him by the Father." In other words, Judas did not believe because "no one can come to me unless it is granted him by the Father"—implying that Judas was *not* granted this. Or, to use the words of verse 44, which Jesus is referring back to, *the Father did not draw Judas.*

This means that not *all* humans are drawn by the Father to Jesus, and therefore that is not what John 12:32 means. Judas wasn't drawn by the Father. So being willing to come to Jesus is not something God *finds* in a group of some humans after he draws all. Rather, being willing to come to Jesus is something God *puts* in a group of humans, which means that God did not choose a group of humans as his own because he saw in them a willingness to come to Jesus. Whatever willingness humans have to come to Jesus is not the *basis* but the *result* of belonging to the Father beforehand. Therefore, the Father does have a people before they come to Jesus.

In Spite of Disqualification

So making it personal again, I ask all of you who belong to Jesus, why were you among those who belonged to God *before* he gave you to Jesus? It was not because you were willing to believe. It was simply because God was willing to *grant* you to believe—to *draw* you to Jesus.

In other words, God *chose you freely* to belong to him. By an act of free grace. You did not qualify for God's choice. Nor did I! It was in spite of *dis*qualification. We were unwilling to come. We loved darkness and hated light and would not come to the light (John 3:19–20). In spite of knowing this about us (far in advance, 2 Tim. 1:9), God chose some darkness lovers to be his. And then, to save us from our rebellion and guilt, he gave us to Jesus. "Yours they were, and you gave them to me" (John 17:6).

What, then, may we hope for—we who have been given to Jesus by the Father? Jesus tells us: "All that the Father gives me will come to me, and whoever comes to me I will never cast out" (John 6:37). The Father's giving us to Jesus secures our coming. All he gives come. And when we come, Jesus receives us—forever. He will *never* cast us out. Instead of casting us out, he dies for us that we may live. "I know my own and my own know me . . . ; and I lay down my life for the sheep" (John 10:14–15).

Dying Uniquely for His Bride, His Sheep

This is why I said earlier in this chapter that God offered Christ as a blood sacrifice "uniquely for his people." There is a sense in which Jesus died for all people (1 John 2:2). God gave his only Son so that whoever believes might have eternal life (John 3:16). The saving achievements of Christ on the cross are offered freely to everyone without discrimination. "Let the one who is thirsty come; let the one who desires take the water of life without price" (Rev. 22:17).

But Christ did not die *in the same way* for everyone. That's the point of 1 Timothy 4:10: "God . . . is the Savior of all people, *especially* of those who believe." Something unique and sure was accomplished in the death of Christ for God's chosen people—the people Jesus is referring to when he says, "I know my own and my own know me . . . ; and *I lay down my life for the sheep*" (John 10:14–15).

This is what Paul meant when he said, "Christ loved *the church* and gave himself up *for her*, that he might sanctify her" (Eph. 5:25–26). And this distinct and sure achievement of the cross for God's elect is why the logic of Romans 8:32 holds true: "He who did not spare his own Son but gave him up for *us all*, how will he not also with him graciously give us all things?" If "us all" refers to the human race rather than the elect (as we are called in the next verse—"Who shall bring any charge against God's elect?"), then the second half of verse 32 veers off in a direction Paul would never approve. He asks, "How will he not also with him graciously give us all things?" We would now need to apply this to the human race. But it doesn't apply to the human race. It only applies to those who cannot be condemned (8:34) and cannot be separated from the love of Christ (8:35). To them—to the elect (8:33)—God will give "all things," that is, all that they need to attain their final glory (8:30).

Immeasurable Benefits Secured for His People

But now back to Jesus's teaching in the Gospel of John. Jesus laid down his life for his sheep (John 10:14–15). The Father gave us to Jesus (17:6). He drew us to him (6:44), and we came to him (6:37). He has kept us (17:12). And he will never cast us out (6:37). No one can snatch us out of his hand (10:28–29). And he will raise us from the dead at the last day (6:39). This relentless divine exertion is what I mean when I say that God is pursuing every providence to bring his people to his final goal.

And I am arguing that my repeated reference to exerting this providence for *his people* is warranted, indeed called for, by the way John describes God's saving work. Every benefit we just described in the preceding paragraph is secure for believers, because *before* we belonged to Jesus, we belonged to the Father (17:6, 9). *Before* we listened to the truth, we belonged to the Father (8:47; 18:37). *Before* we believed, we belonged to the Father (10:26). *Before* we were drawn to the Son, we belonged to the Father (6:44, 65). We were his people before we believed.

Why We Started in the Middle of Christian Experience

I said in chapter 34 that we were jumping into the *middle* of our real existence as Christians rather than starting in eternity past and working forward. So in chapters 34–36 we focused on the question of how providence brought God's people to saving faith. But in using that kind of language (brought *his people* to faith), we now have been driven backward in time from the middle of Christian experience to the prior planning of providence—the planning of God's choosing to save a people from their sin, the planning of *election*. This plan of saving providence stretches back into eternity: "[God] chose us in [Christ] *before the foundation of the world*" (Eph. 1:4).

The reason for starting in the middle of Christian existence was to make clear that the reality of God's providence is not distant, theoretical, academic, or a matter of mere theological analysis or argumentation. It is easier for people to dismiss arguments about election in the distant past than it is for them to dismiss the burning question, How did you come to faith? What hand did God have in that? Did you, or he, have the final, decisive influence in bringing about new life? Will he get all the glory for your repentance and faith, or will you preserve the uncomfortable suspicion (or even conviction) that you should take final, decisive credit for your repentance and faith? Those are the questions that I wanted to put front and center rather than starting with a distant reality (like election) that is more easily set aside as academic.

Of course, we now have seen that it is not academic. Our life hangs on election. *"As many as were appointed to eternal life* believed" (Acts 13:48). *"Yours they were,* and you gave them to me" (John 17:6). And this election provides unfathomably deep roots for the heights of our security in Christ. This is the point of the glorious flow of Paul's Himalayan argument in Romans 8:

> Those whom he predestined he also called, and those whom he called he also justified, and those whom he justified he also glorified. . . . If God is for us, who can be against us? . . . Who shall bring any charge against God's elect? . . . Who shall separate us from the love of Christ? . . . [Nothing] in all creation, will be able to separate us from the love of God in Christ Jesus our Lord. (8:29, 31, 33, 35, 39)

That massive security is rooted in the eternal planning of providence. It may be distant. Many people may argue about it. Many may treat it as theoretical or academic. But it is not. It is a glorious reality. It is precious truth. It is immediately relevant, because our faith (right now) hangs on God's faithfulness to his eternal plan. We are as secure as God is true to the purpose of our election: "He chose us in [Christ] before the foundation of the world . . . to the praise of the glory of his grace" (Eph. 1:4–6, my translation).

Next Burning Question

All of this leads now to the next burning question. Here we are in the middle of God's providence, so to speak, between election in the eternal past and our final glory with God in the eternal future (Rom. 8:17). The burning question is, What about our future between now and then? We have seen how providence omnipotently and unfailingly has brought us to saving faith. But will we make it to the end? Are there not demands put on God's people that they must fulfill? Isn't the statement "no holiness, no heaven" true? Yes, it is true (Heb. 12:14). Well, then, where is our security now? Will God exert the same saving providence in keeping us and transforming us that he exerted in bringing us to faith? That is where we will turn in part 3, section 8.

SECTION 8

Providence over Christian Living

38

Forgiveness, Justification, and Obedience

We began our focus on God's providence in conversion (part 3, section 7) by asking the immediately urgent question, How did you come to believe on Jesus? Or how might you come to believe? Was God the decisive influence in the moment of your conversion, or were you? The answer of chapters 35 and 36 was *God*. Saving faith and repentance are free gifts of God that we do not deserve. Standing at that point in our lives—the point of conversion—we were then driven by the Scriptures to look back in time and see that God was not acting whimsically or on the spur of the moment or without plan and forethought.

We saw that he had acted "according to the purpose of . . . the counsel of his will" (Eph. 1:11)—at the decisive impulse not of *our* will, but of *his*. In other words, the roots of God's providence in our conversion go back into eternity. God "chose us in [Christ] before the foundation of the world" (Eph. 1:4). Converting providence in our lives today brings the ballast of eternal stability because its design goes back as far as God. God's saving love for his elect is as surely without end as it was surely without beginning. God has revealed these mysteries to us to make us unwavering in our confidence amid the unrelenting miseries of history. The eternal roots of providence—the truth of the biblical teachings about election—are revealed to make us humble, and hopeful, and radically risk taking in conformity to Christ's joyful and sacrificial love for his people (Heb. 12:1–2).

About-Face toward Future Providence

Now, in section 8 (chapters 38–43) we do an about-face. Standing at the point of conversion, we turn from looking back at the roots of saving providence in election and look forward at God's saving providence between conversion and eternal glory. If in eternity God planned to save his elect, and if he has brought us to faith in fulfillment of the new covenant ("I will remove the heart of stone . . . and give them a heart of flesh," Ezek. 11:19), what then does he command *from* us and commit to do *for* us so that we will have vigilance and confidence for every hazard? How will providence see to it that all the elect will certainly experience fullness of joy in God's presence and pleasures forever at his right hand (Ps. 16:11)?

Many Are Baffled by the Paradox of Vigilance and Security

To understand what God has committed to do *for* us in this pilgrimage, we must first understand what he commands *from* us. It will be helpful if we can lay down misleading preconceptions about how God's *engagement* to work for us relates to our *efforts* to obey his commands. I say this because we are going to see that at the very heart of how God brings us to glory is a paradox that many people find incomprehensible.

On the one hand, we are going to find that God commands his people to hold fast (Heb. 4:14), to endure (Mark 13:13), to fight (1 Tim. 6:12), to strive (Luke 13:24), to press on (Phil. 3:12), to not grow weary (Gal. 6:9), to be faithful unto death (Rev. 2:10), and to use every means of grace God provides to endure to the end and be saved (2 Cor. 9:8). On the other hand, we are going to find that God is not standing aloof from this struggle, watching for its outcome. Rather, he is working in and through the struggle (1 Cor. 15:10; Phil. 2:13; Col. 1:29) to see to it that we triumph over sin (Rom. 6:14) and Satan (1 John 4:4; 5:18), and that nothing separates us from the love of Christ (Rom. 8:35–37; see chapter 42).

One of the greatest difficulties of the Christian life is to embrace with vigilance and joyful confidence both the seriousness of God's commands and the certainty of God's commitment to bring us home. Despair and presumption are two great enemies to keep us from living in the miracle of this paradox. Despair focuses only on the commandments and feels hopeless that we could ever persevere in the kind of holiness commanded. Presumption focuses only on God's provision and rationalizes indifference to the commands. Both despair and presumption are perilous. God has shown us how his providence will keep us to the end. And it does not include our neglect of his commands. The path to glory is the path he has shown. There is no other. That is what we aim to see in part 3, section 8.

Behind Our Obedience and God's Enabling Power

The provision of God's providence for our perseverance does not begin with either the commandments to persevere, or with God's power to help us. Our obedience to God's commands and God's commitment to help us obey were both secured once for all by the blood of Jesus Christ. And that once-for-all securing was applied to us in the moment when we first believed on Jesus Christ as our Lord, Savior, and treasure of our lives.

So before there is any pursuit of obedience on our part or any empowering of obedience on God's part, two massive events happen to make both his empowering and our pursuit possible. The first is the event of Christ's death and resurrection. The second event is our conversion, when God applies Christ's purchase to us in the forgiveness of sins and imputes Christ's righteousness to us in justification. Without these, God's grace would not flow to his people in sanctifying power. And all obedience would fail. And nobody would be saved.

Purchased Once for All

At the cross, God purchased his people once for all. "You are not your own, for you were bought with a price" (1 Cor. 6:19–20; cf. 7:23). The purchase was complete. As he died, the Lord Jesus said, "It is finished" (John 19:30). Included in that glorious statement was at least this: "No more can be added to the payment I have made for the forgiveness of the sins of my people." That payment was his life: "He obtained [the church of God] *with his own blood*" (Acts 20:28). As we have seen before, this was the enactment of the new covenant, where God had promised, "I will forgive their iniquity, and I will remember their sin no more" (Jer. 31:34). Jesus makes the connection with the new covenant explicit: "This is my blood of the covenant, which is poured out for many for the forgiveness of sins" (Matt. 26:28).

It is true that God's people—the purchased "church of God," as Paul says in Acts 20:28—do not come into the enjoyment of that forgiveness until they believe. "Everyone who *believes* in [Christ] receives forgiveness of sins through his name" (Acts 10:43; cf. 2:38). But it is crucial to emphasize that the great work was finished at the cross. "[Christ] entered once for all into the holy places, not by means of the blood of goats and calves but by means of his own blood, thus securing an eternal redemption" (Heb. 9:12). That redemption is the forgiveness of sins (Col. 1:14). It is finally and decisively purchased and secured. This purchasing and securing does not happen at our conversion. It happened in history, once for all.

Pierced for Our Transgressions

It was the great work of God as he made Christ the substitute for us. God struck Christ, pierced Christ, chastised Christ, laid our sins on Christ:

> Surely he has borne our griefs
>> and carried our sorrows;
> yet we esteemed him stricken,
>> smitten by God, and afflicted.
> But he was pierced for our transgressions;
>> he was crushed for our iniquities;
> upon him was the chastisement that brought us peace,
>> and with his wounds we are healed.
> All we like sheep have gone astray;
>> we have turned—every one—to his own way;
> and the LORD has laid on him
>> the iniquity of us all. (Isa. 53:4–6)

"Christ [was] offered [by the Father] once to bear the sins of many" (Heb. 9:28). "He himself bore our sins in his body on the tree" (1 Pet. 2:24). In this way, the sins of all who come to trust in him—all of them—were punished (before we even existed), and redemption from the curse of God's judgment was secured once for all: "Christ redeemed us from the curse of the law by becoming a curse for us" (Gal. 3:13). The condemnation for which we were rightly destined was endured by Christ: "By sending his own Son in the likeness of sinful flesh and for sin, [God] condemned sin in the flesh" (Rom. 8:3). This was the once-for-all purchase or securing of forgiveness. It happened at the cross, not at our conversion.

Perfect Righteousness Provided Once for All

In the same way, the righteousness we receive through faith was accomplished once for all at the cross. To be sure, we were justified at the moment we first believed, not before. Justification is the reality of God's counting us righteous through faith in Christ on the basis of Christ's perfect righteousness. That divine act of justifying us happens in the moment we believe on Christ. "We have been justified *by faith*"

(Rom. 5:1). "We hold that one is justified *by faith* apart from works of the law" (Rom. 3:28). "A person is not justified by works of the law but *through faith* in Jesus Christ" (Gal. 2:16; cf. 3:8; Rom. 4:5).

But the once-for-all accomplishment of the righteousness—the perfect obedience of Christ—that God counts as ours in justification was completed once for all, long before we ever existed. "[Christ became] obedient to the point of death, even death on a cross" (Phil. 2:8). Just as Adam's sin happened long before we were born, but is counted as ours, so Christ's sinlessness happened long before we were born, but is counted as ours through faith. "As by the one man's disobedience the many were appointed sinners, so by the one man's obedience the many will be appointed righteous" (Rom. 5:19, my translation). The obedience of Christ, the basis of our justification, was completed once for all before we existed.

Counted Righteous in Him Because United to Him

The link between Christ's righteousness and ours is our union with Christ, which we experience by faith in him. Paul describes it, expressing his aim this way: to "be found *in him* [in union with Christ], not having a righteousness of my own that comes from the law, but that which comes through faith in Christ, the righteousness from God that depends on faith" (Phil. 3:9). Since the righteousness depends on faith and on our being "in Christ," we may infer that faith is the way we experience union with Christ (cf. Gal. 3:26).

So there is the historical once-for-all accomplishment of perfect righteousness by Jesus's life and death, and there is the moment when this righteousness is counted as ours (justification). These two events are now separated by thousands of years but are united by our union with Christ through faith. "For our sake he made him to be sin who knew no sin [centuries ago on Golgotha], so that in him we might become the righteousness of God [the moment we believe on Jesus]" (2 Cor. 5:21).

Extra Nos

I conclude, therefore, that being forgiven and counted righteous through faith alone is something that happens to us the moment we believe but that the purchase of it, the securing of it, the provision of it, was accomplished—indeed finished—in the life and death of Jesus, long before we existed. I recall the first time this hit me in a class in seminary, when a professor of counseling, with tremendous earnestness, quoted a Latin phrase from Martin Luther: *extra nos*, "outside of us." He pleaded with us to feel the glory of this: that our purchase, the payment for our forgiveness, the provision for our righteousness was *extra nos*. It was not first something *in* us, but something *outside* of us, once for all in history—unchangeable, fixed, effective. This was a precious realization.

Killing Forgiven Sin, Pursuing Possessed Holiness

Why have I focused on God's provision of forgiveness and justification as foundational for our effort to understand God's providence in bringing his children safely from conversion to glory? The reason is this: the only sin that can be successfully killed in the Christian life is forgiven sin. Or, to put it another way, the only practical, lived-out holiness that pleases God in his children is the holiness we pursue because we are already holy.

Let me try to explain, because this is all-important for living the Christian life in a way that accords with God's providence in bringing us to glory. I am assuming that Christians *must* be on the warpath to kill their own sin. *Must*, not just *should*. And that we *must* be pressing on toward holiness. The *must* of sin-killing is seen in Romans 8:13. Paul says to the church in Rome (not to unbelievers, but to Christians), "If you live according to the flesh you will die, but if by the Spirit you put to death the deeds of the body, you will live" (Rom. 8:13). The death and life in view here are eternal. We know this because everybody dies naturally whether they kill sin or not. And most people go on living naturally whether they put sin to death or not. So Christians *must* be on the warpath to kill sin, if they would live eternally with God.

Similarly, Christians *must* be pursuing holiness, for Hebrews 12:14 says, "Strive . . . for the holiness without which no one will see the Lord." We will not see the Lord as Friend and Savior and treasure at the end of our lives if we have not cared about being like him in this life—if we have not cared about magnifying him with lives of holiness.

Does Necessary Obedience Contradict Justification by Faith?

I am aware that many people hear these things and assume that I now have begun to contradict the teaching of divine forgiveness and justification by faith alone. They think that I have now begun to teach justification by works—by the works of sin-killing and the works of holiness-pursuing.

This misunderstanding of what I am saying is the very reason I have begun by clarifying God's provision of forgiveness and justification as foundational for how Christians kill sin and pursue holiness. For there is no doubt that God commands both, if we would live forever (Rom. 8:13) and see the Lord (Heb. 12:14). The key to killing sin and pursuing holiness, in a way that does not contradict justification by faith, is to realize that the only sin that can be successfully killed is forgiven sin. And the only lived-out holiness that pleases God is the holiness we pursue because we are already holy.

The moment we believe in Christ, we are united to him in such a way that his once-for-all purchase of forgiveness means that every sin we ever commit—past, present, and future—is covered by the blood of Jesus. Therefore, every sin we resolve to kill is a forgiven sin. And the reason I say that *only* forgiven sin can be successfully killed is that if we don't view our sins this way, then our effort to kill them will inevitably be an effort to gain God's acceptance by sin-killing. But if we are trying to gain God's acceptance through sin-killing, we are not trusting Christ as the all-sufficient, once-for-all price that God paid for our forgiveness. We are in fact denying Christ, even as we strive to obey him by killing sin.

That is deadly. It does not accord with the way God's providence brings his children to glory. Therefore, I am not contradicting the precious teaching that by faith alone we have the forgiveness of sins (Acts 10:43) because of Christ's purchase (Eph. 1:7). We *must* kill sin (Rom. 8:13). And the only sin we can successfully kill is forgiven sin.

The same is true of the flip side of killing sin, namely, pursuing holiness. The only lived-out holiness that pleases God and leads to heaven is the holiness we pursue because we are already holy. Or we could say that the only fruit of God-pleasing righteousness (Phil. 1:11) that we can perform is the righteous fruit of already being righteous. Or again, we could say that the only successful path of sanctification is the one that winds through the field of justification. The reason is the same that we saw in the previous paragraph concerning sin-killing. If we try to pursue holiness or righteousness or sanctification without basing this pursuit on the conviction that we are already holy and righteous and sanctified (in Christ through justification by faith, Heb. 10:10), then our effort to be holy in this way will inevitably be an attempt to gain God's acceptance by pursuing holiness.

But if we are trying to gain God's acceptance through pursuing holiness, we are not trusting Christ as the once-for-all provider of a perfect righteousness that God counts as ours by faith alone. We are in fact denying Christ, even as we strive to obey him by pursuing holiness. For on the basis of Christ we are already 100 percent (not 99 percent) accepted by God (Rom. 8:31–34). That's what justification by faith means.

Denying Christ in this way is deadly. It does not accord with the way God's providence brings his children to glory. Therefore, I am not contradicting the precious teaching that justification is by faith alone (Rom. 4:5) on the basis of Christ's finished obedience (Rom. 5:19). We *must* pursue holiness (Heb. 12:14). And the only holiness that pleases God and leads to heaven is the holiness we pursue because we are already holy.

Remove the Leaven, for You Really Are Unleavened

You can see how this sounds in the mouth of the apostle Paul when he says to the Corinthian church in 1 Corinthians 5:7, "Cleanse out the old leaven that you may be a new lump, as you really are unleavened. For Christ, our Passover lamb, has been sacrificed" (1 Cor. 5:7). You can study the details of the context for yourselves. I only want to notice the very strange and uniquely Christian point that, on the one hand, they are told to "cleanse out the old leaven," and on the other hand, they are told that they don't have any leaven in them: "You really are unleavened."

Be holy because you are already holy. Kill the threatening sin because your sin really is already canceled. What does he mean? The ground clause that follows points to the answer. He says, "For Christ, our Passover lamb, has been sacrificed." This is why they "really are unleavened." "Really are" means that because of Christ's blood and righteousness, you really are forgiven and justified in Christ. This is your true standing with God. So kill sin because your sins are forgiven and pursue holiness because you are holy.

No Love without Blood-Bought Promises

I've been trying to answer the question, Why have I focused on God's provision of forgiveness and justification as foundational for our effort to understand God's providence in bringing his children safely from conversion to glory? My first answer has been that if we don't stand in the joyful confidence that we are forgiven and justified, we will inevitably turn holiness and sin-killing into a means of attaining God's acceptance. Such a life denies Christ and dead-ends in destruction, not glory.

There is another reason for focusing on forgiveness and justification as foundational for our effort to fit in with God's providence in bringing us to glory. The reason is that the promises of God are presented again and again in Scripture as the hope-giving means of sustaining costly acts of love, without which our so-called Christian lives will prove abortive. And these promises cannot stand without the blood and righteousness of Christ. "All the promises of God find their Yes in him" (2 Cor. 1:20). God's willingness to "not spare his own Son" for the sake of his elect signals that he will "with him graciously give [them] all things" (Rom. 8:32), that is, he will fulfill every promise for their everlasting good.

These are the promises that sustain the costly acts of love that prove we are born again: "We know that we have passed out of death into life, because we love the brothers. Whoever does not love abides in death" (1 John 3:14). Love is not optional for the Christian. It proves we have eternal life, or it reveals we don't.

Repeatedly in the New Testament God motivates and empowers our love through his promises, that is, through hope. I wrote a book about this called *Future Grace: The Purifying Power of the Promises of God*.[1] The truth it is trying to capture is this: "Faith is the assurance of things hoped for" (Heb. 11:1). And "by faith Abraham [and all the other saints] obeyed" (Heb. 11:8). In other words, faith-sustaining, hope-giving promises are an essential key to the obedience of sin-killing and holiness-pursuing.

How the Promises Empower Love

Without these promises, one essential way that God empowers love is cut off. For example, Jesus says:

> When you give a feast, invite the poor, the crippled, the lame, the blind, and you will be blessed, because they cannot repay you. For you will be repaid at the resurrection of the just. (Luke 14:13–14)

---

1 John Piper, *Future Grace: The Purifying Power of the Promises of God* (Colorado Springs, CO: Multnomah, 2012).

Jesus motivates this sacrificial way of loving the poor by means of a promise: "You will be repaid at the resurrection of the just." That promise is sure only because of the cross of Christ and the forgiveness of sins and the truth of justification by faith.

Again Jesus says:

> Blessed are you when others revile you and persecute you and utter all kinds of evil against you falsely on my account. Rejoice and be glad, for your reward is great in heaven. (Matt. 5:11–12)

How will we return good for evil if our response to being treated badly is only anger? We won't. So one key to returning good for evil is joy and gladness in the face of persecution. And how is that possible? Because of the promise: "Your reward is great in heaven."

This is the way Peter motivated the persecuted believers to return good for evil: "Do not repay evil for evil or reviling for reviling, but on the contrary, bless, for to this you were called, that you may obtain a blessing" (1 Pet. 3:9). How can you be sure there is a blessing in store for you beyond your suffering in this life? Because God promised it. And all those promises are secured by the blood of Christ and its effect in forgiveness and justification.

Central Work of Sustaining Providence

We will turn in the next chapter to see how God actually does require transformed lives of killing sin and pursuing holiness. And we will see how he himself, on the basis of blood-bought forgiveness and Christ-wrought righteousness, sees to it that our obedience comes about.

What we have seen in this chapter is that God's plan to make sin-killing and holiness-pursuing the path that leads to heaven is not inconsistent with his once-for-all provision of the forgiveness of all our sins, or with the imputation of Christ's righteousness as the basis of our being 100 percent accepted by God.

On the contrary, forgiveness and justification are indispensable starting points for the Christian life. And they form the ongoing foundation of every act of Christian obedience. Without them, two catastrophes happen in our experience. First, we dishonor Christ by seeking acceptance with God by supplementing the perfect price he paid for it. And, second, we lose the sure foundation of our hope in the promises of God. In both cases, God-pleasing obedience is undermined.

But we are going to see that God-pleasing obedience is not optional in the way God's providence brings his children to eternal perfection and joy. Therefore, his glorious work in providing his Son's blood and righteousness (securing our forgiveness and justification) proves to be the greatest work of providence designed to bring us to glorification in his presence. The cross is the central answer to the question, What has God's providence done to see to it that his children make it from conversion to glory? We build our Christian obedience and perseverance on that foundation, or we fail.

39

God's Command-and-
Warning Strategy

The all-pervasive, omnipotent, unthwartable providence of God might lead one superficially to infer that he would bring his people from conversion to glory without requiring any resolve, effort, or endurance on their part. That inference would be false. The New Testament paints a very different picture.

The Wholehearted Pursuit of Holiness

Knowing what I would be saying in this chapter, I sought in the previous chapter to avoid misunderstanding by laying a foundation for Christian resolve and effort and endurance in the finished work of Christ. In other words, when I ask how God sees to it that his people are conformed to Christ and make it safely from conversion to glory, my foundational answer has been this: Christ's once-for-all purchase of total forgiveness and once-for-all provision of perfect righteousness.

With that foundation firmly in place, we may now add another biblical answer to the question, How does God see to it that his people are conformed to Christ and make it safely from conversion to glory?

The answer we focus on here is this: God brings us to glory by commanding us to engage all that we are in the wholehearted pursuit of holiness. "Strive for . . . the holiness without which no one will see the Lord" (Heb. 12:14).

There are many other ways to say it. For example, we could say that God "predestined [us] to be conformed to the image of his Son" (Rom. 8:29) and then, as one means to that end, *commanded* us to "put on the Lord Jesus Christ" (Rom. 13:14) and to imitate Christ (1 Cor. 11:1; Phil. 2:5; 1 Thess. 1:6). God's command that his forgiven and justified people pursue heaven by pursuing holiness is part of his strategy to make us holy and bring us to glory. This chapter is about this strategy of providence—how God sees to it that his converted people are conformed to Christ and attain final glorification.

Abundant Commands and the Life of Faith

The New Testament is strewn with hundreds of imperatives addressed to followers of Christ. I wrote a book called *What Jesus Demands from the World* in an effort to synthesize the hundreds of imperatives and implied imperatives in just the four Gospels.[1] The reason I was drawn to do this was that the last thing Jesus said to his disciples before he left the earth was that they were to "make disciples of all nations . . . , teaching them to observe *all that I have commanded* you" (Matt. 28:19–20).

In his final words, Jesus focuses not on all the glorious truths he taught about his heavenly Father or the work of the Spirit or himself or what he accomplished on the cross or the triumphs of his resurrection. The last thing he does is focus on his *commands*. And he tells us to teach *all* of them to the nations. No, not exactly. We are to teach people "to observe" all that he commanded. Not just to know his commands, but to *do* them. So the point of *What Jesus Demands from the*

---

1   John Piper, *What Jesus Demands from the World* (Wheaton, IL: Crossway, 2006).

World is to try to help missionaries, and the rest of us, do that. What is the sum of *all* he has commanded us? And how do we teach it so that people actually are empowered to *observe*—keep, do—all these commands?

I mention this only to draw your attention to the vastness of God's command strategy in bringing his people into conformity to the mind of Christ, and finally to glorification. There are over four hundred imperatives in the writings of Paul and over fifty in the letter of James. I do not believe God is an unwise teacher. He has not blundered in salting his word with imperatives. Clearly, there are times when entreaty is preferable to command (Philem. 8–9). But God knows that balance better than we, especially when the speaker is the Lord of the universe. God has not contaminated the gospel of grace by the abundance of imperatives in the New Testament. He has not distracted us from living by faith. He has guided us.

It is as true as ever that "we walk by faith" (2 Cor. 5:7) and "live by faith" (Gal. 2:20). We "walk by the Spirit" (Gal. 5:16), are "led by the Spirit" (Rom. 8:14), bear "the fruit of the Spirit" (Gal. 5:22), "keep in step with the Spirit" (Gal. 5:25), "[sow] to the Spirit" (Gal. 6:8), and "serve in the new way of the Spirit" (Rom. 7:6). We live under the new covenant. But the mark of that covenant is not the absence of commands, but the blood-bought power to obey them. "I will put my Spirit within you, and cause you to walk in my statutes and be careful to obey my rules" (Ezek. 36:27).

Shall We Ignore the Commands That Grace May Abound?

If we are to appreciate this strategy of God's providence in beautifying his Son's bride (Eph. 5:26–27) and preparing her for the final splendor, we need to see some examples of the abundance and variety of imperatives in the New Testament. And we need to see the warnings that accompany them. The commands I have in mind are not optional. No one should say, "I am justified by faith; therefore, I do not need to obey God's commands." That attitude is a sign that a person's heart has not been penetrated by the true nature of justifying faith.

Already in the first century, the apostle Paul had to deal with this distortion of his teaching on justification: "What shall we say then? Are we to continue in sin that grace may abound?" (Rom. 6:1). Since that day, many Christians have presumed to be wiser than God by drawing out of justification implications for the pursuit of practical holiness that are not there—like the implication that the pursuit of holiness is not essential for being with Christ in the age to come.

So we turn now to consider some of the more prominent imperatives in the New Testament, with the warnings that go with them. This is how we will see what I am calling the command-and-warning strategy of God's providence in conforming his people to Christ and conveying them surely to glory.

Imperative to Hold Fast Our Faith

It is imperative that we not only believe the gospel, but that we keep on believing it:

> I would remind you, brothers, of the gospel I preached to you, which you received, in which you stand, and by which you are being saved, *if you hold fast to the word* I preached to you—unless you believed in vain. (1 Cor. 15:1–2)

If we abandon faith in the gospel, Paul says, then whatever kind of faith we once had, it will not save, because it was "in vain." Surely, the point of saying this is to make us vigilant. The words "if you hold fast to the word" are not designed to make us lackadaisical, but alert. The aim is similar in Colossians 1:21–23:

> You, who once were alienated and hostile in mind, doing evil deeds, he has now reconciled in his body of flesh by his death, in order to present you holy and blameless and above reproach before him,

if indeed you continue in the faith, stable and steadfast, not shifting from the hope of the gospel that you heard.

We will attain the final, glad presentation before Christ *if we continue in the faith, not shifting from the hope of the gospel*. Or as the writer to the Hebrews says it:

Christ is faithful over God's house as a son. And we are his house, *if indeed we hold fast our confidence* and our boasting in our hope. (Heb. 3:6; cf. 3:12–14)

This writer leaves no doubt about God's strategy in telling us that our Christian existence hangs on holding fast. We are God's house—the habitation of his Spirit and the heirs of his treasure—*if we hold fast our confidence*. And the strategy is to make us earnest, rather than cavalier, about our perseverance: "We desire each one of you to *show the same earnestness* to have the full assurance of hope until the end, so that you may not be sluggish, but imitators of those who through faith and patience inherit the promises" (Heb. 6:11–12).

The opposite of earnestness is drifting in the Christian life. "We must pay much closer attention to what we have heard, lest we *drift* away from it" (Heb. 2:1). Most "former Christians" *drifted* away from the faith rather than departing suddenly. As Jesus said, little by little "they are choked by the cares and riches and pleasures of life" (Luke 8:14). One of God's remedies for this dreadful danger of drifting away is the abundance of warnings in his word to make us earnest or vigilant—or, as Jesus said, "awake" (Mark 13:37).

If We Deny Him, He Will Deny Us

Following Jesus's warning not to deny him or be ashamed of him, Paul warns Timothy and his church:

If we have died with him, we will also live with him;
if we endure, we will also reign with him;

if we deny him, he also will deny us;

if we are faithless, he remains faithful—

for he cannot deny himself. (2 Tim. 2:11–13)

Some people try to make this mean that "if we are faithless," God will still save us because "he remains faithful." As we saw in chapter 22, however, that is not what it says or means. It says, "If we deny him, he also will deny us." And the "faithfulness" of God is a faithfulness to his own name, "for he cannot deny himself."

Paul is expressing what Jesus had already said: "Whoever denies me before men, I also will deny before my Father who is in heaven" (Matt. 10:33). "Whoever is ashamed of me and of my words in this adulterous and sinful generation, of him will the Son of Man also be ashamed when he comes in the glory of his Father with the holy angels" (Mark 8:38). These are implicit imperatives: Don't deny Jesus! Don't be ashamed of Jesus! Hold fast to the supreme worth of Jesus! And these implied imperatives are accompanied with the most serious warnings.

Christian Defense: Killing Sin

These same serious warnings accompany the commands to go on the defensive and kill sin and to go on the offensive and pursue love.

We already saw in chapter 38 that failing to kill sin is threatened with death. "If you live according to the flesh you will die, but if by the Spirit you put to death the deeds of the body, you will live" (Rom. 8:13). This death and life are eternal. Making peace with sin in your life, instead of making war, leads to destruction. The apostle John gives the reason: "No one born of God makes a practice of sinning, for God's seed abides in him; and he cannot keep on sinning, because he has been born of God" (1 John 3:9).

We know this does not mean we can attain perfection in this life. John is at pains to oppose perfectionism: "If we say we have no sin, we deceive ourselves, and the truth is not in us" (1 John 1:8). Rather, the point is that "those who belong to Christ Jesus have crucified the flesh with its passions and desires" (Gal. 5:24). A real death has happened. A real new nature has come into being. And the mark of this new nature is hatred of sin. It cannot make peace with sin. It may not always triumph over temptation to sin, but it doesn't "make a practice of sinning." The seed of God abides within. There is a real newness. The imperative "put to death . . . what is earthly in you" (Col. 3:5) is based on the fact that "you have died" (Col. 3:3). There is a new you. Some earthly things remain to be put to death. But the true you hates sin and loves righteousness.

Giving the Rebellious Body a Black Eye

So the strategy of God's providence to make us holy is not to make us passive. The apostle Paul gives himself as a model of putting sin to death:

> Do you not know that in a race all the runners run, but only one receives the prize? So run that you may obtain it. Every athlete exercises self-control in all things. They do it to receive a perishable wreath, but we an imperishable. So I do not run aimlessly; I do not box as one beating the air. But I discipline my body and keep it under control, lest after preaching to others I myself should be disqualified. (1 Cor. 9:24–27)

The word *discipline* is a weak, generic English word for a very colorful, concrete word in Greek (ὑπωπιάζω), which means "to blacken an eye, give a black eye, strike in the face."[2] This is the kind of word Jesus might have used based on his own warnings against lust: "If your right

2   William Arndt, Frederick W. Danker, and Walter Bauer, *A Greek-English Lexicon of the New Testament and Other Early Christian Literature* (Chicago: University of Chicago Press, 2000), 1043.

eye causes you to sin, tear it out and throw it away. For it is better that you lose one of your members than that your whole body be thrown into hell" (Matt. 5:29).

Radical language is not the only thing Jesus and Paul have in common at this point. Jesus warns that failing to make war on lust will lead to hell. And Paul said that he gives himself black eyes (so to speak) "lest . . . I myself should be disqualified." Paul was not a drifter and was not passive. He was in step with the command-and-warning strategy of God's providence.

Strategy Gets Specific

The commands concerning sin do not stay at the level of generalities—such as "kill sin." They get very specific, and so do the warnings. For example, James zeroes in on the sins of the tongue and says, "If anyone thinks he is religious and does not bridle his tongue but deceives his heart, this person's religion is worthless" (James 1:26). Astonishing. An unbridled tongue signals an unsaved person. This is the word of God. It should make us tremble.

Jesus zeroes in on our tendency to love things more than God and depend on things more than the promises of God. So he says, "Any one of you who does not renounce all that he has cannot be my disciple" (Luke 14:33). Surely the aim of this warning is to make us search our hearts with great seriousness to see if our possessions are more precious to us than Christ. This is part of God's strategy to make us Christ-loving and Christlike in our relation to things. It is not comfortable. But it is part of God's providence to bring us to glory.

Three times Paul gives a list of sins that, if they are pursued without repentance, will keep us out of the kingdom of God:

> Do you not know that the unrighteous will not inherit the kingdom of God? Do not be deceived: neither the sexually immoral, nor idolaters, nor adulterers, nor men who practice homosexuality, nor

thieves, nor the greedy, nor drunkards, nor revilers, nor swindlers will inherit the kingdom of God. (1 Cor. 6:9–10)

You may be sure of this, that everyone who is sexually immoral or impure, or who is covetous (that is, an idolater), has no inheritance in the kingdom of Christ and God. (Eph. 5:5)

Now the works of the flesh are evident: sexual immorality, impurity, sensuality, idolatry, sorcery, enmity, strife, jealousy, fits of anger, rivalries, dissensions, divisions, envy, drunkenness, orgies, and things like these. I warn you, as I warned you before, that those who do such things will not inherit the kingdom of God. (Gal. 5:19–21)

What is striking about those lists of sins is that they include both outlandish dissipation (orgies) and garden-variety sins that most of us are familiar with firsthand (greed, strife, enmity, anger, divisions). The point is that *any* sin—because it is *sin* (a preference for something over God)—will destroy us if we cordon it off from opposition, give it amnesty, and keep it as our beloved rebellion against God.

Going on the Offensive: Pursuing Love

We have been focusing on the strategy of God's providence in putting his people on the path of defense against sin. But what God is mainly pursuing in this command-and-warning strategy is even more obvious when he puts us on the offensive in the pursuit of love. I say *love*, when I might have said *holiness* or *obedience*. I highlight love because it is the essence of holiness and the sum of obedience.

Paul prays in 1 Thessalonians 3:12–13 in a way that shows the connection between love and holiness:

May the Lord make you increase and abound in *love* for one another and for all, as we do for you, so that he may establish your hearts blameless in *holiness* before our God and Father, at the coming of our Lord Jesus with all his saints.

Fill them with love *so that* they will be established in *holiness*. Holiness is a quality of heart and life that accords with the infinite worth of God.[3] Love is the form that holiness takes in relation to others. Paul is willing to name love as the aim of all his efforts: "The aim of our charge is *love* that issues from a pure heart and a good conscience and a sincere faith" (1 Tim. 1:5).

And he echoes Jesus when he makes love the sum of all God's commandments: "The commandments, 'You shall not commit adultery, You shall not murder, You shall not steal, You shall not covet,' and any other commandment, are summed up in this word: 'You shall love your neighbor as yourself'" (Rom. 13:9; cf. Matt. 22:39–40).

Love is the essential Christ insignia of all forms of behavior: "Let all that you do be done in love" (1 Cor. 16:14). This pervasive trait of Christian attitude and action was designed by Jesus as the essential meaning of Christlikeness:

> A new commandment I give to you, that you love one another: just as I have loved you, you also are to love one another. By this all people will know that you are my disciples, if you have love for one another. (John 13:34–35; cf. 15:12, 17)

> Walk in love, as Christ loved us and gave himself up for us, a fragrant offering and sacrifice to God. (Eph. 5:2)

Love is the essential insignia of saving faith. "In Christ Jesus neither circumcision nor uncircumcision counts for anything, but only *faith working through love*" (Gal. 5:6). The kind of faith that counts for justification is the faith that is effective in producing love. Without the fruit of love, we know that the tree of faith is dead. As James said, "Faith by itself, if it does not have works, is dead" (James 2:17). And, for James, love is the royal work (James 2:8).

---

3 For a defense and explanation of that definition, see John Piper, *Acting the Miracle: God's Work and Ours in the Mystery of Sanctification* (Wheaton, IL: Crossway, 2013), 33–36.

Providence in Pursuit of Love by Command and Warning

God's providence in shaping a people who love like Christ continues the strategy of command and warning. For example, in 1 John we see both. The *commandment*: "This is the commandment we have from him: whoever loves God must also love his brother" (1 John 4:21). And the *warning*: "We know that we have passed out of death into life, because we love the brothers. Whoever does not love abides in death" (1 John 3:14). "Anyone who does not love does not know God, because God is love" (1 John 4:8, cf. 4:20). If we do not love, we are not born again and we do not know God.

Paul follows the same strategy. The *command*: "You shall love your neighbor as yourself" (Rom. 13:9). "Let love be genuine" (Rom. 12:9). The *warning*: "If I give away all I have, and if I deliver up my body to be burned, but have not love, I gain nothing" (1 Cor. 13:3). Or even worse, "I *am* nothing" (1 Cor. 13:2). Indeed, Paul's warnings can be very specific: "If anyone does not provide for his relatives, and especially for members of his household, he has denied the faith and is worse than an unbeliever" (1 Tim. 5:8). Worse than an unbeliever! Clearly, God's strategy in shaping a people who show practical love to their families includes the warning that if they don't, they are not saved.

Jesus spoke this way regularly. Not only did he say that unchecked lust would destroy us in hell (Matt. 5:27–30) and that greed prevents discipleship (Luke 14:33), but he also spoke the same way about love. For example, in his picture of the final judgment, he said that disciples who show no compassion for the hungry, the thirsty, the stranger, the naked, the sick, or the prisoner "will go away into eternal punishment" (Matt. 25:41–46).

And he said the same thing about an unforgiving spirit:

> If you forgive others their trespasses, your heavenly Father will also forgive you, but if you do not forgive others their trespasses, neither will your Father forgive your trespasses. (Matt. 6:14–15)

Some have tried to say that this unwillingness of God to forgive the unforgiving is only a temporary disruption of fellowship rather than a warning of eternal separation. Certainly if there is repentance, there is forgiveness from God for our temporary failure to forgive. But that is not the point here. The point here is the same as the parable in Matthew 18:21–35. When the wicked servant would not forgive his fellow servant, Jesus said, "In anger his master delivered him to the jailers, until he should pay all his debt. So also my heavenly Father will do to every one of you, if you do not forgive your brother from your heart" (18:34–35). There is no point in trying to weaken Jesus's threat, as if this way of motivating his disciples were foreign to the rest of his teaching, or the rest of the New Testament, when, in fact, it is pervasive.

The strategy of God's providence in creating Christlike Christians who persevere to the end includes what I have called a *command-and-warning strategy*. That is, God brings us to glory by commanding us to engage all that we are in the wholehearted pursuit of holiness. And he infuses tremendous seriousness into this strategy with warnings that the failure to pursue holiness leads to eternal destruction.

One Final Sampling of God's Strategy of Command and Warning

Here are several more examples to show the extent of this command-and-warning strategy in the New Testament.

> Enter by the narrow gate. For the gate is wide and the way is easy that leads to destruction, and those who enter by it are many. For the gate is narrow and the way is hard that leads to life, and those who find it are few. (Matt. 7:13–14)

> Everyone who hears these words of mine and does not do them will be like a foolish man who built his house on the sand. And the rain fell, and the floods came, and the winds blew and beat against that house, and it fell, and great was the fall of it. (Matt. 7:26–27)

Not everyone who says to me, "Lord, Lord," will enter the kingdom of heaven, but the one who does the will of my Father who is in heaven. (Matt. 7:21)

Whoever loves father or mother more than me is not worthy of me, and whoever loves son or daughter more than me is not worthy of me. (Matt. 10:37)

The one who sows to his own flesh will from the flesh reap corruption, but the one who sows to the Spirit will from the Spirit reap eternal life. (Gal. 6:8)

If we walk in the light, as he is in the light, we have fellowship with one another, and the blood of Jesus his Son cleanses us from all sin. (1 John 1:7)

Whoever says "I know him" but does not keep his commandments is a liar, and the truth is not in him. (1 John 2:4; cf. John 14:15; 15:10)

The world is passing away along with its desires, but whoever does the will of God abides forever. (1 John 2:17)

The point of this chapter is that the strategy of God's providence in sanctifying a people and bringing them to final glorification includes commands and warnings. Implicit in the word *commands* are all the biblical instructions to use what are often called the "means of grace." We could also call them the "means of providence." Whole books have been written on this aspect of providence alone.[4] I am only trying to establish the principle: saving, sanctifying, preserving providence uses commands and warnings.

---

4   See especially David Mathis, *Habits of Grace: Enjoying Jesus through the Spiritual Disciplines* (Wheaton, IL: Crossway, 2016); Donald Whitney, *Spiritual Disciplines for the Christian Life* (Colorado Springs, CO: NavPress, 2014).

But these means of providence that God commands include meditation on the Scriptures (Ps. 1:2; Col. 3:16), prayer (Eph. 6:18), membership in the local church (Matt. 18:17; 1 Cor. 12:12; 5:2), corporate worship (Eph. 5:19; Heb. 10:25), participating in baptism and the Lord's Supper (Matt. 28:19–20; 1 Cor. 11:23–26), and mutual exhortation and encouragement with other believers (Heb. 3:12–13).

In all these ways and more, God brings us to glory by commanding us to engage all that we are in the wholehearted pursuit of obedience, holiness, and love. And he warns us that if we don't obey, we don't know God (1 John 2:4); and if we don't pursue holiness, we will not see the Lord (Heb. 12:14); and if we don't love, we abide in death (1 John 3:14). This is God's command-and-warning strategy to prepare and preserve his people for their final glorification.

Strive to Enter through the Narrow Door

Another way to say that God calls us to a wholehearted pursuit of love is to use the words of Jesus: "Strive [Ἀγωνίζεσθε] to enter through the narrow door. For many, I tell you, will seek to enter and will not be able" (Luke 13:24). Or another way to say it is with the words of Hebrews 10:36: "You have need of endurance, so that when you have done the will of God you may receive what is promised."

The word Jesus uses for how Christians enter the final glory is *strive*. "Strive to enter." Or, as you can hear in the Greek (*agōnízesthe*): agonize, struggle, fight, wrestle. If you find the Christian life to be untroubled, without struggle, and without warfare against your own sin, you may not be living the Christian life. If your view of the providence of God is that his promise and power to help us mean there are no commands, no warnings, no threatenings, then your view has probably been more shaped by dubious theological inferences than by specific biblical teachings.

What of Those Who Fall Away from the Living God?

Implicit in this chapter is the heartrending fact that professing believers can and do deny Christ. Jesus spoke of this in the parable of the soils, where he said:

> And the ones on the rock are those who, when they hear the word, receive it with joy. But these have no root; they believe for a while, and in time of testing fall away. And as for what fell among the thorns, they are those who hear, but as they go on their way they are choked by the cares and riches and pleasures of life, and their fruit does not mature. (Luke 8:13–14)

Paul mentions more than one of his partners who abandoned him. Demas was his fellow worker in the gospel (Col. 4:14; Philem. 24), but in his last letter Paul says, "Demas, in love with this present world, has deserted me" (2 Tim. 4:10). This happens not just in individual cases but even in large movements of apostasy (2 Tim. 1:15).

Hebrews 3:12 focuses on the same sad reality of apostasy and turns it into a warning of what really happens: "Take care, brothers, lest there be in any of you an evil, unbelieving heart, leading you to fall away from the living God" (Heb. 3:12). This is the way the New Testament authors talk to the church. In the judgment of charity, they address their hearers as "brothers," knowing that some may be "false brothers" (2 Cor. 11:26).

But both the book of Hebrews and the rest of the New Testament bear witness that those who are truly "in Christ" will never forsake Christ utterly. I use the word *utterly* because temporary lapses of faith do happen. This is why the story of Peter's denial is in the Bible— to show how Christ preserves his own through temporary failures of faith. Jesus said to Simon Peter:

> Simon, Simon, behold, Satan demanded to have you, that he might sift you like wheat, but I have prayed for you that your faith may

not fail. And when you have turned again, strengthen your brothers. (Luke 22:31–32)

Peter's faith *will* fail, but not *utterly*. Why? Because Jesus has laid hold on him and kept him by prayer, as Jesus said in John 17:12: "While I was with them, I kept them in your name, which you have given me." Peter's repentance is certain in the mind of Jesus. "When you have turned again . . ." Not *if*. But *when*. Jesus has prayed for him. And the Father heard his prayer.

This is a preview of what is true for all of God's elect people, according to Romans 8:30–35:

> Those whom he justified he also glorified. What then shall we say to these things? If God is for us, who can be against us? . . . Who shall bring any charge against God's elect? It is God who justifies. Who is to condemn? Christ Jesus is the one who died—more than that, who was raised—who is at the right hand of God, who indeed is *interceding for us*. Who shall separate us from the love of Christ?

Here Paul gives multiple foundations for the certainty that all those who are justified will be glorified. No truly justified person fails to persevere in faith and be glorified. Not one. That's the point of "those whom he justified he also glorified." But here he also shows that the prayers of Jesus in heaven on our behalf are part of that security. "Christ . . . is at the right hand of God . . . interceding for us." Therefore, no one "shall separate us from the love of Christ." Christ kept Peter through his temporary failure. He keeps all God's elect.

Perseverance Proves We Are His

Shift back with me to the warning in Hebrews 3:12. The writer clarifies that no one who is truly in Christ will "fall away from the living God." He says in 3:14, "We have come to share in Christ, if indeed we hold our original confidence firm to the end." The verb tenses are all-important here. He does not say, "We *will* come to share in Christ, if indeed we hold our original confidence firm to the end." He says, "We *have come* to share in Christ, if indeed we hold our original confidence firm to the end." This means that perseverance does not get us into Christ, but proves that we have already come to share in Christ.

This is how the apostle John described apostasy as well. It doesn't happen to those who are truly "of us"—that is, who are truly born again and thus of the family of God:

> Children, it is the last hour, and as you have heard that antichrist is coming, so now many antichrists have come. Therefore we know that it is the last hour. They went out from us, but *they were not of us*; for if they had been *of us,* they would have continued with us. But they went out, that it might become plain that they all are *not of us.* (1 John 2:18–19)

Vigilant and Confident

The fact that professing believers can fall away and be lost, and the fact that God's strategy is to warn us of this and to use commandments to engage us fully in the fight of faith, should sober us and make us vigilant. But the fact that God will not allow any of his children to make shipwreck of their faith, and that he will infallibly bring them all to glory, should make us confident and bold as we embrace him as our supreme treasure and walk in his ways.

What we will see in the next chapter is that the command-and-warning strategy of God's providence goes hand in hand with omnipotent enabling, strong assurance, and unbounded joy. But for now, let us not minimize the sobering truth: "You will be hated by all for my name's sake. But the one who endures to the end will be saved" (Mark 13:13).

40

Those Whom He Called,
He Also Glorified

Without the whole counsel of God, the command-and-warning strategy of God's providence, unfolded in the previous chapter, may give the impression that God's will is not that his people have assurance that they will endure to the end and be saved. That impression would be a serious mistake. God has not left us without the whole counsel of God.

Everything Needed for Your Preservation

That phrase "whole counsel of God" comes from Paul's address to the elders of Ephesus in Acts 20. He said, "I did not shrink from declaring to you the whole counsel of God" (Acts 20:27). The word *counsel* (βουλὴν) refers to a plan or purpose, as when it is used in Acts 4:28 to describe God's *plan* in all the sinful deeds of Herod and Pilate in putting Jesus to death. They were gathered to do "whatever your hand and your *plan* [βουλή] had predestined to take place."

God has a *plan* for his people. Paul says he did not shrink back from declaring *all* of it—the whole plan (πᾶσαν τὴν βουλὴν). What does that mean? We know that God's infinite mind and the totality of his judgments are "unsearchable" (Rom. 11:33; Eph. 3:8). So what does *whole* counsel mean? Paul shows us by using the same language in Acts 20:20 and 27. Both verses say, "I did not shrink from declaring." In verse 20, he did not shrink from declaring "anything that was profitable." In verse 27 he did not shrink back from declaring "the whole counsel of God."

I conclude from this that the "whole counsel of God" is Paul's way of saying at least this: everything you need in order to be saved, to live a life of faith that pleases God, and to persevere to the end, I have declared to you. So when I say that without the whole counsel of God, the command-and-warning strategy of the previous chapter may give the impression that God's will is not that his people have assurance, I mean that there is something utterly crucial in the counsel of God that I now need to make plain, beginning in this chapter and continuing through chapter 43.

All Is Happening according to Plan

God's providence moves according to plan. It is not haphazard or random or whimsical. God does not make his decisions on the spur of the moment. He "works all things according to the counsel [βουλὴν] of his will" (Eph. 1:11). The counsel, or plan, goes back before the foundation of the world (Matt. 25:34; Eph. 1:4; 2 Tim. 1:9). God is never at a loss as to how he will act. The plan does not have holes in it. There were no oversights.

In "bringing many sons to glory" (Heb. 2:10), God knows how he will do it. The plan includes a command-and-warning strategy, but, oh, so much more. And without this *more*, we will not grasp the wisdom and power and unfailing certainty of God's achievement in the preservation, sanctification, and eternal glorification of his people. To that *more* we now turn.

From Bewilderment to Beauty

The essence of the *more* is this: God doesn't just require holiness; he *promises* it to his people, he *bought* it for them, and he *brings it about* in their hearts and lives. Therefore, the holiness that God requires of his people on their path to glory is absolutely certain. It will not fail. We will unfold this from the New Testament in three steps: the *promise* of holiness to us (this chapter), the *purchase* of holiness for us (chapter 41), and the *performance* of holiness in us (chapters 42–43). Each of these is revealed in Scripture with clarity for all to see.

The aim of that clear revelation is joyful, confident, wholehearted, vigilant pursuit of holiness (Heb. 12:14) and glory (Rom. 2:6–7), because God has made it so sure. As Paul says in Philippians 3:12, "Not that I have already obtained this or am already perfect, but I press on to make it my own, *because Christ Jesus has made me his own*." Paul labors to seize Christ as his prize, because Christ has seized him. This is the mystery of sanctification that so many people find incomprehensible—that the *certainty* of belonging to Christ would make us *vigilant* to lay hold on Christ! I am praying that you will find this not bewildering but beautiful. If it starts as an enigma of confusion, I pray it ends as energy for Christ.

Command for Vigilance, Promise for Confidence

What baffles some people about the way God's providence brings his people to glory is that he commands them to hold fast and be holy, and then he sees to it that this will infallibly come to pass. Whether it baffles or not, it is what the Bible teaches. The command awakens vigilance; the promise awakens confidence. In God's design, the command is a means of God's fulfilling the promise. He makes our participation in perseverance essential, but not uncertain.

We tend to think that if God promises to see to something, then we don't have to see to it. That is not the way it is. God has designed that our seeing to it is part of the way he sees to it. "The horse is made ready for the day of battle, but the victory belongs to the LORD" (Prov. 21:31). God could get the victory without the horse. But that is not his way. Nor is it his way of sanctification or glorification.

Greatest Passage on Preservation

The clearest and fullest promise that God will give us all we need and infallibly bring us to glory is Romans 8:28–39. It is manifestly designed to give fearless confidence to God's children in the face of tribulation, distress, persecution, famine, nakedness, danger, and sword (8:35).

The context is the global suffering of all people and the groaning of creation under its subjection to futility and corruption (8:18–25).[1] In this context, Paul speaks of how perplexed Christians can be about how to pray. For example, should we pray for grace to suffer a disease with all the fallen people of the world, or should we lay hold on God for a specific healing? This is the context for saying, "We do not know what to pray for as we ought" (8:26). In this context of universal suffering and perplexity even in prayer, Paul says, in effect, "We may not know how to pray, but we do know something!" "We [do] know that for those who love God all things work together for good" (8:28). That is the beginning of the most exalted of all Scriptures concerning the absolute assurance believers can have in the face of Satan, sin, sickness, and sabotage.

All the universe is groaning. Believers share the pain and perplexity. We often do not know how to pray, but . . .

> we know that for those who love God all things work together for good, for those who are called according to his purpose. For those whom he foreknew he also predestined to be conformed to the image of his Son, in order that he might be the firstborn among many brothers. And those whom he predestined he also called, and those whom he called he also justified, and those whom he justified he also glorified.
>
> What then shall we say to these things? If God is for us, who can be against us? He who did not spare his own Son but gave him up

---

1   See chap. 29 for a fuller treatment of these verses.

for us all, how will he not also with him graciously give us all things? Who shall bring any charge against God's elect? It is God who justifies. Who is to condemn? Christ Jesus is the one who died—more than that, who was raised—who is at the right hand of God, who indeed is interceding for us. Who shall separate us from the love of Christ? Shall tribulation, or distress, or persecution, or famine, or nakedness, or danger, or sword? As it is written,

> "For your sake we are being killed all the day long;
> we are regarded as sheep to be slaughtered."

No, in all these things we are more than conquerors through him who loved us. For I am sure that neither death nor life, nor angels nor rulers, nor things present nor things to come, nor powers, nor height nor depth, nor anything else in all creation, will be able to separate us from the love of God in Christ Jesus our Lord. (8:28–39)

In my judgment (and experience), this is the greatest section of the greatest chapter of the greatest letter in the greatest book in the world. But that's not the point here.

All Things Working for the Good of Whom?

The point here is that God works everything—everything!—for the good of those who love God and are called by him (Rom. 8:28). The beneficiaries of that all-encompassing promise do not include everyone. They are marked by two things—one from us, one from God. From us: love to God. From God: the divine call that we saw in 1 Corinthians 1:22–24, the call that awakens us from death and brings us into new life in Christ.[2] So this promise contains the entire commitment of God to do everything necessary for our eternal good.

---

2 See chap. 35, where we saw the "call" of God as his life-giving summons into existence of the new creature in Christ.

No Links Will Be Broken in the Chain of God's Purpose

We see this in the argument that follows. Paul supports this massive promise in verse 28 with the assertion (in 8:29–30) that, beginning in eternity past (foreknown) and extending to eternity future (glorified), he is committed, at every step of the way, to bringing his people to glory:

> For those whom he foreknew he also predestined to be conformed to the image of his Son. . . . And those whom he predestined he also called, and those whom he called he also justified, and those whom he justified he also glorified.

The point of this golden chain is this: no link breaks. Nobody falls out. Every foreknown one becomes a predestined one. Every predestined one becomes a called one. Every called one becomes a justified one. Every justified one becomes a glorified one. Few things could be clearer or more glorious. Assurance! Confidence! Stability! Courage!

The mention of the "called" in this chain (8:30, "those whom he *called* he also justified and . . . glorified") links back to verse 28, which is a promise to the called (All things work together for good for those who are *called*). That link helps us see that what Paul is describing in this chain is the "good" he had promised in verse 28. God works all things for our *good*. And the *good* is conformity to Christ (8:29) and unfailing glorification (8:30).

Surest Sign That God Is for Us

Then Paul steps back from this massive foundation for our assurance and asks, "What then shall we say to these things?" (Rom. 8:31). That seems to mean that there are scarcely any words good enough to respond to such a solid promise of glory. But he has an answer for his own question. Here's what we shall say: "If God is for us, who can be against us?" Meaning, if, as we can see, the omnipotent, all-planning, all-accomplishing God is committed to our good and not to our harm, then no adversary can succeed in breaking the chain that brings us to glory.

But lest anyone doubt that God is for us, with omnipotent resolve to do everything necessary to conform us to Christ and bring us to glory, Paul invites us to consider once more what Romans has been about for eight chapters: God's giving his Son to bear our condemnation (8:3) and become our righteousness (5:19). So Paul says it again and reveals the indissoluble connection between the death of Christ and the promise of Romans 8:28:

> He who did not spare his own Son but gave him up for us all, how will he not also with him graciously give us all things? (8:32)

This may be the most important verse in the Bible. At least it is for establishing the hearts of God's people in the assurance that he is for us and will use all his infinite wisdom and power to bring us to glory. The logic of the verse is clear and strong: not sparing his own Son is the hardest thing God has ever done. Since he did this hardest thing "for us all"—that is, for all who love God and are called according to his purpose (8:28)—we know that there is nothing he will not do to bring us to himself in glory. Nothing is harder than offering his Son. He did that. For us. It follows that he will not fail to "give us all things"—that is, all that we need in order to be conformed to his Son (8:29) and then glorified (8:30).

The Promise of Glory Does Not Bypass the Provision of Conformity to Christ

The rest of Romans 8:31–39 deepens and broadens the claim that nothing can separate us from the "love of Christ" (8:35) and from the "love of God in Christ" (8:39). The main point of Romans 8:28–39, for our purposes in this chapter, is that "those whom he called . . . he also glorified" (8:30). He sees to it that all of his converted people make it to glory. Our glorification is so sure that Paul speaks of it as accomplished, though it is yet future.

This is not a promise that bypasses God's demand for Christlikeness in holiness and love. God's promise to conform us to Christ is precisely what predestination guarantees. All the foreknown are "predestined to be conformed to the image of his Son" (8:29). This happens through our calling, our justification, and finally our glorification (8:30). The implications for our lives are these: Be strong in faith. Be unshakable in the assurance that God is for you and will bring you to glory. Be done with fear. Be full of joy. Be overflowing with courageous love for others.

Eternal Security Is Not Like an Inoculation

We can think about what Paul has done in Romans 8:28–39 another way: he has established God's faithfulness. From all that Paul has said, it is clear that there is nothing mechanical or natural or automatic about our conformity to Christ and our glorification. All of it is dependent on God's action. Many people have mechanical, or even biological, conceptions of eternal security. They think of once-saved-always-saved similar to the way an inoculation works. They think, "When I was saved, God inoculated me from condemnation. It's built in the way disease-preventing antibodies are in the blood."

That way of thinking about the assurances given by Paul in Romans 8:28–39 is mistaken. Everything hangs on God, not on built-in spiritual antibodies. If God is not faithful to the promises made here, we will perish. Our perseverance in faith, our conformity to Christ, and our final glorification depend on whether God is faithful—day by day and forever.

I often ask people, How do you know you will wake up a Christian tomorrow morning? The bottom-line answer is that God will cause you to wake up a Christian, or you won't. God will be faithful. God will keep you. Everything hangs on the faithfulness of God to his promise: "Those whom he called . . . he also glorified."

God's Faithfulness to His Call

We know Paul thinks this way because twice he rivets our attention on God's faithfulness in promising perseverance in holiness:

> [Christ] will sustain you to the end, guiltless in the day of our Lord Jesus Christ. *God is faithful, by whom you were called* into the fellowship of his Son, Jesus Christ our Lord. (1 Cor. 1:8–9)

> Now may the God of peace himself sanctify you completely, and may your whole spirit and soul and body be kept blameless at the coming of our Lord Jesus Christ. *He who calls you is faithful;* he will surely do it. (1 Thess. 5:23–24)

Both of these texts say that our arriving safe and holy in the presence of Christ depends on God's faithfulness. And 1 Corinthians 1:9 makes the connection with his *calling* explicit: "God is faithful, by whom you were called." The meaning is this: built into our calling is a promise, the promise of Romans 8:30: "Those whom he called . . . he also glorified." Therefore, everything hangs on God's faithfulness to that promise. No doubt this is what Paul had in mind when he said to the Philippians, "I am sure of this, that he who began a good work in you will bring it to completion at the day of Jesus Christ" (Phil. 1:6). Paul is *sure* because the work God had begun was their calling, and "God is faithful, by whom you were called."

"I Will Not Let Them Turn Away from Me"

The roots of this confidence in God's faithfulness go back into the Old Testament, and especially into the new-covenant promises. The most relevant promise for the present point is Jeremiah 32:40, where God says:

> I will make with them an everlasting covenant, that I will not turn away from doing good to them. And I will put the fear of me in their hearts, that they may not turn from me.

There are two ways that God's children could conceivably fail in the Christian life. One is to turn away from God. And the other is for God to turn away from us. Jeremiah, amazingly, says that in the days to come—the days of the new covenant—neither of these will happen. God "will not turn away from doing good to [us]." And he will work in us "that [we] may not turn from [him]." That is the answer to the question, How do you know you will be a Christian when you wake up tomorrow? And it is the answer to how God brings his people to everlasting glory.

"No One Can Snatch Them Out of My Hand"

Jesus gave essentially this same promise in words that many Christians cherish in times of great conflict and fear:

> My sheep hear my voice, and I know them, and they follow me. I give them eternal life, and they will never perish, and no one will snatch them out of my hand. My Father, who has given them to me, is greater than all, and no one is able to snatch them out of the Father's hand. I and the Father are one. (John 10:27–30)

He gives his sheep eternal life. He promises that they will never perish. Never. They will make it to glory. Then he speaks similarly to the way Paul will speak: No one will snatch them out of my hand (10:28). No one will snatch them out of the Father's hand (10:29). Paul said that nothing can separate us from the love of Christ, and nothing can separate us from the love of God in Christ (Rom. 8:35–39). Jesus and Paul and Jeremiah are making the same point: God promises perseverance, holiness, and glorification for his people. They will not fail to attain their inheritance.

Sealed and Guaranteed

Paul speaks of the Christian inheritance being *guaranteed* by the sealing of the Holy Spirit:

> In [Christ] you also, when you heard the word of truth, the gospel of your salvation, and believed in him, were sealed with the promised Holy Spirit, who is the guarantee of our inheritance until we acquire possession of it, to the praise of his glory. (Eph. 1:13–14)

There are two metaphors here to double our sense of assurance that God will not fail to bring us into the full enjoyment of our inheritance (the kingdom of God, 1 Cor. 6:9–10; Eph. 5:5). There is the image of *sealing* and the image of a *down payment* (ἀρραβὼν). This word for *down payment* is translated "guarantee," because it refers to the first installment of a reality that guarantees the rest.

So the Holy Spirit is pictured here as doubly securing our final inheritance. He is like a seal—a sign of God's ownership. And he is himself the firstfruits of a full harvest of his presence and power. Paul is drawing out the inner workings of the new covenant. God promised, "I will put my Spirit within you, and cause you to walk in my statutes" (Ezek. 36:27). And the point is this: "In Christ, you are not left to yourself to attain the inheritance; I will accomplish this by my Spirit within you."

"The Lord Stood by Me"

Paul spoke very personally about his experience of being preserved by the Lord for his entrance into the kingdom of God. He recalled his court appearance with thankfulness:

> At my first defense . . . the Lord stood by me and strengthened me, so that through me the message might be fully proclaimed and all the Gentiles might hear it. So I was rescued from the lion's mouth. The Lord will rescue me from every evil deed and bring me safely into his heavenly kingdom. To him be the glory forever and ever. Amen. (2 Tim. 4:16–18)

The "lion's mouth" may refer to martyrdom. But what Paul seems most thankful for, and confident of, is the assurance that the Lord "will bring me safely into his heavenly kingdom." Martyrdom is no hindrance to this. Unbelief and sin, not martyrdom, keep one out of the kingdom. So when he says, "The Lord will rescue me from *every evil deed* and bring me safely into his heavenly kingdom," his confidence is not that he won't suffer martyrdom but that no evil deed done against him will be allowed to destroy his faith or undermine his obedience. He will be protected from *every* evil deed—his own, and others'. This is the work of the Spirit (2 Thess. 2:13), who guarantees our inheritance (Eph. 1:14).

Required Obedience Is Not Repealed; It Is Promised

In the previous chapter I tried to show that the strategy of God's providence in bringing his people from conversion to glory includes commands and warnings. His design is to engage all that we are in the wholehearted pursuit of holiness. By itself, this strategy of commands and warnings would not succeed. By itself, it would leave us with little assurance that we could ever endure to the end and be saved (Mark 13:13). God never intended for this part of his strategy to be by itself. There is so much more to God's providence in bringing his people to glory.

The present chapter is the first part of this *more*. I said that we will unfold this *more* from the New Testament in three steps: the *promise* of holiness to us, the *purchase* of holiness for us, and the *performance* of holiness in us. This chapter has shown the promise of holiness and its end, eternal glory. The main point has been "those whom God called . . . he also glorified" (Rom. 8:30). None of those who are truly converted to Christ and brought to saving faith will ever be lost.

None of the requirements for making it to glory, which we saw in chapter 39, have been revoked. That is not how God gives assurance. The obedience required has not been repealed. It has been promised. "I will . . . cause you to . . . be careful to obey my rules" (Ezek. 36:27). The conformity to Christ that God commands has not been rescinded.

It has been predestined. "Those whom he foreknew he also predestined to be conformed to the image of his Son" (Rom. 8:29). The fear of failure is not remedied by abolishing obligations. It is remedied by God's faithfulness. "He who calls you is faithful; he will surely do it" (1 Thess. 5:24).

All of God's Majesty Serves Your Keeping

These promises that God will create in us what he commands from us are so magnificent that they elicit from Jude one of the most exalted doxologies in the Bible:

> Now to him who is able to keep you from stumbling and to present you blameless before the presence of his glory with great joy, to the only God, our Savior, through Jesus Christ our Lord, be glory, majesty, dominion, and authority, before all time and now and forever. Amen. (Jude 24–25)

If you woke up a Christian this morning, this is how you should feel. Glory, majesty, dominion, and authority have been at work for you while you slept. Your being kept for a joyful meeting with God has been promised. God is faithful. He will do it. But that is not all. He not only *promised* it; he *purchased* it. To that we now turn.

41

Blood-Bought Zeal for Good Works

God's providence in bringing his people from conversion to glory includes the strategy of issuing commands and warnings designed to engage us in a wholehearted pursuit of holiness (chapter 39). But the stunning thing about God's sanctifying providence is that he sees to it that his people do not fail in keeping these commandments. Not with perfection in this life (Matt. 6:12; Phil. 3:12; 1 John 1:8), but with earnest intent and regular triumphs (Matt. 7:18; Rom. 6:14; Heb. 12:14; 1 John 3:9; 5:4, 18). In other words, God requires obedience from his people, and he makes it certain. Our security lies not in the absence of human conditions but in the presence of divine power. God creates what he commands.

Christ Purchased More Than Forgiveness and Eternal Life

This obedience-producing power is *promised* to us, *purchased* for us, and *performed* in us by God. In chapter 40 we focused on the promise. In this chapter we focus on the purchase. That is, we focus on the effectiveness of the death of Christ in securing for us the life change demanded from us.

Most of us who think about the cross of Christ, and what he achieved by dying there, think about the forgiveness of sin and the gift of eternal life. "In him we have redemption through his blood, *the forgiveness* of our trespasses" (Eph. 1:7). "God so loved the world, that he gave his only Son, that whoever believes in him should not perish but have *eternal life*" (John 3:16). We might also think of the completion of a life of perfect obedience. Christ was "obedient to the point of death, even death on a cross" (Phil. 2:8), so that "by one man's obedience many will be appointed righteous" (Rom. 5:19, my translation).

But what many Christians do not think about is the fact that the blood of Christ purchased, or secured, sanctification as well as justification, faithful obedience as well as forgiven sin, good works as well as eternal life, present transformation as well as final glorification. The practical holiness that leads to heaven (Heb. 12:14), the obedience that enters the kingdom of God (1 Cor. 6:9–10), the fruit that marks every good tree (Matt. 7:18), and the love for people that shows new birth (1 John 3:14)—these realities are not only predestined (Rom. 8:29) and promised (Ezek. 36:27), but also purchased. They are obtained for God's people by the blood of his Son.

Link between Being Forgiven and Being Obedient: Blood

Consider the connection between the blood-bought promise of forgiveness in the new covenant and the promise that God will bring about the obedience of his people. At the Last Supper, Jesus identified his own blood as the price of the new covenant: "This cup that is poured out for you is the *new covenant in my blood*" (Luke 22:20). He made the connection between his blood and the forgiveness of sins promised in the new covenant: "This is my blood of the covenant, which is poured out for many *for the forgiveness of sins*" (Matt. 26:28).

When we read the promise of the new covenant in Jeremiah 31:31–34, we discover that the forgiveness of sins is not simply one of several benefits of the covenant; it is the ground for the others:

> Behold, the days are coming, declares the LORD, when I will make a new covenant. . . . I will put my law within them, and I will write it on their hearts. And I will be their God, and they shall be my people. And no longer shall each one teach his neighbor and each his brother, saying, "Know the LORD," for they shall all know me, from the least of them to the greatest, declares the LORD. *For* [כִּי] I will forgive their iniquity, and I will remember their sin no more.

Notice how the promise of forgiveness is the ground, the basis, of what goes before. "*For* [because] I will forgive their iniquity." In essence, God says, "I will write the law on their hearts, *because* I will forgive their sins." Jesus says that this forgiveness is obtained by his blood (Matt. 26:28). Therefore, the blood of Jesus, through the forgiveness of sins, provides the purchase of the promise "I will write [the law] on their hearts." This is a promise that God will see to it that we obey his word from the heart. "I will . . . cause you to . . . be careful to obey my rules" (Ezek. 36:27).

Saved through Sure and Blood-Bought Sanctification

Indeed, Paul says, "*all* the promises of God find their Yes in him" (2 Cor. 1:20). "In him"—because "*in him* we have redemption through his blood, *the forgiveness of our trespasses*" (Eph. 1:7). Forgiveness is the ground and guarantee of all the benefits of the new covenant. Through blood-bought forgiveness, Christ obtained the surety of every promise of God for his people. And that includes the promise to cause our obedience, our sanctification, our good works, our love, our holiness, without which we will not see the Lord (Heb. 12:14).

Therefore, the fact that sanctification is a necessary part of salvation does not mean that salvation is uncertain or insecure for God's people. It is as sure as the blood-bought promise that God "will remove the heart of stone from their flesh and give them a heart of flesh, that they may walk in my statutes and keep my rules and obey them" (Ezek. 11:19–20). And make no mistake: sanctification is a necessary part of salvation, as Paul says in 2 Thessalonians 2:13: "God chose you as the firstfruits to be saved, *through sanctification by the Spirit* and belief in the truth." The holiness promised in the new covenant is not ancillary to salvation. It is part of what salvation *is*. And it is sure, because Christ died to secure it.

All Things Needed for Our Glorification Are Sure

The fact that all the promises of God—including the promise to cause our obedience—are secured by the blood of Christ has been confirmed already in the previous chapter by the breathtaking logic of Romans 8:32: "He who did not spare his own Son but gave him up for us all, how will he not also with him graciously give us all things?" This *all things* is as certain for God's people as was God's not sparing his own Son. Not sparing his own Son for us sinners was the hardest thing. All the rest of what it takes to get us to glory is easy by comparison.

We saw that the *all things* in Romans 8:32 is similar to the *all things* in Romans 8:28, where God works all things together for our good. What is secured in Romans 8:32 is everything needed to accomplish this *good* in verse 28. And that *good* is defined in 8:29–30 as conformity to Christ and final glorification. Or now to say it another way, God's not sparing his own Son secured for us every promise that God has made to conform us to Christ and bring us to glory. This means that sanctification—the path and appearance of salvation in this life— is purchased and secured by the blood of Christ.

Pardon Unleashes the Power to Love

Confirming that we are in sync with Paul's way of thinking, Romans 8:3–4 says that Christ bore our condemnation precisely so that we might walk in sanctification, that is, in love. The divine power for this obedience was unleashed by the pardon secured on the cross:

> God has done what the law, weakened by the flesh, could not do. By sending his own Son in the likeness of sinful flesh and for sin, he

condemned sin in the flesh, in order that the righteous requirement of the law might be fulfilled in us, who walk not according to the flesh but according to the Spirit.

One could restate the logic this way: Christ accomplished *for* us the condemnation that the law demands *so that* he might accomplish *in* us the sanctification that the law commands. The key phrase for our purpose is the phrase *so that*. When God put Christ in our condemned place, he did this not only to secure heaven, but to secure holiness. Or even more precisely, not only to secure our life in paradise, but also to secure our love for people.

The reason I say that it is more precise to speak of love than of holiness is that, when Paul eventually defines "the righteous requirement of the law" that God secured by putting our condemnation on his Son, the sum of that righteous requirement is love. He writes in Romans 13:8–10:

> The one who loves another has fulfilled the law. . . . [All the commandments] are summed up in this word: "You shall love your neighbor as yourself." Love does no wrong to a neighbor; therefore love is the fulfilling of the law.

So I understand "the righteous requirement of the law" in Romans 8:4 as summed up in "love your neighbor as yourself." This is the love without which we do not have life, for John says, "Whoever does not love abides in death" (1 John 3:14). Therefore, the love for other people that shows life and leads to heaven was secured for us by the death of Christ. When God laid on him our condemnation (Rom. 8:3), his aim was not only to close hell but to cause love.

Reconciled to God for the Sake of Blameless Living

Paul makes the same point with different language in Colossians 1:21–22. He says that we are reconciled to God "in order to" make us holy and blameless. The transaction of being reconciled to God "by [Christ's] death" has this design: our holiness before God:

> You, who once were alienated and hostile in mind, doing evil deeds, he has now reconciled in his body of flesh by his death, in order to present you holy and blameless and above reproach before him.

We might be tempted to think Paul means only that Christ's reconciling death secures our *final* perfection before God rather than our holiness in this life—perhaps a reference to what happens in the twinkling of an eye at the moment of death or at the second coming, when "the spirits of the righteous [are] made perfect" (Heb. 12:23). But that limitation to our final perfecting is unlikely.

The reason it's unlikely is that the very language used to describe the aim of our reconciliation in Colossians 1:22 is used to describe our holiness in this life. Paul says that God reconciled us to himself "in order to present [us] holy and blameless . . . before him." This is also the aim of Paul's prayer in Philippians 1:9–10, where our love and discernment *in this life* are the way God makes us "blameless for the day of Christ":

> It is my prayer that your love may abound more and more, with knowledge and all discernment, so that you may approve what is excellent, and so be pure and blameless for the day of Christ.

In other words, part of the process, in God's providence, for leading us to final perfection in the Lord's presence is that our love abound *now* in knowledge and discernment so that we grow in our ability to approve what is excellent. This is the necessary path to being found pure and blameless at the day of Christ.

So when Paul says in Colossians 1:21–22 that God reconciled us to himself by the death of Christ "in order to present [us] holy and blameless . . . before him," it is unlikely that the design of this reconciliation expressed in the words "in order to" should be limited to the *final* perfecting of the saints. More likely is that it includes the present path of imperfect blamelessness that Paul prays for as the pathway to the perfection of that last day. And if anyone doubts that Paul thought in terms of progressive, *imperfect blamelessness*, consider what he says in Philippians 2:14–15:

> Do all things without grumbling or disputing, *that you may be blameless and innocent*, children of God without blemish in the midst of a crooked and twisted generation, among whom you shine as lights in the world.

This is what he was praying for in Philippians 1:9–10, that we be "pure and blameless for the day of Christ," only it is already happening. Indeed, Paul has no conception of a Christian life lived in unrepentant sin and then suddenly perfected at the judgment day. The achievement and aim of the cross is not just final perfection, but measures of holiness in this life that confirm election (2 Pet. 1:10), show life (1 John 3:14), and glorify Christ (2 Thess. 1:11–12). Christ died for this.

Blood-Bought Zeal for Good Works

One more text from the apostle Paul expresses the sanctifying aim of Christ's self-sacrifice in a unique way. He says that its aim is not just holiness or love or good works, but *zeal* for good works:

> Christ . . . gave himself for us to redeem us from all lawlessness and to purify for himself a people for his own possession who are zealous for good works. (Titus 2:14)

Notice that the design of Christ's self-giving redemption is *from* something and *for* something. He gave himself to redeem us *from* lawlessness and *for* zeal. This is significant, because up till now we have not put our finger on *how* the cross actually creates the good deeds of holiness and love it is designed to create. Here we have a pointer. The effectiveness of the blood of Christ in creating good deeds does not circumvent our zeal. It doesn't bypass our will and our passion. It secures them and awakens them. I said in chapter 39 that God's commands are designed to engage us in a wholehearted pursuit of holiness. Now we can see what this *wholehearted pursuit* is called and where it comes from. It is called *zeal*. And it comes from the death of Jesus.

Ransomed from Futile Ways—by Precious Blood

Paul is not the only one who sees in the death of Jesus the purchase of our obedience, our sanctification, our conformity to Christ, our holiness, and our love. Peter in his first letter teaches the same thing:

> If you call on him as Father who judges impartially according to each one's deeds, conduct yourselves with fear throughout the time of your exile, knowing that *you were ransomed from the futile ways* inherited from your forefathers, not with perishable things such as silver or gold, but with the precious blood of Christ, like that of a lamb without blemish or spot. (1 Pet. 1:17–19)

It is beautiful and profound to discover that two apostles can be so deeply united in what they believe and yet teach it with such different words. Peter says that "with the precious blood of Christ" we are ransomed from "ways inherited from our forefathers" (ἀναστροφῆς πατροπαραδότου). This is unusual language: ransomed from a way of life. But we are not surprised after all we have seen. The aim of God's shedding the blood of his Son was a ransom. And the aim of the ransom was liberation from an empty, futile, dead-end way of living.

Being ransomed from futile deeds is the flip side of being redeemed to make us zealous for good deeds. The Greek word behind "ransomed" (1 Pet. 1:18) and "redeem" (Titus 2:14) is the same (λυτρόω).

Paul and Peter speak with one mind: Christ died not only for our justification and our final glorification, but also for our sanctification in this life. Holiness and love in the most practical and present sense are blood bought.

Bearing Sins to Create Obedience

Then in 1 Peter 2:24–25, Peter says it in another, still different, way:

> [Christ] himself bore our sins in his body on the tree, that we might die to sin and live to righteousness. By his wounds you have been healed. For you were straying like sheep, but have now returned to the Shepherd and Overseer of your souls.

In two different ways Peter makes the same point: Christ's sin-bearing, substitutionary death was designed that we might "live to righteousness." He bore our sin, not only that we might not be condemned by it, but that we might be full of its opposite: righteous living. Living to righteousness is what Paul meant by zeal for good deeds. Both are secured by Christ's sin-bearing death.

The second way Peter makes the point is with imagery taken from Isaiah 53:5: "By his wounds you have been healed." In the flow of Peter's thought, this does not refer to healing from physical diseases (though it can carry that meaning, Matt. 8:17). It refers to the sin-healing flow of blood from Christ's wounds. We can see this from the connection between verses 24 and 25. "By his wounds you have been healed. *For* [γὰρ] you were straying like sheep, but have now returned to the Shepherd and Overseer of your souls."

Peter explains what he means: the healing of Christians by Christ's wounds refers to the fact that they have returned from straying. To be under the "Shepherd and Overseer of your souls [Christ]" is to be made well. This "straying like sheep" probably refers to the "futile ways" we saw back in 1 Peter 1:18. The same point is being made. The wounds of Christ—the precious blood of Christ—have this design and effect: ransom from "futile ways" and returning from futile "straying." What Christ died to purchase was a new way of life with Jesus as guiding and protecting shepherd and overseer.

Peaceful Conscience for a Life of Service

We look at one more representative writer in the New Testament to confirm what we are seeing and to put it in yet another manner of expression:

> If the blood of goats and bulls, and the sprinkling of defiled persons with the ashes of a heifer, sanctify for the purification of the flesh, how much more will the blood of Christ, who through the eternal Spirit offered himself without blemish to God, purify our conscience from dead works to serve the living God. (Heb. 9:13–14)

The main assertion is this: "The blood of Christ [will] purify our conscience from dead works to serve the living God." Here, the blood of Christ has a double design and effect: it clears something away, and it puts something in motion. It clears away the defiling, discouraging, paralyzing effects of "dead works." Nothing but the blood of Jesus can do this the way it needs to be done. To be sure, it is good to live in a way that gives us a clear conscience. But sin is so subtle, and its contaminating effects so pervasive, that without the precious assurance that our sins are purified by the blood of Jesus, the sinfulness of our works will kill us.

But that is not the main point. The main point is that, when the unclean conscience is purified and dead works are dethroned, *a life of service to the living God* is created. That is the aim of God's purifying the conscience. God's aim in the sacrifice of Christ is not a peaceful conscience doing nothing. Serving the living God is the goal of the purified conscience. And the purified conscience is the effect of the blood of Christ. Therefore, Christ died to create a life of service to the living God.

Distinctly Christian Providence

If we do not see the whole counsel of God concerning his providence in bringing his people from conversion to glory, we are likely to take any part of it and misuse it to our hurt. Chapter 39 made clear that part of God's counsel—his plan, his strategy—is to engage our wholehearted pursuit of holiness by issuing commands and warnings. But what makes this strategy distinctly Christian is the fact that this wholehearted pursuit of holiness is *promised* to us through the word of Christ, *purchased* for us by the blood of Christ, and *performed* in us by the Spirit of Christ. We have seen the promise of his word (chapter 40) and the purchase by his blood (chapter 41). In the next two chapters we will see the performance of his Spirit.

42

Working in Us That Which
Is Pleasing in His Sight

In this chapter and the next, we will focus on the biblical teaching *that* God brings about obedience in his people (chapter 42) and *how* he does it through faith and by his Spirit (chapter 43). This aspect of God's providence is the point of immediate contact between his working and our willing. If there had been any question before of whether the transforming effectiveness of God's providence was only a proposal for our acceptance or rejection, he will now make this clear: his transforming providence is not a proposal, but a performance.

Getting Our Bearings in the Book
First, let's get our bearings in the flow of the book. The focus of part 3, sections 7 and 8, has been the nature and extent of God's providence in bringing his fallen, undeserving people out of unbelief into saving faith, which bears fruit in a life of holiness, which leads to eternal glory. In other words, we have been focusing on how God achieves the ultimate goal of creation and history and redemption through his providence.

We concluded in part 2 of this book that the ultimate goal of providence is *to display God's glory with such fullness that it is exalted in the way his people enjoy and reflect his excellencies.* Or to be more precise, we saw that the ultimate goal of providence is *the glorification of God's grace through Jesus Christ in beautifying an undeserving people whose beauty is their enjoyment and reflection of God's beauty.* Or we could say that since God will be thrilled with the work of his hands (Isa. 62:4–5; Jer. 32:41; Zeph. 3:17; Matt. 25:21, 23), the ultimate goal of providence is *the overflowing joy of God himself in the holiness and happiness of his people in the glory of his name.*

Enjoying and Reflecting, Happiness and Holiness

Whatever the precise words we use to describe the ultimate purpose of God's providence, it necessarily includes the Christ-exalting (2 Thess. 1:10, 12), grace-praising (Eph. 1:6), God-glorifying (Phil. 2:11) holiness and happiness of his people. In the previous paragraph, I said the goal of providence includes the destiny of God's people *enjoying* and *reflecting* his excellencies. Those two words correspond to the Christian's happiness and holiness. The Christian's holiness and happiness in God are not two separate realities. Happiness in God is the essence of holiness.

We can see this when we consider that holiness is the opposite of sin, and sin is preferring anything over God. Therefore, holiness is preferring God (for his supreme beauty and worth) over everything, and acting in accord with that preference. But what is happiness in God except that very preference for God over all things, experienced with the intensity it deserves? Therefore, happiness in God as our supreme treasure is the essence of holiness.[1]

---

1   It is not wrong to speak of the essence of holiness as *love*, provided it is viewed biblically. Love for God is, at its heart, happiness in God for who he is. That is, the essence of human holiness is to prize God, treasure God, esteem God, admire God, be satisfied in God, and enjoy God as supremely valuable. The horizontal dimension of this human holiness is to feel and think and act in ways that flow from, and accord with, the heart's treasuring God above all things. Thus, the *essence* of human holiness vertically or horizontally is happiness in (or love for) God as our supreme treasure.

If you think the phrase *happiness in God* is too frivolous, then sub-stitute the reality of *treasuring God*. Sin is treasuring anything above God. Holiness is the opposite of sin. Therefore, treasuring God above all things is the essence of holiness. Jesus said, "Whoever loves father or mother more than me is not worthy of me, and whoever loves son or daughter more than me is not worthy of me" (Matt. 10:37). In other words, if our hearts make peace with the disposition that says, "Our greatest treasures on earth are more precious than Jesus," then we are not Christians.

Satisfy Us in the Morning with Your Steadfast Love

In such a case, not only are *we* not Christians, but *God* is not honored. It is impossible that a heart that prefers the creation to the Creator could honor the Creator by such a preference. God is not glorified by hearts that are more satisfied in his gifts than in him. This is ultimately why the psalmist prayed, "Satisfy us in the morning with your steadfast love, that we may rejoice and be glad all our days" (Ps. 90:14). This prayer was not only for the sake of human happiness. It was also for the sake of the glory of God, because God is most glorified in us when we are most satisfied in him. Being bored with God demeans his beauty. Being satisfied with God magnifies his beauty.

Therefore, when we say that God's ultimate goal in providence nec-essarily includes the Christ-exalting, grace-praising, God-glorifying holiness and happiness of his people, we are saying that Christ will not be exalted, grace will not be praised, and God will not be glorified apart from the holy happiness of his people in God.

Focus of This Chapter: Our Obedience Performed by God

This is why part 3, sections 7 and 8, have revealed a prevailing sancti-fying providence. God is seeing to it that his people enjoy and reflect his glory. God's providence will not reach its goal if his people are not conformed to Christ. I use the word *prevailing* to signify that God's saving and sanctifying and glorifying providence endures and succeeds from eternity to eternity, and at every step in between.

We have seen that our holiness—our conformity to Christ—was predestined from eternity ("Those whom he foreknew he also *predestined* to be conformed to the image of his Son," Rom. 8:29). It was *promised* by God in the new covenant ("I will . . . cause you to walk in my statutes," Ezek. 36:27). The guarantee of our holiness was *purchased* on the cross ("[Christ purified] for himself a people . . . zealous for good works," Titus 2:14). The obstacle of God's wrath and our guilt was removed by the blood of Christ ("He himself bore our sins in his body on the tree," 1 Pet. 2:24). And God engaged our wholehearted pursuit of holiness with *commands* and *warnings* ("Strive . . . for the holiness without which no one will see the Lord," Heb. 12:14). This is what I mean by the *prevailing sanctifying* providence of God. It is designed to guarantee his ultimate purpose: *to display his glory with such fullness that it will be exalted in the way his people enjoy and reflect his excellencies.*

The prevailing thoroughness of God's providence in guaranteeing the Christ-exalting transformation of his people is not yet complete. Besides predestining, promising, purchasing, and commanding this transformation, God performs it. That is the focus of this chapter.

"I Will Cause You to Walk in My Statutes"

When Christ said at the Last Supper, "This cup . . . is the new covenant in my blood" (Luke 22:20), he declared that the decisive moment had arrived in history for the securing of the promises of the new covenant. The promise we are focusing on now is that God would see to it that his people would obey him. "I will put my law within them, and I will write it on their hearts" (Jer. 31:33). "I will . . . cause you to walk in my statutes and be careful to obey my rules" (Ezek. 36:27). In other words, God will create what he commands. That's what Jesus secured by the blood of the covenant.

Fruit of the Spirit

Paul describes this obedience-creating work of providence in several ways. One is with the imagery of the fruit of the Spirit:

> If you are led by the Spirit, you are not under the law. Now the works of the flesh are evident. . . . Those who do such things will not inherit the kingdom of God. But the fruit of the Spirit is love, joy, peace, patience, kindness, goodness, faithfulness, gentleness, self-control; against such things there is no law. (Gal. 5:18–19, 21–23)

Notice three things. First, those who are ruled by the "works of the flesh will not inherit the kingdom of God." Second, those who live by love, joy, peace, and the Spirit's other fruit "are not under the law" but are instead living in a way against which "there is no law." They are fulfilling "the righteous requirement of the law" (Rom. 8:4) through love (Rom. 13:8, 10), with the result that they will "inherit the kingdom of God." Third, this way of life is a "fruit of the Spirit." That is, God is the decisive cause of this new life.

This Comes from the Lord

This Spirit-given transformation of life was promised in the new covenant and purchased by the blood of Jesus:

> A new spirit I will put within you. And I will remove the heart of stone from your flesh and give you a heart of flesh. And I will put my Spirit within you, and cause you to walk in my statutes and be careful to obey my rules. (Ezek. 36:26–27)

Paul makes the connection explicit between the new-covenant promise of the Spirit and the sanctifying work of the Spirit in believers. He sees his own apostolic work as a ministry of the new covenant, serving the work of the Spirit to transform believers into the likeness of Christ:

[God] has made us sufficient to be ministers of a new covenant, not of the letter but of the Spirit. For the letter kills, but the Spirit gives life. . . . The Lord is the Spirit, and where the Spirit of the Lord is, there is freedom. And we all, with unveiled face, beholding the glory of the Lord, are being transformed into the same image from one degree of glory to another. For this comes from the Lord who is the Spirit. (2 Cor. 3:6, 17–18)

"The letter kills, but the Spirit gives life." The letter refers to the old kind of covenant, where the commands were written on stone but not on the heart. Obedience was commanded but not created. As Moses said in Deuteronomy 29:4, "To this day the LORD has not given you a heart to understand or eyes to see or ears to hear."

But now that the new covenant has been inaugurated, the Holy Spirit "gives life" through Christ, frees the heart from bondage to sin, and conforms the believer to Christ "from one degree of glory to another." This process of beholding the glory of Christ and being transformed into his image, Paul says, is "from the Lord who is the Spirit." In other words, the transformation is the "fruit of the Spirit." It is God's keeping his promise: "I will . . . cause you to walk in my statutes" (Ezek. 36:27).

Moved by God to Act of His Own Accord

Here is a little snapshot of the Spirit's producing the fruit of love and how it relates to our own glad willing. Paul says to the Corinthians:

Thanks be to God, who *put into the heart of Titus* the same earnest care I have for you. For he not only accepted our appeal, but being himself very earnest he is going to you *of his own accord*. (2 Cor. 8:16–17)

This earnest care that Titus feels for the Corinthians corresponds to the fruits of love and kindness and goodness in Galatians 5:22. Paul says explicitly "God . . . put [or *gave*, δόντι]" this earnestness into Titus's heart. This is an example of the new-covenant promise "I will put my Spirit within you, and cause you to walk in my statutes" (Ezek. 36:27).

But then notice how Titus *experiences* this work of God in his heart. He does not experience it as bondage or manipulation or something forcing him to do what he doesn't want to do. Rather, he experiences it as what he *wants* to do. This inclination of love that he feels is really *his* inclination; he is going "of his own accord [αὐθαίρετος]." That is what God has *given*—a new inclination. Later, we will focus more fully on this transaction between God and us. We will see that God *caused* this miracle, and Titus *acted* the miracle.

God Works in Us What Is Pleasing to Him

One of the clearest statements in the New Testament that God causes the obedience of believers is Hebrews 13:20–21:

> May the God of peace who brought again from the dead our Lord Jesus, the great shepherd of the sheep, by the blood of the eternal covenant, equip you with everything good that you may do his will, working in us that which is pleasing in his sight, through Jesus Christ, to whom be glory forever and ever. Amen.

Five observations make this an amazing statement of blood-bought, new-covenant obedience in the lives of believers.

First, the writer draws our attention to "the blood of the eternal covenant." It is the means by which God raised Jesus from the dead. "By the blood of the eternal covenant" modifies "brought again from the dead our Lord Jesus." *Through* the perfection of the finished work on the cross, God glorifies Christ with resurrection (as Paul says in Phil. 2:9). Thus, all the triumphs of the resurrection and everything God achieves through the risen Christ is blood bought.

Second, having raised Jesus by his own covenant blood, God now equips believers "with everything good" to do his will. This *everything good* is like the *all things* in Romans 8:32, where God did not spare his own Son but gave him for us, and thus guaranteed *all things* that the elect need to endure trial, be conformed to Christ, and be glorified.[2] The same reality is in the writer's mind here in Hebrews 13:21. God will equip you with all you need to do his will.

Third, this equipping is so decisive and effective that the writer goes beyond the statement of God's providing *equipment* to do God's will, and says God actually *does* his will in us. May God "equip you with everything good that you may do his will, *working in us* that which is pleasing in his sight." The word for *do* (ποιῆσαι) in the phrase "do his will" is from the same verb as the word *work* (ποιῶν) in the phrase "working in us." So it sounds even more striking: "May God equip you with everything good that you may *do* his will, *doing* in us that which is pleasing in his sight." Just as we saw with Titus in 2 Corinthians 8:16–17, God's doing his will *in* us is not a replacement for our doing it, but a gift of our doing it. We act the miracle. He causes it.

Fourth, God "[works] in us that which is pleasing in his sight, *through Jesus Christ*." This circles back to the first part of verse 20, where Jesus was raised by means of his own blood and was installed as "the great shepherd of the sheep." So whether we focus on the efficacy of his blood, the implications of his resurrection, or on the daily help and care of our great shepherd, the point is that God works his will in us "through Jesus Christ." Without the blood, the resurrection, and the shepherding of Jesus, there would be no Christian obedience.

Fifth, the text ends with the ultimate purpose for why God does it this way: "[He works] in us that which is pleasing in his sight, through Jesus Christ, *to whom be glory forever and ever.* Amen." God works his will in us *through Jesus Christ* so that *Jesus will get the glory* for our obedience and everything that led to it. This is another expression of the ultimate goal of providence—the glorification of Christ through the transformation of his people.

---

2 See chap. 37 for the fuller treatment of Rom. 8:32.

What is clear from Hebrews 13:20–21, and from Paul's application of the new covenant to the life of believers in 2 Corinthians 3, is that the transformation that God demands from his people is not just pre-destined concerning them (Rom. 8:29), and promised to them (Ezek. 36:27), and purchased for them (Titus 2:14), but is also *performed in* them (Heb. 13:21). God's providence prevails from predestined obedi-ence to accomplished obedience.

Required Obedience Built on Imputed Obedience

Before we turn in the next chapter to the question of *how* God "[works] in us that which is pleasing in his sight," let's step back for a moment and make sure we do not misunderstand the priority God puts on our transformation as Christians. This transformation—this conformity to Christ that God commands and creates—is required not because the righteousness imputed to us in justification is insufficient to bring us instantly into God's eternal favor. At the moment we are united to Christ through faith, his sin-bearing punishment and perfect obedi-ence are counted as ours. God is at that moment, and forevermore, 100 percent for us and not against us (Rom. 8:31). None of the afflictions that come to us from his hand (and there are many, Acts 14:22) is because he has turned against us. They are purifying love, not punitive wrath. "The Lord disciplines the one he loves, and chastises every son whom he receives" (Heb. 12:6).

Fruitless Faith Is Not Visible, Indeed Not Existent

The reason God requires transformation in his people—conformity to Christ in holiness and love—is to make their faith visible as the public display of the beauty and worth of Christ. Requiring visible obedience is part of God's overarching purpose in creation and redemption. God did not create a visible, material universe in order to hide his glory. "The heavens declare the glory of God" (Ps. 19:1). That was God's idea from the beginning. It is his purpose. What is visible is visible to communicate something about God. Food at mealtime and sex in the marriage bed are created for the sake of thanksgiving to God (1 Tim. 4:1–5)—and not just secret thanksgiving (2 Cor. 1:11).

God's aim is public glory for his name. "[God's] invisible attributes . . . have been clearly perceived, ever since the creation of the world, in the things that have been made" (Rom. 1:20). So it is with the obedience of his people: "Let your light shine before others, so that they may see your good works and give glory to your Father who is in heaven" (Matt. 5:16). Faith without visible fruit in holiness and love would be like a "lamp . . . under a basket" (Matt. 5:15). That is not what lamps are for. Nor what obedience is for.

Actually, faith without the fruit of love is not just invisible. It is nonexistent. God commands and creates the visible fruit of faith not just to make it visible but also to confirm its reality. James says, "Faith by itself, if it does not have works, is dead. . . . As the body apart from the spirit is dead, so also faith apart from works is dead" (James 2:17, 26). This means that faith without love is dead, because the essence of the works that signify living faith is love (James 2:8).

Faith Working through Love

The reason that faith without love is dead is that saving faith is the kind of reality that gives rise to love. It's not that the Spirit simply causes love to exist wherever faith exists. They don't just correlate. Rather, faith itself works through love. This is Paul's massively important point in Galatians 5:6: "In Christ Jesus neither circumcision nor uncircumcision counts for anything, but only faith working through love." Paul's point here is not that love adds to the effectiveness of justifying faith, but rather that justifying faith is the sort of faith that will always bring about love.

He implies the same point in 1 Timothy 1:5: "The aim of our charge is love that issues *from . . . a sincere faith.*" He assumes the same relationship between faith and work when he uses the phrase "work of faith" (1 Thess. 1:3; 2 Thess. 1:11) and when he quotes the risen Jesus to the effect that believers are "sanctified by faith in me" (Acts 26:18). The writer to the Hebrews echoes the same conviction in his hall of fame of faith: "By faith Abraham obeyed" (Heb. 11:8).

Acceptance with God: The Root of Our Obedience

The point we are making, as we transition to the next chapter about *how* God works our obedience through faith, is that the visible transformation God requires of his people is not part of the basis by which God becomes 100 percent for us. That basis is the blood and righteousness of Christ. And the only means of being united to Christ (so that in him God is 100 percent for us) is faith, not faith plus works—not *any* kind of works. From the starting point of our union with Christ by faith alone, every good work that we do is an *effect* of our acceptance with God, not a *means* to it. Our acceptance with God is the *root* of our obedience, not the *fruit*.

This faith that brings us into the favor of God bears the fruit of love. This fruit-bearing connection between faith and love *reveals* and *confirms* the invisible reality of saving faith. This powerful relationship between invisible faith and visible love—call it the "obedience of faith" or the "work of faith" (Rom. 1:5; 16:26; 1 Thess. 1:3)—goes a long way to explaining *how* God performs our obedience within us, as we saw in Hebrews 13:21. That is the focus of the next chapter.

43

Killing Sin and Creating Love— by Faith

The previous chapter revealed that God "[works] in us that which is pleasing in his sight" (Heb. 13:21). Christian obedience is "fruit of the Spirit" (Gal. 5:22). Likeness to Christ is "from the Lord who is the Spirit" (2 Cor. 3:18). It is a fulfillment of the new-covenant promise "I will . . . cause you to walk in my statutes" (Ezek. 36:27). In pursuing the ultimate goal of providence—the creation and transformation of a people who display his glory by enjoying and reflecting his excellencies—God leaves nothing to chance. The great divine declaration in Isaiah is as true now as ever: "My counsel shall stand, and I will accomplish all my purpose" (Isa. 46:10). We saw at the close of the previous chapter that faith is essential in how God fulfills his transforming purpose. We turn now to see this process at work.

Spirit-Supplied Miracles through Hearing with Faith

Perhaps the most helpful window into the relationship between our faith and God's miraculous transforming work within us is Galatians 3:5: "Does he who supplies the Spirit to you and works miracles among you do so by works of the law, or by hearing with faith?" As with other rhetorical questions, Paul assumes that we know how to turn this into an assertion—namely, "God, who supplies the Spirit to you and works miracles among you, does so not by works of the law, but by hearing with faith." Three crucial realities converge here: (1) the work of *the Spirit* producing miracles in and among us; (2) our hearing something, presumably the gospel, or more broadly, the effect of the cross in securing for us all *the promises of God*; (3) our hearing this good news of God's promises *with faith*. Spirit. Word. Faith.

Putting these three together, the point is that God performs miracles for us and in us through faith in his word. He makes faith the instrument of working the miracle of transformation in us. Faith is the link between the work of God and the miracle of obedience. This is why love can be called a fruit of his Spirit and a work of our faith. When we trust the blood-bought benefits of the cross, which God promises to us, a power is at work to produce the holiness and love we could not otherwise perform. Faith is the channel of God's miracle-working power to bring about the transformation God requires.

How Does Faith Produce Love?

We have already described in chapter 39 how faith actually works in producing love.[1] But one brief example might be helpful here. The book of Hebrews illustrates this dynamic as fully as any New Testament book (e.g., 10:32–35; 11:6, 8, 24–26; 12:1–2; 13:12–14). In Hebrews 13:5–6 the author writes:

> Keep your life free from love of money, and be content with what you have, for he has said, "I will never leave you nor forsake you." So we can confidently say,

---

1   The dynamics of how the promises of God and the act of faith and the work of the Holy Spirit come together to produce the transformation God requires is described in great detail in John Piper, *Future Grace: The Purifying Power of the Promises of God* (Colorado Springs, CO: Multnomah, 2012).

"The Lord is my helper;
I will not fear;
what can man do to me?"

This freedom from the love of money is not optional. It is essential. Jesus said we cannot serve two masters (Matt. 6:24). Paul said that "those who desire to be rich . . . plunge . . . into ruin and destruction" (1 Tim. 6:9). So the question is, How does freedom from the love of money come about? How do we obey the commandment "Keep your life free from the love of money"? How does God work this miracle of transformation within us?

The writer expects us to hear with faith (Gal. 3:5) the promises in the text: "I will never leave you. I will never forsake you. I will help you. You do not need to fear. I will not let man do anything to you but what I turn for your good." When we believe these promises, the roots of greed and fear are severed. They are severed by the power of a superior security, a superior helpfulness, and a superior satisfaction.

Money was beckoning us with its promise of security and help and satisfaction. But God speaks: "I will be your security. I will be your help. I will be your satisfaction." Faith *tastes* the reality of this promise. For "faith is the substance [ὑπόστασις, cf. Heb. 1:3] of things hoped for" (Heb. 11:1 NKJV). This taste—this entering into the substance and reality of what God promises—is the power that severs the root of sin. This is what Thomas Chalmers meant by "the expulsive power of a new affection."[2]

Faith by Its Nature Sanctifies, but Only by the Spirit

Two realities must be held together here lest we turn this sanctifying power of faith into a merely psychological process, or into a mere

---

2 Thomas Chalmers, "The Expulsive Power of a New Affection," Monergism, accessed August 6, 2019, https://www.monergism.com/thethreshold/sdg/Chalmers,%20Thomas%20-%20The%20Exlpulsive%20Power%20of%20a%20New%20Af.pdf.

accompaniment of the Spirit's work. Galatians 3:5 holds together the *human* experience of faith and the *divine* work of the Spirit: "Does he who supplies the Spirit to you and works miracles among you do so by works of the law, or by hearing with faith?" The Spirit works the miracle by our hearing with faith. That is, the Spirit is the decisive cause of the miracle. Then faith in God's promise is the instrument of the Spirit. And, finally, our generosity, flowing from freedom from the love of money, is the miracle that we act.

Faith, therefore, is not an isolated psychological power (like the power of positive thinking). To be sure, faith has in it the power to sever the root of sin's deceptive promises by savoring the superior promises of God. But it does so only because the Holy Spirit is wielding that faith and working its miracles.

Putting Sin to Death by the Spirit

When Paul calls us to "put to death the deeds of the body" by the Spirit (Rom. 8:13), he is making the same point: *we* put sin to death. But we do it *by the Spirit*. Faith is not mentioned in this verse. But it is implied. When Paul lists the various parts of the "armor of God" in Ephesians 6:13–17 (belt, breastplate, shoes, shield, helmet, sword), only one is used for killing: the sword. And the sword is called "the sword *of the Spirit*," and "the word of God" (6:17).

So when Paul tells us to *kill* the [sinful] deeds of the body *by the Spirit*, we have good reason to believe he means: "Wield the sword of *the word of God* to kill sin." And how do we wield the word of God to overcome the power of sin's deceitful promises? We put our faith in the promises of God. That is, we savor the reality of what God promises as superior to what sin promises. In this way, the promises of sin lose their compelling power. Or as John says, faith "is the victory that has overcome" the lies of the world (1 John 5:4). But in all of this *human* wielding of the word and savoring of God's superior promises, we are acting, Paul says, "by the *Spirit*."

Opening the Unfathomable Mystery

This is the key that opens the mystery of how God's providence not only predestines, promises, and purchases the holiness of his people, but also decisively *performs* that holiness in them. It is the work of his Spirit, awakening faith in the word of God, that kills sin (Rom. 8:13) and creates love (Gal. 5:6). In other words, faith, which wields God's word to kill sin, is a gift of God—a work of the Spirit.

We saw in chapter 36 that saving faith is a gift of God (Eph. 2:8; Phil. 1:29). This is true not only at the beginning of the Christian life but also at every point afterward. The Spirit of God opens our eyes to see the glory of God in Christ not only at the point of our conversion (2 Cor. 4:6) but also day by day. This is what Paul prays for in Ephesians 1:18–19: may God enlighten "the eyes of [our] hearts" to see and savor the greatness and the riches of his promises.

When God answers this prayer, and awakens our faith to the dangers of sin and unbelief, we embrace some precious, blood-bought promises of God. We taste the reality promised. This is God's way of protecting us and performing in us the persevering holiness that he requires. This is what Peter is referring to when he writes, "By God's power [we] are being guarded *through faith* for a salvation ready to be revealed in the last time" (1 Pet. 1:5). God awakens faith again and again and so guards us from the destruction of unbelief and sin.

Work Out Your Salvation

In this way, God makes full use of our mind and heart and will and affections in the acting of holiness and love, while he himself remains finally decisive as the cause of this obedience. We *act* the miracle. He *causes* the miracle. Probably the most oft-cited text to illustrate this transaction between our willing and God's willing is Philippians 2:12–13:

Work out [κατεργάζεσθε] your own salvation with fear and trembling, for it is God who works in you, both to will and to work for his good pleasure.

The Greek word for *work out* commonly means "produce" or "bring about."[3] It implies conscious effort. And the present tense signifies ongoing, continuous exertion. So, even though the language is risky, Paul is saying, "Join in the work of bringing about your salvation." Salvation, of course, does not refer here to our initial experience of justification. That happened in the past at the point of our conversion. It happened in an instant through faith and is not an ongoing process. Justification is, rather, the unshakable foundation for our ongoing work of pursuing our final salvation and entrance into eternal glory. Paul makes this plain in Philippians 3:12: "Not that I . . . am already perfect, but I press on to make it my own, *because* Christ Jesus has made me his own." His ongoing effort is to seize the prize of glory, *because* he has already been seized by Christ for that very glory.

The logic is the same here in Philippians 2:12–13. We work, *because* God is at work in us. We will and do, *because* God is willing and doing in us. We have seen *how* this works—how God works in us to awaken faith and kill sin and create love. What Paul makes plain here in Philippians is how fully our own effort is called into action. We do not wait for the miracle; we act the miracle. We are not deluded into thinking that our action is unnecessary, or that it is decisive. It is neither. On the contrary, our effort in the pursuit of final salvation is necessary. And God's willing and doing are decisive.

---

3   For example, Rom. 4:15 ("The law *brings* [*about*] wrath"); 5:3 ("Suffering *produces* endurance"); 7:8 ("The commandment . . . *produced* in me all kinds of covetousness); 15:18 (". . . what Christ *has accomplished* through me"); 2 Cor. 4:17 ("This light momentary affliction *is preparing* for us an eternal weight of glory"); 7:10 ("Godly grief *produces* a repentance that leads to salvation"); and others.

I Worked, but It Was Not I

Paul puts it like this in 1 Corinthians 15:10:

> By the grace of God I am what I am, and his grace toward me was not in vain. On the contrary, I worked harder than any of them, though it was not I, but the grace of God that is with me.

This is what Philippians 2:12–13 looks like in retrospect. "I worked [hard] . . . though it was not I, but the grace of God." It is crucial that we realize that *grace* in Paul's vocabulary is not just a divine disposition to pardon sin. It is also a divine power to work in us all that God requires from us. Paul says this in 2 Corinthians 9:8: "God is able to make all grace abound to you, so that having all sufficiency in all things at all times, you may abound in every good work." This was the grace Paul was referring to in 1 Corinthians 15:10, when he said, "It was not I, but the *grace* of God that is with me."

Serve in the Power of Another

Both Paul and Peter labor in their letters to help us act the miracle that God causes. Paul uses his own experience to illustrate it:

> I have been crucified with Christ. *It is no longer I who live, but Christ who lives in me.* And the life I now live in the flesh I live by faith in the Son of God, who loved me and gave himself for me. (Gal. 2:20)

> Him we proclaim, warning everyone and teaching everyone with all wisdom, that we may present everyone mature in Christ. For this I toil, *struggling with all his energy that he powerfully works within me.* (Col. 1:28–29)

Peter says it like this:

> Whoever serves, [let it be] as one who serves *by the strength that God supplies*—in order that in everything God may be glorified through

Jesus Christ. To him belong glory and dominion forever and ever. Amen. (1 Pet. 4:11)

The mystery of the Christian life is that we are called to *serve* and *toil* and *struggle* and *work* and *pursue* and *strive* for the holiness and love that God requires. But we are to do all that through "Christ who lives in me" (Gal. 2:20), "by the strength that God supplies" (1 Pet. 4:11), "with all his energy that he powerfully works within me" (Col. 1:29), by "the grace of God that is with me" (1 Cor. 15:10), "for it is God who works in [us], both to will and to work for his good pleasure" (Phil. 2:13). The wisdom of God's providence in bringing us from conversion to glory engages our wholehearted pursuit of holiness but reserves the decisive power for God himself. We act the miracle. God causes it.

Why Does God Keep the Decisive Power for Himself?

In the text we just cited, Peter made explicit why God does it this way: ". . . in order that in everything God may be glorified through Jesus Christ. To him belong glory and dominion forever and ever. Amen." This is the final and ultimate answer to why God keeps for himself the decisive power of our holiness. The giver of decisive power gets the fullness of glory. We get the help. He gets the glory.

He Glorified in Us and We in Him

We said at the end of the previous chapter that the reason God requires not just faith, but the fruit of faith in holiness and love, is that faith is invisible, but God intends for his glory to be visible in the created universe. He intends for that glory to shine supremely in the person and work of his Son. And he intends for it to shine in the people whom he is conforming to the image of his Son. For this to happen, Christ became a visible man, and his people are becoming visibly holy. This is the glory with which God intends to fill the earth. "All the earth shall be filled with the glory of the LORD" (Num. 14:21).

In one of the most theologically dense descriptions of the Christian life, Paul takes us to this ultimate goal of a glorified people and a glorified Savior. Both come about by the resolves and works of the people and through the grace and power of God:

> To this end we always pray for you, that our God may make you worthy of his calling and may fulfill every resolve for good and every work of faith by his power, so that the name of our Lord Jesus may be glorified in you, and you in him, according to the grace of our God and the Lord Jesus Christ. (2 Thess. 1:11–12)

God calls his people into being (1 Cor. 1:24) and unto glory (2 Thess. 2:14). Then he makes them worthy of that call. That is, he transforms them into the kind of people whose lives reflect the true worth of their calling. The way he does this is through our "[resolves] for good" and "[works] of faith." These resolves and works come to pass "by [God's] power" and "according to the grace of . . . God." In other words, we act the miracle of resolving and doing what is good, but God causes the miracle. He "[fulfills] every resolve for good." That is, he finally and decisively decides if the resolve becomes a work. When it does, it is a "work of faith," because we have relied not on ourselves but on his power and his grace.

All of this divine-human transaction happens in this way for the ultimate goal of a glorified people and glorified Savior: "so that the name of our Lord Jesus may *be glorified in you, and you in him.*" This is the great goal of providence: the visible glorification of Christ and the visible glorification of his people. Christ is glorified by being reflected in his transformed people who are conformed to his image. The people are glorified not with any independent powers or qualities of their own, but only "in him"—that is, only in connection with his saving and sanctifying work.

The Decisive Performer of Our Obedience Gets the Glory

In this way, we see why it is so crucial that the conforming of God's people to the image of Christ is not only predestined (Rom. 8:29) and promised (Ezek. 36:27) and purchased (Titus 2:14) and commanded (Rom. 12:1–2), but also performed *by God*—"working in us that which is pleasing in his sight" (Heb. 13:21). The great goal of providence is the shining forth of the glory of God in the holiness and happiness of his people through Jesus Christ. This could come to pass only if God himself became the decisive strength in all Christian service and obedience. And so it was and is: we serve "by the strength that God supplies—in order that in everything God may be glorified through Jesus Christ. To him belong glory and dominion forever and ever. Amen" (1 Pet. 4:11).

Is It Wise to Sanctify Us So Slowly?

I mentioned above that the way God "[works] in us what is pleasing in his sight" (Heb. 13:21) is a manifestation of the *wisdom* of God's providence. It may be helpful before we leave this chapter to answer one obvious question. Since God keeps for himself the decisive influence in the performing of our obedience, how is it wise that Christians are sanctified so slowly?

The answer is not that God cannot do it more quickly. At the end of our lives, or at the second coming for those who are still alive, God will perfect us in the blink of an eye. We will never sin again. Hebrews 12:23 refers to Christians who have died as "the spirits of the righteous made perfect." We will not be struggling with sin for the rest of eternity. God can and will perfect us quickly. In doing this, he will not turn us into robots or take from us our God-given capacities for thinking and feeling and preferring. Instead, these will be perfected. God will do this when this life is over. And he could do it now.

But he doesn't. In his wisdom, the providence of God works in us a slow transformation that never reaches perfection in this life (Phil. 3:12; 1 John 1:8). He does not hold us back. Left to ourselves, we would not be caught up in the inertia of perfection. Our natural inertia is all in the other direction. Any progress we make in holiness is the fruit of the Spirit, not the fruit of our self-rule. To the degree that the Christians in Rome had "become obedient from the heart to the [the apostles'] standard of teaching," to that degree, Paul says, "thanks be to *God*" for this obedience (Rom. 6:17). Where there is Christian obedience in any degree, there the providence of God is triumphing over the flesh and producing the fruit of the Spirit.

How then is this a wise strategy of God's providence? I am sure that I do not see to the bottom of God's wisdom in any of his acts. But I think there are pointers in the Bible. Essentially, I gave in chapter 19 ("The Ongoing Existence of Satan") the answer that I see. The question there was, Why does God tolerate the ongoing existence of Satan? He could throw him this very day into the lake of fire so that his destructive influence is totally removed. God will do this at the end of history, and Satan will trouble the world no more (Rev. 20:10). God could do this now. But he doesn't. I think the questions of why God endures Satan and why he endures our sinfulness are answered in essentially the same way. Since I devoted an entire chapter to that answer, I will draw out only part of the answer at this point.

If God abolished Satan immediately and totally removed his influence in the world, God would glorify his own power in a marvelous way. But the aim of God's providence is to glorify more than his power. God aims for the fullness of his beauty and worth to be magnified in the way his people prefer him over what Satan offers. God's worth and beauty are magnified in proportion to our preference for them over all that Satan can offer. God intends for Satan to be defeated in this age not merely by being shown to be weaker than Christ, but also by being shown to be less beautiful, less valuable, less desirable, less satisfying.

My point here is that the same reasoning applies to the ongoing existence of temptations to sin in the believer's life. In the course of a lifetime of being a faithful Christian, thousands of thoughts and feelings and deeds are owing to the Christian's blood-bought, Spirit-wrought defeat of temptation by preferring Christ over sin. In other words, every day in which there is any godly fruit of life in Christ, sin is being defeated, and Christ is being magnified. These triumphs in warfare with sin would not happen without the warfare.

Desperation over Sin, Exultation over Grace

This is only part of the answer. Why are there not more triumphs? Why is there not more radical discipleship, more thoroughgoing obedience, and more beautiful maturity in the church? Evidently, God knows that a lifetime of dealing with indwelling sin (Rom. 7:17, 20) is a wise way for us to sense a truer measure of our corruption and a truer measure of God's grace. Truer, that is, than if we were perfected five minutes after our conversion. Paul seems to point in this direction when he correlates the *desperation* we feel because of our ongoing sinfulness and the *exultation* we feel because of the grace that comes to us from God through Christ. "Wretched man that I am! Who will deliver me from this body of death? Thanks be to God through Jesus Christ our Lord!" (Rom. 7:24–25). This double response to the ongoing existence of sin and the fight of faith is the way God aims to bring us finally to complete freedom from all evil. This is the path of the most fitting loathing of sin and treasuring of grace.

Global Goal for All Peoples, and a New Universe

In the next, and final, section, we face the fact that the goal of God's providence is not simply to create and transform worshiping individuals or even gathered churches. His purpose is global. It embraces "every tribe and language and people and nation" (Rev. 5:9). Not only that, but it embraces the gathering of all the redeemed of all the ages. Not only that, but his aim is that their bodies be raised from the dead and that the universe be renovated to share in "freedom of the glory of the children of God" (Rom. 8:21). How will God do this? That is the final focus, in section 9.

The Final Achievement of Providence

44

The Triumph of Missions and
the Coming of Christ

The previous chapter left us with the weighty reminder of the embattled condition of God's people in this fallen age. Sin is unspeakably powerful, not only in unbelievers, but also in the remaining corruption of true Christians (Rom. 7:24). We saw in chapter 13 that this Satan-influenced darkness did not take God off guard but is part of the overall plan. Before the creation of the world, God's only Son was, in the mind of God, "the Lamb who was slain" (Rev. 13:8)—slain because of this darkness of sin and death. Grace, triumphing over sin through blood-bought redemption, was planned for God's people before creation (2 Tim. 1:9). God did not create the world without reckoning how sin and death would fit into his purposes.

Conflict and Confidence
So the weight of sin is with us still. To be sure, in the fullness of time "[Christ] gave himself for our sins to deliver us from the present evil age" (Gal. 1:4). And what he achieved in his life and death and resurrection is glorious beyond description. We saw in part 3, sections 7 and 8, God's great works of providence in saving his people and

bringing them to glory. But it is a long and embattled triumph. Not one Christian is made perfect in this life. God's way is to magnify the patience of grace through the persistence of sin. We have not yet seen the climax of God's saving achievement.

Embattled though we are, the victory is sure—there will be perfect sinlessness in a perfect world, radiant with the glory of God, reflected in the Christ-exalting gladness of his people. Every person known by God—known as his own treasured possession from before the creation—has been predestined for glory and gladness. And all the predestined will be called. And all the called will be justified. And all the justified will be sanctified. And all the sanctified will infallibly be glorified (Rom. 8:29–30).

Ingathering of the Children of God

The omnipotence with which God works obedience in his people guarantees the ingathering of "the children of God who are scattered abroad" (John 11:52). During Jesus's earthly ministry, Caiaphas the high priest was moved by God, John said, to declare this prophecy: "Jesus would die for the nation, and not for the nation only, but also to gather into one the children of God who are scattered abroad" (11:51–52). That these scattered "children of God" will be gathered is as certain as the fact that they have been purchased by the Lamb who was slain and can never die again. This certainty between the blood of the Lamb and the ingathering of the ransomed children is what heaven sings:

> Worthy are you [O Christ] to take the scroll
>   and to open its seals,
> for you were slain, and by your blood you ransomed
>   people for God
>   from every tribe and language and people and
>   nation,

and you have made them a kingdom and priests to our God,
and they shall reign on the earth. (Rev. 5:9–10)

They are already ransomed. From "every tribe and language and people and nation." These are the "children of God who are scattered abroad" and whom Jesus will "gather into one" (John 11:52)—one kingdom, one priesthood, one flock.

I say "one flock" because this is another way that Jesus describes the certainty of the ingathering of his people. He says, "I have other sheep that are not of this fold. I must bring them also, and they will listen to my voice. So there will be one flock, one shepherd" (John 10:16). This is the *must* and the *will* of invincible providence: "I *must* bring them." "They *will* listen to my voice." The mission to gather his sheep—the children of God—from all the nations is as sure as the promise and the purchase and the power of Jesus. It is going to happen.

And all the means needed to bring it about are as sure as God's providence is prevailing. The Great Commission is not just commanded (Matt. 28:18–20); it is promised by Jesus: "This gospel of the kingdom *will* be proclaimed throughout the whole world as a testimony to all nations, and then the end *will* come" (Matt. 24:14). Jesus does not just propose that there be a people gathered from all nations. He promises it and performs it. "I will build my church, and the gates of hell shall not prevail against it" (Matt. 16:18).

He can do this without failing because he is at work in his people "to will and to work for his good pleasure" (Phil. 2:13). He is "[equipping them] with everything good that [they] may do his will, working in [them] that which is pleasing in his sight" (Heb. 13:21). When his emissaries pursue his mission, they are "struggling with all his energy that he powerfully works within [them]" (Col. 1:29). They happily say, "We planted and watered, but God gave the growth" (see 1 Cor. 3:6–7). And even their planting and watering efforts they gladly ascribe to God: "It was not I, but the grace of God that is with me" (1 Cor. 15:10).

The Word of God Is Not Bound

The Lord of the harvest will catapult (ἐκβάλῃ, Matt. 9:38) his workers to the nations. He will give them what they need to say (Mark 13:11). He will protect them (till their work is done) so that not a hair of their head will perish (Luke 21:18). Then, when their assignment is complete, "some . . . they will put to death" (Luke 21:16). The number of the martyrs is appointed. It is part of the plan. John says that those already in heaven who gave their lives for Christ should "rest a little longer, until the number of their fellow servants and their brothers should be complete, who were to be killed as they themselves had been" (Rev. 6:11). The terrors and setbacks of persecutions are no hindrance to the coming triumph. Paul speaks for every imprisoned ambassador of Christ: "I am suffering, bound with chains as a criminal. But the word of God is not bound!" (2 Tim. 2:9).

As long as Christ can say over any unreached city, "I have many in this city who are my people" (Acts 18:10), the unbound word of God will sooner or later penetrate that city, and the Lord will call his sheep by name (John 10:3), open their hearts (Acts 16:14), take a people for his name (Acts 15:14), and as many as are appointed to eternal life will believe (Acts 13:48). His mission cannot fail.

Therefore, God will have his global people—the most diverse gathering ever assembled. There is no partiality with God (Acts 10:34; Rom. 2:11). He will be glorified by the triumphs of his supreme appeal in every ethnic group. In the people he is assembling "there is not Greek and Jew, circumcised and uncircumcised, barbarian, Scythian, slave, free; but Christ is all, and in all" (Col. 3:11). He shuts the mouth of every ethnocentric boast by taking for himself a people from every group, and then "killing the hostility" through the blood of his cross (Eph. 2:16).

Then the End Will Come

When the gospel has done its appointed work in all the nations, the end will come (Matt. 24:14). Not because the clock of the universe was wound only so far and the ticking ceases, but because the ever-present, all-embracing, all-prevailing providence of God set the day. "Concerning that day and hour no one knows, not even the angels of heaven, nor the Son, but the Father only" (Matt. 24:36). He knows it because he planned it. "It is not for you to know times or seasons that the Father has fixed by his own authority" (Acts 1:7).

Suppose someone says, "Where is the promise of his coming, since two thousand years have gone by, and all things are continuing as they were from the beginning of creation?" (cf. 2 Pet. 3:4). The apostle Peter answers, "Do not overlook this one fact, beloved, that with the Lord one day is as a thousand years, and a thousand years as one day" (2 Pet. 3:8; cf. Ps. 90:4). In the Lord's eyes, two days have passed since Jesus was here on earth. The second coming is not slow in coming. It is perfectly timed by the Father.

Then Peter adds, "The Lord is not slow to fulfill his promise as some count slowness, but is patient toward you, not wishing that any should perish, but that all should reach repentance" (2 Pet. 3:9). This verse is often used to argue that God wills all to be saved and that his providence is not able to save all, because unrepentant people have ultimate self-determination when it comes to their saving faith. They, not God, have the final and decisive say over whether they repent. One scholarly commentary on this verse concludes, "God's will may not be done, but it will not be for lack of trying on his part."[1] He tries. They succeed.

We saw in our treatment of 1 Timothy 2:4 (chapter 36) that there is a sense in which God "desires all people to be saved"—a desire

---

1   Peter H. Davids, *The Letters of 2 Peter and Jude*, Pillar New Testament Commentary (Grand Rapids, MI: Eerdmans, 2006), 281.

that he chooses not to put into action. It is possible that 2 Peter 3:9 means something similar. But I doubt it. It seems to me that the focus of the statement is not universal but is on "you"—that is, God's people. "The Lord . . . is patient *toward you*, not wishing that any [of you] should perish." It would be strange if his patience toward "you" did not define the "any" that comes three words later in the Greek (μακροθυμεῖ εἰς ὑμᾶς μὴ βουλόμενός τινας ἀπολέσθαι). Hence Peter is saying, "The Lord is patient toward you, not wishing that any *of you* should perish." It is not awkward or unusual for a writer to refer to *you* as a particular group larger than those in the immediate audience, just as a sergeant should say to his platoon of marines, "Remember, *you* are the finest fighting force in the world," meaning you *as marines*—all marines.

That is the way I take 2 Peter 3:9. "The Lord is . . . patient toward you [elect people of God], not wishing that any [of God's elect] should perish." This is the way we read 2 Peter 1:10: "Brothers, be all the more diligent to confirm *your* calling and election." We read this as applying to Peter's immediate audience, but also to all Christians. We should all confirm our election. So my understanding of 2 Peter 3:9 is that God's timing of the second coming is patient not only for the sake of Peter's audience, but also for the sake of all the elect who are yet to be born and come to repentance.

There is one other reason this interpretation seems right to me. The delay of the second coming century after century is resulting in millions more people perishing than if he came sooner. So to say that he delays the second coming because he does not desire people to perish implies that he is acting in a way that brings about the very opposite of what he desires. I think it is better to take our cue from 2 Peter 1:10, where Peter affirms his belief in election, and then let that be the backdrop of 2 Peter 3:9. God does not desire any of the elect to perish but to reach repentance. This, in fact, is what will happen. And when it does, the end will come (Matt. 24:14).

The End That Is a Beginning

What Jesus means by "the end" (in Matt. 24:14) is the end of this fallen age of sin and death as we know it.[2] The end will come with the return of Jesus Christ bodily from heaven, as Jesus described it:

> Then will appear in heaven the sign of the Son of Man, and then all the tribes of the earth will mourn, and they will see the Son of Man coming on the clouds of heaven with power and great glory. And he will send out his angels with a loud trumpet call, and they will gather his elect from the four winds, from one end of heaven to the other. (Matt. 24:30–31)

This event will mark the beginning of something radically new. It will be the end of history as we know it. But the focus in this text is not on the end but on the beginning. Jesus is coming with power and glory to "gather his elect." He is not gathering them for nothing. This is the beginning of something glorious. This is the consummation of what he has been doing for the elect during all of redemptive history. He has predestined his elect, called them, justified them, and sanctified them, and now he is gathering them for the eternal future of their glorification.

Comprehensiveness of the Gathering

Consider two more descriptions that Paul gives us of this glorious event. One of them shows the comprehensiveness of the gathering, and the other shows the terrible fact that the gathering is a gathering out of and away from those who will perish.

---

2   For the division of history into "this age" and "the age to come," see Matt. 12:32; 1 Cor. 1:20; 2:6, 8; 3:18; Eph. 1:21. "This age" refers to ordinary history as we know it—an age of sin and death. "The age to come" will be radically different and will break in with the resurrection at the second coming, as Jesus says in Luke 20:34–35: "The sons of *this age* marry and are given in marriage, but those who are considered worthy to attain to *that age* and to *the resurrection from the dead* neither marry nor are given in marriage."

> The Lord himself will descend from heaven with a cry of command, with the voice of an archangel, and with the sound of the trumpet of God. And the dead in Christ will rise first. Then we who are alive, who are left, will be caught up together with them in the clouds to meet the Lord in the air, and so we will always be with the Lord. (1 Thess. 4:16–17)

Paul is emphasizing the comprehensiveness of the gathering of the elect to meet the Lord, which includes believers who have died. "The dead in Christ will rise first." Then those who are alive will be gathered up to meet the Lord as he comes.

Don't let the obvious pass by without amazement. Just as Jesus "cried out with a loud voice" at the tomb of Lazarus (John 11:43), and the cry created life, so at the coming of Christ on the clouds there will be a cry of command, and millions upon millions of those who died in Christ will be raised from the dead. Bodily. This is not symbolic speech designed to create a vague sense of hope that somehow there is a better future coming. This is the miraculous reconstituting of whole persons—bodies recreated and reunited to souls. This is a work of omnipotent providence. No one but God can do this. Just as the flood swept the old world clean of sinful people, so the resurrection will fill the new world with the redeemed and renewed people of God.

This is the fulfillment of a predestined future for the elect. "Those whom [God] foreknew he also predestined to be conformed to the image of his Son" (Rom. 8:29). The image of his Son! His Son was raised from the dead. He was visible (John 20:20). He was touchable (John 20:27). He ate fish (Luke 24:42–43). But he was incomprehensibly new and could never die again (Rom. 6:9). To this we will be conformed.

He Will Transform Our Body to Be Like His Glorious Body

The apostle Paul made the connection clear between the resurrection of Jesus and our resurrection. "If the Spirit of him who raised Jesus from the dead dwells in you, he who raised Christ Jesus from the dead will also give life to your mortal bodies through his Spirit who dwells in you" (Rom. 8:11). "Christ has been raised from the dead, the first-fruits of those who have fallen asleep" (1 Cor. 15:20). His resurrection was the first harvesting from the great field of the sleeping children of God. The risen Christ is in heaven today awaiting the great day when he "will transform our lowly body to be like his glorious body, by the power that enables him even to subject all things to himself" (Phil. 3:20–21).

With Mighty Angels in Flaming Fire

So the gathering of the elect at the coming of Christ is comprehensive. It includes the living and the dead. It is also a gathering *out*—out of and away from those who will perish:

> The Lord Jesus [will be] revealed from heaven with his mighty angels in flaming fire, inflicting vengeance on those who do not know God and on those who do not obey the gospel of our Lord Jesus. They will suffer the punishment of eternal destruction, away from the presence of the Lord and from the glory of his might, when he comes on that day to be glorified in his saints, and to be marveled at among all who have believed, because our testimony to you was believed. (2 Thess. 1:7–10)

When Jesus promises that at the coming of the Son of Man, his angels "will gather his elect from the four winds, from one end of heaven to the other" (Matt. 24:31), the implication is clear: the gathering is *out from among others*. He describes this separation in Matthew 25:

> When the Son of Man comes in his glory, and all the angels with him, then he will sit on his glorious throne. Before him will be gathered all the nations, and he will separate people one from

another as a shepherd separates the sheep from the goats. . . . The King will say to those on his right, "Come, you who are blessed by my Father, inherit the kingdom prepared for you from the foundation of the world." . . . Then he will say to those on his left, "Depart from me, you cursed, into the eternal fire prepared for the devil and his angels." . . . And these will go away into eternal punishment, but the righteous into eternal life. (Matt. 25:31–32, 34, 41, 46)

Paul echoed this great separation at the end of the age:

[God] will render to each one according to his works: to those who by patience in well-doing seek for glory and honor and immortality, he will give eternal life; but for those who are self-seeking and do not obey the truth, but obey unrighteousness, there will be wrath and fury. (Rom. 2:6–8)

This is the dark backdrop of the glory of grace and power that appear at the second coming of Christ. "Those who do not know God and . . . do not obey the gospel of our Lord Jesus . . . will suffer the punishment of eternal destruction, away from the presence of the Lord and from the glory of his might" (2 Thess. 1:8–9). It will be eternal, it will be destructive, and it will be without any of the beauty of the Lord.

This Is Not Annihilation

The apostle John gives the bleakest of all descriptions of hell. The person who turns from the true God and walks without faith in his redeeming grace

will drink the wine of God's wrath, poured full strength into the cup of his anger, and he will be tormented with fire and sulfur in the presence of the holy angels and in the presence of the Lamb. And the smoke of their torment goes up forever and ever, and they have no rest, day or night. (Rev. 14:10–11)

This is not annihilation. This is conscious misery forever. Oh, how clear and urgent should be the warning and the pleading and the praying of those who know and believe the truth about hell, and God's ever-available and sufficient salvation! Jesus is the great model for us as he wept over the impending judgment on Jerusalem—temporal and eternal:

> When he drew near and saw the city, he wept over it, saying, "Would that you, even you, had known on this day the things that make for peace! But now they are hidden from your eyes." (Luke 19:41–42)

Warning, Pleading, Praying

The apostle Paul followed his Master's heart. He knew as well as anyone, and taught as clearly as anyone, what Jesus had said about the unbelieving leaders in Jerusalem: "You [O Father] have hidden these things from the wise and understanding and revealed them to little children" (Matt. 11:25). But he joined Jesus in tears (Luke 19:41; Matt. 23:37) and prayers for his perishing kinsmen:

> I have great sorrow and unceasing anguish in my heart. For I could wish that I myself were accursed and cut off from Christ for the sake of my brothers, my kinsmen according to the flesh. . . . My heart's desire and prayer to God for them is that they may be saved. (Rom. 9:2–3; 10:1)

This is the paradoxical path on which we walk toward the great end and the great beginning of the second coming of Christ. "Sorrowful, yet always rejoicing" (2 Cor. 6:10). Weeping for all suffering, especially eternal suffering (Rom. 12:15). Yet always rejoicing in hope (Rom. 5:2; 12:12). All around us are the desolations of sin and the futility of this fallen world (Rom. 8:20). And yet the trumpet sound of triumph and everlasting joy in the presence of our Maker, Redeemer, and Friend can be heard just over the horizon. "The Lord is at hand" (Phil. 4:5). Yes. And we say, "Amen. Come, Lord Jesus!" (Rev. 22:20).

Endlessness after the End

But what is the ultimate effect of the Lord's coming? If omnipotent, all-pervasive, all-embracing providence predestines a people for conformity to the Son of God, promises to work in them the obedience God requires, purchases that holiness at the cost of God's Son, and then gathers them from all the nations and brings this age to climax with the coming of Christ, what are we to expect that providence will bring to pass in the endless ages of eternity? There is one more chapter.

45

New Bodies, New World,
Never-Ending Gladness in God

Coming to the end of part 3 of this book (The Nature and Extent of Providence) brings us back to the end of part 2 (The Ultimate Goal of Providence). The final chapters of part 2 (13 and 14) described the climax of God's ultimate aim in all his works of providence. What we have seen in the intervening chapters is that God's providence is of such an invincible nature and such an all-encompassing extent that he will succeed in the goals that moved him to create and govern the world. This final chapter will echo those earlier discoveries of God's final goal with a focus on five climactic works of providence that grow out of the second coming of Jesus.

Five Climactic Works of Providence

First, at the Lord's coming we will *see* the Lord in the greatness of his glory. Second, we will *be profoundly changed* by that experience, not only bodily, but more essentially, in our capacities to know and love and enjoy God. Third, this transformation will result in *everlasting, ever-increasing measures of pleasure* that are presently inconceivable. Fourth, *the fallen material universe will be set free from its bondage* to futility and corruption and be perfectly adapted to the freedom of the glory of the children of God. Finally, *God himself will be supreme and central*—above all in beauty and worth and greatness, and the all-satisfying focus of all.

1. We Will See the Lord in the Greatness of His Glory

We saw in the previous chapter that even though Jesus describes his coming as "the end"—namely, the end of this fallen age of sin and death as we know it (Matt. 24:14)—he makes clear that it is a glorious *beginning*. He says that he is coming "with power and great glory," and that his angels "will gather his elect . . . from one end of heaven to the other" (Matt. 24:30–31).

The point is full of hope: we will be gathered from the ends of the globe and from the long-forgotten graves and assembled in his presence to see his "great glory." In Jesus's first coming, he had laid aside much of the staggering greatness of his glory. He had "emptied himself, by taking the form of a servant" (Phil. 2:7), manifesting on earth mainly the glory of his grace (John 1:14). But in his second coming, he will not empty himself. He will have his original, eternal, Trinitarian glory with the added accolades of the resurrection and the exalted offices of a perfected redeemer (Heb. 2:10).

OUR BLESSED HOPE

Paul underlines this point—that the second coming is a happy hope and a loved expectation precisely because we will see the glory of Christ. Paul refers to our "blessed hope"—that is, our happy hope (μακαρίαν ἐλπίδα)—namely, "the *appearing* of the glory of our great God and Savior Jesus Christ" (Titus 2:13). It is the *appearing* of the glory, not just the existence of the glory, that makes this event a happy hope.

Then in 2 Timothy 4:8 Paul says that the crown of righteousness will be given at that day to those who "have loved" this appearing:

Henceforth there is laid up for me the crown of righteousness, which the Lord, the righteous judge, will award to me on that day, and not only to me but also to all who have loved his appearing.

In both Titus and 2 Timothy, the emphasis falls on the preciousness of the *appearing*. It is a *happy* hope. It is a *loved* appearing. What appears is the Lord Jesus in "great glory." The happiness of the hope and the love for the appearing do not arise mainly from our subjective response to the Lord's appearing. It is the other way around. Our subjective response—our happiness at his coming—arises from Jesus's *purpose* in coming. He is coming precisely to create this response. "He comes on that day *to be glorified* in his saints, and *to be marveled at* among all who have believed" (2 Thess. 1:10).

His aim is that we see him and marvel at him. We saw already in chapter 2 why this divine purpose to be glorified and marveled at is not egomania. We are not being used for selfish ends. We are being welcomed into the greatest joy possible for a created being—the admiration and reflection of infinite perfection.

"Show Me Your Glory"; Take the Dimness Away

The sight of the glory of God has always been the central longing of the godly heart. Moses cries to God, "Please *show me your glory*" (Ex. 33:18). David prays, "One thing have I asked of the LORD, that will I seek after . . . *to gaze upon the beauty of the LORD*" (Ps. 27:4). Isaiah promises, "The glory of the LORD shall be revealed, and *all flesh shall see it* together" (Isa. 40:5). "*Your eyes will behold the king* in his beauty" (Isa. 33:17). Jesus said, "Blessed are the pure in heart, for *they shall see God*" (Matt. 5:8).

Conversely, one of the greatest burdens of the godly heart in this age is that we see God so dimly. "Now we see in a mirror dimly, but then face to face. Now I know in part; then I shall know fully, even as I have been fully known" (1 Cor. 13:12). Now we "walk by faith, not by sight" (2 Cor. 5:7). Now in all our afflictions we take heart "as we look not to the things that are seen but to the things that are unseen. For the things that are seen are transient, but the things that are unseen are eternal" (2 Cor. 4:18). We "rejoice in hope" (Rom. 5:2). We "*wait* for the hope of righteousness" (Gal. 5:5). We *wait* for the completion of our adoption (Rom. 8:23). But we *wait especially* for "the revealing of our Lord Jesus" (1 Cor. 1:7; cf. 1 Thess. 1:10). "For in this hope we were saved. Now hope that is seen is not hope. For who hopes for what he sees? But if we hope for what we do not see, we wait for it with patience" (Rom. 8:24–25).

But with the coming of Christ in "great glory," the dimness is taken away. The cloudy mirror becomes a window. The waiting is over. We see "face to face" (1 Cor. 13:12). The final and greatest prayer of Jesus for his disciples comes true: "Father, I desire that they also, whom you have given me, may be with me where I am, to see my glory that you have given me because you loved me before the foundation of the world" (John 17:24). Jesus has no greater prayer to pray. No greater gift to give. No greater love to show. He knows that we were created to find our final and greatest destiny in seeing the greatest person in the greatest glory. That is why he prays that God would show them his glory.

2. We Will Be Profoundly Changed

It is not quite accurate to say that seeing Christ in the greatness of his glory, considered apart from its effects, is our greatest destiny. Seeing Christ is great—inexpressibly great—but without its effects, it is not the greatest thing. It is not the ultimate goal of providence. So we turn now to the second climactic work of providence that grows out of the second coming. When we see the Lord in his glory, we will be profoundly changed. We will be like him.

We will speak about our bodily transformation below under the fourth work of providence. Our focus here is the more essential transformation of our capacities to know and love and enjoy God. In his first letter John wrote:

Beloved, we are God's children now, and what we will be has not yet appeared; but we know that when he appears we shall be like him, because we shall see him as he is. (1 John 3:2)

INSTANTLY, NO LONGER IN DEGREES

This is not magic. It is not a merely natural effect of seeing Jesus. It is not like litmus paper changing color when put in the right chemical. This is the work of God's providence. It began in this life at our conversion with the spiritual sight we were given of Christ.

We all, with unveiled face, beholding the glory of the Lord, are being transformed into the same image from one degree of glory to another. For this comes from the Lord who is the Spirit. (2 Cor. 3:18)

"This comes from the Lord who is the Spirit"—it is not automatic or mechanical. It is a work of God. He has ordained and then effected the correlation: beholding yields becoming. At our conversion, God begins a new creation: "If anyone is in Christ, he is a new creation" (2 Cor. 5:17). "We are his workmanship, created in Christ Jesus for good works" (Eph. 2:10). "[We] have put on the new self, which is being renewed in knowledge after the image of its creator" (Col. 3:10). The aim of this creation is our predestined conformity to Christ. "Those whom he foreknew he also predestined to be conformed to the image of his Son" (Rom. 8:29). This happens progressively, "from one degree of glory to another" (2 Cor. 3:18).

But it comes to its climax at the second coming of Christ. What Paul calls *glorification* is consummated there, body and soul. Those whom he predestined to be conformed to Christ, he glorified (Rom. 8:29–30). No longer "from one degree of glory to another" but instantaneously. This is what John meant when he said, "When he appears we shall be like him, because we shall see him as he is" (1 John 3:2). In an astonishing moment at the end of history, the promise will be fulfilled: "Just as we have borne the image of the man of dust [Adam], we shall also bear the image of the man of heaven [Christ]" (1 Cor. 15:49). We will be glorified with his glory. "The righteous will shine like the sun in the kingdom of their Father" (Matt. 13:43).

Perfected Consummation of a Life of Fighting Sin

This will be a physical and a moral brightness. When Paul describes the readiness of the church as a bride for her husband, he mainly has moral perfections in view:

> Christ loved the church and gave himself up for her, that he might sanctify her . . . so that he might present the church to himself in splendor, without spot or wrinkle or any such thing, that she might be holy and without blemish. (Eph. 5:25–27)

This glorification will be the sudden completion of a lifelong warfare with sin and pursuit of holiness. There is a close connection between progressive sanctification now and perfect sanctification when Christ comes. Hence, Paul prays:

> . . . that you may approve what is excellent, and so be pure and blameless for the day of Christ, filled with the fruit of righteousness that comes through Jesus Christ, to the glory and praise of God. (Phil. 1:10–11)

> May the Lord make you increase and abound in love for one another and for all, as we do for you, so that he may establish your hearts blameless in holiness before our God and Father, at the coming of our Lord Jesus with all his saints. (1 Thess. 3:12–13)

> May the God of peace himself sanctify you completely, and may your whole spirit and soul and body be kept blameless at the coming of our Lord Jesus Christ. (1 Thess. 5:23)

In all three of these prayers, Paul is asking that God would cause believers to live in such a pure way that the instantaneous perfecting of our souls at the coming of Christ would be the natural consummation of a lifelong devotion to holy living. It began by spiritually seeing the beauty of Christ imperfectly (2 Cor. 3:18; 4:6), and it will be perfected when we "see him as he is."

The groaning of partial sight will be over. And the accompanying sorrows of falling short will end. This, I believe we may say with confidence, will be greater than having a physical body like Christ's glorious body (Phil. 3:21). "Oh, to be free from sinning!" is a deeper cry in the heart of the saints than "Oh, to be free from physical pain!" We will be given both. But the greatest part of being conformed to the image of God's Son will be spiritual, not physical. We will never sin again! We will be unattracted by what Jesus is unattracted by. We will think the way he thinks. We will prefer what he prefers. We will enjoy what he enjoys.

3. Everlasting, Ever-Increasing Measures of Pleasure

This brings us to the third climactic work of providence that grows out of the second coming of Jesus. The transformation we experience when we see the all-glorious Christ as he is will result in everlasting, ever-increasing measures of pleasure that are presently inconceivable. This is when Psalm 16:11 finds its final fulfillment: "In your presence [O God] there is fullness of joy; at your right hand are pleasures forevermore." After focusing on the work of God in granting us to *see* the glory of Christ at the second coming, I said that this was not the greatest goal of providence if we consider the act of *seeing* without its amazing *effect*—namely, becoming like the risen Christ. "When he appears we shall be like him, because we shall see him as he is" (1 John 3:2).

Now I am going further and saying that it is inadequate to claim that becoming like Christ is the greatest goal of providence, because it does not go to the heart of what that likeness is. The Bible drives us further up and further in. Without doubt, the greatness of our final likeness to Christ will be unfathomably deep and multifaceted. I do not intend to reduce it to one thing. But I do want to follow the prayer of Jesus as far as he takes us in praying for the outworkings of seeing his glory.

Enjoying God with the Very Joy of God in God

One of those outworkings is that we would love Christ with the very love of the Father for his Son. And what is that but the infinite pleasure that the Father has in the perfections of the Son? "This is my beloved Son, with whom I am *well pleased*" (Matt. 3:17). Watch how Jesus prays for us to share in this pleasure:

> Father, I desire that they also, whom you have given me, may be with me where I am, to see my glory that you have given me because you loved me before the foundation of the world. . . . I made known to them your name, and I will continue to make it known, that the love with which you have loved me may be in them, and I in them. (John 17:24, 26)

In making known to his disciples the Father's name, Jesus says, his aim is that the Father's love for his Son *may be in them*: ". . . that the love with which you have loved me may be in them." What does that mean? It means that we are not left to our own finite (even perfected finite) capacities when it comes to loving Christ. The Father puts his own love for Christ in us. Jesus adds, ". . . and I in them." When we are enabled to love Christ with the very love of the Father, the presence of Christ in us will be experienced in a profoundly new way.

Now ponder with me what this actually means—or will mean—in our experience. How does the Father love the Son? What is that love? He does not love him simply in the way he loves us. We are sinners. And the love God has for us, in our sin, is wholly undeserved. "God shows his love for us in that while we were still sinners, Christ died for us" (Rom. 5:8). That is not how the Father loves the infinitely beautiful Son of God. He loves him as perfectly lovely. He loves him as infinitely worthy. He loves him in his immeasurable greatness. But what is the experience of loving the lovely and worthy and great?

God tells us when he says at Jesus's baptism and at the transfiguration, "This is my beloved Son, with whom I am *well pleased*" (Matt. 3:17; 17:5). Or when he announces his servant: "Behold my servant, whom I uphold, my chosen, *in whom my soul delights*" (Isa. 42:1). God's love for his Son is, most deeply and most essentially, his *delight* in the infinite perfections of his Son—his *pleasure* in the beauty and worth and greatness of his Son.

This is what Jesus prayed for us: ". . . that the love with which you have loved me may be in them" (John 17:26). This prayer, coming right after Jesus's prayer that we would see his glory (17:24), surely means that Jesus is praying that we would not only see his glory, and not only be changed by his glory in general, but also that we would love his glory, delight in it, and take pleasure in it with the delight and pleasure that God has in the beauty of his Son.

Loving Like the Father Is Being Like Christ

Loving the Son with the very love of the Father is not essentially different from seeing and becoming like Christ when he appears. This experience of loving with the very love of the Father is one essential dimension of becoming like Christ. Christ and the Father are one (John 10:30). They see the world, and they see each other, and they feel with the same sight and the same feelings. To be so transformed in our perceptions and our affections that we see and feel with the very sight and feeling of the Father is the greatest likeness to Christ possible.

Someone might ask: Isn't it a confused way of thinking, or contradictory, to say that likeness to Christ includes the capacity to admire and enjoy Christ? That would seem to imply that Christ admires and enjoys Christ. No. It is not confused or contradictory. Christ would be sinful if he did not delight in his own excellencies with the very delight of his Father. Indeed, the Son of God would be an idolater if he did not have infinite enjoyment in the Father-reflecting excellency of his own greatness and beauty and worth.

During his ministry on earth, Jesus said, concerning his teachings, "These things I have spoken to you, that my joy may be in you, and that your joy may be full" (John 15:11). This is astonishing. It is not his desire for us to simply have joy, not even joy in Jesus. It is a breathtaking desire—the desire of the Son of God—that we would have the very joy of Jesus himself. It is a desire that we would be made glad with the very gladness of the Son of God.

And when Jesus looked into the future at the great reckoning that would take place at his second coming, he pictured all believers hearing the words of Christ: "Enter into the joy of your master" (Matt. 25:21). Again, he is not merely saying, "From now on your tears are wiped away and you will be happy." He is saying, "Enter *my* joy. Share *my* joy." He is assuring us, just as he prayed in John 17:26, that we will not be left to our own capacities of joy.

I stress this partly because I know that when I preach or write about the immeasurable greatness of the joy we will have in Christ forever, people often despair that they could ever feel the kind of thing I am trying to describe. They look at their own personality, with all its emotional limitations, and they say, "Even at my perfected best, feeling what you describe is unimaginable for me." I have often felt this way myself.

But Jesus prays that we will feel not just with our own perfected feelings but with the very feelings of God (John 17:26). He invites us not simply to have great joy but to have *his* joy (John 15:11). He welcomes us not simply into a happy heaven but into the very experience of his own happiness. We will be so changed at the second coming that we will enjoy the glories of Christ, as much as a finite creature can, with the very joy of God.

Ever-Increasing Joy from Immeasurable Riches of Grace

One more clarification should be added, lest any of us succumb to the foolish thought that this joy in God eventually could become routine and boring, say, after a few million years. Paul put such foolish thoughts out of our minds when he wrote this:

> [God] seated us with him in the heavenly places in Christ Jesus, so that *in the coming ages* he might show the *immeasurable* riches of his grace in kindness toward us in Christ Jesus. (Eph. 2:6–7)

Notice the correlation between "the coming ages" (eternity) and the "*immeasurable* riches of his grace in kindness toward us." In chapter 14 we saw from this correlation that the riches of Christ can never become boring.

The reason the riches of Christ can never be boring is that we are finite, and they are "immeasurable"—infinite. Therefore, we cannot ever take them in fully. There will *always* be more. Gloriously more. Forever. Only an infinite being can fully take in infinite riches. But we can, and we will, spend eternity taking in more and more of these riches. There is a necessary correlation between eternal existence and infinite blessing. It takes the one to experience the other. *Eternal* life is essential for the enjoyment of *immeasurable* riches of grace.[1]

This is why I said that the third climactic providence growing out of the second coming of Christ is everlasting, *ever-increasing* measures of pleasure that are presently inconceivable. Our joy in God will be ever-increasing because it will take eternity to exhaust the new-joy-awakening discoveries of the immeasurable.

4. The Universe Will Be Set Free from Bondage

We have now seen three great works of providence growing out of the second coming of Christ. We might (mistakenly) conclude that the

---

1 See pp. 198–200.

fullness of the purposes of providence has been reached. The people of God have seen the risen King in his power and great glory. They have been changed instantly into sinless persons who will be like their glorious King forever. In that likeness to Christ, their capacities for love—for delighting in what is truly great and beautiful and worthy—have been raised to unimagined heights as they share in the very love of the Father and the Son. And in that supreme, pure, perfected delight in God, the glory of God shines.

But to many people's surprise, God does not intend for our sight of glory, or our likeness to glory, or our praises of glory, to be physically invisible or inaudible. This is why it would be a mistake to think that these three works of providence exhaust the fullness of God's purpose. There is more. The fourth work of providence that grows out of the second coming is the resurrection of the body and the renovation of the universe. God did not create the material universe, including our physical bodies, to be thrown away at the end of this age. That is not what we see in the Bible.

The created universe, and everything in it, is now and always will be (to an infinitely greater degree) a theater of God's glory. "The heavens declare the glory of God, and the sky above proclaims his handiwork" (Ps. 19:1). That is true for the entire material world, from the smallest subatomic particle to the most distant galaxy. The minuteness of the human race within the vastness of the universe is not an incongruity because the vastness of the universe is not about the greatness of man but about the greatness of God. Man has his greatness, but it lies in his capacity to know and worship the God who calls the universe "the work of [his] *fingers*" (Ps. 8:3).

In his work of creation, God has woven a fabric of reality out of the material and the immaterial. He did this in such a way that their interconnectedness is mysterious, yet essential for the maximum display and enjoyment of his glory. By raising the human body from the dead and by renovating the universe for the habitation of those bodies,

God's fourth providence brings into being the final goal of all things—the complete glorification of his people and the fullness of the display of his own greatness and beauty and worth.

Dying Natural Body, Coming Spiritual Body

At the second coming:

> The Lord himself will descend from heaven with a cry of command, with the voice of an archangel, and with the sound of the trumpet of God. And the dead in Christ will rise first. (1 Thess. 4:16)

Paul describes those resurrected bodies:

> What is sown is perishable; what is raised is imperishable. It is sown in dishonor; it is raised in glory. It is sown in weakness; it is raised in power. It is sown a natural body; it is raised a spiritual body. If there is a natural body, there is also a spiritual body. (1 Cor. 15:42–44)

What is a spiritual body? We must be careful not to think of something ethereal or ghostlike. Paul said Christ would make our resurrection body like his own: "[He] will transform our lowly body to be like his glorious body, by the power that enables him even to subject all things to himself" (Phil. 3:21). But the risen Christ was not a ghost. He appeared to his disciples and said, "See my hands and my feet, that it is I myself. Touch me, and see. For a spirit does not have flesh and bones as you see that I have" (Luke 24:39). Then he ate a piece of fish to put it beyond doubt: a spiritual body is not a spirit (24:42–43).

Rather, a spiritual body is a body recreated in a form beyond our comprehension and experience. It is *spiritual* at least in the sense that it is now—not partially, but wholly—fitted for the indwelling of the Spirit of God. It now has Spirit-given capacities that it never had. How else could we look upon one another without being blinded, when each of us is shining like the sun (Matt. 13:43)?

New Universe Made for the New Humanity

To show that the universe exists for man, not man for the universe, something absolutely astonishing then happens. God remakes the universe precisely to accommodate the new humanity with their spiritual bodies. The prophet Isaiah foresaw this day and spoke the word of God: "Behold, I create new heavens and a new earth, and the former things shall not be remembered or come into mind" (Isa. 65:17). The apostle John saw it as well: "I saw a new heaven and a new earth, for the first heaven and the first earth had passed away" (Rev. 21:1). And the apostle Peter described the emergence of the new heavens and the new earth through a cataclysmic purification:

> The heavens will be set on fire and dissolved, and the heavenly bodies will melt as they burn! But according to his promise we are waiting for new heavens and a new earth in which righteousness dwells. (2 Pet. 3:12–13)

But what is astonishing beyond the unimaginable magnitude of this providence is the fact that the entire renovation is carried out so that the universe is adapted to the freedom of the glory of the children of God. Here are the breathtaking words from Paul:

> The creation waits with eager longing for the revealing of the sons of God. For the creation was subjected to futility, not willingly, but because of him who subjected it, in hope that the creation itself will be set free from its bondage to corruption and obtain the freedom of the glory of the children of God. (Rom. 8:19–21)

The picture is not of man standing on tiptoe looking for a new creation. It's the reverse: the creation is standing on tiptoe looking for the day when the children of God will be glorified. When God subjected the creation to its fallen condition of futility and corruption, he had a future day of liberation in mind. That liberation was planned as a response to the glorification of God's people. It was conceived as a participation in the freedom and glory of God's redeemed children. "The creation itself will . . . obtain the freedom of the glory of the children of God" (8:21).

Perfect Home for a Perfect People—Blood-Bought

The children will receive new, free, glorious spiritual bodies, and the whole creation will be transformed into a perfect habitation designed for this new humanity. This means that the original purpose of the creation—to declare the glory of God—will be elevated in proportion as the saints have elevated capacities to see and savor and show the glory of God.

Sin will be completely eliminated. Nothing unclean or immoral or spiritually half-hearted will be there. All thoughts will be true. All desires will be free of any self-exaltation. All feelings will be calm or intense in perfect proportion to the nature of the reality felt. All deeds will be done in the name of Jesus and for the glory of God. Every particle and movement and connection in the material world will communicate something of the wisdom and power and love of God. And the capacity of the glorified minds and hearts and bodies of the saints will know and feel and act with no frustration, no confusion, no repression, no misgiving, no doubt, no regret, and no guilt. All our knowing—whatever we know—will include the knowledge of God. All our feeling—whatever we feel—will include the taste of the worth and beauty of God. All our acting—whatever we do—will comply in sweet satisfaction with the will of God.

We will sing forever the "song of the Lamb" (Rev. 15:3)—the Lamb who was slain (Rev. 5:9)—which means we will never forget that every sight, every sound, every fragrance, every touch, and every taste in the new world was purchased by Christ for his undeserving people. This world—with all its joy—cost him his life (Rom. 8:32; 2 Cor. 1:20). Every pleasure of every kind will intensify our thankfulness and love for Jesus. The new heavens and the new earth will never diminish but only increase our boast "in the cross of our Lord Jesus Christ" (Gal. 6:14). We will never forget that the recreated theater of wonders—this incomprehensible interweaving of spiritual and material beauty—has come into being through Christ and for Christ (Col. 1:16).

God—Father, Son, and Holy Spirit—will behold the finished work of his providence and rejoice over it with singing (Zeph. 3:17). The Father will rejoice over the excellence of the Son and his triumphant achievements (Matt. 17:5; Phil. 2:9–11). The Son, the bridegroom, will rejoice over his immaculate bride—the glorified church (Isa. 62:5). And the joy of the Holy Spirit will fill the saints as the very joy of God in God (1 Thess. 1:6).

5. God Will Be Supreme and Central

The fifth and final work of providence that grows out of the second coming of Christ is not properly a distinct work: God himself will be *supreme* and *central.* He will be *above all* in beauty and worth and greatness, and he will be the all-satisfying *focus of all.* The supremacy of God over all and the satisfaction of the saints in God above all are the unending climactic goals of providence. And the relationship between these two great realities is the final grandeur of God's providence.

The incalculable joy of the saints *in* God is the apex of our glorification *of* God. It would be a serious mistake to think that the magnitude of the Bible's emphasis on the joy of the redeemed means that their happiness is a higher end than God's glory. It is not. God has so designed the world, and human nature in particular, that the essence of praising is prizing. Lips can say words of praise where the heart does not prize. But this is not true praise, and God is not glorified by it. Without prizing, praising is hypocrisy (Matt. 15:7–8).

Paul said that his supreme passion in life was that Christ would be magnified in his body "whether by life or by death" (Phil. 1:20). Then to show how Christ would be magnified by his death, he said that for him to die is *gain* because it would mean being *with Christ*, which is better than life (Phil. 1:21–23). In other words, his cherishing Christ above life was the essence of his magnifying Christ. Christ would be most magnified in Paul's death because Paul was more satisfied in Christ than in life. Prizing Christ supremely was the essence of Paul's highest praise.

So it is clear that the emphasis the Bible puts on the joy of the redeemed does not diminish the glory of God. It reflects the glory. The joy of the redeemed is joy *in God*. It is the prizing of God. It is satisfaction in God. The Bible does not make a god out of joy. It shows that what we take most joy in *is* our God (Col. 3:5). That is how God designed the world. And, therefore, God has made and governed the world to bring the redeemed into the greatest possible pleasure in God. This is the ultimate goal of providence—the glorification of God in the gladness of his blood-bought people in God.

Seeing and Savoring the Providence of God

The providence of God—his purposeful sovereignty—is all-embracing, all-pervasive, and invincible. Therefore, God will be completely successful in the achievement of his ultimate goal for the universe. God's providence is guided by "the counsel of his will" (Eph. 1:11). This counsel is eternal, all-knowing, and infinitely wise. Its plans and goals, therefore, are perfect, and cannot be improved. They never change. Providence is the purposeful sovereignty that carries those plans into action, guides all things toward God's ultimate goal, and leads to the final consummation. Job's prayer is true: "You can do all things, and . . . no purpose of yours can be thwarted" (Job 42:2). Or as God himself states it positively, "My counsel shall stand, and I will accomplish all my purpose" (Isa. 46:10).

Extent of Providence

God's eternal plan includes *everything*—from the most insignificant bird fall (Matt. 10:29), to the movement of stars (Isa. 40:26), to the murder of his Son (Acts 4:27–28). It includes the moral acts of every soul—its preferences, choices, and deeds. Neither Satan at his hellish worst nor human beings at their redeemed best ever act in a way that causes a revision in God's all-wise plan. Whether God planned to permit something or planned to be more directly involved, nothing comes to pass but what God planned as part of the process of pursuing his ultimate goal. Therefore, the extent of his providence is total. Nothing is independent of it. Nothing happens but by "the counsel of his will"—the infinite wisdom of his plan.

Nature of Providence

The nature of this providence is such that the preferences and choices of Satan and man are really their own preferences and their own choices. They are blameworthy or praiseworthy owing to the way they relate to God in faith and to man in justice and love. God's providence is decisive in what Satan and man decide and do. But it is not coercive. That is, its ordinary way of working is to see to it that Satan and man decide and act in a way that is their own preference, while fulfilling God's plan at every moment. *How* God does this may remain a mystery while we "see in a mirror dimly" (1 Cor. 13:12), but *that* he does it is what the Bible teaches. "It is the glory of God to conceal things" (Prov. 25:2). "The secret things belong to the LORD our God, but the things that are revealed belong to us" (Deut. 29:29).

Ultimate Goal of Providence

One essential aspect of the ultimate goal of this all-embracing, all-pervasive, invincible providence is the beautification of the bride of Christ—the church, the people of God, the elect. This is why the final twelve chapters of this book (34–45) have focused on the creation, transformation, and glorification of the bride. But defining the ultimate goal of providence requires more than pointing to the beautification of the bride of Christ. Too much glory is left unexpressed.

What is this beautification? It is her sanctification, her holiness. That is, it is her joyfully obeying all the word of God. It is, most essentially, her love for God, which overflows in God-glorifying love for people. It is her delight in God and her reflection of God. Therefore, to express it more fully, the ultimate goal of God's providence is to glorify his grace in the spiritual and moral beauty of Christ's undeserving, blood-bought bride as she enjoys, reflects, and thus magnifies his greatness and beauty and worth above everything.

But even that expression of God's ultimate goal needs one more expansion in order to have its biblical proportions. We must echo here the climax of part 2. To be sure, the ever-increasing joy of the bride in the inexhaustible riches of the glory of Christ's grace will be the *essence* of how God is glorified in the coming ages. Its essence, not its totality. The bride will inhabit a new creation. And in that new creation, she will see dimensions of the glory of God as never before. The heavens will be glad. The sun and moon and shining stars will praise the Lord. The earth will rejoice. The seas will roar with praise. The rivers will clap their hands. The hills will sing for joy. The field will exult and everything in it. The trees of the forest will chant their praise. The desert will blossom like the crocus. The created world—liberated and perfected—will never cease to declare the glory of God. That will be our dwelling.

But the dwelling is not the family. The beauty of the new world is not the bridegroom. The perfected theater of creation will be glorious, radiant with God. But the drama—the human experience of God in Christ—not the theater, will be foremost in magnifying the God of all-embracing, all-pervasive providence. And the unparalleled beauty and worth of the reigning Lamb who was slain will be the main song of eternity. And the joy of the children of God—the bride of Christ—will be the main echo of the infinite excellencies of God and the focus of his eternal delight.

Ten Effects of Seeing and Savoring This Providence

God did not reveal these glories for nothing. He meant them to be known and loved—or, as I like to say, seen and savored. And he intends that this seeing and savoring would result in showing—showing the greatness and beauty and worth of God in his providence. So before I bid farewell, I offer ten examples of the effects that knowing and loving *this* providence will have. I say *this* providence, meaning the providence we have seen in the forty-five chapters of this book. *This* providence—the all-embracing, all-pervasive, invincible, purposeful sovereignty of God.

1. SEEING AND SAVORING THIS PROVIDENCE AWAKENS AWE AND LEADS US INTO THE DEPTH OF TRUE GOD-CENTERED, CHRIST-EXALTING, BIBLE-SATURATED WORSHIP.

I stand back from the breathtaking panorama of God's glory in the Bible and lift my hands in silence, groping for words that do not feel pitiful before this majesty. He is great beyond our comprehension. Not that our praises ring loudest as we focus on what we do not know. No. God has shown us more of himself, and more of his ways, than we will ever exhaust in this world. I have filled a book by simply tracing his counterintuitive wonders. He has not been sparing in the revelation of his splendors. Before we sing of what we cannot comprehend, let us spend a lifetime singing of what he has revealed.

Those who see and savor this providence sing—not because of ritualistic expectations, but because it's the nature of the God-besotted soul to sing. And how can we not be God-besotted when, every day, we are immersed in an ocean of God-given, God-governed, God-revealing wonders? Did not Hannah sing over this providence?

> The bows of the mighty are broken,
>   but the feeble bind on strength. . . .
> The Lord kills and brings to life;
>   he brings down to Sheol and raises up.
> The Lord makes poor and makes rich;
>   he brings low and he exalts. (1 Sam. 2:4, 6–7)

Did not Miriam sing over this providence?

> Sing to the LORD, for he has triumphed gloriously;
> the horse and his rider he has thrown into the sea.
>> (Ex. 15:21)

Did not Moses sing over this providence?

> I will sing to the LORD, for he has triumphed gloriously. . . .
> Pharaoh's chariots and his host he cast into the sea. . . .
> In the greatness of your majesty you overthrow your
>> adversaries;
>> you send out your fury; it consumes them like stubble. . . .
> Who is like you, majestic in holiness,
> awesome in glorious deeds, doing wonders?
>> (Ex. 15:1, 4, 7, 11)

Did not the psalmists sing over this providence?

> The LORD brings the counsel of the nations to nothing;
>> he frustrates the plans of the peoples.
> The counsel of the LORD stands forever,
>> the plans of his heart to all generations. (Ps. 33:10–11)

> Come, behold the works of the LORD,
>> how he has brought desolations on the earth.
> He makes wars cease to the end of the earth;
>> he breaks the bow and shatters the spear;
>> he burns the chariots with fire. (Ps. 46:8–9)

> Whatever the LORD pleases, he does,
>> in heaven and on earth,
>> in the seas and all deeps. (Ps. 135:6)

Did not Mary sing over this providence?

He has shown strength with his arm;
> he has scattered the proud in the thoughts of their
> > hearts;
he has brought down the mighty from their thrones
> and exalted those of humble estate. (Luke 1:51–52)

And did not Paul sing over this providence?

> Oh, the depth of the riches and wisdom and knowledge of God!
> How unsearchable are his judgments and how inscrutable his
> ways!
>
> > "For who has known the mind of the Lord,
> > > or who has been his counselor?"
> > "Or who has given a gift to him
> > > that he might be repaid?"
>
> For from him and through him and to him are all things. To him
> be glory forever. Amen. (Rom. 11:33–36)

If there are believers or churches whose worship feels thin
and passive and routine, could it be that they do not know this
providence—this God?

2. SEEING AND SAVORING THIS PROVIDENCE MAKES US MARVEL AT OUR OWN SALVATION AND HUMBLES US BECAUSE OF OUR SIN.

God chose us from eternity when he saw that we deserved nothing but
condemnation. He predestined us to be his children and share the likeness of his Son in spite of our unworthiness and treason and redeemed
recalcitrance. He purchased us at the cost of his Son's life. He called
us (the way Lazarus was called) out of death. He caused us to be born
again. He gave us the gift of repentance and faith. He justified us. He
gave us his Holy Spirit as a guarantee.

He is working in us what is pleasing in his sight. He will keep us from falling and bring us to glory. He took away the sting of death and will bring us through it into the presence of Christ. He will perfect our souls, raise us from the dead, give us new bodies like his glorious body, and present us with a new world for our eternal habitation, where his glory is the light and the Lamb is the lamp.

It is a great tragedy that millions of Christians do not know that this is true about them. They have been taught a salvation with themselves as the decisive cause at the point of conversion. This view of their own decisive power obscures the glory of what God has actually done for them, strips them of stunned thankfulness for the gift of faith, dulls the intensity of their amazement that they were raised from the dead, and takes away the wonder that their perseverance is owing to the omnipotent, moment-by-moment keeping of God.

But if we see and savor *this* providence, oh, how we will exult in the freedom and fullness and sovereign effectiveness of our salvation. We will be glad that it is all from God and through God and to God. We will be made humble and happy and hopeful. We will give all the glory to God. The lowliness we feel because of our unworthiness will be accompanied and tempered by the wonder of God's merciful and infinitely loving providence. We saw Jonathan Edwards's beautiful expression of the saints' humility in chapter 10. I love this quote so much, and long for this experience so earnestly, that I give the last sentence again:

> The desires of the saints, however earnest, are humble desires: their hope is a humble hope, and their joy, even when it is unspeakable, and full of glory, is humble brokenhearted joy, and leaves the Christian more poor in spirit, and more like a little child, and more disposed to a universal lowliness of behavior.[1]

---

1 Jonathan Edwards, *Religious Affections,* ed. John E. Smith and Harry S. Stout, vol. 2, *The Works of Jonathan Edwards* (New Haven, CT: Yale University Press, 2009), 348–49.

3. SEEING AND SAVORING THIS PROVIDENCE CAUSES US TO SEE EVERYTHING AS PART OF GOD'S DESIGN— EVERYTHING AS FROM HIM AND THROUGH HIM AND TO HIM, FOR HIS GLORY.

When we hear God say that he "works *all things* according to the counsel of his will" (Eph. 1:11), and then we see him doing this very thing countless times in his word and in his world, we are given a worldview with stunning implications. Everything, absolutely everything, relates to God. As R. C. Sproul would often say, "There are no maverick molecules." Nor are there any maverick athletes or actors or singers or presidents or scholars or street people. All are in the sway of God's all-pervasive providence. All things and all persons fit into God's all-embracing plan.

That is where ultimate meaning is found. If we are going to understand anything, at the most important level, we start with this reality: God created the world, holds it in existence, and governs all of it for his purposes. Everything relates to everything because everything relates to God. The knowledge of this, and the fear of the Lord, is the beginning of wisdom (Ps. 111:12). Where this is denied, all knowledge is enveloped in a cloud of folly. Where it is affirmed, the possibilities of profound, amazing, beautiful, and helpful insights abound.

4. SEEING AND SAVORING THIS PROVIDENCE HELPS PROTECT US FROM THE TRIVIALIZING EFFECTS OF CULTURE AND FROM TRIFLING WITH DIVINE THINGS.

One of the curses of our culture—and it has permeated the church and most Christian communication—is banality, triviality, silliness, superficiality, and an eerie addiction to flippancy and levity. This is accompanied by what to me seems like a baffling allergic reaction to seriousness, dignity, and articulate precision in public speech. Carelessness in speech and casualness in demeanor turn up in times and places where you would expect carefulness, clarity, earnestness, and even gravity.

My impression is that at the root of this culture of inarticulate, casual trifling is a loss of the weight of the greatness and awe-fulness of God. Everything is light and funny because God is a lightweight. The boats of our communication bounce around with a chipper bearing on the waves of cultural trifling because the heavy ballast of a big and holy God has been offloaded at the docks of man-centered theology—and endless screen time.

This is a tragedy not only because it is the fruit of trivializing God, but because it hinders us from seeing him and experiencing him as he really is in the majesty of his providence. My guess is that some who read these lines will have no categories for viewing what I am saying any other way than as a summons to somberness and boredom. We live in a culture that can scarcely imagine something like glad gravity or joyful sorrow. Humor has been so identified with the silliness and levity of slapstick verbal antics that the robust, reality-rooted, natural explosiveness of humor is, for many, inconceivable.

Charles Spurgeon was a very funny man. But he was not a man of levity. He did not trifle with sacred things or think that worship was a place for casual clowning. He was not allergic to seriousness or dignity. Three years after his death, Robertson Nicole expressed my concerns and used Spurgeon as a counter example:

> Evangelism of the humorous type may attract multitudes, but it lays the soul in ashes and destroys the very germs of religion. Mr. Spurgeon is often thought by those who do not know his sermons to have been a humorous preacher. As a matter of fact there was no preacher whose tone was more uniformly earnest, reverent and solemn.[2]

Of course, every mature and healthy person knows that unbroken seriousness of a melodramatic or somber kind will inevitably

---

2 Quoted in Iain Murray, *The Forgotten Spurgeon* (Edinburgh, UK: Banner of Truth, 1966), 38. See other good comments about humor here, and resources for Spurgeon's humor.

communicate a sickness of soul. But that is not our danger in the first half of the twenty-first century. My point here is that seeing and savoring the all-embracing, all-pervasive providence of God has a wonderful effect in helping us recover the gift of authentic earnestness and the beautiful interweaving of gladness and gravity.

5. SEEING AND SAVORING THIS PROVIDENCE HELPS US BE PATIENT AND FAITHFUL AMID THE MOST INEXPLICABLE CIRCUMSTANCES OF LIFE.

When our minds are saturated with Scripture, and day after day we are exposed to God's inscrutable ways in the Bible, we become accustomed to trust him in the dark. It is one thing to be told by God:

> My thoughts are not your thoughts,
>> neither are your ways my ways, declares the LORD. (Isa. 55:8)

But it is even more sobering and peace giving to immerse ourselves in his providence and watch him, time and again, do and say things that are strange and contrary to our ordinary ways of thinking and acting. In this way, the reality of providence shapes our minds and our affections. We become less vulnerable to panic and perplexity and dread—not because there are no perplexing and fearful circumstances, but because we have seen this before in God's word. God has shown us, again and again, that things are not what they seem and that he is always weaving something wise and good out of the painful, perplexing threads that look like a tangle in our lives.

A story may help us grasp how seeing and savoring God's providence helps us deal with the perplexities of life. I created this story based very loosely on a tale from T. H. White's *The Once and Future King*.[3]

---

3 See T. H. White, "The Once and Future King Study Guide: Part 1, Chapters 9–10 Summary," enotes (website), accessed August 14, 2019, https://www.enotes.com/topics/once-future/chapter-summaries/part-1-chapters-9-10-summary.

Once upon a time there was a very wise old man named Job. In his old age, God gave to him a daughter whom he named Jemima, which means "little dove." He loved his little girl, and she loved her daddy.

One day, Job decided to go on a journey and asked Jemima if she would like to go along. "Oh, yes," Jemima said. "I would love to go along."

And so they started off on their journey and walked all day. At sundown they saw a little cottage and knocked on the door. A very poor man and his wife and baby lived there. Job asked if he and Jemima could spend the night there before they continued on their journey in the morning.

The poor man and his wife were very happy to let them stay. They gave Job and Jemima their own room and made them a simple supper. The special treat was fresh milk from their only cow. This was how the poor couple made a living. Their cow gave good milk, which they sold for enough to live on.

In the morning, when Job and Jemima got up, they heard crying. The cow had died during the night. The poor man's wife was weeping. "What will we do? What will we do?" she sobbed. The poor man was about to cut the cow into pieces and sell the meat before it spoiled. But Job said, "I think you should not cut the cow in pieces but bury him by your back wall under the olive tree. The meat may not be good to sell. Trust God, and he will take care of you." So the poor man did as Job suggested.

Then Job and Jemima went on their way. They walked all day again and were very tired when they came to the next town and noticed a fine home. They knocked on the door. A very wealthy man lived in this house, and they hoped that they would not be an inconvenience to one so wealthy.

But the man was very gruff with them and said they could stay in the barn. He gave them water and bread for supper and let them eat it by themselves in the barn. Job was very thankful, and said to the wealthy man, "Thank you very much for the bread and water and for letting us stay in your barn."

In the morning, Job noticed that one of the walls of the house was crumbling. So he went and bought bricks and mortar and repaired the hole in the wall for the wealthy man. Then Job and Jemima went on their way and came to their destination.

As they sat by the fire that night, Jemima said, "Daddy, I don't understand the ways of God. It doesn't seem right that the poor man's cow should die when he was so good to us, and that you should fix the rich man's wall when he was so bad to us."

"Well, Jemima," Job said, "many things are not the way they seem. Perhaps this once I will tell you why. But after this you will have to trust God, who does not usually explain what he is doing."

"The poor man's cow was very sick, but he didn't know it. I could taste it in the milk that he gave us for supper. Soon he would have sold bad milk, and the people would have gotten sick and died, and they would have stoned him. So I told him not to sell the meat, but to bury the cow under the olive tree by his back wall because the Lord showed me that, if he dug the grave there, he would find a silver cup buried from long ago and sell it for enough money to buy two good cows. And in the end things would be better for him and his wife and child.

"When we spent the night at the rich man's house, I saw the hole in the wall, and I saw more than that. I saw that hidden in the wall, from generations ago, was a chest full of gold. If the rich man had repaired the wall himself, he would have found it and continued in his pride and cruelty. So I bought brick and mortar, and closed the wall so that the man would never find this treasure.

"Do you see, Jemima?"

"Yes, Daddy. I see."

6. SEEING AND SAVORING THIS PROVIDENCE SHOWS US THAT THE "PROBLEM" OF GOD'S SOVEREIGNTY IN SUFFERING IS MORE THAN RELIEVED BY THE SUSTAINING PURPOSE AND POWER OF HIS SOVEREIGNTY THROUGH SUFFERING.

I mean this as a theological truth in the ultimate sense, and as a precious, experiential reality for those who trust Christ.

Many people stumble over the conclusion of this book because the all-pervasive providence of God means that his purposeful sovereignty holds sway over all suffering. Satan's power to deceive and destroy is real. Human sin against fellow humans is real. Natural disasters are real. But what we have seen in this book is that neither Satan nor man nor nature ever does anything that was not in the plan of God. In the entire sequence of events in the world, God decides finally which causes will be effective. Therefore, all suffering is in the sway of God's providence. He could always stop it. When he doesn't, his permissions are planned and purposeful and, in his overall design, wise.

This wise, purposeful sovereignty will be the final answer to the justice and goodness of God's painful dealings in this world. As we saw in chapter 22, "All his ways are justice" (Deut. 32:4). "He loves righteous deeds" (Ps. 11:7). "Righteousness and justice are the foundation of his throne" (Ps. 97:2). "He will judge the world with righteousness" (Ps. 98:9). "His righteousness endures forever" (Ps. 111:3). No one will ever be able to rightly accuse God of treating him worse than he deserves. Sin is universal in the heart of man. And its denigration of God is an outrage beyond all its painful consequences.

Why have things come to this? The closest the Bible comes to giving an ultimate answer is Romans 9:22–23:

If God, desiring to show his wrath and to make known his power, has endured with much patience vessels of wrath prepared for destruction, in order to make known the riches of his glory for vessels of mercy, which he has prepared beforehand for glory . . .

How should that sentence be completed? I argued in chapter 7 that Paul's intention was that we complete it with something like this: "then no legitimate objection can be raised." The reason no legitimate objection can be raised is that it is right and fitting that the fullness of the glories of God be manifest, including (as verse 22 says) wrath and power. Therefore, a world exists in which God's holy wrath and righteous judgment fall on guilty sinners. If anyone in this world for whom the painful wrath of God is not fitting is swept away in his judgments, God will "restore, confirm, strengthen, and establish" them in the age to come (1 Pet. 5:10; cf. 4:17).

For those who trust Christ, God's sovereignty in suffering is not an unyielding problem but an unfailing hope. It means that, in the suffering of Christians, neither Satan nor man nor nature nor chance is wielding decisive control. God is sovereign over this suffering, which means it is not meaningless. It is not wrath. It is not ultimately destructive. It is not wanton or heedless. It is purposeful. It is measured, wise, and loving.

Even if (as I have seen personally) the suffering is terrible in the last hour of death, when there is no life left in which the sufferer can be sanctified by it, even then it is eternally purposeful:

> For this light momentary affliction is preparing for us an eternal weight of glory beyond all comparison, as we look not to the things that are seen but to the things that are unseen. For the things that are seen are transient, but the things that are unseen are eternal. (2 Cor. 4:17–18)

If I may bear witness from fifty years of ministering the word of God to many suffering people, here is what I would say. For every *one* person whom I have heard or seen forsaking the truth of God's all-pervasive providence because of suffering—or more often, because of the suffering and death of a loved one—I have seen *ten* others bear witness that the biblical truth of God's absolute sovereignty, in and over their suffering and loss, saved their faith—and some have said, their sanity.

Indeed, it saved not only their faith in God and sanity of mind, but also their love for people. How is that? Love cannot flourish where fear or greed consumes the heart with self-protecting or self-enhancing passions. The heart must be set free from self-focus for the sake of focusing on others (Phil. 2:4). Something must break this double power—fearing loss and craving gain. What breaks this power is the unshakable certainty of hope, warranted by the unstoppable, blood-bought omnipotence of merciful providence. We saw how this works in chapter 43 ("Killing Sin and Creating Love—by Faith").

If our suffering turns us in on ourselves, we will not love well in the midst of affliction. But that is precisely where Christian love should shine. "In a severe test of affliction, their abundance of joy . . . overflowed in a wealth of generosity" (2 Cor. 8:2). Joy, overflowing with generosity in affliction—that is the beauty of Christian love. And how can there be such triumphant joy in affliction? Hope! Certain hope! "We heard of . . . the *love* that you have for all the saints, *because of the hope* laid up for you in heaven" (Col. 1:4–5). "Blessed are you when others . . . *persecute* you. . . . *Rejoice* and be glad, for your *reward* is great in heaven" (Matt. 5:11–12). "Jesus, . . . *for the joy that was set before him* endured the cross" (Heb. 12:2). In every case, hope—the confidence of a joyful future—broke the power of fear and greed and freed the heart for love.

This is how the Christian soul in suffering is saved from bitterness and revenge and self-indulgence and self-pity. God promises to turn every sorrow to joy, every loss to gain, every groan to glory (Rom. 8:18, 28; 2 Cor. 4:17–18; Heb. 12:10; 1 Pet. 1:6–7; 5:10). And this promise does not hang in the air. It is rooted, warranted, secured, and guaranteed "by the power that enables [Christ] even to subject all things to himself" (Phil. 3:21). In other words, for thousands of suffering Christians, the all-pervasive providence of God is not a barrier for faith but the ground of faith-preserving, sanity-sustaining, love-empowering hope.

The all-embracing, all-pervasive, invincible providence of God found in the Bible is theologically more comprehensive, and experientially more comforting and more fruitful, than its denial.

7. SEEING AND SAVORING THIS PROVIDENCE MAKES US ALERT AND RESISTANT TO MAN-CENTERED SUBSTITUTES THAT POSE AS GOOD NEWS.

Indeed, I would say that seeing and savoring this providence sends the roots of countercultural conviction so deeply in the rock of Scripture that lovers of this truth are not easily blown over by the winds of false teaching. Why this is true may be owing mainly to the fact that this providence is so contrary to fallen human nature, and so out of step with self-exalting culture, that if Christians can break ranks with the world on this point, they can on any point, which means they are safe from much deception.

But I think the reason goes deeper than that for why embracing this providence makes us resistant to man-centered substitutes. I think the sheer enormity of God—the sheer weight and seriousness and authority of God—creates in the soul a spiritual sense, a kind of holy acumen, that can detect in any idea or doctrine or behavior a tendency toward exalting man while diminishing God.

8. SEEING AND SAVORING THIS PROVIDENCE MAKES US CONFIDENT THAT GOD HAS THE RIGHT AND THE POWER TO ANSWER PRAYER THAT PEOPLE'S HEARTS AND MINDS WOULD BE CHANGED.

Prayer is one of the great wonders that God has given to the world. That God would plan for his own sovereign hand to be moved by the prayers of his creatures is amazing. It is a thoughtless objection to say, "There's no point in praying, since God has all things planned anyway." It's thoughtless because just a little thought would reveal that God has planned millions of human acts every day that cause other acts to happen.

A nail sinks into a board because God planned for a hammer to hit it. A student makes an A on a test because God planned for the student to study. A jet flies from New York to Los Angeles because God planned for fuel to be available, wings to stay put, engines to thrust, and a pilot to know what he is doing. In none of these cases do we say that the cause was pointless—the hammer, the studying, the fuel, the wing, the engine, the pilot.

Neither is prayer pointless. It is part of the plan. In fact, the all-embracing, all-pervasive, unstoppable providence of God is the only hope for making our most heartfelt prayers effective. What is your greatest longing? Your most heartfelt prayer? Probably it is for the salvation of someone you love. Or it may be for the liberation of your soul from some sinful bondage. When you pray that God would save your loved one or liberate you from bondage to sin, what are you asking God to do? You are asking him to do what he promised to do in the new covenant, which Jesus bought with his blood (which is why we pray in Jesus's name). So we pray:

"God, take out of their flesh the heart of stone and give him a new heart of flesh" (see Ezek. 11:19).

"Lord, circumcise their hearts so that they love you" (see Deut. 30:6).

"Father, put your Spirit within them and cause them to walk in your statutes" (see Ezek. 36:27).

"Lord, grant them repentance and the knowledge of the truth that they may escape from the snare of the devil" (see 2 Tim. 2:25–26).

"Father, open their hearts so that they believe the gospel" (see Acts 16:14).

The only people who can pray like that are people who believe that saving faith is a gift of providence (see chapter 36). Many people do not believe this, because they believe that human beings have the power of ultimate self-determination at the point of conversion. In other words, God can woo sinners, but he cannot create their faith. Man must have the final say. At the point when faith comes into existence, man, not God, is decisive.

My point here is that people who really believe this cannot consistently pray that God would convert unbelieving sinners. Why? Because if they pray for divine influence in a sinner's life, they are either praying for a successful influence (which takes away the sinner's ultimate self-determination), or they are praying for an unsuccessful influence (which is not praying for conversion). So they must either give up praying that God would convert people or give up ultimate human self-determination. Or go on acting inconsistently.

Prayer is a spectacular gift. No one believed more firmly than Paul that humans do not have the final say in their conversion, but that God does. "It depends not on human will or exertion, but on God, who has mercy" (Rom. 9:16). But probably no one prayed with more tears and more urgency than Paul for the conversion of sinners. "I have great sorrow and unceasing anguish in my heart . . . for the sake of my brothers, my kinsmen according to the flesh. . . . My heart's desire and prayer to God for them is that they may be saved" (Rom. 9:2–3; 10:1). He prayed this way because he knew that the new birth is not a mere decision but a miracle. "With man this is impossible, but with God all things are possible" (Matt. 19:26). The providence we have seen in this book does not make prayer a problem. It makes prayer powerful.

9. SEEING AND SAVORING THIS PROVIDENCE SHOWS
US THAT EVANGELISM AND MISSIONS ARE ABSOLUTELY
ESSENTIAL FOR PEOPLE TO BE CONVERTED TO CHRIST,
BECAUSE GOD MAKES THEM THE MEANS OF HIS WORK
IN CREATING SAVING FAITH.

Just as thoughtless as the previous objection about prayer is the objection that says, "There is no point in evangelism and missions since God has planned whom he will save." A moment's thought will reveal that the plan to save people through the word of God includes the plan to send preachers of the word. No one believes and is saved without hearing the gospel. The new birth comes "through the living and abiding word"—the gospel:

> You have been born again, not of perishable seed but of imperishable, through the living and abiding word of God. . . . And this word is the good news that was preached to you. (1 Pet. 1:23, 25)

This gospel is not written in the clouds. It is entrusted to Christians who become witnesses and missionaries. If there were no human witnesses, there would be no salvation:

> "Everyone who calls on the name of the Lord will be saved." How then will they call on him in whom they have not believed? And how are they to believe in him of whom they have never heard? And how are they to hear without someone preaching? And how are they to preach unless they are sent? . . . So faith comes from hearing, and hearing through the word of Christ. (Rom. 10:13–15, 17)

When Paul spoke of his own commissioning from the risen Christ, he described it in the most impossible terms. Jesus commissioned him to the Gentiles to do what only God can do. Jesus said to Paul:

I am sending you to open their eyes, so that they may turn from darkness to light and from the power of Satan to God, that they may receive forgiveness of sins and a place among those who are sanctified by faith in me. (Acts 26:17–18)

Open blind eyes. Liberate from Satan. That's Paul's mission. And ours. This is how the blind see and the enslaved are set free—by evangelism and missions. They are the instruments. But the instruments are not the miracle of conversion. They are another kind of miracle—the miracle of obedience. But we are talking here about evangelism and conversion. When the word is spoken, the Lord opens hearts. That is what we read about Lydia: "The Lord opened her heart to pay attention to what was said by Paul" (Acts 16:14). The word spoken by Paul is the essential instrument. The work of the Lord is the miracle of heart-opening conversion.

As in the case of prayer, the unthwartable providence of God is not a *problem* for evangelism and missions; it is their only *hope* of success. The obstacles to missions around the world today are insurmountable but for one thing: the providence of God is unstoppable. It cannot be stopped by closed countries. It cannot be stopped by hostile religions. It cannot be stopped by difficult languages and cultures. And it cannot be stopped by the ultimate self-determination of the fallen human soul—because in the world of God's purposeful sovereignty, such self-determination does not exist.

We may and we must build our lives and our mission on this confidence. "I will build my church, and the gates of hell shall not prevail against it" (Matt. 16:18). And to that end: "This gospel of the kingdom will be proclaimed throughout the whole world as a testimony to all nations, and then the end will come" (Matt. 24:14). I pray that God will use this book to catapult thousands of new missionaries into God's harvest with undaunted confidence.

10. SEEING AND SAVORING THIS PROVIDENCE ASSURES
US THAT FOR ALL ETERNITY GOD WILL BE INCREASINGLY
GLORIFIED IN US AS WE ARE INCREASINGLY SATISFIED
IN HIM.

Running through this book like a golden thread is the truth that God designed the world and performs his providence so that his glory in saving us and our joy in seeing him would be forever united, as each increases in the increase of the other. When the immeasurable riches of God's glory in saving us through the slaying of the Lamb are forever and continually dispensed from his infinite treasury, our gladness will increase with every fresh sight. And as our gladness in God increases, his worth will be seen as a greater and greater treasure reflected in the pleasures of his people.

The all-embracing, all-pervasive, unstoppable providence of God is precious in proportion as we hope for this day to come. And it will come. God will forever be increasingly glorified as we are increasingly satisfied in him.

> In your presence there is fullness of joy;
> at your right hand are pleasures forevermore. (Ps. 16:11)

> Be exalted, O God, above the heavens!
> Let your glory be over all the earth! (Ps. 57:5)

Our Lord, come!

General Index

Abel, 344
Abimelech, 176
Abiram, 235
Abishai, 457
Abraham: call of, 287–88; choosing of, 71, 72, 112, 562; covenant with, 104–5, 138; obedience of, 139, 645; offspring of, 74, 79n1, 138, 347; promise to, 347–48; sacrifice of Isaac, 30–31
Absalom, 455–56, 459
Achan, 119
acrostic poetry, 489, 490
Adam, sin of, 175, 179, 180, 359–60, 501, 503
adoption, 185
adultery against God, 144
adversary, 480
affections, 147–49
affliction, 140, 491, 705
age to come, 200–201, 672
agnostics, 402
Ahab, 469, 470
Ai, 119
Alford, Henry, 66
alive with Christ, 540–41, 554
"all things," 406–7, 445, 626, 641–62
Amnon, 459
Amorites, 365–66, 391
Amos, 479–80
Ananias and Sapphira, 374
angel of death, 363–64, 500
angels, 174, 226, 495, 669
animals, 244–45, 272
animal sacrifices, 166

annihilationism, 670–71
arm of God's glory, 102
Arminians, 550–55, 557
armor of God, 650
Artaxerxes, 395
asking God to glorify God, 191–92
assurance, 595, 609–10, 612, 614–20
Assyria, judgment on, 320
Assyrian soldiers, struck down, 367–68, 374
attentiveness, to God's providence, 233–49

Babylon, 321–22, 392–93, 482, 491
ballast, of providence, 215, 216
baptism, 604
Bathsheba, 456, 459
beholding, leads to belonging, 182
Belgic Confession, on providence, 33–34
believing, 532–34
belonging to the Father, 567–72
Belshazzar, 291, 292–93, 295, 300, 313
Bethlehem Baptist Church Elder Affirmation of Faith, on providence, 37–38
Bethsaida, 454
Bible: apparent contradictions in, 141, 208, 413, 414, 484, 548; commands in, 592; infallibility of, 413; meditation on, 604; reading into texts, 415–17
birds of the air, 244–45, 246–47
birth, 344, 345–48, 350, 353
bitter providence, 354
blamelessness, 628–29
blessed hope, 675–77

blessing, and obedience, 138–39
blindness, 526, 535, 537, 538
blood of the new covenant, 561, 624, 641
body: reading into texts, 415–17; glorify-
    ing God in, 193; and soul, 342–43;
    transformation of, 668–69. *See also*
    resurrection body
bondage to sin, 523, 526
Bowers, Jim, 377–79
Bowers, Veronica, 377–79
breath and ways of the king, in the hand
    of God, 293, 305–11
bride of Christ, beautification of, 162–63,
    692–93
broken families, 449, 461

Caiaphas, 662
Cain, 344
calamities, 484, 485, 504–7
called, 614, 662
call of God, 529–32, 538, 613
calling, 617; and justification, 531
Calvin, on name of God, 82–83
capital punishment, 357
carelessness in speech, 698–99
certainty, of glorification, 606
Chalmers, Thomas, 649
chance, 405
Chariots of Fire (film), 22
children of Abraham, 74
children of wrath, 518, 522
child sacrifice, 498–501, 506
Chorazin, 454
chosen. See election
Christian: as "the called," 531–32;
    equipped with everything good,
    641–42
Christian life: commands and certainty
    in, 579; drifting in, 595; mystery of,
    654; as struggle, 604
Christian willing, 513
Christlikeness, 616, 676–81, 684
church: creation of, 80–81; as focus of
    Christ's glory, 318; purchased and
    secured, 580
clinging to God, 122, 123

collapse of tower, 505
command-and-warning strategy of
    providence, 593, 594–607, 609–10,
    620, 638
command(s) of God, 483, 486–87,
    578–79, 92
complexity, in desires of God, 548–49
conception, 344, 344–48, 350, 353, 507
condemnation, 360, 501, 626–27
confidence, 595, 607, 611, 614
conformity to Christ, 614, 615–16,
    620, 626, 630, 638, 643; happens
    progressively, 677
conquest of Canaan, 118–23, 157,
    365–67, 374
conscience, 632
consummation, of redemptive history,
    667
contingent reality, 91
conversion, 514–17, 543
corporate worship, 604
counsel, 609
counsel of God's will, 406–7, 691, 698.
    See also whole counsel of God
counterintuitive wonders, in the Bible,
    14–15
courage, 614
covenant keeping, 460
covetousness, 114–15, 123
creation, 59–65, 157; declares glory of
    God, 62, 225–26, 230–31, 687;
    God's joy in, 226–27; groaning of,
    178, 612; liberation from futility
    and corruption, 686–87; overflows
    with "tastes of himself," 227, 229;
    renewal of, 339, 502–3; subject to
    futility, 178, 502
cross of Christ, 580, 623–24
culture, trivializing effects of, 698–700
Cyrus, 309, 393–94, 477–79

Daniel, 262, 291–94, 302, 389–90
Darius, 394–95
Dathan, 235
David, 349; adultery of, 456, 459, 497;
    census of, 470n1; on the exodus,

99–100; and Goliath, 234; as great
psalmist of Israel, 132–33; kingship
of, 316; sought to gaze on the beauty
of the Lord, 675
Davidic king, 297–98
dead in trespasses, 518, 522, 526, 541,
553
death: defeat of, 185, 339–41; as enemy,
360; as God's judgment, 360; and
hand of Satan, 264–65; sorrows of,
372; terrors of, 341–42. *See also* life
and death
deception, 463–73
Declaration of Independence, 337,
355–56
decree, 264, 458, 483, 484
dehumanization, 331, 333
delight: and fear, 160–61; in God, 161,
163, 186, 681, 684, 693
deliverance, through being hated, 444–46
Demas, 605
demeanor, casualness in, 698–99
dementia, 516
demons, 185, 255, 257, 262–63
denying Christ, 595
despair, 579
disasters, 479–81. *See also* natural disasters
discipline, 418, 597
disease: Satan's cause of, 268–71; Satan's
power of, 272
disobedience, 518
Dissertation Concerning the End for
Which God Created the World
(Edwards), 43
divine call, 613
divine hardening, 435–39, 440, 442–43
divine "seeing to it," 411n1, 513
Donaldson, Kevin, 377–80
doubt, 333
down payment, 619
dramatic conversions, 516, 517
dread, in adversaries of God, 391
dullness, of human hearing, 465–66

earnestness, 595
earth, not autonomous, 236

earthquakes, 236
Edwards, Jonathan, 42, 43, 217–18; on
affections, 147–49; on glory of God,
53; on humility, 697; on natural and
moral ability, 508n3
effective call, 531–32
Egypt: death of firstborn, 374; hearts
turned to hate Israel, 431–34; pride
of, 127; plagues of, 92–93, 246,
437–38
election, 443, 515, 559–73; in Gospel of
John, 566–70; of individuals, 109n2
Elihu, 238, 266–67
Eli's sons, 373, 450–52, 453–54, 455
Elizabeth, 349–50
Elliot, Elisabeth, 378, 379–81
Elliot, Jim, 379, 380
emotion(s): divine, 361n5; human, 147,
391
endurance, 591
energy, of providence, 215, 216
Esau, 106, 442; no place of repenting,
452–53
Esther, 444
eternal life, 185, 624, 683
eternal security, 616
ethnic Israel, 71, 74, 106
evangelical humiliation, 147
evangelism, and providence, 709–10
"every tribe and language and people and
mission," 658, 663
evil, 276, 488; God meant for good, 177,
426–27; out of house of David,
459–60
evil spirits. *See* demons
exile, 137–38, 146, 147, 157, 333, 389,
491
exodus, 87–88, 92, 97, 157, 431; and
glory of God, 109–10; and God's
name, 92–94, 103; remembering,
99–110
exorcism, 258
experience, of the riches of grace,
199–200
Ezekiel: on Israel in the wilderness,
116–18; on jealousy of God, 144–45

Ezra, 309

faith: creation of, 532; fruit of, 644; as
a gift, 543–45, 538, 539–45, 651,
708; as instrument of transformation, 648; produces love, 648–49;
and sanctification, 649–50; temporary lapses of, 605–6; unites us to
Christ, 545; working through love,
600, 644–45
faithfulness, 372, 700
faithless, 596
fall, 359–60; ordained by God, 176–77,
180
false brothers, 605
false prophets, 467–71
false teaching, 706
family sorrows, 449, 461
famine, 238, 243, 265, 369, 422–24
fatalists, 402
fate, 35–37, 375, 405
Father: draws those who come to Christ,
568–70; love for the Son, 680–81;
pleasure in the Son, 681
fear of death, 339
fear of the Lord, 96, 160–61
firstborn of Egypt, death of, 363–65,
500–501
first commandment, 113, 122
first creation, 64, 65, 67. *See also* creation
Fleming, Peter, 379
flesh and Spirit, 41, 522, 527
flood, 361–63; death of children in, 500
foreigner, Solomon's prayer for, 134
foreknowledge. *See* God, foreknowledge
of
forgiveness of sin, 56, 156–57, 166, 180,
185, 623–24, 625; and exaltation of
name of God, 134; as starting point
of the Christian life, 589
forming and creating and making,
478–79
freedom from bondage, 275–76
free will, 213–14, 557
fruit bearing, 193

fruit of the Spirit, 593, 639, 640, 647,
657
future providence, 578

Gabriel, 350
Gadites, apostasy of, 392
garden of Eden, 256
gathering of elect, 667–70
general call, 531, 532, 563n1
generosity, in affliction, 705
Gentiles: appointed to eternal life, 80,
565; inherit the blessing of Abraham, 73–75
Gideon, 126–28, 304
glorification, 187, 614, 624, 626, 655,
662, 677–78
glory of God, 53, 185, 195–96, 207, 689;
in creation, 61–62, 225–26, 231;
in nature, 62–63; in providence,
44–45, 101, 314–16; in sanctification, 654
God: absolute being, 90–92; as absolute
reality, 90; as absolute standard of
truth, goodness, and beauty, 91;
active in creation, 222–23; as actor
in Israel's history, 76–79; acts of
deception, 472–74; attributes of,
57n4, 210, 278, 403; cannot deny
himself, 324, 327; condescension of,
300–303; as constant, 91; created
the world for God, 61; creates what
he commands, 638; defeating Satan
with Satan, 280–82; defeating Satan
with savoring, 282–83; defeating
Satan by showing own attributes,
278; defeating Satan with suffering, 278–79; desires all people to
be saved, 547–48, 665–66; does
whatever he pleases, 91, 397–98;
exaltation of, 134, 300–303; faithfulness of, 325, 596, 616–17, 621;
fatherly hand of, 33; foreknowledge
of, 361n5, 472n3, 473, 561–62; glorified in the church, 81; glorified in
history of Israel, 79–80; glorified as
we are increasingly satisfied in him,

711; government of, 247–48, 386, 411–19; greatness and awe-fulness of, 699; hardens whom he will, 107, 109, 110; has mercy on whomever he wills, 107, 109, 110, 123; hates sin, 176; heart of, 493, 495; holiness of, 412–13, 444; independence of, 90; jealousy of, 143, 144–45; joy of, 85–86, 226–27, 515; judgment of, 359–60, 497, 703–4; kingship of, 290–91; knows the way of the righteous, 563; knows the wicked "from afar," 563; levels of motivation, 493; love of, 44, 490, 550, 618; mercy of, 367, 489–92, 550; name's sake of, 101, 116, 119, 131–32, 142, 324–27; never lies, 469, 470–71; no beginning or end of, 90; opens and shuts the womb, 345, 348–49, 353, 355; opposes human pride, 319–23; patience of, 142, 146, 665; "permission" of, 175–76; power of, 33, 315–16; "regretting" of, 361, 471–73; reputation of, 101, 102; righteousness of, 324–28, 369, 412, 703; rights over all life, 355, 359–69; "seeing to it," 411n1, 513; self-exaltation of, 23, 55–56, 208–10; self-sufficiency of, 60, 108, 211; sheer God-ness of, 346; sovereign in hardening, 442–43; sovereign in suffering, 270–71, 704; sovereignty of, 29, 332; supremacy and centrality of, 674, 688–89; supremacy in the law, 112–13; sustaining creation, 223–24; works are right and ways are just, 294, 323–28; at work in us, 651–52

God-centeredness, 372
God-exaltation, 528
"God meant it for good," 422, 426–28, 431
"God's Grandeur" (Hopkins poem), 20
God's workmanship, 543
golden chain, 614
Goliath, 234

good, from evil rulers, 309–10
good works, 193, 543, 624, 645
grace, 56–58, 207, 550; as apex of God's glory, 170; before the ages began, 172–73; and commands, 593–94; confounding, 147–49; exultation over, 658; through faith, 541–42; immeasurable riches of, 198–99; as indispensable, 541–43; precedes faith, 557; sanctifying power of, 580; triumphs through suffering, 179
Great Commission, 663

Haman, 444
hand of God, 293, 305–11
Hannah, 129–30, 345, 346
Hanson, R. P. C., 16
happiness, and holiness, 636
hardening, 431–44
hardness of heart, 388, 526
hardship, enduring, 194
harmony with believers, 193–94
hatred, 433; and hardening, 434–35, 444
healing, 185, 268
hearing the Word, 536
heart of flesh, 159
heart of stone, 158–59, 565
Heidelberg Catechism, on providence, 33, 446n2
hell, 670–71
heretics, use biblical words to defend their heresies, 16
Herod, 374, 403–4, 609
Hezekiah, 138, 140–42
holding fast to the faith, 594–96
holiness, 163, 599; of bride of Christ, 692–93; and happiness, 636; horizontal and vertical dimensions of, 636n1; and new covenant, 158; opposite of sin, 636; performance of, 611, 620, 635, 651–54; predestined from eternity, 638; promise of, 610–11, 620, 638; purchase of, 611, 620, 621, 623–33, 638; pursuit of, 583–87, 588, 591–92, 594, 620, 654; and reconciliation, 628

Holy Spirit: blows where he wills,
527–28; decisive in moment of conversion, 555; and faith, 649–50; in
the new covenant, 158–59; outpouring of, 65–66; sanctifying work of,
639–40; sealing of, 618–19; sent to
glorify Christ, 196; and transformation, 647–48
hope, 674, 676
Hophni and Phineas, 373, 450–52
Hopkins, Gerard Manley, 20
human accountability, 414–18, 429,
440–41, 443–44
human choices, 411, 414
human duty, to glorify God in Christ,
193–94
human kingships. See kingdoms of men
human regret, 472
human responsibility, 411–12n1
human self-determination, 414,
416, 562, 708. *See also* ultimate
self-determination
human self-exaltation, 40–41, 55–56,
331–32, 528
human will, 255, 385–410, 427–29, 513
humility, 330–32, 696–98
humor, 699
hurricanes, 362

I am who I am, 89–90, 93, 105–6, 108,
110, 145, 208–9, 210–11, 290, 399
image of Christ, 668
image of God, 62, 66, 255, 274, 356–57
immeasurable riches of grace, 540, 683
immortality, 228
"immortal until work is done," 376–77
imperatives: in the Gospels, 592; in
James, 593; in Paul, 593
imputed righteousness of Christ, 579,
588, 643
infants, death of, 359n3, 507–8
infertility, 353
ingathering, of people of God, 662–63
inhabitants of the earth, accounted as
nothing, 293, 299–304
innocent blood, 498

iron gate (figure of speech), 236n1
Isaac, 106, 348–49
Isaiah, 302; celebration of exodus, 101–2
Ishmael, 106
"I Sing the Mighty Power of God" (Watts
hymn), 267
Islam, on sovereignty of God, 403
Israel: anarchy in the time of the judges,
125; to be satisfied in God, 113; creation of, 80; in Egypt, 88, 388–89;
election of, 71, 72, 80, 104, 157;
history of, 76–79, 86; judgment on,
320, 371; monarchy of, 128–36,
297–99; pride of, 127; restoration
from exile, 146–50; slavery in Egypt,
88; as treasured possession, 112;
undeserved grace of, 120, 123; in the
wilderness, 116–18, 123, 127

Jacob, 106, 346, 349, 422–23, 426, 442
James: on human willing and doing,
399–402; on new birth, 535–36
Jehoshaphat, 139, 469
Jehovah-jireh (the Lord sees), 31
Jeremiah, 481–95, 549; on double evil of
adultery against God, 144; on the
exodus, 103; hope of, 489–94
Jeroboam, 373
Jerusalem: adultery of, 143–44; destruction of, 447, 475–76, 479, 482; as
a faithless wife, 141; God's defense
for the glory of his name, 137–42;
restored fortunes of, 149
Jesus Christ: abolished death, 361; blood
of, 57, 655–66, 171; bore our
condemnation, 626–27; death of,
180, 183, 278–80, 317, 339, 340,
631–32; enacts new covenant in
his suffering, 162–63; on family divisions, 449–50; fully man
and fully God, 167; glory of, 67,
168–69, 179, 341, 642, 654–55;
as goal of the new covenant, 167,
174; as ground of the new covenant,
166–67, 169, 174; holds all things
together, 248; keen eye for the provi-

dence of God, 245–47; kingship of, 135, 290, 296–99; laid down life for the sheep, 570–71; love of, 618; as mediator of the new covenant, 168; obedience of, 582; pierced for our transgressions, 580–81; resurrection of, 641; righteousness of, 615; second coming of, 197, 200, 665–72, 675–77, 685–88; sinlessness of, 167; as substitute, 520, 521; suffering of, 169–74, 177–79, 180, 183, 317, 278–80, 494; zeal for the glory of the Father, 194–95

Job, 270, 346, 691; bitter providence of, 265–67, 354–55; children of, 470; confession of pervasiveness of providence, 409–10; death of children of, 374; on the Lord giving and taking away, 344; repentance and blessedness of, 249–52

John, Gospel of, on election, 566–70

John the Baptist, 349–50

Jonah, 242, 245, 272

Joram, 346

Jordan, crossing of, 118

Joseph, 177, 386–88, 409, 421–29, 431–32

Joshua, 216

joy, 199–200, 208, 403–4, 682; ever-increasing, 683, 711; and fear, 160–61; as goal of providence, 86, 101, 150, 208; in God's mercy, 149; in the Lord, 84–86, 229–30

joyful worship, 95–97, 280

Judah, firstborn of, 373

Judas: temptation of, 273–74, 281; unbelief of, 569–70

judges, 125–26, 128, 157

judgment: on Assyrians soldiers, 367–68; of conquest, 365–67; in the flood, 362–63; follows unbelief and sin, 139–40; on Israel, 368–69, 476; on the nations, 366; through pagan rulers, 391–93; in Passover, 363–65; on pride, 320–22; and providence, 323; of suffering, 177–79

justification, 185, 531, 581–82, 614, 624, 662; as starting point of the Christian life, 589; and glorification, 606; and obedience, 584–85

killing sin, 583–87, 588, 596–99, 650

kingdom, given to lowliest, 294, 313–18

kings and rulers, 283–84, 287–94, 293, 295–99, 310–11, 313–33, 391–98

kingship of Israel: and glory of God's name, 131–32; and kingship of Christ, 135; as strange providence, 129, 131

knowing God, 22, 63, 156

knowing the providence of God, 294, 328–30

Korah, 235

Lamb who was slain, 172–74

Lamentations, 481–95

Last Supper, 165–66, 624

law: given at Sinai, 111, 122; written on hearts, 156–57, 186, 625

laws of nature, 18, 221, 239, 242

Lazarus, 196, 529, 531, 668

letter vs. Spirit, 640

levels, of God's desires, 548–49

Leviathan, 226, 272

Lewis, C. S., 21, 53–54, 329

Liddell, Eric, 22

life: as gift from God, 337–51; stewardship of, 357–58; as a vapor, 401–2

life and death: misperceptions of, 337, 356; providence over, 333, 350–51, 355, 371–75, 377

light and darkness, 274–75, 478

lilies of the field, 243

logic, 214–15, 415

LORD, 87

Lord's Prayer: first petition, 142; and progressive glorification, 189

Lord's Supper, 604

love, 404; as essence of holiness, 636n1; and freedom from self-focus, 705; for God, 613; and holiness, 599–600; in midst of affliction,

705; for neighbor, 600, 627; not an option for Christians, 587; pursuit of, 599–602
loving the darkness, 519, 523
loving like the Father, 681–82
lowly, exaltation of, 315–17
luck, 405
Luther, Martin, 262
lying spirit, 469–70

McCully, Ed, 379
Manasseh (half-tribe), 392
Manasseh (king), 366
Marshall, Barry, 272
Martyn, Henry, 376–77
martyrdom, 376, 619–20
Mary, 350, 695–96
means of grace, 603
means of providence, 603–4
Melchizedek, 129
membership in the local church, 604
mercy and hardening, 439, 441–43
Micaiah, 469
Michael, 262
Midianites, 126–28
"Mighty Fortress is Our God, A," (Luther hymn), 262
Miriam, 97, 695
miscarriage, 353
missions: and providence, 709–10; triumph of, 661–72
Moab, judgment on, 320–21
modern science, 221; and Satan's deception, 256–57
monarchy, 157
money, love of, 648–49
moral inability, 508n3, 528
Mordecai, 444
more than conquerors, 375, 445
Mosaic covenant, 156
Moses, 88, 346, 695; and hardening of Pharaoh, 431–38; sought to see God's glory, 675
Mount Moriah, 30–31
Mount Sinai, 111
mouth of God, 483, 487

murder, 356
mutual exhortation and encouragement of believers, 604
mystery, of providence, 24, 443, 446, 651, 692
"mystery of Christ," 163

Naaman, 346
Nabal, 373
name of God, 82–83, 324–27; and joy of his people, 82–84
Naomi, 354
narrow door, 604
Nathan, 456, 459
natural inability, 508n3
natural disasters, 265–68, 358–59, 362, 703
natural human willing and acting, 385–410
naturalists, 224
natural life, 342
natural person, 385, 521
natural world, dangers of, 233–34
nature, 221
Nebuchadnezzar, 291–92, 295, 300, 308; beast-like experience, 313; as God's servant, 392–93; homage to Daniel, 389–90; humbling of, 314, 330–31; praise of God, 323, 329; pride of, 313
Nehemiah, 103–4
new birth, 526–29, 532–35, 538
new covenant, 151, 155–63, 492, 494, 560, 564–65; in Christ's blood, 165–66; through death of Christ, 162–63; enactment of, 165, 179, 185–86; as everlasting covenant, 160; obedience commanded and created, 640–41; and power to obey commands, 593; promise of, 617, 624–25, 639; vindicates holiness of God, 158
new creation, 65–66, 536–37, 538, 677, 693; "in Christ," 66; and progressive sanctification, 188–89
new heavens and new earth, 515, 686–88

new life, 275, 529, 534, 613, 639. *See also* new birth
New Testament, on righteousness of God, 326–27
Nicholson, Martha Snell, 381
Nicole, Robertson, 699
northern kingdom, 128–29

obedience, 115–16, 579–80, 589, 599, 620; and blessing, 138–39; and decisive strength of God, 654, 656; through faith, 645; through Jesus Christ, 642; and justification by faith, 584–85; in the new covenant, 157, 159; performed by God, 635, 637–38, 643; rooted in acceptance with God, 645; secured at the cross of Christ, 623–24
"obedience of faith," 138–39, 645
offspring, 344, 347
old covenant, 157, 159, 640
Old Testament, on righteousness of God, 324–25
Olson, Roger, 551–53
orderly arrangement, providence as, 34
ordinary human willing, 513
original sin, 508
outward call. *See* general call
Owen, John, 25n5, 121n3

pain, 275, 276, 282, 380, 503–5, 506–7
parable of the soils, 605
Passover, 363–65, 374
paths of righteousness, 194
patience, and providence, 700
patience endurance, 194
Paul: on Adam's sin, 501; on affliction, 491; on appearing of the glory of Christ, 674–75; on armor of God, 650; before the Areopagus, 347; on call of God, 530; on cleansing out old leaven, 586; commissioning of, 709–10; on creation, 64, 501–2; on deliverance through being hated, 445; on the exodus, 106–8; on glorification, 677; on grace of God, 653; on hardening of Pharaoh, 439–41; on history of Israel, 76–79; on the Holy Spirit, 555–56, 618–19; on human willing and doing, 399; lists of sins that keep unrepentant out of kingdom of God, 598–99; on made alive in Christ, 540–41; on magnifying Christ, 688; on new birth, 536; on new creation, 537; prayer of, 708; on preconversion condition, 518; on providence, 696; on reconciliation, 627–28; on the resurrection, 227–28; on rising from spiritual death, 529–30; thorn in the flesh, 280–81; on whole counsel of God, 609–10; on wrath of God, 519–21
peace, 390, 478
peaceful conscience, 632
penal substitution, 520
people of God: creation and transformation of, 217; gathered into one flock, 663; as multitude of nations, 288–89; peculiar glory of, 318
perfectionism, 596, 656–57
permission. *See* planned permission
persecution, 263–64, 333
perseverance, 514–15, 595, 606–7, 616–18
Peter: on death of Christ, 631; death of, 375; denial of Christ, 605–6; on new birth, 535; on ransom, 630; repentance of, 606; temptation of, 273–74
Pharaoh, 93, 127, 363, 365; God's glory over, 94; hardening of, 429, 431, 435–38; heart turned to bless Joseph, 386–88
philosophy, 212, 213, 215
photosynthesis, 224–25
physical pain, as judgment, 503–7
Pilate, 505
plan, 609, 698. *See also* whole counsel of God
planned permission, 180, 237, 276
planning, 405–6

plants, 242–44, 272
pleasure, 282; everlasting and ever-
increasing measures of, 673, 679–83;
of praising God, 185
poetry, 489
Pontius Pilate, 403–4, 609
Potiphar, 386
potter and clay, 109, 443
power encounters, 258, 259
praise, 53–54, 52–53, 54–55, 56–58,
110, 207, 248–49
praising and prizing, 207, 688–89
prayer, 604; answered and unanswered,
268–70; and providence, 706–8
predestination, 51–52, 561–62, 614, 638,
662
preservation, 612–13
presumption, 579
prevailing sanctifying providence of God,
637–38
prevenient grace, 550–57
pride, 127, 294, 319–23
prizing Christ, 688–89
progressive glorification, 187–93
progressive sanctification, 187–88, 678
promises of God, 347–48, 586–88
propitiation, 183–84
proverb, as general rule or universal truth,
396–97
providence: in age to come, 198; as a
biblical reality, 17; in bringing to
faith, 525–26; and bringing God's
people from conversion to glory,
586; climactic work of, 673–89; and
confident planning, 405–6; in conversion, 514–15; designed to bring
us to glorification, 589; eternal roots
of, 559, 578; and evangelism and
missions, 709–10; in the exodus,
110; and fearless witness, 405; and
glory of God, 44–45; goal of, 23–24,
115–16, 185, 514–15, 635–36, 647,
673, 692–93; as God's purposeful
sovereignty, 18, 29; as God's seeing to, 31; and gospel joy, 403–4;

in hearts of ordinary folk, 398; as
humanizing truth, 332; justice and
righteousness of, 323; as keeping,
574; and love, 404; mystery of, 24,
443, 446, 651, 692; nature and
extent of, 24, 207, 210–11, 216,
514–15, 635, 673, 691–92; and
new birth, 536; and new covenant,
157–58; not haphazard, 610;
over animals, 272; over the earth,
234–36; over hatred, 433; over
hearts of God's enemies, 386–90;
over kings and nations, 283–84,
287–94, 295–98, 310–11, 313–33;
over life and death, 333, 350–51,
355, 371–75, 377; over nature,
221–31, 233–52; over Old Testament nations, 289–90; over Satan,
259–76; over saving faith, 399; over
sin, 411–19, 421, 431, 447, 473,
509; as perfectly righteous, 327–28;
in persevering faith, 514–15; as
pervasive, 409–10; planning of,
572; and prayer, 706–8; presumes
creation, 59; prompts humility,
696–98; as purposeful sovereignty,
691; as saving providence, 513; as
sending, 424–25; stages of, 157; and
suffering, 703–6; in turning foreign
kings against Israel, 306–8; in
turning foreign kings to help Israel,
308–9; and wisdom, 656–57; word
not found in the Bible, 15, 16; and
worship, 694–96
providing, as "seeing forward," 30
psalms: exult in the exodus, 99–101; on
providence, 695
pursuing love, 599–602

quail, 246
quantum mechanics, 484

Rachel, 345, 349
Rahab, 93–94, 95, 368
rain, 238–39
raised with Christ, 554

ransom, 22, 65–66, 535, 630, 632, 662–63

ravens, 245, 246

Rebekah, 348

reconciliation, 193; for sake of holy living, 627–28

redemption, accomplishment of, 582–83

Red Sea, 118

regeneration, partial and complete, 552–53

regret, 361n5

Rehoboam, 451–52

rejoicing, in providence of God, 294, 328–30

repentance, 275–76, 504–7; as a gift, 276, 455; as a gift of providence, 539, 546–47; summons to, 368

resistance, to man-centered substitutes, 706

resurrection, 339, 554, 668

resurrection body, 227–28, 684, 685

Reuben, 423

Reubenites, apostasy of, 392

revealed will of God, 458

righteousness, through faith in Christ, 581–82

right to life, 356–57

rocks of refuge, providence as, 418–19

rulers and authorities. *See* kings and rulers

Ruth, 349

Saint, Nate, 379

Saint, Steve, 378, 379

salvation, 64, 516, 554

Samuel, 130

sanctification, 163, 580, 585, 624; as blood-bought, 625–26; of bride of Christ, 692–93; mystery of, 611; perfection of, 678; as slow process, 656–57

Sarah, 347

Satan, 375; appears to have control over natural world, 252; deceiver of the whole world, 256; ongoing existence of, 277–84; power of, 274–75, 703; as roaring lion, 272; as ruler of this world, 260–62; subject to providence, 276; ten powers of, 260–76; two strategies of, 256–58; will of, 255–76

satisfaction in God, 115, 637

Saul, 130, 316, 361n5, 373, 471–72

savoring, 282–83

Scripture. *See* Bible

sealing, 619–20

seas, obey Christ's command, 237

seated with Christ, 554

second commandment, 113

seeing the Lord in the greatness of his glory, 675–77

seeing and savoring providence of God, 693–711

self-determination. *See* human self-determination; ultimate self-determination

self-exaltation. *See* God, self-exaltation of; human self-exaltation

self-hardening, 435–39

sending, providence, as, 424–25

Sennacherib, 138, 140, 373–74

serving the Lord with gladness, 114–15, 121

Seth, 344

shalom, 478

Shimei, 457–59

Sidon, 453–54, 455

sifting, 273

sin: of deception, 447, 463–73; desperation over, 658; elimination of, 687; of family against family, 447, 449–61; freedom from, 679; as pride, 127; serves God's purposes, 447; and temptation of Satan, 272–74; warfare with, 658. *See also* killing sin

slaves of sin, 518, 522

Solomon, 459; building of temple, 134–35; kingship of, 316; prayer of dedication of the temple, 133–34

Son of David, 290

song of the Lamb, 173–74, 687

song of Mary, 695–96

song of Miriam, 695
song of Moses, 695
Son of God, as Redeemer-King, 302–3
soul, creation of, 342–43
souls, perfected at the coming of Christ, 678–79
southern kingdom, 129
sovereign grace, 131, 519n2
speculation, 212
speech, casualness in, 698–99
"spirit of divination," 258
spiritual body, 685
spiritual bondage, of Satan, 275–76
spiritual death, 541
spiritual life, 342
spiritual resurrection, 518
spiritual warfare, 658
Sproul, R. C., 698
Spurgeon, Charles, 35–36, 699
stability, 614
"staying God's hand," 293, 303–4
stewardship of life, 357–58
stillbirth, 353
"Stone and the Snake, The" (Piper poem), 269–70
strangeness of the ways of God, 15
stumbling stones, providence as, 418–19
suffering, 194, 404, 612; as a gift, 543–44; and providence of God, 703–6; and sovereignty of God, 270–71; terrors of, 341–42; way to glory, 494
sunrise, 21–22
sword of the Spirit, 650

temple, building of, 134–35
temptation to sin, 272–74, 657–58
Ten Commandments, 111, 112
tenth commandment, 114–15
this age, 667
thorn in the flesh, 280–81
"times of ignorance," 75
total depravity, 552, 557
tower of Babel, 67–68
tragedy, 378–80

transformation, 181, 182, 192, 624, 639, 643, 647–48, 656; of the body, 668–69; of God's people, 186; as slow process, 656–57; "will be like him," 676–79
treasure, of providence, 215, 216
treasuring the glory of Christ, 181, 183
treasuring God, 637
trifling with divine things, 698–700
true Israel, 74
truth, of providence, 323
tsunamis, 358, 362
Tyre, 321, 453–54, 455

ultimate self-determination, 212–13, 214–15, 415, 416, 514, 553, 708
unbelief, and judgment, 139
unclean spirits, 262–63
unconditional hardening, 441–43
understanding, 255
UNICEF, 353
union with Christ, 545, 582, 643, 645
universal statements, and specific applications, 482–83
universe: exists for the glory of Christ, 63; renovation of, 658; as secondary to God, 91; set free from bondage, 673–74, 683–88; as theater of God's glory, 198, 684
Uzzah, 373
Uzziah, 480

vigilance, 611
viligance, and confidence, 607
vine and branches, 519n2
virgin birth, 350

walking by faith, 593, 675
warnings. See command-and-warning strategy of providence
Warren, Robin, 272
water, obeys God's command, 235–37
Watts, Isaac, 267
welcoming other believers, 194
well-being and calamity, 478
Wesleyans, 551
Wesley, John, 552

Westminster Confession of Faith, 34–35, 44–45
Westminster Larger Catechism, on providence, 34
Westminster Shorter Catechism, on chief end of man, 38
White, T. H., 700
whole counsel of God, 609–10, 633
wife, supremely satisfied in her husband, 113–14
wilderness wandering, 116–18
will of the flesh, 533
will of God, 156, 186, 255, 270, 405, 433, 443, 458, 687; intersection with human willing, 427–29; and sin, 177
"will of a male," 533–34
wind, providence over, 239–41
wisdom, of providence, 656–57
witness, 405
womb, opening and closing of, 345, 348–49, 353, 355

Word of God, not bound, 664
words, and reality, 15–18
works of faith, 190–91, 645, 655
world: corruption of, 503; and God-entranced, 18–22; judgment on, 322, 503; response to God's providence, 241–42; as theater of God's glory, 227, 228–29; as theater of God's providence, 217–18; as theater of God's wonders, 242
worldliness, oblivious to vastness of God, 509
worship, 95–97
wrath of God, 518, 519–21, 703–4; propitiation of, 183–84

Yahweh, 87–88, 89–90
Youderian, Roger, 379
Young, E. J., 83

zeal for good works, 629–30
Zion, as name of joy, 149–50

Scripture Index

Genesis

1:1	223
1:4	225
1:10	225
1:12	225
1:18	225
1:21	225
1:25	222, 225
1:27	255
1:27–28	62, 182, 360
1:31	360, 502
2:17	179, 359, 360, 503
3	272, 359
3:1–6	65
3:4	337
3:6	503
3:12	503
3:14–19	273, 502, 503
3:15	179
3:16	178
3:17	178
4–11	67
4:1	344
4:25	344
5:20	427
6:5–7	361–62
6:6	361n5
6:7	362
6:13	362
6:17	362
7:22–23	362
8:21	362, 363
9:5–6	356–57
11:4	68
11:7–8	287

11:30	347
12	71
12:1–3	112
12:2	288
12:2–3	72
12:3	73
12:7	289
13:16	347
14:20	129
15:5	347
15:6	105, 139
15:16	120, 365
16:2	348, 353
16:10	347
17:4–5	288
17:6	289, 347
18:10	348
18:11	347
18:13–14	348
18:18–19	562
18:25	413
19:24	242n4
20:6	176
20:18	353
21:1–2	348
22:7	30
22:8	30, 31
22:14	30, 31
22:18	139
25:21	348
26:2	349
26:4	349
28:14–15	349
28:15	347
29:31	349

30:1–2 .... 345, 346
30:2 353
30:22 349
37:2 424
37:4–5 422–23
37:8 422–23
37:18–20 423
37:22 423
37:25–28 423
37:28 425
37:36 424
38:7 373
39:3 409
39:3–4 386
39:20 424
39:21 .... 387, 425
39:21–22 386
39:23 409
41:40–44 387
41:41 424
43:14 388
45:3 424
45:5 425
45:5–8 424
45:7 .... 177, 425, 432
45:8 425
47:1–12 422
50:16–17 426
50:17 .... 426, 429
50:19–21 426
50:20 .... 177, 276, 369, 422,
                      425, 426, 429, 432,
                      433

Exodus
1:8–10 431–32
1:16 432
2:24 104
3:10 88
3:11–12 88
3:13–15 88–89
3:14 .... 89, 110, 113, 123,
                      145, 145n1, 208,
                      210, 290, 399
3:15 89
3:20 246

3:21–22 388
4:3–4 246
4:11 270
4:21 .... 436, 438, 439, 446
4:22–23 .... 363, 365
6:5 104
6:6–7 92
6:7 .... 112, 113
7:1–4 436
7:3 .... 436, 437, 439
7:5 .... 93, 113
7:13 .... 436, 438
7:14 436
7:22 .... 436, 438
8:1–15 246
8:10 93
8:15 .... 436, 438, 439
8:16–17 272
8:16–19 246
8:19 .... 436, 438, 439
8:20–32 246
8:22 .... 93, 246
8:32 .... 436, 438
9:7 436
9:12 .... 436, 438
9:14 .... 93, 95
9:16 .... 93, 94, 95, 100, 107,
                      110, 118, 437, 439
9:34 436
9:35 436
10:1 .... 93, 436, 437
10:1–2 .... 436–37, 439
10:3 127
10:4 246
10:13 240
10:19 240
10:20 436
10:27 436
11:4–8 363
11:5 363
11:7 364
11:9 .... 93, 97, 437, 439
11:10 436
12:7 364
12:13 364
12:23 364

12:29 . . . . 364, 365, 500
12:33 389
12:35–36 388
12:36 389
14:4 . . . . 93, 94, 95, 109, 388, 436
14:8 436
14:17 . . . . 95, 109, 436, 437
14:17–18 . . . . 94, 439
14:18 . . . . 93, 96, 113, 435, 437
14:24–25 248
14:31 96
15:1 695
15:1–3 96
15:4 695
15:7 695
15:10 240
15:11 . . . . 444, 695
15:19 237
15:20 97
15:21 . . . . 97, 695
16:4 248
16:11–13 246
19:1 111
19:4 112
19:4–5 111
19:5 . . . . 112, 234, 343
20:2–3 112
20:3 . . . . 113, 122
20:4–5 113
20:5 113
20:13 . . . . 356, 458n1
20:17 114
21:23–25 497
23:23–24 365
32 116
33:18 675
33:19 107

Leviticus
19:2 457
26:6 246
26:27–29 499
26:29 . . . . 369, 487

Numbers
14:11 120
14:21 . . . . 63, 182, 186, 655
14:21–23 116
16:30–32 235
20:8 238
23:19 . . . . 433, 474n4

Deuteronomy
2:25 391
4:20 112
6:5 159
7:16 366
8:16 127
9:4–7 . . . . 120, 123, 366
9:7 116
10:14 . . . . 105, 234, 343
10:14–15 104
11:4 237
11:6 235
17:14–20 129
17:15 289
17:20 129
19:13 498
28:12 238
28:22 238
28:37 369
28:45 499
28:49 307
28:49–57 476
28:53 . . . . 369, 499
28:53–57 487
28:63 548
29:4 . . . . 161, 640
29:24–25 372
29:29 . . . . 433, 484, 692
30:6 . . . . 161, 492, 561, 707
30:9–10 161
30:20 122
32:4 . . . . 327, 412, 703
32:39 . . . . 264, 346, 355
33:29 . . . . 122, 128

Joshua
2:8–10 368
2:8–11 95

2:9–11 93–94
3:15–17............. 118
4:21–24............. 118
4:24 .... 118, 119, 123, 125, 131
5:13–15............. 216
7:6 119
7:7–9 119
10:12–13 248
11:6 366
11:20............... 366, 450
21:45............... 121
22:5 .... 121, 122, 123, 125, 159
23:9–11............ 121
23:11............... 121, 122, 123
23:14............... 121
23:16............... 139
24:1–13............ 79n1
24:2–3 72
24:7 237
24:19............... 113

Judges
2:11 125
2:16–19............ 126
3:8 306
6:1 126
6:10 126
6:16 126
6:34 126
6:36 304
7:2 .... 127, 128, 131, 304
7:2–3 126–27
7:3 126
7:7 128
7:12 128
7:22 .... 128, 391
7:23–25............ 391
17:6 125
21:25............... 125

Ruth
1:6 243
1:13 354
4:13 349

1 Samuel
1:5 .... 345, 353
1:11 345
1:19–20............ 345
2:4 694
2:5–6 345
2:6 265
2:6–7 694
2:6–8 317
2:7 409
2:10 129–30
2:22–25............ 450
2:25 .... 373, 450, 451, 453
2:34 451
3:9 216
4:11 451
7:10 248
8:11–18............ 130
9:21 316
11:15............... 130
12:12............... 130–31
12:17............... 130–31, 315
12:20–22 130–31
12:22............... 131, 132
13:14............... 132
14:6 303
15:1 130
15:3 471
15:9 471
15:11............... 361n5, 471, 472
15:24............... 471
15:28–29 472
15:29............... 361n5, 433, 472, 473
15:33............... 498
15:35............... 471, 472
16:11............... 316
17:37............... 246
19:5 498
25:38............... 373

2 Samuel
6:7 373
7:8–9 316
7:13–16............ 297
12:9–12............ 456

12:10–12 459
12:11 .... 456, 459
12:11–12 .... 463, 497
12:12 459
13:28–29 459
16:5–7 457
16:9 457
16:11 .... 457, 458
16:22 459
18:14 459
18:33 456
19:18–20 458
22:31 .... 474n4
23:1 132
24:1 .... 470n1

1 Kings
2:23–25 459
3:6 349
3:7 316
9:8–9 372
11:11 451
12:15 451
12:24 451
17:4 246
17:14–16 248
18:38 .... 242n4
20:23 303
20:27–29 303
21:19 469
22 471
22:6 469
22:11 469
22:12 469
22:17 469
22:19–23 469–70
22:22 .... 470, 473
22:34 469
22:38 469

2 Kings
1:10 .... 242n4
3:17 238
3:20 238
4:41 238
5:7 346

6:6–7 238
8:1 243
13:3 307
15:37 307
17:6–8 129
19:6–7 373–74
19:32 367
19:34 138
19:34–35 367
19:36–37 373–74
20:6 138
21:9 366
25:1–12 129

1 Chronicles
5:18 139
5:20 139
5:25–26 392
10:13–14 373
10:14 316
14:17 391
17:16 99
21:1 .... 470n1
29:12 409

2 Chronicles
6:4 347
6:18 133
6:21 133
6:24–25 133
6:26–27 133
6:32 135
6:32–33 134
7:13 238
7:20–22 372
10:7 451
10:15 451
13:20 373
20:6 .... 291, 304
20:15 304
20:20 139
25:8 314
25:20 451
26:5 139
27:6 139
28:6 140

32:8 304

Ezra
1:1–2 309
1:1–3 394
5:13–16 394
6:8 395
6:22 . . . . 309, 395
7:21–22 395
7:27 . . . . 309, 395

Nehemiah
1:9 475
1:11 160
2:8 395
9:7 72
9:8 325
9:9–11 103–104
9:10 . . . . 105, 108, 109, 110,
          127
9:11 237
9:27 308
9:33 176

Job
1:6 470
1:11 265
1:12 . . . . 265, 470
1:15 265
1:16 266
1:17 265
1:18–19 266
1:19 . . . . 252, 354, 470
1:20–21 266
1:21 . . . . 22, 265, 267, 344,
          351, 353, 354, 355,
          374, 381, 470
1:21–22 507
1:22 . . . . 266, 344, 354, 470
2:7 . . . . 252, 270, 354
2:9 . . . . 270, 354
2:10 . . . . 270, 354
5:11 315
6:26 241
7:5 354
9:5 235
9:5–6 235

9:6 236
10:12 . . . . 29n1
12:10 . . . . 244, 305, 357, 375
12:23 . . . . 314, 333
33:4 357
34:14–15 350–51
37:10 237
37:11–13 238–39
37:11–14 266–67
38–41 . . . . 249, 252
38:4 . . . . 226, 234, 249
38:6–7 226
38:8 . . . . 249, 358
38:12 250
38:17 250
38:19 250
38:22 250
38:31 250
38:35 250
38:39 250
38:41 244
39:5 250
39:19 250
39:26 250
40:4–5 . . . . 237, 251
40:8 249
40:15 226
40:20 226
41:6 354
41:11 . . . . 343, 355, 357
42:1 236
42:2 . . . . 251, 319, 355, 410,
          691
42:6 . . . . 251, 252
42:10 252
42:11 . . . . 270, 355, 470

Psalms
1:2 604
1:6 563
2:2–4 261
5:11 150
5:4 412
8:3 . . . . 145, 234, 684
9:5 320
10:16 290

11:7 ...... 327, 703
12:6 ...... 474n4
16:11 ...... 85, 183, 185, 339, 578, 679, 711
18:27 320
19:1 ...... 21, 62, 200, 230, 249, 643, 684
19:4–5 21
20:5 150
22:4 139
22:28 290
23:3 ...... 142, 194, 208
23:5 410
24:1 ...... 234, 343, 357
24:1–2 355
25:10–11 460
25:11 ...... 134, 142, 326, 460
27:4 675
29 248
29:10 290
31:3 194
32:8–9 332
32:9 255
33:4 ...... 474n4
33:10 304
33:10–11 ...... 261, 695
34:19 140
37:4 159
37:40 139
40:8 186
44:22 ...... 140, 390, 445
45:6 167
46:8–9 695
47:8 291
48:11 548
50:6 327
50:12 ...... 234, 343
51 425
51:5 507
57:5 711
58:10 548
60:2 235
62:1 434
63:1 338
63:3 338
66:1–3 96

67 76
67:4 96
68:20 374
72:19 186
73:24–26 338
73:26 122
75:7 314
78:19 246
86:9 ...... 291, 296
86:9–10 95
89:8–9 358
89:11 234
89:14 ...... 325, 412
90:4 665
90:14 637
92:4 330
92:5 434
93:2 290
94:10 320
95:6 343
96:11–13 ...... 200, 548
96:12 63
96:13 355
97:2 ...... 325, 327, 703
97:3 ...... 242n4
98:7–9 200
98:8 63
98:9 ...... 328, 703
100:2 116
100:3 ...... 343, 507
103:22 330
104:8–9 224
104:10 233
104:10–14 223
104:14 ...... 224, 233
104:14–15 242–43
104:24 ...... 176, 229
104:24–25 222
104:24–31 222
104:25–26 226
104:26 272
104:27–29 223
104:27–30 19
104:29 ...... 223, 233
104:30 222

104:31 . . . . .62, 225, 227, 229,
230, 249
104:32 235
104:33–34 . . . . .229, 249
104:34 . . . . .230, 230n1
105 99
105:1 434
105:1–3 434
105:14 320
105:16 243
105:16–17 425
105:17 . . . . .177, 432
105:23–26 432
105:25 . . . . .433, 434, 444, 446
105:29 238
105:32 237
105:36 364
105:41 238
105:42–43 100
105:43–45 434
106:6–10 100–101
106:7 . . . . .105, 109, 112
106:7–8 . . . . .101, 104, 108, 116
106:8 . . . . .131, 142
106:9 237
106:37–38 498
106:40 498
106:41 . . . . .308, 389
106:46 389
107:23–25 240
107:28–29 240
107:31 242
107:39–41 315
109:17 498
110:4 129
110:6 320
111:3 . . . . .328, 703
111:12 698
113:7 409
113:9 345
114:17 238
115:3 . . . . .397, 398
118:6 410
119:73 343
119:91 236
119:137 328

126:3 330
127:3 345
135:3 . . . . .133, 159
135:6 . . . . .364, 397, 398, 695
135:6–7 240–41
135:7 . . . . .19, 221
135:8 364
136:1 322–23
136:17–18 323
137:5–6 475
138:6 563
139:13 224
139:13–14 343–44
139:16 374
143 326
143:1–2 324–25
143:11 . . . . .142, 325
145:7 176
145:9 . . . . .176, 230
145:10 330
145:13 290
145:17 . . . . .176, 328, 412
147:4 234
147:5–6 315
147:8 . . . . .19, 221, 248
147:8–9 224
147:9 244
147:10–11 140
147:16–17 238
148:3 200
148:7–8 241
148:8 267

Proverbs
1:7 396
3:5–6 396–97
3:19 397
6:16–17 319
6:16–19 176
8:13 . . . . .319, 397
12:22 397
14:27 397
16:7 390
16:9 . . . . .406, 409
16:18–19 127
16:33 409

18:10................397
19:21................305, 406, 483
20:12................224
20:24................409
21:1 ....261, 306, 308, 311,
                    396, 397, 398,
                    398n2, 408
21:3 397
21:31................304, 409, 611
25:2 692
25:26...............390
30:5 ....474n4

Ecclesiastes
7:14 488
12:7 357

Song of Solomon
5:13 243

Isaiah
1:3...................332
2:11–12.............322
2:17 322
5:6...................238
5:16 ....319, 355
5:26 306
6:3...................412
6:9–10 464–65
6:10 465
7:18 306
9:6–7...............297–98
9:11 308
10:5–6 307
10:5–7 427
10:15...............307
11:3 160
11:9 63
13:11...............322
13:17...............308
13:19...............308
14:5 320
14:22...............308
14:27...............304
19:3 304
28:9 176
31:2 478

33:17................675
35:1 ....63, 200
36:1–10............138
37:16–17 141
37:20...............141, 142
37:21...............141, 142
37:21–22 141
37:35...............138, 141, 142
37:36...............44, 141
38:7 347
40:2 138
40:5 675
40:11...............300–301
40:15...............300–301, 302
40:17...............91, 300–301, 302
40:22...............302
40:22–23 300–301
40:23...............320
40:26...............234, 300–301, 302,
                    691
40:28...............230
40:28–29 300–301
40:29–31 301
40:31...............300–301
41:4 346
41:16...............84
41:25...............320
41:26...............361n5
42:1 681
42:5 ....365, 375
42:5–6 351
42:9 ....361n5
43:1 342
43:6–7 80
43:7 81
43:10...............346
43:13...............346, 410
43:21...............80, 81
43:25...............208, 346
44:8 211
44:18...............465
45:1 ....477, 478
45:3 477
45:4 477
45:5–7 ....477, 479
45:7 ....477, 484

45:12 234
46:9–10 . . . . 23, 212, 410, 428
46:10 . . . . 361n5, 472, 483,
                                        647, 691
48:3 347
48:9–11 39
48:11 208
48:12 346
49:3 . . . . 80, 81
51:12 346
51:17 520
51:22 520
53:1 465
53:4–6 . . . . 125, 520, 581
53:5 . . . . 185, 268, 631
53:6 520
53:10 . . . . 458n1
55:8 700
55:8–9 14–15
55:12 63
55:12–13 . . . . 82, 83, 85
55:13 82
57:15 302
57:16 . . . . 357, 374
60:21 81
61:1 . . . . 81, 162
61:3 . . . . 81, 162, 194
62:4–5 636
62:5 . . . . 226, 688
63:11–14 101–102
63:12 102
63:14 . . . . 102, 110, 159
65:9 349
65:17 686
65:17–18 84
65:19 85

Jeremiah
1:12 347
2:2 113
2:13 144
2:19 142
2:34 498
3:1 143
4:2 355
5:15 307

5:19 371
8:7 332
10:10 290
13:11 . . . . 80, 81
15:4 369
15:6 139
15:16 150
19:3–6 499
19:7 369
19:9 . . . . 369, 487, 499, 500,
                                        506
21:6 368
22:8–9 371
24:7 158
24:9–10 369
25:9 . . . . 307, 392
25:11 137
27:6 308
28:2–4 309
29:11 410
30:14 143–44
31:3 142
31:31 151
31:31–34 . . . . 155–56, 560,
                                        624–25
31:32 . . . . 156, 157
31:33 . . . . 156, 167, 186, 188,
                                        192, 561, 638
31:33–34 . . . . 174, 560
31:34 . . . . 156, 157, 166, 561,
                                        580
32:20 110
32:20–22 103
32:39–41 . . . . 159–60, 492
32:40 . . . . 160, 561, 617
32:41 . . . . 186, 226, 636
33:9 . . . . 146, 150
34:2 308
43:10 307
48:29–30 321
48:33 321
49:27 . . . . 242n4
50:29–30 322
51:11 . . . . 306, 393
51:20–23 392
51:24–25 393

51:29................393

Lamentations
1:1–2................137, 476
1:7................482
1:8................138, 482, 488
1:17................482, 486
1:18................481, 488, 493
2:2–4................487–88
2:6–7................487–88
2:10................482
2:16................486
2:16–17................485
2:17................486
2:20................485, 487, 490, 500
3................489
3:19–26................490
3:22–23................490
3:23................460
3:24................491
3:28–29................433
3:29................492, 494
3:30................494
3:31................433
3:31–33................492
3:32................492, 494
3:32–33................493, 549
3:37................457, 482, 483, 486
3:37–39................481, 488
3:38................458, 483, 484, 485, 487
3:39................482
3:43................368
3:64–66................486
3:65................464
4:10................487
4:10–11................500
4:11................242n4
4:22................488
5................489
5:16................488
5:21................492

Ezekiel
1:15–19................35
2:3–5................146

5:9–10................499
5:10................487
5:11–13................143
5:13................143, 144
5:16–17................243
9:4–6................368
11:19................561, 578, 707
11:19–20................625
12:15................144
14................471
14:6–11................468
14:7................468
14:9................469, 470, 471, 473
14:10................469
14:11................469
14:13................243
14:15................246
15:7................143, 144
16:8................113
16:14–15................320
16:31–34................143–44
16:37................320, 392
16:39................320
16:62–63................148
18:32................548, 549, 549n1
20:8–10................117
20:9................118, 123, 131
20:13–14................117
20:14................118, 123
20:21–22................117
20:22................118, 123
20:41–44................148
20:44................145
21:26................315
22:31................242n4
28:12................321
28:17................321
30:13................391
31:3................321
31:10–11................321
33:11................416, 548, 549, 549n1
33:29................145
35:6................498
36:20–23................148
36:21–27................158

36:22 146
36:24–36 149
36:26 . . . . 158, 159, 169, 188,
                         561, 564
36:26–27 . . . . 158, 492, 639
36:27 . . . . 23, 158, 561, 593,
                         619, 620, 624, 625,
                         638, 640, 641, 643,
                         647, 656, 707
36:29 243
39:25 113

Daniel
1:9 . . . . 389, 390
2:21 . . . . 261, 296, 314, 333
2:46 389–90
2:48 389–90
3:17 . . . . 242n4
4:16–17 . . . . 291, 328
4:17 . . . . 261, 293, 294, 296,
                         313, 315, 328
4:24–25 291
4:25 293
4:30 . . . . 300, 313
4:32 293
4:32–33 . . . . 294, 330
4:33 . . . . 292, 313
4:34 . . . . 323, 329, 331
4:34–35 . . . . 299–300, 314–15
4:34–37 292
4:35 . . . . 293, 302, 303
4:37 . . . . 294, 319, 323, 329,
                         428
5:20–21 292–93
5:21 . . . . 294, 330
5:22–23 293
5:23 . . . . 293, 305, 375, 507
5:26–28 293
5:30 . . . . 293, 305
6:22 246
6:23 139
7:13–14 298
9:6 138
9:14 . . . . 176, 328
10:13 262
12:2 375

Hosea
9:12 368

Amos
1:1 480
1:14 . . . . 242n4
3:2 . . . . 480, 562
3:3–6 479
3:6 . . . . 236, 479, 480
3:11 480
3:15 480
4:7 238
4:10 368
5:7 480
5:15 480
5:24 480
6:8 319
6:12 480
6:14 306
8:11 464
9:4 368

Obadiah
15 497

Jonah
1:17 . . . . 19, 245, 272
2:10 272
4:6 . . . . 19, 272
4:7 . . . . 19, 221, 272

Micah
1:5 138
4:11–12 427

Habakkuk
1:13 412
2:14 . . . . 63, 182, 186
3:17–18 84

Zephaniah
3:5 412
3:17 . . . . 85, 226, 636, 688

Haggai
1:11 238

Zechariah

2:8 . . . . 150, 476
11:16–17 . . . . 14, 464
12:1 . . . . 357, 374
12:10 75
14:2 308
14:13 391

Matthew

2:16 317
3:8 . . . . 539, 546
3:9 105
3:17 . . . . 200n1, 680, 681
4:3 272
5:5 289
5:8 . . . . 259, 675
5:11–12 . . . . 588, 705
5:15 644
5:16 . . . . 193, 644
5:18 245
5:27–30 601
5:29 598
5:44 404
5:45 238
6:9 . . . . 142, 189
6:12 623
6:14–15 601
6:24 649
6:26 . . . . 18, 223, 244, 245
6:28–30 . . . . 18, 243
6:33 . . . . 19, 244, 245, 410
7:2 497
7:9–10 268
7:13–14 602
7:18 . . . . 623, 624
7:21 603
7:26–27 602
8:17 631
8:24 631
8:25 631
8:26–27 239
8:27 237
9:27 135
9:38 664
10:1 262
10:22 445

10:28 . . . . 339, 343
10:28–29 405
10:28–31 247
10:29 691
10:29–31 18
10:31 405
10:33 596
10:37 . . . . 181, 275, 317, 603, 637
11:20–24 453–54
11:25 . . . . 466, 473, 671
11:25–26 . . . . 318, 466
11:27 245
12:32 . . . . 667n2
12:40 361
13:10–12 466
13:11 466
13:13 526
13:43 . . . . 136, 678, 685
13:44 159
14:13–21 317
14:17–21 245
14:25 237
14:30 237
15:7–8 688
16:17 466
16:18 . . . . 663, 710
17:5 . . . . 681, 688
17:27 245
18:3–4 127
18:4 318
18:17 604
18:21–35 602
18:34–35 602
19:19 404
19:24–26 522–23
19:26 . . . . 319, 708
19:29 365
20:15 454
20:26 318
21:5 135
22:1–14 . . . . 563n1
22:14 . . . . 120n3, 563
22:39–40 600
23:12 318
23:37 . . . . 416, 671

24:9 289
24:14 . . . . 663, 665, 666, 667, 674, 710
24:22 564
24:30 198
24:30–31 . . . . 667, 674
24:31 . . . . 564, 669
24:36 665
25:21 . . . . 136, 200, 636, 682
25:23 . . . . 200, 636
25:31–32 669–70
25:31–34 289
25:34 . . . . 610, 669–70
25:41 . . . . 255, 262, 669–70
25:41–46 601
25:46 . . . . 342, 669–70
26:28 . . . . 166, 580, 624, 625
26:34 273
26:39 520
26:60 473
26:67 494
27:37 135
28:18–20 663
28:19 289
28:19–20 . . . . 592, 604

Mark
1:24 555
1:27 263
6:3 317
8:2 449
8:38 596
9:22 257
9:29 259
10:27 460
10:34 340
13:11 664
13:12–13 450
13:13 . . . . 578, 607, 620
13:37 595
14:50 317

Luke
1:13 349
1:24–25 349
1:32–33 . . . . 136, 290, 296, 298

1:34 350
1:35 350
1:36 350
1:37 350
1:51–52 . . . . 317, 696
1:58 350
2:14 67
2:16 317
3:16–17 . . . . 242n4
3:8 565
4:5–7 260–61
4:18–19 81
5:5–6 245
5:21 56
6:20–21 365
7:13 449
7:21 262
8:3 317
8:9–10 466
8:10 466
8:13–14 605
8:14 595
8:24 . . . . 19, 237, 358
8:29 257
8:30 257
8:32 175
9:58 317
12:20 365
12:24 245
12:27 245
12:50 279
12:51–53 449–50
13:1–5 . . . . 504, 506
13:2 178
13:3 . . . . 178, 505, 507
13:5 . . . . 178, 505, 507
13:10–17 278
13:11 278
13:16 . . . . 268, 278
13:17 278
13:23–24 . . . . 120n3
13:24 . . . . 578, 604
13:32 340
14:13–14 587
14:14 365
14:33 . . . . 598, 601

16:25................365
18:7.................564
18:22...............407, 408
18:24–25............408
18:26...............408
18:27...............408
18:39...............317
19:14...............445
19:41...............671
19:41–42............671
20:34–35............667n2
21:16...............664
21:16–18............212
21:18...............410, 664
22:3................264, 281
22:3–4..............273
22:20...............151, 165, 560, 624,
                    638
22:31...............264
22:31–32............273, 605–6
22:52–53............264
24:27...............151
24:39...............685
24:42–43............668, 685

John
1:11................465
1:11–13.............532–33
1:12–13.............534
1:13................533, 534, 536
1:14................135, 674
1:49................135
2:19................340
3:3.................527
3:6.................533
3:6–8...............527, 538
3:8.................528
3:16................566, 571, 624
3:17................495
3:19................517
3:19–20.............523, 570
3:19–21.............519
3:21................519, 556n8
3:21b...............519n2
3:36................521
5:26................342

5:28–29.............375
5:39................150
6:37................570, 571
6:39................572
6:44................568, 569, 571, 572
6:63................527
6:64................473
6:64–65.............569
6:65................572
7:7.................445
7:15................317
7:30................264
7:46................317
8:20................264
8:31................515
8:44................257, 264, 265, 361
8:47................567, 568, 572
8:54................40, 56
10:3................664
10:14–15............570, 571
10:16...............569, 663
10:17...............340
10:17–18............340
10:18...............264
10:26...............567, 572
10:27–30............618
10:28...............618
10:28–29............572
10:30...............195, 681
10:35...............245
11:1–15.............196
11:4................196
11:43...............531, 668
11:43–44............529
11:51–52............662
11:52...............569, 662, 663
12:27–28............194, 196
12:31...............260
12:32...............569
12:37–40............465
13:3................317
13:11...............473
13:19...............472, 472n3
13:34–35............600
14:15...............603
14:15–18............528

14:16–17 196
14:18 196
14:21–23 259
14:26 528
14:30 260
15:5 .... 519n2
15:8 193
15:10 603
15:11 .... 136, 159, 682
15:12 600
15:16 564
15:17 600
15:18 445
15:20 390
15:26 196
16:11 260
16:14 .... 159, 196
16:21 353
17:2 342
17:5 .... 168, 195
17:6 .... 566, 567, 568, 569,
                       570, 571, 572, 573
17:9 .... 566, 568, 572
17:12 .... 571, 606
17:13 159
17:20 568
17:24 .... 136, 171, 181, 195,
                       338, 676, 680, 681
17:26 .... 159, 181, 200,
                       200n1, 680, 681,
                       682
18:37 .... 567, 572
19:10–11 314
19:30 580
20:20 668
20:27 668
21:5–6 245
21:18–19 375

Acts
1:7 665
1:16 273
2:23 .... 273, 458, 458n1
2:38 580
4:12 75

4:27–28 .... 263, 310, 369, 403,
                       458, 473, 509, 691
4:28 .... 79, 609
5:3–5 374
5:9–10 374
5:19 248
5:31 475
7:9–10 387
10:34 664
10:38 268
10:43 .... 580, 585
12:7 248
12:10 .... 236n1, 248
12:23 374
13 76
13:16–33 76–77
13:17 78
13:18 78
13:19 78
13:20 78
13:21 .... 78, 316
13:22 .... 78, 132
13:23 78
13:26 78
13:27 .... 78, 473
13:30 78
13:32 78
13:33 78
13:48 .... 565, 573, 664
14:16 75
14:17 .... 238, 367
14:22 .... 460, 643
15:14 664
16:14 .... 664, 708, 710
16:18 258
16:31 530
17:24 .... 236, 347
17:24–25 60
17:25 .... 347, 355, 357, 365,
                       375
17:26 287
17:28 248
17:30 75
17:31 .... 328, 355
18:10 664
19:4 .... 539, 546

20:20.................610
20:27.................609, 610
20:28.................580
24:2 ....29n1
24:15.................374
26:17–18 ....258–59, 710
26:18.................645

Romans
1:1–4.................290
1:5...................139, 645
1:7...................532
1:16 ....274, 530
1:19–20..............507
1:19–21..............211
1:20 ....62, 200, 230, 508,
                     644
1:20–21..............249
1:23 327
2:4...................367
2:6–7.................611
2:6–8.................670
2:11 664
2:28–29..............74, 106n1
3:3–4.................467–68
3:4...................474
3:4–6.................413
3:5–6.................520
3:23 ....176, 326, 327
3:23–25..............134
3:24 184
3:24–25..............508
3:25 ....168, 183, 184
3:25–26..............166, 327
3:28 ....508, 531, 582
4:5...................582, 585
4:7...................165
4:13 289
4:13–17..............288
4:15 ....652n3
4:16 ....73, 74
4:16–17..............288
4:20 142
4:25 167
5.....................505, 506
5:1...................503, 508, 531, 582

5:2...................228, 671, 676
5:3...................652n3
5:8...................680
5:9...................184, 274, 521
5:10 ....184, 193
5:12 ....179, 341, 501
5:12–14..............273
5:12–21..............502
5:13–14..............359n3
5:13–21..............65
5:15 501
5:16 501
5:17 ....359, 501
5:18 ....360, 501
5:19 ....185, 501, 507, 582,
                     585, 615, 624
5:21 501
6:1...................594
6:9...................554, 668
6:14 ....579, 623
6:17 ....517, 518, 657
6:23 ....176, 185
7:6...................159, 190, 593
7:8...................652n3
7:17 658
7:20 658
7:24 661
7:24–25..............658
8.....................506
8:1...................228, 520
8:3...................167, 520, 581, 615,
                     627
8:3–4.................626–27
8:4...................627, 639
8:6...................41
8:7...................454, 517
8:7–8.................41, 526
8:9...................41, 522
8:11 ....339, 669
8:13 ....583, 584, 585, 596,
                     650, 651
8:14 593
8:17 ....187, 573
8:18 705
8:18–25..............612
8:19–21..............686

8:20 . . . . 502, 503, 671
8:20–21 . . . . 65, 361
8:20–22 . . . . 178, 228, 273,
        501–2
8:20–23 . . . . 178n1
8:21 . . . . 163, 182, 200, 201,
        227, 229, 339, 502,
        503, 658, 687
8:22 . . . . 502, 505
8:23 . . . . 228, 503, 676
8:24–25 676
8:26 612
8:28 . . . . 268, 333, 445, 561,
        562, 612, 613, 614,
        615, 626, 705
8:28–30 . . . . 531, 562
8:28–32 375
8:28–39 . . . . 460, 612–13, 615,
        616
8:29 . . . . 23, 562, 573, 592,
        614, 615, 616, 621,
        624, 638, 643, 656,
        668, 677
8:29–30 . . . . 614, 626, 662, 677
8:30 . . . . 187, 188, 531, 614,
        615, 616, 617, 620
8:30–35 606
8:31 . . . . 410, 573, 614, 643
8:31–34 585
8:31–39 615
8:32 . . . . 22, 268, 560–62,
        571, 587, 615, 626,
        641, 642n2, 687
8:33 . . . . 564, 571, 573
8:34 571
8:35 . . . . 445, 571, 573, 612,
        615
8:35–37 579
8:35–39 . . . . 23, 375, 618
8:36 . . . . 140, 375, 390, 410,
        445
8:36–37 333
8:37 445
8:39 . . . . 573, 615
9 435
9–11 106

9:1–23 . . . . 109n2
9:2 . . . . 109n2
9:2–3 . . . . 671, 708
9:3 106
9:4 106
9:6 . . . . 106, 109n2
9:6–8 . . . . 74, 289
9:7–8 565
9:8 106
9:9 106
9:10–13 106
9:11 107
9:11–13 442
9:13 442
9:14 . . . . 328, 418, 441
9:15 . . . . 107, 110, 123, 399,
        440, 442
9:15–16 440
9:16 . . . . 107, 110, 399, 406,
        442, 708
9:17 . . . . 107, 108, 110, 440
9:17–18 439
9:18 . . . . 109, 110, 431, 440,
        441, 443, 454
9:19 . . . . 442, 443
9:20 443
9:20–21 109
9:20–23 . . . . 443n1
9:21 443
9:22–23 . . . . 108, 120, 315,
        703–4
9:24 . . . . 109n2, 532
10:1 . . . . 455, 547, 671, 708
10:9 530
10:13–15 709
10:14–15 536
10:17 . . . . 536, 539, 709
10:29 618
11:7 . . . . 443, 564
11:11–16 75
11:12 . . . . 75, 291
11:17 73
11:17–18 73–74
11:20 161
11:25 . . . . 75, 291, 475
11:26 75

11:33................14, 239, 418, 434, 609
11:33–36............15, 549, 696
11:34–36............60
11:36................60, 61, 239
12:1–2..............656
12:2................15, 360
12:9................601
12:12................671
12:15................22, 671
13:1................261, 314
13:8................639
13:8–10............627
13:9................600, 601
13:10................639
13:14................592
14:23................385, 480
15:5–6..............194
15:7................194
15:8–9..............194
15:16................187
15:18................139, 652n3
15:24................405
16:26................139, 645

1 Corinthians
1:2................532
1:7................676
1:8–9................532, 617
1:9................617
1:18–25..............174
1:20................667n2
1:22–24..............530, 536, 613
1:23................530
1:24................531, 532, 538, 563n1, 655
1:26–31..............318
1:27................564
1:27–28..............545
1:29................545
1:30–31..............545
2:6................667n2
2:7–9................174
2:8................340, 667n2
2:9................549

2:14................385, 454, 521, 526
3:6–7................663
3:18................667n2
3:21–23..............23, 289
4:7................211
5:2................604
5:7................586
6:9–10..............598–99, 619, 624
6:19–20..............342, 580
6:20................193
7:23................580
8:6................59, 61, 289
9:24–27..............597
10:24................40, 56
10:31................193
11–14................514
11:1................592
11:23–26............604
11:30................374
12:3................555
12:3a................556
12:12................604
13:2................601
13:3................601
13:4–5..............40
13:5................56
13:12................675, 676, 692
15:1–2..............594
15:10................211, 514, 579, 653, 654, 664
15:20................669
15:22................359
15:26................360
15:32................337
15:42–44............685
15:44................227
15:49................678
15:50................227
15:53................228
15:54–57............168
15:55................228
15:55–57............338
15:56–57............185
16:7................175
16:14................600

2 Corinthians

1:8–9	491
1:11	644
1:20	473, 561, 587, 625, 687
3	643
3:6	156, 640
3:7	156
3:12–16	75
3:14	475
3:16	475
3:17–18	640
3:18	66, 67, 136, 163, 181, 182, 187, 647, 677, 679
3:18b	182
4:4	66, 169, 180, 183, 195, 231, 260, 265, 274, 508n3, 526
4:4–6	537, 538
4:6	182, 195, 274, 537, 538, 539, 651, 679
4:8	433
4:11	16n1
4:15	208
4:17	228, 652n3
4:17–18	704, 705
4:18	676
5:4	228
5:6	338
5:7	513, 593, 675
5:8	338
5:17	66, 537, 677
5:21	582
6:10	22, 228, 671
7:8–10	425
7:9	539, 546
7:9–11	149
7:10	652n3
8:2	705
8:9	208
8:16–17	640, 642
9:8	578, 653
11:23–29	311
11:24	446
11:26	605

12:1–4	280
12:1–10	280
12:7	281
12:7–9	270
12:8–9	281
12:9	282

Galatians

1:4	661
2:16	532, 582
2:20	593, 653, 654
3:2	41
3:5	23, 647, 649, 650
3:7	565
3:7–9	73
3:8	532, 582
3:13	183, 521, 581
3:13–14	73
3:24	532
3:26	582
5:5	676
5:6	600, 644, 651
5:16	593
5:18–19	639
5:19–21	599
5:21–23	639
5:22	159, 593, 640, 647
5:24	597
5:25	593
6:8	593, 603
6:9	578
6:14	231, 688
6:15	66, 537

Ephesians

1	59
1:4	52, 407, 563, 564, 572, 577, 610
1:4–6	51, 131, 170, 171, 175, 573
1:4–7	361n5
1:5	51, 52, 185
1:5–6	52, 57
1:6	51, 53, 54, 56, 105, 170, 195, 199, 207, 280, 320, 525, 636

1:6–7 296
1:7 . . . . 57, 171, 185, 585,
624, 625
1:11 . . . . 105, 176, 210, 236,
319, 398, 406, 407,
409, 439, 440, 577,
610, 691, 698
1:11–12 . . . . 52, 406, 407
1:12 . . . . 52, 53, 54, 56, 170,
199, 207, 280, 407
1:13 536
1:13–14 619
1:14 . . . . 52, 53, 54, 56, 170,
199, 207, 280, 620
1:17–18 157
1:18 . . . . 157, 229
1:18–19 651
1:21 . . . . 667n2
1:22 341
1:22–23 186
2:1 526
2:1–3 . . . . 257, 518
2:2 260
2:2–3 279
2:3 169
2:3–5 168
2:4–10 . . . . 540, 543, 551, 552
2:4–5 . . . . 550, 553
2:5 . . . . 231, 454, 516, 541,
542, 554
2:5–6 543
2:6 . . . . 541, 550, 554
2:6–7 . . . . 198, 683
2:7 . . . . 38n5, 199, 540
2:8 . . . . 542, 543, 551, 554,
651
2:9 543
2:10 . . . . 66, 186, 542, 543,
554, 677
2:12 522
2:16 664
3:4–6 163
3:6 73
3:8 609
4:18 . . . . 517, 522, 526
4:22 257

4:24 537
5:2 600
5:5 . . . . 599, 619
5:6 550
5:14 530
5:19 604
5:25–26 571
5:25–27 . . . . 162, 168, 513, 678
5:26 163
5:26–27 593
6:10–18 259
6:12 . . . . 260, 283
6:13–17 650
6:17 650
6:18 604

Philippians
1:6 617
1:9–10 . . . . 628, 629
1:9–11 191
1:10–11 678
1:11 . . . . 192, 585
1:20 688
1:21 338
1:21–23 689
1:23 338
1:27–30 543
1:29 . . . . 543, 544, 651
2:5 592
2:6–7 167
2:6–8 . . . . 302, 317
2:7 674
2:8 . . . . 360, 582, 624
2:9 . . . . 340, 641
2:9–11 . . . . 168, 688
2:11 636
2:12–13 . . . . 651–52, 653
2:13 . . . . 579, 654, 663
2:14–15 629
3:2 332
3:8 . . . . 275, 282
3:9 . . . . 545, 582
3:12 . . . . 578, 611, 623, 652,
656
3:19 332
3:20 288

3:20–21............669
3:21.................227, 228, 339, 679,
                685, 706
4:4.....................403
4:5.....................672
4:19.................410

Colossians
1:3–4................540
1:4–5................705
1:5.....................536
1:9.....................17
1:13.................57, 515
1:14.................580
1:16.................58, 64, 198, 231,
                341, 688
1:17.................20, 231, 248, 344,
                365
1:18.................198
1:19.................167
1:21–22............627, 628
1:21–23............594
1:22.................628
1:28–29............653
1:29.................579, 654, 663
2:9.....................167
2:10.................341
2:13–14............166
2:13–15............279
2:14.................279
2:15.................168, 179, 185, 279,
                281, 283
3:10.................66, 537, 677
3:11.................289, 664
4:14.................605

1 Thessalonians
1:3.....................139, 645
1:6.....................592, 688
1:10.................676
3:5.....................272, 273
3:12.................159
3:12–13............599, 678
4:16.................685
4:16–17............668
5:9–11.............381

5:23.................678
5:23–24............617
5:24.................621

2 Thessalonians
1:7–10.............669
1:8–9................670
1:9.....................171
1:9–10.............197
1:10.................636, 675
1:11.................139, 645
1:11–12............190–91, 629, 655
1:12.................22, 636
2.......................471
2:9–12.............467
2:10.................258, 467
2:10–11............470
2:11.................467, 473
2:12.................467
2:13.................187, 188, 192, 620,
                626
2:14.................655

1 Timothy
1:5.....................600, 644
1:17.................136, 290
2:1–4................310
2:4.....................416, 547, 548, 549,
                665
3:2.....................16
4:1–5................644
4:10.................571
5:8.....................601
6:9.....................649
6:12.................578
6:15.................129, 135, 209

2 Timothy
1:9.....................171, 172–73, 175,
                180, 361n5, 525,
                570, 610, 661
1:10.................361
1:15.................605
2:9.....................311, 461, 664
2:11–13............595–96
2:12–13............324, 467–68
2:13.................319, 327

2:24–25..............547
2:24–26..............258, 275–76, 455,
            546
2:25..................547, 550
2:25–26..............707
2:26..................454, 547
3:16..................13, 355
4:8...................674
4:10..................605
4:16–18..............619

Titus
1:1–2................467–68
1:2...................469, 470, 471
1:5...................16
2:13..................674
2:14..................23, 342, 629, 630,
            638, 643, 656
3:1...................283
3:5–6................65

Philemon
8–9..................593
24...................605

Hebrews
1:3...................20, 145, 167, 231,
            248, 296, 344, 365,
            649
1:8...................167, 296
1:39.................140
2:1...................595
2:9...................340
2:10.................59, 61, 131, 610,
            674
2:14.................168, 179, 185, 296,
            361
2:14–15.............279, 338
3:6...................595
3:12.................605, 606
3:12–13.............604
3:12–14.............595
3:14.................606
4:14.................578
4:15.................56, 166
6:1–3................175
6:11–12.............595

6:17–18.............467–68
6:18.................319
7:10–11.............129
7:22.................155
8....................155
8:6...................155, 166
9:7...................166
9:12.................580
9:13–14.............632
9:15.................166, 532
9:22.................166
9:26.................166
9:28.................581
10...................155
10:4.................166
10:10................585
10:25................604
10:32–35...........648
10:36................604
11:1.................587, 649
11:6.................480, 648
11:7.................362
11:8.................587, 645, 648
11:24–26...........648
11:31................93, 95, 368
11:33–35a..........140
11:35b–36..........140
12:1–2..............578, 648
12:2.................361, 446, 705
12:6.................643
12:10................705
12:11................418
12:14................515, 574, 584, 585,
            592, 604, 611, 623,
            624, 625, 638
12:15–17...........452
12:17................453
12:23................628, 656
12:24................166
13:3.................509
13:5–6..............648–49
13:6.................410
13:12–14...........648
13:20–21...........190, 192, 641, 643
13:21................23, 642, 643, 645,
            647, 656, 663

James

1:13 412
1:18 .... 535, 539
1:26 598
2:5 .... 318, 564
2:8 .... 600, 644
2:17 .... 600, 644
2:19 262
2:25 .... 93, 368
2:26 644
4:6 .... 318, 319, 557
4:13 .... 400, 401, 402, 405
4:13–16 .... 265, 400
4:13–17 403
4:14 401
4:15 .... 372, 402, 406, 410
4:16 400
5:11 .... 251, 252, 266, 267, 268, 355

1 Peter

1:3 .... 535, 539
1:5 651
1:6 228
1:6–7 705
1:8 199
1:10–11 317
1:11 494
1:16 457
1:17 404
1:17–19 630
1:18 .... 630, 631
1:18–19 535
1:23 .... 455, 536, 539, 709
1:23–25 535
1:25 709
2:9 .... 80–81, 532, 539, 564
2:12 193
2:14 385
2:24 .... 182, 192, 581, 638
2:24–25 631
3:9 588
3:17 .... 263, 404
3:18 .... 183, 185, 211
3:20 363

4:11 .... 189–90, 653–54, 656
4:16 194
4:17 704
4:19 .... 263, 404
5:5 .... 318, 319
5:8 272
5:8–9 263
5:10 .... 532, 704, 705

2 Peter

1:3 532
1:3–4 259
1:10 .... 629, 666
1:11 .... 290, 296
2:5 362
2:12 332
3:4 665
3:8 665
3:9 .... 416, 665, 666
3:12–13 686
3:16 17

1 John

1:5 .... 56, 412
1:7 603
1:8 .... 597, 623, 656
1:9 326
2:2 571
2:4 .... 603, 604
2:12 326
2:17 603
2:18–19 607
3:2 .... 136, 163, 182, 677, 679
3:9 .... 596, 623
3:14 .... 587, 601, 604, 624, 627, 629
4:4 579
4:8 601
4:20 601
4:21 601
5:1 .... 532, 534
5:4 .... 623, 650
5:16 .... 452, 453
5:18 .... 579, 623

Jude
1 532
10 332
24–25 . . . . 453, 621

Revelation
1:5 317
1:17–18 340
2:3 194
2:10 . . . . 264, 578
3:21 299
4:8 412
4:11 . . . . 61, 65
5:9 . . . . 22, 65, 163, 168,
                        173, 180, 291, 340,
                        658, 687
5:9–10 . . . . 64, 169, 288,
                        662–63
5:10 136
5:12 . . . . 65, 208
5:12–13 299
6:4 375
6:8 375
6:10–11 376
6:11 664
7:15–17 136
7:17 . . . . 185, 299
9:18 . . . . 505, 506
9:20 . . . . 368, 506

11:15 . . . . 136, 296
12:9 . . . . 255, 256, 272
12:11 258
13:7 375
13:8 . . . . 171, 172, 175, 180,
                        341, 361n5, 661
14:7 63
14:10–11 670
14:11 342
15:3 . . . . 173, 180, 687
16:9 . . . . 368, 506
16:10–11 506
17:6 375
17:14 . . . . 129, 136, 290, 296,
                        564
17:16–17 467
18:20 548
19:1–3 548
19:11 355
19:15–16 290
19:16 . . . . 129, 296
20:10 . . . . 274, 276, 277, 657
21:1 686
21:23 201
22:1 299
22:16 290
22:17 . . . . 415, 416, 571
22:20 672

desiringGod

Everyone wants to be happy. Our website was born and built for happiness. We want people everywhere to understand and embrace the truth that *God is most glorified in us when we are most satisfied in him.* We've collected more than thirty years of John Piper's speaking and writing, including translations into more than forty languages. We also provide a daily stream of new written, audio, and video resources to help you find truth, purpose, and satisfaction that never end. And it's all available free of charge, thanks to the generosity of people who've been blessed by the ministry.

If you want more resources for true happiness, or if you want to learn more about our work at Desiring God, we invite you to visit us at desiringGod.org.

desiringGod.org